Second Edition

Personal Finance
An Interactive Applications Approach

Dan W. French
University of Missouri

Megan Noel
Johnson County Community College

Kendall Hunt
publishing company

Book Team

Chairman and Chief Executive Officer   Mark C. Falb
President and Chief Operating Officer   Chad M. Chandlee
Vice President, Higher Education   David L. Tart
Director of Publishing Partnerships   Paul B. Carty
Product/Development Supervisor   Lynne Rogers
Vice President, Operations   Timothy J. Beitzel
Senior Production Editor   Mary Melloy
Permissions Editor   Melisa Seegmiller
Cover Designer   Jeni Fensterman

Cover image © Shutterstock, Inc.

Kendall Hunt
publishing company

www.kendallhunt.com
Send all inquiries to:
4050 Westmark Drive
Dubuque, IA 52004-1840

Dedications

To my parents, Burton and Midge, wife Janet (Caya), and children: Dan Brady, Stephanie (Niki), Rachel, Natalie, Cassie, and Aiyana—D.F.

To my daughters: Thea, Desirée, and Shena—M Noel

Brief Contents

Contents

Chapter 3   Housing   65

Chapter 4   Manage Your Credit   99

Chapter 5   Spending Wisely   135

Chapter 6   Tax Planning   159

Chapter 7   Property and Casualty Insurance   191

Chapter 8   Health and Disability Insurance   213

Chapter 9   Life Insurance   243

Chapter 10   Entrepreneurship   271

Chapter 11   Investing   291

Chapter 12   Stocks   325

Chapter 15   Real Estate   413

Chapter 16   Retirement Planning   437

Chapter 17   Estate Planning   473

Preface

Students earn a college degree to increase their earning potential. Most individuals dream of financial independence, the ability to live the life style of their choice. Personal financial planning is a critical step to efficiently obtaining that goal. The ability to manage money and make wise financial decisions is a learned skill which comes with knowledge and practice. This book is designed to provide students with information on how financial instruments work and to provide them with ample opportunity to practice making decisions using their acquired knowledge.

Vision of Text

We designed *Personal Finance: An Interactive Applications Approach* to have its own unique personality.

Student Oriented—The book is written in an open, easy style. Our text is user friendly in its tone, content, and layout.

Applications Approach—The text incorporates case studies, personal financial planning, and reflective thought features. The case studies are inclusive and one is provided for both a college student and a new graduate. The personal financial planning features guide students through the process of creating his or her own financial plan. The reflective thought features ask thought provoking questions to help students incorporate their own personal beliefs as part of the planning process.

Comprehensive—The text provides the tools to allow students to prepare a complete financial plan.

Timely—The text was written with current information, and provides resources for constantly changing financial information.

Organization

The text is organized to build on previously learned concepts and to systematically facilitate the student's ability to develop a financial plan.

Chapter 1 introduces the time value of money concepts critical to many problems in the following chapters. The concepts are explained and examples are used to demonstrate how to solve common financial problems with four popular methods: scientific calculators, financial calculators, tables, and spreadsheets.

Chapter 2 introduces students to the financial planning process. In this chapter students are asked to set goals and develop financial statements: cash flow statement, balance sheet, and budget.

Chapter 3 covers the issues related to housing. It compares and contrasts the benefits of renting versus buying a home. It offers tips for leasing and purchasing. It demonstrates how to determine how much mortgage you can afford and details the items associated with a mortgage payment and closing costs.

Chapter 4 introduces consumer credit. This chapter demonstrates both wise and unwise use of credit cards, explains the difference between revolving and closed end credit, and details the factors that affect your credit (FICO) score.

Chapter 5 introduces comparison shopping. This chapter explains how to comparison shop from the smallest purchases made in the grocery store to large purchases like purchasing an automobile.

Chapter 6 introduces taxes and explains the difference between income and non-income based taxes. It walks students through the process of filing a 1040 form. It highlights tax credits of interest to students and provides information for students to find additional credits through the IRS web site.

Chapter 7 introduces the concepts of insurance and explains how to determine your insurance needs for home and auto insurance.

Chapter 8 covers medical insurance. It starts by introducing the currently available medical care and disability plans and includes healthcare options available under the Affordable Care Act.

Chapter 9 covers life insurance and how to determine which type of policy best covers your personal needs for life insurance. It demonstrates how to select an amount of life insurance appropriate for the number of people you have depending on you for support.

Chapter 10 addresses the issue of how we earn our money. This chapter is titled entrepreneurship and asks the student to be the entrepreneur of their own life. This chapter includes a brief overview of how to write a financial plan, how to write a resume, and how to write a sponsorship request letter.

Chapter 11 introduces the basics of investing and explains the concepts of risk and return. The chapter details the differences among the many financial institutions and financial instruments available to us as investments.

Chapter 12 covers the basics of investing in stocks. It includes the basics of analyzing stocks and shows in examples how someone might analyze a real company.

Chapter 13 covers investing in bonds and interest-paying securities.

Chapter 14 explains investing in mutual funds. It covers the various types of funds and how an individual might select which funds are appropriate for investing.

Chapter 15 introduces real estate as an investment option. It covers some of the terms that are special to real estate investing and shows how even individual investors with a modest amount to invest can purchase an interest in real estate by investing in real estate investment trusts.

Chapter 16 demonstrates how to effectively plan for retirement by using tax-shielded investments and savings plans.

Chapter 17 introduces students to the concept of estate planning. It shows the tax ramifications of different trusts and explains the importance of planning for the final settlement of your estate.

Text Philosophy

We believe financial planning is critical to success. The financial planning process requires accurate knowledge of an ever changing financial world. The best way to learn the skills of financial planning is to create, implement, and adjust a personal financial plan to meet changing desires and needs. This process also involves the ability to reflect on individual definitions of success, personal, moral, spiritual, and ethical beliefs. This text is designed to provide students with accurate information, clear guides, and thought provoking questions to allow them to integrate their personal beliefs into the planning process without requiring them to share that information with others.

Text Features

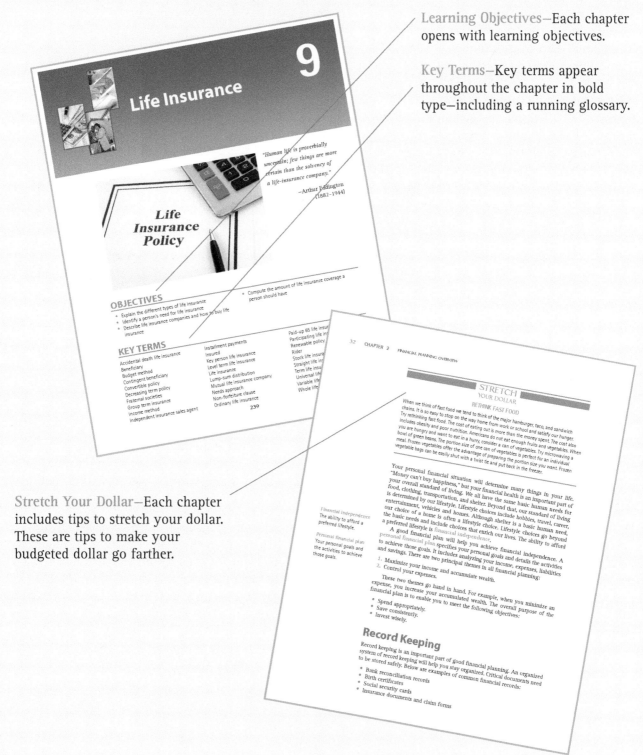

Learning Objectives—Each chapter opens with learning objectives.

Key Terms—Key terms appear throughout the chapter in bold type—including a running glossary.

Stretch Your Dollar—Each chapter includes tips to stretch your dollar. These are tips to make your budgeted dollar go farther.

Financial Equations—The text opens with a solid coverage of the time value of money concepts. We provide examples of how to solve these four main equations with scientific calculators, spreadsheets, tables, and financial calculators. The text provides additional examples of these equations throughout the following chapters. Where appropriate, additional mathematical equations relevant to personal finance are introduced.

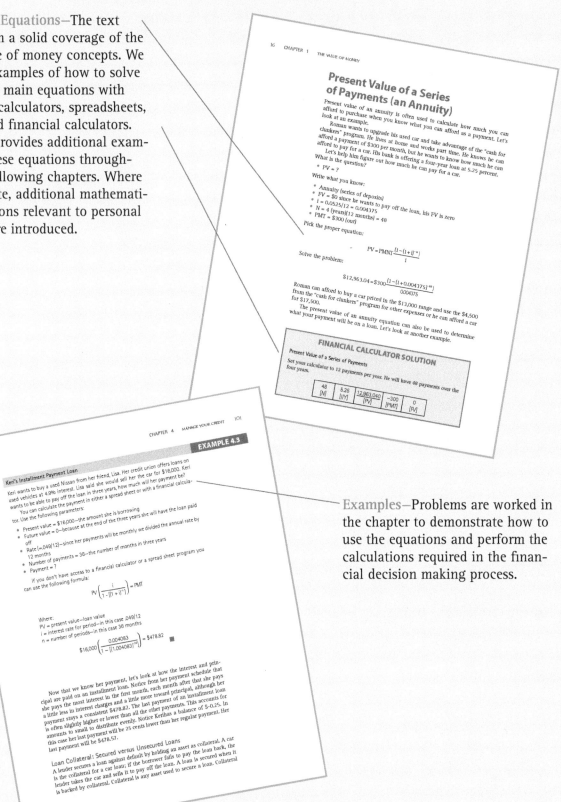

16   CHAPTER 1   THE VALUE OF MONEY

Present Value of a Series of Payments (an Annuity)

Present value of an annuity is often used to calculate how much you can afford to purchase when you know what you can afford as a payment. Let's look at an example.

Roman wants to upgrade his used car and take advantage of the "cash for clunkers" program. He lives at home and works part time. He knows he can afford a payment of $300 per month, but he wants to know how much he can afford to pay for a car. His bank is offering a four-year loan at 5.25 percent. Let's help him figure out how much he can pay for a car.

What is the question?

- PV = ?

Write what you know:

- Annuity (series of deposits)
- FV = $0 since he wants to pay off the loan, his FV is zero
- i = 0.0525/12 = 0.004375
- N = 4 (years)(12 months) = 48
- PMT = $300 (out)

Pick the proper equation:

Solve the problem:

$$PV = PMNT\frac{(1-(1+i)^{-n})}{i}$$

$$\$12,963.04 = \$300\frac{(1-(1+0.004375)^{-48})}{0.004375}$$

Roman can afford to buy a car priced in the $13,000 range and use the $4,500 from the "cash for clunkers" program for other expenses or he can afford a car for $17,500.

The present value of an annuity equation can also be used to determine what your payment will be on a loan. Let's look at another example.

FINANCIAL CALCULATOR SOLUTION

Present Value of a Series of Payments

Set your calculator to 12 payments per year. He will have 48 payments over the four years.

48 [N]	5.25 [I/Y]	12,963.040 [PV]	–300 [PMT]	0 [PV]

CHAPTER 4   MANAGE YOUR CREDIT   101

EXAMPLE 4.3

Keri's Installment Payment Loan

Keri wants to buy a used Nissan from her friend, Lisa. Her credit union offers loans on used vehicles at 4.9% interest. Lisa said she would sell her the car for $16,000. Keri wants to be able to pay off the loan in three years, how much will her payment be?

You can calculate the payment in either a spread sheet or with a financial calculator. Use the following parameters:

- Present value = $16,000—the amount she is borrowing
- Future value = 0—because at the end of the three years she will have the loan paid off
- Rate (=.049/12)—since her payments will be monthly we divided the annual rate by 12 months
- Number of payments = 36—the number of months in three years
- Payment = ?

If you don't have access to a financial calculator or a spread sheet program you can use the following formula:

$$PV\left(\frac{i}{1-((1+i)^{-n})}\right) = PMT$$

Where:
PV = present value—loan value
i = interest rate for period—in this case .049/12
n = number of periods—in this case 36 months

$$\$16,000\left(\frac{0.004083}{1-((1.004083)^{-36})}\right) = \$478.82$$

Now that we know her payment, let's look at how the interest and principal are paid on an installment loan. Notice from her payment schedule that she pays the most interest in the first month, each month after that she pays a little less in interest charges and a little more toward principal, although her payment stays a consistent $478.82. The last payment of an installment loan is often slightly higher or lower than all the other payments. This accounts for amounts to small to distribute evenly. Notice Keri has a balance of $-0.25. In this case her last payment will be 25 cents lower than her regular payment. Her last payment will be $478.57.

Loan Collateral: Secured versus Unsecured Loans

A lender secures a loan against default by holding an asset as collateral. A car is the collateral for a car loan; if the borrower fails to pay the loan back, the lender takes the car and sells it to pay off the loan. A loan is secured when it is backed by collateral. Collateral is any asset used to secure a loan. Collateral

Examples—Problems are worked in the chapter to demonstrate how to use the equations and perform the calculations required in the financial decision making process.

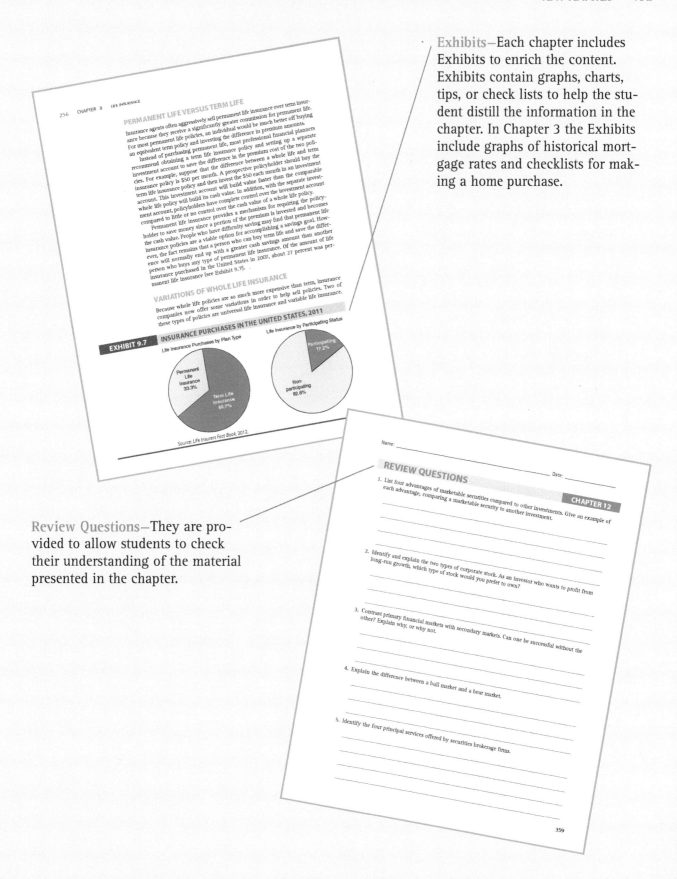

Exhibits—Each chapter includes Exhibits to enrich the content. Exhibits contain graphs, charts, tips, or check lists to help the student distill the information in the chapter. In Chapter 3 the Exhibits include graphs of historical mortgage rates and checklists for making a home purchase.

Review Questions—They are provided to allow students to check their understanding of the material presented in the chapter.

---

256   CHAPTER 9   LIFE INSURANCE

PERMANENT LIFE VERSUS TERM LIFE

Insurance agents often aggressively sell permanent life insurance over term insurance because they receive a significantly greater commission for permanent life. For most permanent life policies, an individual would be much better off buying an equivalent term policy and investing the difference in premium amounts.

Instead of purchasing permanent life, most professional financial planners recommend obtaining a term life insurance policy and setting up a separate investment account to save the difference in the premium cost of the two policies. For example, suppose that the difference between a whole life and term life insurance policy is $50 per month. A prospective policyholder should buy the term life insurance policy and then invest the $50 each month in an investment account. This investment account will build value faster than the comparable whole life policy will build its cash value. In addition, with the investment account, policyholders have complete control over the investment account compared to little or no control over the cash value of a whole life policy.

Permanent life insurance provides a mechanism for requiring the policyholder to save money since a portion of the premium is invested and becomes the cash value. People who have difficulty saving may find that permanent life insurance policies are a viable option for accomplishing a savings goal. However, the fact remains that a person who can buy term life and save the difference will normally end up with a greater cash savings amount than another person who buys any type of permanent life insurance. Of the amount of life insurance purchased in the United States in 2007, about 27 percent was permanent life insurance (see Exhibit 9.7).

VARIATIONS OF WHOLE LIFE INSURANCE

Because whole life policies are so much more expensive than term, insurance companies now offer some variations in order to help sell policies. Two of these types of policies are universal life insurance and variable life insurance.

EXHIBIT 9.7   INSURANCE PURCHASES IN THE UNITED STATES, 2011

Life Insurance Purchases by Plan Type

Permanent Life Insurance 33.3%
Term Life Insurance 66.7%

Life Insurance by Participating Status

Participating 17.2%
Non-participating 82.8%

Source: *Life Insurers Fact Book, 2012.*

REVIEW QUESTIONS

CHAPTER 12

1. List four advantages of marketable securities compared to other investments. Give an example of each advantage, comparing a marketable security to another investment.

2. Identify and explain the two types of corporate stock. As an investor who wants to profit from long-run growth, which type of stock would you prefer to own?

3. Contrast primary financial markets with secondary markets. Can one be successful without the other? Explain why, or why not.

4. Explain the difference between a bull market and a bear market.

5. Identify the four principal services offered by securities brokerage firms.

Problems—Allow the students to apply the concepts related to mathematical problems (quantitative analysis) discussed in each chapter.

Case Studies—Chapters 2–17 include two case studies each. There is a case study for:

- A new college student
- A new college graduate

The individuals are introduced in Chapter 2. Realistic occupation incomes, and expenditures are provided for each cases study. The students are asked to perform a task related to the text content, for example in Chapter 2 they are asked to create goals, cash flow statements, balance sheets and budgets. In Chapter 3 they are asked to qualify the individuals in their case study for a mortgage and help them select a home. Each chapter builds on the information covered previously. We have also included a recap of the financial information needed to make the decision for that chapter's case study so they can be assigned independently.

Cases contain a note asking students to use accumulated information if they are working the same case throughout the book. Each case was developed with poor financial management in Chapter 2 to stress the points of common financial mistakes people make. The instructor's manual includes complete recommended solutions for each case study. These can also be used as examples in lecturers for instructors who want to demonstrate the concepts and use the development of a personal financial plan for student assignments.

CHAPTER 2   FINANCIAL PLANNING OVERVIEW   57

Balance risk and reward to optimize your savings. The right savings vehicle for you will depend on the risk you are willing to assume, the intended use for the savings, and the length of time you have to save.

PROBLEMS

1. Connie is trying to calculate her personal wealth and is having a difficult time. She has:

   - $2,000 in a savings account
   - A car valued at $15,000
   - A car loan with a balance of $9,000
   - Stocks worth $4,000
   - Credit card balance of $1,000

   What is Connie's current net worth?

2. Jerry struggles to save money. Last month he had:

   - Gross monthly income $5,000
   - Monthly tax deduction $800
   - Health insurance $300
   - Rent and utilities $1,000
   - Car payments and expenses $1,200
   - Food $900
   - Miscellaneous $500

   Create a personal cash flow statement for him. Make recommendations to help him save $400 next month.

CASE STUDIES

COLLEGE STUDENT

Kevin Maedor is a 19-year-old college student. He still lives at home with his parents, and he works part time at Vapor's Lane. He started his financial plan in the spring semester of 2014. He plans to graduate with a B.S. in engineering in May 2017. He has the following financial information:

- He brings home $760 a month from his job; he currently has $174 in his checking account.
- He asks his parents for $50 cash a week.
- He has a Visa card with a balance of $1,700 and a MasterCard with a balance of $800. He makes the minimum monthly payment of $15.00 on each of them.
- His cell phone bill is $85 a month.

Create Your Financial Plan—Chapters 2–17 contain activities designed to help students create their own financial plan. These can be used throughout the course as assignments. Instructors can use the case studies as group activities in class to demonstrate how to create a financial plan, then assign these activities for students to create their own plan. If instructors don't assign a personal financial plan, students can use these on their own.

Make It Personal—These are not found in every chapter, but they are found in key chapters in the text. They are thought provoking questions designed to allow students to incorporate their own personal values into their financial plan. They are reflective activities that encourage students to consider what is important to them from a personal, moral, spiritual or political point of view. They are not designed to be graded. Each one tells the student this is a private matter for their consideration and they should not feel obligated to share these. They are free to share them if they wish.

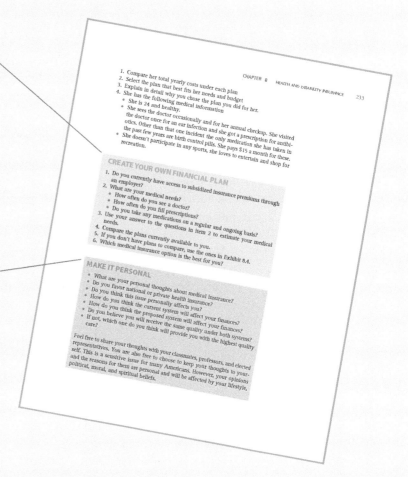

Instructional Resources

We have developed an interactive website with:

Survey Questions—These are questions designed to answer chapter-specific questions. For example, in the chapter on housing, the survey questions provide students with feedback on the rent versus buy issues based on their answers to a set of question derived from their personal preferences.

Poll Questions—These are designed to provide the instructor feedback at the opening of a chapter. In Chapter 1 students are asked which they would rather have a penny that doubles in value everyday for a month or $1,000,000.

PowerPoint Presentation—Chapter outlines are provided in a PowerPoint presentation.

Interactive Exercises—In Chapter 2 a drag and drop game is used to teach the skills of developing a financial statement. Students are given a set of financial items and asked to drag them to the appropriate financial statement. Students receive immediate feedback and can increase their ability to accurately write cash flow statements and balance sheets in a fun and entertaining way.

Videos—These are provided to explain complex information. For example, in Chapter 1 videos are provided to show students step-by-step how to set up an Excel spread sheet to solve time value of money problems. In Chapter 3 on housing, videos are provided to explain how to calculate how much mortgage a person can afford.

Test Questions—Both pre-test and post-tests are provided. Test questions for each chapter are provided in a variety of formats, true or false, multiple choice, essay and short answer.

Sample Syllabi—We have provided sample syllabi designed to be used with a standard 16-week course. We have provided them for both Monday/Wednesday/Friday and Tuesday/Thursday course schedules.

Solutions—We have provided complete solutions for all review questions, problems, and case studies.

Stock Trak—Each text comes with access to Stock Trak.

Acknowledgments

Danny Phillips, Vice President of Mortgages, Capitol Federal Savings, for his generous input to Chapter 3 on housing.

Ken Coffey, retired Assistant Dean, Business Division, Johnson County Community College, for his support and encouragement in the development of this book.

Reviewers

Robert Atra
Lewis University

Mark Bell
MaysvilleCTC

Pam Bennett
University of Central Arkansas

Anne Berre
Schreiner University

Ted Berzinski
Mars Hill College

Yvette Swint-Blakely
Lansing Community College

Dr. George Boulware
Lipscomb University

John Brady
Ohio State University, Lima

Todd Brown
Stephen F. Austin State University

Bill Brunsen
Eastern NM University

Nicholas A. Daves
Winston-Salem State University

Pierre David
Baldwin-Wallace College

Cristine M. Elliott
Pittsburg State University

Len Eichler
Western Dakota Tech

Harry Fisher
Eureka College

Caroline Fulmer
The University of Alabama

Dr. Georg Grassmueck
Lycoming College

Timothy Green
North Georgia Technical College

Melodi Guilbault
Warner Southern College

Charles Hennon
Miami University

Cindy L. Hinz
Jamestown Community College

Joe Howell
Salt Lake Community College

Jeanette Klosterman
Hutchinson Community College

Lauri Kremer
Lycoming College

Junnae Landry
Pratt Community College

Thomas Largay
Thomas College

Greg Lindeblom
Broward Community College

Diana Watson-Maile
East Central University

James Malia
University of Tennessee

Pam McGlasson
College of San Mateo

Zack McNeil
Longview Community College

Jim Meir
Cleveland State Community College

Deborah Myers
Bluffton University

Kevin Nguyen
Lone Star College–Montgomery

Merlene Olmsted
Eastern New Mexico University

Mary Pickard
East Carolina University

Michael Phillips
California State University, Northridge

Barbara Poole
Roger Williams University

Dave Rath
Roane State Community College

Susan Reichelt
East Carolina University

Howard V. Roberts
Pikeville College

Cheryl Malone Robinson
The University of Tennessee
at Chattanooga

Thomas L. Severance
MiraCosta College

Grover Sheffield
University of West Alabama

Howell Sheffield
University of West Alabama

Lakshmy Sivaratnam
Kansas City Kansas Community College

Don Skousen
Salt Lake Community College

Anthony W. Slone
Elizabethtown Community & Technical
College

Suresh Srivastava
University of Alaska, Anchorage

William A. Steiden, Ph.D.
Jefferson Community College

Dr. Jesse Stevens
Nyack College

Patricia Stevens
University of Memphis

Denise Deason-Toyne
Northeastern State University

Dr. Paula Tripp
Sam Houston State University

Steve Wages
Abilene Christian University

Sinan Yildirim
University of North Carolina, Pembroke

Baomei Zhao
University of Akron

About the Authors

Dan W. French

Dan W. French received a Bachelor of Arts degree in Economics from Lamar University in 1973 and a Ph.D. in 1979 from Louisiana Tech University. He joined the faculty of the University of Missouri as Professor of Finance and Chair of the Department of Finance in 2003. He teaches courses in investments, personal finance, real estate, and business finance. After receiving his BA degree, he began a career in the banking industry but soon realized that teaching at the college level was his passion. He has previously held teaching positions with New Mexico State University, Texas Christian University, Texas A&M University, Corpus Christi State University (now Texas A&M University–Corpus Christi), Jackson State University, and Lamar University.

Professor French's minor as an undergraduate student was Spanish, and he has enjoyed assignments in Ecuador, Mexico, Puerto Rico, and Venezuela where he was able to teach his finance courses in the Spanish language. He is a member of the American Finance Association, Financial Management Association, and National Association of Real Estate Investment Trusts.

Megan Noel

Megan Noel received a Bachelor of Science Degree in Civil Engineering from Kansas State University and a Masters of Business Administration from Baker University. She is an associate professor of Business Administration for Johnson County Community College. She teaches courses on savings and investments, personal finance, introduction to business, and business communications. She has been a professor at Johnson County Community College since the spring of 2001. She was a committee member of the Business and Industrial Technology Division Curriculum Committee from 2001–2003. She served as chair of the committee in 2003.

She began her teaching career at Brown Mackie Business College in 2000. She taught as an adjunct professor while working as an engineer. In her career as an engineer she managed multiple million dollar projects, but if you asked her where she learned to manage money she would say in the school of hard knocks. Although she was once a foster child, child bride, and 8th-grade dropout, she learned to set clear goals and put herself through college as a single parent of three. Well defined goals and careful budgeting are the tools she used.

She is an advocate for women's and children's rights. She served as a volunteer for Safe Home from 2002–2006. She worked both as a hotline counselor and as a court advocate. She is also actively involved in Quality Matters and was a presenter at the 5th Annual National Conference in 2013.

The Value of Money

"Time is money."

—Benjamin Franklin
(1706–1790)

OBJECTIVES

- Differentiate between simple and compound interest
- Explain the concepts of the time value of money
- Calculate future and present values for lump sums
- Calculate future and present values of annuities
- Perform calculations using equations, financial calculators, financial tables and spread sheets

KEY TERMS

Annuity
Annuity due
Compound interest
Future value

Interest rate (rate)
Opportunity cost
Ordinary annuity
Present value

Principal
Return on investment
Simple interest

STRETCH
YOUR DOLLAR

SELECTING SAVINGS ACCOUNTS

Select savings accounts with the highest compounding frequency. A savings account with monthly compounded will grow faster than one with quarterly compounded at the same interest rate.

This is a personal finance book; designed to help you understand the different aspects of the financial decisions you will make in your life. You will learn how to answer the following questions:

- What is the most economical purchase?
- Which mortgage is best for me?
- Do I need insurance?
- Which loan fits my budget?
- Can I reduce what I owe in taxes?
- How much do I need to save for retirement?

These topics and more are covered in the following chapters, but before we delve into these topics, you need to understand the time value of money. This chapter covers basic time value of money along with some general examples. Individual chapters that follow will use time value of money concepts where appropriate and build on the lessons here with additional examples to illustrate points in that chapter.

The time value of money deals with interest, return on investments, and inflation. Time is money; $100 today is worth more than $100 tomorrow.

Why do most people take out a mortgage to purchase their first home? If you want to buy a new home, with three bedrooms and two bathrooms in a nice neighborhood, how much would that cost you today where you live? In most Midwest metropolitan areas it would cost about $200,000. If you saved $10,000 a year for 20 years could you pay cash for a new home? Probably not. Time plays a role in the cost of goods. A new home in a nice area with three bedrooms and two bathrooms sold for $85,000 20 years ago in the Midwest. Money's value or buying power changes with time. Cost increases of goods and services over time is called inflation.

Inflation The increase in the cost of goods and services over time.

Interest, Rate of Return, and Inflation

The principles of the time value of money are the same regardless of whether we are computing interest (on debt), return on investment (profit from stocks), or inflation (the increase of cost in goods and services).

Examples in this chapter use the computation of interest to illustrate the principles of time value. However, the same methods apply for the other applications.

Return on investment Profit per period for each dollar invested. Often expressed as a percentage.

INTEREST CALCULATIONS

The interest rate (or simply the rate) is the amount of interest per year expressed as a percentage of the principal. The principal is the amount owed on a loan if you paid it off today. The original principal balance is the amount borrowed. Interest rates are stated as an annual rate. If the lender says they are charging 6 percent, it means they are charging 6 percent of the funds borrowed as a fee to use their money for one year. The equation to calculate the interest is:

$$\text{interest} = \text{principal} \times \text{rate} \times \text{time} \qquad \textbf{Equation 1.1}$$

The time variable in **Equation 1.1** correlates with the interest rate, and is expressed in years. The interest rate is expressed as a decimal. Always use the decimal equivalent of the interest rate in your equations. Example 1.1 provides an illustration.

Interest rate Amount of interest per year expressed as a percentage of the amount borrowed.

Principal The amount borrowed.

Calculating Interest	**EXAMPLE 1.1**

You deposit a $1000 in a savings account; it pays 4 percent interest annually. How much interest will you receive at the end of the year? Note the decimal equivalent of 4 percent, is .04.

$$\begin{aligned}
\text{interest} &= \text{principal} \times \text{rate} \times \text{time} \\
&= 1000 \times .04 \times 1 \\
&= 40
\end{aligned}$$

You earn $40 at the end of the year ■

CALCULATING INTEREST FOR LESS THAN ONE YEAR

When the time period is less than one year, time is expressed as a fraction of a year. Example 1.2 provides a sample calculation.

Sample Interest Calculation	**EXAMPLE 1.2**

You deposit a $1000 in a savings account; it pays 4 percent interest and pays interest earned at the end of each month. How much interest will you receive at the end of the month?

Now our time is a fraction of a year, specifically one month or 1/12 of a year, so the interest for one month is:

$$\begin{aligned}
\text{interest} &= 1000 \times .04/12 \\
&= 3.33
\end{aligned}$$

You earn $3.33 at the end of the month. ■

Both Examples 1.1 and 1.2 show the computation of simple interest. Simple interest is interest paid one time on the principal for one period of time, usually a year or less.

Interest rates are always stated as an annual rate and need to be divided by the number of compounding periods per year.

.04/12 is the same as .04 × 1/12

Simple interest Interest paid one time on the principal. The time period is usually one year or less.

Start out saving small amounts and watch your money grow over time.

COMPOUND INTEREST CALCULATIONS

Compound interest
Interest paid on the
previous interest.

In contrast to simple interest, compound interest applies when either:

- The time period is greater than one year
- The payment period for interest is less than one year and the principal accumulates interest for multiple periods

In either of these situations, the interest paid in one period becomes part of the principal in the next period. When interest is paid on interest it is called compound interest.

EXAMPLE 1.3	Compound Interest

Let's use the savings account in Example 1.2 and calculate the balance at the end of two months.

The interest you earned last month becomes part of the principal in the second month. In Example 1.2 the balance at the end of one month was $1,003.33.

$$\text{interest} = 1003.33 \times .04 \times 1/12$$
$$= 3.34$$

Add $3.34 to the $1,003.33 you had at the beginning of month. Your new account balance is $1,006.67. ■

Example 1.3 illustrates compounded interest. At the end of two months the account has $1,006.67. Note: the first month's interest was $3.33; two months' interest at that rate would be $6.66. However, at the end of two months, the account accumulates interest of $6.67, an extra $.01. While this extra penny may seem insignificant, over time the accumulative effects of compounding make a big difference in the total return an investment earns.

Exhibit 1.1 shows the cumulative effects of compounded interest. A hundred dollars at 9% interest multiplies over 5 times in 20 years.

The bank adds $9 to the account at the end of the first year. At the end of the second year, the bank pays interest on the new balance of $109. The interest for the second year is $9.81. Notice the amount of interest added increases each year. This is the result of compound interest.

The effect of compounding is powerful. The original balance of $100 almost doubles by the eighth year and more than triples by the end of year 13. At the end of the 20 years, the account contains $560.41, more than 5½ times the original beginning balance.

If interest had not compounded (and the first year's interest of $9 was added to the account 20 times) the balance at the end of 20 years would be $280.

Exhibit 1.2 shows graphically the power of compounding interest. Note how the balance grows exponentially.

END OF YEAR BALANCE		EXHIBIT 1.1

Interest rate = 9%

Year	Interest	Balance
		100.00
1	9.00	109.00
2	9.81	118.81
3	10.69	129.50
4	11.66	141.16
5	12.70	153.86
6	13.85	167.71
7	15.09	182.80
8	16.45	199.25
9	17.93	217.18
10	19.55	236.73
11	21.31	258.04
12	23.22	281.26
13	25.31	306.57
14	27.59	334.16
15	30.07	364.23
16	32.78	397.01
17	35.73	432.74
18	38.95	471.69
19	42.45	514.14
20	46.27	560.41

| EXHIBIT 1.2 | ILLUSTRATION OF COMPOUND INTEREST |

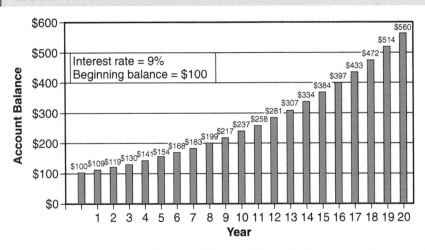

In the illustration provided by Exhibit 1.1, interest is compounded annually. Many financial institutions compound interest more often; and the balance of the account will grow even faster. However, even when compounding periods are less than a year (for example, monthly compounding), we always state interest rates on an annual basis.

Example 1.4 demonstrates compound interest for compounding periods of less than one year. Interest compounds each month at the annual rate of

| EXAMPLE 1.4 | Compound Interest, Compounding Periods Less Than One Year |

The Parkway Savings Bank pays 12 percent interest on its savings accounts compounded monthly. (Interest rates are not that high these days, but they have been in the past. A higher interest rate provides a faster growth rate.) If you deposit $100 in an account at the beginning of the year, how much will you have in your account at the end of the year?

Using   interest = principal × rate × time   **Equation 1.1**

the interest for the first month is:

$$\text{interest} = 100 \times .12 \times 1/12$$
$$= 1.00$$

At the beginning of month 2, the account has a total of $101.00. Computing the interest for month 2:

$$\text{interest} = 101 \times .12 \times 1/12$$
$$= 1.01$$

Thus, at the beginning of month 3, the account contains $102.01, or $.01 cent more than if there were no compounding. Continuing this process would yield the interest payments and account balances shown in Exhibit 1.3. ■

12 percent, and by the end of the year the account has accumulated a total of $112.67. If the account had paid 12 percent simple interest for the year (rather than compounded monthly), only $12 in interest would have been added at the end of the year.

As in Example 1.2, the additional interest accumulated by compounding in Example 1.4 seems small. However, over time, compound interest becomes substantial.

Note that $12.67 in interest accumulates in the account over the year in Exhibit 1.3. This is equivalent to an account paying a simple annual interest rate of 12.67 percent. An account that pays interest only at the end of the year (instead of compounding monthly) would have to pay 12.67 percent interest to yield the same profit as the account that pays 12 percent interest compounded monthly. Therefore, the effective interest rate of 12.67 percent (considering compounding) is greater than the annual interest rate of 12 percent.

SIMPLIFYING THE TASK OF COMPUTING COMPOUND INTEREST

Calculating compound interest by using sequential computations as in the previous examples is a tedious and time-consuming process. There are easier ways, and this book demonstrates four ways to simplify calculations of compound interest:

1. Time value of money equations
2. Financial calculators
3. Spread sheets
4. Present value tables

ILLUSTRATION OF INTEREST COMPOUNDED MONTHLY		EXHIBIT 1.3

Interest rate = 12%

Month	Interest	Balance
		100.00
1	1.00	101.00
2	1.01	102.01
3	1.02	103.03
4	1.03	104.06
5	1.04	105.10
6	1.05	106.15
7	1.06	107.21
8	1.07	108.28
9	1.08	109.36
10	1.09	110.45
11	1.10	111.55
12	1.12	112.67

The time-value-of-money equations calculate compound interest in one computation. Financial calculators, spread sheets and tables are based on the equations and further simplify the process of calculating compound interest. In this chapter we will demonstrate how to use the equations. For each problem we solve we will show you the key strokes for using a financial calculator in the margins next to the problems. You will find the financial tables in the Appendix of your book. The first two examples we work will also demonstrate how to use the tables. Spread sheets work similar to a financial calculator. We will explain how to use Microsoft Excel 2007 to solve time value of money problems at the end of the chapter. You can find example spread sheets with the solutions to the problems presented in this chapter on the accompany student web site. Experiment with the different methods and use the one you are most comfortable with. Before we can use the equations or the financial aids based on them, you need to understand the variables used in the equations.

Time Value of Money Variables

There are five variables, or pieces of information you need to solve time value of money problems:

1. Number of periods, (N)
2. Interest rate, (i)
3. Present value, (PV)
4. The payment amount, (PMT)
5. Future value, (FV)

The Number of Periods, (N)

The number of periods, (N), is the number of times interest is compounded. The period can be any time frame. Common periods are daily, monthly, quarterly, or yearly. There are 20 periods in 20 years compounded annually. There are 48 periods in four years compounded monthly.

$$N = (years)(periods\ in\ a\ year)$$

Calculate the number of quarters in 3 years.

$$N = (3\ years)(4\ quarters) = 12\ periods$$

The Interest Rate, (i)

The interest rate, (i) is stated as an annual interest rate. The interest rate for the calculations needs to correlate with periods, and should be entered into the equations as a periodic rate.

If you are calculating a payment on a loan that has 48 payments over four years, you are using a period of a month. If the bank is charging you 5 percent interest, they are quoting you an annual rate. To compute the (i) for the equation divide the annual rate by the number of periods per year. Always use the decimal equivalent of percents in the calculations.

$$i = \frac{\text{annual interest rate}}{\text{periods per year}}$$

$$i = \frac{.05}{12\,\text{months}} = 0.004167$$

Present Value, (PV)

The present value, (PV) is the current amount. This can be the amount borrowed at the beginning of a loan. The PV can be zero if you are starting a new savings account and plan to make future deposits. The present value can also be your current savings account balance you intend to add to, or it can be the current payoff on a loan you have held for a while.

Payment Amount, (PMT)

The payment amount, (PMT) is the amount of periodic payments or deposits. This can be a loan payment or it can be a regular deposit to savings.

Future Value, (FV)

The future value, (FV) is the value of the loan or investment in the future. The future value is the value of a savings account in the future, or it can be zero if you are calculating a loan. The amount borrowed for a loan is typically its present value, but its future value is zero when it is paid off.

Future value The ending balance in an account or the future worth of a present balance.

TIME VALUE OF MONEY EQUATIONS

Whether you use a financial calculator, a spread sheet, or present and future value tables, all time value of money calculations are based on the following equations:

- Future Value of a Single Deposit (lump sum)
- Present Value of a Single Deposit (lump sum)
- Future Value of a Series of Deposits (an annuity)
- Present Value of a Series of Payments (an annuity)

Table 1.1 lists the equations used in time value of money calculations.

TABLE 1.1 Table of Time Value Equations

	Lump Sum	Annuity
Future Value	$FV = PV(1+i)^n$	$FV = \left(\dfrac{(1+i)^n - 1}{i} \right)(PMT)$
Present Value	$PV = \dfrac{FV}{(1+i)^n}$	$PV = PMT\dfrac{(1-(1+i)^{-n})}{i}$

TIME VALUE OF MONEY CONVENTIONS

Before you can use the above equations properly, you need to understand the conventions used to determine when an amount is considered negative and when it is considered positive. The general convention is:

- Money that flows in is positive.
- Money that flows out is negative.

If you don't indicate the direction flow of money when using spread sheets and financial calculators you will get an incorrect answer.

Pick a checking account, your purse or wallet as a reference point. If you use your checking account as a reference point, what direction is the money flow when you make a deposit to your savings? The direction is out of your checking account, so a savings deposit is negative. You would indicate this in a spread sheet or financial calculator input by entering a negative number. What direction of money flow is a loan? When you take out a loan, the money flows into your checking account. Money flow into your checking account is positive. A consistent reference point will help you keep the direction of money flow correct. Remember money in is positive, money out is negative.

The term financial calculator here is used to indicate when you are using the time value of money keys on a calculator. If you enter the values according to the equations yourself (on a scientific or basic calculator) these conventions aren't used. These conventions are required when a calculator or spread sheet has the equations stored internally so you don't have to remember the equation.

Calculating Time Value of Money

Time value of money calculations are useful in a variety of applications. If you want to buy a new car and know your budget will only handle a $300 a month payment. You can use these calculations to determine how much you can afford to spend before you go shopping. This gives you a bargaining advantage. There are many applications for these equations, but before we work several examples let's look at how to solve a problem in general.

There are four basic steps that can be applied to solve any problem:

1. What is the question?
2. Write what you know.
3. Pick the proper equation.
4. Perform the calculation. (Solve the problem.)

These steps will help you solve problems consistently and accurately. Now let's look at our first example, how to solve for the future value of a single deposit.

FUTURE VALUE OF A SINGLE DEPOSIT

Compounded Annually
Let's use the problem in Exhibit 1.1. We had a single deposit of $100. The bank was paying 9 percent interest. How much is in the account at the end of 20 years?

What is the question?

- FV = ?

While it is convenient, and many times necessary, to compute finances on a calculator, it is important to understand how to use tables to calculate interest. Compound Interest Tables can be found in the Appendix of this text.

© Pressmaster, 2014, Shutterstock, Inc.

FINANCIAL CALCULATOR SOLUTION

Future Value of a Single Deposit Compounded Monthly

Set the payments per year key to 1. Set the contents of the time value of money keys as follows and then press the [FV] key for the solution.

20	9	−100	0	560.44
[N]	[I/Y]	[PV]	[PMT]	[FV]

The content of each key appears above the key, and the solution shows as underlined. You do not need to enter the 0 values if you have cleared all of the time value keys prior to beginning to entering the values. It is good practice to always clear the time value key memories before starting a new problem.

Write what you know:

- Single deposit (lump sum calculation)
- PV = $100 (out)
- i = 0.09 –remember use the decimal form
- N = 20 (years)

Pick the proper equation:

$$FV = PV(1 + i)^n$$

Solve the problem:

$$\$560.44 = \$100(1 + 0.09)^{20}$$

Did you notice the solution was slightly different from the answer in Exhibit 1.1? The account balance at the end of 20 years in the exhibit is $560.41, three cents less that the balance indicated by this calculation. In the exhibit, the bank computes the interest each year, rounds the amount off to the nearest cent, and adds it to the account. The calculator doesn't round until the end of the calculation. This results in a small difference in the answer.

Financial institutions do not keep track of any fraction of a cent you might lose (or gain) in a given year due to rounding, so the actual account balance and the result from a financial calculation may differ by a few cents in any one situation. For simplicity's sake, accept the financial calculation solution and realize it may be off by a small amount.

How to Use Financial Tables

Appendix A of your book has tables you can use to solve simple future value problems. The formula for use with a table is:

$$FV = PV \times FVF_{N,1\%} \qquad \text{Equation 1.2}$$

Where $FVF_{N,I\%}$ is the future value *factor* for N periods and I% rate from the table. A simpler version of the equation is:

$$FV = PV \times factor$$

Exhibit 1.4 shows you how to use the table in Appendix A.

To solve the same problem we just worked with the equations, find the factor that corresponds to 20 periods (years) at 9 percent interest. The factor value corresponding to 9 percent for 20 years is 5.6044. The factor in the table is the value of $1 if it were invested at 9 percent interest for 20 periods. Multiply that factor by your present value to get the answer. In our case we invested $100.

$$FV = PV \times factor$$

$$FV = \$100 \times 5.6044$$

$$= \$560.44$$

Compounded Monthly

The bank from Exhibit 1.1 decides to pay interest more often in order to attract more savings deposits. The bank's marketing department announces the bank will pay interest on savings accounts compounded monthly. What will the balance be after 20 years? We had a deposit of $100 and the bank is paying 9 percent interest compounded monthly.

What is the question?

- FV = ?

Write what you know:

- Single deposit (lump sum calculation)
- PV = $100 (out)
- i = 0.09/12 = 0.0075
- N = 20 (years) × 12 months = 240 months

Pick the proper equation:

$$FV = PV(1 + i)^n$$

EXHIBIT 1.4	PRESENT VALUE OF $1 PER PERIOD AT THE END OF EACH PERIOD (ORDINARY ANNUITY)

	Interest rate (i)		
Periods (n)	8%	9%	10%
19			
20		5.6044	
21			

FINANCIAL CALCULATOR SOLUTION

Future Value of a Single Deposit Compounded Monthly

Set your calculator to 12 payments per year, this step is important.

240	9	−100	0	600.92
[N]	[I/Y]	[PV]	[PMT]	[FV]

Note when using a financial calculator you enter the annual interest rate. With the tables, spread sheets and equations the interest rate must be adjusted to match the compounding frequency. This adjustment with a financial calculator is taken care of when you set the number of payments per year.

Solve the problem:

$$\$600.92 = \$100(1 + 0.0075)^{240}$$

Note the change from annual to monthly compounding yields an extra $40.48 in interest.

Compound Interest Tables Solution

Look up the factor that corresponds to 0.75 percent for 240 periods. The resulting factor is 6.0092.

$$FV = 100 \times 6.0092$$
$$= 600.92$$

PRESENT VALUE OF A SINGLE DEPOSIT

Nancy inherited $20,000 from her Great Aunt Mattie. Aunt Mattie left the money to Nancy to use as a down payment on her first home. Nancy is currently a sophomore in college. She plans to get a Master's Degree and hopes to graduate in six years. Nancy plans to work a full year after graduation before she purchases a home. Nancy wants to use the $20,000 her Aunt left her for a down payment, but she also needs extra cash now for books. How much should Nancy put into a CD now so it is worth $20,000 in seven years? The CD pays 4.25 percent interest and compounds interest quarterly.

What is the question?

- PV = ?

PRESENT VALUE OF A SINGLE DEPOSIT

Set the payments per year key to 4.

7	4.25	14,876.78	0	20,000
[N]	[I/Y]	[PV]	[PMT]	[FV]

Write what you know:

- Single deposit (lump sum calculation)
- FV = $20,000 (in)
- i = 0.0425/4 = 0.010625
- N = 7 (years)(4 quarters) = 28 periods

Pick the proper equation:

$$PV = \frac{FV}{(1+i)^n}$$

Solve the problem:

$$\$14,876.78 = \frac{\$20,000}{(1+0.010625)^{28}}$$

Nancy can deposit $14,876.78 now in a CD and when she is ready to buy a house she will have a $20,000 down payment. That leaves her with $5,123.22 to use now.

Future Value of a Series of Deposits (an Annuity)

Annuity A series of periodic payments.

Ordinary annuity An annuity in which payments occur at the end of each period.

Annuity due An annuity in which payments are at the beginning of each period.

A series of periodic payments is an annuity. An ordinary annuity is one in which payments occur at the end of each period. An annuity due exists when payments take place at the beginning of each period. For simplicity, this book only works with ordinary annuities. Financial calculators and spread sheets can handle both types of annuity, and the default modes are for an ordinary annuity. Let's look at an example to illustrate the future value of an (ordinary) annuity.

Tom receives an annual Christmas bonus of $1,000. He deposits his bonus each year in a savings account paying 6 percent interest compounded annually. How much does he have in his account in five years?

What is the question?

- FV = ?

Write what you know:

- Annuity (series of deposits)
- PV = $0
- i = 0.06
- N = 5 (years)
- PMT = $1,000 (out)

Pick the proper equation:

$$FV = \left(\frac{(1+i)^n - 1}{i} \right)(PMT)$$

Solve the problem:

$$\$5,637.09 = \left(\frac{(1+0.06)^5 - 1}{0.06} \right)(\$1,000)$$

FINANCIAL CALCULATOR SOLUTION

Future Value of a Series of Deposits (an Annuity)

Set your calculator to 1 payment per year.

5	6	0	−1000	5,637.09
[N]	[I/Y]	[PV]	[PMT]	[FV]

If your calculator displays "BEGIN" or some abbreviation such as "BEG" or "BGN," it is probably in the annuity due mode. If so, you should change it to the ordinary annuity mode.

Compound Interest Tables Solution

Use the future value of an annuity table in the Appendix A. The value corresponding to 6 percent for five years is 5.6371.

$$FVA = 1,000 \times 5.637$$

$$= 5,637.10$$

Note that there is a slight difference of 0.01 between the calculated solution and the solution provided from the tables. This difference is caused by the table's limit of four significant digits.

Present Value of a Series of Payments (an Annuity)

Present value of an annuity is often used to calculate how much you can afford to purchase when you know what you can afford as a payment. Let's look at an example.

Roman wants to upgrade his used car and take advantage of the "cash for clunkers" program. He lives at home and works part time. He knows he can afford a payment of $300 per month, but he wants to know how much he can afford to pay for a car. His bank is offering a four-year loan at 5.25 percent.

Let's help him figure out how much he can pay for a car.

What is the question?

- PV = ?

Write what you know:

- Annuity (series of deposits)
- FV = $0 since he wants to pay off the loan, his FV is zero
- i = 0.0525/12 = 0.004375
- N = 4 (years)(12 months) = 48
- PMT = $300 (out)

Pick the proper equation:

$$PV = PMNT \frac{(1-(1+i)^{-n})}{i}$$

Solve the problem:

$$\$12{,}963.04 = \$300 \frac{(1-(1+0.004375)^{-48})}{0.004375}$$

Roman can afford to buy a car priced in the $13,000 range and use the $4,500 from the "cash for clunkers" program for other expenses or he can afford a car for $17,500.

The present value of an annuity equation can also be used to determine what your payment will be on a loan. Let's look at another example.

FINANCIAL CALCULATOR SOLUTION

Present Value of a Series of Payments

Set your calculator to 12 payments per year. He will have 48 payments over the four years.

48	5.25	12,963.040	−300	0
[N]	[I/Y]	[PV]	[PMT]	[FV]

Karen is a friend of Roman's and now she wants to take advantage of the cash for clunkers program. She found a great little car for $24,000 and she wants to know what her payment would be. She plans to get a six-year loan at 6 percent. She doesn't want to use the $4,500 toward the car; she wants to use it to take a trip for spring break.

Let's help her figure out how much her payment will be.

What is the question?

- PMT = ?

Write what you know:

- Annuity (series of payments)
- FV = $0 since she wants to pay off the loan, her FV is zero
- i = 0.06/12 = 0.005
- N = 6 (years)(12 months) = 72
- PV = $24,000 (in) this is her loan amount

Pick the proper equation:

$$PV = PMNT \frac{\left(1-(1+i)^{-n}\right)}{i}$$

This is the right equation, but we need to rearrange it so we can solve for the payment.

$$PV\left(\frac{i}{1-\left[(1+i)^{-n}\right]}\right) = PMT$$

Solve the problem:

Now that we have it arranged to solve for payment we can use it finish our problem.

$$\$24,000\left(\frac{0.005}{1-\left[(1+0.005)^{-72}\right]}\right) = \$397.75$$

FINANCIAL CALCULATOR SOLUTION

Present Value of a Series of Payments

Set your calculator to 12 payments per year. He will have 48 payments over the four years.

72	6	24,000	397.75	0
[N]	[I/Y]	[PV]	[PMT]	[FV]

Solutions with Excel

Spread sheets are a great place to create your own financial plan. You can use one "book" to store all your financial statements and calculations. In the next chapter you will learn how to create goals, balance sheets, cash flow statements and a budget. This book will demonstrate the use of Excel, but any spread sheet software you use will do the same task. Using a spread sheet to calculate future and present values will make setting accurate goals easier. You can easily calculate how much to budget for each goal you set, and link the goals to your budget.

Excel uses the same input as the equations, the main difference between the equations in this chapter and Excel are the names used for the variables. Table 1.2 shows the nomenclature Excel uses.

TABLE 1.2 Excel Table

Name	Equations	Excel
Number of Periods	N	Nper
Interest rate	i	rate
Present Value	PV	PV
Future Value	FV	FV
Payment	PMT	PMT

- N becomes Nper
- i becomes rate.
- The present value, future value and payment variables stay the same.

To solve a problem in Excel, use the function (fx) tool. A dialogue box will open and you will select the function for the unknown. In our examples we wrote the unknown under the heading "What is the question?" So if you want to find the present value you select "PV" from the list in the dialogue box.

Each function has a brief description displayed in the lower portion of the box. The description explains what the function does and lists the variables needed for the calculation. Highlight the function and the description will be displayed.

Select the function by clicking the "OK" button. Once you select a function another dialogue box will open, this is where you will enter your values. The second dialogue box will list all the variables you need to solve the problem. Type in the information and hit enter. Excel will calculate both ordinary annuities and annuities due. It defaults to ordinary annuities. You tell Excel which you want to calculate in the dialogue box where you enter the variables. The last variable listed in that dialogue box will be "type", its asking which type of annuity you want to calculate. A zero is entered for an ordinary annuity and a 1 is entered for an annuity due. If you enter nothing it will default to an ordinary annuity. You can ignore this input box unless you want to calculate an annuity due, then you would enter a 1.

PROBLEMS SOLVED IN EXCEL

Let's use the previous examples and solve them in Excel.

Future Value of a Single Deposit

You deposit $100 in an account paying 9 percent interest, compounded monthly. How much is in the account at the end of 20 years?

What is the question?

- Select FV from the list in the f_x dialogue box

Enter what you know:

- rate = "0.09/12" Excel displays 0.0075 to the left of the entry box
- NPER = "20*12" Excel displays 240 to the left of the entry box
- PMT = "0" zero, because it is a single deposit
- PV = "-100" (out)
- Type = you don't need to make an entry

The answer will be displayed at the bottom of the dialogue box, "600.9151524".
Hit enter:

$600.92

Excel will place the answer (formatted in currency) in the cell that was selected
when you opened the function dialogue box.

Present Value of a Single Deposit
Nancy wants to use the $20,000 her aunt left her for a down payment, but she
also needs extra cash now for books. How much should Nancy put into a CD
now, so it is worth $20,000 in seven years? The CD pays 4.25 percent interest
and compounds interest quarterly.
What is the question?

- Select PV from the list in the f_x dialogue box

Write what you know:

- rate = "0.0425/4" Excel displays 0.010625 to the left of the entry box
- NPER = "7*4" Excel displays 28 to the left of the entry box
- PMT = "0" zero, because it is a single deposit
- FV = "20,000" (in, since she will withdraw it in the future)
- Type = you don't need to make an entry

Hit enter:

- $14,876.78

Nancy has $5,123.22 to use now.

Future Value of a Series of Deposits (an Annuity)
Tom deposits $1,000 each year in a savings account paying 6 percent interest
compounded annually. How much does he have in five years?
What is the question?

- Select FV from the list in the f_x dialogue box

Write what you know:

- rate = ".06" Excel displays 0.06 to the left of the entry box
- NPER = "5" Excel displays 5 to the left of the entry box
- PMT = "−1000" Excel displays −1,000 to the left of the entry box
- PV = "0" (his beginning balance)
- Type = you don't need to make an entry

Hit enter:

- $5,637.09

Present Value of a Series of Payments (an Annuity)

Roman can afford a payment of $300 per month, but he wants to know how much he can afford to pay for a car. His bank is offering a four-year loan at 5.25 percent. How much can he afford to borrow?

What is the question?

- Select PV from the list in the f_x dialogue box

Write what you know:

- rate = ".0525/12" Excel displays 0.004375 to the left of the entry box
- NPER = "4*12" Excel displays 48 to the left of the entry box
- PMT = "−300" Excel displays −300 to the left of the entry box
- FV = "0" (the balance when he pays the loan off)
- Type = you don't need to make an entry

Hit enter:

- $12,963.04

Roman can afford a loan in the $13,000 range.

What Will My Payment Be?

Karen wants to buy a car for $24,000. She plans to get a six-year loan at 6 percent. What will her payment be?

What is the question?

- Select PMT from the list in the f_x dialogue box

Write what you know:

- rate = ".06/12" Excel displays 0.005 to the left of the entry box
- NPER = "6*12" Excel displays 72 to the left of the entry box
- PV = "24000" Excel displays 24,000 to the left of the entry box
- FV = "0" (the balance when she pays the loan off)
- Type = you don't need to make an entry

Hit enter:

- $397.75

Why Does Money Have a Time Value?

There are two main reasons money has a value over time:

1. The opportunity cost of money
2. The risks of holding (or not holding) money

THE OPPORTUNITY COST OF MONEY

Opportunity cost The value of foregoing the opportunity to have a given good, service, or activity.

An opportunity cost is the value of foregoing the opportunity to have a given good, service, or activity. For example, suppose you have two alternatives for this afternoon. You could take a nap or you could work on your project for sociology class. Taking a nap has a certain appeal, but there is a cost of doing so. The opportunity cost of taking the nap is the progress you don't make on your sociology project.

The opportunity cost of money is the gain you would receive if you put the money to a different use. Suppose you won $1,000 with your college essay in a competition sponsored by a local civic club. The club offers you the $1,000 cash today, or you can wait a year to collect your money. Ask yourself this question: "Would I rather have $1,000 immediately or $1,000 a year from now?" Most people would prefer the $1,000 today, because money now is worth more than the same amount later.

The opportunity cost of waiting a year to collect the prize is equal to what you could earn by investing the $1,000 for a year. There are many alternative investments you could choose. For estimating the opportunity cost of money, we usually choose a safe and easily identifiable investment such as a savings account. If the bank offers 5 percent interest on a savings account, the $1,000 deposited now would grow to $1,050 at the end of the year. The opportunity cost of not taking the winnings is $50.

RISKS OF HOLDING (OR NOT HOLDING) MONEY

What if the civic organization offered to pay you $1,000 now or $1,050 a year from now?

In addition to opportunity cost, there is a risk of not collecting the $1,000 prize money now. The civic organization might not be in the greatest financial condition. What happens if they spend all of their money on projects over the next year and can't raise additional funds? The organization might just fold, and you would lose your $1,000 prize. The risk might be small, but you should consider the risk before you decided to take the future payment. If you allow someone else to use your money, you are an investor. You should get paid for the time value of your money.

SUMMARY

There is a "time value" of money that represents the opportunity cost of money and the risk of holding money. Inflation decreases the buying power of money and interest increases the accumulation of money. Interest on the original principal for one period is simple interest. Interest paid on previous interest earnings is compounded interest.

There are five variables used in the time value of money equations:

1. N the number of periods
2. I the interest rate
3. PV the present value
4. FV the future value
5. PMT the payment.

A single deposit or payment is a lump sum. A series of deposits or payments is an annuity. Time value of money calculations are simplified by the use of tables, calculators and spread sheets. The method you use to solve the problem is not as important as being able to identify and use the concepts for wise financial planning.

PROBLEMS

1. You deposit $800 in a savings account that pays 2 percent interest. What is the balance in your account at the end of one year?

2. Chris deposits $3,000 in a savings account that pays 2 percent, compounded annually. Calculate the interest he is paid for **each** of the three years.

3. Tammy deposits $4,000 in a savings account that pays 2 percent interest, compounded quarterly. What is her balance at the end of 20 years?

4. Lynn invests $250 a month in a mutual fund with an average yearly return of 11 percent. What is Lynn's balance in 7 years?

5. Emma won $150,000 in the lottery. She wants to have $300,000 in 15 years. How much does she need to invest today at 10 percent interest, compounded monthly, to reach her goal?

6. Joe saves $500 per year. He puts his money in a credit union account that yields 1 percent interest, compounded annually. What is Joe's balance at the end of 10 years?

7. Katie deposits $600 a year at 2 percent, compounded monthly. What is her balance after 10 years? (Hint: Divide her deposit into monthly deposits.)

8. Rick borrows $20,000 from his credit union. He chooses a 6-year loan at 8 percent. What is his monthly payment?

9. Amy wants to pay cash in six years for a $45,000 new car. Her savings account pays 3 percent, compounded quarterly. She wants to have her savings taken out of her check automatically. She gets paid on the 1st and 15th of every month. How much is her paycheck deduction? (Hint: Calculate her quarterly savings first; then covert that into a bi-monthly deposit.)

10. Michael puts $100 in a CD for his newborn daughter. The CD pays 3 percent compounded monthly. What is the CD worth on her daughter's 21st birthday?

11. Mae opened a new savings account with $1,500. She faithfully deposited $200 per month into the account for 10 years. The account paid 5 percent, compounded quarterly. What is the balance in Mae's account at the end of the 10 years? (Hint: Convert her $200 per month deposit into quarterly deposits.)

12. Ruth's employer contributes $100 a month to her retirement plan. It yields an average yearly return of 10 percent. How much is in the account when Ruth receives her 20-year service pin? (Hint: Compound monthly.)

13. Shane put $500 in a 20-year savings bond that yields 4 percent. What is his savings bond worth at the end of 20 years?

14. Paul borrows $3,000 for two years. The finance company charges him 10 percent interest. What is his monthly loan payment?

15. Kelly plans to take a cruise in two years. The cruise costs $4,000. How much should Kelly save each month? Her account pays 1 percent interest compounded quarterly. If Kelly failed to save, how much would her payment be on a 2-year loan at 6 percent?

16. Kim contributes $300 per month to her retirement account. In addition, she deposits her $5,000 year-end bonus to the account. Kim receives an average return of 10 percent. What is her balance in 25 years? (Hint: Break this problem into two parts. The $300 compounded monthly and the $5,000 compounded annually. Then add the two figures together)

ADDITIONAL HELP   CHAPTER 1

Using a Financial Calculator

Excellent financial calculators are available for a modest cost of $25 to $35, and more expensive ones are available that allow users to solve even more complicated financial problems. For this text, a financial calculator with the five basic keys for simple time value calculations is sufficient.

The instructions presented here are generic for a number of different calculator models. Each different manufacturer and often each different model for a given manufacturer has instructions specific to its calculators. Instructions for time value of money computations are no exception. It would be impossible to detail the steps that each different model uses.

While there is no substitute for being familiar with your own calculator and having its instruction manual handy, the use of the five basic time value keys is sufficiently consistent across brands and models to allow presentation of generic instructions for these keys that should be useful for all financial calculators. If you are interested in becoming proficient with financial computation, you should learn how to use all of the financial functions available on your particular model.

The five time value of money keys on financial calculators and the symbols used for them in this book are:

The number of periods: [N]

The interest rate per year: [I/Y]

The present value: [PV]

The payment: [PMT]

The future value: [FV]

To solve time value of money (compound interest) problems, you enter values for any four of the keys, and the calculator then solves for the value of the remaining fifth key. (Sometimes you only enter values for three of the keys, assuming that the fourth key has a value of zero.)

THE NUMBER OF PERIODS KEY

This key represents the number of periods for the calculation. For example, for a problem with four years of annual payments or compounding, you would enter 4 with the [N] key. For a problem with four years of monthly compounding, you need to remember that the compounding period is a month. There are 48 months in four years, so you would enter 48 with the [N] key by taking the following steps:

1. press 48
2. press [N]

THE INTEREST RATE KEY

The [I/Y] key holds the interest rate expressed as a percent. When 6 percent is the stated annual interest rate, use the [I/Y] key with the following key sequence:

1. press 6
2. press [I/Y]

THE PRESENT VALUE KEY

Present value The beginning balance or the present worth of a future balance.

The beginning value, balance, or principal of an investment or sum of money is the present value. Sometimes this will be called the time period zero value. When dealing with the present value key [PV] and the next two keys, both of which deal with amounts, we have to identify the "direction" of the amount.

The direction tells us whether the cash flow is positive (+, or inflow) or negative (-, or outflow). To correctly identify the direction, consider which way the cash is flowing in relation to you. If you are setting up a savings account, you are paying the money into the account. It is a cash outflow for you (but it is an inflow to the account), so you must be sure to enter the number and include the "-" sign.

For example, you deposit $500 into a savings account. To record that transaction on the calculator, follow this sequence:

1. press 500
2. press the positive/negative key [+/-] to change the 500 from a positive to a negative number
3. press [PV]

If you withdraw $500 from your savings account, you would enter the $500 cash inflow as:

1. press 500
2. press [PV]

THE PAYMENT KEY

Up to this point, we have discussed the simple time value situation of only a beginning and ending sum of money. In some situations there are additional payments or withdrawals between the beginning and the end time. This is where the payments key [PMT] applies.

If you want to analyze the situation in which someone deposits $500 into an account and then continues to deposit $500 at the end of each year for the next four years, you would record the annual payments using the [PMT] as follows:

1. press 500
2. press [+/-], (remember, this is a cash outflow, so the payment has to be entered as negative)
3. press [PMT]

Suppose that you are receiving a payment of $300 per year for the next 12 years. Since you are receiving money, this is a cash inflow (positive) to you. You would enter these into your calculator as follows:

1. press 300
2. press [PMT]

THE FUTURE VALUE KEY

The amount left at the end of the time in a time value problem the future value, and the [FV] key applies. As with the present value, we need to consider the direction of the cash flow. If we end up with a balance of money in an account, then we can withdraw that money and have a cash inflow. If, for example, you wanted to calculate how much money you would have to deposit each year so that you would have $500 in an account at the end of four years, you would enter the $500 future value with the following key sequence:

1. press 500
2. press [FV]

THE PAYMENTS PER YEAR KEY

There is one more important key for the time value of money computations, the payments per year key. This key sets the number of payments per year or the number of compounding periods per year. For annual compounding, set the value to one. The most common value other than one is 12 for monthly payments or compounding.

For accessing the payments per year, most calculators make use of the "shift" or "2ND" key. These keys allow users to access a secondary function attached to a key. For example, the primary function of the [FV] key is future value, but the secondary function for the key might be to clear all the time value memory in the calculator as it is for the Texas Instruments brand of financial calculators.

The payments per year key may have a secondary function label of [P/Y] or [P/YR]. For example, suppose that you want to set the calculator to compute monthly car loan payments. On the Hewlett-Packard financial calculator, press the following key sequence:

1. press 12
2. press "shift"
3. press [P/YR]

For a Texas Instruments calculator, the sequence is:

1. press [2ND]
2. press [P/Y]
3. press 12
4. press [ENTER]

Always be sure that the payments-per-year key is set to the appropriate number. It is a good habit to keep the key set to one and change it only when using other compounding periods. Making time value of money calculations with the number of payments per year set to the wrong number is one of the most common sources of errors in computations.

Some calculator users never change the payments per year from one. They account for compounding by adjusting the interest rate per period and the number of periods before they input these numbers in a process similar to the adjustment explained for using compound interest tables.

COMPUTING THE ANSWER

Once you have entered all of the values you need for solving your present value problem, you instruct your calculator to compute the answer by pressing the key for which you need the answer. For Texas Instruments calculators, you must press the compute key [CPT] before pressing the key to compute the answer. There is no need to press a compute key (indeed, there is no compute key) on a Hewlett-Packard calculator.

For example, suppose that you want to know the future balance in an account. You have entered the number of periods, the interest rate, and the present value. (There will be no payments, so you leave the payment at zero.) You then press the future value [FV] key (or [CPT] [FV] if you have a Texas Instruments calculator), and the answer appears in the calculator display.

USING PRESENT VALUE TABLES

The other method to compute time value of money problems (other than using long formulas or a computer spreadsheet) utilizes look-up factors in a table. These factors represent the "per dollar" values of the present and future values of $1.00 for various periods and interest rates.

Before the advent of calculators, bankers carried around books containing nothing but a huge set of time value of money tables. They used these tables to compute payments on loans. Today, the use of calculators makes computing time value and interest rate problems much easier and faster. In addition, calculators have the following advantages over the use of tables:

- Tables are restricted only to a given set of interest rate values.
- Tables are restricted only to a given set of periods.
- The decimal precision of tables is limited.

Because of the advantages that calculators offer, the answers you get using a financial calculator will be right on the money. The result using a table will be rounded only to the precision in the table.

Why, then, does this text demonstrate the use of tables for computing compound interest problems? The answer is that the use of tables is still common. You might find yourself wanting to analyze a compound interest situation but find you only have a simple four-function calculator and a finance book with some interest tables.

REVIEW QUESTIONS

1. Which of the following quotes do you think best describes the time value of money? "Time is Money" or "It Takes Money to Make Money". Explain your answer.

   _____

   _____

   _____

   _____

   _____

   _____

2. Would you rather borrow money that is compounded daily or monthly? Assume both loans have the same interest rate.

   _____

   _____

   _____

3. Would you rather invest money that is compounded quarterly or annually? Assume both accounts pay the same interest rate.

   _____

   _____

   _____

4. What is the interest rate for the magic penny example?

   _____

   _____

   _____

Financial Planning Overview

2

"Plans are nothing: planning is everything."

–Dwight D. Eisenhower

OBJECTIVES

- Set well-defined goals
- Determine your current financial position
- Prepare a budget
- Use creative solutions to stay on budget
- Select the right savings instrument for your goals

KEY TERMS

Assets
Balance sheet
Bonds
Cash flow statement
Certificates of deposit (CDs)
Current liabilities
Financial assets
Financial independence
FDIC

Individual retirement account (IRA)
Laddering
Liabilities
Liquidity
Long-term liabilities
Money markets
Money market accounts
Mutual funds
Net worth

Opportunity costs
Personal financial plan
Roth IRA
Savings account
Security
Stock
Tangible assets
Tax deferred
Tiered interest schedule

STRETCH
YOUR DOLLAR

RETHINK FAST FOOD

When we think of fast food we tend to think of the major hamburger, taco, and sandwich chains. It is so easy to stop on the way home from work or school to satisfy our hunger. Try rethinking fast food. The cost of eating out is more than the money spent. The cost also includes obesity and poor nutrition. Americans do not eat enough fruits and vegetables. When you are hungry and want to eat in a hurry, consider a can of vegetables. Try microwaving a bowl of green beans. The portion size of one can of vegetables is perfect for an individual meal. Frozen vegetables offer the advantage of preparing the portion size you want. Frozen vegetable bags can be easily shut with a twist tie and put back in the freezer.

Your personal financial situation will determine many things in your life. "Money can't buy happiness," but your financial health is an important part of your overall standard of living. We all have the same basic human needs for food, clothing, transportation, and shelter. Beyond that, our standard of living is determined by our lifestyle. Lifestyle choices include hobbies, travel, career, entertainment, vehicles and homes. Although shelter is a basic human need, our choice of a home is often a lifestyle choice. Lifestyle choices go beyond the basic needs and include choices that enrich our lives. The ability to afford a preferred lifestyle is financial independence.

Financial independence
The ability to afford a preferred lifestyle.

A good financial plan will help you achieve financial independence. A personal financial plan specifies your personal goals and details the activities to achieve those goals. It includes analyzing your income, expenses, liabilities and savings. There are two principal themes in all financial planning:

Personal financial plan
Your personal goals and the activities to achieve those goals.

1. Maximize your income and accumulate wealth.
2. Control your expenses.

These two themes go hand in hand. For example, when you minimize an expense, you increase your accumulated wealth. The overall purpose of the financial plan is to enable you to meet the following objectives:

- Spend appropriately.
- Save consistently.
- Invest wisely.

Record Keeping

Record keeping is an important part of good financial planning. An organized system of record keeping will help you stay organized. Critical documents need to be stored safely. Below are examples of common financial records:

- Bank reconciliation records
- Birth certificates
- Social security cards
- Insurance documents and claim forms

- Tax records
- Credit agreements
- Retirement account statements
- Warranty information
- Titles and deeds

Set up a filing system for your documents so you can stay organized and easily find your documents when they are needed. There are three main types of filing systems:

- Home files
- Electronic files
- Safety deposit boxes

Home files are the most common and are used to store paper copies of documents. You can use a filing cabinet, plastic storage box, or even a cardboard box. If you use only a home filing system, you may want to consider buying a firesafe box. A firesafe box will protect your documents in case of a fire. Passports, wills, and prenuptial agreements are examples of documents you would want to protect, because they are either time-consuming or impossible to replace.

Electronic filing systems store electronic documents on a computer, flash drive, or network. Many financial institutions, credit companies, and utilities offer online services, statements, and billing. Set up a filing system for these electronic documents.

Exhibit 2.1 shows an example filing system. You can use this one or modify it to fit your personal situation.

EXAMPLE FILE SYSTEM	EXHIBIT 2.1

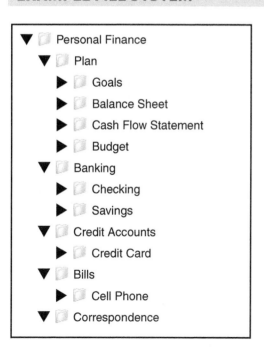

> ### TIP ON FILING
>
> Card board boxes that are used for 8.5 x 11 copy paper make excellent storage boxes for files. Hanging files will easily fit in them. Colleges use substantial amounts of paper in their copiers each year. Check with your department office to see if they will give you one of the boxes that copier paper comes in.

Safety deposit boxes are rented secure storage. They require two keys to open, the one you are issued when you rent the box and one held by the financial institution. Use a safety deposit box to store the same documents you would store in a firebox. They can also be used to store a variety of items including family heirlooms. In some circumstances the cost of safety deposit boxes are tax deductible. If you don't want to invest in a firesafe box, consider asking a parent or grandparent to store your items in a safety deposit box.

Records should generally be kept for two years. You don't need all your old records, but it is a good idea to keep a two-year record of your bank and credit accounts. There are some exceptions to this rule. Tax records need to be kept for seven years. Some records like birth certificates and social security cards need to be kept for life. Titles and deeds are kept as long as you own the property. Dispose of old records safely. Shred all documents that contain your personal and financial information to protect yourself against identity theft.

Creating a Financial Plan

Creating a financial plan is a critical step to achieve financial independence. It serves as a map to help you obtain your desires. If you decide you want a steak and a baked potato for dinner, how do you make that happen? Would you go to a restaurant? Would you go to the grocery store? Would you cook it yourself? If you choose to eat at a restaurant, which one would you choose? If you chose to cook, do you need anything other than the steak and potatoes at the grocery store? In this case a written plan isn't needed, but if you don't make these decisions and just get in the car and drive aimlessly, you may and may not arrive where you can get a steak and baked potato. You might end up at the post office instead. Knowing where you are going and how you intend to get there is a large part of arriving at the correct destination.

For most people managing our finances is not as easy as selecting where to eat dinner. The funny thing about money is it tends to disappear as fast as we earn it, unless we have a plan in place to save it. Creating a financial plan will help you achieve your goals. The financial planning process is broken into six steps:

1. Create a list of financial goals.
2. Analyze your current financial situation.
3. Create a budget.
4. Select appropriate savings vehicles.
5. Measure the performance of your plan.
6. Adjust the plan as necessary.

Using these steps you can create a personal financial plan that will guide you to financial independence.

STEP 1: CREATE A LIST OF FINANCIAL GOALS

What do you want in life? Would you like to retire early and play golf every day? Would you like to purchase your first home? Do you want to fund your children's college education? Whatever your desires are, saving is easier when you have clear goals. Goals motivate us to save. The development of a set of financial goals is critical to the planning process.

Approach the task of setting financial goals seriously. It takes some time to develop a good goal. Start with general ideas and then work to make a specific plan to achieve the desire. Start by asking yourself what you want and when you want to achieve it.

A good financial plan will include goals to be achieved in different time frames. A short-term goal is one you plan to achieve in one year or less. A long-term goal is one you plan to achieve in 10 or more years. Mid-term goals would fall somewhere in between a short-term and a long-term goal. The exact time definition of a short-term goal is not near as important as whether you have goals set to be achieved in varying time frames. You may have a goal to accomplish in 20 months rather than in under a year. This too is a reasonable time frame for a short-term goal. Regardless of how you define short term and long term, make sure you set goals for the near future, the next stage of your life, and for the distant future.

Brain Storm

A good way to begin setting financial goals is by brain storming. Brain storming is the process of generating ideas without censoring your thoughts. We censor our thoughts when we tell ourselves we can't afford that, or we won't be able to achieve that. We may also censor our thoughts through someone else's definition of success. It is important that your plan fits your lifestyle and will lead you to where you wish to be in life. To brain storm just get a pad of paper and a pen and write down any thoughts that come to mind. Don't censor your thoughts. Then go over your list of ideas and select the ones you would like to turn into goals.

Turn Desires into Measurable Goals

Once you use brain storming techniques to decide what you want, it is time to turn your desires into well-defined goals. A goal is more specific than a wish; it includes an action plan of how to obtain the desire. A well-defined goal is specific, measurable, action oriented, realistic, and includes a time frame. A good way to remember the criteria for a well-defined goal is the acronym SMART.

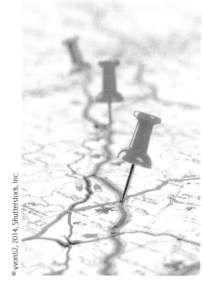

© yvon52, 2014, Shutterstock, Inc.

A solid financial plan acts as a roadmap for reaching your goals.

- Specific. Be as specific as you can. I want to save money is too general. I want to save money for a down payment on a home is better, but it can still be more specific. I will save $15,000 for a 10 percent down payment on a home that costs $150,000 is specific.

- Measurable. It's important to have goals you can measure. I want to save some money for a down payment is hard to measure. How much is some? Is 2 cents enough—obviously not. In the above example, we stated that we need $15,000 for a down payment. This is measurable. We can measure our progress. When we have $5,000, we have accumulated one-third of our goal.
- Action oriented. I will save $300 a month by having $150 per paycheck direct deposited in my savings account. This action tells how to save $15,000 for the down payment on a $150,000 home. This assumes you get paid twice a month.
- Realistic but challenging. If you are single and make $75,000 per year, a goal to save $100 per month is not a challenge. On the other hand, if you are married with two kids and have a household income of $50,000, a goal to save $10,000 per year is not realistic. Goals in the middle of this spectrum are best.
- Time-focused. Set a period of time to reach a goal. I will save $300 a month for 50 months to accumulate $15,000 for a down payment on a $150,000 home.

When you put all the pieces together, you have a well-defined goal. I will save $300 a month, by having $150 per pay period direct deposited into my savings account. I will save for 50 months to accumulate $15,000 for a 10 percent down payment on a $150,000 home.

You need a set of goals for a good financial plan. You can have short-term, intermediate, and long-term goals. Develop a series of goals to provide a set of milestones to reach. When developing your goals, think about what you would like in the next year or two. What you would like in the next stage of your life? Where would you like to be five years from now? When do you want to retire? How would you like to spend your retirement years?

| EXAMPLE 2.1 | Jade's Financial Goals |

Jade Rodell is a 21-year-old college student from Des Moines, Iowa. She still lives at home and she works part time at Java Cup. She started her financial plan in the spring semester of 2013. She plans to graduate with a B.A. in architecture in May 2015. She set the following goals for herself:

Short-Term Goals

1. Payoff my MasterCard balance of $456 in 3 months by paying $152 a month.
2. Pay Mom back the $800 I borrowed in 10 months by paying her $80 a month.

Mid-Term Goals

3. Accumulate $5,000 in my savings account by May 2015. The money will be used for moving expenses to get my own apartment after graduation. I will save for 26 months. I currently have $400 dollars in my account, so I need to save an additional $4,600. I need to save $177 a month.
4. Buy a home 2 years after I graduate. I will need to save $12,500 between 2015 and 2017 to pay for the down payment and closing costs. I plan to buy a small house

for about $150,000. I will put 5% down. I will save $521/month from my salary from my first full-time job after graduation.

Long-Term Goals

5. I plan to retire at 65. I would like to stay in the Midwest where I hope to someday own some acreage. When I begin working after college, I will take advantage of any company-sponsored pension plan or company match to a 401K. After I purchase a home in 2017, I will put the $521 a month in my Roth IRA. This will allow me to save the maximum current allowable amount in my Roth IRA.

Notice Jade's short-term goals are more specific than her long-term goals. Since she is still a college student, she doesn't know what her future income or expenses will be. Still, she set clear goals for the long term. Each year as she works toward her goals and revises them, she will be able to become more specific with her long-term goals. Even though her long-term goals don't set an exact amount for her 401K, she will be better prepared to make wise decisions when she first starts out on her own. Instead of spending the maximum amount she can afford on an apartment or buying a new car immediately, she will be thinking about her retirement and saving to buy a house. Her goals will help her avoid some of the common pitfalls of overspending in the first years of her career.   ■

Calculate Savings Amounts

Accurately calculating savings amounts will depend on how long you intend to save. With low interest rates and short-term goals you can simply divide the dollar amount by the number of months. With longer-term goals, compounding of interest will make a significant difference. To calculate projected retirement amounts use the time value of money equations in Chapter 1.

Jade's Projected Retirement Savings	EXAMPLE 2.2

Jade currently has a Roth IRA she started with $2,500 she had in a savings account when she graduated from high school. She has $1,500 in a money market account and $1,034 of it in a mutual fund. Her account pays 1.05% interest on the money market account and the mutual fund fluctuates with the stock market. Assume she can average 7% on the mutual fund for the next 4 years. How much will Jade's Roth IRA be worth when she can afford to start making contributions to it again?

Jade's future value of the $1500 in cash:

$$PV = \$1,500$$

$$i = 1.05\%$$

$$n = 4 \text{ years}$$

$$PV(1 + i)^n = FV$$

$$\$1,500(1 + 0.105)^4 = \$1,564$$

Jade's future value of $1,034 in mutual funds:

$$PV = \$1,034$$

$$i = 7\%$$

$$n = 4 \text{ years}$$

$$\$1,034(1 + .07)^4 = \$1,355.36$$

Jade's future value of her Roth IRA = $1,564 + $1,355.36 = $2,919.36

Now if Jade deposits $6,252 a year starting when she is 25, how much will she have in her Roth IRA when she is 60? Since Jade will have 35 years to save, she will invest in mutual funds. Use the historical stock market return rate of 10% annually.

Solution: Jade will make monthly deposits of ($6,252/12) = $521
She will make (35 years)(12 months) = 420 deposits
She will earn (10% annually)/(12 months) = 0.83% monthly i = 0.0083
Using the equation for a FV of a series of deposits.

$$FV = \left(\frac{(1+i)^n - 1}{i} \right) \text{(Periodic deposit amount)}$$

$$\$1,978,048.43 = \left(\frac{(1+.0083)^{420} - 1}{.0083} \right) (\$521)$$

If Jade's monthly deposits of $521 for 35 years grow to be $1,978,048.43, what is her total Roth IRA balance at that time? Remember she had $2,919.36 when she started making these additional deposits. Assume she decided to invest the whole $2,919.36 in mutual funds that earn a 10% return annually when she begins making her additional deposits.

Solution:

$$\$2,919.36(1 + .10)^{35} = \$82,041.13$$

Jade's Roth IRA is worth $1,978,048.43 + $82,041.13 = $2,060,089.55

If Jade decided the future values calculations weren't worth the time to calculate, she would have multiplied the $521 by 420 deposits. She would have calculated a savings of $218,820. She then would have added her $2,534. She would have calculated her total Roth IRA balance as $221,354, which is a miscalculation of approximately $1.8 million. ■

STEP 2: DETERMINE YOUR CURRENT FINANCIAL POSITION

Have you ever been lost? Have you ever used a map in the mall to find your favorite store? The mall directory lists the stores in the mall and shows a color-coded map of the stores. On the map there is a sticker that says, "You are here." Knowing where you are helps you map your path to where you want to be. Financial planning is no different. The first step in mapping a path to where you want to be is determining where you are. Setting goals in the last section was the process of determining where you want to be, now in this step you are going to find out where you are. The first step in determining how to get to your goals is to analyze your current financial situation so you know where you are. Personal financial statements (see Exhibit 2.2) are the tools we will use to determine your current financial situation.

PERSONAL FINANCIAL STATEMENTS   EXHIBIT 2.2

Budget

For the Month of

Cashflow statements

For the Month of Ending

Balance sheet for Name

as of date

Assets			
Liquid Assets			
Checking Account			
Savings Account			
Stocks			
Bonds			
	Total		Liquid Assets
Tangible Assets			
House			
Car 1			
Car 2			
Furniture			
Guns			
Electronics			
Jewelry			
Furs			
Collectibles			
Other			
	Total		Tangible Assets
Financial Assets			
401K			
IRA			
Roth IRA			
Pension			
Life Insurance (Cash Value)			
	Total		Financial Assets
	Total		Assets
Liabilities			
Current Liabilities			
Credit Card 1			
Credit Card 2			
Loan	Total		Current Liabilities
Long-term Liabilities			
Mortgage			
Car Loan			
Car Loan			
Student Loan			
	Total		Long-term Liabilities
	Total		Liabilities
Net Worth		0	
Net worth equals total assets – total liabilities			

Personal Financial Statements

Step 2 of the financial planning process is to analyze your current financial situation. An important part of this analysis is the creation of personal financial statements. Personal financial statements list in detail your income, expenses, assets, and liabilities. A cash flow statement lists your income and expenses, while a balance sheet lists your assets and liabilities.

Cash flow statement Lists your income and expenses.

Balance Sheet

The balance sheet lists your assets and liabilities on a specific date. The balance sheet is used to determine a person's net worth. Net worth equals total assets minus total liabilities. The date you write your balance sheet is the date listed on the balance sheet. It will say "Your name's balance sheet as of current date." The balance sheet is accurate on the day it is written. As you use your debit card or make a payment on your credit card, you change the amounts you own or owe. Think of a balance sheet like a snapshot. When you take a picture of a child, you capture all the growth to that moment. The next day the picture still resembles the child, but subtle changes have taken place since the picture was taken. Balance sheets capture the net worth of a person at a given moment (see Exhibit 2.3). The next day the balance sheet will still resemble the person's financial situation, but subtle changes will have occurred.

Balance sheet Lists your assets and liabilities on a specific date.

EXHIBIT 2.3	BALANCE SHEET

Balance sheet for Jade Rodell			as of 2-Mar-2013
Assets			
Cash Assets			
Checking Account	$230.00		
Savings Account	$400.00		
	Total	$630.00	Cash Assets
Property			
2006 Nissan Sentra	$10,615.00		
Personal Items	$1,500.00		
	Total	$12,115.00	Property
Investments			
Roth IRA - C.U.			
Mutual Fund	$1,034.00		
Cash	$1,500.00		
	Total	$2,534.00	Investments
	Total	$15,279.00	Assets
Liabilities			
Current Liabilities			
Master Card	$456.00		
Mom	$800.00		
	Total	$1,256.00	Current Liabilities
Long-term Liabilities			
Car Loan-C.U.	$9,680.00		
Student Loan	$11,500.00		
	Total	$21,180.00	Long-term Liabilities
	Total	$22,436.00	Liabilities
Net Worth		($7,157.00)	
Net worth equals total assets – total liabilities			

Your possessions are your personal assets. Your debts are your personal liabilities. Exhibit 2.3, illustrates a personal balance sheet. A balance sheet is broken into three main parts, assets, liabilities and net worth. The balance sheet lists the assets at the top, liabilities in the middle and net worth at the bottom of the sheet. The assets and liabilities sections of a balance sheet are then further divided into sub-sections.

Assets

Assets include everything you own with value. Common assets are checking or savings accounts, stocks, bonds, mutual fund investments, automobiles, homes, and household items. Assets are commonly broken into two main categories tangible assets and financial assets. Tangible assets are those you can touch—they have a physical form. Examples of tangible assets are your automobile, home, computer, stereo, and cash in your pocket. Financial assets are typically represented by a written document. Financial assets are an interest in something of value. Examples of financial assets are stocks, bank statements showing your balance in an account, bonds, or the amount your brother owes you for a loan.

Tangible assets are less liquid than financial assets. Liquidity is the ability to turn an asset into cash quickly at the current market value. Stocks are liquid assets and can be sold and converted to cash in a matter of minutes if not seconds. A home is not a liquid asset, because it typically takes three to six months or longer to sell a home and convert it to cash at the current market value.

Unlike business balance sheets that use standard accounting terminology, a personal balance sheet should be set up with headings that make sense to the individual. One person may use the "liquid asset" heading and another may feel more comfortable with the "cash" heading.

Notice in Becky's balance sheet she used the heading "cash," "property," and "investments," for her assets. She was specific about her automobile and listed it as a 2006 Nissan Sentra, but was general about her clothing, CDs, stereo, and computer, which she grouped together and called personal items. She used the generic balance sheet shown above, but customized it to fit her financial situation.

Every semester students ask the question, "What if I don't have any assets?" I always ask them how they would react if I took a sibling into their bedroom and told them they could have anything they wanted. You may not own much, but anything you own with a market value is an asset. You do not need to take an inventory of all of your belongings in order to total your assets. Your old shoes have some value to you, but have little market value. However, your entire wardrobe probably does have a market value. If you are a traditional college student, you can break your possessions into categories: clothing, CDs, collectibles. Estimate how much you could earn if you sold all your clothing at a garage sale. How much would you make if you sold all your DVDs? If you are a nontraditional student who owns a home and one or two cars, you may not want to break out your household and personal items into different categories. Adjust the balance sheet to fit your current financial situation. Use the examples of balance sheets given in this book and on the web as a guide, but personalize it to clearly reflect your current financial situation.

Assets Everything you own with value.

Tangible assets Assets you can touch—they have a physical form.

Financial assets Typically represented by a written document, an interest in something of value.

Liquidity The ability to turn an asset into cash quickly at the current market value.

If you need help estimating the value of your belongings, you can use Internet sources to find the value of many items. Goodwill lists values of common household and personal items (www.goodwillwm.org). *Kelley's Blue Book* (www.kbb.org) estimates the value of automobiles. To estimate the value of specialty items and collectables, try using eBay (www.ebay.com).

Liabilities

Liabilities Debt.

Liabilities are your debt. Liabilities are commonly divided into two categories:

1. Current liabilities
2. Long-term liabilities

Current liabilities Debts you expect to pay off within the next year.

Long-term liabilities Debts you expect to pay off more than one year from now.

Current liabilities are debts you expect to pay off within the next year. The most common current liabilities are credit card debts.

Long-term liabilities are debts you expect to pay off more than one year from now. Student loans, car loans, and home loans are the most common long-term liabilities. Car loans are typically financed for three to six years, while homes are typically financed for 15 to 30 years.

Liabilities are the debt or total amount owed, not the monthly payments. If you bought a home today for $200,000 and put 20 percent down, you would have a loan for $160,000. Your mortgage payment for a 5 percent, 30-year fixed loan would be about $860. Your liability would be the $160,000 you owe the bank. The asset would be the $200,000 market value of the home. The mortgage payment does not go on the balance sheet. The mortgage payment will go on the cash flow statement as an expense.

Net Worth

Net worth The value of your total assets minus the value of your total liabilities.

The purpose of calculating your assets and liabilities is to find your current net worth. Your net worth is the value of your total assets minus the value of your total liabilities.

The net worth amount represents the amount of your current wealth and can be either positive or negative. A negative net worth means that you owe more than you own. A new graduate who had to borrow to pay for her college education may graduate from college with a negative net worth. However, the new graduate has just increased her earning power substantially by obtaining an education. Typically, though, a negative net worth is a sign of poor financial decisions. Whether the negative net worth is the result of a wise investment in education or excessive use of credit, the goal is the same: Increase net worth over time. A balance sheet should be updated at least once a year. The goal is to determine what your net worth is and to increase your net worth from year to year.

Cash Flow Statement

The cash flow statement shows your income and expenses over a period of time, typically a month (see Exhibit 2.4). You can write a cash flow statement for any period of time: a day, a week, a year, but a month is the most common time frame for a personal cash flow statement. At the top of the cash flow statement, it typically says "For the month ending," followed by a date. The cash flow statement can be written for the month ending January 31st, which

CASH FLOW STATEMENT

EXHIBIT 2.4

Jade Rodell's Cash Flow Statement			
For the Month Ending			as of 31-Mar-2013
Income			
Java Cup	$758.00		
Total	$758.00		Income
Expenses			
Fixed Expenses			
Nissan Payment	$222.49		
Master Card	$15.00		
Cell Phone	$49.02		
	$286.51		
Total			Fixed Expenses
Variable Expenses			
Gas	$174.28		
Movies	$78.00		
Restaurants	$184.69		
Total	$436.97		Variable Expenses
Total	$723.48		Expenses
Net Income		$34.52	
Net Income = Total Income – Total Expenses			

obviously means for January 1st–31st. The cash flow statement can also be written for the month ending March 15th, which means it covers the period from February 16th to March 15th.

Notice the preceding cash flow statement is divided into two main categories—income and expenses. The cash flow statement (sometimes called an income statement) was so named because it records your cash flows in and out. Regardless of what you call it, it records your income at the top followed by your expenses. At the bottom of the statement you calculate your net cash flow by subtracting your total monthly expenses from your total monthly income. A positive net income is the amount saved for the month. A negative net income indicates the amount of increased debt for the month.

Income

For most people, their paycheck is their largest source of income. Other sources of income are interest on savings accounts, unemployment benefits, child support, and alimony. You should record all of your monthly net income in this portion of the cash flow statement. Net income is your gross income minus taxes and other paycheck deductions for insurance or retirement accounts. Although your paycheck may have deductions, your other income may not. Record the dollar amount of the payments you receive. The cash flow statement is a look back at the month that just ended in terms of actual amounts received, not estimated amounts.

What will you do to reach your financial goals? It's not enough to just dream about your goals, you have to write them out to see them and become accountable for them.

Expenses

Expenses are broken into two categories—fixed expenses and variable expenses. Fixed expenses are expenses that don't change from month to month. Mortgage payments and car loan payments are examples of fixed expenses. Variable expenses are expenses that vary in amount from month to month. Food expenditures and utility bills are examples of common variable expenses. However, if you pay your electric bill on a cost average basis, then it would be a fixed expense. If you pay your electric bill based on the usage per month, then it would be a variable expense.

Exhibit 2.4 shows an example cash flow statement. Notice the example breaks variable expenses into multiple categories: groceries, personal items, and household maintenance. This breakdown may work well for you; if it does, use it. However, if you purchase your groceries, personal items, and most of your household maintenance items in the same discount store, breaking these items into three categories may not work well for you. It is easiest to record and monitor your spending if you create categories that allow you record all items on one receipt under the same category.

Net Cash Flow

Net cash flows are your income minus expenses. This amount can be positive, negative, or zero. A positive net cash flow is an amount saved for the month and would increase your net worth. A negative net cash flow indicates you spent more than you earned. The only way to do this is to either increase your debt or reduce your savings, both of which will decrease your net worth. A zero net cash flow means you either budgeted precisely or you allocated your savings under your fixed expenses. Another way to have a zero net cash flow would be to allocate excess cash to pay down debt.

A negative net cash flow typically indicates a person is living beyond his means and needs to adjust his spending habits. There are exceptions to this, and occasionally everyone will experience a month with a negative net cash flow. It is wise to have an emergency fund to cover expenses during these times. Sometimes it is as simple as a major repair on an automobile, and the net negative cash flow may only be a few hundred dollars for one month. Other times it may be a prolonged period of being out of work with a net negative cash flow of $1,000 or more for more than one month. Everyone should have an emergency fund to cover at least two months' worth of living expenses. However, people who work in seasonal jobs, or for companies who tend to have frequent layoffs, may want to have an emergency fund to cover expenses for four to six months.

STEP 3: CREATE A BUDGET

In Step 1 you determined where you want to go. In Step 2, you found out where you are. In Step 3 you will plan how to get there. A budget is similar to a cash flow statement. The two look alike, but they look in opposite directions. A cash flow statement is a look back at what you earned and spent last month. A budget is an estimate of what you will earn and spend next month.

Jade's Budget Goals	**EXAMPLE 2.3**

Jade Rodell recorded her income and expenses for March 2013. She calculated her net cash flow and realized she spent more than she made. To create a budget for April, Jade used March's cash flow statement and her top 3 goals.

- Payoff my MasterCard balance of $456 in 3 months by paying $152 a month.
- Pay Mom back the $800 I borrowed in 10 months by paying her $80 a month.
- Accumulate $5,000 in my savings account by May 2015. The money will be used for moving expenses to get my own apartment after graduation. I will save for 26 months. I currently have $400 dollars in my account, so I need to save an additional $4,600. I need to save $177 a month.

Last month Jade paid only the minimum payment on her credit card. She didn't make a payment to her mom. For her budget she increased her MasterCard payment to $152 and added an $80 payment to her mom.

Next she looked at variable expenses. She went to the movies every weekend last month. Each time she paid $9.50 for her movie ticket and $10 for a drink and popcorn. Jade decided to cut down to one trip to the movies next month. She budgeted $19.50 for this item. Last month Jade also spent several evenings a week riding around in her car with her friends. Each time they stopped for either fast food. Jade decided to cut back on the leisure activity also. She figured she wasted at least one tank of gas. She adjusted her gas budget to $125 and cut her restaurant budget to $80. Jade then added $100 for savings to her variable expenses. With her earnings from Java Cup she didn't have enough income to cover her expenses and include all her goals.

She could adjust her goals, but she decided they were the most important expenditures to her. She considered cutting movies and restaurants completely from her budget, but knew she wouldn't want to stick to such a tight budget. Last month Jade turned down several offers to babysit for her neighbor. She decided to accept those offers this month. Babysitting would earn extra income and cut down on her available free time to drive around with friends. Jade added $80 to her estimated income. This created a surplus of $9.99. She adjusted her estimated savings to 109.99. ■

The best way to make a budget is to start with last month's cash flow statement and your written goals. Add a line item for each of your goals and record the dollar amount per month. If you have a goal of saving $50 a month to build an emergency fund, then add "Savings for emergency fund" as a fixed expense. Once you add in your goals, recalculate your net income. If your net income is still positive or zero you can afford your current goals. If your net income is now negative, you need to readjust your goals and/or your spending.

Don't think of a budget like a financial diet. A budget is a tool used to control spending. When you control spending, you increase savings. Most excessive spending is wasted on items we don't remember buying. In a *Sex and the City* episode, Carrie was wondering where all her money went. She couldn't figure it out. Then Miranda reminds her she bought 100 pairs of Manolo Blahnik shoes for $400 a pair. That is $40,000! Carrie loves shoes, but do you think she would have budgeted $40,000 for them? We all spend money on unnecessary items, be it clothes, videogames, concerts, or green fees. A budget helps us minimize those fluff expenses. The two most common areas for excessive spending are restaurants and leisure activities. When you waste less on frivolous items, you retain more money for your goals.

EXHIBIT 2.5	JADE'S APRIL BUDGET

Budget			Jade Rodell	
	For the Month of		April, 2013	
Income				
Java Cup	$758.00			
Babysitting	$80.00			Income
Total	$838.00			
Expenses				
Fixed Expenses				
Nissan Payment	$222.49			
MasterCard	$152.00			
Cell Phone	$49.02			
Mom	$80.00			
	$503.51			
Total				Fixed Expenses
Variable Expenses				
Gas	$125.00			
Movies	$19.50			
Resturants	$80.00			
Savings	$109.99			
Total	$334.49			Variable Expenses
Total	$838.00			Expenses
Surplus/Deficit		$0.00		
Surplus/Deficit = Total income – Total expenses				

Characteristics of a Good Budget

A good budget accurately portrays your current financial situation and wisely plans for future expenditures. The following are some characteristics of good budgets:

- Well-planned. A good budget takes some time and thought to create. Start by adding your goals to your cash flow statement. Adjust the numbers as needed to make the budget work. Consider any changes you know would affect the budget. For example, if you just moved into your first apartment, you need to add several new expenses that weren't recorded on last month's cash flow statement.
- Practical. If you make the budget too tight, you won't stick to it. It is often tempting when adjusting the numbers to cut leisure to zero. Although it looks good on paper, it isn't practical. Allow yourself at least one leisure or fun expense a month. Pick your leisure activity with care and make it something that will serve you well as a reward for staying on your budget. Know what you intend to do and estimate that cost.
- Open to the family. The family budget should not be a secret. Everyone needs to understand the family goals. It is easier for everyone to make sacrifices when they know what reward they will receive for the effort.
- Flexible. A good budget needs to change as life's circumstances change.

> ### A TIP ON SAVING
>
> Have your budgeted savings direct deposited to a savings or money market account. You can allocate either a flat amount to go to your savings or you can allocate a percentage of your pay be direct deposited to your savings account.

Making a Budget Work

Carrie in *Sex and the City* has more expendable cash than most people. Most of us could not spend $40,000 a year on our favorite past time. The hardest part about budgeting is making a tight budget work. When you are well established and can afford a generous leisure budget, it is much easier. However, in the college years and the first years of raising a family, staying on a budget while providing for all of your needs can be difficult. There are many ways to reduce the expenses of day-to-day living. Convenience foods cost more, so preparing your food from basic ingredients is a good way to cut down on food costs. However, preparing your meals from scratch takes more time than warming up a prepackaged meal. The trade-off of cutting costs versus saving time is called an opportunity cost.

Opportunity Costs

Opportunity costs are the consequences of our choices. If we choose to save time and eat out, the price difference between the restaurant and home-cooked meal is the cost of our choice. If we choose to comparison shop to find the best price, the cost of our time is the price we pay for the savings. Each time we

Opportunity costs The consequences of choices.

make a choice, we also forgo its alternative choices. These alternative choices are the opportunity cost we pay for the choice we make. If we choose to save for a future purchase, we pay the price of not gratifying our immediate desires to spend the money now.

Most cost-saving methods to stretch your monthly budget will come with the opportunity cost of time. The following are a few suggestions for ways to stretch your budget dollars.

Buy Used

Buying a gently used item can save you substantial cash outlays. An automobile that is two years old will hold its value longer than a brand new car. When you buy a brand new car, you pay the new price. The moment you drive that new car off the dealer's lot, it is a used vehicle and its price depreciates by 10 percent. A car depreciates most rapidly in the first two years. Buying a used vehicle that is two years old with low mileage will stretch your car-buying power.

Furniture and appliances also depreciate substantially from new to used prices. Buying used furniture and appliances will help stretch your budget. Craig's list is a web site that list items for sale. Sometimes you can even find free items on Craig's list (http://www.craigslist.org/about/sites). The owner will just give the item away if you will come pick it up. Craig's list is national, but sorts the listings by metropolitan area. Other places to shop for used furniture and appliance are garage sales and thrift stores.

Buy Staples

Staples are the basic ingredients needed for a household kitchen. Staples include items like salt, pepper, sugar, flour, butter, eggs, and milk. These basic ingredients are needed for most meals. Staples along with meat, cheese, fruit, and vegetables are all that is needed to feed a family well. The basic ingredients are less expensive per unit weight than prepackaged items. Unit weight is the cost per ounce or pound.

© Robert Kneschke, 2014, Shutterstock, Inc.

Stock your pantry with staple items since most are the basic ingredients in many meals. Comparison shop, the generic alternative is usually just as good if not better than the name brand counterpart; in some instances, they are manufactured by the same company.

Make Gifts

Holidays are stressful for many people. Those who struggle financially may find themselves overwhelmed with stress. A meaningful gift doesn't have to cost a small fortune. It really is the thought that counts. Use what you have available and be creative to make gifts. This can save a substantial amount of money. Consider gifts of home-baked goods. Use your computer and digital photos to make personalized calendars. You can even include birthdays and anniversaries for family and friends on the calendar. Use flower pots and plant seeds to make a living bouquet. The best way to come up with great gifts to make is to think about the person the gift is for. Think about what he or she enjoys or treasures. Be creative and use whatever you can find.

Several years ago when my children were small I went through a financially difficult time around Christmas. I had three little girls and only $9.00 to spend on Christmas. I thought about what they would like and came up with new teddy bears and denim skirts. Both of these items were popular at the time. I went to the library and searched for books on teddy bears. I found a book that included the pattern for the original teddy bear, which was named after Theodore Roosevelt. I traced those patterns on grocery sacks, so I could cut the patterns out and use them. I used old velour sweaters, jeans, and corduroy pants for the fabric. The teddy bears were jointed and needed cotter pins to hold their jointed parts together. I spent my $9.00 on cotter pins, which cost only a few pennies, polyester fiberfill to stuff the bears, and candy for the girls' Christmas stockings. I used old buttons and broken jewelry pieces to make the bears' eyes and embroidered the bears' noses and mouths. I had patterns for the skirts, and I cut up old blue jeans to make them new skirts. At the time I worried they would be disappointed in what they received that year for Christmas, but to this day that is still their favorite Christmas of all time. You can do the same. Be creative. It really is the thought that counts.

Go Back to the Basics

In a world of new and improved products, we sometimes forget the basics. Instead of buying expensive bathroom cleaning products, try vinegar to remove soap scum. Chlorine bleach kills mold and mildew. Ammonia will cut through grease. Either vinegar or ammonia will clean glass. These basics are inexpensive and effective at most household cleaning jobs. Old newspapers clean windows to a streak-free shine and don't leave the lint that paper towels do. Newspaper will also make a wonderful dust pan. Wet one edge of a single sheet of newspaper and stick the wet edge to the floor. The wet edge will hold the newspaper in place as you sweep the dirt onto the paper. Just pick up the newspaper and toss it in the trash. You don't even need to buy the newspaper, save the free ones that come in the mail with weekly coupons.

Plant a garden. There is nothing as tasty as fresh vegetables from the garden. Instead of paying higher prices for organically grown vegetables, plant some yourself. If you don't have a yard, you can grow many vegetables in containers on a balcony or patio.

Shop Off Season

Shopping off season is a good way to buy clothing at a discount. Winter coats and sweaters are usually deeply discounted in the late winter and early spring. Swimsuits and shorts are usually discounted in the late summer to early fall. You can stretch your wardrobe dollars by purchasing your clothing off season.

Shop Thrift Stores and Garage Sales

Another way to stretch your wardrobe dollars is to shop garage sales and thrift stores. Avoid the urge to buy in quantity because it is cheap. Take your time, examine the clothing carefully, try it on, and only make purchases you will actually wear. You may be surprised at the treasures you find.

Use Coupons

Coupons are a great way to reduce your grocery bill. Be careful, though, that you don't buy products just because you have a coupon. Make a grocery list first, and then cut coupons for those items on your list. Use a file system to store coupons you don't need. Instead of buying expensive coupon sorting systems, you can use basic envelopes. This makes a great inexpensive way to organize your coupons. Take advantage of double coupon deals. Also make sure that the price of the item using a coupon is less than a similar item in a generic brand. For example, a can of brand-name corn at $.99 with a $.20 cents-off coupon will still be more expensive than a generic brand of corn that sells for $.69. More on generics follows.

Buy Generics

Buy generics or store brands instead of national brand products. When comparing vegetables, salad dressings, and other food items, you will find some store brands are better than name brands. Remember generics are packaged by name-brand manufacturers, only under store labels, so often the quality is not compromised. Sometimes you will prefer a name brand. You will have to experiment a little to find which products you like. Over-the-counter medicine is a great place to save by purchasing the generic. Acetaminophen is a pain reliever that is sold under the brand name Tylenol®. Ibuprofen is another pain reliever sold under the brand names Advil® and Motrin®. These are examples of items that are marked up substantially because of brand name recognition. Often a store will carry a store brand next to the major name brand. Read the label of the name brand product and compare it to the label of the generic product. Compare both the ingredients and amounts of the drugs in over-the-counter medicines.

Play Together

To stretch your family leisure budget consider a game night. This will also work with friends if you are single. Play cards or board games instead of going out to the movies. You can make snacks. Consider popping popcorn instead of buying the microwavable varieties. You can also obtain free videos from the library instead paying to rent movies.

STEP 4: SELECTING THE RIGHT SAVINGS VEHICLE

A building block for achieving financial goals is successfully investing your savings. Successful investing means choosing the investments that are appropriate for you and that will yield an optimum rate of return for your ability to accept risk. Once you have a functioning budget and are saving toward your goals, the next step is to determine where to put your savings. There isn't one correct answer. Savings instruments are not one size fits all. The best place for your savings will depend on the intended use of the money and your personal comfort level with risk.

In this section we will briefly introduce you to your savings options, then we will explain the relationship between risk and reward. The second half of this book is dedicated to detailed coverage of investing. If you want more information on a specific investment vehicle, flip to the chapter on that topic.

The most popular investments vehicles are:

- Savings accounts
- Money market accounts
- CDs (certificates of deposit)
- IRAs
- Roth IRAs
- Money market funds
- Mutual funds
- Bonds
- Stocks

Savings accounts: (as of March 2013, a typical interest rate 0.02–0.04 percent).

A savings account is an account at a commercial bank that pays the depositor interest. Credit Unions call these accounts share accounts, but they both work the same way.

Savings account An account at a commercial bank that pays the depositor interest.

- Accounts require small minimum deposit to open, typically from $50–$100.
- There is no limit on the number of deposits or withdrawals.
- No fees are associated with the account as long as the balance does not fall below the minimum.
- Accounts compound interest quarterly, monthly, daily, or annually (typically quarterly).
- Accounts are FDIC/NCUA insured.

Interest rates, minimum deposits, and methods of compounding vary from one financial institution to the other. To find the best rate, it is wise to shop around. These accounts are the lowest interest-bearing investment tool, but they are safe and allow unlimited access to your funds. They are FDIC insured at commercial banks and NCUA insured at credit unions. This insurance protects the depositor against loss in the event the financial institution was to fail. The funds are insured up to $100,000. During the market crash of 2008, the insured amounts were increased temporarily to $250,000 through December 31, 2009.

FDIC Insurance that protects the depositor against loss in the event the financial institution was to fail.

Money Market Accounts

Money market account
Savings account that bear a higher interest rate than standard savings accounts.

Tiered interest schedule
As you reach a higher level of minimum deposit, you earn a higher interest rate.

Money market accounts are savings accounts that bear a higher interest rate than a standard savings account. They require a higher minimum deposit than a regular savings account and limit the number of withdrawals that can be made a month. Most financial institutions offer a tiered interest rate schedule for their money market accounts. A tiered interest schedule means that as you reach a higher level of minimum deposit you earn a higher interest rate. Most banks start the second tier of the schedule at $10,000. Money market accounts:

- Pay higher interest rates than standard savings accounts.
- Offer tiered interest rate schedules.
- Require minimum deposits to open, typically from $1,000 to $2,500.
- Require minimum deposits be maintained.
- Limit the number of withdrawals per month, typically two to six allowable.
- Charge fees for each withdrawal in excess of limit, typically $5 to $10 per transaction.
- Compound interest daily, monthly, or quarterly (typically daily).
- Are FDIC/NCUA insured.

CDs Certificates of Deposit

Certificate of deposit (CD) A savings instrument issued through a financial institution. It is issued for a specified amount of time, typically 90 days to five years.

Certificates of deposit (CDs) are savings instruments issued through financial institutions. They are issued for a specified amount of time, typically 90 days to five years. They pay a higher interest rate than savings accounts. Short term CDs pay interest rates similar to those of a money market account. Longer term CDs will typically pay a higher interest rate than a money market account. CDs do not allow withdrawals. If you take your money out of the CD before its maturity date, you will pay a penalty. Typical penalties for early withdrawal range from 31 to 91 days of interest. CDs:

- Require minimum deposits, typically $500 to $1,000.
- Pay interests that is compounded quarterly, monthly, or daily (typically monthly).
- Do not allow withdrawals of principal.
- Are offered in a variety of maturities: 91 day, 180 days, 1 year, 18 months, 2 year, 3 year, and 5 year.
- Charge penalties of 30 to 90 days interest for early withdrawal of principal.
- Often allow withdrawal of accrued interest.
- Are FDIC/NCUA insured.

Laddering A process of buying staggered maturity date CDs.

Certificate of deposits can be laddered to allow both the higher returns and some access to your money. Laddering is a process of buying staggered maturity date CDs. You can ladder CDs to time their maturity at convenient intervals. This technique is commonly used with conservative retirement accounts. It allows the investor to earn higher interest on his or her funds, while still having access to a portion of his or her cash every month, quarter, or year. This process can also be used for short-term savings like an emergency fund.

| Irene's CD Ladder | **EXAMPLE 2.4** |

Irene Hanover is an IT technician for a large telecommunications company. She enjoys her job and loves the working environment, but her company tends to overhire during busy times and lay off workers in down times. She has been laidoff for at least 2 months at time for the past 2 years. She has an emergency fund to cover living expenses during these layoffs, but would like to earn more interest on them. She decided to ladder CDs.

Irene brings home $3,800 a month when she is working, but only makes $2,100 when she is collecting unemployment. That is a difference of $1,700 a month. She scales back her leisure spending and savings during times when she is laid off and can manage her budget on $2,700 a month. She currently has $8,000 in a money market account. She decides to leave $2,000 in the money market account and put the other $6,000 in a CD ladder. She deposits $2,000 each in a 90-day, 180-day, and 1-year CD. The table below shows how her CD ladder matures.

CD	Purchase Date	Maturity Date
A	3/1/14	6/1/14
B	3/1/14	9/1/14
C	3/1/14	3/1/15
A	6/1/14	12/1/14
B	9/1/14	9/1/15
A	12/1/14	6/1/15
C	3/1/15	3/1/16

When her first CD matures 3 months later, she buys another 6-month CD with those funds. Notice her second CD will now mature in 3 months. Since she has funds to cover 2 months of expenses in her money market account, she is comfortable with the funds being available in 3 months. In September when her second CD matures, she purchases a 1-year CD with those funds. She notices the pattern:If each time CD A matures, she reinvests it for 6 months, she can reinvests the other two CDs for a year at a time and still always have funds available in 3 months. ∎

IRAs

IRAs are individual retirement accounts that allow the investor to deposit money tax deferred. Tax deferred means the depositor doesn't have to pay taxes on the amount deposited until it is withdrawn. These accounts offer a tax savings in the year deposits are made and allow for retirement savings. The amounts deposited cannot be withdrawn until the investor reaches the age of 59½. Early withdrawals carry heavy penalties and are taxed in the year they are withdrawn.

An IRA account can be opened at most banks, credit unions, and brokerage firms. Typically, banks and credit unions limit the investment options with the IRA to mutual funds, money market accounts, and CDs. IRAs opened at a brokerage firm allows the investor more options, such as purchasing individual stocks and bonds as well as investing in mutual funds.

Individual retirement account (IRA) Account that allows the investor to deposit money tax deferred.

Tax deferred Depositor doesn't have to pay taxes on the amount deposited until it is withdrawn.

Roth IRAs

Roth IRA After-tax investment.

Roth IRAs are not tax deferred, since they don't offer any tax savings in the year deposits are made. These are after-tax investments, but they offer the benefit of tax-free withdrawals. Roth IRAs also provide tax-free growth as long as the gains are not withdrawn before the depositor reaches the age of 59½. These accounts are ideal for individuals in a low tax bracket. The funds deposited can be withdrawn anytime, but the gains cannot.

Roth IRAs are similar to IRAs in the opportunities for opening an account and the investment choices associated with where an account is opened.

Money Market Funds

Money markets Pooled funds that are invested in short term securities.

Security Documented financial interest in a company or fund.

Money market funds are not savings accounts and are not typically guaranteed. They are investments that bear a minimal risk of loss to premium. Money markets funds are pooled funds that are invested in short term securities. A security is a documented financial interest in a company or fund. Individual investors' funds are pooled together and used to buy U.S. Treasury securities, jumbo CDs, and commercial paper. These are low-risk, short-term loans to the government, banks, and companies. The fund pays the accumulated interest earned back to the investors. Jumbo CDs and commercial paper often have minimum investment amounts of $10,000 to $100,000, which make it hard for the average investor to participate in these higher interest-bearing loans. Money market funds allow the average investor to participate in these through the pooled resources of multiple investors. Money markets:

- Are offered through banks, credit unions, brokerage firms, and employer-sponsored retirement accounts.
- Allow for withdrawals and may have check writing privileges.
- Require a minimum deposit of $500 to $3,000 typically.
- Are not insured (temporary exception in market crash of 2008–2009).
- Are mutual funds invested in high-quality debt to be paid back in one year or less.

Mutual Funds

Mutual funds Pooled investments; funds take deposits from multiple investors and use the combined funds to purchase stocks, bonds, or short-term securities.

Mutual funds are pooled investments. These funds take deposits from multiple investors and use the combined funds to purchase stocks, bonds, or short-term securities. A money market fund is a mutual fund that must invest in high-quality, short-term debt. Mutual funds are also offered in stock funds, bond funds, or combination funds that buy a variety of securities. These funds allow investors to benefit from stock and bond investments without having to manage their investments themselves. Mutual funds are popular investment tools in retirement accounts like 401ks. Investors buy shares in the fund, and the fund invests in the stock and bond market.

Bonds

Bonds Issued debt from a government or company.

Bonds are issued debt from a government or company. Bonds have maturity dates ranging from 90 days for T-bills to 10 years for the average corporate bond. They pay higher interest rates than short-term debt. Bonds are traded on the secondary market, and their face value will fluctuate with raising and falling interest rates. Bonds will be discussed in more detail in a later chapter.

- Corporate bonds are typically sold in 1,000 to 10,000 denominations.
- Corporate bonds typically have 10-year maturity dates.
- Bonds offer higher rates of return.
- Bonds are frequently packaged in mutual funds.

Stocks

Stocks are ownership in a company. Shares of stock are sold on the secondary market to the average investor through a brokerage account. Stocks carry the highest risk and provide the highest return rates historically. If the company makes a profit, the stockholder shares in those profits. If the company loses money, the stockholder shares in those losses. Stocks will be discussed in more detail in a later chapter.

Stock Ownership in a company.

- Stocks are frequently packaged in mutual funds.
- Stocks bear the highest risk.
- Stocks bear the highest rate of return.
- Stocks are typically a long-term investment.

Risk Versus Reward

Investing risk and reward are directly proportional. The more risk you take, the greater the possible reward. If you want to get the best interest rate on a good loan, you need a good credit rating. Those who do not have a good credit rating pay higher interest on the loans they take out. This is the same principal, since someone with a good credit rating is less of a risk because she is more likely to pay the loan back on time and in full, she can borrow money for a cheaper rate. The reward for lending that person money is less, but the risk of lending that person money is also less.

In general, you can assume more risk with long-term savings. Stocks are the riskiest investments, but they also yield the highest rates of return. Long term they are a good investment if you hold them and don't sell them after the market has turned down. Ideally, you want to sell them before the market takes a dive. Since no one has a crystal ball to predict the future, it is easy to miss that timing. Once the market has already crashed, it is better to hold them than to cash out and realize the loss. Individuals who have 15 or more years to retirement can weather these downturns with plenty of time for the market to recover before they need their money. However, you wouldn't want to invest the money you saved for next month's rent in stocks.

It is unwise to risk the principal of your savings for short-term goals. You will forgo some interest for the safety of preserving your principal. The most common method for short-term savings is a standard savings account. The standard savings account typically pays the lowest interest rate, but the depositor may withdrawal his funds without penalty as often as he likes. This is a good place to start, but as your savings grow, you may want to consider a higher interest-bearing money market account or CD.

When deciding where to invest your money you need to ask yourself the following questions:

- When do I need the money back?
- How much interest do I need to earn to achieve my goal?
- How frequently will I need to make withdrawals from this savings?
- What is the purpose of my investment?
- How much risk am I comfortable with?

For short-term savings, consider a savings accounts, money market accounts, and CDs. For mid-term savings goals, consider money market accounts, CDs, or a Roth IRA. For long-term goals try an IRA or Roth IRA. Financial institutions vary greatly in their offerings of interest rates, minimum deposits, and terms. Take the time to do a little research to find the best fit for your financial needs.

STEP 5: MEASURE THE PERFORMANCE OF THE PLAN

Now that you have a plan in place, it is important to review it periodically. Review your plan every quarter, six months, or year as is appropriate to how rapidly your finances change. Everyone should review his or her financial plan at least annually. A good review will include updating your balance sheet and cash flow statement. If you have been using your budget and comparing your actual amounts to your budgeted amounts, your cash flow statement is already updated. Look at the new balance sheet. Check to see that your net worth is increasing.

Take a careful look at your plan. Are you saving your planned amounts each month? If not, are there expenses you can cut out or ways you could earn extra money? Are your investments yielding the returns you hoped they would? Have unplanned expenses arisen? Are you reducing you debt? A yearly review will allow you to determine where you need to make adjustments.

For example, if you saved $50 a month, at the end of one year you have $600. Last year your only choice might have been a savings account, because you couldn't meet the minimum deposit for a money market account or CD. Now that you have a higher balance, you could move the money to a higher interest account.

STEP 6: MAKE CHANGES AND ADJUSTMENTS TO THE PLAN

The purpose of reviewing your financial plan is to make adjustments. You may want to move money from one form of savings to another as your accrue higher account balances. If you paid off a debt last year, you will want to adjustment your plan to reallocate those funds.

Life and our personal circumstances are constantly changing. Your goals will probably change with every major life change: new career, marriage, birth of a child, child going off to college, divorce, or death of a spouse. Your financial plan will go through many changes: Don't be afraid to scrap old goals or do a complete overhaul of your financial plan.

How It All Ties Together: Planning and Budgeting

Let's look back at the six steps to financial planning. You started by determining what you wanted and developed a set of goals. In Step 2 you analyzed your current financial situation by creating a balance sheet and cash flow statement. In Step 3 you combined your goals and cash flow statement to create a budget. With a good budget in place, you chose the best place for your savings (Step 4).

In Step 5 you measured the performance of your plan. For example, you budgeted savings of $500 a month, but after a year you find you are actually saving $200 each month. Go back and analyze the cause of this discrepancy in your budget. In the final step you will make any needed changes and adjustments. A well-planned budget anticipates and prepares for the unexpected.

SUMMARY

Financial planning sets personal and financial goals and then lists the steps to achieve these goals. The process consists of six steps:

1. Create a list of financial goals.
2. Analyze your current financial situation.
3. Create a budget.
4. Select appropriate savings vehicles.
5. Measure the performance of your plan.
6. Adjust the plan as necessary.

An integral part of financial planning is the preparation of a personal balance sheet, cash flow statement, and budget. The balance sheet shows your assets and liabilities. Your personal net worth equals your total assets minus your total liabilities. Your net worth is your accumulated wealth.

Both cash flow statements and budgets can be written for any time frame, but they are commonly written for a month. Cash flow statements are a look back. They show actual income and expenses for the previous period. Budgets are an estimate of expected income and expenses in the future. A good budget should be well-planned, flexible, openly communicated to the family, and practical.

Although they are separate financial statements, the cash flow statement and balance sheet work together. Your cash flow statement shows your monthly savings and debt reduction. Both increased savings and reduced debt increase your net worth on the balance sheet. The opposite is also true; if you spend your savings or increase your debt, you reduce your net worth.

Balance risk and reward to optimize your savings. The right savings vehicle for you will depend on the risk you are willing to assume, the intended use for the savings, and the length of time you have to save.

PROBLEMS

1. Connie is trying to calculate her personal wealth and is having a difficult time. She has:

   - $2,000 in a savings account
   - A car valued at $15,000
   - A car loan with a balance of $9,000
   - Stocks worth $4,000
   - Credit card balance of $1,000

   What is Connie's current net worth?

2. Jerry struggles to save money. Last month he had:

   - Gross monthly income $5,000
   - Monthly tax deduction $800
   - Health insurance $300
   - Rent and utilities $1,000
   - Car payments and expenses $1,200
   - Food $900
   - Miscellaneous $500

   Create a personal cash flow statement for him. Make recommendations to help him save $400 next month.

CASE STUDIES

COLLEGE STUDENT

Kevin Maedor is a 19-year-old college student. He still lives at home with his parents, and he works part time at Vapor's Lane. He started his financial plan in the spring semester of 2014. He plans to graduate with a B.S. in engineering in May 2017. He has the following financial information:

- He brings home $760 a month from his job; he currently has $174 in his checking account.
- He asks his parents for $50 cash a week.
- He has a Visa card with a balance of $1,700 and a MasterCard with a balance of $800. He makes the minimum monthly payment of $15.00 on each of them.
- His cell phone bill is $85 a month.
- His parents bought him a 2011 Jeep Wrangler worth $23,730. They still pay the insurance on it for him.
- He owns $1,100 in golf equipment, $1,200 in electronics, a jet ski worth $5,500, and personal items worth $1,650.
- Last month he spent $450.00 on gas, $375.00 on golf, and $490.69 at restaurants.

Help Kevin create his financial plan by completing the following tasks:

1. Set goals for Kevin.
2. Create a balance sheet (April 3, 2014).
3. Create a cash flow statement (month ending March 2014).
4. Create a budget (May 2014).

Adjust his budget and goals as needed.

NEW GRADUATE

Rene Harris recently graduated with a B.S. in nursing. She lives by herself in a modest apartment. Her annual salary is $76,000 a year. Rene loves to entertain, but her apartment is too small and the neighbors complain about the slightest noise. Rene is a good neighbor, so she has been going out with friends instead. She has the following financial information:

- She brings home $4,433.33 a month from her job.
- She pays $1,125.00 a month for her apartment, which includes trash service and cable.
- She used her new Visa last month for the first time and charged $600. She also opened a new Macy's charge and charged $762.78. She hasn't received her first bill for either of them; assume her minimum monthly payment will be $15.00 on each.
- She owes $30,000 in student loans and makes a monthly payment of $151.47.
- Her cell phone bill is $105.00 a month.
- She owns a 2011 Kia worth $7,085. It is paid for but she pays $65.44 a month in insurance. It has 87,000 miles on it.
- She has $1,804.12 in her savings account.
- She owns $2,100 in furniture, $1,800 in electronics, and personal items worth $2,900.
- Last month she spent $275.00 on gas, $398.63 on food, $32.17 for her water bill, $76.18 for her electric bill, $49.98 for Internet service, $820 at restaurants, $357.82 on entertainment, $762.78 on clothing (this is her Macy's charge), and $152.75 on hair and nail services.
- Her checking account balance is $124.18 and she has $33.17 in her billfold.

Help Rene create her financial plan by completing the following tasks:

1. Set goals for Rene.
2. Create a balance sheet and cash flow statement for her.
3. Create a budget for her and incorporate the goals you made for her.
4. Adjust her budget and goals as needed.

CREATE YOUR OWN FINANCIAL PLAN

1. Goals are specific, measurable, action oriented, realistic and time-focused. Create three financial goals for yourself. Write one short-term goal, one intermediate-term goal, and one long-term goal.

2. Create a personal balance sheet. Be sure to label it with a date. Remember a balance sheet is a snapshot in time. Divide your balance sheet into three main sections: Assets, Liabilities, and Net Worth.

3. Create a personal cash flow statement for last month. Cash flow statements show actual expenditures and income received. The general categories for a cash flow statement are Income, Expenses, and Net Cash Flow. Customize the sub-sections to fit your personal financial situation.

4. Create a budget for next month. Budgets estimate expected income and expenses. They follow the general format of Income, Expenses, and Surplus or Deficit.

5. Adjust the budget you made in activity 4 to include the goals you made in activity 1. Check to see if you can afford your current goals. Adjust your goals and budget to allocate all your expected income. Make sure you don't have any deficits. If you don't have enough money, adjust your goals so they are realistic. If you have money left over, allocate it to savings, debt pay down, or leisure. You should have zero for you surplus or deficit and the end of this activity.

6. Research the available savings instruments at two local banks. Select the account(s) that best fit your goals. Write two to four paragraphs describing the results of your research and your reasoning for your choice(s). Items to include:

   • Name of financial institution
   • Type of account (savings, CD, money market)
   • Minimum deposit
   • Interest rate
   • Period of compounding

7. Create a financial plan by completing activities 1–6.

MAKE IT PERSONAL

"To thine own self be true." William Shakespeare wrote it first, but it has become a common adage in our lives. What are your personal beliefs about money? How can you incorporate your values into your financial plan?

For example, three of the world's major religions—Judaism, Christianity, and Islam—believe the Torah or Old Testament is the word of God. Proverbs 3:9-10 says "Honor the LORD with thy substance, and with the first fruits of all thine increase: So shall thy barns be filled with plenty, and thy presses shall burst out with new wine." If you hold one of these faiths, what does this passage say to you? If you hold a different view or adhere to a different religion, does that belief system hold any shared beliefs about wealth?

What is the cost of honoring your own beliefs with your money? What is the cost of not honoring your own beliefs with your money?

Remember that a personal financial plan is personal. Our lives are not separated into isolated departments. Your personal beliefs should and do affect how you spend and manage your money. This is not something you have to share with your classmates or instructor, but it is something you should consider as you build a plan for your own financial well-being.

REVIEW QUESTIONS

1. Summarize the main purpose of a financial plan.

   _____

   _____

   _____

2. List the six steps of financial planning.

   _____

   _____

   _____

   _____

   _____

   _____

3. How does the time value of money relate to financial planning?

   _____

   _____

   _____

4. Which asset is more liquid—a car or a stock traded on the NYSE?

   _____

   _____

   _____

5. What does the acronym SMART stand for?

   _____

   _____

   _____

6. Which two financial statements show you where you are? Discuss how they are different and how they work together.

_____

_____

_____

7. Identify the following as an asset, a short-term liability, or a long-term liability.

- Savings account _____

- 36-month car loan _____

- Student loan _____

- Money your parents gave you that you have to pay back in three months _____

- Clothing _____

- Credit card balance _____

8. What is the main difference between a cash flow statement and a budget?

_____

_____

_____

9. List three characteristics of a good budget.

_____

_____

_____

10. Summarize the role of budgeting in the overall financial planning process.

_____

_____

_____

Housing

"Mid pleasures and palaces though we may roam, be it ever so humble, there's no place like home."

—John Howard Payne
(1791–1852)

OBJECTIVES

- Compare and contrast the benefits of renting versus buying a home
- Explain and negotiate the terms of a lease
- Select the best mortgage for the current situation
- Determine how much mortgage you qualify for
- Adjust your personal financial plan to accommodate your home decision

KEY TERMS

Adjustable rate mortgage (ARM)
Closing costs
Collateral
Debt-to-income ratio
Escrow account
Eviction
Fixed-rate mortgage (FRM)
Homeowners' insurance

Housing-expense ratio
Landlord
Lease
Loan application fee
Loan origination fee
Mortgage loan
Points
Preapproval

Prequalified
Private mortgage insurance (PMI)
Property taxes
Security deposit
Sublet
Tenant
Title insurance

65

A home purchase is an important financial decision. The largest single investment you make in your life will probably be your home. Home ownership is a symbol of the American dream; it symbolizes success and stability. Both the decision to buy a home and the choice of your new home should be given careful consideration before you make the purchase.

In this chapter, we will use the word *home* to indicate your primary residence. It may be a free-standing house, a duplex, an apartment, a condo, or another option. We will discuss the benefits and disadvantages of both renting and buying a home.

Renting a Home

Tenant A person who rents and occupies rental property.

Lease A legal document specifying the terms of rental of a property.

Landlord The owner of rental property.

A tenant is a person who rents a home; they have no ownership in the residence. The tenant pays rent for the right to occupy the home. Renters sign a rental agreement called a lease with the owner. A lease is a legal document; it protects both the tenant (the renter) and the landlord (the owner) of the property. Exhibit 3.1 provides tips on renting a home.

THE LEASE AGREEMENT

The principal provisions of a lease identify the following:

As a tenant, you have no ownership in the property. Many people rent at some time in their lives so it's beneficial to have a basic understanding.

© Philip Lange, 2014, Shutterstock, Inc.

- The term of the lease and the conditions for extension of the lease. Most lease agreements are for one year; shorter leases are often available for higher rent. The lease may be renewable or it may terminate at the end of the year. The term of the lease will show the specific dates: month, day, and year for the start and end of the lease agreement.
- The rent payments and due dates. Most lease agreements require monthly rent payments due sometime around the third day of each month. The lease agreement usually specifies when the rent is considered late and the amount of the late fee. It is common to allow a three to five days grace period before assessing a late fee.

TIPS FOR RENTING A HOME   **EXHIBIT 3.1**

1. Make a list of potential rental properties. Check newspapers, Internet rental sites, and local neighborhoods for yard signs.
2. Check the fundamental characteristics of a property. Eliminate any properties that are not:

- **Safe**. Your personal safety is important. Check for:
  - Appropriate locks
  - Adequate lighting
  - Open layout and well maintained grounds
  - Secure clean buildings. Is the condition of the property up to building and safety codes?
- **Clean**. A clean property indicates the degree of care the property receives. Check for:
  - Broken windows, locks, or lights
  - Clean unobstructed pathways, hallways, and public areas
  - Normal wear and tear on sidewalks, walls, and gates
- **Pleasant**. The design of the property adds to your enjoyment of your home. Check for:
  - Adequate number of entrances
  - Adequate convenient parking
  - Do you like the look of the property?
- **Quiet**. Check for noise. Are there any airports or trains? Can you hear someone's stereo? Is there loud entertainment: a bowling alley in a nearby commercial center or nightclub?

3. Once you narrow you choices with the fundamental property characteristic, compare specific items:

- Rent amount
- Size of the home
- Number of rooms
- Condition of kitchen and bathroom(s)
- Utilities: are they included in the rent?
- Type of heat and air conditioning
- Laundry facilities
- Appliances
- Furnished or unfurnished

4. Rent the smallest place to meet your needs. This will save you money in both rent and utilities.
5. If the rent is more than you can afford, ask the landlord if you can work in exchange for part of the rent. Apartment complexes hire part-time managers. If you are renting an apartment, maybe the homeowner needs assistance with lawn care.

- **The security deposit.** A security deposit is money you pay the landlord to cover the cost of any damages you might do to the property. The landlord holds the security deposit for the duration of the lease. Security deposits discourage abuse of the property. The amount of security deposit is usually equal to one month's rent. Renters who take good care of their rental home should be refunded their security deposit at the end of the lease. When you

Security deposit A deposit paid at the beginning of a lease to deter renters from abusing the premises.

first move in, it is important to take a detailed inventory of any existing damage. Make a detailed list of scratches, stains, broken fixtures, or missing parts. Check the shades and inside closets. If the apartment is in good condition, these should be minor, but you don't want to be blamed for them. Give a copy of the list to the landlord. It is a good idea to have the landlord sign a copy. Keep it for your records.

- **Responsible party for utilities on the property.** Some rentals include payment of water, electricity, gas, trash, Internet or cable. The lease will specify who is responsible for these payments.
- **Any restrictions.** For example, the lease may not allow pets in the home. It may also restrict the renter from painting walls.
- **The ability to sublet the unit to another individual.** If a tenant rents the home to another person, it is called a sublet. An example of a common sublet would be to rent the home to someone while you were out of the country for two months. The lease will state whether you are allowed to sublet.
- **The conditions for eviction.** The landlord has the right to evict a tenant who violates certain provisions in the lease. Eviction is the process of forcibly removing a tenant. Eviction in most states requires the landlord to give the tenant notice, in many states it also requires the landlord to be granted the right to evict from a court. Common reasons for eviction are:
  - 30–90 days behind on rent payments
  - Significant damages to the apartment
  - Noise or police complaints
  - Illegal activities at the place of residence
- **Notice to vacate.** Many lease agreements require you (the tenant) to give written notice 30 to 60 days prior to moving out. When you move out, you vacate the premises. The most common mistake renters make is failing to give *written* notice. If you don't give notice, the landlord can charge you for an additional one or two months rent. If you plan to move out at the end of your lease, you still need to give the notice required in the lease. It is not assumed the tenant is vacating because the lease expired.

Sublet A lease contracted by a person who is also a tenant of the property.

Eviction The process of forcibly and immediately removing a tenant from the rental property for violation of the lease.

ADVANTAGES AND DRAWBACKS OF RENTING

The advantages of renting include the following:

- **Lower initial cost and monthly cash payments.** Security deposits and the first month's rent are normally lower than a down payment and closing costs to purchase a home. Rent is often cheaper than a house payment, because renters tend to rent smaller homes than they buy.
- **Mobility.** Renters have increased mobility. It is easier to move when you rent. At the end of a lease, you can choose to extend the lease or move with no obligation. By contrast, a homeowner has to sell his or her existing home when moving.
- **Lower maintenance requirements.** Renters are not responsible for repairs. Most apartments, duplexes, and town homes provide lawn care and snow removal. However, if you rent a house you may be required to provide your own lawn care and snow removal.

The drawbacks of renting include:

- Fewer financial benefits. Long term, renting is usually more expensive than owning a home. Homeowners receive tax benefits that renters don't and also benefit from appreciation in property values.
- Uncertainty. You may not be able to live in the rental home as long as you want. The landlord can raise rent or rent to someone else at the end of a lease. The owner could sell the house to a person who wants to live in the house, or the owner can sell apartment units as condos, which would also force a tenant to move.
- Restrictions. Renters are limited by the terms of the lease. You may not be allowed to have pets, paint, or redecorate. Residents of an apartment building have to consider the proximity of neighbors when they entertain or play music.

Home Ownership

You purchase a home to have a desirable place to live, but a home is also a good financial investment. Home prices historically increase at a steady rate. Most purchases depreciate in value. A new car loses 10 percent of its value when you drive it off the dealer's lot. It is no longer new and now is valued at the used car price. A home appreciates in value. Recently, however, home prices have fallen. Let's take a look at why before we move on to our discussion of buying a home.

Rapidly rising home prices and loose lending standards contributed to the economic crisis that made front page news for most of 2009. Home prices rose too quickly. The lending standards for mortgages were relaxed, in some instance to a point where a borrower didn't have to prove his or her income or put any money down. This led to an increase in the number of home buyers. As the number of buyers increased, so did home prices. The overinflated housing market is what the news calls the housing bubble. When borrowers failed to keep up with their payments, the bubble burst. Lending standards were tightened, so there were fewer buyers. Foreclosed homes began to flood the market. As the number of homes for sale increased and number of buyers decreased, home prices plummeted because they were overpriced. Historically, home prices have increased at a rate of about 4 percent a year. However, during the housing boom, home values increased at a rate of 10 to 12 percent a year.

© MaxyM, 2014, Shutterstock, Inc.

Owning a home is a big responsibility; however, among the advantages are tax benefits and the ability to create your living space the way you choose.

The collapse of the housing market rippled through our financial world. Its effects devastated many people. As bad as it was, it doesn't change the basic principles of home ownership. The process to purchase a home is more complicated than signing a lease. Home ownership also carries higher risks than renting. There is a relationship between risk and reward in finances: the higher the risk, the higher the potential reward.

PROS AND CONS OF HOME OWNERSHIP

There are both benefits and drawbacks in home ownership. The benefits of home ownership are the following:

- Pride of ownership. The home is yours. You can design and decorate your home as you wish to fit your lifestyle. If you want a swimming pool, and have the space and money, you can build a pool.
- Financial benefits. You profit from any increase in value. Homeowners are allowed to deduct the interest and property taxes (or the taxes based on the value of the real estate) they paid during the year from their income taxes. When the home is paid off, they don't have to continue to make payments.
- Fewer restrictions. If you want a pet, you can have a pet. It is easier and more convenient to entertain.
- Privacy. You don't have to allow a landlord in to periodically inspect your home. You don't have to worry about the neighbors overhearing your conversations.
- Stability. The home is yours. No one can sell it or terminate your lease.

Property taxes Taxes based on the value of real estate.

The drawbacks of home ownership are the following:

- Risk. The home could decrease in value. Although historically real estate values increase, they are cyclical with ups and downs as economic and local conditions change. Homeowners can suffer a decline in property values due to national conditions like the sub-prime lending fiasco of 2007. Local conditions can also create property value declines; for example, when a major employer in the area closes its doors.
- Limited mobility. Mobility is a plus for renters, but it is not for a homeowner. If you want to move, you have to sell or rent your home.
- Property insurance. Mortgage lenders require homeowners to insure the property against loss with a hazard insurance policy, typically called homeowners insurance.
- Regular maintenance. Homeowners are responsible for maintenance. Maintenance items such as lawn care and annual furnace checks take time and money, as do repairs to plumbing, electrical, or other systems.
- Major repairs. Homeowners are responsible for major repairs. For example, a roof lasts about 20 years and replacement is expensive.

Some homeowners may view repairs and regular maintenance as too much work, especially if time is an issue. However, for others, putting work into their investment is an enjoyable task.

HOW TO BUY A HOME

This section presents nine steps to buy a home. The nine steps are in a good order, but you may use a different order. For example, you may want to shop

STEPS TO HOME OWNERSHIP

EXHIBIT 3.2

1. Know your rights.
2. Learn about home buying programs.
3. Shop for financing.
4. Determine how much you can afford.
5. Shop for a home.
6. Make an offer.
7. Get a home inspection.
8. Shop for homeowners insurance.
9. Close the mortgage (Sign the papers).

for your home first. Sometimes a buyer finds his dream home when he isn't looking for it. However, it is a good idea to have a mortgage preapproval before you shop. Exhibit 3.2 lists the nine steps.

Know Your Rights

Home buyers have certain rights they can expect when they purchase a home, and all home buyers should familiarize themselves with their rights. The U.S. Department of Housing and Urban Development (HUD) has a number of informative publications. Its web site is www.hud.gov. Two important federal acts provide rights to home buyers:

1. Fair Housing Act. Prohibits discrimination in housing for reasons of race, national origin, religion, sex, familial status, or handicap. http://www .usdoj.gov/crt/housing/title8.htm
2. Real Estate Settlement Procedures Act. Requires that home buyers receive disclosures at various times in the transaction and outlaws kickbacks that increase the cost of settlement services. http://www.hud.gov/offices/hsg/ sfh/res/respa_hm.cfm

Learn About Home Buying Programs

There are several programs that offer assistance to home buyers. These programs are usually available for first-time and lower-income buyers. Some programs are available to all buyers in a specified area. Examples of popular programs include the following:

- The Federal Housing Administration (FHA). The FHA provides mortgage insurance on loans made through approved lenders. FHA loans often require very little down, and buyers face less stringent credit requirements than for a conventional mortgage.
- HUD programs. HUD has several programs that offer assistant to home buyers. For example, the Officer Next Door program offers incentives to law enforcement officers to purchase homes in certain areas. The program allows officers who agree to occupy their home for at least three years to purchase an approved home for 50 percent of its value.

- State programs. Many states run their own programs. For example, Missouri's First Place Program offers first-time home buyers affordable mortgage financing, often at an interest rate below that offered by market rate loans. Home buyers may also be eligible for a subsidy equal to 3 percent of the loan amount to help pay the down payment or other loan closing expenses.
- USDA rural development. The United State Department of Agriculture offers loan guarantees to individuals living in small communities and rural areas. A loan guarantee allows a bank to offer the loan under the USDA guidelines without assuming all the risk of the loan. This loan program is available to low- to moderate-income families. The program offers zero down payments and no private mortgage insurance premiums (PMI) on 30-year fixed rate loans.

Shop for Financing

You can save money and frustration by doing your homework. Talk to several lenders; compare costs, terms, and interest rates. Negotiate the best deal.

- Check online lenders.
- Visit local banks.
- Visit local savings associations.
- Visit local mortgage companies.
- Ask friends, family, and coworkers about their lenders.
- Know which type of mortgage you want.

Loan rates can vary one-quarter percent or more on otherwise identical loans. You will pay $6,247 more over the 30-year life of a 6 percent loan than you will pay if you get a 5.75 percent loan. Customer service varies widely between lenders as well. Quality customer service is important; ask around and see what other borrowers say about their experience before you settle on a lender.

Mortgages

Mortgage loan A loan with the home serving as collateral; the type of loan used to purchase a house.

Collateral An item of value used to secure a loan. The lender has the right to repossess collateral if the borrower fails to pay the loan back.

A mortgage loan provides financing for real property. It is often called a mortgage for short. Technically, the mortgage is a legal document that names the property as collateral for the loan. The loan itself is a separate document. Collateral is an item the lender has the right to repossess if the borrower fails to pay the loan back.

With a home mortgage you make monthly payments to a lender. The lender is typically a financial institution such as a bank, savings and loan association, or mortgage company. However, the lender can also be an individual. As with any loan, the amount of the monthly payment depends on three factors:

1. The amount of your loan
2. The interest rate on your loan
3. The length of time you will be making payments

Loan Amount

The loan amount is the purchase price minus your down payment. Under special circumstances you may be able to finance all of the purchase. Typically, lenders require a down payment of at least 5 percent of the purchase price.

Financing a Home

An important factor in the down payment is private mortgage insurance (PMI). Private mortgage insurance is an insurance policy that the home buyer purchases for the lender. It insures the lender against default on the loan. In other words, if you fail to make your mortgage payments, the insurance company will cover any loss that the lender might incur when foreclosing on the mortgage loan.

Private mortgage insurance (PMI) Insurance purchased by the borrower that covers the lender in case of default.

In general, lenders require mortgage insurance whenever a buyer puts less than 20 percent down on a home purchase. Rates vary, but on average PMI costs about one-half of 1 percent of the loan amount annually. Insurance on a $150,000 home loan would be about $750 per year. Lenders usually allow borrowers to finance the cost of the insurance with the loan, so PMI would increase the monthly payment by about one-half of 1 percent. PMI raises the cost of a home to the borrower, but it does allow lenders to make loans that require only 10 percent, 5 percent, and sometimes even zero down. Paying 20 percent down is often difficult for a first-time home buyer.

MORTGAGE INTEREST RATES

The interest rate on your home mortgage has a tremendous effect on how much your loan payment will be. A small difference in the interest rate creates huge payment variances with a six-figure loan amount. Several factors affect your interest rate. They all deal with the risk of the loan from the lender's perspective. If a lender views you as a low-risk borrower, you will get a lower mortgage rate. These factors are the following:

- Fixed versus adjustable rate mortgages
- Default risk
- Length of the loan

Fixed versus Adjustable Rate Mortgages

A fixed rate mortgage has a constant interest rate for the life of the loan, hence the term fixed. The monthly payment for principal and interest on the loan will always stay the same. With a fixed rate mortgage, the lender carries the interest rate risk. Interest rates change, sometimes dramatically. When interest rates rise, lenders are in an unfavorable position. They pay higher rates to obtain funds, but the revenue they receive from fixed rate loans remains constant. However, when interest rates fall, borrowers have the option to refinance at a lower rate.

Fixed rate mortgage A mortgage with a fixed interest rate for the life of the loan.

Adjustable rate mortgage (ARM) A mortgage with an initial fixed rate for 3, 5 or 7 years which adjust annually after the initial period. The new interest rate is calculated based on the index, the lenders margin, and the caps associated with the loan.

An adjustable rate mortgage (ARM) is not fixed over the life of the loan. After the initial period with a fixed rate, the interest rate adjusts up or down based on current market conditions. ARMs have these main characteristics:

- Initial fixed rate period and frequency of adjustment: Common adjustable rates mortgages are:
 7/1 ARMs
 5/1 ARMs
 3/1 ARMs

The first number indicates the initial fixed rate period and the second number indicates the frequency of adjustment. A 7/1 ARM has a fixed rate for the first seven years and adjust every year after that. Since most ARMs have an adjustment frequency of one year, the rest of our text will assume this frequency rate.

- Index. The index is the base rate used to set a lender's interest rate. There are many indexes, but the LIBOR rate is commonly used for adjustable rate mortgages. The LIBOR rate is the rate banks pay when they borrow money from other banks.
- Margin. The margin is the percentage above the index that the lender charges to loan money to you. The margin is the lenders profit. Since the bank borrowed the money it loaned, it is paying interest as well and adds a margin to make a profit. For example, if the index the lender is using is the LIBOR rate and it is at 2.5 percent and the lender's margin is 3 percent, then the interest charged to the consumer is:

$$2.5\% + 3.0\% = 5.5\%$$

- Annual cap. An annual cap limits the amount the rate can adjust in one year. The annual cap is set and won't change over the life of the loan. If the annual cap is 2 percent, then your loan rate can't increase or decrease by more than 2 percent a year.
- Lifetime cap. The lifetime cap limits the amount the rate can adjust over the life of the loan. If the cap is 4 percent, then your loan rate can't increase or decrease by more than 4 percent from its starting rate.
- Floor. The floor is the interest rate your loan can't go below. If the floor is 2 percent, your interest rate can fall to 2 percent, but not below 2 percent.

If you take out a 5/1 ARM at 4.75 percent with a 2 percent annual cap and a 4 percent lifetime cap, how would your mortgage adjust if interest rates rose to 8.5 percent over the next five years?

Assume the bank has a margin of 2 percent and the current index rate is 6.5 percent. This would lead to a current interest rate of 8.5 percent. It is time for your mortgage to adjust for the first time.

1. Current rate = 8.5 percent
2. Your rate plus annual cap = 4.75 percent + 2 percent = 6.75 percent

Since you cap is reached, your mortgage will adjust to 6.75 percent for the next year. If the current rate had been lower than your cap, your rate would have adjusted to the current rate. If rates continued to increase over the next year, when it is time to adjust your rate again, the current rate is 9.25 percent. Your rate would be 8.75 percent, but the mortgage holder could not increase further because that is 4 percent above your starting rate, the lifetime cap.

The borrower assumes the interest rate risk with adjustable rate mortgages. If interest rates rise, the loan payments increase. There is less interest rate risk for the lender, so lenders charge lower interest rates on ARMs than on fixed-rate mortgages. For example, a typical rate in early 2006 for a 20-year fixed-rate mortgage was 6 percent, which would give a monthly payment of $716. The corresponding 3/1 ARM carried a rate of 5.675 percent, with a monthly payment of $698. This provides a savings of $18 a month to assume the interest rate risk past the third year of the loan.

So is a fixed or adjustable rate mortgage better for you? Clearly, if you think interest rates will increase over time, then a fixed rate mortgage is better, and vice versa. If you do not have a clear prediction of future interest rates, which is the safe way to go? The length of time you plan on staying in a home becomes an important factor. Many first-time home buyers plan on staying in the home for only several years. If this is true for you, a shorter-term ARM makes sense. If you intend to sell the home in two years, then you will sell during the initial fixed rate period of a 3/1 ARM. If you think that you might settle in the house for years to come, the safe bet is to take the fixed-rate mortgage and the peace of mind that comes with it.

Interest rates on mortgages have varied significantly over the past 25 years, ranging from a high of about 18 percent to a low of a little over 5 percent. However, the last decade has seen relative stability, as the chart of historical mortgage rates in Exhibit 3.3 shows.

AVERAGE RATES ON 30-YEAR CONVENTIONAL HOME MORTGAGES

EXHIBIT 3.3

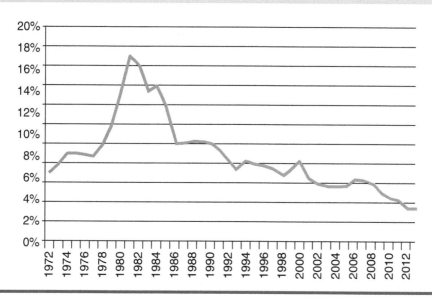

LOAN MATURITY

Mortgages are typically for a period of 15, 20, or 30 years. The shorter your loan is, the lower the interest rate. Of course, shorter loans will have greater monthly payments because repayment is divided over a fewer number of years. Exhibit 3.4 shows the monthly payment for an 8 percent fixed-rate mortgage loan for $100,000 over 15, 20, 30, and 40 years. With a 30-year mortgage, you cut your payments, but the decrease in monthly payment is not as much as you might expect. For example, you pay a 15-year mortgage for half the number of years as a 30-year loan, but the payment on the 30-year loan ($734) is quite a bit more than half the payment on the 15-year loan ($956).

Taking a shorter-term mortgage loan can dramatically decrease the interest that you pay over the life of the loan. A 30-year mortgage is the most common maturity, but a 15-year loan is more economical. Historically, the longest mortgage loan had a maturity of 30 years, but now 35- and 40-year mortgages are becoming more common. Longer terms make a home more "affordable" because they decrease each monthly payment, but they make the home more expensive over the life of the loan. The interest on longer-term loans is significantly more than for the shorter-term ones as Exhibit 3.5 illustrates. The total interest on an 8 percent 15-year loan is $72,017. Double the loan term to 30 years, and you have to more than double the total interest cost to $164,155. By taking the 15-year loan, you save $92,138!

EXHIBIT 3.4	MONTHLY PAYMENT OF PRINCIPAL AND INTEREST FOR $100,000, 8 PERCENT MORTGAGE LOANS OF 15-, 20-, 30-, AND 40-YEAR TERM

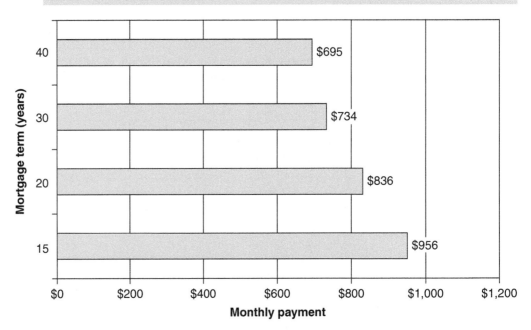

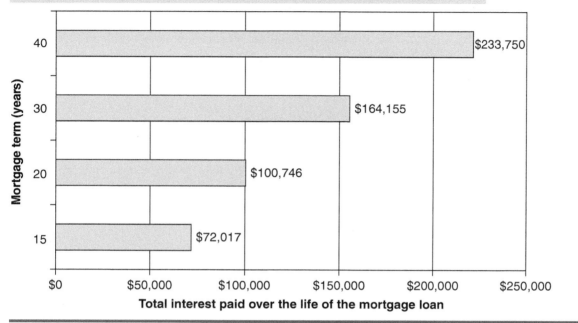

TOTAL INTEREST PAID OVER THE LIFE OF $100,000, 8 PERCENT MORTGAGE LOANS OF 15-, 20-, 30-, AND 40-YEAR TERMS   **EXHIBIT 3.5**

Good advice is to get as short a mortgage as you can afford. This will result in higher payments each month but will save you tens of thousands of dollars in the long run.

MORTGAGE PAYMENTS

Mortgage payments typically include the following:

- Principal
- Interest
- PMI—0.75% of sales price annually (0.0075)
- Property Insurance—0.5% of sales price annually (0.005)
- Property Taxes—1.3% of sales price annually (0.013)

The principal payment is the part of the loan you pay off that month. The interest payment is the accumulated interest for that month.

PMI is private mortgage insurance. Lenders require buyers with a down payment of less than 20 percent to carry PMI. If you want to buy a home with a 5 percent down payment, PMI allows you to qualify for the loan.

Property insurance and property taxes are added to the mortgage payment. You pay one month's worth of each, and the lender holds the money in an escrow account. Escrow occurs when a trustee holds funds earmarked for a certain use. When the annual bills for the insurance and property taxes come due, the mortgage lender will pay them from the escrow account. If you have a 20 percent down payment or more, you will have the option to not pay your taxes and insurance as part of your mortgage. You will make a smaller monthly payment, but you will still need to budget for these expenses.

Escrow account An account to hold funds for a future use. The escrow account on a mortgage is used to pay real estate taxes and homeowners' insurance.

Estimate:

- PMI at 0.75% of sales price annually
- Property Insurance at 0.5% of sales price annually
- Property Taxes at 1.3% of sales price annually

Computing Mortgage Payments

The principles of compound interest apply to mortgages. You can use any of the methods described in Chapter 1 for solving time value of money problems. For your convenience we have included a simplified mortgage payment table in Exhibit 3.6.

Mortgage Payments Using the Table

The payment factors in Exhibit 3.6 give the monthly payment per dollar of mortgage loan. To compute the monthly payment of a mortgage, follow these steps:

EXHIBIT 3.6	MONTHLY MORTGAGE PAYMENT FACTORS

Multiply the amount of the mortgage loan by the factor in the table to find the monthly payment of principal and interest on a mortgage loan.

INTEREST RATE (PERCENT)	MORTGAGE TERM (YEARS)				
	15	20	25	30	40
5.00	0.0079079	0.0065996	0.0058459	0.0053682	0.0048220
5.25	0.0080388	0.0067384	0.0059925	0.0055220	0.0049887
5.50	0.0081708	0.0068789	0.0061409	0.0056779	0.0051577
5.75	0.0083041	0.0070208	0.0062911	0.0058357	0.0053289
6.00	0.0084386	0.0071643	0.0064430	0.0059955	0.0055021
6.25	0.0085742	0.0073093	0.0065967	0.0061572	0.0056774
6.50	0.0087111	0.0074557	0.0067521	0.0063207	0.0058546
6.75	0.0088491	0.0076036	0.0069091	0.0064860	0.0060336
7.00	0.0089883	0.0077530	0.0070678	0.0066530	0.0062143
7.25	0.0091286	0.0079038	0.0072281	0.0068218	0.0063967
7.50	0.0092701	0.0080559	0.0073899	0.0069921	0.0065807
7.75	0.0094128	0.0082095	0.0075533	0.0071641	0.0067662
8.00	0.0095565	0.0083644	0.0077182	0.0073376	0.0069531
8.25	0.0097014	0.0085207	0.0078845	0.0075127	0.0071414
8.50	0.0098474	0.0086782	0.0080523	0.0076891	0.0073309
8.75	0.0099945	0.0088371	0.0082214	0.0078670	0.0075217
9.00	0.0101427	0.0089973	0.0083920	0.0080462	0.0077136
9.25	0.0102919	0.0091587	0.0085638	0.0082268	0.0079066
9.50	0.0104422	0.0093213	0.0087370	0.0084085	0.0081006
9.75	0.0105936	0.0094852	0.0089114	0.0085915	0.0082956
10.00	0.0107461	0.0096502	0.0090870	0.0087757	0.0084915
10.25	0.0108995	0.0098164	0.0092638	0.0089610	0.0086882
10.50	0.0110540	0.0099838	0.0094418	0.0091474	0.0088857
10.75	0.0112095	0.0101523	0.0096209	0.0093348	0.0090840
11.00	0.0113660	0.0103219	0.0098011	0.0095232	0.0092829
11.25	0.0115234	0.0104926	0.0099824	0.0097126	0.0094826
11.50	0.0116819	0.0106643	0.0101647	0.0099029	0.0096828
11.75	0.0118413	0.0108371	0.0103480	0.0100941	0.0098836
12.00	0.0120017	0.0110109	0.0105322	0.0102861	0.0100850

1. Find the factor that corresponds to the interest rate and term (in years) of the mortgage.
2. Multiply that factor by the amount of the mortgage. The result will be the monthly payment of the mortgage.

$$\text{monthly mortgage payment} = \text{mortgage payment factor} \times \text{loan amount}$$

Equation 3.1

Example 3.1 illustrates how to use the table in Exhibit 3.6 to compute a mortgage payment.

Using the Mortgage Table to Compute a Monthly Mortgage Payment	**EXAMPLE 3.1**

Kim and CodyMarlow have been approved for a 5-percent 30-year mortgage. The home they chose is priced at $265,000. They will put 10 percent down. Compute their monthly payment.

The mortgage payment factor for a 5-percent 30-year loan is 0.0053682. Kim and Cody will borrow 90 percent of the home price, $148,500.

$$\text{payment} = \text{mortgage payment factor} \times \text{loan amount}$$
$$= 0.0053682 \times \$238,500$$
$$= \$1,280.32$$

You can also use the present value of an annuity equation
  or
The payment function in Excel or on a financial calculator

Notice this only calculates the principal and interest payment. The mortgage payment also includes taxes, insurance, and PMI. To get a better idea of what the monthly payment will be, we need to add these payments to our principal and interest payment.

You can estimate the property taxes, insurance and PMI with the following:

- Property taxes = 1.3% of sales price annually (0.013)
- Insurance = 0.5% of sales price annually (0.005)
- PMI = 0.75% of sales price annually (0.0075)

Sales price $265,000

$$\text{Property tax} = \frac{\$265,000 \times 0.013}{12} = \$287.08 \text{ a month}$$

$$\text{Insurance} = \frac{\$265,000 \times 0.005}{12} = \$110.42 \text{ a month}$$

$$\text{PMI} = \frac{\$265,000 \times 0.0075}{12} = \$165.63 \text{ a month}$$

Their total monthly mortgage payment will be:

$$\$1,280.32 + \$287.08 + \$110.42 + \$165.63 = \$1,843.45$$

This is what their actual payment will be. If they had estimated it with a mortgage calculator, they would have received the same answer we did before we added in the insurance, taxes, and PMI. If you have less than 20 percent down, always add at least $300 per $100,000 of the selling price to cover the insurance, taxes, and PMI in your estimates. ■

Determine How Much You Can Afford

Some people are able to pay cash for their home without having to finance any portion of the home price. For them, determining how much home they can afford is easy; it is the amount they have available for the home purchase.

If you need a mortgage to purchase your home, what you can afford depends on your income, credit rating, current monthly expenses, down payment, and the interest rate.

To get a quick idea of what you can afford to spend, multiply your annual gross income (before taxes) by 2.5. For example, if your annual household income is $50,000, you might be able to qualify for a $125,000 home. This is just a rough estimate; to determine an accurate amount you will need the financial information on your cash flow statement. Your mortgage lender will calculate the maximum loan amount for you. However, calculating it for yourself will aid in your understanding of the process. To calculate the home you can afford, follow these steps:

1. Using the lender's loan ratios, determine your maximum monthly mortgage payment.
2. Use your maximum monthly payment to determine the amount of the loan. (Use the present value of an annuity equation from Chapter 1.)
3. Add your down payment to the loan amount—this is the maximum home price you can afford.

Mortgage lenders use two ratios to determine your maximum monthly mortgage payment.

Housing-expense ratio
The total housing payment, including insurance and property taxes as a percent of the borrower's income.

- Housing-expense ratio (front-end ratio) 25–38 percent of gross monthly income (GMI)
- Debt-to-income ratio (back-end ratio) 30–45 percent of GMI

Debt-to-income ratio
Total monthly debt payments divided by gross monthly income.

The housing-expense ratio determines the maximum mortgage payment. The mortgage payment includes principal, interest, PMI, hazard insurance, and property taxes. The ratio is the maximum percentage of a borrower's gross monthly income that can be consumed by the mortgage payment. Housing expense ratio requirements vary by lender. Some lenders use a set of ratios depending on the applicant's credit score. They allow a higher ratio for applicants with excellent credit.

The debt-to-income ratio determines the maximum total monthly debt payments. This includes all payments the borrower is required to make. Common debt payments include student loan payments, car payments, and credit card payments. Utilities and food are not debt; they are expenses and are not included in this calculation. This ratio is the maximum percentage of a borrower's gross monthly income that can be consumed by debt payments.

Example 3.2 shows how to use these ratios to determine the monthly payment a loan applicant can afford and the price of house for which the person can shop.

How Much House Can Zach Afford?

EXAMPLE 3.2

Zach Quang has a monthly income of $5,000 and has saved $15,000 as a down payment for a house. Zach has a $540 a month car payment and a $150 student loan payment.

Zach's bank requires a housing expense ratio of 0.25and a debt to income ratio of 0.38. Itoffers a 30-year fixed rate mortgage for4.5 percent. Zach's monthly insurance and property taxes on a house will be about $300. How much can Zach afford to pay for a house?

Follow the three steps:

1. Use the lender's ratios to determine the maximum monthly payment the lender will allow Zach to make on his mortgage.
   Multiply Zach's gross monthly income by 0.25 the housing-expense ratio.

$$\$5,000 \times 0.25 = \$1,250$$

Zach could afford a mortgage payment of $1,250. Subtract his insurance and taxes.

$$\$1250 - \$300 = \$950.$$

Now check his debt-to-income ratio. Multiply his income by 0.38

$$\$5,000 \times 0.38 = \$1900$$

Subtract his monthly debt payments from this amount.

$$\$1900 - (\$540 + \$150) = \$1210 - 300 \text{ taxes} = \$910$$

Compare the two payments $950 or $910; select the smaller of the two. This is the maximum mortgage payment the bank will allow. We will use $910 to calculate his maximum loan amount.

2. Use the maximum monthly payment to determine the amount of the loan.

$$PV = \$910 \; \frac{\left(1 - \left(1 + \frac{.045}{12}\right)^{-360}\right)}{\frac{.05}{12}}$$

$$\$179,596.65 = \$910 \; \frac{\left(1 - \left(1 + \frac{.045}{12}\right)^{-360}\right)}{\frac{.05}{12}}$$

3. Add Zach's down payment to the loan amount, and you have the price of the house he can buy.
   Round to the nearest $1,000.

$$\$180,000 + 15,000 = \$195,000 \quad \blacksquare$$

Did you know that most lenders sell your mortgage once the paper work is complete? Some lenders maintain the servicing on the loan. If the lender maintains the servicing on the loan, you will deal with your lender when making payments, or with any other issue related to the mortgage. If it does not maintain the servicing on the loan, you will be notified where to send your payment. A loan and its servicing can be sold multiple times over the life of a loan. Choosing a lender who maintains the servicing of the loan is more convenient.

Preapproval A guarantee for a mortgage loan for a specified amount of time.

Prequalification An estimate of what you might be able to afford for a mortgage payment.

PREAPPROVAL VERSUS PREQUALIFIED

You have a negotiating advantage if you get preapproved for a loan before you make an offer. Preapproval means you have completed the application and been approved for a specified amount based on your financial documentation. The lender actual approves your loan before you select a home. A preapproved loan is usually good for a minimum of 90 days. You have the option to lock the current interest rate, which means you will take the interest rate the day the loan was approved. If interest rates go up, you don't have to worry; your loan will be at the rate you locked. You also have the option to float the rate, which means you will use the rate at the time you close the loan. If you are preapproved for a $160,000 loan, then you can purchase a home up to $160,000. The final loan will be based on your purchase price. If you find a home for $140,000, your loan will be based on that amount. The preapproval allows you to purchase a home up to the pre-approved amount. Preapproval is a guarantee for a loan for a specified amount of time.

Prequalification is an estimate of what you might be able to afford. It is not a guarantee you will get a loan. Prequalification takes a few minutes to do and is based on what you tell the lender. If you are honest, prequalification is an accurate estimate of what you can afford, if you get approved for a loan.

Shop for a Home

Finding a home that meets your needs and fits your budget is a time-consuming task. You shouldn't feel like you need to "settle" on an unsatisfactory place. There are several questions you need to answer as you begin even looking for a home.

- **What features would you like?** Do you care about parking, off-street parking, garage? Do you want a single garage or a double-car garage? Does it need to be attached or detached? Would you like a basement? Should the basement be for storm shelter, or should it be finished for extra living space? What type of kitchen do you want: eat in, galley, oversized? To start, you should list all the things you would like in the home. Which items are a must, and which would be nice to have? This will help you narrow your search and make a final decision that is best for you.
- **How much space do you need?** If you are single or married with no kids, you probably don't need a mansion as your first home. You should figure out how many bedrooms and bathrooms you need. Also, try to think about any changes that might occur during the time you plan on living in the home. If you are thinking about having children in the near future or know that relatives plan on visiting you often in your new home, you probably need some extra space.
- **How long do you plan on living there?** If you are planning on living in your home for 10 years or more, you will want to consider your future needs when you select your home. If you know you will sell the house in

two to five years, long-term needs are not a priority. However, for short-term ownership, you need to carefully consider your resale opportunities. Your home is an asset you will sell in time, hopefully for a nice profit. If you plan on putting your home back on the market in the near future, you want to purchase a home you will be able to sell quickly and easily. For example, a home with neutral wall colors located in a good school district will be easier to sell than a home in a neighborhood with less desirable schools and cutting edge decor.

- **What about location?** Consider all of the characteristics of your desired location. Do you want a home near your place of employment, favorite shopping areas, or parks? Do you prefer the city, suburbs, or country living? Is the school district or proximity of schools an important consideration?

- **How good are you at repairs and maintenance?** If your only home improvement skills are from watching reruns of *Home Improvement,* you are probably not going to be able to fix many things around the house. Hiring people to fix things in your house can be expensive, so if you can't do it yourself, you might want to pass up the fixer uppers and look for homes in good repair. By contrast, if you enjoy doing repairs yourself, you can save some money by purchasing a home that needs some work.

- **Checklists.** It is easy to forget to check items in the excitement of home shopping. Use a checklist like the one in Exhibit 3.8 to help you thoroughly check out each property.

- **Real estate agents** earn their living from commissions. Traditionally, the seller pays the real estate agent's commission. However, most sellers take the commission into account when they price the home. You can save some or all of the commission by purchasing a home advertised as "FSBO," for sale by owner.

- **The real estate contract, title insurance, and title companies.** Every real estate contract that involves a mortgage requires two title insurance policies, one to cover the lender, purchased by the buyer, and one to cover the buyer, purchased by the seller. Title companies will provide their customers with free documents for extending an offer to buy. This offer, when accepted by the seller, becomes a legally binding contract known as the real estate contract. This is the part most new home owners need help with. Real estate agents take care of this paper work for you. If you don't use a real estate agent, your title company will help you with this document. You will pay the title company's fees regardless of whether you use a real estate agent.

Should you use a real estate agent? That is a personal choice. Real estate agents offer services of convenience:

- Perform home searches and identify homes you might like.
- Schedule appointments to view homes.
- Present your offer to the seller's agent.
- Recommend inspectors; some may even set up the appointment for you.
- Schedule the closing of the transaction (your lender can also perform this task for you).

EXHIBIT 3.8   HOME SHOPPING CHECKLIST

The Home	Good	Avg	Poor
Square footage	___	___	___
Number of bedrooms	___	___	___
Number of baths	___	___	___
Practicality of floor plan	___	___	___
Interior walls condition	___	___	___
Closet/storage space	___	___	___
Basement	___	___	___
Fireplace	___	___	___
Cable TV	___	___	___
Basement: dampness, odors	___	___	___
Exterior appearance, cond.	___	___	___
Lawn/yard space	___	___	___
Fence	___	___	___
Patio or deck	___	___	___
Garage	___	___	___
Energy efficiency	___	___	___
Screens, storm windows	___	___	___
Roof: age and condition	___	___	___
Gutters and downspouts	___	___	___

The Neighborhood	Good	Avg	Poor
Conditions of nearby homes	___	___	___
Traffic	___	___	___
Noise Level	___	___	___
Safety/Security	___	___	___
Age mix of inhabitants	___	___	___
Number of children	___	___	___
Pet restrictions	___	___	___
Parking	___	___	___
Zoning regulations	___	___	___

The Neighborhood (cont.)	Good	Avg	Poor
Restrictions/covenants	___	___	___
Fire protection	___	___	___
Police	___	___	___
Snow removal	___	___	___
Garbage service	___	___	___

Schools	Good	Avg	Poor
Age/condition	___	___	___
Reputation	___	___	___
Quality of teachers	___	___	___
Achievement test scores	___	___	___
Play areas	___	___	___
Curriculum	___	___	___
Class size	___	___	___
Busing distance	___	___	___

Convenience to	Good	Avg	Poor
Supermarket	___	___	___
Schools	___	___	___
Work	___	___	___
Shopping	___	___	___
Child care	___	___	___
Hospitals	___	___	___
Doctor/dentist	___	___	___
Recreation/parks	___	___	___
Restaurants/entertainment	___	___	___
Church/synagogue	___	___	___
Airport	___	___	___
Highways	___	___	___
Public transportation	___	___	___

If you choose to use a realtor, know whom the realtor is representing, you or the seller. In most cases, realtors represent the seller. There are buyers agents, which work on the buyer's behalf. However, most real estate agents, if not specifically contracted by the buyer, are sellers' agents, and they are bound by law to look after the sellers' best interests. Know who you are dealing with: If you tell a seller's agent you will offer $130,000 but would go to $138,000, it is likely the agent will share that information with the seller.

Make an Offer

Negotiating to buy a home is much like buying any other major asset; negotiation can play a major part in setting the transaction price. As the Internet has grown, buyers have become more informed regarding the market value of homes and can use this knowledge to their benefit in the negotiation.

The market value of a home is normally determined by an appraisal based on recent sales prices of comparable nearby homes. If the asking price for a home is reasonably close to its market value, that home should sell within a relatively short time (one to three months). Even if a home is over-priced, it may sell quickly if the seller is motivated to sell and the buyer is anxious to buy. Negotiations often break down, however, when one or both parties want to make the sale only at a price that is advantageous for them. Here are some points to keep in mind when preparing and making an offer for a home. Your real estate agent can help you with these items.

- Know market values of comparable homes in the area. This will prevent you from overpaying and help you in making a reasonable offer on the home.
- Find out the seller's motivation. The seller's motivation may give you information about his or her inclination to accept a low offer (if the seller needs to move quickly) or ability to hold out (a couple has just retired and is thinking about moving near a lake).
- Avoid becoming emotionally involved in the negotiation. Sellers may hold out for top price if, for example, they sense you have just found your dream home and are excited to buy and move in as soon as possible. However, do not become offended by a seller who wants a top asking price for a home in a desirable area where sales usually occur rapidly.

When shopping for a home, don't get caught up in the decorations and furniture. These things add charm to a home, but they are not significant in the long run. It is a relatively minor thing to paint, but a new coat of paint and a bit of organization will often sell a home. Before you seriously shop for a home, watch some home improvement shows, like HGTV's Designed to Sell. By viewing the process from the seller's perspective, you may save considerable money by purchasing a home that has a better floor plan for your needs but needs just a little TLC.

When looking at a home, take a tape measure, flashlight, level, and pen and paper with you. You can quickly check to see if floors and walls are level and take notes about room dimensions and major appliances. Check the furnace and water heater; there is usually a label on them that will tell you the make, model, and year. Knowing the age of major items will help you determine the timeframe for their eventual replacement.

Once you have decided to make an offer on a home, your real estate agent will prepare contracts and present the offer to the seller's agent. The real estate sales contract is not the actual sale of the property but rather it is an agreement to make the transaction if the conditions of the contract are met (see Exhibit 3.9). If you are not working with an agent, your title company will help you prepare the documents. If you do a "for sale by owner" and prepare your own paperwork, do your research carefully. If you are unsure, consult an attorney. Be sure to make the contract contingent upon financing. This means if for some reason the lender will not make a loan on the property, you are not obligated to purchase the home. Know that the offer is a contract and binding, don't make a written offer unless you intend to buy the home. In real estate transactions verbal offers are not offers, they must be written.

EXHIBIT 3.9	ITEMS INCLUDED IN AN OFFER

- Names of the buyer(s) and seller(s).
- Legal description of the property. Be specific and attach an addendum if necessary. You can often get the legal description from county appraiser's web site. It is part of the property tax documents.
- Earnest money deposit. While there is no legal requirement to provide a good faith deposit for a real estate contract, most sellers will want one. A deposit of 1 percent of the price should be sufficient. If you are making an offer well below the asking price, a large deposit may encourage the seller to accept your offer.
- The purchase price and the terms of sale. Specify the price you are offering. If you are financing the home, you should make the sale contingent on your qualifying for a specific (for example, 7 percent 30-year mortgage.)
- Personal property to be included. Specify if you want any personal property, such as the refrigerator, to remain.
- Time to respond to the offer. Specify a relatively short time (24 to 48 hours) for the seller to accept or respond to your offer. The seller may respond with a counteroffer.
- A professional inspection. An inspection by a licensed inspector can give a buyer the ability to get a refund of the earnest money should an inspector discover defects that the seller is unwilling to correct.
- Other items. Consult with your real estate agent and/or attorney for any additional items that you should include in a contract.

Get a Home Inspection

One of the best bits of advice to a home buyer is to get an inspection of the home before the purchase is final. Your home is one of the most important purchases you will make in your lifetime, so you should be sure the home you want to buy is in good condition. A home inspection provides an evaluation of a home's condition by a trained expert. During a home inspection, a qualified inspector takes an in-depth and impartial look at the property you plan to buy. The inspector will do several things:

- Evaluate the physical condition of your home, including the structure, construction, and mechanical systems.
- Identify items that should be repaired or replaced.
- Estimate the remaining useful life of the major systems (such as electrical, plumbing, heating, air conditioning), equipment, structure, and finishes.
- Identify any rodent or bug infestations.

Following the inspection, the inspector will provide a detailed report showing the condition of the home and property. A smart home buyer will include a clause in the real estate sales contract that allows the buyer to back out of the contract should the seller refuse to fix any items that the inspector finds to be in need of repair.

Shop for Homeowners' Insurance

Most lenders require you to obtain homeowners insurance in order to get approved for a home mortgage. Homeowners' insurance protects your home and your belongings inside your home in case they are damaged. The most typical damages would be from a fire or weather-related incident, like strong winds or hail. The cost of your insurance will depend on the carrier, home value, types of coverage (like additional flood, hurricane, or earthquake), and deductible amount.

Even if you are not required to purchase homeowners' insurance, it is a good idea to protect your investment.

Homeowners' insurance Insurance that covers a homeowner for damage to the home. Homeowners' insurance can also cover personal property in the home.

Sign the Papers

Purchasing a home with a loan takes the help of several different people, each of whom gets paid for his or her work. You pay these costs at closing when your lender funds your loan and the title for the property is transferred to you. Both the buyer and seller are responsible for various closing costs, and some costs are split between buyer and seller. Common closing costs are:

- Lender fees
- Third-party fees
- Prepaids
- Miscellaneous fees

Closing costs Unsettled costs associated with the loan and title transfer of the property. These are paid when the final documents are signed.

LENDER FEES

Typical lender fees include the loan application fee, the loan origination fee, and points.

The loan application fee is a specified dollar amount you pay the lender when you apply for the loan. The application fee covers the cost associated with processing your loan application and checking your credit report. This fee is typically between $75 and $100.

The loan origination fee covers (also called the underwriting, processing, or administration fee) the lender's cost associated with preparing your loan and mortgage documents. The loan origination fee may be a flat rate charge of a few hundred dollars or based on a percent of your loan. Common fees are $350 or 1 to 1.5 percent of your loan. You can save thousands by shopping around. One percent of a $100,000 is $1,000. A lender who charges a flat rate of $350 would save you $650 on this loan. Typically, the better your credit score, the more selective you can be when it comes to choosing a lender.

Points are used to lower the interest rate. For example a lender may offer a 5.5 percent fixed 30-year mortgage with zero points or a 5.25 percent fixed 30-year mortgage with 1 point. In essence you purchase a lower interest rate buy paying 1 percent interest up front. If you intend to keep your home and pay it off in 30 years, the lower interest rate is worth the upfront cost. You will save money after the fourth or fifth year.

Loan application fee A fee paid to the lender for loan application and documentation costs.

Loan origination fee A percent of the amount of the loan paid at the beginning of the loan. The fee is extra interest on the loan.

Points Interest paid up front on a loan to buy down the interest rate offered on the loan.

© Gajus, 2014, Shutterstock, Inc.

Signing papers at closing usually involves several parties; the buyer, seller, banker and sometimes an agent or representative.

Application fees, origination fees, and points are calculated as interest on the loan. For this reason, the APR on a mortgage is greater than the stated interest rate. These fees are also deductible on your federal income tax for your primary residence.

THIRD PARTY FEES

Appraiser/inspector costs. The home will be appraised to determine its value. Lenders want to make sure the home is worth at least as much as the amount they are lending. Most lenders also require a wood-destroying insect inspection. This can be included in your home inspection. If you did not pay for the inspection separately, the cost of a wood-destroying insect inspection will be added to the closing costs. If the home has a well or a septic system, these will also require an inspection. These inspections are for the benefit of the lender; they may not indicate the quality of the water but only that there is an adequate supply. These combined fees can range from $300 to $1,000 depending on your lender and the property you select.

Title insurance protects you against losing your home if someone with a prior financial interest in your home makes a claim against your property. It is important to ensure no unknown person has a financial interest in your property. Title insurance protects you against any historical claims against your property. A title is "free and clear," when all former financial interests are settled. A title company will issue a title insurance policy to insure you. The seller will pay for the policy that covers you. You will pay for title insurance to protect the lender. This cost may be paid prior to closing.

Flood inspection fees cover the cost of research associated with determining if your home is located in a FEMA-designated flood zone. Federal law prohibits lenders from granting mortgages in areas with federally subsidized flood insurance programs unless the borrower has flood insurance. The fee for the research is typically $15 to $50. This does not buy the flood insurance. It is a fee to check if flood insurance is required. Flood insurance would be an additional cost under your homeowners insurance policy.

Survey fees are charged to cover the cost of a survey of the property you intend to finance. This is not a complete boundary survey. This is for the lender's benefit to ensure the home and any other structures are where you say they are. This checks for appropriate setbacks from property lines and often includes information about easements or rights of way.

PRE-PAID ITEMS

Interest. The buyer usually has to pay interest on the mortgage loan for the time between closing and the date when the first payment is due. This is called prepaid interest.

Homeowners insurance premiums. The lender usually requires the first six months to a year's policy to be paid in advance. Often lenders require you have a policy in place before you close. You will pay your insurance agent to

Title insurance Insurance coverage against losing property, should issues arise concerning the legal ownership of the property.

obtain a policy. At closing you will pay any addition amount required to meet the lender's minimum.

Property taxes. The lender often requires one to three months of property tax payments to be made up front. This is a prepaid item.

Mortgage insurance or guarantee fees. If you get a conventional loan with less than a 20 percent down payment, your lender will require you to carry PMI. The lender often requires you to pay one year's premiums in advance. This is typically 0.5 percent of the sale price of the home. FHA (Federal Housing Authority), VA (Veteran's Administration), and USDA (United State Department of Agriculture) loans offer no or low down payments with no PMI. This can be misleading; although they don't charge PMI, they do charge similar fees. FHA loans have an FHA insurance premium and VA and USDA loans have loan guarantee fees. FHA insurance premiums are about 1.5 percent of the loan amount per year. VA guarantee fees range from 1.25 to 2 percent of the loan amount a year. USDA guarantee fees are 1.75 percent of the loan amount a year. Like PMI, under federal law these fees are required to be removed once a borrower obtains 22 percent equity in their home.

MISCELLANEOUS FEES

Brokerage fees. A mortgage broker is not a lender; it is a third party who finds a lender for you. It charges you a fee for its service. Fees range from 1 to 5 percent of the loan amount. Mortgage brokers often tack their fee onto the loan amount or the back of the loan. You can save thousands of dollars by going directly to the lender instead of using a mortgage broker.

Assumption fees. When you take over an existing loan, you assume the loan. Most lenders will charge you a fee to assume an existing loan. This is advantageous when you can assume a loan with a lower interest rate than is currently available.

Inspections for your benefit. If you have the home inspected after you make an offer, you will have to pay these costs. These costs are associated with the purchase of the home, but are typically paid to the inspector directly and are not a part of the closing cost.

SUMMARY

Housing is one of the most important personal financial decisions people make. The choice of renting or owning a home is complex. Advantages of renting include a lower initial cost, greater mobility, and less maintenance. Drawbacks of renting are fewer financial benefits, greater uncertainty, and more restrictions when compared to owning.

The legal document between the tenant and the landlord is the lease. Main provisions of a lease specify the lease terms, rent amount, security deposit, utility payments, restrictions, sublets, and eviction.

Most people want to own their home in the United States. Benefits of home ownership are pride of ownership, tax breaks, appreciation, fewer restrictions, privacy, and stability. Drawbacks of ownership include financial risk, less mobility, and increased maintenance responsibilities.

Most homes are financed with a mortgage. Most lenders require a down payment. Private mortgage insurance covers the lender against loss in case of default on the loan. Home buyers who pay 20 percent or more down do not have to purchase mortgage insurance.

A fixed rate mortgage has a constant interest rate for the life of the loan. An adjustable rate mortgage (ARM) has a fixed rate for an initial period of three, five, or seven years then it adjust annually.

Lenders typically offer 15-, 20-, and 30-year term mortgages, although terms up to 40 years are now available. While the longer-term mortgages have lower monthly payments, the total interest paid over the life of a longer-term loan is significantly greater. Monthly mortgage payments are computed with the time value of money equations. Solve them with your favorite method from Chapter 1.

The loan amount you can qualify for depends on your income, credit rating, monthly debt payments, down payment, and the interest rate. Lenders use the housing expense ratio and the debt-to-income ratio to qualify a buyer for a home.

Before you apply for a mortgage, you should know your rights, and you should check for available home buying programs. You can save thousands of dollars in interest over the life of a loan if you carefully select your lender.

Both a real estate agent and the title company will help you prepare an offer for a home. Real estate agents will also help you select your home, set times to show you homes, and facilitate other appointments like the closing.

Which home is best for you is a personal choice. When you make your selection, consider the home's size, location, condition, and the length of time you plan to own the home. Before you make an offer on a home, familiarize yourself with market prices of comparable homes in the area, consider the seller's motivation, and don't become emotional about the negotiation.

Once you have a sales contract, get a home inspection from a qualified inspector and shop for homeowners' insurance. Closing is the final step. At the closing you will pay any unsettled costs associated with the loan and title transfer.

PROBLEMS

1. Joan and Perry found a new home for $230,000. They have a 5 percent down payment. They want a 30-year fixed-rate mortgage at 4 3/4 percent interest. What is their monthly principal and interest payment? What is their total monthly payment?

   (**Hint:** Calculate their insurance, taxes, and PMI by multiplying the sale price by the appropriate percent [1.3 percent taxes, 0.5 percent insurance, and 0.75 percent PMI] then divide that amount into 12 monthly payments.)

2. Joan and Perry (previous problem) decide to tighten their budget and take out a 15-year mortgage with a 4 1/4 percent interest rate instead. What will their new payment be?

   (**Hint:** Recalculate principal and interest and add the insurance, taxes, and PMI for problem 1.)

3. What is the monthly principal and interest payment on a $150,000 40-year mortgage at 5 1/2 percent?

4. Stacy Hova wants to purchase a home for $200,000. She has $10,000 to put down. She also has a $417 car payment. She makes $82,000 a year. Her lender is offering a 4.25-percent 30-year loan and uses a housing expense ratio of 28 percent and a debt-to-income ratio of 33 percent. Determine whether Stacy will qualify for this loan. Show your work and calculations to explain your answer. Don't forget to include insurance, taxes, and PMI in her house payment.

CASE STUDIES

Although the following cases have been solved to show the maximum house payment for each case study, ask students to consider the individual's or family's overall financial situation. Ask them to consider buying a house for less than the maximum. Ask them to discuss why it may not be wise to buy at the maximum allowable price range.

COLLEGE STUDENT

We met Kevin Maedor in Chapter 2. He is a 19-year-old college student. He still lives at home with his parents, and he works part time at Vapor's Lane. He started his financial plan in the spring semester of 2014 and will graduate with a B.S. in engineering in May 2017. Help Kevin by creating a goal for him to move out of his parent's house. Remember goals are specific, measurable, action oriented, realistic, and time focused.

Determine:

1. When will Kevin move out?
2. Will he rent or buy?
3. How much can he afford to pay for housing? (Hint: Assume he makes $45,000 a year once he graduates.)

Help Kevin calculate the house payment he will be able to afford when he graduates, then determine how much he can afford to borrow. Finally, help him find a house.

What payment can he afford?

1. His gross monthly income = His annual salary/12 months
2. His bank uses a housing expense ratio of 38 percent. Multiply his gross monthly income by this ratio. Then subtract an estimated $300 for his taxes, insurance, and PMI from this figure.
3. His bank uses a debt-to-income ratio of 42 percent. Multiply his gross monthly income by this ratio. Then subtract his total monthly debt payments from this figure.
4. Select the smaller of the two numbers in (2) and (3). This is his maximum allowable house payment.

How much can he afford to borrow?

5. You now know the payment and want to know how much he can afford to borrow. Use the present value of an annuity equation or your favorite method from Chapter 1 to calculate the amount he could afford to borrow.

   Select the best loan for him by researching local banks in your area. Use the interest rate and term associated with the loan you pick.

How much house can he afford? What price range should he shop for?

6. Add any down payment he has available to the amount he can borrow; this is the amount he can spend on a home. Assume he needs $1,500 for closing costs when you determine how much down payment he has available.
7. Go to www.realtor.com and shop for a house you think would fit his needs and lifestyle.
8. Use the payment you calculated for him as an affordable house payment and research what he could rent for that price. Select a possible rental unit for him.
9. Compare his options for buying and renting. Which do you think he should do?

- Assume he receives $5,000 in cash for graduation and he pays off his credit cards. He has a Visa card with a balance of $722.42 and a Master-Card with a balance of $471.96. He has no other debt payments.
- See case studies in Chapter 2 for additional financial information.
- Are there any loan programs available that would help him?

NEW GRADUATE

We met Rene Harris in Chapter 2. She is a nurse. Her annual salary is $76,000 a year. Rene loves to entertain, but her apartment is too small. She wants to buy a home.

Help Rene calculate the house payment she can afford, then determine how much she can afford to borrow. Finally, help her find a house.
What payment can she afford?

1. Her gross monthly income = Her annual salary/12 months
2. Her bank uses a housing expense ratio of 38 percent. Multiply her gross monthly income by this ratio. Then subtract an estimated $300 for her taxes, insurance, and PMI from this figure.
3. Her bank uses a debt to income ratio of 42 percent. Multiply her gross monthly income by this ratio. Then subtract her total monthly debt payments from this figure.
4. Select the smaller of the two numbers in (2) and (3). This is her maximum allowable house payment.

How much can she afford to borrow?

5. You now know the payment and want to know how much she can afford to borrow. Use the present value of an annuity equation or your favorite method from Chapter 1 to calculate the amount she could afford to borrow.

   Select the best loan for her by researching local banks in your area. Use the interest rate and term associated with the loan you pick.

How much house can she afford? What price range should you shop for?

6. Add any down payment she has available to the amount she can borrow; this is the amount she can spend on a home. Assume she needs $1,500 for closing costs when you determine how much down payment she has available.
7. Go to www.realtor.com and shop for a house you think would fit her needs and lifestyle.

- She has monthly debt payments of $15 each on her Visa and Macy's credit cards and $151.47 in student loans.
- She has $1,804.12 in her savings account.
- See case studies in Chapter 2 for additional financial information.
- Are there any loan programs available that would help her?

CREATE YOUR OWN FINANCIAL PLAN

1. Find a home you could buy.
   Determine the payment you could afford. You can use either your current income or your projected income when you graduate. If you don't know what you will make in your chosen career field, visit Bureau of Labor Statistics *Occupational Outlook Handbook*

2. Use the annual salary you selected in question 1 to determine the payment you can afford.

   - Your gross monthly income = Your annual salary/12 months.
   - Ask your bank what ratios it uses to qualify home buyers or assume a housing expense ratio of 38 percent and a debt-to-income ratio of 42 percent. These ratios will depend on your credit score. The ones given here would typically require a credit score of 720 or higher.
   - Multiply your gross monthly income by the housing expense ratio. Then subtract an estimated $300 your taxes, insurance, and PMI from this figure. You can adjust this later to be more accurate based on the price of the home you select.
   - Multiply your gross monthly income by the debt-to-income ratio. Subtract your total monthly debt payments from this figure.
   - Select the smaller of the two numbers in (C) and (D). This is your maximum allowable house payment.

3. How much can you afford to borrow?

   - Research local banks in your area and select the best type of mortgage for you.
   - Use the interest rate and term associated with that loan to calculate how much you can afford to borrow.
   - You now know the payment from part 2; use the present value of an annuity equation or your favorite method from Chapter 1 to calculate the amount you can afford to borrow.

4. Add your down payment to the loan amount you calculated in question 3. This is the amount you can spend on a home. Assume you need $1,500 for closing costs when you determine how much down payment you have available.

5. Go to www.realtor.com and shop for a house that will fit your needs and lifestyle.

6. Refine your estimates. Assume you need 1 percent of the loan value for closing costs. If you have less than 20 percent for a down payment, estimate you PMI, property insurance, and tax payments:

$$\text{Property tax} = \frac{\text{sales price} \times 0.013}{12}$$

$$\text{Insurance} = \frac{\text{sales price} \times 0.005}{12}$$

$$\text{PMI} = \frac{\text{sales price} \times 0.0075}{12}$$

MAKE IT PERSONAL

Your home is a personal reflection of you. Consider the style you would most enjoy. If you aren't sure, look through architecture magazines and real estate listings. If you aren't ready to buy now, that is OK. A specific list of features and styles you like will help you narrow your search when you are ready.

REVIEW QUESTIONS

1. Define a lease and list the principal provisions of a lease.

   _____

   _____

   _____

   _____

2. Identify ways you can increase your chances of getting your security deposit at the end of a lease.

   _____

   _____

   _____

3. Outline the advantages and drawbacks of renting a home.

   _____

   _____

   _____

   _____

4. Outline the advantages and drawbacks of owning a home.

   _____

   _____

   _____

   _____

5. What three factors determine the monthly payment amount of a mortgage?

   _____

   _____

   _____

6. Define private mortgage insurance. Tell how mortgage insurance helps borrowers even though it insures lenders.

_____

_____

_____

7. Differentiate between a fixed-rate and a variable rate mortgage. Identify which type would most likely have a lower interest rate at the beginning of the loan. Identify which type is riskier for the borrower.

_____

_____

_____

8. What items are included in a monthly mortgage payment?

_____

_____

_____

9. What is the difference between a preapproval and prequalification?

_____

_____

_____

10. List nine steps in buying a home.

_____

_____

_____

_____

_____

_____

_____

_____

_____

11. What factors influence a lender's decision to grant a mortgage to an applicant?

_____

_____

_____

12. List two features of an FHA loan.

_____

_____

_____

13. What services do real estate agents offer home buyers?

_____

_____

_____

14. List three key things to do before you make an offer on a home.

_____

_____

_____

15. Why is it important to request a home inspection?

_____

_____

_____

16. What are closing costs for mortgage? List the costs associated with closing a mortgage.

_____

_____

_____

Manage Your Credit

"Credit is like a looking-glass, which when once sullied by a breath, may be wiped clear again; but if once cracked can never be repaired."

–Walter Scott
(1771–1832)

OBJECTIVES

- Distinguish between revolving and closed-end credit accounts
- Describe the various characteristics of consumer loans
- Create an amortization table
- Use credit cards with wisdom
- Describe the elements of a loan contract
- Understand how your FICO (credit) score is calculated

KEY TERMS

Closed-end credit
Credit
Fixed interest loan
General credit card

Home equity loan
Inflation
Installment loan
Interest

Principal
Revolving credit
Variable rate loan

STRETCH
YOUR DOLLAR

CREDIT CARDS

Pay your credit card balance on time and in full every month. This eliminates interest charges. If you use a credit card with bonus points and pay no interest charges, the card company pays you to borrow its money.

In the years preceding the crash of the 2007–2008, credit flowed freely: Credit cards and mortgages were handed out like Halloween candy. Interest rates were low. Borrowers took advantage of offers with zero down payments and no closing costs on mortgages; they borrowed more than they could afford to pay back. Consumers and businesses alike borrowed more than they saved. But when default rates began to skyrocket on loans to sub-prime borrowers, it produced a domino effect that brought the availability of credit to a screeching halt. Banks held onto their funds to prop up their balance sheets, and individuals and businesses who had used credit wisely suddenly were unable to continue to obtain credit. The wise use of credit is critical to the world economy, and the wise use of credit starts with the individual.

Credit

Credit A contract that allows the borrower to accept something of value with the promise to pay the lender back later.

Principal Amount of money borrowed or the dollar amount of the goods or services sold.

Interest The cost of credit. The interest rate is expressed as a percentage per year.

Revolving credit A credit line that allows the borrower to borrow up to a maximum limit.

Closed-end credit A loan for a specific amount that must be paid back on or before an agreed upon date.

Credit is a contract that allows the borrower to accept something of value with the promise to pay the lender back later. The item of value can be goods, services, or money. The lender makes a loan as an investment with the anticipation of being paid back all the principal plus interest. Principal is the amount of money borrowed or the dollar amount of the goods or services sold. Interest is the cost of credit. The interest rate is expressed as a percentage per year. The concepts of calculating interest on loans are the same as those for computing interest for savings accounts and investments.

Credit is available in two forms: revolving credit and closed-end credit. Revolving credit is a credit line that allows the borrower to borrow up to a maximum limit. A revolving credit account stays open after the borrower has paid off the balance and can be used again for new borrowing needs. Credit cards and home equity loans are common types of revolving credit. Closed-end credit is a loan for a specific amount that must be paid back on or before an agreed upon date. Closed-end credit accounts close when the borrower pays off the balance. Car loans and home mortgages are common closed-end credit accounts. Most closed-end credit is offered in the form of installment loans. Installment loans are loans where the borrower pays the loan back in equal payments periodically. For example, the borrower pays the lender $200 every month for 36 months.

Credit is also categorized by who the borrower is. Personal loans are those made to individuals or families. Business loans are those made to companies, including sole proprietors for the purpose of business operations. Loans made to individuals or families fall under one of two categories: consumer loans or mortgages. This broad category differentiation deals with government regulations that govern lending practices. Mortgages were covered in the chapter on housing. Consumer loans are offered in a variety forms and are covered in this chapter.

CONSUMER LOANS

Consumers choose from several credit options to finance their purchases. Loans are offered with the following characteristics:

- Credit type. Closed end credit versus revolving credit
- Number of payments. Single-payment versus installment loans
- Loan collateral. Secured versus unsecured loans
- Interest rates. Variable rate versus fixed rate loans

Closed-end Credit

Personal loans are either single payment or installment loans. Both single payment and installment loans are offered in secured or unsecured loans. Interest rates and options vary widely between lenders. Both fixed and variable rates are available on all types of loans; however, not every lender offers every option.

Single-Payment versus Installment Loans

A single-payment loan has one lump-sum payment at the end of the loan. This payment includes the initial principal (face value of the debt) plus the interest accrued during the life of the loan. Single-payment loans are typically short-term loans, one year or less. Sometimes a borrower obtains a single-payment loan until he can arrange long-term financing. A bridge loan is a typical single-payment loan. A new home construction loan is often a bridge loan during the construction phase of the house. After the construction is complete, the bridge loan is paid off with a traditional mortgage.

Single-payment loans are offered by some college financial aid departments. These single-payment loans are often secured against pending financial aid payments. The borrower takes out a loan to cover education expenses and pays the loan back in one lump sum payment, typically within the semester and often with the proceeds of a financial aid check. These loans are typically offered for either tuition or the purchase of textbooks and supplies.

| Kathy's Single Payment Loan | **EXAMPLE 4.1** |

Kathy Hampton wants to borrow $10,000 to go to Europe during summer break. Her dad agrees to lend her the money at 3.5 percent for one year, at which time she will pay back the entire balance of the loan, plus interest. How much will she owe her dad at the end of the year?

The basic formula to calculate interest is:

$$\text{interest} = (P) \times (i) \times (t)$$ **Equation 6.1**

Where:

Interest: is the total amount of interest to be paid on the loan

    P: is the principal amount of the loan

    I: is the interest rate expressed as a decimal

    t: is time in years

$$\text{Interest} = \$10,000 \times 0.035 \times 1 = \$350$$

At the end of the year Kathy owes the principal + interest, so she owes:

$$\$10,000 + \$350 = \$10,350. \quad\blacksquare$$

| **EXAMPLE 4.2** | Leon's Single Payment Loan |

Leon Fitzgerald doesn't have enough cash to buy his textbooks this semester. He applies for financial aid and is awarded a $2,500 grant, but his check won't be in until late in the semester so he takes out a short-term loan. Ben borrows $650 at 5 percent interest and agrees to pay back the loan in 3 months. How much will he owe in three months?

$$\text{Interest} = \$650 \times 0.05 \times 1/4 = \$8.13$$

Notice that since Leon is borrowing the money for 3 months, the timeframe is ¼ of a year. At the end of three months he owes the principal + interest, so he owes:

$$\$650 + \$8.13 = \$658.13 \quad\blacksquare$$

Installment Loans

Installment loan Loan that is paid back in periodic payments for a specified period of time until paid off.

Installment loans are paid back in periodic payments for a specified period of time until the loan is paid off. Car loans are typical installment loans. The borrower takes out the loan and agrees to pay it back in equal monthly payments. The equal monthly payments are periodic payments, although the most common period for payments on installment loans is a month, they are also offered in bi-weekly periods.

Installment loans are the most common type of loan used for large consumer purchases.

Each monthly payment pays that month's interest and a portion of the balance on the loan. The payment stays the same for the life of the loan, but the amount of principal or interest that is paid each month will change during the course of the loan. Initially, a greater portion of the monthly payment is applied to interest. This changes as the loan balance decreases. By the end of the loan term, payments are predominantly principal.

| Keri's Installment Payment Loan | **EXAMPLE 4.3** |

Keri wants to buy a used Nissan from her friend, Lisa. Her credit union offers loans on used vehicles at 4.9% interest. Lisa said she would sell her the car for $16,000. Keri wants to be able to pay off the loan in three years, how much will her payment be?

You can calculate the payment in either a spread sheet or with a financial calculator. Use the following parameters:

- Present value = $16,000—the amount she is borrowing
- Future value = 0—because at the end of the three years she will have the loan paid off
- Rate (=.049/12)—since her payments will be monthly we divided the annual rate by 12 months
- Number of payments = 36—the number of months in three years
- Payment = ?

If you don't have access to a financial calculator or a spread sheet program you can use the following formula:

$$PV \left(\frac{i}{1 - [(1 + i)^{-n}]} \right) = PMT$$

Where:
PV = present value—loan value
i = interest rate for period—in this case .049/12
n = number of periods—in this case 36 months

$$\$16,000 \left(\frac{0.004083}{1 - [(1.004083)^{-36}]} \right) = \$478.82$$

Now that we know her payment, let's look at how the interest and principal are paid on an installment loan. Notice from her payment schedule that she pays the most interest in the first month, each month after that she pays a little less in interest charges and a little more toward principal, although her payment stays a consistent $478.82. The last payment of an installment loan is often slightly higher or lower than all the other payments. This accounts for amounts to small to distribute evenly. Notice Kerihas a balance of $-0.25. In this case her last payment will be 25 cents lower than her regular payment. Her last payment will be $478.57.

Loan Collateral: Secured versus Unsecured Loans

A lender secures a loan against default by holding an asset as collateral. A car is the collateral for a car loan; if the borrower fails to pay the loan back, the lender takes the car and sells it to pay off the loan. A loan is secured when it is backed by collateral. Collateral is any asset used to secure a loan. Collateral

EXHIBIT 4.1	KERI'S PAYMENT SCHEDULE

$16,000 loan to purchase Nissan

Payment	Interest	Principal	Balance
1	$65.33	$413.49	$15,586.51
2	$63.64	$415.18	$15,171.33
3	$61.94	$416.88	$14,754.45
4	$60.24	$418.58	$14,335.87
5	$58.53	$420.29	$13,915.59
6	$56.82	$422.00	$13,493.59
7	$55.09	$423.73	$13,069.86
8	$53.36	$425.46	$12,644.40
9	$51.63	$427.19	$12,217.21
10	$49.88	$428.94	$11,788.27
11	$48.13	$430.69	$11,357.59
12	$46.37	$432.45	$10,925.14
13	$44.61	$434.21	$10,490.93
14	$42.83	$435.99	$10,054.94
15	$41.05	$437.77	$9,617.17
16	$39.27	$439.55	$9,177.62
17	$37.47	$441.35	$8,736.27
18	$35.67	$443.15	$8,293.12
19	$33.86	$444.96	$7,848.16
20	$32.04	$446.78	$7,401.39
21	$30.22	$448.60	$6,952.79
22	$28.39	$450.43	$6,502.36
23	$26.55	$452.27	$6,050.09
24	$24.70	$454.12	$5,595.97
25	$22.85	$455.97	$5,140.00
26	$20.99	$457.83	$4,682.16
27	$19.12	$459.70	$4,222.46
28	$17.24	$461.58	$3,760.88
29	$15.36	$463.46	$3,297.42
30	$13.46	$465.36	$2,832.06
31	$11.56	$467.26	$2,364.80
32	$9.66	$469.16	$1,895.64
33	$7.74	$471.08	$1,424.56
34	$5.82	$473.00	$951.56
35	$3.89	$474.93	$476.62
36	$1.95	$476.87	-$0.25

can be a savings account or a vehicle you bought new and paid off, but if you need cash you can take out a new loan against the vehicle and use it as collateral again. However, as the vehicle ages you won't be able to borrow as much against it, since the collateral is decreasing in value.

Loans can be secured by any item the lender appraises to have value. Normally, the lender will loan less than the collateral's value. If the borrower defaults on the loan; the lender needs to pay off the debt with the proceeds from the sale of the collateral.

Unsecured loans have no specific asset backing the loan. If the borrower defaults on the loan, the lender cannot repossess any of the borrower's assets. Unsecured loans are typically offered to customers with excellent credit history. These loans usually bear higher interest rates than secured loans. An unsecured loan bears higher risk for the lender because the lender holds no claim on a specific asset.

Interest Rates: Variable Rate versus Fixed Rate Loans

Fixed interest loans have a constant interest rate throughout the life of the loan. If interest rates rise, the lender does not receive a higher rate, and if interest rates fall the borrower doesn't receive a lower rate; both agree to a rate, and it does not change with fluctuating economic conditions. The rate is fixed.

Variable rate loans are not fixed, and the interest rate can adjust both up or down over the life of the loan. If the rates go up, the lender benefits; if the rates go down the borrower benefits. Variable rate loans are based on an index. There are many indexes, but the prime rate and the London InterBank Offered Rate (LIBOR) rate are two common indexes used in variable rate loans. They both are indexes or rates that banks use to loan money. The LIBOR rate is a rate used when banks loan money to other banks. The prime interest rate is the rate banks use to loan money to the most credit worthy customers. The prime rate is the rate large well-financed corporations pay for short-term loans. Banks use this rate as an index and add a margin or premium to set the rate for all other types of loans. The margin is the percentage above the index that the lender charges to loan money to the borrower. The margin is the lender's profit. Since the bank borrowed the money it loaned, it is paying interest as well and adds a margin to make a profit. For example, if the index the lender is using is the LIBOR rate, which is at 2.5 percent, and the lender's margin is 3 percent, then the interest charged to the consumer is the following:

$$2.5\% + 3.0\% = 5.5\%$$

A premium is added to compensate for the risk related to the loan based on the borrower and the type of loan. Two common types of variable rate loans are adjustable rate mortgages and credit cards. Credit cards often list the rate charged on outstanding balances as a percentage above the prime rate. These are higher risk loans, and they carry a higher interest rate. It is not uncommon to see rates between 14 to 19 percent above the prime rate.

Fixed interest loan Has a constant interest rate throughout the life of the loan.

Variable rate loan Loan where the interest rate can adjust both up or down over the life of the loan.

COMPUTING LOAN PAYMENTS AND AMORTIZATION

To amortize a loan is to make regular equal payments to pay off the loan. Each payment pays the current interest due and pays down the principal amount of the loan. Installment loans are amortized loans. An amortization table is a complete listing of the scheduled payments of a loan, the amount of each payment's interest, principal, and the new loan balance. Keri's payment schedule is an amortization table.

Adam is a college student, and his car just blew a head gasket. He decided the old car isn't worth the cost of the repair, and he needs to buy another used vehicle. He has three years of college left, and he wants to buy a used car he can pay off by graduation. He plans to ask his grandfather for a loan and offer to pay him 3 percent interest. Adam works part time and can afford a payment of $240 a month. He has found a car he would like to buy for $14,500. Can Adam buy this car?

Let's start by calculating what his payment will be on a $14,500 loan with 3 percent interest.

$$PV\left(\frac{i}{1-[(1+i)^{-n}]}\right)=PMT$$

Where:

PV = present value—loan value

i = interest rate for period—in this case .03/12

n = number of periods—in this case 36 months

$$\$14,500\left(\frac{\frac{.03}{12}}{1-\left[\left(1+\frac{.03}{12}\right)^{-36}\right]}\right)=PMT$$

$$\$14,500\left(\frac{0.0025}{1-[(1.0025)^{-36}]}\right)=\$421.68$$

Adam's payment would be $421.68 if he buys the car he wants. Since this is more than he can afford, he needs to determine how much he can afford. We can use the same equation, but we need to rearrange it so we are solving for the PV now instead of the payment.

$$PV=PMNT\frac{(1-(1+i)^{-n})}{i}$$

Where:

PV = present value—loan value

i = interest rate for period—in this case .03/12

n = number of periods—in this case 36 months

PMNT = the payment—Adam can afford $240 a month

$$PV=\$240\frac{\left(1-\left(1+\frac{.03}{12}\right)^{-n}\right)}{\frac{.03}{12}}$$

$$\$8252.75=\$240\frac{(1-(1.0025)^{-36})}{0.0025}$$

Adam can afford to buy a car for $8252.75. He shops around and finds another dependable car for $7,500. His grandfather agrees to loan him the money. Adam makes an amortization table to track his payments and to monitor his payoff value on his loan.

Compute Loan Amortization

To make a loan amortization or a payment schedule Adam needs to know what his payment will be. He calculates his payment as the first step:

$$PV\left(\frac{i}{1-[(1+i)^{-n}]}\right)=PMT$$

Where:

PV = present value–loan value of $7,500

  i = interest rate for period–in this case .03/12

 n = number of periods–in this case 36 months

$$\$7,500\left(\frac{0.0025}{1-[(1.0025)^{-36}]}\right)=\$218.11$$

Adam's monthly payment will be $218.11. Now he can create a table (see Exhibit 4.2) to calculate his principal and interest portions of his payment. He will also have a column for his new balance at the end of each month. A spreadsheet makes these calculations easy, but you can also do them with a calculator.

If you use a spreadsheet to track your payments, the spreadsheet will recalculate your balance, principal, and interest if you make a larger or smaller payment. If you choose to hand write your payment schedule, you may want to calculate each month's new balance as you make your payment.

ADAM'S PAYMENT SCHEDULE   EXHIBIT 4.2

$7,500 loan to purchase car

No.	Payment	Interest	Principal	Balance
1	$218.11	(.03/12) x (balance) (0.0025)($7,500) = $18.75	Payment - interest $218.11 – 18.75 = $199.36	prior balance-principal $7,500 – $199.36 = $7,300.64
2	$218.11	(0.0025)($7,300.64) = $18.25	$218.11 – 18.25 = $199.86	$7,300.64 – $199.86 = $7,100.78
3	$218.11	(0.0025)($7,100.78) = $17.75	$218.11 – 17.75 = $200.36	$7,100.78 – $200.36 = $6,900.42

Exhibit 4.3 shows Adam's amortization table for both his minimum payment and his affordable payment side by side. If Adam makes the $240 payment he can afford each month, he will save $32.92 in total interest and pay off his loan three months early.

EXHIBIT 4.3	ADAM'S PAYMENT SCHEDULE

$7,500 loan to purchase car

	Minimum Payment				Affordable Payment			
No.	Payment	interest	principal	7500	Payment	interest	principal	7500
1	$218.11	$18.75	$199.36	$7,300.64	$240.00	$18.75	$221.25	$7,278.75
2	$218.11	$18.25	$199.86	$7,100.78	$240.00	$18.20	$221.80	$7,056.95
3	$218.11	$17.75	$200.36	$6,900.42	$240.00	$17.64	$222.36	$6,834.59
4	$218.11	$17.25	$200.86	$6,699.56	$240.00	$17.09	$222.91	$6,611.68
5	$218.11	$16.75	$201.36	$6,498.20	$240.00	$16.53	$223.47	$6,388.20
6	$218.11	$16.25	$201.86	$6,296.34	$240.00	$15.97	$224.03	$6,164.18
7	$218.11	$15.74	$202.37	$6,093.97	$240.00	$15.41	$224.59	$5,939.59
8	$218.11	$15.23	$202.88	$5,891.09	$240.00	$14.85	$225.15	$5,714.43
9	$218.11	$14.73	$203.38	$5,687.71	$240.00	$14.29	$225.71	$5,488.72
10	$218.11	$14.22	$203.89	$5,483.82	$240.00	$13.72	$226.28	$5,262.44
11	$218.11	$13.71	$204.40	$5,279.42	$240.00	$13.16	$226.84	$5,035.60
12	$218.11	$13.20	$204.91	$5,074.51	$240.00	$12.59	$227.41	$4,808.19
13	$218.11	$12.69	$205.42	$4,869.09	$240.00	$12.02	$227.98	$4,580.21
14	$218.11	$12.17	$205.94	$4,663.15	$240.00	$11.45	$228.55	$4,351.66
15	$218.11	$11.66	$206.45	$4,456.70	$240.00	$10.88	$229.12	$4,122.54
16	$218.11	$11.14	$206.97	$4,249.73	$240.00	$10.31	$229.69	$3,892.84
17	$218.11	$10.62	$207.49	$4,042.24	$240.00	$9.73	$230.27	$3,662.58
18	$218.11	$10.11	$208.00	$3,834.24	$240.00	$9.16	$230.84	$3,431.73
19	$218.11	$9.59	$208.52	$3,625.71	$240.00	$8.58	$231.42	$3,200.31
20	$218.11	$9.06	$209.05	$3,416.67	$240.00	$8.00	$232.00	$2,968.31
21	$218.11	$8.54	$209.57	$3,207.10	$240.00	$7.42	$232.58	$2,735.73
22	$218.11	$8.02	$210.09	$2,997.01	$240.00	$6.84	$233.16	$2,502.57
23	$218.11	$7.49	$210.62	$2,786.39	$240.00	$6.26	$233.74	$2,268.83
24	$218.11	$6.97	$211.14	$2,575.25	$240.00	$5.67	$234.33	$2,034.50
25	$218.11	$6.44	$211.67	$2,363.57	$240.00	$5.09	$234.91	$1,799.59
26	$218.11	$5.91	$212.20	$2,151.37	$240.00	$4.50	$235.50	$1,564.09
27	$218.11	$5.38	$212.73	$1,938.64	$240.00	$3.91	$236.09	$1,328.00
28	$218.11	$4.85	$213.26	$1,725.38	$240.00	$3.32	$236.68	$1,091.32
29	$218.11	$4.31	$213.80	$1,511.58	$240.00	$2.73	$237.27	$854.05
30	$218.11	$3.78	$214.33	$1,297.25	$240.00	$2.14	$237.86	$616.18
31	$218.11	$3.24	$214.87	$1,082.38	$240.00	$1.54	$238.46	$377.72
32	$218.11	$2.71	$215.40	$866.98	$240.00	$0.94	$239.06	$138.67
33	$218.11	$2.17	$215.94	$651.04	$139.01	$0.35	$138.66	$0.00
34	$218.11	$1.63	$216.48	$434.55				
35	$218.11	$1.09	$217.02	$217.53				
36	$218.08	$0.54	$217.54	$0.00				

REVOLVING CREDIT

Revolving credit is a credit line; the borrower may spend up to a maximum limit. A revolving credit account stays open after the borrower has paid off the balance and can be used again for new borrowing needs. Credit cards and home equity loans are common types of revolving credit.

Credit Cards

Credit cards are the most popular form of revolving credit. Credit cards are popular, because they are easy use. MasterCard, Visa, American Express, and Discover are accepted around the world. Credit cards eliminate the need to carry cash or personal checks. Credit cards make it easy to borrow, and with that ease comes the risk of borrowing too much. Credit cards should be used wisely. There are two main types of credit cards: general credit cards and retail credit cards. Credit cards are normally unsecured debt.

General credit cards. General credit cards are issued by finance companies, credit unions, or banks. The four largest general credit cards in the United States are MasterCard, Visa, Discover, and American Express. The services offered by these different issuers vary somewhat, but they all are accepted worldwide.

General credit card
Credit issued by finance companies, credit unions, or banks.

Credit card companies generate income from two main sources:

1. They charge a discount to the merchant.
2. They charge interest and/or annual fees to their cardholders.

Merchants with higher charge volumes and larger average charges pay smaller discounts to the credit card. For example, a restaurant with an average charge of $56 might pay a discount of 3 percent while a jewelry store with an average sale of $300 might pay a discount of 2 percent. Exhibit 4.4 shows how the discount affects the net amount that the merchant receives for its sales from the credit card company. Retail merchants are willing to pay credit card fees and discounts because accepting credit cards can significantly increase their sales.

The second source of revenue for the credit card companies is the interest they charge cardholders who carry a balance at the end of the month. Interest rates vary depending on both the company who issued the card, and the customer who carries the card. Effective annual rates typically range between 6 and 24 percent.

Retail credit cards. Some stores offer their own credit cards, called a retail (merchant) credit card. They work just like a regular credit card except they are only good at the issuing store. For example, a Shell credit card can only be used at Shell gas stations. Stores prefer issuing their

© Phase4Photography, 2014, Shutterstock, Inc.

Credit can be a convenient way to pay for unexpected expenses; however, be cautious and use credit cards wisely.

EXHIBIT 4.4   CREDIT CARD DISCOUNTS

Merchant	Average Sale	Discount
Restaurant	$ 56	3%
Jewelry store	$312	2%

Discount on a $100 sale

Merchant	Discount	Net Sale
Restaurant	$3.00	$97
Jewelry store	$2.00	$98

own credit cards because they avoid the discount fee of a general credit card issuer such as MasterCard.

Retail stores often offer discounts to their retail credit card holders. For example Shell gas stations may offer a 5 cent per gallon discount for gas purchases charged on a Shell gas credit card. Many stores also offer instant cash back on purchases if you apply for one of their cards.

The disadvantages of retail cards are that they can only be used at the issuing store; they charge higher interest rates; and there can be a possible negative impact on your credit score if you have too many cards.

CREDIT CARD BASICS

Credit cards have the same basic features. Compare the following features before selecting a credit card:

- Credit limit
- Annual fees
- Card reward systems
- Grace period
- Cash advances
- Interest rate
- Minimum payment due
- Late fees

Credit Limit

The credit limit is the maximum allowable balance. If the credit card has a limit of $1,000, you can carry a balance of up to $1,000. Credit limits typically range from a few hundred dollars to several thousand dollars. Your credit limit will depend on your current financial situation and your credit history. Most credit card companies automatically increase your limit as you use the card and pay off the balance in full.

If you have a $1,000 credit limit and make $800 in purchases, you will have an available credit limit of $200. As you pay down your balance, your available credit limit increases.

If you exceed your credit limit, your account will be charge an over the limit fee. The over the limit fee is typically $30 or more. Transactions that cause a card to be severely over its limit will be rejected by the card company. If you go over your credit limit, you must make a payment large enough to bring your balance under the credit limit in the next billing cycle if you want to remain in good standing. If you fail to correct the over the limit situation, your card will be suspended.

Annual Fees
Some credit cards charge an annual fee of $50 to $100 for the use of their credit card. Other credit cards have no annual fees. Shop around for a card with no annual fee.

Card Reward Systems
Some credit cards offer incentives or rewards. These incentives include airline miles, cash back, merchandise, and discounts on major purchases. Card companies offer incentives to encourage and reward the use of their credit cards.

Grace Period
The grace period is the length of time you have to pay off your balance before interest accrues. Most companies allow a 25-day grace period on new purchases. If the balance is paid in full within 25 days of the billing statement date, no interest is charged.

Most credit card statement periods are 30 days long—for example, from March 15 to April 13. All purchases made during this period will appear on the monthly statement. The statement will show a closing date of April 13th. The grace period begins after the closing statement date. Day 1 of the grace period is April 14th. The grace period runs from April 14th to May 8th, as long as you pay off your balance by May 8th you won't be charged interest on your new purchases.

Cash Advances
Cash advances allow the cardholder to take cash, deposit cash in an account, or write checks against that person's credit limit. Cash advance limits may differ from your total credit line limit. There are several ways to access cash advances:

- Withdraw funds in person at a financial institution such as a bank that offers cash advance services for the card. This option is usually best for withdrawing large amounts.
- Use the card to withdraw funds from an automated teller machine (ATM). Most cards have account information encoded on them and, by using a PIN (personal identification number) or password, a cardholder can withdraw funds subject to the teller machine's and the card's cash limit.
- Use paper checks supplied by the card issuer. Many credit card companies send personalized checks to their customers. If you use these checks, they are considered a cash advance. You can use these checks to write a check for cash to yourself or to make any other purchase (except to pay your monthly payment on that card).

Although the ability to take a cash advance from credit cards may come in handy in emergency situations, there are additional costs associated with cash advances, and they are an expensive source of credit. Costs of taking a cash advance include the following:

- Interest charges. There is no grace period for cash advances, and interest begins accumulating on the date of the advance. In addition, some cards levy a higher interest rate on cash advances than on purchases.
- Cash advance fees. Cards usually charge an additional cash advance fee at the time of the cash advance. This fee typically ranges from 2 to 4 percent of the amount of the cash advance and is added to the card balance at the time of the cash advance.

Interest Rate

The interest rate, or APR, a credit card charges is either the most important or the least important feature of the card, depending on how you use the credit card. If you always pay the entire credit card balance before the end of the grace period, then the interest rate doesn't matter since you won't pay any interest. However, individuals who pay off their total bill every month are in the minority. The majority of households use credit cards to finance purchases they couldn't otherwise afford. If you use credit cards this way, the interest rate is the most important feature of the card.

Credit cards bear a higher interest rate compared to other forms of debt. Interest rates for the average user range from 12 to 30 percent.

Minimum Payment Due

Each month there is a balance on a credit card, the cardholder must make at least a minimum monthly payment. The minimum monthly payment is typically the larger of either 4 percent of the balance or $15.

If you have a balance of $150, you would be required to make a minimum payment of $15, since 4 percent of $150 is only $6.

If you have a balance of $5,000, you would be required to make a minimum monthly payment of $200.

© euroshot, 2014, Shutterstock, Inc.

Shop around for the best deals in a credit card. The better your credit, the more leverage you have when negotiating annual fees and interest rates.

One in six U.S. families pay only the minimum payment due each month. This habit leads to ever-increasing debt balances. You should always strive to pay off the balance in full. If you can't pay it off in full, pay as much as you can to avoid the high interest charges.

Late Fees

If you fail to make at least the minimum payment by the due date, you will be charged a late fee. Late fees typically range from $29 to $45.

Failure to pay by the due date has the following consequences:

- You will be charged a late payment fee, which significantly increases the cost of credit.
- Your credit score will be adversely affected.

Credit Card Statements

You will receive a credit card statement at the end of each billing cycle. Exhibit 4.5 contains an example of a credit card statement. The key pieces of information on the statement are the following:

- Previous balance. The amount due from the previous credit card statement.
- Purchases. The statement should list all purchases during the statement period, as well as the total amount of purchases during the period.
- Cash advances. The amount of any cash advances taken during the billing cycle.
- Credits. Credits include payments you made plus any refunds from returned merchandise since the last billing cycle.
- Finance/interest charges. The amount of interest accrued on cash advances or outstanding balances from the previous period.
- New balance. The total amount due from this statement. The balance is calculated by the following formula:
  New balance = Previous balance
  + Purchases
  + Cash advances
  – Payments
  – Credits/refunds
  + Finance charges
- Minimum payment. The minimum payment due.

Most credit card companies now offer online and secure access to account information. You can opt to receive statements electronically through e-mail or a paper copy through U.S. mail. Online access allows customers to track purchases during a billing cycle. It also allows cardholders to identify mistakes or potential fraud items quicker.

Lori Richards, like the rest of us, has the potential to be both wise and unwise with the use of credit. Lori opens a new credit card in March. Exhibit 4.6 shows the charges she made the first month.

Lori's new card has an 11.49 percent interest rate on new purchases. She has a 28-day billing cycle and is allowed a 25-day grace period on new purchases. As long as she pays off her balance in full by the due date, she pays no finance charges. In addition, her new card offers a reward incentive. The reward earns

EXHIBIT 4.5	EXAMPLE CREDIT CARD STATEMENT

Summary Activity

Statement date	4/9/2014
Previous balance	$0.00
+ purchases	$1,545.48
+ cash advances	$0.00
– payments payment recv'd	$0.00
Late Fee	$0.00
+ finance charges	$0.00
New Balance	$1,545.48
Minimum payment	$62.00
Date Due	5/4/2014
bonus earned	$15.00
bonus available cash back available	0

Detailed Activity

23-Mar-14	Supermarkets	$40.72
24-Mar-14	Supermarkets	$12.14
25-Mar-14	Merchandise/ Retail	$122.65
26-Mar-14	Merchandise/ Retail	$190.00
27-Mar-14	Supermarkets	$69.13
28-Mar-14	Merchandise/ Retail	$92.14
29-Mar-14	Merchandise/ Retail	$66.75
30-Mar-14	Gasoline	$53.17
31-Mar-14	Restaurants	$124.75
1-Apr-14	Supermarkets	$42.34
2-Apr-14	Supermarkets	$198.17
3-Apr-14	Restaurants	$42.00
4-Apr-14	Home Improvement	$53.98
5-Apr-14	Restaurants	$72.16
6-Apr-14	Merchandise/ Retail	$54.17
7-Apr-14	Supermarkets	$178.45
8-Apr-14	Restaurants	$34.00
9-Apr-14	Merchandise/ Retail	$98.76
		$1,545.48

1 percent of all new purchases. It is unlimited in the number of rewards she can earn. To redeem her rewards she must redeem them in amounts of $20 or more for merchandise from the card's sponsors or, she may redeem them for cash in equal increments of $50. For example she can redeem $50, $100, or $150 at a time. She cannot redeem $52. As long as she pays at least her minimum balance by the due date each month, she is in good standing. If she fails to pay her minimum balance by the due date, she does not earn reward points for purchases in that billing cycle. If she does not make her minimum payment by the due date, she loses her good standard, and her interest rate on new purchases increases to 28.99 percent.

LORI'S JULY CREDIT CARD CHARGES   EXHIBIT 4.6

Date	Category	Amount
2-Jul	Supermarkets	$90.90
3-Jul	Supermarkets	$27.22
4-Jul	Merchandise/ Retail	$78.14
5-Jul	Merchandise/ Retail	$100.54
6-Jul	Supermarkets	$36.09
8-Jul	Merchandise/ Retail	$138.74
10-Jul	Merchandise/ Retail	$42.99
11-Jul	Gasoline	$46.08
13-Jul	Restaurants	$60.93
14-Jul	Supermarkets	$10.71
15-Jul	Supermarkets	$65.25
16-Jul	Restaurants	$11.05
17-Jul	Home Improvement	$28.65
19-Jul	Restaurants	$20.85
20-Jul	Merchandise/ Retail	$28.99
23-Jul	Supermarkets	$24.97
24-Jul	Restaurants	$17.94
28-Jul	Merchandise/ Retail	$69.13
	Total	$899.17

Wise Lori reads all the information about her new account. She understands how her account works. She decides to take advantage of the cash back bonuses and begins using her new card for her regular budgeted purchases. Her first statement with her July charges closes on August 2nd; her first payment is due 25 days later on August 27th. She pays her balance in full each month and earns $50 cash back by the end of six months. Exhibit 4.7 shows a summary of the first six months of Wise Lori's credit card statements.

WISE LORI'S MONTHLY SUMMARY CREDIT CARD STATEMENT   EXHIBIT 4.7

Statement Date	8/2/2014	8/30/2014	9/27/2014	10/25/2014	11/22/2014	12/20/2014
Previous balance	$0.00	$899.17	$899.17	$899.17	$899.17	$899.17
+ purchases	$899.17	$899.17	$899.17	$899.17	$899.17	$899.17
+ cash advances	$0.00	$0.00	$0.00	$0.00	$0.00	$0.00
– payments	$0.00	–$899.17	–$899.17	–$899.17	–$899.17	–$899.17
payment recv'd		25-Aug	22-Sep	20-Oct	17-Nov	15-Dec
Late Fee	$0.00	$0.00	0	0	0	0
+ finance charges	$0.00	$0.00	0	0	0	0
New Balance	$899.17	$899.17	$899.17	$899.17	$899.17	$899.17
Minimum payment	$40.00	$40.00	$40.00	$40.00	$40.00	$40.00
Date Due	8/27/2014	9/24/2014	10/22/2014	11/19/2014	12/17/2014	1/14/2015
bonus earned	$8.99	$8.99	$8.99	$8.99	$8.99	$8.99
bonus available			$26.97	$35.96	$44.95	$53.94
cash back available						$50.00

Unwise Lori receives her card and makes the same charges in the first month that Wise Lori made. She doesn't read the cardholder's agreement and doesn't understand how her card works. She fails to notice she has a 28-day billing cycle or that her bill is due 25 days after the close of the statement. Unwise Lori gets her first bill and is excited to see she is only required to pay $40. Unwise Lori makes the minimum payment and continues to make equal charges on her card the following month. Unwise Lori notices she has plenty of extra cash in her checking account and spends it shopping and going out with friends. Unwise Lori is thrilled with the new credit card. She continues to make only the minimum monthly payments. She doesn't reconcile her statement or even bother to read it beyond a quick glance to see what her minimum payment is. Exhibit 4.8 shows a summary of the first six months of Unwise Lori's credit card statements.

Unwise Lori assumed since her August bill was due on the 27th, that her September bill would also be due on the 27th. This assumption causes Lori to make her second payment late. The credit card company charges her $29.95 in late payment fees and increases her interest rate to 28.99 percent. Lori doesn't notice because she just quickly glanced at the statement to see her minimum payment is now $120. In just six short months Lori owes almost $6,000. She has only earned $20.02 in bonus points but isn't qualified to redeem any as cash. Her finance charges are now accruing at a rate of over $150 a month and she still hasn't noticed she is being charged late fees.

Unwise Lori made some common assumptions and mistakes.

HOW TO PROPERLY USE CREDIT CARDS

Credits cards make buying easy–too easy, for many people. Monitor your credit spending as if you were spending your cash, because you are.

EXHIBIT 4.8   UNWISE LORI'S MONTHLY SUMMARY CREDIT CARD STATEMENT

Statement Date	8/2/2014	8/30/2014	9/27/2014	10/25/2014	11/22/2014	12/20/2014
Previous balance	$0.00	$899.17	$1,777.55	$2,649.32	$3,537.34	$4,407.48
+ purchases	$899.17	$899.17	$899.17	$899.17	$899.17	$899.17
+ cash advances	$0.00	$0.00	$0.00	$0.00	$0.00	$0.00
– payments	$0.00	–$40.00	–80	–120	–160	–200
payment recv'd		27-Aug	27-Sep	27-Oct	27-Nov	27-Dec
Late Fee	$0.00	$0.00	29.95	29.95	29.95	29.95
+ finance charges	$0.00	$19.21	22.65	78.9	101.02	122.66
New Balance	$899.17	$1,777.55	$2,649.32	$3,537.34	$4,407.48	$5,259.26
Minimum payment	$40.00	$80.00	$120.00	$160.00	$200.00	$235.00
Date Due	8/27/2014	9/24/2014	10/22/2014	11/19/2014	12/17/2014	1/14/2015
bonus earned	$8.99	$8.99	0	0	0	0
bonus available			$17.98	$17.98	$17.98	$17.98
cash back available	0	$0.00	0	0	0	0

- Don't buy what you can't afford. Make sure you can pay off the entire balance every month. Use credit cards for their convenience, not to finance unnecessary items. Do you really want to pay 20 percent interest on a new pair of shoes?
- Budget credit card spending like cash each month. Balance and reconcile your credit card statements at least once a month, like any other account.
- Always pay on time. Late fees are like bounced check fees–avoid them. They are expensive and damage your credit rating.
- Emergency use. If you have an emergency expenditure you can't pay off all at once, pay as much as you can the first month. Reallocate your budget to pay off the credit card as quickly as possible. Always pay more than the minimum balance.
- Read the cardholder statement; make sure you fully understand how your card works.

DEALING WITH CREDIT CARD DEBT

Credit card debt affects tens of millions of households across the country. If you have excessive credit card debt, there are steps you can take to pay it off.

1. Correct your spending habits.
2. Create a payment plan. Set a goal to pay off the debt. You can decrease your debt as long as you pay more than the accrued interest each month.

The key to dealing with credit card debt is to reduce the principal amount of the debt as quickly as possible. This isn't easy if interest is compounding at 18 or 22 percent. As interest accumulates on credit card debt, the balance grows at an ever-increasing pace.

Pay your credit card bill off before you invest. If you have $1,000 in credit card debt and $1,000 in a savings account, use the $1,000 to pay off the debt. If your credit card charges 18 percent interest, paying off your debt yields an effective18 percent return.

Home Equity Loans

Home equity loans are revolving credit accounts available to homeowners. The equity in a home is the portion the homeowner has paid off. To calculate home equity, subtract the debt on the home from the fair market value of the home.

Home equity loan
Revolving credit account available to homeowners.

$$Equity = Market\ value - Mortgage$$

If you bought a home for $150,000 and you currently owe $135,000, how much is the equity in the home? There isn't enough information to answer the question. It doesn't matter what you paid for the home. The important factor is fair market value, or how much would the house sell for in the current market. During the housing boom, home prices rose at record rates, sometimes by as much as 10 percent a year. However, when the bubble burst, home prices fell dramatically, in some states by as much as 50 percent. Let's say for our example your house is currently worth $175,000. Your amount of equity in the home is:

$$\$175,000 - \$135,000 = \$40,000$$

Banks offer home equity loans on a percentage of the equity in your home. Like credit cards, the loan has a maximum limit. Most banks will loan you up to 80 percent of your equity. You only owe interest on amounts you actually borrow, usually at a variable rate. This type of loan is popular with homeowners because the loan is easy to get, and the rates are often comparable or better than other types of consumer loans. In addition, the interest paid is usually deductible for federal income tax purposes. These are secured revolving credit accounts. The home is the collateral for the loan.

Regardless of the form the loan takes, they all have one thing in common; the lender is required to disclose the APR. Whether you have secured or unsecured credit, revolving credit or installment loans, a fixed rate or variable rate—the lender is required to disclose the APR before you sign the loan agreement.

APR VERSUS INTEREST RATE

The Truth in Lending Act, originally enacted by Congress in 1968, requires all consumer loan agreements to clearly state the APR. The APR is the annual percentage rate, expressed as the true interest charged over the life of the loan. The APR includes fees associated with the loan. These fees are often called finance fees, origination fees, or points. This requirement protects the consumer from abusive lending practices.

Joe Quince borrows $1,000 for 7.9 percent interest and pays a $19.95 origination fee. He takes the loan out for one year. How much is he really paying in interest?

For simplicity sake, let's assume he makes one single payment at the end of the year. He would pay the bank back $1079 at the end of the year, but he also paid $19.95 up front. To calculate his APR, total his interest payments and finance charges and divide by his net loan value.

$$(\$79 + \$19.95)/(\$1,000 - \$19.95) = 10.1\%$$

For this loan the lender is required to clearly state an APR of 10.1 percent. Most lenders show this as 7.9 percent interest, APR 10.1 percent. The interest rate quoted is the nominal rate, in this case the nominal rate is 7.9 percent.

The above example is a simple illustration of the APR, but most loans are not made as a single payment loan with one payment at the end of the loan term. The most common loan would require equal monthly payments. Let's look at how this same loan for Joe Quince would work with monthly payments. His payment schedule is shown in Exhibit 4.9.

If you sum his payments they total $1,043.30. That means over the course of the year he paid $43.30 in interest. We can use the average monthly balance

JOE QUINCE'S PAYMENT SCHEDULE

EXHIBIT 4.9

$1,000 loan at 7.9 percent

	Payment	Interest	Loan Principal	Balance 1000
1	86.94	6.58	80.36	919.64
2	86.94	6.05	80.89	838.75
3	86.94	5.52	81.42	757.33
4	86.94	4.99	81.95	675.38
5	86.94	4.45	82.49	592.89
6	86.94	3.9	83.04	509.85
7	86.94	3.36	83.58	426.27
8	86.94	2.81	84.13	342.14
9	86.94	2.25	84.69	257.45
10	86.94	1.69	85.25	172.2
11	86.94	1.13	85.81	86.39
12	86.96	0.57	86.39	0
Totals	1,043.30	43.30	1,000	6,578.29

method to estimate the interest rate he was charged. First, sum the balances for each month of the loan and divide by the number of payments.

$$\$6,578.29/12 = \$548.19 \quad \text{average monthly balance}$$

Next divide the total amount of interest he paid by his average monthly balance.

$$\text{interest rate} = \frac{\text{Total interest paid}}{\text{average periodic balance}}$$

This is an estimated value.

$$\$43.30/548.19 = 7.9 \text{ percent}$$

He paid the stated interest rate on his payments, but this doesn't include the $19.95 he paid up front for his loan. Let's use the same average method to estimate his APR.

$$\text{APR} = \frac{\text{Total finance charges}}{\text{average periodic balance}}$$

This estimates the interest rate:

$$(\$43.30 + \$19.95)/\$548.19 = 11.53\%$$

This is the reason the law requires lenders state the APR, because when you factor in the fees paid up front, the interest rate can be substantially higher than the rate you are charged

Note that there isn't a formula given to calculate the interest rate for a series of payments, in terms of the present value and the future value. The interest rate cannot be solved for algebraically using these calculations. The interest rate must be solved by iteration, which is a method of making guesses in smaller increments until the right number is selected. Tables are published with interest rates, spreadsheets and calculators have the ability to iterate rapidly, or we can come up with a close approximation using the average periodic balance method.

over the course of your payments. The average method gives a good estimate and is relatively easy. You can also calculate the interest rate using a spreadsheet or financial calculator.

Joe took out a loan for $1,000, but he had to pay $19.95 to receive that loan. So the day he received his loan he actually only got to borrow:

$$\$1,000 - \$19.95 = \$980.05$$

Now plug in the following values

- Present value = $980.05
- Future value = 0
- Payment = (–86.94)
- Number of payments = 12
- Rate = ?
- This calculates an APR of 11.7 percent, which is slightly higher than our estimated value.

The APR is the true interest rate charged over the life of a loan. This rate factors in all applicable costs and fees associated with the loan and expresses those costs on an annualized basis. Use the APR to compare loans with different credit terms. For example, if you compare a five-year auto loan to a seven-year auto loan, it is tempting to look at the payments and choose the seven-year loan. You should compare the APRs not the payments. The seven-year loan will typically have a higher APR. For example, a quick look at the APRs for the following 30-year fixed-rate mortgages indicates which lender offers the lowest upfront costs.

Lender	Interest Rate	Points	APR
A	5.125%	0	5.213%
B	5.125%	0	5.123%
C	5.0%	0	5.167%
D	5.0%	0	5.088%

If you look at the rates for Lenders A and B, you will see they are charging the same interest rate and no points, but the APR is higher for Lender A than it is for Lender B. This indicates Lender A charges more for the fees associated with processing the loan and will have higher closing costs than the same loan from Lender B. APR helps the consumer compare loans and find the best value for their borrowing needs.

Sometimes a borrower can negotiate an interest-only loan. Let's look at using this method for Joe's loan of $1,000 at 7.9 percent for one year. He is still required to pay the $19.95 processing fee. What is his APR on the loan? (See Exhibit 4.10.)

Using the same average monthly balance method we can estimate his APR.

$$9.9\% = \frac{(\$78.96 + \$19.95)}{\$1,000}$$

INTEREST ONLY LOAN   EXHIBIT 4.10

	Payment	Interest	Loan Principal	Balance 1000
1	6.58	6.58	0	1000
2	6.58	6.58	0	1000
3	6.58	6.58	0	1000
4	6.58	6.58	0	1000
5	6.58	6.58	0	1000
6	6.58	6.58	0	1000
7	6.58	6.58	0	1000
8	6.58	6.58	0	1000
9	6.58	6.58	0	1000
10	6.58	6.58	0	1000
11	6.58	6.58	0	1000
12	1,006.58	6.58	1,000	0
Totals	1,078.96	78.96	1,000	12,0000

Joe's APR for both the lump sum loan and the interest-only loan are both 9.9 percent. At first glance it may appear they are equal; however, although the APR is a good place to start when comparing loans, it isn't the only consideration. Notice Joe pays a total of $1,043 in payments with the standard installment loan but he pays $1,078.96 for the interest only loan. Exhibit 4.11 shows a comparison of the two types of loans.

In order for Joe to pay back the $1,000 in one lump sum payment at the end of the year he needs to set aside $83.33 a month for the principal; add this to his interest payments. He needs to budget for $89.91 a month. If he pays down the balance with a regular installment loan, his payment is $86.94. Joe's total cost for the loan and his monthly budget expenses are both higher with the interest-only loan, although the APR on both are equal. This type of loan is not wise for most consumers, and should be avoided. It is attractive to those who cannot afford the loan to begin with. There are some exceptions.

If you receive the bulk of your income in one lump sum annual payment, it may be a good alternative; however, if you receive regular income in weekly or monthly intervals this type of loan should be avoided. Budgeting for one

COMPARISON OF INTEREST COSTS FOR AN INTEREST-ONLY LOAN TO A STANDARD LOAN   EXHIBIT 4.11

Type	Principal	Interest	APR	Total Cost to Borrow
Standard	$1,000	43.30 +19.95	9.9%	63.25
Interest Only	$1,000	78.96 + 19.95	9.9%	98.91

large payment at the end of a loan can be difficult, so most borrowers and lenders prefer installment loans that pay off the principal over the life of the loan rather than in one balloon payment at the end.

THE LOAN CONTRACT

The loan contract is a binding legal document that details the terms of the loan. The borrower and lender both sign the contract. The contract includes the following:

- Amount of the loan. Typically, this is the purchase price of the item you are buying with the loan. The loan may be less than the purchase price if a down payment is required.
- Payment schedule to repay the loan. This includes the maturity of the loan. The maturity is the time duration of the loan. Car loans are offered in standard maturities of 36, 48, 60, or 72 months. The payments are calculated by the amortization of the loan based on the loan amount, interest rate, and maturity.
- Interest rate on the loan. The lender is required to state the APR. Many contracts will show both the nominal rate and the APR.
- Security agreement. If the loan has collateral, the details of the security agreement will be included in the loan contract.

Exhibit 4.12 shows an example of a consumer loan agreement. In addition to the standard features of a loan contract, the contract may contain one or more clauses. There are several common clauses you might find in your loan agreement:

- Insurance agreement clause
- Acceleration clause
- Deficiency payments clause
- Recourse clause
- Prepayment penalties clause

INSURANCE AGREEMENT CLAUSE

Applicants for consumer loans are often asked if they would like to purchase credit insurance along with their loan. Credit insurance makes the loan payments if you become unable to do so. Credit insurance is usually optional. Federal law prohibits lenders from deceptively including credit insurance in any loan without the borrower's knowledge and consent.

Types of Credit Insurance
There are four main types of credit insurance:

1. Credit life insurance will pay off all or part of the remaining loan balance if you die.
2. Credit disability insurance makes loan payments while you are injured or sick and unable to work. Credit disability insurance is also called credit accident and health insurance.

CONSUMER LOAN AGREEMENT   **EXHIBIT 4.12**

CONSUMER LOAN AGREEMENT

1. Parties: The undersigned is _____, the Borrower, and the Lender is _____.

2. Date of Agreement: _____.

3. Promise to Pay: Within _____ months from today, Borrower promises to pay to Lender_____ dollars ($_____) and interest and other charges stated below.

4. Responsibility: Although this agreement may be signed below by more than one person, each of the undersigned understands that they are each as individuals responsible and jointly and severally liable for paying back the full amount.

5. Breakdown of Loan: Borrower will pay:

   Amount of Loan $_____

   Other (Describe) $_____

   Amount financed: $_____

   Finance charge: $_____

   Total of payments: $_____

   ANNUAL PERCENTAGE RATE _____%

6. Repayment: Borrower will repay in the following manner: Borrower will repay the amount of this note in _____ equal uninterrupted monthly installments of $_____ each on the _____day of each month starting on the ____day of _____, 20____, and ending on _____, 20____.

7. Prepayment: Borrower has the right to prepay the whole outstanding amount at any time. If Borrower pays early, or if this loan is refinanced or replaced by a new note, Lender will refund the unearned finance charge, figured by the Rule of 78-a commonly used formula for figuring rebates on installment loans.

8. Late Charge: Any installment not paid within ten (10) days of its due date shall be subject to a late charge of 5% of the payment, not to exceed $_____ for any such late installment.

9. Security: To protect Lender, Borrower gives what is known as a security interest or mortgage in: [Describe:]

   _____

   _____

   _____

   _____

10. Default: If for any reason Borrower fails to make any payment on time, Borrower shall be in default. The Lender can then demand immediate payment of the entire remaining unpaid balance of this loan without giving anyone further notice. If the Borrower has not paid the full amount of the loan when the final payment is due, the Lender will charge Borrower interest on the unpaid balance at _____ percent (%) per year.

11. Right of Offset: If this loan becomes past due, the Lender will have the right to pay this loan from any deposit or security Borrowed has with this lender without notice to him/her.

    If the Lender gives Borrower an extension of time to pay this loan, he/she still must repay the entire loan.

12. Collection fees: If this note is placed with an attorney for collection, then Borrower agrees to pay an attorney's fee of fifteen percent (15%) of the unpaid balance. This fee will be added to the unpaid balance of the loan.

13. Co-borowers: Any Co-borrowers signing this agreement agree to be equally responsible with the borrower of this loan.

    Agreed To:

    _____

    Lender

    _____

    Borrower

    _____

    Borrower

    _____

3. Involuntary unemployment insurance will continue to make your loan payments while you are unemployed following the loss of your job through no fault of your own, such as a layoff.
4. Credit property insurance provides insurance coverage for any property used to secure the loan if damaged or lost by events such as theft or natural disasters.

Consumers pay for credit insurance in one of two ways:

1. They can make periodic (for example, monthly) payments that pay the insurance premium.
2. They can finance the insurance premium as part of the loan by increasing the loan balance to cover the premium.

The second method is usually more expensive because the borrower has financed the insurance premium with the loan, meaning that interest will be paid on the insurance premium.

Should You Get Credit Insurance?

Credit insurance is an expensive alternative. Other methods, such as obtaining a regular life insurance policy instead of credit life, are less costly. Exhibit 4.13 provides a list of questions to help you determine if credit insurance is appropriate for a particular loan.

Acceleration Clause

An acceleration clause gives the lender the right to demand full immediate payment if the borrower misses one or more loan payments. If you do not pay the entire balance in full, then any collateral is subject to repossession. This clause is common; however, most lenders will work with you. If you have a problem, contact the lender and ask for an altered payment schedule. Your chances for working out a satisfactory arrangement are best before a payment is late. As soon as you know you won't be able to make a payment on time, call the lender and discuss the situation.

EXHIBIT 4.13	QUESTIONS TO ASK BEFORE BUYING CREDIT INSURANCE

- How much is the premium?
- Will the premium be financed as part of the loan?
- Can you pay monthly instead of financing the entire premium as part of your loan?
- How much lower would your monthly loan payment be without the credit insurance?
- Will the insurance cover the full length of your loan and the full loan amount?
- What are the limits and exclusions on payment of benefits—that is, spell out exactly whats covered and what's not.
- Is there a waiting period before the coverage becomes effective?
- If you have a co-borrower, what coverage does he or she have and at what cost?
- Can you cancel the insurance? If so, what kind of refund is available?

Source: www.ftc.gov/credit

Deficiency Payments Clause

This clause states that if you default on a loan, the lender may collect payments in addition to the collateral. Lenders protect themselves with this clause in case the value of the collateral decreases and is insufficient to pay off the balance of the loan. If this occurs, then the lender can bill you for the amount of the deficiency. If you default on a loan with an outstanding balance of $8,000, the bank can repossess your car and sell it. If the current market value of the car is $6,000, the bank can collect the $2,000 difference plus its costs for the repossession, sale, and attorney's fees. The lender is not allowed to sell the car at a reduced rate from market value, if it does, it must credit you the reasonable market value. Most states recognize the Gold Book Value as the current market value. The Gold Book is published monthly, and many public libraries carry it in their reserve collections. Get an attorney if a lender repossesses your property. Most collections are handled by collection companies, not the lender. Collection companies are in business to make money on bad debt and do not represent the borrower's interest. An attorney will represent your interest in such a situation, and although you will probably still owe some money, an attorney can protect you from excessive charges.

Recourse Clause

This clause states what actions the lender can take against you in case you default on a loan. This is necessary for unsecured loans, but it is also included in secured loan contracts.

Prepayment Penalty Clause

This part of the loan states whether you have to pay any penalties in case you pay off a loan early. If you think you may not need the loan for the entire period of time, you should make sure there are no penalties for paying off your loan early. Some states prohibit prepayment penalty clauses.

SOURCES FOR CONSUMER LOANS

Several types of financial institutions offer consumer loans:

- Commercial banks
- Credit unions
- Consumer finance companies

Commercial banks and credit unions are depositary institutions that accept deposits from customers and then lend a certain portion of the funds they have on deposit. A finance company also makes loans, but it has sources of funds other than deposits.

Interest Rates on Consumer Loans

The interest rate a borrower pays on a consumer loan varies widely from person to person and from year to year. The interest rate an individual pays is determined by both economic factors and credit risk. Interest rates for loans are affected by four factors:

- Inflation
- Monetary policy of the central bank

- Maturity risk
- Default risk

As a consumer, you have no control over the first two factors, which are the broad economic variables. You do have some control over maturity and default risks. If you minimize these risks, you reduce your costs to borrow money.

Inflation

Inflation The increase in the price of goods over time.

Inflation is the increase in the price of goods over time. Higher inflation causes higher interest rates.

Monetary Policy of the Central Bank

The central bank in the United States is the Federal Reserve Bank, or simply the Fed. The Fed has the responsibility of monitoring the overall health of the economy and regulating the money supply in the economic system. The Fed's decisions impact interest rates across the country.

The interest rate the Fed controls is the federal funds rate. The federal funds rate is the interest rate one bank charges another to borrow funds overnight. Banks adjust the rates they charge their customers based on what it cost the bank to borrow money. As the Fed raises rates, banks raise rates. When the Fed lowers rates, banks lower rates.

Rates on car loans in 1981, when the Fed funds rate was 19 percent, were substantially higher than they are today. Unfortunately, individuals have no control over this rate or the Fed's actions, but it is important you understand how changes in this rate affect the interest rates you pay.

Maturity Risk

In the financial world, risk and reward are directly proportional—the greater the risk, the greater the reward. From a lender's perspective, loans are investments. The lender will ask for a higher interest rate as the risk of the loan increases. Maturity of loan influences the risk of a loan. The longer the borrower has to repay, the greater the risk the lender will lose money. If interest rates increase, the lender loses potentially higher earnings. The lender could have loaned the same money to another borrower for a higher rate of return. Lenders compensate for maturity risk by charging higher interest rates for longer loans.

Other factors equal, a lender would prefer to make short-term loans rather than long-term loans. As a lender with two potential borrowers, who would you rather loan money to, the one who will repay the loan in six months or the one who wants 10 years to repay the loan?

When shopping for a loan, take the loan with the shortest maturity you can afford. The higher monthly payments are worth the long-term savings.

Default Risk

A loan is in default when the borrower does not make a scheduled payment on time. Lenders consider default risk when they select the interest rate on a loan. Lenders offer lower rates to borrowers with lower risk of default. Loan applications are evaluated on the borrower's FICO score, income, current debt level, and current debt payments. A borrower's history of timely repayment and the borrower's available expendable income are good predictors of his or her ability and willingness to repay the loan.

Loan defaults are costly for lenders. They stop the flow of income to the lender, and they force the lender to take actions to collect the debt from the borrower. Legal actions include foreclosing on the loan and repossessing collateral. Lenders increase the interest rate as the risk of default increases.

FICO SCORE

What is your credit score? Your credit score is the FICO score, and it is a compiled score that reflects your credit history. The three credit bureaus, TransUnion, Experian, and Equifax, assign a credit score to all individuals with a credit history. FICO scores range from 300 to 900. Your credit scores from each of the three agencies may differ slightly, based on different information listed with the agency.

FICO scores influence both your ability to obtain a loan and the interest rate you pay for a loan. A score greater than 720 is considered excellent. Individuals with scores above 700 have no problem getting new credit, and they are offered the best interest rates. A score between 600 and 700 is good, but may be rejected by some creditors. Interest rates offered on loans increase as the FICO scores decreases. A score between 500 and 600 is considered fair, and individuals with scores in this range have a tougher time getting a loan. An individual with a score less than 500 is considered to be a high credit risk and will have a difficult time obtaining a loan.

The best way to maintain a good credit score is to pay your bills on time. Although this is a key factor in your credit score, it is not the only factor.

Factors That Affect Your Credit Score

There are five main factors that affect a person's credit score. Exhibit 4.14 illustrates these five variables.

Exhibit 4.15 explores common myths about credit.

How to Check Your Own Credit Report

The Fair Credit Reporting Act protects consumers. It allows the consumer to have fraudulent and false information removed from their credit report. It is important to check your credit report periodically to make sure all the information in your credit report is accurate. You may choose to receive a report from each TransUnion, Experian, and Equifax once each year or you can space your requests out and receive a report from one agency at a time, one every four months. You may request your free credit reports at

© Feng Yu, 2014, Shutterstock, Inc.

Checking your credit report periodically allows you to look for mistakes or dispute uninitiated accounts.

EXHIBIT 4.14   FACTORS THAT AFFECT CREDIT SCORE

1. Past payment history (35%). Missed payments will reduce a person's credit score. The more recent the missed payment, the more it influences the score.

2. Outstanding debt (30%). The amount of an individual's debt affects the credit score. It is not simply the total amount of debt but rather the amount of debt as a portion of the person's credit limits. Outstanding debt greater than 75 percent of a person's credit limit will significantly reduce the credit score.

3. Length of time with credit (15%). The longer a person has an established credit history, the greater the credit score. This criterion hurts young people like. A 22-year-old with a new credit card does not yet have a well-established credit history; this lowers his or her score. For this reason, many financial professionals encourage individuals to start a credit history as soon as possible.

4. New applications for credit (10%). If you apply for several different loans (credit cards, car loans, etc.) in a short period of time, it will lower your score. It is best to space out these credit requests, even if they are for a good reason.

5. Types of credit (10%). The more types of credit you have, the higher your score. Credit cards, student loans, car loans, and house mortgage are all types of credit. Established credit with different types of loans is beneficial.

---

www.annualcreditreport.com. This web site was created under the Fair Credit Reporting Act and is sponsored by the three main credit bureaus—TransUnion, Experian, and Equifax. It is the only official site of the credit bureaus. There are many web sites offering you your credit score, but for your safety use the official site.

To request a copy of your credit report from one or all of the credit bureaus:

1. Go to www.annualcreditreport.com.
2. Select your state of residence.
3. Fill out the form with your personal information (the web site is VeriSign secured).
4. Select which of the three credit bureaus you would like to receive the report from.
5. At this time you will be taken to the web site for whichever bureau you selected in Step 4.
6. Answer the series of questions regarding your credit history. The questions may be about where you have lived, current payments you are making—anything about your personal or credit history. These questions are designed to make sure it is really "you" requesting the report.
7. Your credit report should be ready!

The credit report will include your:

- Personal information
- Account information
- Accounts in good standing (satisfactory accounts)
- Past-due accounts
- Credit inquiries within the last 12 months

EIGHT MYTHS ABOUT CREDIT	EXHIBIT 4.15

Myth 1   Everyone has only one credit score. Each of the three credit bureaus computes its own score. These three scores may differ by as many as 50 points.

Myth 2   Checking your own credit will reduce your credit score. Checking your credit score through a credit bureau will not affect your score.

Myth 3   Age, income, and gender will influence your credit score. Not true; these factors are not used to compute a credit score.

Myth 4   A higher salary will increase your credit score. Credit history will impact your credit score, not income. An individual lender may use your income when making a credit decision, but income is not part of your credit score.

Myth 5   You can remove unfavorable information in your credit report by disputing it. Credit bureaus will remove inaccurate information from your credit report. If you see an inaccuracy on your report, inform the credit bureau. It must investigate claims within 30 days. However, if you have unfavorable information that is accurate, chances are that the credit bureau will retain that information on your record.

Myth 6   Shopping around for the best deal on a loan will adversely affect your credit score. Actually, shopping around for a loan is a good idea. While credit bureaus do reduce your score when you apply for too many loans, they generally count inquiries within two weeks as one application, which will not hurt your score.

Myth 7   Credit card solicitations hurt your credit record. Mailings soliciting a credit card application may be annoying, but they do not reduce your credit score. On the other hand, actually making applications for too many of them will lower your score.

Myth 8   Getting married combines your credit score with your spouse's. Nope, your credit score is yours. Any account set up jointly with your spouse, however, will affect both of your credit ratings.

Source: CNNMoney.com

You want to make sure there are no items on the credit report you did not initiate. If there are such items, you need to immediately dispute them (a link is provided on the web site). The report will also show any accounts not in good standing. Finally, the report will include a list of inquiries into your credit report. These inquiries should reflect your recent credit applications. A sample credit report is available at: http://www.experian.com/credit_report_basics/pdf/samplecreditreport1.pdf.

Your actual FICO score can also be obtained from the web site with your report, but the bureaus charge a fee of $5 for the score. If it is your first time on the web site and you do not know your score, it may be worth $5 to find out. After you know your score, it is not necessary to check your score unless there are significant changes in your credit situation.

SUMMARY

 Credit is a contract that allows the borrower to accept something of value with the promise to pay the lender back later. The item of value can be goods, services, or money. Consumers choose from several credit options to finance their purchases. Loans are offered with the following characteristics:

- **Credit type.** Closed-end credit versus revolving credit
- **Number of payments.** Single-payment versus installment loans
- **Loan collateral.** Secured versus unsecured loans
- **Interest rate.** Variable rate versus fixed rate loans

Revolving credit is a credit line that allows the borrower to borrow up to a maximum limit. A revolving credit account stays open after the borrower has paid off the balance and can be used again for new borrowing needs. Credit cards and home equity loans are common types of revolving credit. Closed-end credit is a loan for a specific amount; it must be paid back on or before an agreed upon date. Closed-end credit accounts close when the borrower pays off the balance. Car loans and home mortgages are common closed-end credit accounts.

The wise use of credit cards includes:

- **Don't buy what you can't afford.** Make sure you can pay off the entire balance every month. Use credit cards for their convenience, not to finance unnecessary items.
- **Budget credit card spending like cash each month.** Balance and reconcile your credit card statements at least once a month, like any other account.
- **Always pay on time.** Late fees are expensive and damage your credit rating.

"Credit Crunch" littered the headlines in the fall of 2007. By 2008 the talk turned to the devastation of the world's financial system as the U.S. government poured billions of tax dollars into a failing financial system. How did individuals contribute to the crisis?

The APR is the real cost of credit and the lender must disclose the APR to the borrower. The APR factors in all fees and finance charges associated with the loan and states the total finance charge on an annualized basis.

Interest rates on consumer loans are affected by both economic conditions and loan risk factors.

Your credit score, known as a FICO score, influences both your ability to get a loan and the rate you will pay on the loan.

PROBLEMS

1. Mary applies for an $8,000 loan at her bank. The bank approves of the 1-year loan at an interest rate of 3 1/2 percent. The terms of the loan state that she will repay the principal and interest at the end of the year. How much will Mary owe the bank at the maturity of the loan?

2. Kyle gets a $600 3-month loan from a finance company at 10 percent interest payable at the end of the 3 months. Compute Kyle's interest.

3. Kim borrows $3,000 and pays it back in a year. Use the following payment schedule to calculate her interest rate.

	Payment	Interest	Principal	3,000
1	$261.66	21.25	240.41	2,759.59
2	$261.66	19.55	242.11	2,517.48
3	$261.66	17.83	243.83	2,273.65
4	$261.66	16.11	245.55	2,028.09
5	$261.66	14.37	247.29	1,780.80
6	$261.66	12.61	249.05	1,531.75
7	$261.66	10.85	250.81	1,280.94
8	$261.66	9.07	252.59	1,028.36
9	$261.66	7.28	254.38	773.98
10	$261.66	5.48	256.18	517.80
11	$261.66	3.67	257.99	259.81
12	$261.65	1.84	259.81	0.00

4. Greg is considering two different credit cards that charge the same interest rate. Card A has a $50 annual fee and offers a 1 percent rebate on all purchases. Card B has no fee. Greg normally charges about $1,300 per month on his card. Which card should he get?

5. Everett has a credit card that has an interest rate of 14 percent and requires him to pay a minimum of 4 percent of the balance. His previous balance was $1,200, and he made the minimum payment and made new purchases of $700 since his last statement. Compute Everett's new minimum payment. (Round up to the nearest dollar)

CASE STUDIES

COLLEGE STUDENT

Kevin Maedor is a 19-year-old college student. He still lives at home with his parents, and he works part time at Vapor's Lane. He started his financial plan in the spring semester of 2014. He plans to graduate with a B.S. in engineering in May 2017. He has the following financial information:

- He brings home $760 a month from his job.
- He has a Visa card with a balance of $1,700 and a MasterCard with a balance of $800. He makes the minimum monthly payment of $15.00 on each of them.
- His cell phone bill is $85 a month.

Help Kevin assess his use of credit:

1. What is he doing that he shouldn't be doing?
2. What should he be doing that he isn't?
3. Create a plan to help him reduce his credit card debt.

NEW GRADUATE

Rene Harris recently graduated with a B.S. in nursing.

- She brings home $4,433.33 a month from her job.
- She used her new Visa last month for the first time and charged $600. She also opened a new Macy's charge and charged $762.78. She hasn't received her first bill for either of them; assume her minimum monthly payment will be $15.00 on each.
- She owes $30,000 in student loans and makes a monthly payment of $151.47.
- She has $1,804.12 in her savings account.

Help Rene assess her use of credit:

1. What is she doing that she shouldn't be doing?
2. What should she be doing that she isn't?
3. Create a plan to help her reduce her credit card debt.

CREATE YOUR OWN FINANCIAL PLAN

Use your balance sheet and cash flow statement to assess your own use of credit.

- Do you have any bad credit habits?
- Are you ready to develop new credit habits?
- If you wanted to open your first credit card account, what limits and rules should you follow to prevent running up excessive debt?

REVIEW QUESTIONS

1. Explain why interest is defined as the cost of money.

   _____

   _____

   _____

2. List the two principal parties in a loan transaction and describe the overall loan process.

   _____

   _____

   _____

3. Will a credit card normally have a different interest rate than a home mortgage? Why or why not?

   _____

   _____

   _____

4. Is APR or the nominal rate more effective in identifying the true cost of a loan?

   _____

   _____

   _____

5. What is the difference between a merchant credit card and a general credit card?

   _____

   _____

   _____

6. List six basics characteristics of any credit card and give a brief description of each.

   _____

   _____

   _____

_____

_____

_____

7. Identify a benefit from the use of a credit card, as opposed to using a debit card or cash to make purchases.

_____

_____

_____

8. List the five variables that affect your credit score.

_____

_____

_____

_____

_____

9. How does a good FICO credit score save you money?

_____

_____

_____

10. Name the potential pitfalls of using a credit card for all of your purchases.

_____

_____

_____

Spending Wisely

5

"A penny saved is a penny earned."

—Benjamin Franklin

© Natali Glado, 2014, Shutterstock, Inc.

OBJECTIVES

- Select the best value in: groceries, phone service, Internet service, television service, appliances and automobiles
- Compare values using unit weights and nutritional information

- Read an Energy Guide Label
- Analyze financing options for vehicles
- Negotiate for a reduced price
- Differentiate between written and implied warranties
- Differentiate between service contracts and warranties

KEY TERMS

Brands
Captive finance company
Car leasing
Dial up
DSL (digital subscriber line)

Energy guide label
Implied warranty
National brands
Net weight
Service contract (extended warranty)

Unit price
Warranty
Warranty of fitness
Warranty of merchantability

STRETCH
YOUR DOLLAR

COMPARING INGREDIENTS

Compare ingredients on over the counter medicines. If the ingredient list and percentages are the same, the medicine will work identically. Name brands are often several dollars higher due to advertising costs.

You earned it. You set goals, created a budget, stashed away savings, and now you are ready to spend. Spending wisely is as important as saving. The best way to spend wisely is to comparison shop. Before you shop, clearly identify what you want, what you need, and what you can afford. Once you clearly identify those three parameters, you are ready to shop. As you shop, compare purchases against each other and against your list.

Expensive purchase like automobiles, appliances, and dream vacations take more time to research and compare than smaller daily purchases. Don't think the small purchases don't matter though: If you watch the pennies, the dollars will take care of themselves. It won't take as long to choose which package of corn to buy as it does to decide which vehicle to purchase, but consistently spending wisely is as good as saving.

In the Grocery Store

Wise spending involves comparing like products for price, value, and features while filtering your choices through your wants, needs, and budget. In the grocery store compare unit price, nutritional information, and quality, but filter your food selections by your personal tastes and your budget.

BRANDS

Brands Indicate who the product was manufactured by or for.

National brands Common household name brands.

Brands indicate who the product was manufactured by or for. National brands are the common household name brands. They are well advertised and typically are more expensive. Keebler®, Folgers®, and Frito Lay® are examples of national brands. Store brands are items manufactured for a specific grocery store. Dillon's grocery stores have Kroger and private selections store brands. Price Chopper sells products under a Price Chopper brand. Generics are those items that either are not sold under a store or private label brand and are not a national brand. They may be labeled generic or carry a label like always save or Best Choice. It always helps to remember that generics and store brands are often manufactured by the national brand companies, only under store or generic labels. For this reason, there also is not a lot of difference between items in some cases.

The cost of advertising plays the largest roll in the additional cost of the product. National brands are often perceived to be higher quality because they cost more—this is not always the case. Each consumer has personal preferences, for example an Oreo cookie may be the only chocolate sandwich cookie you want. In that case, you may not want to compare other cookies if you know only an Oreo will do. However, there are some generic or store products that surpass their name brand counterparts. Compare the unit cost of items and try the lowest cost product. If you like the flavor and quality of the product, continue to buy it; if you don't, move up to the next expensive brand. You may be surprised how many items you will find that you prefer over their national brand counterparts.

PRICE

Price is easiest to compare on a unit cost basis. Which is more economical, a 12 oz. package for $2.99 or a 14 oz. package for $3.19. The unit price is the price per ounce (oz.), pound (lb.), or some other measurement (such as per 100 in tissues). To calculate the unit price, divide the price by the weight or volume.

Unit price The price per ounce (oz) or pound (lb).

$2.99/12 oz. = 24.9 cents per oz.

$3.19/14 oz. = 22.7 cents per oz.

In this case the 14 oz. package for $3.19 is the most economical buy because it cost only 22.7 cents an ounce compared to 24.9 cents an ounce for a 12 oz. package.

LABEL INFORMATION

Product

The label must clearly state the common name of the product, for example, cereal or coffee. Most labels are easy to read and understand. Cheese is a good example of labeling that isn't always clear to the consumer. Cheese is cheese, right? What is the difference between cheddar and muenster? Cheese comes in many varieties, but all cheeses share some commonality. To be labeled cheese, the product must be a dairy product, made basically from milk. Cheese is classified by its moisture content and its milk fat content. Typically, as the milk fat content increases, so does its calcium content. Harder cheeses tend to be higher in milk fat content, lower in moisture, and higher in calcium.

What is the difference between cheese, pasteurized process cheese, and pasteurized process cheese food?

Cheese is the basic dairy product, made from milk, and is classified by its moisture content and milk fat content.

Cheese	Milk Fat Content	Moisture Content
Cheddar	50%	39% or less
Munster	50%	46%
Mozzarella	45%	52–60%

Pasteurized process cheese is a mixture of one or more cheeses and emulsifiers. The cheese is heated and ingredients are added to soften the cheese. The product is still predominantly cheese. Pasteurized process cheese food is a mixture that is only part cheese—the FDA requires products with this label be at least 51 percent cheese. You may also see products labeled imitation cheese: These products are not made from milk or cheese; they are made from oil.

Most product labels are obvious, but not all product names are clearly understood by the consumer. If you are not sure of the difference between butter and margarine, check the nutritional information and the ingredients list.

Net Weight

Net weight The total weight minus the weight of the package.

The net weight tells you the amount of product in the package, computed as the total weight minus the weight of the package. In a can of tomatoes, the net weight would include the weight of both the tomatoes and the liquid they are packaged in but not the weight of the can. The net weight is listed by either a dry ingredient measure or a liquid ingredient measure in both U.S. and metric units.

- Dry product: Net wt. 12 oz. (340 g)
- Liquid product: Net wt. 32 fl. oz. (1qt.) 946 ml

Nutritional Information

The Federal Food and Drug Administration (FDA) requires all food products be labeled with the same basic nutritional information. The FDA suggests you minimize your intake of the items shown in yellow and maximize your intake of the items shown in blue. When comparing products, your personal dietary needs and lifestyle are also an important part of comparison shopping.

Ingredients

Ingredients are listed in the order of quantity, from highest to lowest. If a product contains 4 ounces of sugar, 2 ounces of flour, and 1 ounce of butter, the ingredients would be listed as sugar, flour, and butter. A typical package of cheddar cheese lists the ingredients as: pasteurized milk, cheese culture, salt, enzymes, and vegetable coloring.

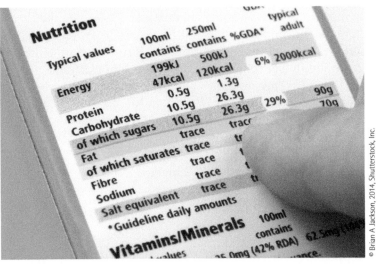

Take into consideration dietary needs when shopping; while cost is important to consider, don't skimp on nutrition because something is less expensive.

It takes time to compare labels, unit prices, and nutritional information, but the time you spend comparing products in the grocery store is an investment for future savings. Once you determine which brand and package size of a product is best for you needs, you can repeat the purchase and the savings without continually repeating the process.

Household Services

Do you use the Internet? Carry a cell phone? Have a home phone? Do you have a choice of which trash service to use? Do you prefer cable, satellite, or an antenna for TV reception?

Most U.S. citizens don't have a choice when it comes to main utilities like water, gas, and electric. With deregulation, this may change in the future. However, most of us do have a choice when it comes to an Internet service provider, a phone provider, and TV reception. Like other purchases, the best way to determine what to buy is to start with what you need.

TELEVISION PROVIDERS

There are three basic choices for TV reception:

1. Antenna requires digital TV or converter box and antenna, free service.
2. Cable requires digital TV or converter box, $30 to $120 month.
3. Satellite requires satellite receiver for each TV and satellite, $50 to $120 month.

To determine which choice is right for you, begin by asking some basic questions.

- How often do you watch TV?
- What is your favorite channel(s)?
- Which providers carry those channels?
- What is the monthly cost of the service?
- What is the installation charge for that service?
- What is the monthly equipment charge?
- What is available in my area?
- How much am I willing to spend for TV?

If you typically watch the big three TV stations, ABC, NBC, and CBS you will save $600 or more a year with the free service choice of an antenna. If you live in a rural area, you may only have the choice of antenna or satellite. Consider what you watch and avoid paying for channels and services you won't use.

INTERNET SERVICE PROVIDERS

You have four basic choices with Internet service providers:

1. Dial-up. With dial-up, your computer literally places a call or dials up a local server. Once the connection is established with the local server, you access the Internet through that connection. Dial-up requires the use of a land line, which is a typical home phone line. With dial-up you can use the phone or

Dial-up An internet service provider. Your computer literally places a call or dials up a local server.

© Odua Images, 2014, Shutterstock, Inc.

Know the difference in Internet providers and understand your needs before committing to a plan. Do your research to determine if it is more cost effective to bundle your options such as phone, Internet, and cable service.

DSL (Digital subscriber line) Like dial up requires the use of a phone line, but unlike dial up DSL allows the consumer to use both their phone and connect to the internet at the same time.

Broadband is sometimes used to refer to cable connections to the Internet. Cable connections do use broadband, but DSL and wireless connections are also broadband technologies. Broadband means multiple channels using different frequencies are being transmitted over the same line.

the Internet, but not both at the same time. Dial-up connections use a standard 56 kilobyte modem, and thus are slow compared to other connections, but they are also less expensive. It is often not possible to access large or complicated files, such as games and some types of video and artwork. Dial-up service ranges from $7 to $20 a month.

2.   DSL. DSL stands for digital subscriber line. DSL, like dial up, requires the use of a phone line, but unlike dial up, DSL allows the consumer to use both phone and Internet at the same time. With DSL the Internet connection is made on a high-frequency channel, and the phone or voice connection is made on a lower frequency channel. Both channels are carried on the same line; this frequency channel separation allows both the Internet and the phone to operate simultaneously. Filters are used on each phone jack in the house; the filters reduce interference between the two channels. (Michigan Public Service Commission)

DSL connections require a DSL modem and filters for each phone jack in the home. DSL is offered in two configurations, ADSL and SDSL. The "A" standards for asymmetrical, and the "S" stands for symmetrical. Asymmetrical DSL is the common residential consumer configuration; with asymmetrical DSL the upload speed is slower than the download speed. SDSL offers upload speeds equal to download speeds.

The typical residential consumer speed for DSL is 512 Kbps/256 Kbps. The first number, 512 Kbps is the download speed, and the second number, 256 Kbps is the upload speed. DSL is offered in a variety of speeds, though, depending on the carrier offering the service. Typically you pay more for higher speeds. DSL service costs range from $20 to $50 a month and is available in the following speeds.

- 256 Kbps/128 Kbps
- 512 Kbps/128 Kbps
- 1 Mbps/256 Kbps
- 2 Mbps/512 Kbps
- 8 Mbps/1024 Kbps

3. Cable connections. Cable Internet connections use your cable TV provider's line to provide Internet access. Cable connections require a splitter that turns the incoming cable line into two lines. One line is used to service the TVs in the home, and the other line is used to service the modem for the Internet connection.

Unlike dial up and DSL lines, which are dedicated lines for the user, cable connections share the line for access with other subscribers in the same general area or neighborhood. This sharing makes speeds vary dramatically. These connections tend to be quick during off-peak hours and slow in neighborhoods with heavy subscribers during peak hours of use. Typically, cable download speeds range from 1.5 Mbps to 3.0 Mbps. However, most companies limit upload speeds from 128 Kbps to 256 Kbps. Typical costs for cable Internet connections range from $30 to $50 a month.

4. Wireless. Wireless connections for residential customers typically mean Internet service provided through a satellite TV provider or through your cell phone carrier. In this case it means the service to your home is wireless. Service within your home can be made wireless with the use of a router with both DSL and cable connections. Here we distinguish wireless as the means of transmitting the signal to your home.

With a satellite connection, the transmission to your home is wireless, but the connection within your home uses a coaxial cable connected to a modem. Cell phone providers also provide wireless connections. Cell phone companies use a wireless modem that connects to a USB port on your computer or an adapter that connects your phone to your computer. If the cell phone company uses an adapter and your phone, your phone is serving as the modem.

Wireless download speeds range from 768 Kbps to 1.5 Mbps. Upload speeds are typically limited to 256 Kbps. The cost for monthly service ranges from $30 to $70.

When shopping for internet service, ask the following questions:

- How do I use the internet? Do I need rapid download speeds for music and videos?
- Do I need internet access for work or school?
- What new equipment do I need to buy or rent? What is the cost of the equipment?
- Is a contract required with the service?
- What is the cost of installation?
- What is the monthly cost?
- Is the price quoted a promotional price? Will the price increase and if so when?

TELEPHONE SERVICE

Long distance calls used to be the main concern with phone bills. In the last decade cell phones have become so common that long distance plans on land lines have become reasonable. Today the big phone bill killer is minute overages on cell phones. Although cell phones offer convenience and security for a society constantly on the go, a basic home phone service may be more economical. Consider a basic home phone service if you need to adjust a tight budget.

The competition between phone services is good for the consumer. Competition tends to drive the prices down. Ask the following questions to determine which plan is best for you.

- How many text messages do you send and receive a month?
- Do you make more calls during peak hours or during off peak hours?
- Peak hours are typically from 6:00 am to 9:00 pm Monday through Friday.
- Which carriers do most of your friends and family use?

Since many companies offer mobile-to-mobile minutes, this can help reduce your need for anytime minutes. Mobile-to-mobile minutes are those calls placed between mobile phones with the same service carrier. For example, when a Verizon wireless customer calls another Verizon wireless customer those calls are not charged against either person's available minutes.

Exhibit 5.1 shows a comparison of three major cell phone providers in the United States. At first glance, there appears to be little difference between the services provided. However, depending on what part of the country you live in, you may find the signal strength and reliability varies greatly. Customer service is another important factor to consider. Ask around and find out what your friends and family think of the customer service provided by the companies in your area.

Periodically review your phone bills for the previous three months. Check your minutes used each month, number of text messages, and optional services. If you have a plan with 600 anytime minutes but over the past three months have averaged 280 anytime minutes a month, you can save by switching to a cheaper plan with fewer anytime minutes. Most carriers will allow you to switch between plans; however, if you switch plans, it may restart a new contract.

BUNDLING

Many companies offer packages of bundled services. You can save by purchasing your phone, cable, and Internet services as a bundle.

EXHIBIT 5.1	COMPARISON OF THREE MAJOR CELL PHONE COMPANY		
Plan Name	AT&T Nation 450 w/ Rollover	T-Mobil Individual Value	Verizon Wireless Nationwide Basic 450
Plan Type	Individual	Individual	Individual
Coverage	National	National	National
Contract Term	2 Years	2 Years	2 Years
Monthly Rate	$39.99	$39.99	$39.99
Included Minutes	450	600	450
Mobile-to-Mobile Minutes	Unlimited	None	Unlimited
Night and Weekend Minutes	5000 Nights (9 p.m. to 6 a.m.) Weekends (Fri. 9 p.m. to Mon. 6 a.m.)	Unlimited Nights (9 p.m. to 6:59 a.m.) Weekends (12 a.m. Sat. to 11:59 p.m. Sun.)	Unlimited Nights (9:01 p.m. to 5:59 a.m.), Weekends (Sat. 12 a.m. to Sun. 11:59 p.m.)
Off-Network Roaming	None	None	None
Activation Fee	$36.00	$35.00	$35.00

Source: Phonedog.com

Appliances

Appliances come in a wide range of prices. A washer with basic features starts around $350, and one with the latest colors and advanced features cost around $1,700. Think about both the upfront cost and the long-term cost when purchasing appliances. Most major appliances come with an energy guide label. The energy guide label shows estimated energy consumption, estimated annual energy cost for the appliance, and a comparison of energy costs to other similar appliances with the same features. The following appliances have energy labels: washers, dishwashers, refrigerators, freezers, water heaters, window air conditioners, central air conditioners, furnaces, boilers, heat pumps, and pool heaters. However, the Federal Trade Commission (FTC) does not require energy labels on these appliances: televisions, ranges, ovens, clothes dryers, humidifiers, and dehumidifiers. Exhibit 5.2 shows an energy guide label and explains its features.

Energy guide label A label on an appliance that shows estimated energy consumption, estimated annual energy cost for the appliance, and a comparison of energy costs to other similar appliances with the same features.

HOW TO USE THE ENERGY GUIDE LABEL

EXHIBIT 5.2

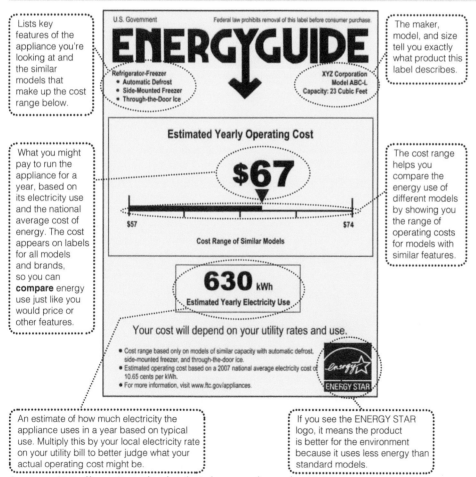

Lists key features of the appliance you're looking at and the similar models that make up the cost range below.

The maker, model, and size tell you exactly what product this label describes.

What you might pay to run the appliance for a year, based on its electricity use and the national average cost of energy. The cost appears on labels for all models and brands, so you can **compare** energy use just like you would price or other features.

The cost range helps you compare the energy use of different models by showing you the range of operating costs for models with similar features.

An estimate of how much electricity the appliance uses in a year based on typical use. Multiply this by your local electricity rate on your utility bill to better judge what your actual operating cost might be.

If you see the ENERGY STAR logo, it means the product is better for the environment because it uses less energy than standard models.

Courtesy of http://www.ftc.gov/bcp/edu/pubs/consumer/homes/rea14.shtm

When shopping for appliances make sure you make a list of features you want and a general price range before you shop. Do some research first so you know what is available? *Consumer Reports* offers independent ratings on many consumer goods. Most libraries will carry *Consumer Reports* or you can access its information online, for a fee. Don't forget to check the dimensions of an appliance before you buy. Measure the space available in your home for the appliance and make sure your new appliance will fit into the available space. You can save time and money by calling several stores for price comparisons before you go shopping.

Buying a Vehicle

A vehicle purchase is the first big financial decision in most people's lives. The process can be both exciting and overwhelming. The prevalence of the Internet as a research tool often leads to information overload. In this section we will discuss the general steps to buy a vehicle. For simplicity, we will use the word car instead of vehicle.

Purchase a car in five steps:

1. Choose the right car.
2. Negotiate the price of the car.
3. Decide if you want to trade in another vehicle.
4. Select the best way to finance the car.
5. Stay firm after the deal.

CHOOSE THE RIGHT CAR

You may not be able to afford your dream car, but you should like the car you choose, and it should fit your needs. Use magazines like *Consumer Reports* or

You should comparison shop before you make a major purchase. Use resources such as the Internet to find the best deal, educate yourself before setting foot on a car lot.

online resources like www.cars.com or www.kbb.com to gather information. Consider the following to help make the best choice:

- Gas mileage. The more miles you put on your car in a week, the more important gas consumption will be to your budget.
- Size. The size of the car you need will depend on how you intend to use it. If you want to car pool, a comfortable back seat is more important than if you are its main passenger.
- Style or type. Strictly personal preference.
- New or used. A new car depreciates (loses its value) fastest in the first two years. The best value is often a two-year-old certified used car with low mileage. A new car will be covered under a warranty and should have little or no repair expenses in the first few years. Many dealers offer certified used cars with the warranty advantages of a new car. Have a used car inspected by a qualified mechanic before you agree to buy the car.
- Insurance costs. Insurance costs vary widely based on the car's performance in crash testing, the cost of vehicle repairs, the vehicle's reputation, and the individual insurance company's claims experience with that car. A sporty car will often have higher insurance premiums than its plain-Jane counterpart. The best way to compare insurance costs is to narrow your search to two or three cars and call your insurance agent for a quote on each.
- Property taxes. These taxes are based on the car's assessed value by the municipality, county, or state. Like insurance the best way to compare is to call the appraiser's office where you will tag the car and ask about property tax cost on two or three preferred cars. Costs vary by location, some states have low taxes and others high. These taxes are also called by different names in different areas.
- Resale value. Some brands have a reputation for reliability and longevity; they hold their resale value. This becomes less important as the time you intend to own the car increases. However, if you want to purchase a new car every two or three years, this becomes a critical consideration.

Use Online Resources

Find the invoice price of the vehicle you are interested in at www.cars.com. The invoice price is the price the dealer paid when it purchased the car from the manufacturer; it is the dealer's cost. If you see the Manufacturer's Suggested Retail Price (MSRP or sticker price) is $19,000 and the invoice price $16,000, you know there is $3,000 of profit in the MSRP. If a dealer is listing the car for $21,500, you know you can negotiate for a lower price. Use this online information to inform yourself before you negotiate.

DECIDE IF YOU WANT TO TRADE IN A CAR

If you currently own a car, you have the option of trading the vehicle in or selling it yourself. Trading the vehicle in is quicker, but you will normally get more for it if you sell it yourself. You can estimate your car's trade in and resale value with Kelly's Blue Book web site, www.kbb.com. The difference is often several thousand dollars. However, selling the car yourself takes time, effort, and commitment.

Even if you don't trade in a vehicle, you can make a down payment on the car. This decreases the loan amount and your monthly payment. Down payments are more important on high interest rate loans. However, if you use 0 percent financing, there is no reason to make a down payment.

SELECT THE BEST WAY TO FINANCE A CAR

If you buy a car from a dealer, you have two main options. You can use a traditional lending source, like a bank, or you use the dealer's financing. A captive finance company is a finance company owned by the manufacturer, for example, Ford Motor Credit. Captive finance companies provide manufacturers with additional revenue sources and allow them to offer customers low rates and convenience. If you buy a used car from a private party, you will have to use the traditional sources.

Captive finance company A finance company owned by a parent company. The purpose of the finance company is to provide financing to customers of the parent company for purchase of the parent company's products or services.

Use your knowledge of the time value of money to determine how much you can afford to pay for a car. Focus on the price and the interest rate to adjust your payment to fit your budget. Don't negotiate the monthly payment with the car dealer. This is a trick dealers use sell you a more expensive car. They will extend a loan from 48 months to 60 or 72 months to make a payment fit your budget. This decreases your monthly payment, but increases your total cost. If a dealer asks you for a "payment range." Tell them you prefer to negotiate price.

Lease or Purchase?

Car leasing When you lease a car you agree to pay for the value of the vehicle used during the lease.

Car leasing is another way of financing a car. When you buy a car, you agree to pay for the entire cost of the car. When you lease a car, you agree to pay for the value of the vehicle used during the lease. If you buy a car today for $25,000 and 24 months from now it is worth $16,000, then it depreciated in value by $9,000. Depreciation is the value used during a lease. There are two basic components to a lease payment: a depreciation charge and a finance charge.

The depreciation charge compensates the leasing company for the depreciation, and the finance charge pays the interest on the cost of the car during the lease period. This is similar to a monthly car loan payment; a portion of the payment covers the interest and a portion is applied to the principal.

In the short-term, leasing is less expensive than buying. In the long-term, the cost of buying is less than the cost of leasing. In the long-term, the depreciation is spread out over many years; this reduces the effective cost of operating a car. Short-term leasing is always more expensive than long-term buying. While buying a car for the long-term is the best financial alternative, there are other motivating factors such as convenience, pleasure, and utility. Leasing is an attractive option to many people. The decision to lease or buy can be complicated. You can use a "lease versus buy" calculator to help you make a decision. Try the one at www.leaseguide.com/leasevsbuy.htm. Everyone has different priorities in life, and you need to choose a vehicle and financing to fit your situation. Note also that many dealers have stopped offering leasing plans in the recent economic downturn.

Exhibit 5.3 summarizes the differences between leasing and buying.

	PURCHASE	LEASE
Payment	Higher	Lower
You Pay for	Principal & Interest	Depreciation & Interest
In the End	You own the car	You return the car
Long Term	Economical	Expensive
Short Term	Less budget friendly	More budget friendly
Ideal for	Wealth accumulation	People who want to drive a new car every two or three years

DIFFERENCES BETWEEN LEASING AND BUYING   **EXHIBIT 5.3**

NEGOTIATE THE PRICE OF THE CAR

Car dealers prefer to negotiate at their dealerships. This gives the salesperson more control of the situation. It is to your advantage to negotiate over the phone or online. Many dealers post their inventories and prices online. These prices are a starting point for negotiations. Call or e-mail an offer to the dealer. A growing number of dealers have salespeople devoted to online requests.

You can also use the technique companies and government agencies use when they make a major purchase. Start with a list detailing the car's specifications. For example, you want a 2010, full size, short wheel base, Dodge Ram 2500. You prefer a black or blue truck. You want automatic transmission, an AM/FM radio with 6-changer CD, AC, cruise control, and power windows and locks. Call several dealerships and ask to speak to their sales manager. This is important: the sales manager is the one with the authority to alter the list price of a vehicle. Tell the manager you intend to buy a vehicle no later than 5:00 pm. Give him or her a genuine and short time limit. State you are calling several dealers in the area, and will purchase the vehicle from the dealer who offers you the best price. Give your list of specifications. The sales manager

How Much Can You Afford   **EXAMPLE 5.1**

You need a new car and can afford a payment of $450. You have a $7,000 trade-in. Your bank offers a 48-month loan at 4 percent interest. How much car can you afford to finance? Buy?

Solution: How much can you finance?

$$PV = PMNT\frac{(1-(1+i)^{-n})}{i}$$

$$PV = \$340\frac{\left(1-\left(1+\frac{0.04}{12}\right)^{-48}\right)}{\frac{0.04}{12}i} = \$19,929.98$$

Add your trade in value to your loan amount.

$$\$20,000 + \$7,000 = \$27,000$$

It makes sense to round to the nearest $100 in these calculations. ∎

will typically need time to research the vehicle you asked for, and will ask if he or she can call you back. Take notes when each dealer calls back. Compare the offers and test-drive the vehicle from the dealer with the best offer. If you are satisfied with the vehicle, purchase it. This is the best way to get the lowest price. If a dealer asks you to come in or test drive a vehicle before he quotes a price to you, tell him you only intend to visit the dealership that quotes you the best price. You will be surprised how well this process works. You can save thousands with this simple technique.

Stay Firm after the Deal

When you sign the documents to purchase the car, beware of additional charges. The sales manager will offer you rustproofing, extended warranties, credit life, or additional parts. None of these extras are necessary; they are high-profit sales for the dealer. Be polite, be patient, and just say no after the pitch.

Warranties

Warranty A promise by the manufacturer or merchant to stand behind their product.

A warranty is a promise by the manufacturer or merchant to stand behind their product. There are two categories of warranties: written warranties and implied warranties. Federal law requires merchants to allow you to read the written warranties before you buy a product. Compare the warranty coverage just as you would the style, price, and other characteristics of products.

WRITTEN WARRANTIES

Written warranties come with most major purchases. When you compare written warranties, ask the following questions:

- How long does the warranty last? Check the warranty to see when it begins and when it expires, as well as any conditions that may void coverage.
- Who do you contact to get warranty service? It may be the seller or the manufacturer who provides you with service.
- What will the company do if the product fails? Read to see whether the company will repair the item, replace it, or refund your money.
- Which parts and repairs are covered? Are parts or repairs excluded from coverage? For example, some warranties require you to pay for labor charges. Are there expensive or inconvenient conditions? For example, are you required to ship a heavy object to a factory for service or return the item in the original carton?
- Does the warranty cover "consequential damages?" Consequential damages are damages caused by the product. For example, if a freezer breaks and the food spoils, the consequential damage is the spoiled food. Most companies don't cover consequential damages.
- Are there any conditions or limitations on the warranty? Some warranties provide coverage only if you maintain or use the product as directed. For example, a warranty may cover only personal uses—as opposed to business uses—of the product. Make sure the warranty will meet your needs.

IMPLIED WARRANTIES

Implied warranties are created by state law, and all states have them. Almost every purchase you make is covered by an implied warranty.

The most common type of implied warranty is a warranty of merchantability. This warranty implies the product will do what it is supposed to do. For example, a car will run and a coffee pot will brew coffee.

Another standard implied warranty is the warranty of fitness for a particular purpose. When you buy a product on the seller's advice, the implied warranty holds the seller accountable for a particular use. For example, a person who suggests you buy a certain sleeping bag for zero-degree weather warrants the sleeping bag will be suitable for zero degrees.

Many stores and manufacturers offer product warranties on appliances. For example, Sears® offers protection agreements on their appliances that cover "preventative" maintenance. Once a year, a technician services your appliance to make sure it's working properly; any problems with the product are also covered.

If your purchase does not come with a written warranty, it is still covered by implied warranties unless the product is marked "as is," or the seller otherwise indicates in writing that no warranty is given. Several states, including Kansas, Maine, Maryland, Massachusetts, Mississippi, Vermont, West Virginia, and the District of Columbia, do not permit "as is" sales.

If you have problems not covered by a written warranty, you should investigate the protection given by the implied warranty. Implied warranty coverage can last as long as four years, although the length of the coverage varies from state to state. A lawyer or a state consumer protection office can provide more information about implied warranty coverage in your state.

Preventing Problems

To minimize problems:

- Read the warranty before you buy. When online, look for hyperlinks to the full warranty or to an address where you can write to get a free copy. Understand exactly what protection the warranty gives you. If a copy of the warranty is available when shopping online, print it out when you make your purchase and keep it with your records.
- Consider the reputation of the company offering the warranty. Look for an address to write to or a phone number to call if you have questions or problems. If you're not familiar with the company, ask your local or state consumer protection office or Better Business Bureau if they have any complaints against the company. A warranty is only as good as the company that stands behind it.
- Save your receipt and file it with the warranty. You may need it to document the date of your purchase or prove you are the original owner in the case of a nontransferable warranty.

Implied warranty
A product warranty created by state law, and all states have them. Almost every purchase you make is covered by an implied warranty.

Warranty of merchantability A warranty implies the product will do what it is supposed to do.

Warranty of fitness
A warranty for a particular purpose. When you buy a product on the seller's advice, the implied warranty holds the seller accountable for a particular use.

- Perform required maintenance and inspections.
- Use the product according to the manufacturer's instructions. Abuse or misuse may void your warranty coverage.

Resolving Disputes

If you have problems with a product or with getting warranty service:

- Read your product instructions and warranty carefully. Don't expect features or performance your product wasn't designed for, or assume warranty coverage that was never promised in writing. A warranty doesn't mean you'll automatically get a refund if the product is defective—the company may be entitled to try to fix it first. On the other hand, if you reported a defect to the company during the warranty period and the product wasn't fixed properly, the company must correct the problem, even if your warranty expires before the product is fixed.
- Try to resolve the problem with the retailer. If you can't, write to the manufacturer. Your warranty should list the company's mailing address. Send all letters by certified mail, return receipt requested, and keep copies.
- Contact your state or local consumer protection office. It can help you if you can't resolve the situation with the seller or manufacturer.
- Research dispute resolution programs that try to informally settle any disagreements between you and the company. Your local consumer protection office can suggest organizations to contact. Also, check your warranty; it may require dispute resolution procedures before going to court.
- Consider small claims court. If your dispute involves less than $750, you can usually file a lawsuit in small claims court. The costs are relatively low, procedures are simple, and lawyers usually aren't needed. The clerk of the small claims court can tell you how to file your lawsuit and your state's dollar limits.
- If all else fails, you may want to consider a lawsuit. You can sue for damages or any other type of relief the court awards, including legal fees. A lawyer can advise you how to proceed.

Courtesy of Federal Trade commission http://www.ftc.gov/bcp/edu/pubs/consumer/products/pro17.shtm

SERVICE CONTRACTS

Service contract (extended warranty)
A promise to perform (or pay for) certain repairs or services. Sometimes called an "extended warranty," a service contract is not a warranty as defined by federal law.

A service contract is a promise to perform (or pay for) certain repairs or services. Sometimes called an "extended warranty," a service contract is not a warranty as defined by federal law. A service contract may be arranged at any time and always costs extra; a warranty comes with a new car and is included in the original price. The separate and additional cost distinguishes a service contract from a warranty. If you're told you must purchase an auto service contract to qualify for financing, contact the lender yourself to find out if this is true. Some consumers have had trouble canceling their service contract after discovering the lender didn't require one.

Before deciding whether to buy an auto service contract, ask these questions:

Does the service contract duplicate any warranty coverage? Compare service contracts with the manufacturer's warranty before you buy. New cars come with a manufacturer's warranty, which usually offers coverage for at least one year or 12,000 miles, whichever comes first. Even used cars may come with some type of coverage.

You may decide to buy a "demonstrator" model—a car that has never been sold to a retail customer but has been driven for purposes other than test drives. If so, ask when warranty coverage begins and ends. Does it date from when you purchase the car or when the dealer first put the car into service?

Who backs the service contract? Ask who performs or pays for repairs under the terms of the service contract. It may be the manufacturer, the dealer, or an independent company.

Many service contracts sold by dealers are handled by independent companies called administrators. Administrators act as claims adjusters, authorizing the payment of claims to any dealers under the contract. If you have a dispute over whether a claim should be paid, deal with the administrator.

If the administrator goes out of business, the dealership still may be obligated to perform under the contract. The reverse also may be true. If the dealer goes out of business, the administrator may be required to fulfill the terms of the contract. Whether you have recourse depends on your contract's terms and/or your state's laws.

Learn about the reputation of the dealer and the administrator. Ask for references and check them out. You also can contact your local or state consumer protection office, state Department of Motor Vehicles, local Better Business Bureau, or local automobile dealers' association to find out if they have public information on the firms. Look for the phone numbers and addresses in your telephone directory.

Find out how long the dealer or administrator has been in business and try to determine whether they have the financial resources to meet their contractual obligations. Individual car dealers or dealer associations may set aside funds or buy insurance to cover future claims. Some independent companies are insured against a sudden rush of claims.

Find out if the auto service contract is underwritten by an insurance company. In some states, this is required. If the contract is backed by an insurance company, contact your state insurance commission to ask about the solvency of the company and whether any complaints have been filed.

How much does the auto service contract cost? Usually, the price of the service contract is based on the car make, model, condition (new or used), coverage, and length of the contract. The upfront cost can range from several hundred dollars to more than $1,000.

In addition to the initial charge, you may need to pay a deductible each time your car is serviced or repaired. Under some service contracts, you pay one charge per visit for repairs, no matter how many. Other contracts require a deductible for each unrelated repair.

You also may need to pay transfer or cancellation fees if you sell your car or end the contract. Often, contracts limit the amount paid for towing or related rental car expenses.

What is covered and not covered? Few auto service contracts cover all repairs. Indeed, common repairs for parts like brakes and clutches generally are not included in service contracts. If an item isn't listed, assume it's not covered.

Watch out for absolute exclusions that deny coverage for any reason. For example:

- If a covered part is damaged by a non-covered component, the claim may be denied.
- If the contract specifies that only "mechanical breakdowns" will be covered, problems caused by "normal wear and tear" may be excluded.
- If the engine must be taken apart to diagnose a problem and it is discovered that non-covered parts need to be repaired or replaced, you may have to pay for the labor involved in the tear-down and reassembling of the engine.

You may not have full protection even for parts that are covered in the contract. Some companies use a "depreciation factor" in calculating coverage: the company may pay only partial repair or replacement costs if they consider your car's mileage.

How are claims handled? When your car needs to be repaired or serviced, you may be able to choose among several service dealers or authorized repair centers. Or, you may be required to return the vehicle to the selling dealer for service. That could be inconvenient if you bought the car from a dealership in another town.

Find out if your car will be covered if it breaks down while you're using it on a trip or if you take it when you move out of town. Some auto service contract companies and dealers offer service only in specific geographical areas.

Find out if you need prior authorization from the contract provider for any repair work or towing services. Be sure to ask:

- How long it takes to get authorization;
- Whether you can get authorization outside of normal business hours;
- Does the company have a toll-free number for authorization. Test the toll-free number before you buy the contract to see if you can get through easily.

You may have to pay for covered repairs and then wait for the service company to reimburse you. If the auto service contract doesn't specify how long reimbursement usually takes, ask. Find out who settles claims in case you have a dispute with the service contract provider and need to use a dispute resolution program.

Are new or reconditioned ("like") parts authorized for use in covered repairs? If this concerns you, ask. Some consumers are disappointed when they find out "reconditioned" engines are being used as replacement parts under some service contracts. Also ask whether the authorized repair facility maintains an adequate stock of parts. Repair delays may occur if authorized parts are not readily available and must be ordered.

What are your responsibilities? Under the contract, you may have to follow all the manufacturer's recommendations for routine maintenance, such as oil and spark plug changes. Failure to do so could void the contract. To prove you have maintained the car properly, keep detailed records, including receipts.

Find out if the contract prohibits you from taking the car to an independent station for routine maintenance or performing the work yourself. The contract may specify that the selling dealer is the only authorized facility for servicing the car.

What is the length of the service contract? If the service contract lasts longer than you expect to own the car, find out if it can be transferred when you sell the car, whether there's a fee, or if a shorter contract is available.

Courtesy of the Federal trade commission http://www.ftc.gov/bcp/edu/pubs/consumer/autos/aut02.shtm

SUMMARY

Wise spending involves selecting the lowest price product that meets your needs and fits in your budget. Comparison shopping is the technique used to determine the best product for you. Make a list of what you need, what you would like, and how much you can afford before you talk to a salesperson. Do your research ahead of time; you will make the best choice when you have all the necessary information.

In the grocery store compare unit costs and label information. For service like your phone, Internet, and cable, compare the price of equipment and installation as well as the monthly service price. Check to make sure the price you are offered is not a promotional price subject to increase once you sign a contract.

When shopping for appliances consider both the upfront and long-term costs. Use the energy guide label to help you determine the energy costs associated with a particular appliance.

Car purchases are major commitments of your financial resources and should be carefully considered before you make your final selection. Compare gas mileage, style, size, price, and financing options. A long-term purchase is always more economical than a short-term lease, but other factors play into the decision. If you intend to replace the car every two or three years, a lease may be a better option for you.

Every product sold comes with an implied warranty. Written warranties are a promise by the manufacturer or merchant to stand behind its product. Extended warranties are not warranties at all—they are service contracts. Carefully read warranty information because many warranties have clauses and exclusions that will void the warranty if they are not followed.

PROBLEMS

1. Which is more economical, a 10 oz. package for $1.49 or a 16 oz. package for $2.29?

2. Which is more economical, a 40 lb bag of dog food for $19 or a 25 lb bag for $15.25?

3. Hank wants to buy a new washer. He has narrowed his choice to two models. One is $1,098 and the energy guide label says it costs $26 a year to operate. The other is $848 and the energy guide label says it costs $30 a year to operate. Which is the most economical long term? Assume he owns the washer 20 years.

4. In problem 3, the $1,098 washer is red, and the $848 washer is white. Which would you buy? (Hint: There is no right or wrong answer here)

5. Don can afford a car payment of $600 per month. He wants a 4-year loan at 3.25 percent. He does not have a down payment. How much car can he afford to buy?

6. Kim can afford a car payment of $300. She intends to use a 5-year loan for 6 percent. How much can she afford to pay for a car? She has a trade-in worth $1,500.

CASE STUDIES

COLLEGE STUDENT

We met Kevin Maedor in Chapter 2 and helped him find a home in Chapter 3, although he is a 19-year-old college student who still lives at home with his parents. We are helping him plan for after graduation in May 2017.

Help Kevin find a washer and dryer for his new home.

1. He has doorways that are 36 inches wide and a laundry room that is 8 ft by 6 ft. The washer and dryer hookups are along the long wall. There are cabinets mounted above the hookups so stackable units won't fit.
2. He has $2,000 to furnish his home with the necessities and would like to spend no more than $800 on the washer and dryer.
3. He will use the washer and dryer for his casual clothes, mostly jeans and t-shirts. His dress clothes for work will go to the cleaners. He isn't fully convinced his mother's opinion on sorting clothes is necessary.

Shop at least three places and look at as many washer and dryers as you can. Narrow your list to three choices and then do a detailed comparison on those three sets. Compare upfront costs (price) and long-term cost (energy usage).

Estimate the life of the machines you pick. Compare functions and indicate why you think he does or doesn't need those functions.

Make a final selection for Kevin and explain why you chose that washer and dryer.

NEW GRADUATE

We met Rene Harris in Chapter 2 and helped her buy a home in Chapter 3. Rene loves to entertain and is learning to manage her spending. She wants to take advantage of buying in bulk, but needs a refrigerator for her new home.

Help Rene find a refrigerator.

1. She would like a modern refrigerator with the latest features but she isn't sure what is available. She loves to serve cheese and wine and uses lots a fresh fruits and vegetables when she cooks.
2. She has budgeted $3,000 for this purchase.
3. Research refrigerators and determine what features are available on the latest models.

Shop at least three places and look at as many refrigerators as you can. Narrow your list to three choices and then do a detailed comparison on those three. Compare upfront costs (price) and long-term cost (energy usage). Compare features and indicate why you think she does or doesn't need them.

Make a final selection for Rene and explain why you chose the refrigerator you did for her.

CREATE YOUR OWN FINANCIAL PLAN

Pick an item you would like to buy, either now or in the future. This can be any item from a top-of-the-line appliance to a dependable, practical car. It can be as simple as the best pair of jeans for you. It can be an item you hoped to buy in a year or in five years. Make it personal and pick an item you would enjoy.

- Make a list of the features you want.
- Set a price range you are willing to spend on the item
- Research the item; look at at least 20 items.
- Narrow your selection to three items and compare price, features, warranty, and other critical information. Make a final selection. Use the information you gathered to write a goal to obtain this item. Add the goal to your financial plan.

REVIEW QUESTIONS   CHAPTER 5

1. Describe the information found on a food label and briefly explain how you would use the information.

   _____

   _____

   _____

2. List the five steps to buy a car.

   _____

   _____

   _____

   _____

   _____

3. Describe the major difference between leasing and purchasing a car.

   _____

   _____

   _____

4. What information is provided on an energy guide label?

   _____

   _____

   _____

5. Describe a technique that is advantageous to the buyer when negotiating the price of a car.

   _____

   _____

   _____

6. Describe a technique that is advantageous to the dealer when negotiating the price of a car.

_____

_____

_____

7. What is an implied warranty? List two common implied warranties.

_____

_____

_____

8. What is another name for an extended warranty? Is it a warranty? Why or why not?

_____

_____

_____

Tax Planning

"The hardest thing to understand in the world is the income tax."

—Albert Einstein (1879–1955)

OBJECTIVES

- Understand how to reduce your tax burden
- Fill out a federal income tax form
- Differentiate between tax deductions and credits
- List the variety of taxes citizens pay
- Learn to maximize credits and deductions

KEY TERMS

Adjusted gross income (AGI)
Basis
Capital gain
Dependent
Dividend income
Estate tax
Excise tax
FICA
Form 1040
Gift tax

Hope Credit
Inheritance tax
Interest income
Itemized deductions
Lifetime Learning Credit
Long-term gain
Personal property tax
Progressive
Real estate tax
Sales tax

Schedule A
Schedule B
Schedule D
Short-term gain
Social Security
Standard deduction
Taxable income
Tax liability
W-2

What scares you the most about personal finance? The most common answer is taxes and the IRS. Taxes are everywhere in our lives. You pay sales tax at the grocery store. You pay personal property taxes on the vehicles you own and real estate taxes on your home. And, of course, you pay income tax on your earnings. Taxes take a big bite out of your budget. You can legally reduce your tax liability with careful planning and a clear understanding of the tax codes.

Tax Overview

Taxes are the main revenue source for governments. The U.S. economy is a free enterprise system, but we still depend on the government to provide common services. Schools, roads, and clean water are funded by taxes. Exhibit 6.1 shows tax sources for the U.S. government. The 2012 actual revenues are shown in the first chart, and the projected 2018 revenues are shown in the second chart. Personal income taxes are projected to rise by 5 percent over the next few years. This data was taken from the White House web site, http://www.whitehouse.gov/omb/budget/Historicals

The 2013 federal budget was $2.7 trillion. State and local governments have smaller budgets, but they also rely on taxes for their revenue. We pay a variety of taxes:

- Social Security and Medicare taxes
- Non–income-based taxes
- State and federal income taxes

Social Security An insurance program run by the government that provides for everyone in the case of death, disability, health issues, or retirement.

Medicare A government-sponsored health insurance program for individuals over 65.

FICA The combination of Social Security and Medicare taxes.

Social Security and Medicare Taxes

Social Security is a federal insurance program that provides benefits in the event of death, disability, or retirement. Medicare is a government-sponsored health insurance program for individuals over 65. Both Social Security and Medicare taxes are paid by employees and employers at a rate of 7.65 percent each, for a total of 15.3 percent. Combined, these taxes are referred to as FICA, or Federal Insurance Contributions Act, and they are automatically deducted from your paycheck.

The taxes for Social Security, which represent 6.2 percent of the 7.65 percent, are paid on income up to a maximum cap (113,700 in 2013). The Medicare tax of 1.45 percent has no salary cap, so it is paid on all earnings by both the employee and employer.

2012 U.S. FEDERAL BUDGET REVENUE   EXHIBIT 6.1

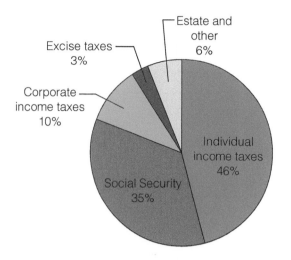

2018 U.S. FEDERAL PROPOSED BUDGET REVENUE

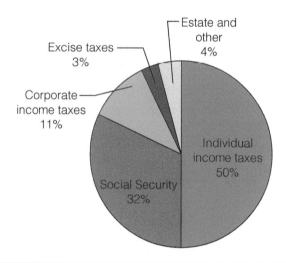

An individual with an income of $50,000 will pay $3,825 in FICA taxes ($50,000 x 7.65%). Of this amount, $3,100 (6.2%) goes to Social Security while the remaining $725 (1.45%) is for Medicare. Employers make matching contributions on their employees' behalf.

Self-employed workers are responsible for both the employee- and employer-paid portions of the taxes, so they pay 15.3 percent of their income as Self-employment taxes, which is used for the same purpose as FICA taxes. They are allowed to deduct half of this as an expense for federal income taxes, which will be discussed in greater detail later in the chapter.

The Social Security program is a controversial political issue. Workers pay taxes into the system, and people who are disabled or retired draw the benefits from the system. As Exhibit 6.2 illustrates, the cost of supporting one retiree is now spread over fewer current workers. The money you put into the system

EXHIBIT 6.2   HOW MANY WORKERS ARE PROVIDING FOR EACH RETIREE

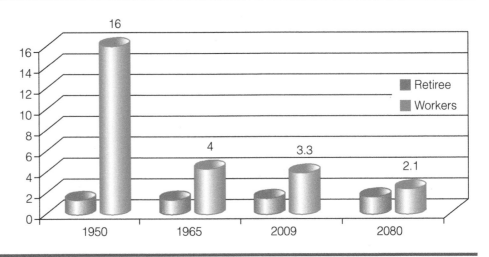

is not saved for you in a personal account. The taxes Social Security currently collects are used to cover the benefits for current retirees. Any extra revenue is put in a Social Security trust fund. The Social Security system is comprised of four trust funds:

1. Old-Age and Survivors Insurance (OASI)
2. Disability Insurance (DI)
3. Hospital Insurance (HI)
4. Supplemental Medical Insurance (SMI)

The Old-Age, Survivors, and Disability Insurance (OASDI) programs pay monthly cash benefits to workers and their families when they retire, become disabled, or die. Many references to "Social Security" specifically mean the OASDI portion.

The health care portion of the system is Medicare. Medicare has both Part A, Hospital Insurance (HI), and Part B, Supplemental Medical Insurance (SMI). Part A pays for inpatient hospital and skilled nursing facility expenses. Part B provides coverage for doctor bills and other outpatient expenses.

Changing demographics creates a potential problem. Life expectancy in the United States is increasing. People are living longer after retirement and continuing to draw benefits longer than originally planned. In 1950, there were 16 workers for every retiree. Now, there are only three workers per retiree, and experts' project this downward trend will continue.

Estimates on the future viability of the Social Security program differ based on political views, but most economic forecasts show the program will need to cut benefits if the system isn't changed. The American Association of Retired Persons (AARP) estimates the Social Security system will begin drawing down trust funds around 2015 and will run out by 2035.

President Bush introduced a plan to privatize Social Security in 2005. In a private Social Security plan, part of your FICA taxes would go into a personal account you "own" that could be invested in different securities. This plan did not pass Congress, but it will not be the last plan set forth by current and future lawmakers to change the system. The current program will lead to higher taxes and/or reduced benefits. The future of Social Security is an important issue. To learn more, visit the Social Security web site www.socialsecurity.gov. Here are links to two articles you may find interesting to compare and contrast the proposed changes.

http://www.socialsecurity.gov/OACT/solvency/provisions/wagebase.html
http://www.socialsecurity.org/pubs/articles/tanner-050114.html

Your income is not the only place you are taxed. Taxes are imposed on almost everything in your daily life, such as a new pair of jeans, attending a movie with some friends and even your monthly electric bill.

Non-Income-Based Taxes

Several taxes are not based on income:

- Sales taxes
- Personal property and real estate taxes
- Excise taxes
- Gift and estate taxes

SALES TAXES

Sales taxes are paid on purchases. These taxes are collected for the benefit of the city, county, or state where the transaction occurs. Sales tax rates differ from one location to another, but are typically between 6 and 8 percent. Some states exempt necessities, like groceries or prescription drugs, from sales tax. Some states do not have a sales tax.

Sales tax Tax paid on all purchases that you make. This tax goes to the city, county, or state where you are making the purchase.

PERSONAL PROPERTY AND REAL ESTATE TAXES

Personal property such as automobiles and recreational vehicles are taxed annually. Personal property taxes are paid to the municipality or county and are based on the assessed value of the property. The assessed value is less than the market value. Real estate taxes are similar to personal property taxes. They are collected by the municipality or county and based on an assessed value, but they are taxes on land or homes you own.

Personal property tax Tax paid to your municipality or county of residence that are based on the assessed value of real property like motor vehicles and boats.

Real estate tax Similar to personal property taxes but for land or homes that you own.

EXCISE TAXES

Excise taxes are additional taxes imposed on certain purchases, like gasoline, alcohol, or cigarettes. Some states or municipalities call the personal property tax an excise tax. The government uses taxes to encourage or discourage some activities, such as drinking and smoking. These taxes are often called sin tax. Excise taxes on gasoline encourage fuel economy.

Excise tax Tax imposed on certain purchases, such as gasoline, alcohol, or cigarettes.

GIFT AND ESTATE TAXES

Gift tax A federal tax on gifts received. Gifts valued over $13,000 in 2009 are subject to gift tax.

Estate tax Tax based on the value of the total estate of a deceased person.

Inheritance tax A tax on a deceased person's property based on who receives the bequest and the amount of the bequest.

Gift and estate taxes are imposed on the transfer of property. The IRS limits the monetary amount of gifts you are allowed to give to one person in a year tax free. The limit is called an exclusion. The IRS states all gifts are taxable, but allows you to exclude a limited amount per donee (the person who receives the gift) per year. You may give $14,000 (2014) to each donee tax free, but gifts over this amount will be taxed.

The estate tax is a federal tax. Your estate is all you own. The IRS uses the current market value to assess the value of a person's estate after his or her death. In 2013 an estate of $5.25 million or less can be transferred tax free. Estates worth more than $5.25 million are taxed at rates from 41 to 50 percent of their value over $5.25 million. There is an exception to the estate taxes for married couples. Whenever a husband or wife dies, the surviving spouse can receive the entire estate with no tax consequences. Some states also impose an estate tax. Depending on the state the "estate tax" can be a tax on the value of the deceased's estate or it can be another name for an inheritance tax.

Inheritance taxes are state taxes paid by the heir(s). An heir is the person who receives the money after the person dies. Each state handles these taxes differently, but most use multiple tax rates depending on the relationship of the deceased to the heir. For example, a son or daughter is usually taxed at a lower rate than a friend or nephew.

Income Taxes

PERSONAL INCOME TAXES

Personal income taxes are the heaviest tax burden for most people. Income taxes are collected by federal, state, and local governments. Federal income tax is paid by everyone who earns an income. Only seven states have no income tax: Alaska, Florida, Nevada, South Dakota, Texas, Washington, and Wyoming. The states of New Hampshire and Tennessee only tax investment income. If you are unfortunate enough to live in a city like Kansas City, Missouri, you also have to pay city income tax. Contact your state or city to obtain forms and instructions to file state or local income tax. You can use the IRS's state tax web site link for more information.

FEDERAL INCOME TAXES

Federal income taxes started in 1913 with the Sixteenth Amendment, which gave Congress the power to impose an income tax. Back then, the tax was 1 percent on any income greater than $3,000 if you were single, or $4,000 if you were married. Since then, many legislatures and federal administrations have changed the tax system. The current U.S. tax code is complex. For this reason, most Americans are intimidated by the thought of planning for income taxes. Taxes paid are true cash outflows. If you reduce your taxes, you have more money. The best way to reduce your taxes is to use the tax laws to their full advantage.

The federal income tax is progressive; as your income increases, you will pay a higher percent of income in tax. This assumes people with higher incomes can afford a greater tax burden. For example, a single person in 2012 with net income of $20,000 paid 15 percent in federal income taxes, while a single person with a net income of $100,000 pays 28 percent in income taxes.

> **Progressive** A tax characteristic, meaning that as you have greater income, you will pay a higher percent of income tax.

Federal income taxes are governed by the Internal Revenue Service, or IRS. Every year individuals with income have to file tax forms with the IRS. This government agency is in charge of preparing citizens to file their personal income tax forms as well as making sure that everyone has prepared taxes correctly. The most common federal tax form is the Form 1040, which is included as Exhibit 6.3. This two-page form will be used to demonstrate how to fill out a tax form. Each line on the form is given a line number, and this number is often used as a reference point. For example, line 7 is where you input your wages and salaries. There are simpler forms for those who qualify to use them. The 1040EZ and 1040A will be discussed later in the chapter in the section on simplified tax forms. All tax forms are also available on the IRS's web site, www.irs.gov.

> **Form 1040** The standard tax form used to file an individual federal tax return.

The 1040 is divided into eight sections:

1. Label
2. Filing status
3. Exemptions
4. Income
5. Adjusted gross income
6. Tax and credits
7. Payments
8. Refund or amount you owe

If you understand these categories, you can plan your federal income taxes.

Label. The label at the top of the form is administrative. Fill out your name, address, and Social Security numbers (SSN).

Filing status. Filing status affects your applicable tax rates. The filing status choices are:

- Single
- Married filing joint return (mfj)
- Married filing separate return (mfs)
- Head of household (hoh)
- Qualifying widow(er) with dependent child

EXHIBIT 6.3   EXAMPLE FORM 1040

Form **1040** Department of the Treasury—Internal Revenue Service (99) **U.S. Individual Income Tax Return** **2012** OMB No. 1545-0074 | IRS Use Only—Do not write or staple in this space.

For the year Jan. 1–Dec. 31, 2012, or other tax year beginning _____ , 2012, ending _____ , 20 ___

See separate instructions.

Your first name and initial Last name	Your social security number
If a joint return, spouse's first name and initial Last name	Spouse's social security number
Home address (number and street). If you have a P.O. box, see instructions. Apt. no.	▲ Make sure the SSN(s) above and on line 6c are correct.
City, town or post office, state, and ZIP code. If you have a foreign address, also complete spaces below (see instructions).	**Presidential Election Campaign** Check here if you, or your spouse if filing jointly, want $3 to go to this fund. Checking a box below will not change your tax or refund. ☐ You ☐ Spouse
Foreign country name Foreign province/state/county Foreign postal code	

Filing Status

Check only one box.

1 ☐ Single
2 ☐ Married filing jointly (even if only one had income)
3 ☐ Married filing separately. Enter spouse's SSN above and full name here. ▶
4 ☐ Head of household (with qualifying person). (See instructions.) If the qualifying person is a child but not your dependent, enter this child's name here. ▶
5 ☐ Qualifying widow(er) with dependent child

Exemptions

6a ☐ **Yourself.** If someone can claim you as a dependent, **do not** check box 6a . . . . .
b ☐ **Spouse** . . . .

c **Dependents:**

(1) First name Last name	(2) Dependent's social security number	(3) Dependent's relationship to you	(4) ✓ If child under age 17 qualifying for child tax credit (see instructions)
			☐
			☐
			☐
			☐

If more than four dependents, see instructions and check here ▶ ☐

d Total number of exemptions claimed . . . .

Boxes checked on 6a and 6b ___
No. of children on 6c who:
• lived with you ___
• did not live with you due to divorce or separation (see instructions) ___
Dependents on 6c not entered above ___
Add numbers on lines above ▶ ___

Income

Attach Form(s) W-2 here. Also attach Forms W-2G and 1099-R if tax was withheld.

If you did not get a W-2, see instructions.

Enclose, but do not attach, any payment. Also, please use Form 1040-V.

7	Wages, salaries, tips, etc. Attach Form(s) W-2	7
8a	**Taxable** interest. Attach Schedule B if required	8a
b	Tax-exempt interest. **Do not** include on line 8a . . . 8b	
9a	Ordinary dividends. Attach Schedule B if required	9a
b	Qualified dividends 9b	
10	Taxable refunds, credits, or offsets of state and local income taxes	10
11	Alimony received	11
12	Business income or (loss). Attach Schedule C or C-EZ	12
13	Capital gain or (loss). Attach Schedule D if required. If not required, check here ▶ ☐	13
14	Other gains or (losses). Attach Form 4797	14
15a	IRA distributions . 15a b Taxable amount . . .	15b
16a	Pensions and annuities 16a b Taxable amount . . .	16b
17	Rental real estate, royalties, partnerships, S corporations, trusts, etc. Attach Schedule E	17
18	Farm income or (loss). Attach Schedule F	18
19	Unemployment compensation	19
20a	Social security benefits 20a b Taxable amount . . .	20b
21	Other income. List type and amount _____	21
22	Combine the amounts in the far right column for lines 7 through 21. This is your **total income** ▶	22

Adjusted Gross Income

23	Educator expenses 23	
24	Certain business expenses of reservists, performing artists, and fee-basis government officials. Attach Form 2106 or 2106-EZ 24	
25	Health savings account deduction. Attach Form 8889 . 25	
26	Moving expenses. Attach Form 3903 26	
27	Deductible part of self-employment tax. Attach Schedule SE . 27	
28	Self-employed SEP, SIMPLE, and qualified plans . . 28	
29	Self-employed health insurance deduction 29	
30	Penalty on early withdrawal of savings 30	
31a	Alimony paid b Recipient's SSN ▶ _____ 31a	
32	IRA deduction 32	
33	Student loan interest deduction 33	
34	Tuition and fees. Attach Form 8917 34	
35	Domestic production activities deduction. Attach Form 8903 35	
36	Add lines 23 through 35	36
37	Subtract line 36 from line 22. This is your **adjusted gross income** . . . . . ▶	37

For Disclosure, Privacy Act, and Paperwork Reduction Act Notice, see separate instructions.   Cat. No. 11320B   Form **1040** (2012)

Form 1040 (2012) Page **2**

Tax and Credits	38	Amount from line 37 (adjusted gross income)	38	
	39a	Check if: ☐ **You** were born before January 2, 1948, ☐ Blind. ☐ **Spouse** was born before January 2, 1948, ☐ Blind. } **Total boxes** checked ▶ **39a**		
Standard Deduction for—	b	If your spouse itemizes on a separate return or you were a dual-status alien, check here ▶ **39b**☐		
• People who check any box on line 39a or 39b or who can be claimed as a dependent, see instructions.	40	**Itemized deductions** (from Schedule A) **or** your **standard deduction** (see left margin) . .	40	
	41	Subtract line 40 from line 38	41	
	42	**Exemptions.** Multiply $3,800 by the number on line 6d	42	
	43	**Taxable income.** Subtract line 42 from line 41. If line 42 is more than line 41, enter -0- .	43	
• All others: Single or Married filing separately, $5,950	44	**Tax** (see instructions). Check if any from: **a** ☐ Form(s) 8814 **b** ☐ Form 4972 **c** ☐ 962 election	44	
	45	**Alternative minimum tax** (see instructions). Attach Form 6251	45	
Married filing jointly or Qualifying widow(er), $11,900	46	Add lines 44 and 45 . . . . ▶	46	
	47	Foreign tax credit. Attach Form 1116 if required . . .	47		
	48	Credit for child and dependent care expenses. Attach Form 2441	48		
Head of household, $8,700	49	Education credits from Form 8863, line 19	49		
	50	Retirement savings contributions credit. Attach Form 8880	50		
	51	Child tax credit. Attach Schedule 8812, if required . .	51		
	52	Residential energy credits. Attach Form 5695	52		
	53	Other credits from Form: **a** ☐ 3800 **b** ☐ 8801 **c** ☐	53		
	54	Add lines 47 through 53. These are your **total credits**	54	
	55	Subtract line 54 from line 46. If line 54 is more than line 46, enter -0- . . . . ▶	55	
Other Taxes	56	Self-employment tax. Attach Schedule SE	56	
	57	Unreported social security and Medicare tax from Form: **a** ☐ 4137 **b** ☐ 8919 . .	57	
	58	Additional tax on IRAs, other qualified retirement plans, etc. Attach Form 5329 if required . .	58	
	59a	Household employment taxes from Schedule H	59a	
	b	First-time homebuyer credit repayment. Attach Form 5405 if required	59b	
	60	Other taxes. Enter code(s) from instructions _____	60	
	61	Add lines 55 through 60. This is your **total tax** . . . . ▶	61	
Payments	62	Federal income tax withheld from Forms W-2 and 1099 . .	62		
	63	2012 estimated tax payments and amount applied from 2011 return	63		
If you have a qualifying child, attach Schedule EIC.	64a	**Earned income credit (EIC)**	64a		
	b	Nontaxable combat pay election **64b**			
	65	Additional child tax credit. Attach Schedule 8812	65		
	66	American opportunity credit from Form 8863, line 8	66		
	67	Reserved	67		
	68	Amount paid with request for extension to file	68		
	69	Excess social security and tier 1 RRTA tax withheld	69		
	70	Credit for federal tax on fuels. Attach Form 4136	70		
	71	Credits from Form: **a** ☐ 2439 **b** ☐ Reserved **c** ☐ 8801 **d** ☐ 8885	71		
	72	Add lines 62, 63, 64a, and 65 through 71. These are your **total payments** . . . . . ▶	72	
Refund	73	If line 72 is more than line 61, subtract line 61 from line 72. This is the amount you **overpaid**	73	
	74a	Amount of line 73 you want **refunded to you.** If Form 8888 is attached, check here . ▶☐	74a	
Direct deposit? See instructions.	b	Routing number ▶		
		▶ **c** Type: ☐ Checking ☐ Savings		
	d	Account number		
	75	Amount of line 73 you want **applied to your 2013 estimated tax** ▶	75		
Amount You Owe	76	**Amount you owe.** Subtract line 72 from line 61. For details on how to pay, see instructions ▶	76	
	77	Estimated tax penalty (see instructions)	77		

Third Party Designee

Do you want to allow another person to discuss this return with the IRS (see instructions)? ☐ **Yes.** Complete below. ☐ **No**

Designee's name ▶	Phone no. ▶	Personal identification number (PIN) ▶

Sign Here

Under penalties of perjury, I declare that I have examined this return and accompanying schedules and statements, and to the best of my knowledge and belief, they are true, correct, and complete. Declaration of preparer (other than taxpayer) is based on all information of which preparer has any knowledge.

Joint return? See instructions.
Keep a copy for your records.

Your signature	Date	Your occupation	Daytime phone number
Spouse's signature. If a joint return, **both** must sign.	Date	Spouse's occupation	If the IRS sent you an Identity Protection PIN, enter it here (see inst.)

Paid Preparer Use Only

Print/Type preparer's name	Preparer's signature	Date	Check ☐ if self-employed	PTIN
Firm's name ▶		Firm's EIN ▶		
Firm's address ▶		Phone no.		

Form **1040** (2012)

If you are single with no dependents, you must file a single return. If you are married, you can file either a joint return with your spouse or separate returns. Filing separate returns is rarely the economical choice if you are married, and it complicates the return. You may select the head of household status if you are single and have qualifying dependents. If your spouse died within the past two years and you have dependent children, you may file as a qualifying widow(er). This status uses the same tax rate as married filing jointly.

Exemptions. An exemption is the amount of your income that is exempt from tax. The federal government allowed a $3,800 exemption for each dependent in 2012. Dependents are yourself, your spouse, and anyone whom you supported in your household, typically your children. However, your dependent can be anyone who lived with you if you provided over 50 percent of that person's support. There are a few exceptions to this rule:

> **Dependent** Normally applied to children or family members for which a taxpayer is providing at least half of the living expenses.

1. The dependent cannot be a qualifying child of another taxpayer for that tax filing year. For this purpose, a person is not a taxpayer if he or she is not required to file a U.S. income tax return and either does not file such a return or files only to get a refund of withheld taxes.
2. The dependent did not earn more than $3,800 (2012).
3. There cannot be a decree of divorce that grants the other parent the right to claim the child as a dependent.

If you are single with no dependents, you will have one exemption. On line 42 of the 1040 form, you will multiply $3,800 for each exemption you listed here. This amount is deducted from your income before you figure the amount of taxes you owe.

INCOME

Lines 7 through 22 of the 1040 form are used to record your annual income. Lines 7 through 21 list different types of income, and line 22 shows your total income from all sources. The most common types of earned income are the following:

- Wages and salaries (line 7)
- Taxable interest (line 8)
- Dividend income (line 9)
- Capital gains (line 13)

Wages and Salaries

For most taxpayers the greatest portion of their income comes from their employment. You will receive a W-2 from each employer you worked for during the past year. Box 1 of the W-2 shows the income you earned which is subject to federal income taxes. If you worked for only one employer, record this amount on line 7 of your 1040 (see Exhibit 6.4). If you worked for more than one employer total the amounts in Box 1 of each W-2 and record the total on line 7 of the 1040.

> **W-2** A federal tax sheet that you receive from any employer that you worked for during the year that lists your income and other tax amounts.

EXAMPLE OF W-2 FORM

EXHIBIT 6.4

a Employee's social security number			

OMB No. 1545-0008   Safe, accurate, FAST! Use   IRS e-file   Visit the IRS website at www.irs.gov/efile

b Employer identification number (EIN)	1 Wages, tips, other compensation	2 Federal income tax withheld
c Employer's name, address, and ZIP code	3 Social security wages	4 Social security tax withheld
	5 Medicare wages and tips	6 Medicare tax withheld
	7 Social security tips	8 Allocated tips
d Control number	9	10 Dependent care benefits
e Employee's first name and initial Last name Suff.	11 Nonqualified plans	12a See instructions for box 12
	13 Statutory employee Retirement plan Third-party sick pay	12b
	14 Other	12c
		12d
f Employee's address and ZIP code		

15 State Employer's state ID number	16 State wages, tips, etc.	17 State income tax	18 Local wages, tips, etc.	19 Local income tax	20 Locality name

Form **W-2**   Wage and Tax Statement   **2013**   Department of the Treasury—Internal Revenue Service

Copy B—To Be Filed With Employee's FEDERAL Tax Return.
This information is being furnished to the Internal Revenue Service.

The amount shown in box 1 of the W-2 may be different from your gross salary. If you made contributions to a company-sponsored retirement plan, like a 401(k), the amount shown in box 1 will be reduced by the amount you contributed to your retirement plan. These contributions are tax deferred, and you will not owe federal taxes on them until you withdraw them.

Your employer also sends a copy of your W-2 to the IRS. After you file your return, the IRS compares your return to their records. Verify the amount you claim on line 7 matches the amounts shown on your W-2s.

Taxable Interest

Most interest income is taxable. If you were paid interest you are required to pay taxes on that interest. Common sources of taxable interest are:

- Savings account
- Checking account
- CD
- Corporate bond
- Federal bond
- Loans you made

Interest income Taxable interest you received, common sources of taxable interest are savings accounts, tax accounts, personal loans you made, CDs, federal and corporate bonds.

You will receive a Form 1099-INT from any financial institution where you earned interest during the year. Interest from state or municipal bonds is usually exempt from federal income tax.

Dividend Income

Dividend Income received from companies or mutual funds that you have invested in.

A dividend is a payment made to stockholders. When a company makes a profit, it can choose to reinvest all of its profit in the company or share some of the profit with its stockholders. When the company chooses to share the profit with its stockholders, it pays a dividend. Dividends paid to stockholders are taxable income. However, if the dividends are paid to a tax deferred account like a 401(k), 403(b), or an IRA, then they are not taxable until they are withdrawn.

If you invest in stocks or mutual funds outside of a tax-deferred plan, you will receive a Form 1099-DIV from each brokerage firm where you received dividends on your investments. Box 1a on the 1099-DIV form will show the amount of ordinary dividends you were paid. If the total amount of dividend and interest income you made during the year is less than $1,500, you record the amounts on the appropriate line. If the total of your dividends and interest for the year is more than $1,500, you must also include Schedule B with your tax return. This form is shown in Exhibit 6.5.

Schedule B The federal tax schedule for totaling your interest and dividend income amounts.

Capital Gains

Capital gain Whenever you sell an asset for more than you paid for it, a tax is owed on this gain.

Many people purchase financial securities like stocks or mutual funds. You may also be involved in other types of financial assets like rental real estate property. Whenever you sell an asset for more than you paid for it, you have to pay tax on the capital gain. The capital gain is calculated by your proceeds from the sale minus your basis in the security. Basis typically means what you paid for the asset. For example, if you made a $3,000 investment three years ago and you sold it this year for $4,000, your capital gain is $1,000. You will owe tax on this $1,000.

Basis The amount you paid for a security; used in the capital gain calculation.

Short-term gain A capital gain that occurs when you hold the security for less than one year.

Long-term gain A capital gain that occurs when you hold the security for more than one year.

Capital gains are taxed based on whether they were short-term gains or long-term gains. Short-term gains are profits made from assets you owned for one year or less. Long-term gains are profits made from assets you owned for more than a year. Short-term gains are taxed at the marginal income tax rate. The marginal income tax rate is the tax rate you pay based on your income. Long-term gains are taxed at the capital gains rate, which starting in 2013 is based on the following table.

Capital Gains Tax Rate Starting January 1st 2013 Marginal Tax rate in the year of the sale							
	10%	15%	25%	28%	33%	35%	39.60%
Held investment less than 1 year	10%	15%	25%	28%	33%	35%	39.60%
Held investment more than 1 year	0%	0%	15%	15%	15%	18.80%	23.80%

EXAMPLE SCHEDULE B **EXHIBIT 6.5**

SCHEDULE B (Form 1040A or 1040) Department of the Treasury Internal Revenue Service (99)	**Interest and Ordinary Dividends** ▶ Attach to Form 1040A or 1040. ▶ Information about Schedule B (Form 1040A or 1040) and its instructions is at *www.irs.gov/form1040*.	OMB No. 1545-0074 20**12** Attachment Sequence No. **08**
Name(s) shown on return		Your social security number

				Amount	
Part I **Interest** (See instructions on back and the instructions for Form 1040A, or Form 1040, line 8a.) **Note.** If you received a Form 1099-INT, Form 1099-OID, or substitute statement from a brokerage firm, list the firm's name as the payer and enter the total interest shown on that form.	1	List name of payer. If any interest is from a seller-financed mortgage and the buyer used the property as a personal residence, see instructions on back and list this interest first. Also, show that buyer's social security number and address ▶ -- -- -- -- -- -- -- -- -- -- -- -- --		**1**	
	2	Add the amounts on line 1	**2**		
	3	Excludable interest on series EE and I U.S. savings bonds issued after 1989. Attach Form 8815	**3**		
	4	Subtract line 3 from line 2. Enter the result here and on Form 1040A, or Form 1040, line 8a . . . . ▶	**4**		
		Note. If line 4 is over $1,500, you must complete Part III.		**Amount**	
Part II **Ordinary Dividends** (See instructions on back and the instructions for Form 1040A, or Form 1040, line 9a.) **Note.** If you received a Form 1099-DIV or substitute statement from a brokerage firm, list the firm's name as the payer and enter the ordinary dividends shown on that form.	5	List name of payer ▶ ----------------------------------- -- -- -- -- -- -- -- -- -- -- -- -- --		**5**	
	6	Add the amounts on line 5. Enter the total here and on Form 1040A, or Form 1040, line 9a . . . . ▶	**6**		
		Note. If line 6 is over $1,500, you must complete Part III.			

		You must complete this part if you **(a)** had over $1,500 of taxable interest or ordinary dividends; **(b)** had a foreign account; or **(c)** received a distribution from, or were a grantor of, or a transferor to, a foreign trust.	Yes	No
Part III **Foreign Accounts and Trusts** (See instructions on back.)	7a	At any time during 2012, did you have a financial interest in or signature authority over a financial account (such as a bank account, securities account, or brokerage account) located in a foreign country? See instructions		
		If "Yes," are you required to file Form TD F 90-22.1 to report that financial interest or signature authority? See Form TD F 90-22.1 and its instructions for filing requirements and exceptions to those requirements		
	b	If you are required to file Form TD F 90-22.1, enter the name of the foreign country where the financial account is located ▶ ---------------------------------		
	8	During 2012, did you receive a distribution from, or were you the grantor of, or transferor to, a foreign trust? If "Yes," you may have to file Form 3520. See instructions on back		

For Paperwork Reduction Act Notice, see your tax return instructions.   Cat. No. 17146N   Schedule B (Form 1040A or 1040) 2012

Schedule D The federal tax schedule used to input capital gains.

Capital gains are recorded on Schedule D of the 1040, shown in Exhibit 6.6. If your capital gains were from the sale of securities you will receive a 1099-B from your brokerage firm.

EXHIBIT 6.6	EXAMPLE SCHEDULE D

SCHEDULE D (Form 1040)

Department of the Treasury
Internal Revenue Service (99)

Capital Gains and Losses

► Attach to Form 1040 or Form 1040NR.
► Information about Schedule D and its separate instructions is at *www.irs.gov/form1040*.
► Use Form 8949 to list your transactions for lines 1, 2, 3, 8, 9, and 10.

OMB No. 1545-0074

2012

Attachment
Sequence No. **12**

Name(s) shown on return

Your social security number

Part I   Short-Term Capital Gains and Losses—Assets Held One Year or Less

Complete Form 8949 before completing line 1, 2, or 3. This form may be easier to complete if you round off cents to whole dollars.	(d) Proceeds (sales price) from Form(s) 8949, Part I, line 2, column (d)	(e) Cost or other basis from Form(s) 8949, Part I, line 2, column (e)	(g) Adjustments to gain or loss from Form(s) 8949, Part I, line 2, column (g)	(h) Gain or (loss) Subtract column (e) from column (d) and combine the result with column (g)
1 Short-term totals from all Forms 8949 with **box A** checked in **Part I**				
2 Short-term totals from all Forms 8949 with **box B** checked in **Part I**				
3 Short-term totals from all Forms 8949 with **box C** checked in **Part I**				

4 Short-term gain from Form 6252 and short-term gain or (loss) from Forms 4684, 6781, and 8824	**4**	
5 Net short-term gain or (loss) from partnerships, S corporations, estates, and trusts from Schedule(s) K-1	**5**	
6 Short-term capital loss carryover. Enter the amount, if any, from line 8 of your **Capital Loss Carryover Worksheet** in the instructions	**6**	( )
7 **Net short-term capital gain or (loss).** Combine lines 1 through 6 in column (h). If you have any long-term capital gains or losses, go to Part II below. Otherwise, go to Part III on the back	**7**	

Part II   Long-Term Capital Gains and Losses—Assets Held More Than One Year

Complete Form 8949 before completing line 8, 9, or 10. This form may be easier to complete if you round off cents to whole dollars.	(d) Proceeds (sales price) from Form(s) 8949, Part II, line 4, column (d)	(e) Cost or other basis from Form(s) 8949, Part II, line 4, column (e)	(g) Adjustments to gain or loss from Form(s) 8949, Part II, line 4, column (g)	(h) Gain or (loss) Subtract column (e) from column (d) and combine the result with column (g)
8 Long-term totals from all Forms 8949 with **box A** checked in **Part II**				
9 Long-term totals from all Forms 8949 with **box B** checked in **Part II**				
10 Long-term totals from all Forms 8949 with **box C** checked in **Part II**				

11 Gain from Form 4797, Part I; long-term gain from Forms 2439 and 6252; and long-term gain or (loss) from Forms 4684, 6781, and 8824	**11**	
12 Net long-term gain or (loss) from partnerships, S corporations, estates, and trusts from Schedule(s) K-1	**12**	
13 Capital gain distributions. See the instructions	**13**	
14 Long-term capital loss carryover. Enter the amount, if any, from line 13 of your **Capital Loss Carryover Worksheet** in the instructions	**14**	( )
15 **Net long-term capital gain or (loss).** Combine lines 8 through 14 in column (h). Then go to Part III on the back	**15**	

For Paperwork Reduction Act Notice, see your tax return instructions.   Cat. No. 11338H   Schedule D (Form 1040) 2012

OTHER TYPES OF INCOME

Form 1040 lists many other types of income. Include any income you made during the year. If you were self-employed, you record your income on line 12. You will use schedules C and SE. Schedule C documents your profit or

---

Part III   **Summary**

16	Combine lines 7 and 15 and enter the result	**16**

- If line 16 is a **gain**, enter the amount from line 16 on Form 1040, line 13, or Form 1040NR, line 14. Then go to line 17 below.
- If line 16 is a **loss**, skip lines 17 through 20 below. Then go to line 21. Also be sure to complete line 22.
- If line 16 is **zero**, skip lines 17 through 21 below and enter -0- on Form 1040, line 13, or Form 1040NR, line 14. Then go to line 22.

17   Are lines 15 and 16 **both** gains?

☐ **Yes.** Go to line 18.
☐ **No.** Skip lines 18 through 21, and go to line 22.

18   Enter the amount, if any, from line 7 of the **28% Rate Gain Worksheet** in the instructions . . ▶ | **18** |

19   Enter the amount, if any, from line 18 of the **Unrecaptured Section 1250 Gain Worksheet** in the instructions . . . . ▶ | **19** |

20   Are lines 18 and 19 **both** zero or blank?

☐ **Yes.** Complete the **Qualified Dividends and Capital Gain Tax Worksheet** in the instructions for Form 1040, line 44 (or in the instructions for Form 1040NR, line 42). **Do not** complete lines 21 and 22 below.

☐ **No.** Complete the **Schedule D Tax Worksheet** in the instructions. **Do not** complete lines 21 and 22 below.

21   If line 16 is a loss, enter here and on Form 1040, line 13, or Form 1040NR, line 14, the **smaller** of:

- The loss on line 16 or
- ($3,000), or if married filing separately, ($1,500)   . . . . | **21** ( )

Note. When figuring which amount is smaller, treat both amounts as positive numbers.

22   Do you have qualified dividends on Form 1040, line 9b, or Form 1040NR, line 10b?

☐ **Yes.** Complete the **Qualified Dividends and Capital Gain Tax Worksheet** in the instructions for Form 1040, line 44 (or in the instructions for Form 1040NR, line 42).

☐ **No.** Complete the rest of Form 1040 or Form 1040NR.

loss from operating your business and Schedule SE is used to compute your self-employment tax. On line 22 enter the sum of lines 7-21 this is your gross (total) income.

Adjusted Gross Income

Lines 23 through 36 are special deductions. The deductions on lines 23 through 36 are associated with the cost of employment. These deductions are subtracted from your gross income to obtain your adjusted gross income (AGI) on line 37. AGI is used as a limit for other tax computations. Credits and deductions offered later in the return may require you to have an AGI under a certain amount. Some states ask for your AGI on the state income tax return. If you don't take any of deductions listed here, your gross income will equal your adjusted gross income. Notice there is a deduction here for tuition and fees you paid to a college or university. There is also a deduction listed here for interest paid on student loans. Other common deductions include alimony paid, moving expenses, IRA deductions, and one-half of your self-employment tax deduction.

Adjusted gross income (AGI) The amount of income that you have after taking into account any applicable adjustments on the first page of the 1040 form.

Taxes and Credits

The tax and credits section begins on page two of the 1040. This section includes:

- Standard or itemized deductions
- Exemptions
- Tax
- Credits

Standard deduction A fixed amount that is subtracted from AGI before you arrive at taxable income.

Standard or Itemized Deductions

The standard deduction is a fixed amount. This deduction depends on your filing status. For 2012 the deduction was the following:

- $5,950 if you are single or married filing separately
- $11,900 if you are married filing jointly or a qualifying widow(er)
- $8,700 if you are head of household

Itemized deductions Specific expenses that you can deduct before arriving at taxable income; used when their total is greater than the standard deduction.

Schedule A The federal tax schedule for itemized deductions.

You may also choose to itemize your deductions. Itemized deductions are specific expenses you deduct to calculate your taxable income. Taxpayers may use either the standard or itemized deduction—they cannot receive both.

Tax deductions reduce your taxable income. Tax credits reduce your taxes. If you have a $2,000 deduction and are in a 25% tax bracket, this reduces the taxes you owe by $500. If you have a $2,000 tax credit, it reduces the taxes you owe by $2,000, regardless of your tax bracket.

The schedule for itemized deductions is Schedule A, shown as Exhibit 6.7. If you itemize your deductions, you must include this schedule with your return. You should calculate your itemized deductions; if they are higher than the standard deduction for your filing status, you should itemize. If not, take the standard deduction.

EXAMPLE SCHEDULE A

EXHIBIT 6.7

SCHEDULE A (Form 1040)	**Itemized Deductions**	OMB No. 1545-0074
Department of the Treasury Internal Revenue Service (99)	► Information about Schedule A and its separate instructions is at *www.irs.gov/form1040.* ► Attach to Form 1040.	20**12** Attachment Sequence No. **07**
Name(s) shown on Form 1040		Your social security number

Medical and Dental Expenses	**Caution.** Do not include expenses reimbursed or paid by others.		
	1 Medical and dental expenses (see instructions)	**1**	
	2 Enter amount from Form 1040, line 38 **2**		
	3 Multiply line 2 by 7.5% (.075)	**3**	
	4 Subtract line 3 from line 1. If line 3 is more than line 1, enter -0-		**4**
Taxes You Paid	5 State and local (**check only one box**):		
	a ☐ Income taxes, **or** }	**5**	
	b ☐ General sales taxes }		
	6 Real estate taxes (see instructions)	**6**	
	7 Personal property taxes	**7**	
	8 Other taxes. List type and amount ► _____		
	_____	**8**	
	9 Add lines 5 through 8		**9**
Interest You Paid **Note.** Your mortgage interest deduction may be limited (see instructions).	10 Home mortgage interest and points reported to you on Form 1098	**10**	
	11 Home mortgage interest not reported to you on Form 1098. If paid to the person from whom you bought the home, see instructions and show that person's name, identifying no., and address ►		
	_____		
	_____	**11**	
	12 Points not reported to you on Form 1098. See instructions for special rules	**12**	
	13 Mortgage insurance premiums (see instructions)	**13**	
	14 Investment interest. Attach Form 4952 if required. (See instructions.)	**14**	
	15 Add lines 10 through 14		**15**
Gifts to Charity If you made a gift and got a benefit for it, see instructions.	16 Gifts by cash or check. If you made any gift of $250 or more, see instructions	**16**	
	17 Other than by cash or check. If any gift of $250 or more, see instructions. You **must** attach Form 8283 if over $500 . . .	**17**	
	18 Carryover from prior year	**18**	
	19 Add lines 16 through 18		**19**
Casualty and Theft Losses	20 Casualty or theft loss(es). Attach Form 4684. (See instructions.)		**20**
Job Expenses and Certain Miscellaneous Deductions	21 Unreimbursed employee expenses—job travel, union dues, job education, etc. Attach Form 2106 or 2106-EZ if required. (See instructions.) ► _____	**21**	
	22 Tax preparation fees	**22**	
	23 Other expenses—investment, safe deposit box, etc. List type and amount ► _____		
	_____	**23**	
	24 Add lines 21 through 23	**24**	
	25 Enter amount from Form 1040, line 38 **25**		
	26 Multiply line 25 by 2% (.02)	**26**	
	27 Subtract line 26 from line 24. If line 26 is more than line 24, enter -0-		**27**
Other Miscellaneous Deductions	28 Other—from list in instructions. List type and amount ► _____		
	_____		**28**
Total Itemized Deductions	29 Add the amounts in the far right column for lines 4 through 28. Also, enter this amount on Form 1040, line 40		**29**
	30 If you elect to itemize deductions even though they are less than your standard deduction, check here . . . . ► ☐		

For Paperwork Reduction Act Notice, see Form 1040 instructions.   Cat. No. 17145C   Schedule A (Form 1040) 2012

Itemized Deductions

Here are the common itemized expenses:

- Medical and dental expenses. If your medical and dental expenses are more than 10 percent (.1%) of your AGI, you can deduct the amount in excess of 10 percent of your AGI. Qualified medical and dental expenses are ones you paid for. If you were reimbursed for them, they are not tax deductible. These expenses can include your accident or health insurance premiums paid.
- State income or sales tax. You can deduct either your state and local income tax or the sales tax you paid for the year. Allowing sales tax as a deduction was new to the tax code in 2004. Don't worry—you do not have to keep track of all the sales tax you paid during the year. The IRS provides charts for each state based on income ranges and you are allowed to simply use the sales tax figure for your state and income. Normally, the income tax is greater than the sales tax, but if you live in a state without a state income tax, you can use the sales tax deduction. Or if you made a large purchase during the year, like a car or boat, the sales tax amount may provide a larger deduction.
- Real estate taxes. If you own a home or any land, you pay real estate taxes on the property. You can deduct real estate taxes you paid on line 6 of Schedule A.
- Personal property taxes. If you own a vehicle, boat, or piece of large equipment, you pay personal property tax. You can deduct these taxes on Schedule A, line 7.
- Mortgage interest. If you have a mortgage on your home, you can deduct the interest you paid on line 10. You cannot deduct interest on automobile loans or credit card debt.
- Gifts to charity. Any charitable contributions you make can be deducted on line 15. Gifts to churches and most nonprofit organizations are allowed. Political contributions are not deductible. Noncash contributions can also be included here. If you donate clothes or furnishings to the Salvation Army, that's considered a contribution. The allowable deduction is the fair market value of the items donated. Ask for a receipt when you donate items, you will need it if you are ever audited.

Total your itemized deductions; compare this number to your standard deduction. Choose whichever is higher and record it on line 40 of the 1040.

Exemptions

Near the beginning of the tax return, you listed your dependents. You receive an exemption for each dependent. On line 42 you calculate the deduction for your exemptions. For 2012, you were allowed a $3,800 exemption for each dependent. If you claimed five exemptions, your deduction on line 42 would is $3,800 × 5 = $19,000. You qualify for additional exemptions if you are blind or over the age of 65.

Tax and Credits

Your adjusted gross income minus your deductions and exemptions is your taxable income. Taxable income is the amount on which you calculate federal income taxes. Taxable income is your AGI less deductions and exemptions. Tax rate schedules are included as Exhibit 6.8. The tax is progressive, which means the rate increases as your income increases.

Taxable income The income on which you owe federal income tax.

2012 TAX RATE SCHEDULES

EXHIBIT 6.8

Schedule X—If your filing status is Single

If your taxable income is over:	But not over:	The tax is:	Of the amount over:
$0	$8,700	10%	$0
$8,700	$35,350	$870.00 + 15%	$8,700
$35,350	$85,650	$4,867.50 + 25%	$35,350
$85,650	$178,650	$17,442.50 + 28%	$85,650
$178,650	$388,350	$43,482.50 + 33%	$178,650
$388,350	no limit	$112,683.50 + 35%	$388,350

Schedule Y-1—If your filing status is Married filing jointly or Qualifying widow(er)

If your taxable income isover:	But not over:	The tax is:	Of the amount over:
$0	$17,400	10%	$0
$17,400	$70,700	$1,740.00 + 15%	$17,400
$70,700	$142,700	$9,735.00 + 25%	$70,700
$142,700	$217,450	$27,735.00 + 28%	$142,700
$217,450	$388,350	$48,665.00 + 33%	$217,450
$388,350	no limit	$105,062.00 + 35%	$388,350

Schedule Y-2—If your filing status is Married filing separately

If your taxable income isover:	But not over:	The tax is:	Of the amount over:
$0	$8,700	10%	$0
$8,700	$35,350	$870.00 + 15%	$8,700
$35,350	$71,350	$4,867.50 + 25%	$35,350
$71,350	$108,725	$13,867.50 + 28%	$71,350
$108,725	$194,175	$24,332.50 + 33%	$108,725
$194,175	no limit	$52,531.00 + 35%	$194,175

Schedule Z—If your filing status is Head of household

If your taxable income isover:	But not over:	The tax is:	Of the amount over:
$0	$12,400	10%	$0
$12,400	$47,350	$1,240.00 + 15%	$12,400
$47,350	$122,300	$6,482.50 + 25%	$47,350
$122,300	$198,050	$25,220.00 + 28%	$122,300
$198,050	$388,350	$46,430.00 + 33%	$198,050
$388,350	no limit	$109,229.00 + 35%	$388,350

Tax liability The amount of federal income taxes that you owe for the year.

The schedule for determining your tax liability is straightforward to use. Your tax liability is the amount of federal income taxes you owe for the year. The liability is calculated by the formula:

$$\text{Tax liability} = \text{Tax on base} +$$
$$[\text{Percentage on income over base} \times (\text{taxable income} - \text{base})]$$

If you are single with $40,000 in taxable income, your tax liability will be equal to:

$$\$4,386.25 + [(0.25)(40,000 - 31,850)] = \$6,423.75$$

However, if you prepare your tax return and calculate your tax liability is $6,423.75, you do not write the IRS a check for that amount. You first check if you have any available tax credits and subtract the federal taxes withheld from your paycheck during the year.

Tax credits are offered by the government in several areas and directly offset taxes owed. If you have $2,000 in credits, this lowers the amount of taxes you pay by $2,000. Credits are better than deductions and exemptions. A $2,000 deduction lowers your taxable income by $2,000, but may only decrease your taxes by $500. Tax credits are a dollar-for-dollar reduction in taxes.

Tax Credits

Credit for child and dependent care expenses. If you pay expenses to provide care for a child under 13 or a disabled dependent, you will be eligible for this credit. This credit has a maximum of $1,000 per child. The percent of your expenses you are allowed to use when you calculate your credit decreases as your adjusted gross income increases. The highest wage earner are allowed to use 20 percent of their expenses. If this credit applies to you, you need to prepare Form 2441 in order to calculate the value of your credit.

Educational credits. Educational credits are available if you paid for any post-secondary education. This includes colleges, universities, or vocational schools. You cannot take the credit if:

- You are claimed as a dependent on someone else's tax return.
- Your adjusted gross income is greater than $53,000 if single, or $107,000 if married filing jointly.

Hope Credit An educational credit that is available to use for the first four years of college if the student is full-time.

Lifetime Learning Credit An educational credit that is available for any college student who doesn't claim the Hope Credit.

The IRS offers two educational credits, the Hope Credit and the Lifetime Learning Credit. The Hope Credit is for full-time students in their first four years of college. The maximum hope credit is $2,500 per student. The Lifetime Learning Credit is for all other students. The maximum Lifetime Learning Credit is $2,000, but this is not a per student limit. The maximum a taxpayer can claim a year in Lifetime Learning Credits is $2,000. You may take either the Hope or Lifetime Learning Credit, but you cannot take both in the same year for the same student.

Qualifying expenses for the educational credits are tuition, books, supplies, and mandatory activities or university fees. It does not include payments for room and board. You may take the credit if you paid education expenses for yourself, your spouse, or any dependent claimed on your tax form. Form 8863 is used to calculate the credit amount.

© rSnapshotPhotos, 2014, Shutterstock, Inc.

Depending on your situation, there are several different tax credits available to families.

Child tax credit. If you have dependent children under the age of 17, you may qualify for the child tax credit. This credit is up to $1,000 per child. The credit is not allowed if your adjusted gross income is greater than $75,000 if single or $110,000 if married filing jointly. This is a refundable credit. Refundable credits are credits you can take as a refund even if you do not owe taxes.

Earned income credit. The earned income credit is for low-income households. This is a refundable credit for those who meet the guidelines. The largest credits go to families with two or more children who are working but well below the poverty guidelines.

Payments

Federal income tax is withheld from your paycheck. Federal income tax withholdings are based on your estimated tax liability for the year. Box 2 on the W-2 form lists the amount of federal taxes withheld from your paycheck. Write this amount on line 64 of the 1040 as your payment.

If you are self-employed or receive substantial investment income, you need to make quarterly estimated tax payments to the IRS. If you don't make quarterly payments and owe at the end of the year, you will be charged penalties.

Refund or Amount You Owe

You are finally at the end of the federal return. Here you calculate whether you owe money to the IRS or if it owes you a refund. Whether you owe is based on the following:

Tax liability from line 46
– Credits
– Tax payments

= Amount you owe or the amount of your refund

If your credits and payments are greater than your tax liability, you will receive a refund. If your credits and payments are less than your tax liability, you owe money to the IRS. This money is due, along with your tax return, on April 15th after the end of the tax year. Individuals who are unable to complete their tax return by April 15 may file for an extension. The extension allows you until August 15 to file your return. The extension of time is automatic, and it is an extension only for filing. You must estimate the amount of taxes you owe and include the payment with your extension request. Failure to accurately estimate and pay taxes due results in a penalty assessment plus interest on the penalty.

A Comprehensive Income-Based Tax Example

Let's work through a sample tax return. Anthony Robinson and his wife, Charlotte, are working on their tax return. They have two dependent children in the household, ages 6 and 10. Charlotte works full-time as a lawyer and makes $60,000 per year. Anthony works part-time as an accountant and makes $15,000 annually. Charlotte contributes $3,000 to an employee-based retirement account that is not subject to federal income tax.

FICA taxes. Anthony and Charlotte each owe 7.65 percent of their income for FICA taxes.

Charlotte	$60,000 × .0765 = $4,590
Anthony	$15,000 × .0765 = $1,148
	$5,738 total FICA taxes

Their FICA taxes were withheld from each of their paychecks. Note that Charlotte paid FICA taxes on her retirement contribution.

Personal taxes. Anthony and Charlotte will use the 1040 form to file their federal income tax return.

Gross income. Salary:

Charlotte	$57,000
Anthony	$15,000
Total	$72,000

Charlotte's contribution of $3,000 is not included as income here. They also have $1,000 in interest income, so their gross income on line 22 is $73,000. They do not need to file Schedule B since their investment income is less than $1,500.

Adjusted gross income. They contributed $4,000 to a traditional IRA, which is an allowable adjustment on line 32. This brings their adjusted gross income amount on line 37 down to $69,000.

Standard or itemized deduction. They need to decide which deduction to use. The standard deduction for their filing status of married filing jointly is $11,900. Their allowable itemized expenses are:

Mortgage interest	$9,000
State income taxes	$3,000
Real estate and personal property taxes	$1,500
Charitable donations	$2,000
	$15,500

Their itemized deductions are greater than the standard deduction, so they will itemize.

Exemptions. The Robinsons have four exemptions (one for Anthony, Charlotte, and each of the two children), so their exemptions amount is $3,800 × 4 = $17,200.

Taxable income. Their taxable income is their adjusted gross income minus their deductions and exemptions.

$$\text{Taxable income} = \$69,000 - \$15,500 - \$17,200$$
$$= \$36,300$$

Tax liability. Use the tax rate schedule (Exhibit 6.8) to determine the Robinsons' tax liability.

$$\text{Tax liability} = \$1,740 + [(\$36,300 - \$17,400)(0.15)]$$
$$= \$4,575$$

Tax credits and payments. The Robinsons were able to take a $1,000 child tax credit for each of their two children, for a total credit of $2,000. They had no additional credits.

Both Anthony and Charlotte had federal tax withheld from their paychecks. Anthony had $500 in federal taxes withheld and Charlotte had $4,000 withheld. So their total credits and payments are $6,500.

Refund amount. Since their total payments and credits are greater than their tax liability, the Robinsons file for a refund of $6,500 − $4,575 = $1925.

Help filing tax returns. You can get help with your taxes from a variety of sources. Use the IRS's web site, www.irs.gov, to gather necessary forms and instructions. Tax software, like TurboTax, is popular and easy to use, or you can hire a professional to prepare your taxes for you. Accounting firms and CPAs are tax specialists, but they are an expensive option for a basic return. Tax preparers like H&R Block charge lower rates for standard returns. Exhibit 6.9 lists some common mistakes made by taxpayers.

| EXHIBIT 6.9 | SEVEN BIGGEST TAXPAYER MISTAKES |

1. **Bad math.** Simple math errors are common.
2. **Not reporting all interest and dividends.** Many taxpayers forget about a savings account here or a dividend there. The IRS receives this information and will flag your return.
3. **Not keeping accurate records to track the cost basis of your investments.** In order to correctly compute the profit from selling an investment, you need to know just what it cost you.
4. **The marriage penalty.** In many cases, a married couple pays more in taxes than they would if single. While this should not discourage marriage, it might be wise to postpone a December wedding until January. This can also be offset by increasing the amount of taxes withheld.
5. **Losing receipts.** Keeping track of everything is difficult, but the IRS will ask for proof of deductions if it audits your return.
6. **Failure to plan deductions to their maximum.** For example, it may be advantageous to go ahead and pay an expense before December 31 so that you get the deduction in the current year.
7. **Failing to donate unwanted items to charity by year end.** You can take a deduction equal to the market value of items donated to charity, but be sure to get and keep a receipt.

Source: http://moneycentral.msn.com/content/Taxes/Cutyourtaxes/P41352.asp

Tax Planning Strategy

Use deductions, exemptions, and credits to your advantage. If you increase these, you will lower your tax liability. Defer taxes as long as possible; don't intentionally have more taxes withheld than you owe. Remember the time value of money concepts. Hold financial securities longer to defer capital gains tax. You do not owe the tax until you sell the asset. Invest in tax-free bonds; most municipal and state bonds are exempt from federal income taxes.

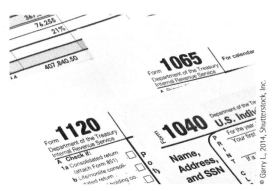

Should you decide to prepare your own taxes, educate yourself on the basic forms to use and know where to look if you need help.

SIMPLIFIED TAX FORMS

The IRS has two simplified versions of the 1040 tax form: the 1040A and the 1040EZ. The 1040EZ is the simplest form and is ideal for most students.

Form 1040EZ and IRA instructions on how to use the form can be found at: http://www.irs.gov/pub/irs-pdf/f1040ez.pdf

Who Can Use Form 1040EZ

You can use Form 1040EZ if all the following items apply:

- Your filing status is single or married filing jointly.
- You do not claim any dependents.
- You do not claim any adjustments to income.
- You can claim only the earned income credit and the recovery rebate credit.
- You (and your spouse if filing a joint return) were under age 65 and not blind at the end of 2008.
- Your taxable income is less than $100,000.
- You had only wages, salaries, tips, taxable scholarship or fellowship grants, unemployment compensation, or Alaska Permanent Fund dividends, and your taxable interest was not over $1,500.
- You did not receive any advance earned income credit.
- You do not owe any household employment taxes on wages you paid to a household employee.
- You are not a debtor in a Chapter 11 bankruptcy case filed after October 16, 2005.
- You are not claiming the additional standard deduction for real estate taxes or disaster losses.

Who Can Use Form 1040A?

You can use Form 1040A if all six of the following apply:

1. You only had income from the following sources:

   a. Wages, salaries, tips
   b. Interest and ordinary dividends
   c. Capital gain distributions
   d. Taxable scholarship and fellowship grants
   e. Pensions, annuities, and IRAs
   f. Unemployment compensation
   g. Taxable Social Security and railroad retirement benefits
   h. Alaska Permanent Fund dividends

2. The only adjustments to income you can claim are:

   a. Educator expenses (see Publication 525)
   b. IRA deduction
   c. Student loan interest deduction
   d. Tuition and fees deduction, earned income credit (EIC) payments (You can also use Form 1040A if you received advance earned income credit payments), dependent care benefits, or if you owe tax from the recapture of an education credit or the alternative

3. You do not itemize deductions.
4. Your taxable income (line 27) is less than $100,000.
5. The only tax credits you can claim are:

   a. Child tax credit
   b. Additional child tax credit
   c. Education credits
   d. Earned income credit
   e. Credit for child and dependent care expenses
   f. Credit for the elderly or the disabled
   g. Retirement savings contributions credit
   h. Recovery rebate credit

6. You did not have an alternative minimum tax adjustment on stock you acquired from the exercise of an incentive stock option.

SUMMARY

Taxes are the largest expense for most households. Taxes are the main income producer for our federal, state, and local governments. You learned about three main types of taxes:

- Social Security and Medicare taxes
- Non–income-based taxes
- State and federal income taxes

Social Security and Medicare taxes are combined into a tax called FICA. This tax is 7.65 percent of our wages if we are employed by someone else, and it provides for individuals who are retired or disabled.

Non–income-based taxes are based on your purchases and property. They include sales taxes, personal property taxes, and real estate taxes.

Federal income taxes are administered by the Internal Revenue Service, a government agency. You owe taxes on your income, less deductions, exemptions, and credits. The standard tax form used to file an individual return is the 1040.

Income refers to earnings you received during the year. You can deduct mortgage interest, charitable contributions, real estate/personal property taxes, and state income taxes. The Hope and Lifetime Learning educational credits, child tax credit, and earned income credit are examples of credits. A credit is more desirable than a deduction because the credit offers a dollar-for-dollar reduction in taxes.

In addition to your federal income taxes, you may also be subject to state and local income taxes.

PROBLEMS

1. How much FICA tax will be withheld from your paycheck if your gross income is $30,000?

2. Using Exhibit 6-8, compute the amount of tax due for a single taxpayer with $28,000 in taxable income.

3. Using Exhibit 6-8, compute the amount of tax due for a married couple with $100,000 in taxable income.

4. If you are in a 25% tax bracket, how much will a $1,000 deduction reduce your taxes?

5. If you are in a 25% tax bracket, how much will a $1,000 credit reduce your taxes?

CASE STUDIES

COLLEGE STUDENT

Kevin Maedor is a 19-year-old college student. He still lives at home with his parents and he works part time.

Kevin's 2012 W-2 shows:

- He earned $9,120.
- $912 was withheld in federal income tax.
- $150 was withheld in state income tax.
- $565.44 was paid to social security.
- $132.24 was paid to Medicare.
- He is still a dependent and claimed on his parents' income tax.

1. Select the easiest federal income tax form he is allowed to use.
2. Complete his 2012 tax return, including any required schedules.

NEW GRADUATE

Rene Harris recently graduated with a B.S. in nursing.

Rene's 2012 W-2 shows

- She earned $76,000.
- $13,734.10 was withheld in federal income tax.
- $1,322.48 was withheld in state income tax.
- $4,712.00 was paid to social security.
- $1,102.00 was paid to Medicare.

1. Select the easiest federal income tax form she is allowed to use.
2. Complete her 2012 tax return, including any required schedules.

CREATE YOUR OWN FINANCIAL PLAN

1. Research current credits and determine which ones apply to your situation.
2. Use the information presented in this chapter and create a plan to reduce your taxes. You can use either your current financial information or your projected future income when you graduate.
3. Determine which income tax form is the best for you this year.
4. Organize receipts you will need for tax purposes. Create a file for tax-related documents.

REVIEW QUESTIONS

1. Discuss how the Social Security system works and how the current system will fail if changes are not made.

   _____

   _____

   _____

2. Describe the four non–income-based taxes discussed in the book.

   _____

   _____

   _____

   _____

3. How does a taxpayer's filing status affect the amount he or she owes in taxes?

   _____

   _____

   _____

4. If you owned stock, what two types of income would you receive and how would they be taxed?

   _____

   _____

   _____

5. What is the purpose of the following federal tax schedules?
   • Schedule A

   _____

   _____

   _____

   • Schedule B

   _____

   _____

   _____

   • Schedule D

   _____

   _____

   _____

6. Why is it important to keep good records?

   _____

   _____

   _____

7. When is it beneficial to itemize deductions? Give examples of items that would make it beneficial to itemize.

   _____

   _____

   _____

8. What is the difference between a tax credit and a tax deduction?

   _____

   _____

   _____

9. What is earned income credit?

_____

_____

_____

10. What are the total taxes (as a percent) for Social Security and Medicare and who pays them?

_____

_____

_____

Property and Casualty Insurance

7

"No man acquires property without acquiring with it a little arithmetic also."

—Ralph Waldo Emerson

OBJECTIVES

- Define insurance terms: premium, deductible, claim, and risk
- Understand liability insurance and its coverage limits
- Distinguish between comprehensive and collision coverage
- Understand the difference between cash value, replacement value, and extended value coverage

KEY TERMS

Actual cash value	Hazard	Premium
Automobile insurance	Liability coverage	Property and casualty insurance
Claim	Medical payments coverage	Renters' insurance
Collision insurance	Mitigate	Replacement cost
Comprehensive insurance	No-fault insurance	Risk
Deductible	Personal injury protection (PIP)	Uninsured motorist coverage
Extended replacement cost	Personal property rider	

▰ STRETCH ▰
YOUR DOLLAR
SELECT HIGHEST DEDUCTIBLE

Select the highest deductible you can to save on premiums. Set a goal to save the deductible amount and deposit it in a savings account in case you ever need it. When you have saved the full amount, put it in a CD to earn a higher return. Let the deductible accumulate wealth while it protects you in case you are in an accident.

Risk The danger of a loss.

Hazard Increases the chance of a risk occurring, such as icy roads and drunk drivers.

Mitigate To transfer all or part of the risk to another.

Premium The amount you pay an insurance company for an insurance policy.

Claim The official process of notifying the insurance company you have suffered a loss.

Deductible The amount of money the policyholder pays for a loss before the insurance coverage takes over.

Severe storms ravaged the Midwest from May to August 2008. Tornados and floods left residents in 235 Midwest counties in a disaster area. Like hurricane Katrina in 2005, the financial loss was devastating and the cleanup was heart breaking. You may not live in a disaster area, but we all face risks everyday of our life.

When you drive, you face the risk of a possible accident. A risk is the danger of a loss; the accident is the risk. A hazard increases the chance of a risk occurring. Icy roads and drunk drivers are both hazards, which increase the chances of the risk of an accident. How much would it cost if you had a car accident? The answer depends on the extent of the damage. The uncertainty of the financial costs coupled with the inability to completely avoid accidents gives rise to the need for insurance. Insurance is designed to mitigate risk. Mitigate means to transfer all or part of the risk to another.

Insurance companies assume the risk in return for a payment, called a premium. The insurance premium is the amount you pay the insurance company for your insurance policy. The basic insurance process is that you pay premiums to an insurance company, which will issue you insurance coverage documented in your insurance policy. If you suffer a loss your insurance policy covers, you file a claim with the insurance company.

An insurance claim is the formal notice you give your insurance agent when you suffer a loss. Claims can usually be filed by calling your agent, who will fill out the claim forms. However, with some insurance companies, you may have to fill out a claim form and submit it to your insurance agent.

Most insurance policies have a deductible. The deductible is the amount of money the policyholder pays for a loss before the insurance coverage takes over. For example, you might be insured against hail damage to your home with a $500 deductible. If you then sustain damage of $5,000 during a hailstorm, the insurance company pays a claim of $4,500 ($5,000 – $500 deductible). Premiums and deductibles have an inverse relationship. Higher policy deductibles reduce the price of the premium, and vice versa.

You can get insurance on virtually anything. During Matt Leinart's senior year as quarterback at USC, he insured his ability to play football for several million dollars. If he had been seriously injured and could not continue to play football, the insurance company would have paid him for his loss. Have you ever seen one of those "half-court-shot for a million dollars" basketball contests? The sponsoring organizations don't pay if someone makes the shot. They buy an insurance policy to pay if someone hits the miracle shot. In all of these cases, insurance is used to decrease the risk of a financial loss.

Why People Buy Insurance

For consumers (the policyholders), insurance is a money-losing business. If policyholders received more in claims than they paid in premiums, insurance companies would be out of business. Why then, do people buy insurance? Why not just hope nothing bad happens? People are risk averse. When people are risk averse, they are willing to pay to reduce their risk.

Consider this example. In a room of 100 college students, auto insurance costs $1,000 per year for each student. The insurance company will receive $100,000 ($1,000 × 100) in premiums from these students. Odds are they won't all have claims during the year. Maybe 80 out of the 100 will have no problems at all and will not receive any benefit from their insurance. Eighteen students will have some small claim and will receive $500 in benefits from the insurance company. Two individuals have severe accidents during the year and get $30,000 in benefits covered by the insurance.

This example illustrates key points about insurance. First, it shows how the insurance company profits. This hypothetical company takes in $100,000 in premium revenue and pays $69,000 in claims. That is $31,000 in profits. The second key point is the average policyholder pays more in premiums than he or she receives in benefits. Ninety-eight out of the 100 people would have spent less money if they had not purchased insurance.

So why do we need insurance? We do not want to be one of the two people who found themselves in the position of needing the benefits of the insurance policy. Imagine if one of those two people with $30,000 in damages did not have insurance. Insurance coverage provides a safety net for situations like this.

Property and casualty insurance Broad terms describing insurance that provides compensation for loss due to damage, theft, or liability.

Property and Casualty Insurance

Property and casualty insurance policies insure personal assets from financial loss. This type of insurance protects your most valuable assets, such as your home and automobile.

Property and casualty insurance are broad insurance terms used to describe insurance coverage for loss, damage, or liability. Consider the destruction Hurricane Katrina caused in 2005. Those who were prepared for such a disaster with property insurance received insurance money to help them rebuild. What would happen to you if you had no insurance on your home (probably your largest personal asset), and it was destroyed by a tornado, a fire, or a flood? Obviously, none of these events are likely to happen to you, but they do happen to somebody, and you need to protect your assets in case of a catastrophe.

© Pattie Steib, 2014, Shutterstock, Inc.

Homes in the ninth ward area in New Orleans post Hurricane Katrina.

EXHIBIT 7.1	TOP TEN WRITERS OF PROPERTY/CASUALTY INSURANCE BY DIRECT PREMIUMS WRITTEN, 2012 *($000)*

Rank	Group/company	Direct premiums written (1)	Market share (2)
1	State Farm Mutual Automobile Insurance	$53,654,237	10.3%
2	Liberty Mutual	28,297,511	5.4
3	Allstate Corp.	26,652,040	5.1
4	American International Group	23,596,418	4.5
5	Travelers Companies Inc.	22,695,958	4.3
6	Berkshire Hathaway Inc.	20,236,495	3.9
7	Farmers Insurance Group of Companies (3)	18,311,402	3.5
8	Nationwide Mutual Group	17,042,933	3.3
9	Progressive Corp.	16,559,746	3.2
10	USAA Insurance Group	13,286,274	2.5

(1) Before reinsurance transactions, includes state funds.
(2) Based on U.S. total, includes territories.
(3) Data for Farmers Insurance Group of Companies and Zurich Financial Group (which owns Farmers' management company) are reported separately by SNL Financial LC.
Sources: SNL Financial LC, courtesy of the Insurance Information Institute. ISO, a Verisk Analytics company, courtesy of the Insurance Information Institute. © 2012 National Association of Insurance Commissioners (NAIC), courtesy of the Insurance Information Institute.

There are two main kinds of property and casualty insurance most individuals need to purchase:

1. Automobile insurance
2. Homeowners' insurance or renters insurance

Both of these types of insurance policies are common and widely available. Exhibit 7.1 shows the largest property insurance companies in the United States.

Automobile Insurance

Automobile insurance
Protects the policyholder in the event that his or her vehicle is damaged or he or she is in an accident that damages another car.

Automobile insurance provides financial protection for the policyholder's automobile in the event of damage to the vehicle. It also provides liability coverage for damage to another automobile in the event of a collision and for medical expenses for occupants involved in a collision.

Most states require automobile owners and licensed drivers to purchase at least the liability portion of auto insurance. They enforce the requirement by requiring people to provide proof of insurance before they are issued license plates or drivers' licenses. Most states also require drivers to keep proof of insurance in their vehicle at all times. These cards provide a basic description of the coverage in the policy.

TYPES OF AUTOMOBILE INSURANCE COVERAGE

There are four basic auto insurance provisions:

1. Collision and comprehensive
2. Liability coverage

3. Medical payments coverage
4. Uninsured motorist coverage

Collision and Comprehensive Coverage (C&C)

Collision and comprehensive insurance protects against damage to the covered vehicle. Collision insurance protects your car if you are in an accident, while comprehensive insurance protects your car from other types of damage, such as weather-related events, theft, or vandalism. Most states do not require you to maintain collision and comprehensive insurance, but if you financed your car with a loan, your lender will likely require you to maintain collision and comprehensive coverage on your car until the loan is paid.

The decision to obtain collision and comprehensive coverage typically depends on the value of your car. An expensive car should be insured for the full value of the car. However, if you're driving your parents' old 1994 Dodge Neon, the car is not worth much, and you probably need little or no collision and comprehensive coverage.

Collision and comprehensive insurance typically covers the car and its accessories. It does not cover the replacement of any personal items damaged in the car.

Collision insurance A type of automobile insurance that provides compensation if the covered vehicle is involved in a collision.

Comprehensive insurance A type of automobile insurance that provides compensation in case of losses stemming from non-collision events such as weather, theft, or vandalism.

> **Example:**
> Ellen has a collision and comprehensive insurance on her car with a $500 deductible. She slides on the ice and hits a tree, doing $2,400 worth of damage to her car. How much will her insurance pay?
> They will pay for her damages minus her deductible.
>
> $$\$2,400 - \$500 = \$1,900$$

Liability Coverage

Liability coverage protects you from financial claims from others in case you have an accident that injures someone or causes damage to his or her property. This is a necessary component of auto insurance for everyone, and it is required by most states. Your insurance policy provides payments if the accident is your fault. If the accident is the other driver's fault, their carrier will cover the applicable costs.

If you are involved in an automobile accident, you can be sued by any other parties involved. If a court finds you to be at fault, you are liable for the damages you caused. For that reason, you should carry a sufficient amount of liability insurance to cover the damages from an automobile accident including:

Liability coverage A type of automobile insurance that pays for damages to another person's vehicle and/or medical bills should the insured be at fault in an automobile accident.

- Individual. The amount of medical coverage for any one person involved.
- All persons. The total amount of medical coverage for all individuals involved.
- Property. The amount of coverage for property damage.

The state you live in determines the minimum amount of coverage you must maintain by law. All states have passed legislation to require liability insurance. Exhibit 7.2 shows state required liability insurance and the amount required.

EXHIBIT 7.2	AUTOMOBILE FINANCIAL RESPONSIBILITY LIMITS AND ENFORCEMENT BY STATE

State	Insurance required (1)	Minimum liability limits (2)	Insurer verification of insurance (3)
AL	BI & PD Liab	25/50/25	c, d
AK	BI & PD Liab	50/100/25	a
AZ	BI & PD Liab	15/30/10	a, b
AR	BI & PD Liab, PIP	25/50/25	b, d
CA	BI & PD Liab	15/30/5 (4)	a, b, d
CO	BI & PD Liab	25/50/15	a, d
CT	BI & PD Liab	20/40/10	a
DE	BI & PD Liab, PIP	15/30/10	a, b, c, d
DC	BI & PD Liab, UM	25/50/10	a, c, d
FL	PD Liab, PIP	10/20/10 (5)	a, d
GA	BI & PD Liab	25/50/25	a, d
HI	BI & PD Liab, PIP	20/40/10	a
ID	BI & PD Liab	25/50/15	none
IL	BI & PD Liab, UM	20/40/15	a, b, c
IN	BI & PD Liab	25/50/10	a
IA	BI & PD Liab	20/40/15	a
KS	BI & PD Liab, PIP, UM	25/50/10	a,c
KY	BI & PD Liab, PIP	25/50/10 (5)	a, d
LA	BI & PD Liab	15/30/25	a, d
ME	BI & PD Liab, UM, UIM	50/100/25 (6)	b
MD	BI & PD Liab, PIP (7), UM, UIM	30/60/15	a
MA	BI & PD Liab, PIP, UM, UIM	20/40/5	a, d
MI	BI & PD Liab, PIP	20/40/10	a
MN	BI & PD Liab, PIP, UM, UIM	30/60/10	a, c
MS	BI & PD Liab	25/50/25	a, d
MO	BI & PD Liab, UM	25/50/10	a, c, d
MT	BI & PD Liab	25/50/10	d
NE	BI & PD Liab, UM, UIM	25/50/25	a, b, d
NV	BI & PD Liab	15/30/10	a, d
NH	FR only, UM	25/50/25 (6)	a
NJ	BI & PD Liab, PIP, UM, UIM	15/30/5 (8)	a, d
NM	BI & PD Liab	25/50/10	a, c
NY	BI & PD Liab, PIP, UM	25/50/10 (9)	a, d
NC	BI & PD Liab, UM, UIM (10)	30/60/25	a, d
ND	BI & PD Liab, PIP, UM, UIM	25/50/25	c
OH	BI & PD Liab	12.5/25/7.5*	a, c
OK	BI & PD Liab	25/50/25	a, c, d
OR	BI & PD Liab, PIP, UM, UIM (11)	25/50/20	a, c
PA	BI & PD Liab, PIP	15/30/5	a
RI	BI & PD Liab	25/50/25 (5)	c

(cont.)

State	Insurance required (1)	Minimum liability limits (2)	Insurer verification of insurance (3)
SC	BI & PD Liab, UM	25/50/25	a, d
SD	BI & PD Liab, UM, UIM	25/50/25	a
TN	BI & PD Liab	25/50/15 (5)	a, d
TX	BI & PD Liab	30/60/25	a, d
UT	BI & PD Liab, PIP	25/65/15 (5)	d
VT	BI & PD Liab, UM, UIM	25/50/10	c
VA	BI & PD Liab (12), UM, UIM	25/50/20	a, b, c, d
WA	BI & PD Liab	25/50/10	a
WV	BI & PD Liab, UM	20/40/10	a, d
WI	BI & PD Liab, UM, UIM	25/50/10	a
WY	BI & PD Liab	25/50/20	c, d

(1) Compulsory Coverages:
   BI Liab=Bodily injury liability
   PD Liab=Property damage liability
   UM=Uninsured motorist
   PD=Physical damage
   Med=First party (policyholder) medical expenses
   UIM=Underinsured motorist
   PIP=Personal Injury Protection. Mandatory in no-fault states. Includes medical, rehabilitation, loss of earnings and funeral expenses. In some states PIP includes essential services such as child care.
   FR=Financial responsibility only. Insurance not compulsory.

(2) The first two numbers refer to bodily injury liability limits and the third number to property liability. For example, 20/40/10 means coverage up to $40,000 for all persons injured in an accident, subject to a limit of $20,000 for one individual, and $10,000 coverage for property damage.

(3) a. Insurer must notify Department of Motor Vehicles or other state agency of cancellation or nonrenewal.
   b. Insurer must verify financial responsibility or insurance after an accident or arrest.
   c. Insurer must verify randomly selected insurance policies upon request.
   d. Insurers must submit entire list of insurance in effect, which may be compared with registrations at a state agency. Also known as a computer data law. Also includes cases where insurers are required to report new issues and/or renewals.

(4) Low-cost policy limits for low-income drivers in the California Automobile Assigned Risk Plan are 10/20/3.

(5) Instead of policy limits, policyholders can satisfy the requirement with a combined single limit policy. Amounts vary by state.

(6) In addition, policyholders must also carry at least $2,000 for medical payments.

(7) May be waived for the policyholder but is compulsory for passengers.

(8) Basic policy (optional) limits are 10/10/5. Uninsured and underinsured motorist coverage not available under the basic policy but uninsured motorist coverage is required under the standard policy.

(9) In addition, policyholders must have 50/100 for wrongful death coverage.

(10) Mandatory in policies with UM limits exceeding 30/60.

(11) Mandatory when UM liability limit is greater than required FR.

(12) Compulsory to buy insurance or pay an Uninsured Motorists Vehicle (UMV) fee to the state Department of Motor Vehicles.

*Effective December 22, 2013, Ohio's limits will rise to 25/50/25.

Sources: SNL Financial LC, courtesy of the Insurance Information Institute. ISO, a Verisk Analytics company, courtesy of the Insurance Information Institute. © 2012 National Association of Insurance Commissioners (NAIC), courtesy of the Insurance Information Institute.

In general, insurance experts recommend you maintain more liability coverage than the state minimums. Financial judgments can easily exceed the minimum, and the party at fault is liable for any amount not covered by insurance. General recommendations for coverage amounts are $100,000 for individuals, $500,000 for "all persons," and $50,000 for property liability. Insurance companies typically identify the coverage for liability by specifying those three numbers in sequence, so the general recommendations are 100/500/50 (individual/all persons/property) liability coverage.

Example:
Karen carries only liability insurance of 100/500/50. Karen runs a red light and hits Jim's car. Jim is not hurt, but his two passengers Lisa and Adam both suffer injuries. Lisa has medical bills of $1,400, and Adam is seriously injured. He spends a month in the hospital and has medical bills of $625,000. Karen's car has $4,500 in damages, and Jim's car has $12,000 in damages.
What does the insurance company pay? What is Karen's liability?

	Karen's Insurance Company	Karen
1. Karen's car	$0	$4,500
2. Jim's car	$12,000	$0
3. Lisa's injuries	$1,400	$0
4. Adam's injuries	$100,000	$525,000

1. Karen's car isn't covered under her liability.
2. Karen's policy covers the property damage up to $50,000. The insurance covers all damages.
3. Karen's policy covers injuries for the individual up to $100,000 and for all parties combined to $500,000, so it pays all of Lisa's bills and $100,000 of Adam's.

You may think that because Jim wasn't at fault, he is safe and his insurance doesn't have to pay. If Adam sues, Jim can be forced to pay.

Jim is well off. He has $700,000 in assets. Karen isn't; she lives from paycheck to paycheck. Adam sues both Jim and Karen for the $625,000 in medical bills. The court finds Jim is three percent and Karen is 97 percent responsible for Adam's injuries. This means Jim is liable for $18,750 and Karen is liable for $606,250.

However, the victim gets paid now if it is possible. Under the "deep pocket rule" the "at fault" party with the ability to pay must pay now and recoup his or her loss from the other at-fault parties. Since Jim can pay, he would have to and try to recover Karen's portion from her later. Karen's insurance paid $100,000. If Jim's insurance has the same liability limits, then his insurance would also pay $100,000. Jim would pay $425,000. For this reason it is important to carry liability insurance limits that equal or exceed your assets.

Medical Payments Coverage

Accidents can often require medical care for some or all of the passengers involved. Liability coverage only encompasses occupants of other vehicles or pedestrians. Medical payments coverage provides compensation to anyone riding in your vehicle and when you are driving someone else's vehicle. Coverage for potential medical bills for these people is therefore an appropriate portion of your liability coverage.

How much medical payments coverage you need with this portion of your auto insurance depends on your health insurance and who normally rides in your car. Your health insurance should generally cover your own costs arising from an auto accident, so you may not need to include this coverage on yourself. However, you should consider your passengers. If you are driving around friends, colleagues, or family who may not have sufficient health insurance, their medical bills from an accident in your car may not be covered unless you have medical payments liability coverage.

Medical payments coverage Provides compensation to anyone riding in your vehicle and when you are driving someone else's vehicle.

Uninsured Motorist Coverage

Unfortunately, in spite of state laws requiring it, many drivers do not maintain auto insurance. The next person who speeds past you with a cell phone glued to her ear may be an uninsured driver. Uninsured motorist coverage gives you protection in case you are in an accident through the fault of an uninsured driver. This type of coverage also protects you from hit-and-run injuries or from an accident where the other driver's insurance carrier is unable to pay a claim due to bankruptcy or other financial distress.

Uninsured motorist coverage A form of automobile insurance that provides compensation should the policyholder or passengers suffer from injuries in an accident with an uninsured driver who is at fault.

© CandyBox Images, 2014, Shutterstock, Inc.

Unfortunately, there are drivers on the road without insurance. Protect yourself and your passengers financially by carrying coverage on your vehicle.

You can also purchase underinsured motorist insurance, which protects you if the driver who caused the accident does have liability coverage, but not enough to cover your medical bills. For instance, the other driver may have the state minimum liability coverage of $10,000, while your bills total $30,000. If you have purchased the underinsured motorist coverage, the other driver's insurance would pay $10,000 and your policy would pick up the remaining $20,000.

NO-FAULT INSURANCE

No-fault insurance
A system of automobile insurance that requires drivers to carry insurance for themselves and places limits on their ability to sue other drivers for damage.

No-fault insurance states require drivers to carry insurance for their own protection and places limitations on their ability to sue other drivers for damages.

In an accident under no-fault laws, your auto insurance company will pay for your damages (up to your policy limits), regardless of who was at fault for the accident. Any other drivers involved will be covered by their auto insurance policies. Under a pure no-fault system, drivers would be completely covered by their own policy and would be barred from suing another driver for damages.

Although no state has a pure no-fault system, states that have no-fault insurance actually use parts of both the no-fault system and the standard liability system (under which you're financially responsible for the cost of damages you cause to others). States do this by permitting lawsuits in certain cases.

Personal injury protection (PIP) No-fault insurance coverage.

The actual no-fault part of your auto insurance policy is usually called personal injury protection, or PIP. Different states' PIP packages cover different things, but in general benefits will include most injury-related expenses. The most common benefits are medical costs, loss of wages, compensation for loss of services, funeral expenses, and death benefits.

The amount and type of PIP required varies from state to state. For example, in Pennsylvania, Kentucky, and the District of Columbia, drivers can choose whether they want to purchase PIP and drive under the no-fault system. If not, they operate under the standard liability system. However, because no state is pure no-fault, drivers can always be held financially responsible for the cost of injuries they cause in certain circumstances. It is important to understand your state's requirements before you shop for insurance.

Factors That Influence Your Auto Insurance Premium

Insurance companies base the premiums they charge on their claim experience. Auto insurance premiums vary widely from driver to driver and for policies with different types of coverage. Several parameters influence the price of automobile insurance premiums:

- Types of coverage and amounts
- Deductibles
- Type of car
- Personal characteristics
- Driving record
- Location
- Discounts

TYPES OF COVERAGE AND AMOUNTS

The cost of the premium rises as the coverage limits are increased. For example, a policy with coverage limits of 100/300/50 will cost more than one with limits of 50/100/20.

DEDUCTIBLES

Deductibles and premiums have an inverse relationship. A deductible is the amount that you pay out of pocket before your insurance pays a claim. Selecting higher deductibles will decrease your insurance premiums.

TYPE OF CAR

The make and model of the car affects the insurance premium. A higher-priced car will result in higher premiums, since the covered amount will be greater. Some vehicles are also more expensive to repair than others, which would result in higher premiums.

Is your vehicle a sports car or a minivan? The sportier the car, the higher the premium. Statistics show sportier cars are more likely to be involved in an accident. Insurance companies obtain historical information on automobile accidents and the damage resulting from them. They price their policies based on this information.

PERSONAL CHARACTERISTICS

Your personal characteristics influence your automobile premiums. For example:

- Younger drivers generally pay higher premiums than older drivers.
- Males have higher premiums than females.
- Singles have higher premiums than those who are married.

The number of miles you drive a year will also affect your premium. The more you drive, the more likely you are to be involved in an accident. If you drive less than the average, your premium will decrease; if you drive more than the average, your premiums will increase.

© Lisa S, 2014, Shutterstock, Inc.

Your vehicle type and distance you drive daily are just a couple of factors considered when premiums are determined.

DRIVING RECORD

If you have not had any moving violations or traffic accidents in the past five years, you will be rewarded with a lower premium. Insurance companies tag drivers who receive tickets as riskier. If you have more than three combined tickets or accidents within a year, your premiums will increase dramatically. Being labeled a high-risk driver is expensive, and it normally takes three years without a ticket or accident before you will be offered standard insurance rates.

LOCATION

Insurance premiums vary by state and locality. Proportionally, many more claims occur in larger cities. If you live in an urban, congested area, your premiums will be higher than if you are living in a more rural area. Exhibit 7.3 shows the five most expensive cities and the five least expensive cities for car insurance in the United States. Note what a difference location makes! Average annual premiums for a car in Detroit are $5,072 compared to $869 in Eau Claire, Wisconsin.

DISCOUNTS

Your insurance provider may offer various discounts on your policy. An example is a good student discount, where if you are a young driver but are receiving good grades in high school or college, you will get a discount on your auto insurance. Another common discount is the multiline discount, in which your insurance company offers a discount if you have more than one policy with the company. For example, you would be offered a discount on both your homeowners and automobile policies if you have both types of insurance through the same company.

EXHIBIT 7.3	TOP TEN MOST EXPENSIVE AND LEAST EXPENSIVE STATES FOR AUTOMOBILE INSURANCE, 2010 (1)

Rank	Most expensive states	Average expenditure	Rank	Least expensive states	Average expenditure
1	New Jersey	$1,157.30	1	South Dakota	$525.16
2	D.C.	1,133.87	2	North Dakota	528.81
3	Louisiana	1,121.46	3	Iowa	546.59
4	New York	1,078.88	4	Idaho	547.78
5	Florida	1,036.76	5	Maine	582.29
6	Delaware	1,030.98	6	Nebraska	592.69
7	Rhode Island	984.95	7	North Carolina	599.90
8	Connecticut	965.22	8	Wisconsin	613.37
9	Maryland	947.70	9	Ohio	619.46
10	Michigan	934.60	10	Wyoming	621.08

(1) Based on average automobile insurance expenditures.
Sources: SNL Financial LC, courtesy of the Insurance Information Institute. ISO, a Verisk Analytics company, courtesy of the Insurance Information Institute. © 2012 National Association of Insurance Commissioners (NAIC), courtesy of the Insurance Information Institute.

INSURANCE CLAIMS

If you are in an accident, you will need to file an insurance claim. After an accident, always get the other driver's insurance information. Many states assign percents to each driver in an accident, accounting for their percent of the fault. For example, if you receive 80% of the blame for an accident, your insurance provider will be responsible for paying for most of the damages. If the other driver is at fault, then his or her insurance will pay.

If an event other than an accident causes damage to your vehicle, like a hailstorm, you also need to notify your insurance provider, who will send an agent to inspect your car for damage and then award any settlement. With most providers you will have the option of having a garage or mechanic fix your vehicle for you and then directly bill the insurance company, or you can just receive a check in the amount of the damage estimate.

Homeowners' and Renters' Insurance

Homeowners' insurance covers your home against damage from natural disasters such as wind, hail, or fire. It also provides liability protection in case someone is injured on your property. Homeowners' policies also cover personal property in the house against damage or theft.

If you rent, you do not need to insure the residence, but you can insure your personal property with renters' insurance. Renter's insurance policies also provide liability coverage.

Homeowners' insurance Insurance policy that protects against damages, theft, or liability on your home.

Renters' insurance An insurance policy that covers the personal property in a rented residence.

TYPES OF HOMEOWNERS' INSURANCE POLICIES

There are six main types of homeowners' insurance policies:

1. HO-1. Limited coverage, protects against the first 10 events listed in Exhibit 7.4. This coverage is no longer available in many states.

© Benjamin Simeneta, 2014, Shutterstock, Inc.

Homeowners insurance covers your home and belongings in case of a natural disaster or theft.

EXHIBIT 7.4	TYPES OF DISASTERS THAT HOMEOWNERS' INSURANCE MAY COVER

Coverage of damage or loss from:

1. Fire or lightning
2. Windstorm or hail
3. Explosion
4. Riot or civil commotion
5. Aircraft
6. Vehicles
7. Smoke
8. Vandalism
9. Theft
10. Volcanic eruption
11. Falling object
12. Weight of ice, snow, or sleet
13. Accidental discharge or overflow of water
14. Breach of hot water heating, air conditioning, or automatic fire-protective system
15. Freezing of plumbing, heating, air conditioning, automatic, fire-protective sprinkler system, or household appliance
16. Generated electrical current
17. All other perils except excluded items such as flood, earthquake, war, nuclear accident, landslide, mudslide, sinkhole, and others specified in your policy. Check your policy for a complete list of perils excluded.

2. HO-2. Basic coverage, protects against the first 16 events in Exhibit 7.4. A version of this type is also available for mobile home owners.
3. HO-3. Comprehensive coverage, protects against the first 16 disasters plus others not specifically excluded in your policy. This is the most comprehensive and popular policy.
4. HO-4. Provides renters' insurance for your personal belongings.
5. HO-5. Protects your personal belongings in a condo you own and occupy.
6. HO-8. Policy designed for older homes, provides benefits as cash damages rather than what you initially paid for the home.

Actual cash value
Insurance coverage that pays the cost of replacing a loss less any depreciation.

Replacement cost
Insurance coverage that covers the full cost of replacing a loss.

Extended replacement cost Insurance coverage that compensates for the full replacement value even when that value exceeds the maximum coverage of the policy.

Earthquake or flood damages are not typically covered by standard homeowner's insurance policies. Insurance for earthquakes and floods are sold in supplemental insurance policies.

Regardless of the type of homeowners' policy, there are three different options that describe your type of coverage, starting with the least amount of coverage:

1. Actual cash value. Pays the cost of replacing your home and personal property minus depreciation from the wear and tear of use.
2. Replacement cost. Covers the full cost of replacing the damage with no deduction for depreciation.
3. Extended replacement cost. Extended coverage, pays the cost of rebuilding or replacing your home even if it exceeds your policy limits.

Suppose you bought a home three years ago for $130,000, and it was destroyed in a tornado yesterday. You had a coverage maximum of $160,000 on your home, and it will cost $170,000 to rebuild your home as it was before the catastrophe. If you had an actual cash value policy, you would be awarded $130,000 (less a little bit for depreciation) to rebuild your home. A replacement cost policy would award you $160,000 (up to your coverage limits), while the extended replacement cost policy would give you $170,000. The extended policy is the only one in which you would not have any financial "loss" from the event, since the other two policies do not provide enough to rebuild in the current environment.

PROVISIONS IN HOMEOWNERS' INSURANCE POLICIES

A policy typically covers property damage, the loss of personal belongings, and personal liability. The type of coverage you have will depend on your policy (like HO-1 or HO-3), but the following discussion will give standard coverage items.

Property Damage

Property damage is typically what enters your mind when you think of homeowners' insurance. Property damage represents damage to the home itself. Your policy will state whether your policy covers other structures on your property, such as barns, sheds, or swimming pools. Most homeowners' insurance claims result from property damage of some sort. Exhibit 7.5 illustrates the makeup of claims for homeowners' insurance. The four categories of property damage in the chart (wind and hail; water and freezing; fire, lightning, and debris removal) made up 93.7% of the total amount of claims against homeowners' policies in 2008.

BREAKDOWN OF CLAIMS FOR PROPERTY INSURANCE, 2011   EXHIBIT 7.5

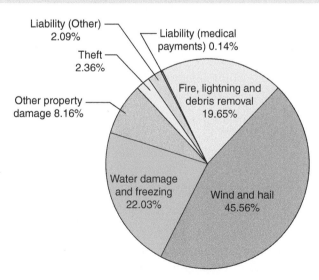

Sources: SNL Financial LC, courtesy of the Insurance Information Institute. ISO, a Verisk Analytics company, courtesy of the Insurance Information Institute. © 2012 National Association of Insurance Commissioners (NAIC), courtesy of the Insurance Information Institute.

The vast majority of lenders require mortgage holders to maintain at least 80% of the home's value in insurance. Lenders do not want one of their mortgages to become a partial or total loss because the borrower had no insurance.

Personal Property

Homeowners' insurance also covers personal goods that could be damaged or stolen. Standard policies list a maximum coverage amount for personal goods, which will then be used to replace the loss of furniture, computers, jewelry, and other household items.

You need to document the items, especially those of value, in your home. If you lost your entire home to a fire tonight, would you be able to remember all the items that were destroyed? Take an inventory of your belongings and photograph them or take a video of your home. You need to keep your inventory lists or video in a safe place, such as a safety deposit box or another family member's home.

You can choose whether to have your personal property coverage at actual cash value or replacement cost. This choice is independent of your choice of replacement value for the structure.

Personal property rider
If your personal property is worth more than the insurance cap, a rider will cover the excess.

Some items may require additional coverage. You may need to obtain a personal property rider policy. Most homeowners' policies set the maximum amount of personal property coverage at one-half of the structural property coverage. If your personal property is worth more than this cap, the rider will cover the excess.

Some individuals have an office in their home. Homeowners' policies normally do not cover the portion of a residence used for business, so additional coverage would be necessary to provide protection for property used for business.

Liability

You are liable for another person's injuries while he or she is on your property. For example, if someone slips or falls on your steps, he could sue you for his medical bills. For this reason, homeowners' policies include a liability portion in their coverage. Homeowners' liability also covers damage to someone else's property. If another person's car is struck by a gutter that falls off your roof, your liability insurance will cover the damages. The amount of liability coverage is not tied to the value of your home; you must identify the amount of liability coverage you want with your policy. As usual, higher coverage amounts will produce higher premiums.

HOMEOWNERS' INSURANCE PREMIUMS

Homeowners' insurance policies are actually less expensive than most automobile policies. Your home is worth more than your car, but the chances of your car getting damaged are much greater, so home insurance premiums are lower. Many factors affect the premiums on a homeowners' policy.

Factors Affecting a Homeowners' Insurance Policy

- Value of the home and personal property. The higher the value of the home and goods, the greater the premium will be.
- Type of coverage. An extended replacement cost policy will be the most expensive, while an actual cash value will be the cheapest.
- Geography. Some locations are simply more prone to damage than others, and this will increase the annual premium. Weather-related damages are the highest percentage of homeowners' insurance damages, so homes that are in Tornado Alley or along the coast have higher premiums.
- Deductible amount. As with all insurance policies, the higher the deductible, the lower your premium.

There are ways to control some of the costs of a homeowners' insurance policy. Exhibit 7.6 lists some ways to help reduce the premiums on home insurance.

SUGGESTIONS FOR REDUCING THE COST OF HOMEOWNERS' INSURANCE	**EXHIBIT 7.6**

1. **Shop around for the best prices and terms.** Check prices from several sources. Ask your friends for referrals, check out websites of insurance companies and organizations, and read to consumer guides available at your library.
2. **Increase your deductible.** Policies with higher deductibles have lower premiums.
3. **Insure only your building.** You do not need insurance on your land. Only pay for insurance on the building. (Fire can destroy your building, for example, but not your land.)
4. **Buy multiple policies from the same insurance company.** Insurance companies often offer multiline discounts to policyholders with more than one type of policy from the company. For example, you might save 5 to 15% if you purchase both your automobile insurance and homeowners' policy from the same company.
5. **Protect your home from disasters.** There are many things a homeowner can do to reduce the probability of making a claim on the policy, and doing these can reduce insurance premiums. For example, the owner of an older home can often reduce the possibility of a fire by replacing old wiring, and the insurance company might recognize this by offering a break on premiums.
6. **Improve your home security.** Installing security devises such as smoke detectors, burglar alarms, or dead-bolt locks can yield a savings in premiums. Check with the insurance company to see what it offers.
7. **Look for other discounts.** Companies sometimes offer miscellaneous discounts such as for senior citizens or for members of a particular organization.
8. **Maintain good credit.** Insurers often use an applicant's credit record in setting premium rates, so maintaining a good credit standing can save you money.
9. **Reward for loyalty.** Some insurance companies offer a special discount for long-term policyholders. For example, policyholders receive a 5% discount after having held a policy with the company for three years.

10. **Review your policy and values annually.** Check to make sure that you do not have any unnecessary coverage and that you are not paying for more coverage than you need on your insured items.

11. **Check for government plans.** Property in certain high-risk areas is often eligible for government-sponsored coverage at a lower cost than available from strictly private plans. For example, there may be federally sponsored flood insurance available in a river flood plain.

12. **Consider insurance cost when shopping for a home.** Insurance premiums may be less for homes located in certain areas. For example, a home in a community close to a fire station may receive reduced premiums.

Exhibit *Source:* Insurance Information Institute.

SUMMARY

Property and casualty insurance offers financial protection from losses due to natural disasters, theft, accidents, and liability. The two major assets most people need property insurance for are their car and home.

Automobile insurance is a requirement in most states. The four key provisions in an automobile insurance policy are coverage for collision and comprehensive, liability, medical payments, and uninsured motorists.

Collision insurance offers payment for damage to the policyholder's automobile because of an accident. Comprehensive covers damage for other causes, such as weather or vandalism. A liability and medical payments provision covers medical cost for injuries sustained in an accident. Uninsured motorist offers coverage in case the other driver in an accident does not have automobile insurance.

Premiums for car insurance depend on several factors, which include the types and amount of coverage, deductibles, make and model of car, personal characteristics of the insured, driving record, location, and discounts. You can reduce car insurance premiums by maintaining a clean driving record, making good grades in school, and increasing the deductible.

Homeowners' insurance offers compensation in case of damage to the home or its contents. Although the likelihood of significant damage to a home is small, a home is such a large investment most homeowners carry homeowners' insurance. A homeowners' insurance policy also provides compensation for theft and liability coverage in case someone is injured on the insured property. Renters can purchase a special form of insurance called renters' insurance, which covers property in a rental residence.

PROBLEMS

1. Mr. Jones collides with another car. The accident is Mr. Jones's fault, and Mr. Jones has the minimum liability coverage in his state, 25/50/10. Fortunately, no one was injured in the accident, but the other driver's car was a total loss valued at $45,000. What is Mr. Jones's financial responsibility? (Hint: The value of the loss not covered by insurance)

2. Ken's home was damaged in a hailstorm. He needs a new roof, which will cost $10,000. His roof has a life expectancy of 40 years, and the existing roof is 30 years old. He has an actual cash value homeowner's policy. How much will his insurance company pay? How much would it have paid if he had replacement cost coverage?

CASE STUDIES

COLLEGE STUDENT

In the previous chapters you helped Kevin Maedor create a financial plan, select housing, make a major purchase, and manage his credit. Now help him select property insurance. Review the financial information you have for him from previous chapters and select insurance to cover his home and automobile.

1. Use the home you selected for him in Chapter 3.
2. He owns a 2011 Jeep Wrangler worth $23,730.

NEW GRADUATE

In the previous chapters you helped Rene Harris create a financial plan, select housing, make a major purchase, and manage her credit. Now help her select property insurance. Review the financial information you have for her from previous chapters and select insurance to cover her home and automobile.

1. Use the home you selected for her in Chapter 3.
2. She owns a 2011 Kia worth $7,085. It is paid off.

CREATE YOUR OWN FINANCIAL PLAN

List the items you own and determine which types of property insurance you need.

Do you own?

1. A vehicle
2. A home
3. Household items
4. Guns, jewelry, or electronics that would require a rider

- Do you know what your liability coverage is?
- Are you currently covered for your state's minimum?
- Are those minimums adequate? Why or why not?
- Are you covered too heavily? Why or why not?

Compare premium rates and service from several insurance providers. Pick the lowest premiums and minimum coverage that adequately protects you.

REVIEW QUESTIONS

1. What are the four major provisions of automobile insurance coverage? Describe an event that would be covered under each type of provision.

_____

_____

_____

2. Why is it important to maintain automobile and homeowners' insurance?

_____

_____

_____

3. What actions can you take to reduce premiums on automobile insurance?

_____

_____

_____

4. What are the coverage limits for an auto insurance policy with 200/600/100?

_____

_____

_____

5. What does no-fault automobile insurance cover?

_____

_____

_____

6. How do you file an automobile insurance claim?

_____

_____

_____

7. What is covered under actual cash value, replacement cost, and extended replacement cost coverage insurance?

_____

_____

_____

8. What assets does renter's insurance cover?

_____

_____

_____

9. If you have personal property valued at $150,000 and a homeowners' policy with a maximum coverage of $100,000 on personal property, what insurance could you get to provide financial compensation for the entire value of your personal property in the event of a loss?

_____

_____

_____

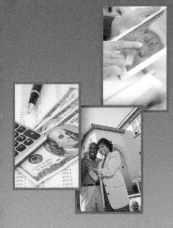

Health and Disability Insurance

"If you have health, you probably will be happy, and if you have health and happiness, you have all the wealth you need, even if it is not all you want."

—Elbert Hubbard

OBJECTIVES

- Differentiate between health insurance and medical insurance
- Define indemnity, HMO, PPO, and POS plans
- Explain HDHPs and their relationship to HSAs
- Evaluate which medical insurance in best for a given situation
- Explain disability income insurance
- Differentiate between public and private health insurance

KEY TERMS

Any-occupation disabled
COBRA Act of 1986
Co-insurance
Co-payment
Dental insurance
Disability income insurance
Elimination period
Flexible spending account
Health insurance
Health maintenance organization (HMO)

Health savings account (HSA)
High deductible health plan (HDHP)
Income replacement policy
Indemnity plan
Insurance policy
Lifetime maximum benefit
Long-term disability policy
Managed health care plan
Medicaid
Medical insurance

Medicare
Out-of-pocket limit
Own-occupation disabled
Point-of-service (POS) plan
Preferred provider organization (PPO)
Presumptive disability
Private health insurance
Probationary period
Short-term disability policy
Vision insurance

Having adequate health insurance coverage is an important piece of anyone's overall financial situation. The probability of a serious accident or illness occurring might be small, but the financial consequences of such an event are disastrous. In addition, costs of healthcare have been increasing at a rapid rate in recent years, and forecasts show those increases to continue for the foreseeable future. Health insurance provides a way for individuals and families to control and plan annual medical expenses and to avoid financial catastrophe in the case of an extended medical situation.

Health Insurance

Health insurance Provides benefit payments for health care expenses.

Health insurance provides benefit payments for health care expenses. Health insurance includes medical, disability, and long-term care insurance. The exact coverage depends on the particular insurance plan.

You can obtain health insurance in four ways:

- Purchase private health insurance via your employer's group plan.
- Purchase private insurance as an individual.
- Purchase insurance from one of the providers on the Health Insurance Marketplace created by the Affordable Health Care Act.
- Qualify for coverage in one of the government-sponsored programs.

Insurance companies negotiate prices with doctors and hospitals for various health care services. Exhibit 8.1 lists some popular insurance companies.

PRIVATE HEALTH INSURANCE

Private health insurance Any health insurance policy purchased from a private insurance company.

Private health insurance is available from a number of insurance companies and offered through employers and to individuals. Both life and property insurance companies can underwrite health insurance policies. Normally, you should take advantage of any health insurance offered through an employer, especially a large employer. Large companies or groups have more leverage when they negotiate premiums with insurance companies. However, your employer may offer only one or two insurance plans, which limits your options.

Exhibit 8.2 presents the percentage of employers who offer health insurance coverage to their employees. As this exhibit shows, only a minority of small organizations (less than 10 employees) offer health insurance. Larger organizations increasingly offer insurance coverage to employees, with almost all of the very large ones (1,000 employees or more) offering insurance.

EXHIBIT 8.1	**POPULAR MEDICAL INSURANCE PROVIDERS**

Blue Cross and Blue Shield
Aetna
Humana
Cigna
HealthOne

PERCENTAGE OF EMPLOYERS OFFERING HEALTH CARE INSURANCE IN THE UNITED STATES, 2012

EXHIBIT 8.2

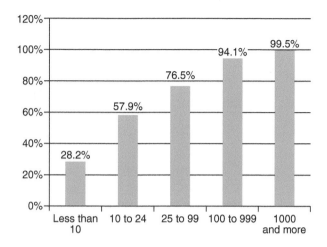

Exhibit 8.3 shows the average total medical insurance premiums charged for both individual and family coverage in the United States. These costs reflect the total premium for employer group plans. Employees' personal costs are lower if the employer pays part of the premiums as an employee benefit.

In health insurance plans where the employer makes a contribution toward the total cost of health insurance coverage, employees typically cover only a small part of the total cost of coverage. In 2012, employees paid on average 20.8 percent of the cost of individual coverage and 27.4 percent of the cost for family coverage. The employer paid the remaining amounts.

AVERAGE ANNUAL COST PER EMPLOYEE FOR EMPLOYER GROUP HEALTH INSURANCE, 2000 TO 2012

EXHIBIT 8.3

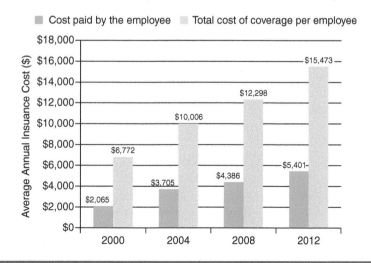

If your employer does not offer health insurance, you may obtain health insurance coverage on your own; however, it is typically more expensive than the group rates employers negotiate. Before you decide which health insurance is best for you, educate yourself about what is available. Whether you purchase health insurance through your employer or on your own, it is important to understand what you are purchasing. Compare:

- Options
- Costs
- Benefits

When you compare costs, consider total costs, not just premium cost. When you compare benefits, check which services are covered. Drug prescriptions, psychiatric care, and fertility treatments are benefits where providers offer vastly different levels of coverage. Web sites such as www.insure.com allow consumers to compare plans and rates online.

MEDICAL INSURANCE

Medical insurance
An insurance plan that covers medical expenses; often called health insurance.

Medical insurance covers medical expenses and is often called health insurance. Health insurance actually includes disability and long-term care insurance as well; it is a broad category of insurance. You can purchase medical insurance either for yourself or your family. All medical insurance companies offer individual and family plans. Some companies offer more plans; common options are the following:

- Individual
- Individual plus spouse
- Individual plus one
- Individual plus two
- Individual plus children (regardless of the number of children)
- Individual plus family (spouse and children)

Medical insurance coverage has several parts:

- Hospital insurance covers stays in hospitals and related costs.
- Physician insurance covers physician's care and visits to doctors.
- Surgical insurance includes certain types of procedures.

Insurance policy Lists covered services and maximum benefit amounts.

Medical insurance coverage varies from plan to plan. The insurance policy lists covered services and maximum benefit amounts. The plan also lists deductibles, co-insurance, and co-payment amounts. If you receive a medical service your insurance does not cover, you have to pay for it.

Components of Health Insurance Plans

- Deductible. The deductible is the amount the policyholder (insured person) must pay, each year, before the insurance company begins to pay benefits.

Co-insurance The percent of cost sharing between the policy holder and the insurance company.

- Co-insurance. The percent of cost sharing between the policyholder and the insurance company. A common co-insurance is 20 percent. If a policy has a $300 annual deductible with a 20/80 co-insurance, then the first $300 is paid by the policyholder. Additional covered medical expenses are paid 20 percent by the policyholder and 80 percent by the insurance company

- Co-payment. Preset amounts the policyholder must pay each time he or she uses a service. These are also often called co-pays. If your policy has a co-pay of $25 for an office visit, then for each office visit you pay $25 and the insurance company pays the additional charges.

- Annual out-of-pocket limit. The maximum out of pocket expenses you must pay for covered services before your insurance pays 100 percent of your covered medical expenses for the rest of the year. If the policy used as an example under co-insurance had an out-of-pocket limit of $1,000, then you would pay $300 in deductibles and 20 percent of covered cost for the next $3,500 of covered medical expenses. Twenty percent of $3,500 is $700. $300 + $700 = $1,000, your maximum required expense for the year. Covered charges in excess of $3,500 would be paid 100 percent by your insurance company.

- Lifetime maximum benefit. The maximum amount the insurance company will pay for claims over the policyholder's life. If the policy has a $1,000,000 lifetime maximum benefit, then once the insurance company has paid $1,000,000 in medical claims, it will no longer pay additional medical expenses for that insured individual. The company would cancel the insurance policy.

Types of Private Medical Insurance Plans

Private insurance plans are categorized as either indemnity (traditional) plans or managed health care plans. Managed health care plans, the more common type, require you to choose medical providers who are a part of your provider's network. With these plans, medical providers bill the insurance company for the medical work and then you pay the uncovered portion. Managed plans are classified as health maintenance organizations, preferred provider organizations, or point-of-service plans.

Indemnity Plans

Indemnity plans are the less common type of the two. With an indemnity plan, or traditional plan, you are free to select your own health care provider, and your insurance company reimburses you for all or a portion of the costs. The heath care provider bills you directly; you fill out medical claim forms to get reimbursed from your insurance company. Indemnity plans typically require an annual deductible and co-insurance payments after you meet your deductible. You can buy indemnity plans where the company pays 100 percent, 80 percent, 60 percent, or 50 percent of the co-insurance.

These plans offer greater flexibility. You decide who provides medical services; you select your physicians and specialists. You can change physicians as you wish. You do not need to preapprove services. These plans charge higher premiums.

Health Maintenance Organizations

Health maintenance organizations are commonly called HMOs. HMOs provide health care to their members through a medical provider network. Networks are

Co-payment A payment the policyholder makes for each medical service received.

Out-of-pocket limit The maximum out-of-pocket expenses you must pay for covered services before your insurance pays 100 percent of your covered medical expenses for an entire year.

Lifetime maximum benefit The maximum amount the insurance company will pay for claims over the policy holder's life.

Managed health care plan A plan that requires you to choose medical providers who are a part of your provider's network.

Indemnity plan A private health care plan in which the policyholder is free to select his or her own health care provider.

Health maintenance organization (HMO) A managed health care plan that allows its members medical services performed by approved doctors and hospitals.

Many insurance companies cover preventative health care in their plans. It costs less to prevent an illness than to treat it.

groups of doctors, hospitals, and other health care specialists who agree to provide services to the HMO members. Services are provided for a co-pay, as long as you use in-network providers. HMOs don't require deductibles or coinsurance payments. You must select a primary care physician, PCP, from a list of in-network doctors. Your primary care physician provides the majority of your medical care, and you must have a referral from him or her before you can see a specialist. If you visit a doctor or specialist without a referral from your primary care physician, you have to pay the entire cost.

The providers in the HMO (doctors, hospitals, etc.) are paid a set amount to cover the costs of medical care for the HMO members assigned to them. If the costs of providing medical service exceed the payments they receive, they lose money. This creates an incentive to control costs. Some critics of HMOs claim they provide less than optimal care to control costs. Although this may be true for some HMOs, there are many who provide good service. Before you join an HMO plan, research the doctors and hospitals in the plan. See if you are comfortable with the hospital and doctors available under the plan. Ask other plan members about their experience with the HMO.

HMOs often focus on preventive care, because it costs less to prevent illness than to cure it. An annual checkup is normally included as a part of the plan. HMOs offer the lowest premiums and the least flexibility.

Preferred Provider Organizations

Preferred provider organization (PPO) A managed health care plan that offers medical benefits through a list of approved providers.

A preferred provider organization (PPO) is similar to an HMO but offers more flexibility. With a PPO you choose any doctor from a list of approved plan physicians. You also can choose any approved specialists if you need a specialist's care. You do not need a referral, and you do not have to maintain a primary care physician. PPOs typically offer a large selection of doctors. These plans offer more flexibility than HMOs, but they also have higher premiums.

PPOs are like HMOs for in-network services and like indemnity plans for out-of-network services. Normally, you will have a co-pay for in-network services and a deductible and co-insurance payment for out-of network services.

Point-of-Service (POS) Plans

A point-of-service (POS) plan offers a combination of the other types of plans. When medical care is needed, a member of a POS plan typically has three choices.

1. The plan member can choose to go through his or her primary care physician, in which case services will be covered under HMO guidelines (i.e., usually a co-payment will be required).
2. The plan member can access care through a PPO provider, and the services will be covered under in-network PPO rules (i.e., usually a co-payment or co-insurance will be required).
3. The plan member may choose to obtain services from a provider outside of the HMO and PPO networks, and services will be reimbursed according to out-of-network rules (i.e., usually a deductible and co-insurance charge will be required).

If you have a POS plan, you are responsible for deciding where to seek care. You need to understand the financial implications of your choices when you seek medical care.

Dental and Vision Insurance

Insurance for dental and optometry services, not usually covered by regular medical insurance, is available. Employers often offer dental and vision insurance employees can purchase in addition to their health insurance. It is also available to individuals from private insurance companies. Dental insurance covers expenses like dental checkups, miscellaneous dental work, or orthodontics. Vision insurance provides coverage for visits to an optometrist, contacts, glasses, and other eye-care needs.

The premium costs and benefits provided for both dental and vision insurance vary greatly from plan to plan.

Health Coverage under the Affordable Health Care Act

The Patient Protection and Affordable Healthcare Act (usually shortened to the Affordable Care Act) became law in the United States on March 23, 2010. This law signaled a new era in healthcare in the United States by guaranteeing the availability of medical insurance coverage to all U.S. residents. Individuals and small businesses began to enroll in plans created by the act, and coverage began on January 1, 2014.

Point-of-service (POS) plan A health insurance plan with combined components of indemnity plans, HMOs, and PPOs.

Dental insurance Covers expenses such as dental checkups, miscellaneous dental work, or orthodontics.

Vision insurance Provides coverage for optometry visits, contacts, glasses, and other eye-care needs.

CHANGES INSTITUTED BY THE ACT

The most sweeping change brought about by the Affordable Care Act is the institution of universal medical insurance coverage for virtually all individuals in the United States. This universal coverage is not a national healthcare system as in many other countries, but it is a system requiring almost everyone to obtain coverage either through an employer-sponsored group plan or from a private insurance company.

Medical coverage for the plans offered covers from less than 60 percent (for the lower-cost plans) up to 90 percent of the average total cost of care (for the more expensive plans). Exhibit 8.4 shows the categories of plans and the average percent of total care coverage that the plans in each category cover. Some of the other important features of the act are

- Coverage
  - Ends pre-existing conditions for children. Benefits can no longer be denied to children because of a condition that existed before the policy became effective.
  - Extends coverage of young adults under parents' plan to age 26.
  - Ends arbitrary termination of insurance coverage by insurance companies.
  - Guarantees that policyholders have the right to appeal any denial of benefits payment.
  - Allows emergency care at any provider, even those that are outside of the health plan's network.

- Cost
  - Ends lifetime limits of coverage.
  - Requires insurers to justify any unreasonable rate increases.

The only factors that insurance companies can consider to determine premiums for any individual (or family) premiums is through family structure, geography, tobacco use, participation in a health promotion program, and age.

EXHIBIT 8.4   **CATEGORIES OF MEDICAL INSURANCE OFFERED IN THE HEALTH INSURANCE MARKETPLACE CREATED BY THE AFFORDABLE HEALTH CARE ACT**

Category	Percentage of Total Average Care Cost Covered
Catastrophic	Less than 60%
Bronze	60%
Silver	70%
Gold	80%
Platinum	90%

Source: HealthCare.gov, October 12, 2013

MEDICAL INSURANCE AND THE HEALTH INSURANCE MARKETPLACE

The law requires all individuals to have medical insurance coverage, so those who do not have coverage from their employer must purchase an approved policy. Individuals or families who remain without coverage (or who do not receive an exemption) face paying a penalty. The penalty is phased in until 2016, when it will be the greater of 2.5 percent of taxable income or $695 per adult plus $347.50 per child, subject to a maximum of $2,085 per family. Families in lower-income brackets qualify for government subsidies to help cover the cost of the health insurance.

Under the act, each state chooses how it wants to offer health insurance. On one side are the states that opt to have their own insurance exchange that contracts with insurance companies to offer qualifying policies. At the time of the writing of this book, 16 states had chosen this method. At the other end, states choose to participate in the federally facilitated marketplace. Nineteen states had elected that option. The remaining states have chosen an alternative with features of both state exchanges and the federal exchange. These state exchanges together comprise the Health Insurance Marketplace at www.healthcare.gov. The HealthCare.gov website provides a friendly gateway for individuals to learn about health insurance, get quotes for specific policies in their state, and enroll in the program.

Exhibit 8.5 shows the range of average monthly premiums for a sampling of the various policy categories in the Health Care Marketplace in 2013. Plans that cover a smaller portion of average annual healthcare costs but that do protect the insured for a catastrophic health care illness or accident are the cheapest. Moving up the scale, plans that cover on average a greater portion of average annual medical costs are progressively more expensive.

MONTHLY COST OF MEDICAL INSURANCE COVERAGE FROM THE HEALTH CARE MARKETPLACE, 2013

EXHIBIT 8.5

| Category | Monthly Cost for | | |
	Individual Age < 50	Individual Age ≥ 50	Family
Catastrophic	$140 to $165	$239 to $281	$474 to $557
Bronze	$195 to $223	$333 to $381	$659 to $754
Silver	$242 to $274	$412 to $467	$816 to $925
Gold	$297 to $348	$507 to $594	$1004 to $1177

Range of monthly costs for medical insurance policies in the Health Care Marketplace on HealthCare.gov (www.healthcare.gov) for persons in Boone County, Missouri, October 2013.

Source: HealthCare.gov, October 12, 2013

Ways to Save Money on Health Insurance

The costs of insurance premiums and unreimbursed medical bills can take a big chunk out of your gross income. There are a few ways to reduce your health insurance costs. Some examples are the following:

- High-deductible insurance
- Flexible spending accounts
- Health savings accounts

HIGH-DEDUCTIBLE INSURANCE

High deductible health plan (HDHP) This health insurance is also referred to as catastrophic health insurance, since it pays only if you have a medical catastrophe. It is best for healthy individuals who don't require frequent doctor visits.

For healthy individuals who don't require frequent doctors visits, high deductible health plan (HDHP) insurance can significantly reduce your cost. This high-deductible health insurance is referred to as catastrophic health insurance since it pays if you have a medical catastrophe. To qualify for tax savings through a health savings account, your HDHP must have at least an individual deductible of $2,100 or a family deductible of $4,200 per year (Publication 969). Some providers offer policies with higher deductible amounts. Qualified HDHPs have maximum out-of-pocket expenses of $4,200 for individual plans and $6,750 for family plans. These are 2012 figures and since they are part of tax regulations they are subject to change annually. Check with the IRS web site to find the limits for years after 2012.

The premiums for HDHPs are typically less than 50 percent of more conventional medical insurance plans. This insurance provides medical benefits for large expenses, and you pay out-of-pocket up to your deductible amount. You save on premiums with this type of insurance, yet you are covered for catastrophic illness or injury. You need to save enough money to pay the deductible amount if it becomes necessary.

STRETCH
YOUR DOLLAR

SELECT YOUR COVERAGE

Select the lowest amount of coverage to meet your needs. Consider your need first then premiums. If you are a healthy individual, consider a HDHP and a HSA.

FLEXIBLE SPENDING ACCOUNTS

Flexible spending account An employer-offered benefit allowing employees to contribute tax-deductible dollars to an account to be used for medical expenses.

A flexible spending account allows you to pay medical bills tax free. Some employers offer flexible spending accounts as an employee benefit. The amount you deposit in your flexible spending account is not taxed. You must estimate your annual out of pocket medical costs. You use your account to pay for these costs; however, if any money is left in the account at the end of the year, you forfeit that money.

The savings from a flexible spending account can be substantial. If you are in the 25 percent income tax bracket and use a flexible spending account to cover $1,000 in medical expenses, you will save $250.

HEALTH SAVINGS ACCOUNTS

Health savings accounts (HSAs), created in Congress in 2003, are available to individuals with a qualified HDHP. They work similarly to flexible spending accounts; they offer a tax-free way to pay for medical expenses not covered by your insurance. However, they offer benefits flexible spending accounts don't:

1. Funds in the account can be invested to earn a return.
2. Any unused funds at the end of the year continue in the account from year-to-year.

The health savings accounts are relatively new. If an HDHP makes sense for your situation, you should consider setting up a health savings account. Exhibit 8.6 shows the 2012 limits for HDHPs and HSAs. If you withdraw the funds for a purpose other than a qualified medical expense, they are taxed as income in the year they are withdrawn.

Let's look at an example. Sandy is a 26-year-old graduate student. She is healthy and rarely goes to the doctor. She uses the local health department for her annual checkup and buys a year's supply of birth control pills at her annual visit. She pays $40 for the office visit and $60 for the birth control pills. Last winter she had strep throat and went to a local doctor. She paid $80 for the office visit and $4.00 for a generic prescription at Walmart. She was billed $76 for lab work a week after her office visit. Sandy does not have insurance and pays all her medical expenses when she needs them. She is considering purchasing medical insurance when she graduates.

First let's compare the cost associated with insurance for her now, without an employer subsidy. Exhibit 8.7 shows the comparison of insurance plans and benefits.

Health savings account (HSA) A savings account funded with tax-deductible dollars to be used for medical expenses for people who have a catastrophic health insurance plan (HDHP).

2012 HDHP AND HSA LIMITS   EXHIBIT 8.6

	HDHP Min. Deductible	HDHP Max. Out-of-Pocket	HSA Max. Contribution
Individual	$2,100	$4,200	$3,100
Family	$4,200	$6,700	$6,250

Data compiled from IRS publication 969(201).

EXHIBIT 8.7   MEDICAL PLAN COMPARISON

	HMO	Indemnity	PPO		HDHP
			In network	Out of network	
Monthly Premium					
Individual	$600	$1,000	$500		$150
Family	$1,600	$2,500	$1,250		$300
Deductible per Year					
Individual	$0	$250	$0	$150	$2,100
Family	$0	$500	$0	$300	$4,200
Out-of-Pocket Maximum per Year					
Individual	$0	$1,000	$0	$3,000	$4,200
Family	$0	$2,000	$0	Not applicable	$6,750
Doctor's Office Visit					
You pay	$15	20% (A)	$25	20% (A)	All (B)
Specialist's Office Visit					
	$15	20% (A)	$25	20% (A)	All (B)
Prescription Drugs					
	$15	$15	$15		All (B)
Hospitalization					
	$0	20% (A)	$300	20% (A)	20% (A)
Emergency Room					
	$50	20% (A)	$50	$50	20% (A)
Out-Patient Surgery					
	$0	20% (A)	$100	20% (A)	20% (A)
Lab and X-ray					
	$0	20% (A)	$0	20% (A)	20% (A)

Now we will input Sandy's typical medical costs in the applicable line items.

Sandy's Cost with No Employer Subsidy of Premiums					
	HMO	Indemnity	PPO		HDHP
			In network	Out of network	
Monthly Premium					
Individual	$600	$1,000	$500		$150
Annual cost	$7,200	$12,000	$6,000	$6,000	$1,800
Deductible per Year					
Individual	$0	$250	$0	$150	$2,100
Out-of-Pocket Maximum per Year					
Individual	$0	$1,000	$0	$3,000	$4,200
Doctor's Office Visit					
Sandy pays	$15(2)	$40 + $80	$25(2)	$40 + $80	$40 + $80
Prescription Drugs					
	$15(12)	$15(12)	$15(12)	$30 + $20(12)	$5(12)
Total	$7,410	$12,300	$6,230	$6,360	$1,980

Notice her prescription costs assume that if she uses out-of-network providers, she pays the full price for her birth control. Under her HDHP, she continues to buy birth control through the health clinic. Sandy is healthy and has birth control as her only regular prescription. Without an employer subsidy, the HDHP is less than a third of the cost of the cheapest other options.

Now let's compare her costs if her future employer subsidizes 100 percent of individual coverage.

Sandy's Cost with 100 Percent Employer Subsidy of Premiums					
	HMO	Indemnity	PPO		HDHP
			In network	Out of network	
Monthly Premium					
Individual	$600	$1,000	$500		$150
Annual Cost	$0	$0	$0	$0	$0
Deductible per Year					
Individual	$0	$250	$0	$150	$2,100
Out-of-Pocket Maximum per Year					
Individual	$0	$1,000	$0	$3,000	$4,200
Doctor's Office Visit					
Sandy pays	$15(2)	$40 + $80	$25(2)	$40 + $80	$40 + $80
Prescription Drugs					
	$15(12)	$15(12)	$15(12)	$30 + $20(12)	$5(12)
Total	$210.00	$300.00	$230.00	$360.00	$180.00

TEN THINGS TO CONSIDER ABOUT HEALTH INSURANCE   EXHIBIT 8.8

1. Health insurance is expensive, but not having it can be disastrous. Even one minor car accident or other medical emergency can deplete your entire savings. The best way to save on insurance is to purchase insurance to fit your medical needs.
2. Take advantage of employer-sponsored health insurance. Employee group coverage is cheaper than an individual plan, especially if it is subsidized by your employer.
3. Freedom costs more. HMO or PPO plans cost less than plans with more freedom to choose any doctor or hospital you want.
4. The insurance with the lowest premium is not necessarily the cheapest plan. When you consider health insurance, compare both the cost of the premium and the benefits you need to receive from the plan. A plan with a higher premium may cost you less if it covers your prescription medicine and you need medication on a continuous basis.
5. Compare all plans available to you; determine which one best fits your needs.
6. Research HMOs and other networks before signing up. A growing number of public and private sources compile and distribute information about individual physicians and providers, hospitals, and health plans.
7. Married couples in which both partners work for an employer with a health plan should consider how to structure their coverage between one or both plans.
8. Know your plan and the procedures to follow before you seek routine medical care.
9. Medical expenses are itemized tax deductions if they exceed 7 1/2 percent of your income.
10. You can continue your insurance coverage with COBRA if you lose your job.

Now although the cheapest is still the HDHP, there is only $30 difference between it and the HMO. If she has one more office visit a year, the HMO would be her most economical option.

The decision about which health care plan is best for you should be based on your medical needs. Use your medical needs to compare the plans available to you. If you know what your typical medical service needs are for a year, you can compare costs for yourself, like we did for Sandy. Exhibit 8.8 lists ten things to consider before you decide which medical insurance plan is best for you.

Insurance Continuity

COBRA Act of 1986
Requires companies to allow employees to continue in a company-sponsored health insurance plan for 18 months to three years after leaving the company.

The COBRA (Consolidated Omnibus Budget Reconciliation Act) Act of 1986 requires companies with at least 20 employees to allow former employees to continue to participate in company-sponsored health insurance plans for 18 months to three years after they leave the company. Employers are not required to pay any part of the premium cost for COBRA recipients. Under COBRA coverage the monthly premium you pay will be greater if your employer subsidized your insurance.

Government Medical Insurance

If you cannot afford health insurance, are retired or disabled, you may be able to receive health insurance coverage from one of two government-run insurance programs, Medicare or Medicaid.

MEDICAID

Medicaid A government-sponsored health insurance plan for individuals and families with limited income and assets.

Medicaid is government-sponsored health insurance for individuals and families with limited income and assets. This program is run by each individual state but must conform to federal guidelines. The plan has limited options as to where covered individuals can receive medical care, and it is intended for the neediest individuals and families.

MEDICARE

Medicare A government-sponsored health insurance plan for qualified older and disabled persons.

All employees have a portion of their income deducted from their paychecks for Medicare tax. The tax is 1.45 percent of earned income and supports the Medicare health insurance program. Medicare provides health insurance for qualified older and disabled persons.

Medicare consists of four parts, Parts A, B, C, and D. Part A covers hospital stays, surgeries, and home health care. There is no cost to members to receive benefits under Part A. Part B is optional insurance; it provides for additional health care services such as physical therapy and outpatient hospital care. In 2014 the monthly cost of Medicare Part B was $104.90 plus an additional amount of up to $200.80 for individuals with an annual income greater than $80,000.

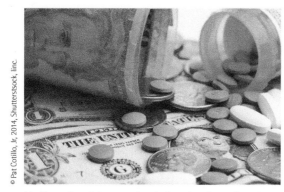

Medicare Part D is an optional plan aimed to offset the cost of prescription medication.

Part C allows Medicare recipients to receive all of their medical services from one provider organization, which may help lower overall medical costs. To sign up for Part C a participant must be enrolled in both parts A and B and be willing to pay an additional monthly fee. Part D is another optional plan to help pay the costs for prescription medications.

Private health insurance companies also get in the mix with Medicare. These companies offer a type of insurance called *medigap,* which provides additional health insurance for individuals who want more coverage than Medicare offers. Typically, there are 10 types of medigap policies available, called plans A through J. The policies become more and more comprehensive moving through the alphabet, and of course the premium costs increase as well.

Disability Insurance

Medical insurance reduces out-of-pocket medical expenses if you become ill or have an accident. It does not provide coverage, however, from the lost wages if your illness or injury prevents you from working.

Disability income insurance provides income in the event the policyholder becomes disabled. Exhibit 8.9 shows the percent of disability claims by category, in the United States in 2008.

Disability income insurance An insurance policy that provides income to an individual in the event that he or she becomes disabled.

CHARACTERISTICS OF DISABILITY INSURANCE

To compare disability insurance from various insurance companies you need to understand the basic characteristics of disability insurance. Disability insurance policies include the following:

- Disability income payment
- Definition of disability
- Elimination (waiting) period
- Benefit period
- Probationary period
- Non-cancellable or renewable provisions
- Exclusions and optional riders

EXHIBIT 8.9	PERCENT OF NEW DISABILITY CLAIMS BY CATEGORY (2008)

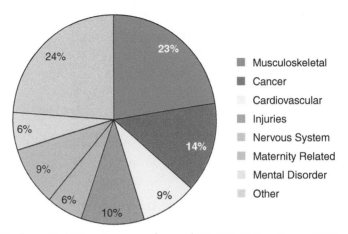

Data source http://www.disabilitycanhappen.org/surveys/CDA_LTD_ Claims_Survey_2008.asp

Disability Income Payment

This is the payment you receive from your insurance if you are disabled. This is set at the time you buy the policy. It is typically 45 to 60 percent of your earnings at the time the policy is written. However, you can purchase a policy for a specified monthly payment. The greater the coverage, the higher the insurance premiums will be. This amount is fixed unless otherwise stated in your policy. Adjustments to your income disability payments will be discussed in the optional riders section.

To determine the amount of coverage you need consider your:

- Monthly financial shortfall from your regular pay
- Emergency fund savings
- Taxes

When the employer pays the disability insurance premiums, disability income benefits are taxable income. If you pay the premiums, your benefits are not taxed.

DEFINITION OF DISABILITY

What does it mean to be disabled? The answer to that question depends on the particular policy. There are three standard definitions used to write disability income insurance policies.

The first is own-occupation disabled. A policy with this definition provides income if the policyholder is unable to perform the job duties of his or her current occupation. If you have an own-occupation disability policy, the insurance company will consider you totally disabled if you cannot perform in the occupation in which you were employed when you became disabled. It will pay disability benefits even if you go to work in another occupation. This

Own-occupation disabled
A policy that provides income if the policyholder is unable to perform the job duties of his or her current occupation.

This pharmaceutical sales representative may not make as much as he would as a surgeon. However, own-occupation disability insurance is available to compensate him for his career loss.

© EDHAR, 2014, Shutterstock, Inc.

is the most comprehensive coverage you can purchase. You might think you wouldn't need disability insurance if you can work. However, consider the case of a surgeon who develops a medical condition that prevents him or her from safely performing surgery. Perhaps he or she wants to stay busy and takes a job as a sales representative for a medical company. Although he or she can perform those duties, it wouldn't come close to compensating him or her for the career loss. In a situation like this, an own-occupation policy allows the most freedom without forgoing benefits.

The second is income replacement policy. A policy with this definition provides income if the policyholder is unable to perform the job duties of his or her current occupation, and he or she is not employed in another occupation. If you have an income replacement policy, the insurance company will consider you totally disabled if you cannot perform in the occupation in which you were employed when you became disabled, as long as you are not employed in another occupation. This is similar the own-occupation policy, but you wouldn't be allowed to work at a less strenuous job for personal satisfaction or to supplement your income.

The third definition is any-occupation disabled. This policy defines totally disabled as being unable to perform any job the policyholder is capable of doing for his or her education and background. Under an "any-occupation" disability policy, you will not be considered totally disabled if you can work in another occupation.

The most comprehensive coverage is offered by an own-occupation defined policy. The income replacement policy will qualify the policyholder by the same definition as an own occupation policy, but will not allow him or her to work in another occupation to supplement his or her income. Policies offering this type of coverage are more expensive. Disability qualification by the any-occupation definition forces policyholders to seek other types of jobs to determine if they can work in their "disabled" condition.

Income replacement policy This policy provides income if the policyholder is unable to perform the job duties of his or her current occupation and he or she is not employed in another occupation.

Any-occupation disabled Under this policy you will not be considered totally disabled if you can work in another occupation.

Elimination Period

Elimination period
A waiting period that is the length of time from the original disability-causing event to the time when the policy begins to make payments.

The elimination period is a waiting period. It is the length of time from the original disability-causing event to the time when the policy begins to make payments. The most common elimination period is 90 days. However, for a higher price you can purchase policies with elimination periods of 30 or 60 days. You can also purchase policies for longer elimination periods like 180 days or as long as 720 days. However, the premium discount for an extended elimination period is substantially less than the increase for a shorter elimination period. The standard elimination period is 90 days; during this period you will not receive any disability income under your insurance. Once the elimination period passes, you will be paid your monthly income at the end of the next month. Although your elimination period is 90 days, you won't receive your first check until the end of the fourth month.

You should have an emergency savings account to cover expenses during the elimination period. This "waiting" period discourages policyholders from making small claims when they miss work for a short period of time. It reduces premiums significantly.

Presumptive disability
A provision that provides immediate benefits for severe and sudden disabilities, such as loss of sight, hearing, speech, or two limbs.

The elimination period is waived for a presumptive disability. A presumptive disability provision provides immediate benefits for severe and sudden disabilities, such as loss of sight, hearing, speech, or two limbs. Most policies offer a presumptive provision but vary on their definition. Some may pay for either a total and/or permanent loss. A total loss is not the same as a permanent loss. For example, two broken limbs is a total but temporary loss. The amputation of two limbs is a total and permanent loss.

Benefit Period

Short-term disability policy Disability insurance policy with a waiting period of 0 to 14 days that pays benefits for up to two years.

Once the elimination period passes, how long will you continue to receive benefits? That depends on the benefit period. The benefit period defines the maximum amount of time you can draw disability income. The standard times are two years, five years, to age 65, to age 67.5, or lifetime. Policies differ greatly on how long disability income will continue. A short-term disability policy has a benefit period up to two years. Long-term disability policies pay benefits from several years to the remainder of the policyholder's life. As you extend the benefit period, the premiums increase.

Long-term disability policy Disability insurance policy with a waiting period of several weeks to several months that pays benefits for periods from several years to as long as the lifetime of the insured.

Probationary Period

Probationary period The length of time from initial application for disability insurance to the time when coverage takes effect.

A probationary period states the length of time from the original application for disability insurance to the point at which coverage begins. This length of time is usually only a few months. The purpose of the probationary period is to deter fraud. Unscrupulous people might have an injury, get disability insurance, and then immediately file a claim.

Non-cancellable or Renewable Provisions

Policies can either be non-cancellable or renewable. A non-cancellable policy allows the holder to renew coverage each year for the same premium amount. A renewable policy allows continued coverage each year with the same benefits, but the insurance company has the right to increase the premium amount. Policies with the non-cancellable provisions have a higher premium.

Exclusions and Optional Riders

Exclusions limit your benefits under certain conditions. Common exclusions are:

- Alcohol and drugs claims. Some policies limit your benefit period to one year for disability claims related to alcohol or drug claims.
- Mental disorders and nervous conditions. Some policies limit your benefit period to two years for disabilities related to stress, anxiety, depression, dementia, or other mental disorders and nervous conditions.
- Crime related. Most policies exclude coverage for disabilities that were caused while you were committing a felony.
- Acts of war. Some policies exclude disabilities caused by acts of war.

Optional riders are a way to add additional coverage to you policy. Common riders are:

- COLA, cost of living adjustments. This rider takes effect after you have collected benefits for one year. Each year after that you will receive a cost of living adjustment to offset the effects of inflation.
- Automatic increase rider. This rider automatically increases your coverage and premiums for five years. You coverage is increased about 25 percent automatically over a five-year period. This allows you to adjust your disability income payment automatically.
- Future increase rider. This allows you to increase your coverage to equal your current income regardless of your health to age 55. To increase your coverage, you have to verify your current income. Increases in your disability income payment will increase your premiums.

SOURCES OF DISABILITY INSURANCE

Companies that offer health insurance also offer disability insurance. Following are the potential sources for disability benefits.

Private Insurance Policies

Insurance companies make disability insurance available to individuals. By comparison shopping, you should be able to find a policy to fit your coverage needs. Premiums depend on provisions in the policy and the job occupation of the applicant—a coal miner's insurance will be much greater than an office secretary's.

Employer Provided Disability Insurance

Many employers will offer disability insurance to their employees as a benefit. Premiums of such group policies will be lower than those from a policy purchased as an individual. In addition, some employers subsidize or pay disability insurance premiums for their employees. Employer-provided disability insurance may provide limited options. Before you sign up for employer-sponsored disability insurance, make sure it offers sufficient coverage for your family's needs.

Worker's Compensation

Employees who are injured on the job are usually entitled to worker's compensation benefits. Workers' compensation benefits are administered and set at the state level. It normally pays for medical expenses and provides minimal income for a job-related injury or illness.

Social Security

Social Security also provides disability income benefits. The amount you receive depends on how much and how long you paid into the Social Security system through FICA taxes. Consider Social Security benefits as a supplement to disability insurance income because the amount of the Social Security benefit is not likely to provide sufficient income.

To be eligible for disability income from Social Security you have to be disabled for at least five months with a condition that lasts at least 12 months. You must also meet the definition of disability set by the Social Security administration:

Social Security pays only for total disability. **No benefits are payable for partial disability or for short-term disability.**

"Disability" under Social Security is based on your inability to work. We consider you disabled under Social Security rules if:

- You cannot do work that you did before;
- We decide that you cannot adjust to other work because of your medical condition(s); **and**
- Your disability has lasted or is expected to last for at least one year or to result in death.

This is a strict definition of disability. Social Security program rules assume that working families have access to other resources to provide support during periods of short-term disabilities, including workers' compensation, insurance, savings and investments. (Disability Planner)
From the Social Security web site http://www.ssa.gov/dibplan/dqualify4.htm

Exhibit 8.10 shows the number of Social Security disability insurance applications filed and approved.

SOCIAL SECURITY APPLICANTS COMPARED TO THE NUMBER OF APPROVED APPLICATIONS

EXHIBIT 8.10

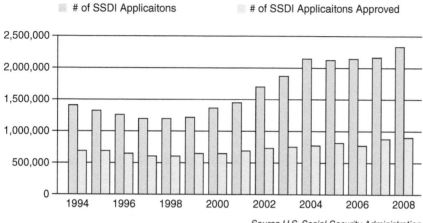

Source U.S. Social Security Administration

From http://www.disabilitycanhappen.org/surveys/CDA_LTD_Claims_Survey_2008.asp

SUMMARY

Insurance is an important aspect of proper financial planning. Insurance mitigates the risk of financial loss by transferring the risk to the insurance company. You purchase an insurance policy with insurance premiums. The insurance company pays benefits according to the specifics of your policy.

Medical insurance pays a predetermined portion of medical care costs. It is available from private insurance companies and for qualified applicants from government-sponsored plans. Private health insurance is normally offered in employee benefit packages. The employer negotiates for a group policy with lower premiums. Self-employed individuals and those whose employers do not offer a group policy can purchase medical insurance on their own.

The main types of private medical insurance plans are indemnity plans, health maintenance organizations (HMOs), preferred provider organizations (PPOs), and point-of-service (POS) plans. An HMO is usually the least expensive choice but has the least flexibility. An indemnity plan is the most expensive but allows the most freedom of choice. PPO and POS plans offer degrees of flexibility and cost between those of HMO and indemnity plans.

The Patient Protection and Affordable Care Act contains a number of provisions that protect insured persons such as prohibiting non-coverage because of pre-existing medical conditions, guaranteeing the right to appeal any decision to not pay a benefit, and ending lifetime coverage limits. The most far-reaching change in the act was to require medical insurance coverage for everyone. Persons not covered by employers' group plans can access the Health Care Marketplace to enroll in insurance coverage available through their state's insurance exchange. Costs of the plans available vary by extent of coverage, and individuals and families in the lower-income brackets can qualify for subsidies to help pay the cost.

There are strategies to reduce medical care costs. One option is to purchase a catastrophic health insurance policy with a high deductible and low premium. This, combined with a flexible spending account or health savings account, can provide cost savings along with tax benefits.

Disability insurance provides income to policyholders if they become disabled and are unable to return to work. Social Security and worker's compensation both provide some income, but it is usually not sufficient to cover the needs of most workers. Disability insurance provides a necessary supplement to the government benefits. Employers often offer disability insurance as a group plan. Sometimes they will even subsidize the premiums.

PROBLEMS

1. Kim has an HMO with a $15 co-pay for office visits and a $10 co-pay for prescriptions. She pays $350 a month in premiums through her employer. She visits the doctor six times and has 14 prescriptions filled. How much are her medical expenses for the year?

2. John has an indemnity plan with a $250 deductible. His insurance pays 20 percent of his medical expenses after his deductible is met. He has a maximum out of pocket limit of $1,000. He pays $150 a month in premiums through his employer. He visits the doctor four times; each office visit costs $80. He has four prescriptions filled at Walmart for $4.00 each. How much are his medical expenses for the year?

3. Sam and Lynn have three children. They have a family indemnity plan with the following provisions:

   - There is a $250 individual and a $500 family deductible.
   - Their insurance pays 20 percent of medical expenses after the deductible is met.
   - They have a maximum out-of-pocket limit of $1,000 individual and $2,000 family.
   - They pay $450 a month in premiums through Lynn's employer.
   - Each office visit costs $80, and they fill their prescriptions at Walmart for $4.00 each.
   - Sam visits the doctor one time.
   - Lynn visits the doctor twice and has two prescriptions filled.
   - Their middle child visits the doctor 14 times and has seven prescriptions filled.
   - The oldest and youngest each visit the doctor three times and each have two prescriptions filled.

   How much are their medical expenses for the year?

CASE STUDIES

COLLEGE STUDENT

Assume Kevin Maedor graduated and he makes $65,000 a year. He is no longer covered under his parent's insurance. Use the plans in Exhibit 8.4. Assume an office visit under the indemnity or out of network plan costs $80 and prescriptions without co-pays are $4 for generic and $25 for non generic.

1. Compare his total yearly costs under each plan
2. Select the plan that best fits his needs and budget
3. Explain in detail why you chose the plan you did for him.
4. He has the following medical information
   - He is 23 and healthy.
   - He hasn't seen a doctor for anything other than a check-up since he started college
   - He plays basketball and loves water sports especially his jet ski

NEW GRADUATE

Rene Harris has decided to purchase medical insurance. Use the plans in Exhibit 8.4. Assume an office visit under the indemnity or out of network plan costs $80 and prescriptions without co-pays are $4 for generic and $25 for non generic.

1. Compare her total yearly costs under each plan
2. Select the plan that best fits her needs and budget
3. Explain in detail why you chose the plan you did for her.
4. She has the following medical information
   - She is 24 and healthy.
   - She sees the doctor occasionally and for her annual checkup. She visited the doctor once for an ear infection and she got a prescription for antibiotics. Other than that one incident the only medication she has taken in the past few years are birth control pills. She pays $15 a month for these.
   - She doesn't participate in any sports, she loves to entertain and shop for recreation.

CREATE YOUR OWN FINANCIAL PLAN

1. Do you currently have access to subsidized insurance premiums through an employer?
2. What are your medical needs?
   - How often do you see a doctor?
   - How often do you fill prescriptions?
   - Do you take any medications on a regular and ongoing basis?
3. Use your answer to the questions in item 2 to estimate your medical needs.
4. Compare the plans currently available to you.
5. If you don't have plans to compare, use the ones in Exhibit 8.4.
6. Which medical insurance option is the best for you?

MAKE IT PERSONAL

- What are your personal thoughts about medical insurance?
- Do you favor national or private health insurance?
- Do you think this issue personally affects you?
- How do you think the current system will affect your finances?
- How do you think the proposed system will affect your finances?
- Do you believe you will receive the same quality under both systems?
- If not, which one do you think will provide you with the highest quality care?

Feel free to share your thoughts with your classmates, professors, and elected representatives. You are also free to choose to keep your thoughts to yourself. This is a sensitive issue for many Americans. However, your opinions and the reasons for them are personal and will be affected by your lifestyle, political, moral, and spiritual beliefs.

REVIEW QUESTIONS

1. What is the relationship between insurance deductibles and premiums?

   _____

   _____

   _____

2. What are the four main types of private medical insurance plans?

   _____

   _____

   _____

3. Identify the main patient protection provisions of the Patient Protection and Affordable Care Act.

   _____

   _____

   _____

4. Outline the medical coverage system created by the Affordable Care Act.

   _____

   _____

   _____

5. How can you reduce your after-tax medical costs?

   _____

   _____

   _____

6. What is an HDHP? Who is most likely to benefit from this type of insurance?

_____

_____

_____

7. What is the difference between a health savings account and a flexible spending account?

_____

_____

_____

8. What are the two federally funded medical insurance plans? Who is eligible under these plans?

_____

_____

_____

9. What types of insurance are included under the broad category of health insurance?

_____

_____

_____

10. What tool would you use to prepare for the high deductible under an HDHP plan?

_____

_____

_____

11. What are the pros and cons of an HMO?

_____

_____

_____

12. What are the pros and cons of an indemnity plan?

_____

_____

_____

13. Which plans offer a mix of the benefits and costs offered by HMOs and indemnity plans?

_____

_____

_____

Life Insurance

"Human life is proverbially uncertain; few things are more certain than the solvency of a life-insurance company."

—Arthur Eddington
(1882–1944)

OBJECTIVES

- Explain the different types of life insurance
- Identify a person's need for life insurance
- Describe life insurance companies and how to buy life insurance
- Compute the amount of life insurance coverage a person should have

KEY TERMS

Accidental death life insurance
Beneficiary
Budget method
Contingent beneficiary
Convertible policy
Decreasing term policy
Fraternal societies
Group term insurance
Income method
Independent insurance sales agent

Installment payments
Insured
Key person life insurance
Level term life insurance
Life insurance
Lump-sum distribution
Mutual life insurance company
Needs approach
Non-forfeiture clause
Ordinary life insurance

Paid-up 65 life insurance policy
Participating life insurance policy
Renewable policy
Rider
Stock life insurance company
Straight life insurance
Term life insurance
Universal life insurance
Variable life insurance
Whole life insurance

© Andy Dean Photography, 2014, Shutterstock, Inc.

Life insurance can provide a financial safety net for dependants in case the main wage earner dies.

For many people, one of the least desirable financial planning topics to consider is life insurance. Considering and planning for life insurance forces you to think about what will happen in the case of your death. Although unpleasant to contemplate, it is important to do proper and appropriate life insurance planning. With appropriate planning, your loved ones and others important to you will have adequate financial support should you die. Having to deal with an unexpected death is difficult enough, so those close to you and those who depend on you should not also be placed in a situation of added financial difficulty. Life insurance helps you avoid those financial difficulties.

Life Insurance

Life insurance Insurance that provides a monetary payment to a specified beneficiary in the event that the policyholder dies.

Insured The person whose life is covered by a life insurance policy.

Beneficiary The person or organization designated to receive the death benefit of a life insurance policy.

Life insurance provides a monetary payment to a specified beneficiary in the event that the insured person dies. Imagine a household with one family member who is the main breadwinner earning the majority of household income. If that person dies, who will provide the income for the family? This is a situation in which life insurance can provide a safety net by making financial resources available that can hopefully replace the income of the deceased.

The beneficiary (or primary beneficiary) of a life insurance policy is the person or organization named in the policy to receive the policy's benefits. While beneficiaries are usually related to the insured, or they are close friends, a beneficiary can be any person or other legally formed organization. However, should the beneficiary be a minor at the time the policy pays benefits, the minor's parent or guardian will control the benefits. Beneficiaries can also be organizations such as a business, church, charity, or trust.

Life insurance policyholders also often name a contingent beneficiary. The contingent beneficiary receives the policy benefit if the primary beneficiary died before the policyholder died.

One distinctive feature of life insurance benefits is that they are usually nontaxable. A person receiving a $200,000 life insurance benefit will receive the entire $200,000 payment and owe no income taxes on the amount received.

Providing life insurance is a major business. As Exhibit 9.1 shows, at the end of 2007, there were 374 million life insurance policies in force in the United States through private insurers. These policies represented total life insurance of about $19.5 trillion.

Contingent beneficiary A person who receives policy benefits if the primary beneficiary is not able to receive benefits.

LIFE INSURANCE POLICIES IN FORCE IN THE UNITED STATES THROUGH PRIVATE INSURERS, 1990–2007

EXHIBIT 9.1

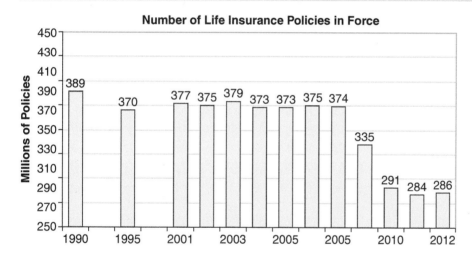

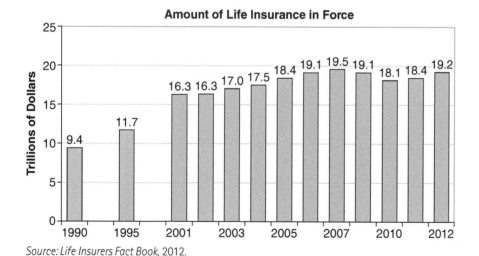

Source: Life Insurers Fact Book, 2012.

Who Needs Life Insurance?

Not everyone needs life insurance. People who are independently wealthy or who have guaranteed incomes (for example, from a retirement plan) may have little or no need for life insurance. Typically, the following groups of people may need little or no life insurance:

- Single people
- Married couples with no dependents who both work in well-paying jobs
- Children
- Retirees

The common element among individuals in these "little-need-for-life-insurance" groups is that they have no one else who is dependent on their income. While the loss of a member of one of these groups is certainly a sad event, it normally will not create a financial burden for surviving family members or friends.

It is not unusual, however, to see advertisements by life insurance companies targeting sales at any of the above groups. These companies are in business, after all, to make a profit. However, it is important that consumers or any organization considering the purchase of life insurance be aware of the factors that really create a true need for life insurance so that they can make an informed decision of any insurance purchase.

So who *does* need life insurance? In general, the following could benefit from having a life insurance policy:

- Individuals who have others dependent on their income
- Individuals who have significant debt that would become the responsibility of others
- Businesses that depend on key people whose loss would mean a financial loss for the business
- Individuals for whom life insurance would favorably meet an estate planning or charitable giving objective

It is common for business partners to have life insurance to protect against financial loss. A death of a key employee can be detrimental to the business.

WHO NEEDS LIFE INSURANCE?

Scenario

Kerri and Paul are a married couple with two children in elementary school. They both have jobs, each contributing about half of the annual household income. They make monthly payments of $1,250 on their home mortgage.

Recommendation

Both Kerri and Paul should have an adequate amount of life insurance to cover the financial needs of their survivors.

Scenario

Lisa and Gabriela run a small business firm manufacturing parts for custom product builders. Their partnership has been in operation and successfully profitable for ten years, and they now employ 24 workers in the facility and have a sales staff of four. Lisa, who has a degree in engineering, designs the parts, and Gabriela takes care of managing the business.

Recommendation

Both Gabriela and Lisa appear to be important to the business. While either could probably be replaced after some time, the business would likely suffer through a transition period. Key person life insurance could help ease that burden.

Scenario

Carl is a single professional in his early thirties, making $140,000 per year. No one is dependent on Carl for income. Carl is free of financial obligations except for a $160,000 loan that he had to take out to cover some gambling losses he had during a spree last year. The bank required Carl to have a cosigner on the loan, and Carl's father agreed to cosign as long as Carl entered treatment for his gambling problem. Carl is participating in a treatment program at the local medical school.

Recommendation

Although no one is dependent on Carl for regular income, should Carl die, his father becomes liable for the balance of the $160,000 loan. Carl should purchase a policy to cover the loan and name his father as beneficiary.

For families, life insurance should be important for anyone who makes a significant contribution to the family's welfare, regardless of whether that contribution is monetary or in kind. We usually think of support in financial terms. For example, it is obvious that a family with three children would have a financial burden if the income-earner for the family were to pass away.

Note that it is important to consider that a parent who is not employed outside of the home can contribute just as much as an income-earner to the operation and lifestyle of a family. What would happen if a parent dies who

> ### LIFE INSURANCE FOR CHARITABLE GIVING
>
> Kevin has had a career as a successful mid-level supervisor at a small manufacturing company. Kevin, now 52 years old, is divorced and has two grown children. The manufacturing company job has provided steady income, and although Kevin is not wealthy, he will have a comfortable retirement. Kevin has recently become involved with the local food bank and often spends his Saturdays or evenings helping out at the warehouse. In addition, Kevin makes regular contributions to the food bank, but he would like to do more.
>
> One of Kevin's friends, who is a financial advisor, explains to Kevin how he can set up a future sizable gift to the food bank and at the same time take current tax deductions. Kevin purchases a $500,000 life insurance policy, names the food bank as beneficiary, and also makes the food bank the owner of the policy. Kevin's monthly premiums on the policy are $98, and he can deduct these payments from his taxable income for U.S. income tax purposes.

cares for three children, cooks most of the family's meals, and takes care of the household? It certainly would be an expensive proposition to hire a person (or persons) to assume those responsibilities. In other words, if anybody depends on you financially or otherwise, maintaining proper life insurance is very important.

Key person life insurance Life insurance policy on an important employee or owner of a business, and the business is the beneficiary.

Life insurance is also useful to protect a business against the loss of a key person with key person life insurance. For example, suppose two individuals own a small manufacturing business as a partnership. One is in charge of production and manufacturing, and the other takes care of sales and promotion. The business might purchase key person life insurance policies on each. In case of the death of either partner, the life insurance benefits could provide funding to help find and hire a replacement to keep the business going. Or, should it not be possible to continue the business, the life insurance could continue the living partner's income. Although businesses often use life insurance, this chapter focuses on the types of life insurance policies that individuals use to protect their families.

Sometimes life insurance can be helpful for charitable giving or for estate planning purposes even when there is no obvious financial need. For example, a person might want to leave sufficient funds in the event of death to pay a granddaughter's college tuition for four years. The granddaughter's parents are financially able to send the girl to college, so there is no financial need in this case. Life insurance would provide a way to ensure that the gift would be available in the future.

Life Insurers

Most life insurers fall into one of four different organizational types:

1. Stock life insurance companies
2. Mutual life insurance companies
3. Fraternal societies
4. U.S. federal government veterans and uniformed service life insurance

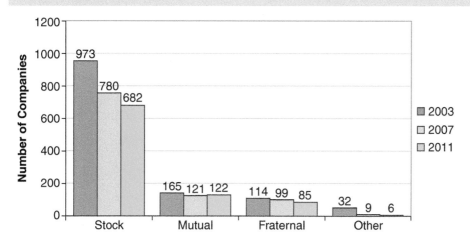

LIFE INSURANCE PROVIDERS IN THE UNITED STATES, 2002, 2007, AND 2011

EXHIBIT 9.2

Source: *Life Insurers Fact Book*, 2012.

The first three issuers in the above list are private organizations, while the last is a part of the federal government.

Stock life insurance companies issue shares of stock to represent their ownership and are therefore owned by their stockholders. Most life insurers in the United States are stock companies, as is evident in Exhibit 9.2, which shows the number of U.S. life insurers categorized by issuer type.

The policyholders in a mutual life insurance company are the owners of the company and share in any profits of the company. A mutual insurance company can legally own a stock company by owning all its stock, but that stock life insurance company then falls into the mutual category.

Fraternal societies also offer life insurance to their members. Fraternal societies are organizations whose membership is based on a common tie or pursuit of a common objective. They also must operate under the lodge system in which there is a parent organization and a number of subordinate lodges (usually the local branches). Examples of fraternal societies include the Knights of Columbus and the Freemasons.

Over the past several decades there has been a trend of consolidation in the life insurance industry. This trend is evident in the decline in the number of all of the types of private insurers from 2003 to 2011, as shown in Exhibit 9.2.

The U.S. federal government also serves as a life insurer by making insurance available under nine different programs. These programs provide life insurance for veterans and members of the uniformed services.

In 2007, As Exhibit 9.3 shows, these issuers combined had life insurance policies in force totaling $20.9 trillion in benefits. Stock companies accounted for 75 percent of that total.

To sell life insurance, a company must be licensed in the state in which the sale takes place. The states place certain regulations and requirements on life

Stock life insurance company A life insurance issuer owned by stockholders.

Mutual life insurance company Life insurance issuer owned by its policyholders.

Fraternal societies Organizations whose members have a common pursuit.

EXHIBIT 9.3	TOTAL LIFE INSURANCE IN FORCE IN THE UNITED STATES, 2007

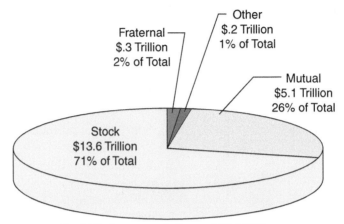

Total Life Insurance in Force: $19.2 Trillion

IS YOUR LIFE INSURANCE POLICY SOUND?

You trust your bank with your money, and if the bank becomes insolvent, the FDIC steps in with its insurance to keep depositors from losing money. What about your life insurance policy? Suppose you have taken care to pay the premiums on your permanent life insurance policy for many years, and your policy has built up a cash value of $50,000. How safe is your money.

Unlike bank accounts, there is no federally sponsored agency to guarantee the safety of the balance in a life insurance policy, or to guarantee the payment of a claim when that time arrives.

So, how do you know your money is safe if held in an insurance policy?

Fortunately there are third-party rating firms that assess the financial strength of life insurance companies and issue their opinions, or ratings, regarding the insurance companies' ability to pay off their policies. Some of the major insurance company rating firms and their rating scales are:

- A.M. Best   A++ (best) to F (worst)
- Moody's   Aaa (best) to C (worst)
- Fitch Ratings   AAA (best) to D (worst)
- Standard & Poor's AAA (best) to D (worst)

These companies analyze factors like the quality of the life insurance company's assets, the adequacy of its capital, and profitability to arrive at their rating.

Insurance policyholders and consumers wanting to know an insurance company's rating can consult publications from the ratings first available in most public libraries.

Most financial planners recommend a rating of at least A with A.M. Best, Aa2 with Moody's, or AA with Fitch or Standard & Poor's. Some of the more conservative planners recommend one notch higher on the rating scale.

insurance companies. The purpose of this licensing and the requirements is to make sure that life insurance companies meet a minimum level of financial health, and that they provide certain information to consumers about their business.

Even though the states do regulate life insurance companies, bankruptcies of life insurance companies occur from time to time. It is therefore advisable to check out the financial stability of any company from which you might be purchasing insurance. The A.M. Best Company is an independent firm that provides ratings of the financial condition of insurance companies. Other financial service rating firms, such as Standard & Poor's Corporation and Moody's, also rate insurance companies. Before purchasing any insurance policy, you should investigate the insurance company's financial position by accessing material from one of the rating firms at a local library or online.

BUY DIRECT OR FROM A SALES REPRESENTATIVE

Many life insurance companies employ sales personnel as their strategy for selling policies, while other companies sell directly to consumers. Companies that employ a sales force rely on the sales agents to generate sales by calling on prospects, which they do via a combination of efforts such as contacting people they know, cold calling (calling on people whom they do not know and asking for an appointment to make a sales presentation), and advertising.

Life insurance sales representatives collect their compensation by receiving a commission on every policy they sell, and they continue to receive a portion of the premium paid each year that the insured continues to pay the premiums. Companies that sell directly to consumers generate their sales leads through print and other media advertising and make their sales via the mail or Internet. When companies sell directly to policyholders, they avoid the costs of paying commissions to sales agents, so policies sold directly usually have lower premiums than comparable policies sold by sales representatives.

Independent insurance sales agent An insurance sales agent who represents more than one insurance company.

Dealing with Life Insurance Sales Representatives
There are two types of insurance salesperson:

1. Sales representatives employed by the company. Sales personnel who are employees of the insurance company and sell only policies issued by that company. These sales representatives are sometimes called "agents," although they are not truly agents in the strict definition of the word.
2. Independent insurance sales agents. Sales personnel who are independent agents, usually selling policies from more than one company. They may therefore offer their clients a wider selection of policies than an agent who represents only one company.

Life insurance sales personnel must be awarded a license from the state. License requirements obligate

An informed life insurance agent can assist you in choosing the best policy for your needs.

applicants to meet minimum levels of knowledge and competency regarding financial needs of clients and insurance.

There are some advantages of dealing with a sales representative or agent for making a life insurance decision. These advantages include the following:

- Life insurance is not an item that a person typically thinks about buying, so a salesperson can stimulate an interest in purchasing a policy that the insured needs.
- Life insurance representatives offer their assistance as trained professionals to suggest the type of policy and the amount of coverage that best fit the client's needs.
- Sales representatives and agents are usually available to personally assist in filing claims on a policy.

Life insurance sales people receive all or part of their compensation in the form of a commission on the policies they sell. The commission usually continues as long as the policyholder pays the premiums on the policy, although the commission paid on a given policy typically falls as the policy ages.

One problem with commissions is that they provide an incentive to sales personnel to act in their own interest rather than the interest of the client. Sales representatives' income increases as they sell more policies. So, commissions might encourage a sales person to sell a policy that the client may not need, or to sell an amount of insurance beyond what the purchaser needs.

Buying Directly

Purchasing insurance directly from the company can save a significant amount of money, but insurance buyers have to take the initiative themselves. They have to seek out the different companies and policies available and be willing to take the time to compare the alternatives. Because of the need to choose the best type of policy and optimal amount of coverage, insurance buyers also need to be familiar with the different types of life insurance coverage and to be able to estimate the amount of coverage needed. Fortunately, most direct-sale insurance sales literature and Internet sites publish guidelines for prospective policyholders to follow.

STRETCH
YOUR DOLLAR

TIPS ON SAVING MONEY WHEN BUYING LIFE INSURANCE

- Buy only the amount of insurance you need; consider all factors to estimate how much coverage you should have and avoid sales representatives who try to persuade you to purchase more.
- Shop around. There are many different insurers and representatives; the more quotes you obtain the more likely you are to save money.
- Stay healthy by maintaining a reasonable weight and avoiding use of tobacco products.
- Consider the benefits and costs of any additional riders recommended for your policy (such as adjustments for inflation) before agreeing to them.

HOW CAN I FIND THE BEST PRICES ON DIRECTLY SOLD LIFE INSURANCE?

With life insurance, shopping around for the best prices or service usually pays off. To find life insurance offers from companies selling directly to policyholders, the following sources are useful:

- Check out financial publications such as *Money* magazine for advertisements.
- Do an Internet search with the phrase "life insurance."
- Check out some of the Internet sites that compare different life insurance policies from different providers. Examples of such sites include www.IntelliQuote.com and www.SelectQuote.com.
- Ask friends if they have found reasonably priced life insurance directly from an insurance company.

There are some advantages of shopping to purchase life insurance directly from the company:

- Purchasing directly offers the ability to consider a wider range of different policies from different companies.
- Prices of policies sold directly to policyholders tend to be lower than prices of policies sold through agents.
- Prospective policyholders do not have to deal with a sales representative who may try to aggressively sell a policy, although careful selection of an agent can help avoid this problem.

How Much Life Insurance Coverage to Buy

"How much life insurance do I need?" The answer depends on the situation, but a general rule says that a person should have sufficient life insurance so that the earnings on the proceeds of the policy are similar to the person's current salary. For example, a person currently earning $50,000 per year should consider a life insurance policy whose proceeds would be able to generate about $50,000 in annual income. The proceeds of a $1 million life insurance policy in an account earning 5 percent simple interest would yield $50,000 per year income.

Taxes are an important consideration when planning for life insurance needs. The proceeds of a life insurance policy are generally exempt from income taxes to the beneficiary. However, income subsequently earned from those proceeds is taxable, so planning can be important.

Using the previous example, the person receiving $50,000 annually as earnings on the proceeds of the insurance policy would pay taxes each year on the $50,000 income. In many cases, beneficiaries have the option from the insurance company of receiving a payout over time (an annuity, or series of payments in the future) rather than a lump sum. For example, the insurance company may offer to pay $75,000 per year for the next 20 years (for a total of $1,500,000) instead of a lump-sum $1,000,000 payment at the death of the insured. In such a case, a portion of the $75,000 annual payment represents earnings or interest on the benefit and is taxable; the portion that represents the benefit only is nontaxable.

There are two common methods for estimating the amount of recommended life insurance coverage for an individual: the income method and the budget method.

INCOME METHOD

Income method (needs approach) A method of estimating life insurance needs applying a multiple to a person's annual earnings.

The income method (also known as the needs approach) is a useful technique that states that a person needs a certain multiple of his or her income in life insurance. Typical recommendations range from 10 to 20 times a person's annual salary in life insurance. Some quick mental math quickly reveals that a person earning $50,000 per year needs between $500,000 and $1,000,000 in life insurance. This may seem like very high and expensive coverage, but life insurance is very affordable for young, healthy people.

The income method gives a ballpark number for life insurance needs. It is not meant to provide an exact number, but it does give a quick and easy estimate. The income method provides a useful beginning basis that you can augment with further investigation and other methods of estimating insurance needs.

Exhibit 9.4 shows an example worksheet for applying the income method. It indicates that a 25-year-old should use an income multiplier of 15. If she were earning $38,000 per year, she should target a life insurance policy of about $570,000.

Budget method A method of calculating how much life insurance coverage a person needs by taking into account expected future income and expenses.

BUDGET METHOD

The budget method takes into account expected future household income and expense amounts to calculate any shortfall that a family might encounter

EXHIBIT 9.4	WORKSHEET FOR THE INCOME METHOD OF ESTIMATING RECOMMENDED LIFE INSURANCE COVERAGE

Age	Recommended Income Multiple
20–30	15x
31–40	15x
41–50	10x
51–60	7x
61–65	5x
66 or older	3x

1. Age of person seeking life insurance coverage   _____
2. Recommended multiple from table above   _____
3. Annual income   _____
4. Recommended amount of life insurance (multiply lines 2 and 3)   _____

without income from a wage earner. This approach should take into account the following questions:

1. **How much are expected household expenses?** Life insurance proceeds should cover living expenses for all dependents. The household budget is a good place to start and should show how much income is necessary to cover basic living requirements. It is important to account for the possibility of expenses increasing in the future. Increasing expenses are especially relevant for families with young children whose financial support needs will increase as they get older.

2. **Will another wage earner contribute to family income in the future?** If there is a family member who plans to continue or begin earning in the future, the income provided will reduce the need for life insurance coverage. However, it is important to consider that such employment probably creates a need for this other person to carry life insurance coverage.

3. **Are there any current debts or savings?** Anyone with debt that might fall on others to pay in case of death will probably want sufficient life insurance coverage to pay off those debts. On the other side, any savings or balances in investment accounts would reduce the need for life insurance.

4. **Are there any large extra expenses expected in the future?** Sometimes there are large extra expenses expected in the future. An example of such an expense would be college tuition for a child. If these expenses are present, extra life insurance to cover those expenses should be considered.

Exhibit 9.5 provides an example of the type of worksheet that is useful for applying the budget method. It shows some sample expense categories and

WORKSHEET FOR THE BUDGET METHOD OF ESTIMATING RECOMMENDED LIFE INSURANCE COVERAGE

EXHIBIT 9.5

Expense Description	Amount
Annual family expenses needed to cover normal living:	
1. Housing	$20,000
2. Food	10,000
3. Clothing	3,000
4. Transportation	5,000
5. Education	2,000
6. Other	5,000
7. Total (sum lines 2 to 6)	45,000
8. Rate of return on invested funds	0.05
9. Amount of life insurance needed to cover normal expenses (divide line 7 by line 8)	900,000
Other one-time anticipated expenses:	
10. College education expenses	80,000
11. Funeral expenses	10,000
12. Paying off debts	10,000
13. Total (sum lines 10 to 13)	100,000
14. Total recommended life insurance (add lines 9 and 13)	$1,000,000

numbers for an individual who would need about $1,000,000 in life insurance to cover the present and estimated future needs of survivors.

Forms of Life Insurance

Life insurance can take many forms, but all policies fall into one of two main categories:

1. Term life insurance
2. Permanent life insurance

Term life insurance is always cheaper than permanent life insurance. The decision of which type to purchase should consider all of the benefits and costs of the type of insurance under consideration, but the price advantage of term life insurance usually gives it quite an advantage over other types.

TERM LIFE INSURANCE

Term life insurance
Provides life insurance for a certain amount of years, usually ranging from ten to thirty years, at one constant premium.

Level term life insurance
Term life insurance with constant coverage amount over the life of the policy.

Term life insurance provides life insurance coverage for a certain number of years, usually 10–30 years. The amount of coverage remains fixed over the life of the policy, so this type of term policy is level term life insurance. If the insured person dies during this time period, the beneficiaries will receive the amount of coverage specified in the policy (sometimes called the face amount). Term is the most basic form of life insurance; its only purpose is to provide a financial benefit upon the death of the insured. If the insured policyholder survives the term of the policy, the policy expires with no benefit payable.

Term life insurance is the most cost-effective in terms of the amount of coverage that a dollar's worth of premium will buy. With term insurance, you select the term of the policy—how long the policy will provide coverage—and how long you will pay premiums.

What Will Term Insurance Cost?

Exhibit 9.6 shows some example annual premiums for different amounts of coverage of term life insurance. The actual premium that any one applicant for insurance will pay depends on the following factors:

- **Amount of coverage.** The greater coverage amount you want, the higher your premium will be. However, twice the coverage will cost less than twice the price. For example, a 25-year-old nonsmoking male 5 ft. 10 in. tall and weighing 175 lbs. would expect to pay about $17 per month for $500,000 of 10-year term life insurance (from Exhibit 9.6). A policy for $1,000,000 would cost $27 per month (not in Exhibit 9.6).
- **Length of term insurance.** Life insurance premiums depend on the probability that a person of a given age and health characteristics will die while the policy is in effect. Since it is more likely that someone will die within the next 20 years compared to only the next 10 years, a 20-year policy will have a higher premium. Exhibit 9.6 shows that the 25-year-old male's monthly premium would be $17 on a 10-year policy and $23 on a 20-year policy.

THE COST OF TERM LIFE INSURANCE

EXHIBIT 9.6

	Monthly Premium on a $500,000 Term Life Insurance Policy							
	Male (Height = 5′ 10″)				Female (Height = 5′ 5″)			
	Nonsmoker		Smoker		Nonsmoker		Smoker	
	Weight		Weight		Weight		Weight	
Age	175 lbs.	225 lbs	175 lbs	225 lbs	135 lbs	185 lbs	135 lbs.	185 lbs
10-year level term								
25	$17	$30	$52	$70	$14	$24	$40	$50
40	19	42	82	83	17	34	63	82
55	69	132	275	376	53	102	192	266
70	371	675	1218	1563	211	379	707	864
15-year level term								
25	20	37	63	81	17	30	47	59
40	22	53	99	100	21	35	79	103
55	93	185	386	462	60	127	259	332
70	579	1148	1750	2082	340	626	1076	1378
20-year level term								
25	23	44	72	89	20	34	53	63
40	32	63	127	128	27	52	102	122
55	122	245	484	598	89	162	327	403
70	850	1334	–	–	527	1002	–	–

Table contains average representative premiums. Quoted premiums for a given policy can vary significantly by company.

- **Current health situation.** Before issuing a life insurance policy, insurance companies usually require a medical exam to assess the applicant's current level of health. The extent of this exam will depend on the amount of coverage requested. A $1,000,000 policy will have a much more detailed exam than a $50,000 policy. Smoking, being overweight, having high cholesterol, and having a family history of medical problems are among the health-related factors that will increase life insurance premiums. The $23 monthly premium of the nonsmoking 25-year-old male compares to a monthly cost of $52 if he had been a smoker.
- **Age.** Other factors being equal, older individuals are more likely to die than younger individuals, so the older a person is when beginning a term life insurance policy, the higher the premiums will be. A 40-year-old nonsmoking female weighing 135 lbs. could expect to pay around $17 a month for a 15-year $500,000 policy (see Exhibit 9.6). Fifteen years later, when that policy expires, she would have to pay $53 per month for the same coverage.

- Gender. Since females live longer than males on average, they have lower life insurance premiums, all other factors being equal. From Exhibit 9.6, a 25-year-old male would pay $17, while a female receives the same coverage for $14.
- Special extra features of the policy. Life insurance policies may have options or a rider. A rider is an attachment to an insurance policy that adds or removes features of the policy. For example, a rider to a term policy might increase the benefit each year as a result of inflation. Options and riders can change the cost of insurance.

Rider An addendum to an insurance policy that changes the features of the policy.

Term Insurance Options

There are a number of options that term life insurance policies commonly offer. A basic term policy has duration of a fixed number of years and a level premium payment over those years.

A decreasing term policy reduces coverage as time passes. The reason for purchasing this type of policy would be in a situation in which the insured person's financial situation is likely to strengthen as the years pass and income and savings increase. A person typically will not need as much life insurance 10 years from now as today. The person will likely have more accumulated wealth by then—and, possibly, fewer dependents. With a decreasing term policy, the premiums stay the same during the life of the term, but the benefit decreases. The first year's premium on a decreasing term policy is less than that of a level term policy with the same amount of coverage.

Decreasing term policy A term insurance policy in which coverage decreases.

A renewable policy gives the holder the guarantee of being able to purchase a new life insurance policy after the current one expires. This new policy in the future may have a very different premium amount based the insured's age and health status at that time, but it is often comforting to an insured person to know that coverage is guaranteed in the future. The extension or renewal of the policy is optional for the insured person. A renewal feature increases the premium of a policy.

Renewable policy A term life insurance option that offers a guaranteed life insurance policy, albeit at higher premiums, after your current one expires.

A participating policy allows the insured to participate in surplus profits that the company makes. A well-run, profitable insurance company usually has extra profits left over at the end of the year after covering all death benefits to beneficiaries, administrative expenses, and a reserve account. These leftover funds are surplus, and each year the company pays a cash dividend from any surplus to policyholders who have participating policies.

Participating policy Policy that pays a dividend to its policyholder when the insurance company has a surplus.

A convertible policy offers the option of converting the policy to a different type of policy after it expires. Holders of convertible policies usually may convert their policy to some type of permanent life insurance that is covered in the next section. The premium under the new converted policy will likely be much higher than the earlier term insurance rate.

Convertible policy Provision that allows a term life insurance policy to be converted into some kind of whole life plan.

Individuals can often purchase group term insurance either from their employer or an organization to which they belong. This is regular term insurance, but it is sold to members of a defined group of people rather than to just one individual. Groups are often able to negotiate rates lower than an individual can obtain. Employers who offer group life insurance to their employees often pay a portion of the premium, so the cost of this coverage may be an even greater bargain to the employee.

Group term insurance Term insurance that is offered to individual members of a group.

PERMANENT LIFE INSURANCE

Whole life insurance provides insurance coverage for the insured person and in addition accumulates a cash value. Upon the death of the insured, the benefit payable is equal to the amount of insurance coverage plus the accumulated cash value of the policy.

The advantage that permanent life insurance carries is that it guarantees insurance coverage for a person. With term insurance, an insured person has to seek a new policy when a current policy expires. A person whose health has declined might not be able to purchase a new term life policy when an old one expires. In any case, the new policy will be much higher in cost than the previous policy because the insured will be older. Permanent life insurance provides insurance coverage over a person's whole life, so it is also often called permanent life insurance.

The premiums on permanent life insurance remain the same, so the insured has the protection of not having to worry about increased premiums in the future. With a whole life policy (also called straight life or ordinary life), the insured pays premiums over his or her life. With a paid-up 65 life insurance policy, policyholders pay premiums up to age 65, at which time they owe no more premiums, and the life insurance remains in effect for the rest of their life. Should the insured cease paying premiums on a permanent life policy, the insurance company will continue the coverage by reducing the cash value of the policy by the amount of the premium.

The cost of permanent life insurance is significantly greater than that of term life. Premiums are higher for two reasons:

1. Coverage continues on the insured as long as the premium payments are current. Coverage does not stop at some future date as with term policies.
2. A portion of the premium goes into an investment account that builds the cash value of the policy.

Whole (permanent) life insurance Permanent life insurance that accumulates a cash value and has a level premium. Also known as ordinary life insurance or straight life insurance.

Straight life insurance (ordinary life) Permanent life insurance that accumulates a cash value and has a level premium. Also known as whole life insurance or ordinary life insurance.

Paid-up 65 life insurance policy Life insurance with premiums paid up to the age 65 after which the life insurance continues in effect.

© kurhan, 2014, Shutterstock, Inc.

Permanent, or whole life insurance, covers the insured for the span of their life. The policy will pay out the amount of coverage plus any accumulated cash value upon the insured's death.

The cash value of whole life policies represents a benefit to policyholders by providing a loan source. Most policies allow the insured to borrow amounts up to the current cash value at a specified interest rate. This interest rate is usually well below market rates of interest that the policyholder would expect to pay on a loan from a bank or other source.

A whole life policy may also include a non-forfeiture clause. A non-forfeiture clause states that the cash value of the policy belongs to the policyholder. If the policyholder decides to cease making payments and cancel the policy, the insurance company will pay the cash value to the policyholder. An insurance policy with a non-forfeiture clause will have a higher premium than one without it.

Non-forfeiture clause
A provision in a whole life policy stating that the cash value in the account is owed the policyholder even if the policy is canceled.

PERMANENT LIFE VERSUS TERM LIFE

Insurance agents often aggressively sell permanent life insurance over term insurance because they receive a significantly greater commission for permanent life. For most permanent life policies, an individual would be much better off buying an equivalent term policy and investing the difference in premium amounts.

Instead of purchasing permanent life, most professional financial planners recommend obtaining a term life insurance policy and setting up a separate investment account to save the difference in the premium cost of the two policies. For example, suppose that the difference between a whole life and term insurance policy is $50 per month. A prospective policyholder should buy the term life insurance policy and then invest the $50 each month in an investment account. This investment account will build value faster than the comparable whole life policy will build its cash value. In addition, with the separate investment account, policyholders have complete control over the investment account compared to little or no control over the cash value of a whole life policy.

Permanent life insurance provides a mechanism for requiring the policyholder to save money since a portion of the premium is invested and becomes the cash value. People who have difficulty saving may find that permanent life insurance policies are a viable option for accomplishing a savings goal. However, the fact remains that a person who can buy term life and save the difference will normally end up with a greater cash savings amount than another person who buys any type of permanent life insurance. Of the amount of life insurance purchased in the United States in 2007, about 27 percent was permanent life insurance (see Exhibit 9.7).

VARIATIONS OF WHOLE LIFE INSURANCE

Because whole life policies are so much more expensive than term, insurance companies now offer some variations in order to help sell policies. Two of these types of policies are universal life insurance and variable life insurance.

Universal Life Insurance

Universal life insurance
A hybrid of a term insurance policy and whole life policy.

Universal life insurance is a hybrid of the term insurance policy and whole life policy. Premiums during the life of the policy may change over time, and a certain amount of each premium goes to cover term life insurance. The

INSURANCE PURCHASES IN THE UNITED STATES, 2011   EXHIBIT 9.7

Life Insurance Purchases by Plan Type

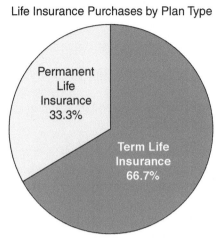

Permanent Life Insurance 33.3%

Term Life Insurance 66.7%

Life Insurance by Participating Status

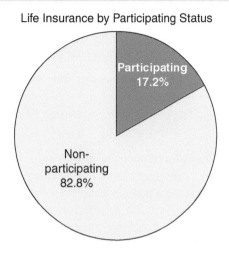

Participating 17.2%

Non-participating 82.8%

Source: Life Insurers Fact Book, 2012.

remainder is invested into a savings account. Depending on the policy, there may be different investment choices in which to invest this balance, such as stocks or high-yielding bonds.

Universal life policies vary from insurer to insurer, but a feature of these policies is that each provides policyholders with a separate accounting of the amount of premiums that go to pay for the insurance component of the policy, the charges made by the insurance company (commissions, fees, etc.), and the return on the investment portion of the policy. The rate of return is flexible and depends on the investments that the policyholder chooses to allocate to the policy. There is often a minimum guaranteed return for the policy, regardless of the performance of the investments.

Variable Life Insurance

Variable life insurance is a type of universal life that allows policyholders to make their own selections regarding investments. A regular universal life policy does offer some choice of investment alternatives, but a variable policy will allow more flexibility.

Variable life insurance A type of universal life that lets the policyholder make certain investment decisions.

Accidental Death Insurance

In addition to regular life insurance, which pays out a benefit no matter how the policyholder dies (except in case of suicide), there is also accidental death life insurance. This insurance only pays out a benefit if the cause of death is an accident. Accidental death insurance is attractive because the premiums are much lower than term life insurance. Although it is not a good idea to rely solely on accidental death insurance, it can be a nice supplement to regular life insurance, especially for young and healthy individuals who want to increase their coverage without raising premiums significantly.

Accidental death life insurance A special form of term life insurance in which the beneficiary receives payment only if the insured's death was the result of an accident.

Ways of Receiving a Life Insurance Settlement

There are two events that can cause the payment of a life insurance benefit:

1. The insured person dies, and the beneficiary receives the life insurance benefit.
2. The owner of a permanent life policy (normally the insured person) requests a withdrawal of a portion or all of the cash value.

Changes that occur in any policyholder's life can lead to the need to change the beneficiary or beneficiaries on a life insurance policy. Policyholders should always keep their beneficiaries current. For example, divorce may necessitate the change of a beneficiary from an ex-spouse to someone else.

Should an insurance policy pay a benefit, the recipient typically can choose one of two ways to receive the distribution:

1. A lump-sum distribution
2. An annuity or installment payments

LUMP-SUM DISTRIBUTION

Lump-sum distribution
Life insurance proceeds received in one payment.

With a lump-sum distribution, a beneficiary receives the entire benefit up front in one payment. This can be advantageous because it allows a beneficiary control over the investment of the proceeds of the life insurance. Investment in a portfolio of securities or mutual funds should allow the recipient to maximize investment income from the life insurance settlement. For example, a $750,000 distribution invested at a 10 percent return generates $75,000 per year in income. If this covers living expenses, then the principal balance of $750,000 will stay the same or even grow. Keep in mind that while the distribution is tax-free, the earnings received from investing it will be taxed for income tax purposes.

A lump-sum distribution normally makes the most sense from a financial standpoint. However, if a policyholder is unsure about a beneficiary's ability to handle responsibility investing and managing a lump sum, an installment payment might make more sense.

INSTALLMENT PAYMENTS

Installment payments
Life insurance proceeds received as an annuity.

With the installment payments plan, a beneficiary can choose to receive a series of future payments: an annuity. The number of payments will differ from plan to plan, but one usually has the option to receive a monthly payment for a few years up to 30 years. These payments are usually equal, but an option may be offered that allows payments to increase at the rate of inflation. When considering the purchase of life insurance, it is a good idea to find out the settlement payment options that are available to beneficiaries and, if possible, make sure that they are specified in the policy.

SUMMARY

Life insurance provides a payment to beneficiaries in the event of the insured person's death. Life insurance provides financial support to one's dependents and offers peace of mind about the future. Because consumers often purchase a life insurance product that does not fit their particular needs, knowledge of the different types of life insurance is very important.

The income method and the budget method are both good procedures for estimating the amount of life insurance coverage you need. The income method says that you should have a multiple of your salary—probably between 10 and 20 times—in life insurance. With the budget method, you estimate how much future income your dependents will need to cover future expenses (after considering your dependents' own future earnings) and purchase life insurance to provide that income. You need an adequate amount of life insurance to fill the gap between your dependents' future expenses and income.

There are two main types of life insurance—term and whole-life. Term life insurance is true life insurance, and provides a benefit in case of death during a certain time period. This type of insurance is probably the optimum selection for most households. Term insurance premiums are relatively low and depend on several factors:

- Amount of coverage
- Length of term policy
- Current health situation of the insured
- Insured's age
- Insured's gender

Accidental death life insurance is even cheaper than regular term insurance but only provides a benefit in the case of death by accident.

Permanent life insurance provides life insurance for as long as the policyholder continues to pay the premiums, and it includes a cash savings value that accumulates over time. The premiums for whole life insurance are much higher than for term life insurance. The problem with whole life insurance is that the fees are typically high and limited flexibility on the types of investments allowed often limits the return on the cash accumulation. Most individuals are probably better off purchasing a term insurance policy and investing a budgeted amount in a separate investment account.

Universal life and variable life are two variations of whole life that give policyholders more control of their savings and investments, but they still do not make financial sense for most consumers.

PROBLEMS

1. Manny is 31 years old and has decided to shop around for some life insurance. He wants to estimate the amount of coverage he needs based on both the income method and the budget method.

    Manny is married and has a 5-year old daughter. His annual salary is $65,000. First of all, he wants his life insurance to pay off the mortgage on his family's home. The remaining balance on their loan is $116,000. He analyzed his family's expenses and estimates that that his wife will need $25,000 per year in housing expenses (after the mortgage is paid off), food, transportation, and other expenses.

He also wants to have a college fund of $90,000 for his daughter, $20,000 to cover costs of his burial and legal fees, and an emergency fund of $50,000. He also would like a fund of $50,000 to help out his parents. He believes that his life insurance proceeds will yield 6 percent.

a. Using Exhibit 9.4 in the text, estimate the amount of life insurance coverage that Manny needs using the income method.
b. Using the budget method and Exhibit 9.5 as a guide, estimate the amount of life insurance that Manny needs.

CASE STUDIES

COLLEGE STUDENT

We've met Kevin before; below you will find a recap of his original financial information. If you have worked on this case study from the beginning of the book, use the current financial data you have for him. If you set goals for him to pay off his credit cards, he may now have a lower balance on them. If you haven't worked on this case study through the entire book, use the financial information below.

Kevin Maedor is a 19-year-old college student. He still lives at home with his parents, and he works part time at Vapor's Lane. He started his financial plan in the spring semester of 2014. He plans to graduate with a B.S. in engineering in May 2017. He has the following financial information:

- He brings home $760 a month from his job.
- He asks his parents for $50 cash a week.
- He has a Visa card with a balance of $1,700 and a MasterCard with a balance of $800. He makes the minimum monthly payment of $15.00 on each of them. His cell phone bill is $85 a month.

Answer the following questions for Kevin.

1. Does he need life insurance?
2. Which type of life insurance would you recommend for him?
   - Term Life
   - Whole Life
   - Universal Life
3. How much life insurance should he purchase?
4. Select his beneficiary(s).

NEW GRADUATE

We've met Rene before below you will find a recap of her original financial information. If you have worked on this case study from the beginning of the book, use the current financial data you have for her. If you set goals for her to pay off her debts, she may now have a lower balance on them. If you helped her purchase a home in Chapter 3, include her mortgage information. Don't forget any debt she acquired in Chapter 4. If you haven't worked on this case study through the entire book, use the financial information below.

Rene Harris recently graduated with a B.S. in nursing. She lives by herself in a modest apartment. Her annual salary is $76,000 a year. Rene loves to entertain, but her apartment is too small and the neighbors complain about the slightest noise. Rene is a good neighbor, so she has been going out with friends instead. She has the following financial information:

- She brings home $4,433.33 a month from her job.
- She used her new Visa last month for the first time and charged $600. She also opened a new Macy's charge and charged $762.78. She hasn't received her first bill for either of them; assume her minimum monthly payment will be $15.00 on each.
- She owes $30,000 in student loans and makes a monthly payment of $151.47.
- Her cell phone bill is $105.00 a month.
- She has $1,804.12 in her savings account.

Answer the following questions for Rene.

1. Does she need life insurance?
2. Which type of life insurance would you recommend for her?
   - Term Life
   - Whole Life
   - Universal Life
3. How much life insurance should she purchase?
4. Select her beneficiary(s).

CREATE YOUR OWN FINANCIAL PLAN

1. Do you need life insurance at this time?
2. Will your need for life insurance increase or decrease in the next stage of your life?
3. Which type of life insurance fits your needs?
   - Term life
   - Whole life
   - Universal life
4. Why did you select the type of life insurance you chose in 3? List the pros and cons you used to make your decision
5. How much life insurance should you purchase?
   - Consider others who are financial dependent on you.
   - Consider debt others are liable to pay.
   - Consider burial costs.
6. Who will you name as beneficiary(ies)?

MAKE IT PERSONAL

Preparing for your own death is a generous act. The loss of a loved one isn't compensated for with money. What other things can you do to ease the sorrow of your loved ones? What are your views of death? What would you like to leave behind? If you died suddenly tomorrow is there anything left unsaid in your life? Who will take care of your children? Who will take care of your pets?

The following are some additional items for you to consider. Take what applies and ignore what doesn't. This is a personal issue; how you prepare for it will reflect your own views on death.

1. Do you want to be kept on life support? Are there conditions that apply to this decision?
2. Do you want to donate any or all of your organs?
3. Do you want to leave a final letter, video, or personal message to anyone? Who will keep this message for you until the proper time? Do you want the message to be delivered at your funeral, upon your death, at some future date?
4. How do you want your remains handled? Do you want to be buried, cremated, or entombed?

There are no right or wrong answers to these questions. These are for your personal reflection. You should not feel obligated to share this with anyone else.

REVIEW QUESTIONS

1. Define life insurance.

   _____

   _____

   _____

2. Describe key person life insurance and relate a situation in which key person life insurance would be useful.

   _____

   _____

   _____

3. Identify sources that you might access to determine the financial soundner of a life insurance policy and explain the rating system they use.

   _____

   _____

   _____

4. Identify advantages of buying life insurance through an agent and advantages of buying it directly from the company.

   _____

   _____

   _____

5. Summarize the two methods of calculating how much life insurance coverage a person might need. Identify the more detailed and accurate way of calculating life insurance coverage needs.

   _____

   _____

   _____

6. "The goal of proper life insurance coverage is to be able to live off of the income derived from the principal of the policy." Interpret this statement and provide an example.

_____

_____

_____

7. Define term life insurance and list the variables that determine the cost of a person's policy.

_____

_____

_____

8. Describe several of the options you may get to choose from when choosing a term life policy. Which options are most important?

_____

_____

_____

9. Differentiate between a group term policy and an individual term policy.

_____

_____

_____

10. Define permanent life insurance and identify two different types of permanent life insurance policies.

_____

_____

_____

11. Contrast permanent and term life insurance policies.

_____

_____

_____

12. Explain the difference between participating and non-participating life insurance policies. Which type has higher premiums?

_____

_____

_____

13. Identify the two ways that life insurance beneficiaries can receive their settlement. What factors might make a person choose one method over the other?

_____

_____

_____

Entrepreneurship 10

"For every failure, there's an alternative course of action. You just have to find it. When you come to a roadblock, take a detour."

—Mary Kay Ash

OBJECTIVES

- Redefine the term *entrepreneur*
- Apply entrepreneurial characteristics to your career choice
- Describe the components of a business plan
- Discuss the importance of career choice
- Discuss the purpose and components of resumes and cover letters
- Explain when and how to ask for a sponsorship

KEY TERMS

Career test
Corporate sponsorship
Cover letter
Chronological resume
Endorsement

Entrepreneur
Entrepreneurial spirit
Executive summary
Functional resume
Income statement

Owner's equity
Private sponsorship
Sponsorship

Each semester more students ask if they can forgo writing a resume. They never intend to apply for a job; they each tell me a dream—some dream of owning a business; some want to develop a multimillion dollar conglomerate; others dream of a small boutique. Some dream of freelancing as photographers or writers. Some students dream of a bass fishing circuit or becoming a billiards champion or a rodeo cowboy. Yet most of my students still plan to enter the workforce as employees. Regardless of how you plan to earn your money, the first step to financial security is to earn a good living.

Entrepreneur Person who takes a vision and makes it a reality.

Entrepreneurs are people who take a vision and make it a reality. Entrepreneurship traditionally implies success in a business venture. We think of entrepreneurs as people who own and operate their own businesses. Let's expand our idea of an entrepreneur to include someone who makes a good income doing what they love. Most of us pick our career based predominantly on income. When we start out young and hungry, we need to meet our basic needs for shelter and food. We tend to think of our careers in the early stage of life strictly on a "how much can I earn" philosophy. After we have satisfied our needs for a safe place to live and we have enough money to eat something other than noodles, we realize how important personal satisfaction is in our careers. True success, however you define it, is always more than how much you earn. If you work 80 hours a week at a job you hate, it doesn't matter how much money you earn. You still won't feel successful. Success, like beauty, is in the eyes of the beholder; we each have our own definition of success. Finding the career that allows you to earn the income you desire while working at a task you find rewarding and satisfying takes careful consideration and planning.

The Entrepreneurial Spirit

Entrepreneurial spirit The drive behind a successful person.

The entrepreneurial spirit is the drive behind a successful person. It is often broken down into a set of characteristics. Many resources on entrepreneurship give a set of characteristics followed by a series of questions so you can assess your ability to be an entrepreneur. These are helpful, but they shouldn't be used to deter you. Everyone is born with a different set of talents. We all have natural strengths and weaknesses, but no one is born with a completely developed set of talents. We all must learn and develop our natural talents. We all have weak areas where we must struggle to gain proficiency. Successful entrepreneurs are people who developed these characteristics over time, and you can, too. Most entrepreneurs are:

- Passionate
- Persistent
- Adventurous
- Positive
- Self-aware
- Focused
- Flexible
- Honest

PASSIONATE

If you do what you love, the money will follow. Pursuing your own personal passion is critical to success. You don't want to just earn money, you want to enjoy life. When you are passionate about something, you bring all of yourself to the endeavor. You will naturally work longer when you are working on something you enjoy doing. If you love what you do, work is like play. If you love to fix cars, the choice to be a mechanic may be obvious. But what if you love to shop and the choice isn't so obvious? Jennifer Aniston's character on *Friends*, Rachel, had the same problem. She loved to shop and struggled to find a career in the early years of the sitcom. She did find her ideal job, and she didn't give up her passion for shopping. She became a buyer for a high-end fashion store. Success will come if you are passionate about what you are doing.

PERSISTENT

Persistence pays; don't give up. Many childhood stories teach the lesson of persistence. *The Little Engine That Could* tells the story of a small train engine that carries a heavy load up a hill by repeating the words "I think I can," "I think I can." We all experience setbacks; it is a normal part of life. Success comes with persistence.

ADVENTUROUS AND POSITIVE

Risk evokes ideas of fear; adventures evoke ideas of a journey. Both deal with the unknown. Entrepreneurs are willing to take risk; they are adventurous. When you are faced with a new opportunity, you can choose to focus on the fear of "what if," or you can choose to focus on the excitement of the challenge and the journey. The difference between being fearful and adventurous is a simple matter of how you look at new challenges. A positive outlook can be developed if you weren't born with one naturally.

SELF-AWARE, FOCUSED, AND FLEXIBLE

To develop new strengths, you need to know what your current limitations are. Self-awareness is an important part of being successful. Listening to yourself and trusting your instincts are part of self-awareness. Most successful people have learned to listen to their instincts. Self-awareness also contributes to the discovery of our passions. Self-awareness helps us to overcome our limitations. Take the time to reflect on your hopes, dreams, fears, strengths, and limitations. Once you know what you are passionate about, what strengths will help you achieve success with your passion, and what limitations will hold you back, it is easier to stay focused. Entrepreneurs are focused on the goal, and they are flexible enough to find new paths when they run into dead ends.

© Jarous, 2014, Shutterstock, Inc.

If you have a passion for rock climbing, what is one way you can turn that into a career?

HONEST

The last but certainly not the least characteristic of being an entrepreneur is honesty. Honesty develops trust. Great entrepreneurs surround themselves with good people. Success is built on relationships, and relationships are built on trust. Good relationships allow you to delegate tasks you are weak at to those who are talented in those areas.

BE THE ENTREPRENEUR OF YOUR LIFE

The entrepreneurial spirit will bring success in any endeavor. You can be the entrepreneur of your own life. How you put the entrepreneurial spirit to work in your life is up to you. If you dream of owning your own business, you need to learn about creating a business plan. If you dream of climbing to the top of the corporate ladder, you need to learn about employment trends. If your dream of being a star athlete, you need to learn about sponsorships. The rest of this chapter is broken into sections so you can focus on your area of interest.

Business Plans

If you want to finance your business venture, you will need a business plan. A business plan is used to obtain a loan. Even if you are lucky enough to have your own finances, you will still want to take the time to write a business plan. A good plan is the starting point for any new business. Here we will provide a general overview of a business plan. If you want more information, use the references we've provided through this text's accompanying web site. There are also courses you can take dedicated to the development of a business plan. Check with your college or university to see if it offers one. A business plan contains the following:

- Executive Summary
- Description
- Marketing
- Competition
- Development
- Management
- Finances

EXECUTIVE SUMMARY

Executive summary The first page of the business plan that clearly highlights all the important points of your entire plan.

The executive summary is the first page of the business plan, but it will be the last one you write. The executive summary should be one page or less. It clearly highlights all the important points of your entire plan. A potential partner or financial backer will typically decide whether he or she is interested from reading this one page. If he or she is interested, he or she will read the rest of your plan. This is the most important part of your plan since it is the first impression. The executive summary should summarize the business description, show how you will make a profit, and describe how the business will be funded and structured.

In the first paragraph describe the business. Clearly state what the business will provide, who the customers will be, and what makes this business competitive. Next, describe your business's financial information. What are your projected sales, profits, cash flows, and your return on investment? Follow the financial information with how your business will be funded. This is where you tell the reader how much of your own money you are investing and ask for how much you need. Include how your company will be structured. Will it be a sole proprietorship, a partnership, or a corporation? Include any additional information that is critical to the business; for example, do you have a patent or an exclusive contract?

DESCRIPTION

The description here will be longer than the description in the executive summary. Start with the industry your business is in. Is it food service or industrial manufacturing? Is this industry growing; is it expected to continue growing? What makes this a good industry to start a new business in for your location? Describe your business within the industry. What will you produce or provide and who are your customers? Include how your business will be structured; is it a corporation or a partnership? What gives your business a competitive edge? For example, you make and sell fresh ice cream in a boutique with a porch-like atmosphere; your competition sells prepackaged ice cream in a franchised store.

MARKETING

You can probably think of one or two great commercials. When you think of marketing, you may think of advertising, and that is one piece of a marketing plan. Although you will address advertising as part of the promotional aspect of your product, it is one of the last items in a marketing plan. A marketing plan requires you to study your competition and your customers. A careful analysis of your competition and future customers is called a market analysis. You will want to research the desires of the customers as well as the available services and products provided by your competition. Once you know your market, you will need to decide how you will distribute, price, and promote your product. There are an infinite number of combinations, and your marketing plan will depend a great deal on your product, business structure, the market, and your instincts. However, determining exactly how you will market your product in clear precise detail is essential to a good plan. Once you determine how you will market your product, you can project how much market share you can capture. Market share is the percentage of customers who use your product or service and will become your customers. This information is needed so you can project sales and profits. Your pricing strategy will also affect your projected profits.

COMPETITION

Who is your competition and how is your product or service better for the customer? This is the question you want to answer in this section of your business plan. Most of the groundwork for this section is accomplished in your marketing plan. This section compares your marketing strategy to your competition's marketing strategy. Clearly state your product, distribution, pricing, and/or promotion beats your competition's. Although it may seem redundant to you, it is important that you concisely spell out how your product or service provides your business with a competitive edge.

DEVELOPMENT

How will your business grow and change? What is your vision for the next year, the next five years? There are three main areas of development you will want to address:

- Product
- Market
- Business structure

Will you add or change your product? Do you plan on developing a new product? This can be as simple as adding new flavors to the menu of our ice cream boutique or as complex as developing a hybrid vehicle. If you plan to develop new products, you need to include the cost of product development in your financial plan. You will need to set clear goals with timelines and budgets for the new product.

If you develop a new product, you will also need to consider how to market the product and how your business structure will be changed by the addition of the new product. Will you need to add a new facility or hire new personnel?

Even if you don't intend to develop a new product in the next five years, you need to address how your business will grow. How will you develop new markets or new customers? Will you hire new employees? Once you decide how to grow your company, whether through new products, new marketing strategies, or additional locations, you need to budget for this growth. If you sell more ice cream, you will have to make more ice cream. Ingredients come with a cost, so it is important to plan for the development and growth of your business. The cost of making the ice cream is incurred before you can sell it. If you fail to plan for growth, your business will not be able to grow.

MANAGEMENT

Who will operate your business, how many employees do you need, and how much will it cost for day-to-day operations? These are the questions you want to answer in this section. You will want to detail your business operations here and the expenses associated with them. A large company would be divided into operational units such as:

- Customer service
- Marketing
- Product development
- Sales
- Administration

Will your business plan account for employees? To secure financing, make sure to incude resumes for any key personnel.

Within each unit you would list key personnel and develop spreadsheets for operating costs. For a small family-run business, you wouldn't need to break the business into operating units, since one or two people are likely to handle all aspects of the operation. You still need to develop operational costs for the business and break them into categories that make sense for you business. For our ice cream boutique example, we might want to break the operational costs into categories for

- Supplies
- Equipment
- Overhead

The supplies would include the ingredients to make the ice cream plus the cups, cones, dishes, spoons, napkins, and miscellaneous preparation items we would need to operate. Equipment would include freezers we need to buy to start our business, cash register, counters, tables, and chairs or stools, for example. Overhead would include rent and utilities. How you divide the operation costs depends greatly on how you operate your business, but it is important to carefully plan for all costs. For business plans intended to secure financing, you also want to include the names and resumes of the key personnel in this section.

FINANCES

The financial section of a business plan is comprised of three financial statements, each followed by a brief analysis. The three financial statements are remarkably similar to the three financial statements you developed in Chapter 1 for your personal financial plan. The main difference is a business plan includes an income statement instead of a budget. The three financial statements to include in your business plan are the balance sheet, the cash flow statement, and the income statement.

Balance Sheet

A balance sheet for a business is developed just like a personal balance sheet. It lists assets in the top section, liabilities in the middle section, and owner's equity at the bottom of the statement. Owner's equity is similar to net worth in a personal balance sheet. For a personal balance sheet we used the equation:

$$\text{Assets} - \text{liabilities} = \text{net worth}$$

The same equation is used in business but it is rearranged. First, let's substitute the business language of owner's equity for net worth:

$$\text{Assets} - \text{liabilities} = \text{owner's equity}$$

Now we have the same equation with business terminology, but for standard accounting practices the equation is rearranged so assets are on one side of the equation. Add liabilities to both sides of the equation and you get:

$$\text{Assets} = \text{liabilities} + \text{owner's equity}$$

For a business balance sheet use the equation in this form.

Owner's equity Net worth in a personal balance sheet.

Cash Flow Statement

The cash flow statement for business use is prepared like the cash flow statement for personal use. It shows the cash flow in and out for a given time period, typically a month. For a new business, a cash flow statement would be generated every month. The difference between the cash flow statement for personal and for business use is how you label your income and expenses. For a personal cash flow statement, you would list salary or wages; for a business cash flow statement, the most common income would be from sales. As a personal cash flow statement has multiple types of income—for example salary, alimony, interest income, or gifts—so a business cash flow statement has multiple types of income. Common types of income for a business are the following:

- Cash on hand
- Sales or service charges
- Receivables
- Interest from investments
- Cash received from the liquidation of assets

The cash flow statement for a business is used to determine if a business has enough cash to continue operations. Since it takes money to produce a product before it is sold, or it takes cash to pay salaries for employees who offer a service before the customer is charged, it is important for a business to maintain adequate operating capital to continue business. When investors look at a business's cash flow statement, they are assessing a company's ability to pay its bills and suppliers.

Cash outflows for a business will typically include any or all of the following:

- Supplies
- Labor
- Overhead

- Advertising
- Administration
- Professional services
- Loan payments
- Equipment
- Taxes

Like a personal cash flow statement, a business lists the actual income it received and the expenses it paid during the past month.

At the bottom of the cash flow statement the total expenses are subtracted from the total income.

$$\text{Income} - \text{expenses} = \text{current cash flow}$$

The current cash flow is carried over to the next month as cash on hand. This number can be positive or negative, just like a checkbook balance can be positive or negative. Although both are possible, a positive cash flow is preferred.

Income statement

The income statement is used to show a company's profitability. It is similar to the cash flow statement, because it lists both income and expenses; however, it is different from the cash flow statement because it includes deductions for tax purposes, and it includes taxes that have accrued but that have not yet been paid.

The income statement is written in the following pattern:

Revenue: Total income generated by the business

Cost of goods sold: Cost of materials or ingredients to produce a product or cost you paid for items you sold

Gross profit: Revenue minus cost of goods; for service industries, revenue equals gross profit

Operating expenses: Cost of labor and overhead to operate the business

Net profit: Gross profit minus operating expenses

Depreciation: The decrease in value of using a piece of equipment or building. These are known as capital assets. Depreciation is a deduction for tax purposes and an expenses that isn't true cash outlay

Interest: The interest cost for all debt

Net profit before taxes: Net profit minus depreciation and interest

Taxes: All taxes levied against the business

Profit after taxes: Net profit before taxes minus taxes; this is a company's bottom line

Income statement Financial statement reporting a company's profits.

Income statement A financial statement used to show a company's profitability.

A well-written business plan takes a substantial amount of time to write. It involves researching the market and projecting future sales. A good business plan is crucial to the success of a business. Most startup business failures happen in the first five years, and they fail because they did not have enough money to continue to operate. A good plan will project future operating costs and sales, which will allow you to determine whether you have enough capital to get the business off the ground in those early lean years. A business plan can be either formal or informal. A formal plan is used to obtain financing and is an external document. It often includes color graphics and charts and is bound and printed professionally. An informal business plan is an internal document, and although the aesthetics of the informal plan are less important, the details of an informal plan are as important, if not more important. Your business plan maps out how you will use your resources to generate a profit.

Corporate World

If you want to use your entrepreneurial spirit in the corporate world, you'll need to decide on a career path. When considering a career path, you should not make your decision based solely on income; also consider your life style and passions.

Two main factors influence earning potential in the corporate world:

1. Level of education
2. Choice of career

A direct correlation exists between higher education and higher earnings. Exhibit 10.1 shows the average annual earnings by education level for the U.S. population. The income differences are striking. A person who graduates from high school makes on average $27,280, 45 percent more than someone who doesn't have a high school diploma. A bachelor's degree increases the average income to $51,194, an additional 88 percent over a high school graduate.

The second factor that affects a person's capacity to earn income is career choice. Of course, since many careers require a minimum level of education, your career choices are limited or enhanced by your education. Exhibit 10.2 shows the highest and lowest paying occupations by education and training.

EXHIBIT 10.1	AVERAGE ANNUAL EARNINGS BY DEGREE LEVEL ($1,000)

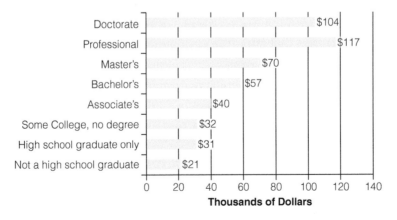

Data compiled from U.S. Census Bureau, Current Population Survey.

HIGHEST AND LOWEST PAYING OCCUPATIONS BY EDUCATION AND TRAINING CATEGORY, MAY 2007

EXHIBIT 10.2

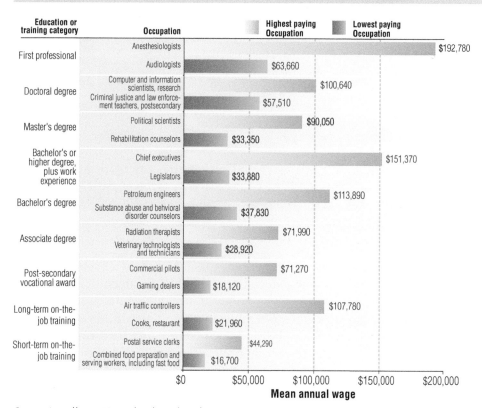

Source: http://www.bls.gov/oes/2007/may/figure9.pdf

Naturally, occupations that require higher levels of education in general pay higher salaries. However, this is not always the case. Notice the highest paid profession for long-term on-the-job training is an air traffic controller, and the pay is higher than the highest paid occupation that requires a master's degree.

LIFESTYLE

Do you want to live in the country or the city? Do you prefer to travel or stay close to home? The variety of occupations available in the city is far greater than those available in rural communities. Engineers and corporate buyers have more opportunities to travel on a business expense account than mechanics and elementary school teachers. Your career should enhance your life, not rule it, so make sure your career choice fits well with your lifestyle.

PASSIONS

What are you passionate about? When you incorporate your passions into your career choices, you are more likely to enjoy your job. Ask yourself, "What

What would you do with your life if money were not an issue?

would you do all day if money was not an issue?" Take your answer to the previous question and ask how you can turn that into a career.

If you aren't sure what you want to do for a living, you aren't alone. The average American changes careers completely three times in his or her adult life. We grow and change through life. Take a chance and try a career; if you don't like it you can always try another one. Many college degrees will open more than one door.

CAREER TESTING

If you need help deciding which career to pursue, take a few career tests. Most colleges and universities offer free career tests through their career placement or student services. You can also take free career tests online. Career tests ask you a series of questions about your preferences between specific tasks. For example:

Which of the following would you prefer the most? Which would your least enjoy doing?

- Bake a cake
- Mow the yard
- Read a book

Career test Tests that ask you a series of questions about your preferences between specific tasks. They use your interests to suggest appropriate careers that would utilize those interests.

Your answers are compared against required skills sets for occupations, and you are given a report that tells you which careers are best suited to your interests. When taking career tests, remember they are designed to be a guide, not a definitive answer. Take several and compare the suggestions against your own list of ideas. To help you get started try a few of these web sites:

http://www.livecareer.com
http://www.careerexplorer.net
http://www.careerplanner.com
http://www.questcareer.com

Resumes and Cover Letters

Your resume and cover letter introduce you to a prospective employer. Its appearance is a direct reflection on you. You would carefully consider what to wear and how you wanted to present yourself for an interview. The same is true for you first introduction through your resume and cover letter. You want it to be neat, free of errors, and organized to present you in the best possible light. Here we will provide a brief summary of what is included in a resume and cover letter. For more detailed guidance to write your own, please visit the companion web site for this text. There you will find links to web sites with detailed resume and cover letter writing information.

RESUMES

A resume summarizes your skills, education and work experience. The most common format for a resume is chronological. A chronological resume lists your information from most recent to the oldest. A functional resume does not use chronological order; it highlights specific skills aimed at a specific occupation. Functional resumes are often used to draw attention away from large gaps in work history. This is not necessary for new college graduates, since most employers expect new graduates to have limited work history directly related to their new degree. A functional resume is also a good choice for a major career change. It allows you to highlight skills from the former occupation to emphasize their fit in the new occupation. You can also include a section on work history to demonstrate you are not using the format to hide a gap in work history.

> **Chronological resume** Lists your information from most recent to the oldest.

> **Functional resume** Resume that does not use chronological order; it highlights specific skills aimed at a specific occupation.

The standard chronological resume for a new graduate includes the following:

1. Personal Information: name, address, contact information
2. Objective: specific objective you hope to achieve with this resume
3. Education: degrees earned, course of study, university name and address, graduation date
4. Employment: job title, company information, hire and leave dates
5. Other: affiliations, organizations, awards, certifications, special training, or any other information to showcase your qualifications

Once you acquire some work experience directly related to your degree, you would list employment above the education. You always want to show the most current information first.

COVER LETTERS

A cover letter is your resume's introduction; it states which position you wish to apply for, tells how you fit the position, and asks for an interview. A cover letter is brief, but clearly identifies which position you wish to apply for in the opening. In the body of the cover letter you can expand on your qualifications to show how you would benefit the company if you were hired. Here you can tell more about an award you won or why you chose the field of study you did. You also

> **Cover letter** A resume's introduction; it states which position you wish to apply for, tells how you fit the position, and asks for an interview.

want to tell the company specifically why you are interested. You will need to research the company if you want to make your cover letter shine. Knowing more about a company improves your chance of correctly stating why it is a great company to work for. How do its objectives and goals align with yours? In the last paragraph you want to specifically ask for an interview and thank the reader for his or her consideration. Include specific information on how to contact you.

STRETCH
YOUR DOLLAR

PURSUE YOUR PASSION

Select a career to allow you to pursue a passion of yours. When your job aligns with your interest, you naturally work longer and make more money.

Sponsorships

If you answered the question in the previous section, "What would you do all day if money wasn't an issue?" with an answer like fish or play pool, you may need a sponsor. You could turn those answers into careers, such as becoming a mechanical engineer and designing better pool cues. If you want to fish, you could become a marine biologist. But if you consider your answer and decide you want to play pool or participate in bass tournaments for a living, then sponsorships are a great way to increase your income.

For athletes who participate in sports that don't pay substantial salaries, sponsorships provide money for their training, travel, and living expenses. Sponsorships come in a variety of sizes. They can be as small as a single entry fee for a single event or as large as a good annual salary. Sponsorships are typically either private or corporate.

If your passion is to compete for a living, it may be possible to obtain a sponsorship.

Private sponsorships include financial support from family, friends, and fans. They typically are provided without a business agreement. The sponsor provides financial backing for pleasure of participating in the athlete's success. There are some wealthy individuals who follow sports who have provided substantial financial support to athletes. The athletes who receive these types of sponsorships are usually approached by the fan.

Corporate sponsorships come in one of two forms: sponsorships and endorsement contracts. Both are business arrangements where the athlete receives funds, and the business receives advertisement. In a sponsorship the advertisement comes in the form of the athlete's displaying the business's name or logo on the equipment, gear, or clothing. With endorsement contracts the athlete actually participates in ad campaigns in commercials, print advertising, or even product packaging. Wheaties is famous for the athletes it puts on its boxes. Endorsement contracts are more prestigious and lucrative, and they are typically offered to the top athletes in any given sport.

So if you are just starting out, how do you obtain sponsorships? Start close to home. Ask local businesses you frequent if they would like to sponsor you. Offer to wear their logo and name when you participate in the event. You can start small and ask them to sponsor one event, for example, one bass tournament. Plan ahead and have a list of tournaments you would like to participate in, make a chart with the tournament names, dates, locations, entry fees, travel expenses, and any other pertinent costs. Make a list of companies that sell goods related to your sport. For example if you play pool, which brand of pool cue do you use? Which brand of pool cue do you wish you could afford? What companies supply chalk, pool balls, and pool tables? Research the companies on your list so you have a clear understanding of what each company offers and what its business philosophy is. Then write each one a letter asking them for a sponsorship. Sponsorship letters are similar to resumes. They should be brief, clear, and concise. They should start with an introductory sentence that asks for what you want, a sponsorship. Next tell them what you can offer them—for example, you will wear their logo at the following tournaments. In the second paragraph list your accomplishment in the sport. For example, you have participated in 14 tournaments this year, won seven first-place trophies and two second-place trophies. The third paragraph should include your contact information. Close the letter politely.

Private sponsorship Financial support from family, friends and fans.

Corporate sponsorship Business arrangement where an athlete receives funds and the business receives advertisement.

Sponsorship Money provided for education, travel, and living expenses for students, often athletes.

Endorsement A type of corporate sponsorship where the athlete actually participates in ad campaigns.

SUMMARY

Entrepreneurs are people who take a vision and make it a reality. We tend to think of our careers from a "how much can I earn" viewpoint. True success, however you define it, is always more than how much you earn. Finding the career that allows you to earn the income you desire while working at a task you find rewarding and satisfying takes careful consideration and planning. The entrepreneurial spirit is the drive behind a successful person. Entrepreneurs possess the following characteristics:

- Passion
- Persistence
- Adventurousness
- Positive outlook
- Self-awareness
- Focus
- Flexibility
- Honesty

The entrepreneurial spirit will bring success in any endeavor. You can be the entrepreneur of your own life. How you put the entrepreneurial spirit to work in your life is up to you. If you dream of owning your own business, you need to learn about creating a business plan. If you dream of climbing to the top of the corporate ladder, you need to learn about employment trends. If you dream of being a star athlete, you need to learn about sponsorships.

If you want to finance your business venture, you will need a business plan. A business plan is used to obtain a loan. Even if you are lucky enough to have your own finances, you will still want to take the time to write a business plan. A good plan is the starting point for any new business. Business plans contain the following sections:

- Executive summary
- Description
- Marketing
- Competition
- Development
- Management
- Finances

If you intend to enter the corporate world, you need to select a career to fit your lifestyle and passions. Career tests are useful tools to help you research career options to match your interest. The first introduction to an employer is usually made through your cover letter and resume. They should be well written to represent you in the best possible light.

If you are more interested in a sport or freelance activity as a profession, sponsorship can bridge the income gap. There are both private and corporate sponsorships available to help you pay for expenses, travel, and fees related to you activity. A sponsorship letter is similar to a cover letter, but written with a different request. Instead of requesting an interview you request a sponsorship.

CASE STUDIES

COLLEGE STUDENT

If Kevin Maedor wants to work in the corporate world as an engineer, what should he do to prepare?

1. Which documents does he need to write?
2. As a new graduate, which type of resume should he use?
3. Draft an outline of a resume for him with headings in the proper order for his stage in his career.

NEW GRADUATE

Rene Harris would like to apply for a nursing position at a clinic.

1. Which documents does she need to write?
2. Which type of resume should she use?
3. Draft an outline of a resume for her with headings in the proper order for her stage in her career.

CREATE YOUR OWN FINANCIAL PLAN

1. What are your passions in life?
2. How can you use your passions as a part of your career?
3. Depending on your answers, use the web site for this text and explore the tools to help you write a business plan, write a cover letter and resume, or write sponsorship requests.
4. Break you career goal into smaller steps, make each step a SMART goal.

REVIEW QUESTIONS   CHAPTER 10

1. What is an entrepreneur?

   _____

   _____

   _____

2. What is the entrepreneurial spirit?

   _____

   _____

   _____

3. What are the common characteristics of an entrepreneur?

   _____

   _____

   _____

4. If you weren't born with all the strengths of an entrepreneur, does that mean you won't be a success?

   _____

   _____

   _____

5. What are the main components of a business plan?

   _____

   _____

   _____

6. If a new owner has personal finances to cover the costs of operating a business does she still need a business plan? Why or why not?

_____

_____

_____

7. What serves as your first introduction to an employer?

_____

_____

_____

8. What factors should you consider when you select your career?

_____

_____

_____

9. Who would want to apply for a sponsorship?

_____

_____

_____

10. What is the main difference between a corporate sponsorship and an endorsement contract?

_____

_____

_____

Investing

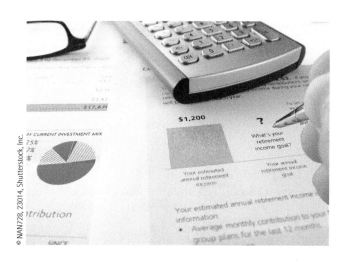

"The question isn't at what age I want to retire, it's at what income."

—George Foreman (1949–)

OBJECTIVES

- Describe the main vehicles for saving and investing.
- Define the types of financial institutions and describe how each is useful for saving and investing money.
- Summarize the key elements in an investment program.
- Compute holding period return on investment.
- Define risk and expected return and explain the relationship between the two.
- Analyze methods for holding cash in money market investments.

KEY TERMS

Asset allocation decision
Bond
Cash
Cash equivalent
Certificate of deposit
Commercial bank
Commercial paper
Commission-based investment advisor
Credit union
Depositary financial institution
Equity
Expected return
Fee-based investment advisor

Finance company
Financial institution
Financial intermediary
Financial intermediation
Interest-bearing checking account
Investment bank
Investment monitoring
Marketable securities
Money market mutual fund
Money market security
Mutual fund
Negotiable certificate of deposit
Non-depositary financial institution

Pension fund
Precautionary motive
Real estate investment trust (REIT)
Retirement funds
Risk
Riskless investment
Risky investment
Securities brokerage firm
Securities firm
Security
Speculative motive
Transactions motive
U.S. Treasury bill

A successful investing program is essential to your financial well-being. There are a large number of possible investments, and there is certainly no end of people wanting to advise you on where, when, and how to invest your money. Of course, those people usually have a financial product to sell you or want to earn a commission on your investment. That does not mean that you should avoid them; it simply means that in today's world, you need to have some level of financial education in order to survive.

While you do not necessarily have to know how to select the best investments for you and your family, you should know enough to be able to:

- Distinguish the pros and cons of different types of alternative investments.
- Select an appropriate investment advisor or manager should you decide not to make investment decisions yourself.

Saving and Successful Investment

One of the important building blocks for achieving financial goals is saving a part of your income and successfully investing it. Successful investing means choosing the investments that are appropriate for you and that will yield you an optimum rate of return for your ability to accept risk. The rate of savings in the United States is not high. According to a recent survey, only 52 percent of all U.S. families saved any portion of their income in 2010. Exhibit 11.1

EXHIBIT 11.1	PERCENTAGE OF FAMILIES WHO SAVED DURING THE PREVIOUS YEAR BY INCOME, 2010

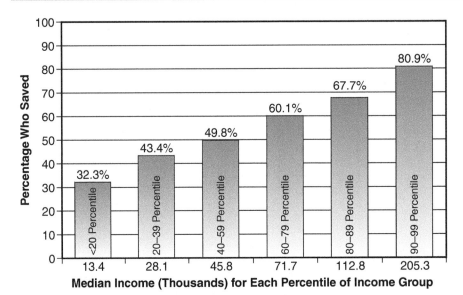

Source: Jesse Bricker, Arthur B. Kennickell, Kevin B. Moore, and John Sabelhaus, "Changes in U.S. Family Finances from 2007 to 2010: Evidence from the Survey of Consumer Finances," *Federal Reserve Bulletin* (June 2012).

presents this data broken down by income percentile. For example, 49.8 percent of families with incomes in the fortieth to fifty-ninth percentiles saved at least some money. This group had a median family income of $47,300 per year. Even 19.1 percent of the families with the highest incomes (the top 10 percent, with a median income of $205,300) were unable to save any of their earnings.

Individuals with higher levels of education tend to save more, but the relationship is not as strong as it is with income and saving. Exhibit 11.2 shows the percentage of people who save by education level. In general, the higher the education level, the more likely that a person added to their savings. The exception is the group with "some college," which is less likely to save than the "high school diploma" group. While this might seem contradictory at first glance, it is not so surprising since most of those in the "some college" group are still in school and less likely to be able to add to their savings.

People save for a variety of reasons, chief among them:

- Planning for retirement
- Providing liquidity and an emergency fund for the family
- Preparing for education
- Saving for major purchases such as a home

Exhibit 11.3 shows survey responses given by individuals when asked why they save. Note the percentage of families who saved fell in all categories from 2007 to 2010.

PERCENTAGE OF FAMILIES WHO SAVED DURING THE PREVIOUS YEAR BY EDUCATION, 2007 AND 2010   EXHIBIT 11.2

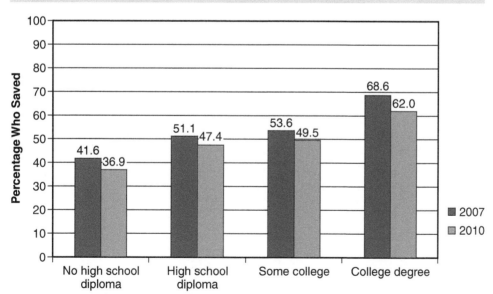

Source: Jesse Bricker, Arthur B. Kennickell, Kevin B. Moore, and John Sabelhaus, "Changes in U.S. Family Finances from 2007 to 2010: Evidence from the Survey of Consumer Finances," *Federal Reserve Bulletin* (June 2012).

EXHIBIT 11.3	REASONS PEOPLE SAVE

Responses indicating the most important reason for their family's saving

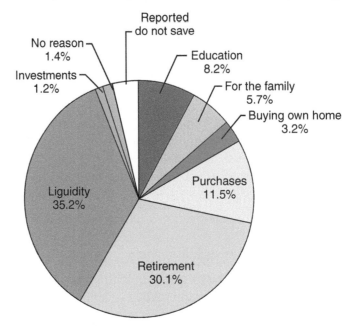

Source: Jesse Bricker, Arthur B. Kennickell, Kevin B. Moore, and John Sabelhaus, "Changes in U.S. Family Finances from 2007 to 2010: Evidence from the Survey of Consumer Finances," *Federal Reserve Bulletin* (June 2012).

Vehicles for Saving and Investing

Financial institution A business that accepts funds from investors and provides these funds to users of capital.

There are many types of vehicles for saving and investing your money. Each has pros and cons for the individual investor. There are two principal avenues for investing: You can invest your money directly with the party that plans to use it, or you can place your money with an institution that will then invest your money for you. Businesses and other organizations that deal in money and securities rather than goods and services are called financial institutions.

Financial intermediaries Any financial institution that collects funds from investors and supplies these funds to businesses and other entities (e.g., a government) that need funds.

INVESTING THROUGH FINANCIAL INSTITUTIONS

Most financial institutions are also financial intermediaries. Financial intermediaries perform a very valuable function in the economy. They accept funds and channel them to the users of these funds in a process called financial intermediation.

Financial intermediation The process by financial institutions of acquiring funds and channeling them to users of funds.

Financial intermediation is important to the smooth functioning of an economy because it facilitates the accumulation of capital and allows this capital to be put to productive use. Exhibit 11.4 provides an illustration of financial intermediation. Investors who have funds to invest do not want their money lying idle; they want it to earn a return.

Investors have a choice. They can invest their money directly in a business—for example, by buying and operating a business. But not everyone wants to own a business, much less have the problems of operating one. Many investors take the easier route. They go to a financial institution and invest their money. The financial institution collects funds from a number of investors and then makes these funds available to businesses and others who need funds. For example, the institution may lend the money to a business at some specific interest rate. Or the institution might purchase part ownership in the business. In any case, funds flow from investors to users of capital, as Exhibit 11.4 illustrates.

This process is very important in developed economies. It makes investing easier for those who have excess funds, and it makes obtaining funds easier for those who need funds and can use them in a productive fashion, such as to build a new factory that will employ more workers. Financial intermediation thus facilitates employment and economic growth.

Financial institutions are generally of the depositary type or the non-depositary type. Depositary financial institutions get their funds by accepting deposits from customers. Non-depositary financial institutions raise funds through other means such as selling stocks to investors or selling insurance policies.

Depositary financial institution Raises funds by accepting deposits from customers.

Non-depositary financial institution Obtains funds by methods other than accepting deposits.

The major types of financial institutions are as follows:

- Commercial banks
- Savings institutions
- Credit unions
- Finance companies
- Securities firms
- Mutual funds
- Pension funds
- Insurance companies

Of this group, the first three are depositary institutions; the remaining are non-depositary.

FINANCIAL INTERMEDIATION: FLOW OF FUNDS FROM INVESTORS TO USERS OF CAPITAL THROUGH FINANCIAL INSTITUTIONS

EXHIBIT 11.4

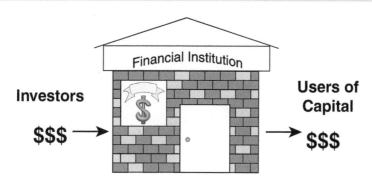

Commercial Banks

Commercial bank A financial institution that accepts deposits and makes loans.

Commercial banks are financial institutions that accept deposits and make loans. In order to make loans, banks need to have sources of funds. The most important source of funds for banks is deposits. Banks attract deposits by offering to pay interest to depositors on their deposits or by offering them some other type of financial service such as checking accounts. The checking, debit card, and savings accounts that most people and businesses have add up to billions of dollars in deposits at commercial banks. Banks have to keep some of these deposits in cash and ready for withdrawal at the Federal Reserve Bank, but they make loans with a large portion of those deposits.

Exhibit 11.5 shows the breakdown of the various sources of funds in commercial banks in the United States. The greatest portion of funds in commercial banks (70 percent) is from deposits. Banks borrow from other sources another 11 percent of their funds.

EXHIBIT 11.5	SOURCES AND USES OF FUNDS FOR U.S. COMMERCIAL BANKS, 2013

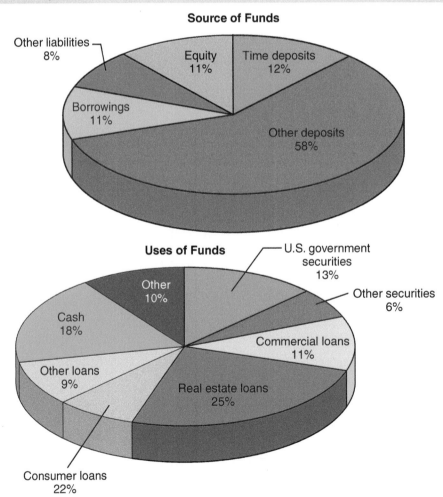

Source: Board of Governors of the Federal Reserve System, Assets and Liabilities of Commercial Banks in the United States, Weekly Report October 4, 2013.

The owners of the banks have put up 11 percent of the funds that banks have available. The slice in the "Sources" section of Exhibit 11.5 labeled equity represents the owners' interests in the banks. Equity is the funds that owners have invested in their business. The equity that owners have in a business can represent funds they originally invested to set up the business, additional capital they may have contributed as needed since beginning the business, and any profits the business made and then retained in the business (instead of distributing it to the owners).

Banks also supply funds to businesses and to individuals by making loans. They make a number of different types of loans as Exhibit 11.5 shows. The largest portion of loans (25 percent) goes to finance real estate purchases. Loans to consumers take 8 percent of bank funds, and commercial loans occupy another 11 percent.

Equity Funds that owners have invested in their business.

Savings Institutions

Savings institutions such as savings and loan associations or mutual savings banks attract deposits and make loans. In today's economy, there is not much difference between the basic services offered by commercial banks and these savings institutions. In past years, savings institutions generally only offered savings accounts and made mortgage loans to finance housing purchases, but changes in the laws and regulations affecting savings institutions and banks since about 1980 have virtually eliminated those differences.

Credit Unions

Credit unions are financial institutions that are owned by their member-depositors. They accept deposits and make loans to their members. The original idea behind credit unions was to facilitate the availability of credit and loans

Credit union A financial institution that is owned by its members. Members finance the credit union by making deposits, and the credit union extends loans to its members.

STRETCH
YOUR DOLLAR

CREDIT UNIONS CAN BE A SMART CHOICE
FOR CONSUMERS

It pays to shop around for financial services. Credit unions are very consumer-oriented and often offer individuals lower rates on loan and higher rates on savings accounts than do commercial banks.

Comparison of Average Rates Offered by Credit Unions and Banks, December 2008:

Product	Credit Unions	Banks
5-year $10,000 certificate of deposit	3.81%	3.12%
30-year fixed rate home loan	5.44%	5.58%
48-month new car loan	5.46%	6.91%

That difference between the credit union and bank interest rates on a 30-year home loan may look small (only 0.14%). But over the life of the loan, you would pay the bank a total of $3,162 more in interest charges than you would the credit union.

Source: National Credit Union Administration.

---

to individuals during a time (early to mid-1900s) when banks often ignored the interests of small depositors and offered them few opportunities to borrow money. Although today's banks are very consumer-oriented and offer services to all individuals, credit unions do continue to thrive in a competitive environment. At the beginning of 2006, U.S. credit unions had total deposits of more than $575 billion and loans of more than $450 billion. Credit unions are typically small institutions serving a relatively small number of individuals when compared to banks. For example, as illustrated in Exhibit 11.6, almost

EXHIBIT 11.6	NUMBER OF FINANCIAL INSTITUTIONS AND THEIR TOTAL ASSETS IN THE UNITED STATES, 2007

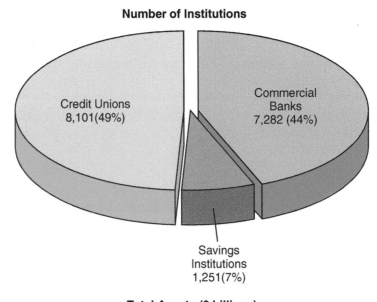

Number of Institutions

Credit Unions
8,101(49%)

Commercial Banks
7,282 (44%)

Savings Institutions
1,251(7%)

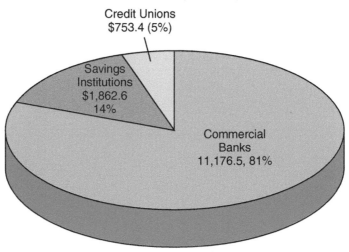

Total Assets ($ billions)

Credit Unions
$753.4 (5%)

Savings Institutions
$1,862.6
14%

Commercial Banks
11,176.5, 81%

Source: Statistical Abstract of the United States, 2009.

than half (49 percent) of the depository institutions in the United States are credit unions, but they have a relatively small percentage of assets (5% percent).

Credit unions often offer their members advantages over terms that they might receive for financial products from a bank. For example, a credit union might offer automobile loans at a lower interest rate and more favorable terms (such as no penalty for early repayment) than a bank. Credit unions often also pay higher interest rates on savings accounts.

Finance Companies

A finance company is a financial service firm that extends credit and makes loans to customers. However, unlike banks, savings institutions, and credit unions, finance companies do not receive their funds by taking deposits. Instead, they borrow funds from other sources. Sometimes they borrow from banks, but more often they borrow directly from investors.

Securities Firms

A security is a financial instrument that provides evidence of some claim representing a financial interest. Securities might be evidence of ownership of part of a business or of debt, an amount that the business owes the holder of the security.

Securities firms sell securities to investors. Securities firms can be securities brokerage firms that transact securities from one investor to another. In this case, the firm serves as an agent in the transaction. Securities firms can also be investment banks. An investment bank represents companies (or other entities) that need to raise capital. It sells a company's securities to raise that capital.

For example, suppose that a corporation needs $10 million to finance the purchase of a new manufacturing operation. There are a number of ways that the corporation could obtain those funds, such as borrowing from a bank, but the corporation may decide to offer ownership in the corporation by selling shares of stock to investors. Stock is a security that represents ownership in the corporation.

The investment banking firm would sell shares—say 1 million shares of stock at $10 per share—to investors and pay the $10 million to the company. (Actually, the investment banker would pay somewhat less than $10 million to the company after subtracting the fee for its services.)

Mutual Funds

Mutual funds are financial firms that raise funds by selling their own stock to investors. They then use the money they raise via the sale of their stock to buy stocks or other securities of other companies. The mutual fund becomes a part owner of the companies in which it invests its funds, and the shareholders of the mutual fund have indirectly invested in the portfolio of stocks owned by the mutual fund.

Individual investors find mutual funds to be a convenient way to invest. They offer benefits such as diversification and professional money management that might otherwise be difficult or expensive for a small investor to obtain. In mid-2013, investors had more than $27 trillion invested in mutual funds of various types worldwide.

Finance company A financial institution that extends loans to its customers but raises funds from investors rather than accepting deposits.

Security An instrument that provides evidence of a financial claim.

Securities firm Financial service firms that sells securities to investors.

Securities brokerage firm Securities firms that acts as an agent to transact securities from one investor to another.

Investment bank A securities firm that assists corporations and other entities to raise capital by selling the corporations' securities to investors.

Mutual fund Financial institution that raises funds by selling its stock to investors and investing those funds in securities such as stocks and bonds of other companies.

Pension Funds

Companies and their employees often pay into a fund that accumulates to provide a regular income for the employee at retirement. These funds are pension funds, and they are sponsored and set up by the employer. The employer sponsor of a pension fund can be a business or government employer.

Pension fund A fund holding and investing funds contributed by companies and/or their employees to provide an income for employees who retire.

Retirement funds include pension funds but also include all funds set aside for retirement. For example, an individual can make tax-deferred contributions to a retirement account under various types of plans. These accounts can be set up, for example, as a savings account at a bank or an account with a mutual fund. Although these accounts certainly are part of an individual's retirement planning and may even provide all of a person's retirement income, they are not considered to be a pension fund.

Retirement funds Accounts that hold investments to provide retirement income.

At the end of 2006, pension funds held more than $12.1 trillion in investments. Exhibit 11.7 breaks this total down by pension funds sponsored by private businesses, state and local governments, and the federal government (not including social security).

Insurance Companies

Insurance companies are financial institutions because they accept money from policyholders, invest that money for a financial return, and then end up paying back some or all of that money if the policyholder collects on the policy. The average length of time between the receipt of a premium by an insurance company and the payment of claims represents a period during which the insurance company needs to invest the premiums. It would be foolish for an insurance company not to invest its accumulated insurance premiums, thereby not earning any money. Insurance companies therefore act as financial intermediaries by collecting premiums, investing those premiums, and liquidating investments to pay policyholders when they make claims.

EXHIBIT 11.7	PENSION FUND ASSETS IN THE UNITED STATES BY TYPE OF FUND SPONSOR, 2006

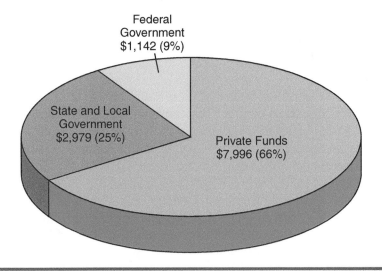

Federal Government $1,142 (9%)

State and Local Government $2,979 (25%)

Private Funds $7,996 (66%)

INVESTING DIRECTLY IN A BUSINESS OR OTHER INVESTMENT

Rather than investing your money through a financial intermediary, you might choose to invest directly in a business or other asset.

Invest in a Business

As an individual, you have the opportunity to buy directly into a business by owning it outright or owning part of it by being a shareholder. Being an owner or part owner of a business can be an exciting and profitable venture. It also takes significant expertise and lots of hard work if you are involved in the operation and management of the business. Business owners sometimes take on partners in the business who only supply capital to the business. If you invest in a business as a partner, you avoid having to run the business, but you place your trust (and your money) in the hands of another person.

Personal investment in a property or business is another way to diversify. In fact, every homeowner is considered an investor.

Marketable securities provide an excellent opportunity for individuals to own part of a business, even part of a major business in the economy. Marketable securities are securities that investors trade on open markets so that anyone can buy or sell these securities. So, for example, if you wanted to be a part owner of Intel Corporation, the firm that manufactures semiconductor chips such as the microprocessors that are the central part of every computer, you could do so.

Marketable securities Securities that trade on open financial markets.

Anyone can buy shares of Intel Corp. The easiest way is to buy them through a securities brokerage firm, which will charge a small commission for providing the service. After purchasing one share of Intel, you are a part owner of the Intel Corporation. One share does not give you much of a percentage of ownership because Intel is so large. There are 4.9 billion shares of Intel in the market, but owning even one of them does give you ownership of a portion of Intel.

Investing in Your Government

Governments need to raise funds just as businesses do, which, of course, provides opportunity for investors. Governments only borrow money, so investors can only buy the debt of governments. That is, while you might want to, you cannot buy a portion of Chicago's city government—at least not legally. Government debt is often in the form of bonds that are marketable securities. A bond is a financial instrument that represents an amount owed by the issuer. Bonds usually pay interest periodically (possibly monthly but usually every six months) on the amount owed.

Bond A security representing debt of the issuer.

In 2013, the investing public held debt securities of the U.S. federal government totaling $12 trillion. The easiest way for an individual to invest in the U.S. government is to buy U.S. savings bonds. You can do this at any bank or online. Many people find U.S. savings bonds a convenient way to save; by mid-2013

---

they were holding savings bonds worth a total of $658 billion. Note that savings bonds are not marketable securities because there is no market where investors buy and sell them. If you want to buy a bond, you purchase it from the Treasury. When you need your money, the Treasury will redeem your bond.

Investing in Real Estate

Buying real estate is another way to invest your money. In fact, homeowners are real estate investors from the standpoint that their house is an investment. Many people own rental property as an investment. Of course, owning rental property carries many responsibilities and duties, such as property maintenance.

Real estate investment trust (REIT) A company that invests in income-producing real estate property.

For those who are interested in profiting from real estate investment but who have neither the time nor inclination to manage property, there is a publicly traded marketable security available. These are real estate investment trusts (called REITs, rhyming with *beets*). A real estate investment trust (REIT) is a company that invests in real estate. REITs lease and manage properties that they own, and they often sell properties for a profit and reinvest the proceeds by investing in other properties. You can buy shares of REITs just like you can buy shares of Intel.

Other Assets

Other types of assets sometimes present opportunities for investment. One example is precious metals such as gold or silver. For example, some individuals invest in gold by purchasing American Eagles. American Eagles are gold coins produced every year and sold by the U.S. mint in denominations of $50 (1 ounce of gold), $25 (1/2 ounce), $10 (1/4 ounce), and $5 (1/10 ounce). Of course, the mint sells them for a price somewhat above the price of gold, not for the stated denomination. For example, if gold is selling for $1500 per ounce, a one-ounce ($50) gold American Eagle would sell for around $1575. Some people combine investing with a hobby by investing in collectibles. Stamp and coin collecting have long been hobbies that have provided some of their followers a nice investment return in addition to offering hours of collecting and educational pleasure. Rare art is also often on the list of collectibles that also might appreciate in value. Investing in collectibles requires knowledge of the market, just as knowledge is important for investing in businesses and other investments.

Your Investment Program

Regardless of whether you decide to select and manage your own investments or seek partial or complete outside counsel and management, you should have a formal framework identified as your investment program.

Exhibit 11.8 illustrates the four elements of an investment program:

1. Setting goals
2. Identifying strategies
3. Implementing strategies
4. Monitoring progress

Note how Exhibit 11.8 shows the flow of decisions and actions in an investment program. An investment advisor or financial planner can assist you with any phase of your investment program.

INVESTMENT ADVISORS AND YOUR INVESTMENT PROGRAM

Investment advisors can take much of the responsibility of selecting and administering your investments. They can save you considerable time and effort, and they can add their expertise to the strategy.

However, you should remember that investment advisors receive payment for their services. Investment advisors receive their compensation in two ways:

Consider hiring an investment advisor or financial planner to assist you in choosing the right investment vehicle to reach your goals.

1. Fee-based investment advisors charge a fee for their services. The fee is usually based on the amount of money under their management. For example, a fee might be 0.75 percent of total assets, so a client with a portfolio valued at $1 million would pay $7,500 for investment management.
2. Commission-based investment advisors receive commissions from the investments they sell you. For example, the commission for selling a mutual fund can be as high as 8 percent of the price of the fund.

Fee-based investment advisor Advisor who charges a fee for services rendered.

Commission-based investment advisor Advisor compensated by commissions from the investments sold to clients.

FLOWCHART OF AN INVESTMENT PROGRAM	EXHIBIT 11.8

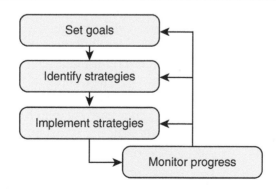

Keep in mind that all fees serve to reduce your net return on your investments. If a manager charges a 0.75 percent fee, then your net returns will be 0.75 percent less. If you pay a commission, your returns are also reduced. The question that you have to answer is whether the fees you pay are worth the services that you receive from an investment advisor.

Commission-based advisors have an incentive to sell you more investment product than you might need, because the more they sell, the more they earn. Fee-based advisors do not have this conflict of interest and may be preferable. However, fee-based advisors do not usually accept smaller accounts; $50,000 would probably be the minimum, with many advisors taking only accounts of $500,000 or more. Commission-based advisors do accept smaller accounts.

SETTING GOALS

Setting realistic and achievable goals for your investment program is the starting point. This is investment, so these goals represent some type of financial gain or position. There are generally two benchmarks for identifying goals: net wealth (or dollar) achievement, and return on investment.

Net Wealth or Dollar Goals

One way to specify a financial goal is to identify a specific dollar target for the investment or group of investments. For example, Erica Gardiner has an account with a mutual fund. She has designated the account as her supplemental retirement account; she has this account to supplement her company-sponsored pension plan. Her present age is 32, and she wants to have a balance of at least $800,000 in the account at age 55.

Erica has specified a dollar amount that she wants to have at a future date. She then must identify the combination of investments for the account and the periodic contributions that she will need to reach her goal.

Return on Investment

Another way to specify investment goals is to identify a target return for the investments. Investors state the profits (or losses) they make in terms of return on investment (ROI). Return is the profit per period for each dollar invested. For example, a person who invests a dollar and receives $1.05 makes five cents profit, or a return of $0.05. Since we often state return in percent, we could say the return is 5 percent.

A person might set a goal of achieving a 9 percent return on his or her portfolio of investments. However, it is not a simple matter of setting return goals as high as possible, because those return goals will have a big influence on the investment strategies designed to reach that goal.

Note that return is per time period. It may be over (for example) one month, six months, or one year. Because it is not very meaningful to compare a three-year return to a seven-year return, we typically state return on an annual basis.

The formula for computing return is

$$\text{holding period return} = \frac{\text{price}_{\text{end}} - \text{price}_{\text{beginning}} + \text{income}}{\text{price}_{\text{beginning}}}$$

There are three components of calculating the return for a given period (the holding period):

1. *Price*$_{beginning}$ is the price of the investment at the beginning of the period.
2. *Price*$_{end}$ is the price at the end of the period.
3. *Income* is any income that the investment produced during the holding period.

Example 11.1 shows an investment that returns 10 percent to an investor over a one-year holding period. In the example, we have a holding period of one year, so the annual return is 10 percent.

Short-Term versus Long-term Goals

It is important to include a time horizon associated with all of your investment goals. Note how Erica, in the example of setting a dollar goal, identified a time for her goal. She wants $800,000 at age 55. Her present age is 32, so her time horizon is 23 years.

Investment goals can be of a short-term nature or a long-term nature. For example, you might establish a savings account for accumulating a down payment on a car with the goal of having a $4,000 balance in one year. Or, having just purchased a car, you might begin saving and investing to buy the next one

---

Kerri's Return on Investment	**EXAMPLE 11.1**

Kerri Gardiner purchased 100 shares of Intel Corp. for $24 per share. During the year, Intel paid her a cash dividend of 40 cents per share, and Intel was selling for $26 one year later. Compute Kerri's return on her investment in Intel.

$$\text{holding period return} = \frac{26-24.40}{24}$$

$$= \frac{2.40}{24}$$

$$= .10 \text{ or } 10 \text{ percent}$$

Compute her return if the stock had fallen to $20 per share.

$$\text{holding period return} = \frac{20-24.40}{24}$$

$$= \frac{-3.60}{24}$$

$$= -.15 \text{ or } -15 \text{ percent}$$

With investment returns, it is important to remember the principles of compound interest. For example, a person who owns an investment for two years cannot simply add up the two one-year returns to compute the two-year return. ■

EXHIBIT 11.9	DIAGRAM OF AN INVESTMENT STRATEGY

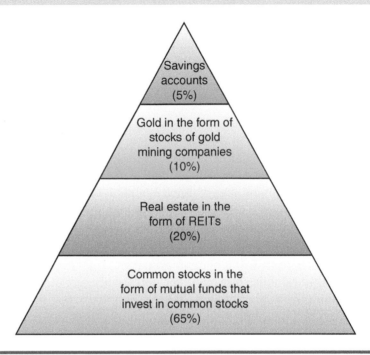

for cash without having to borrow any funds. You could set up a plan to have $35,000 at the end of 6 years.

IDENTIFYING STRATEGIES

After setting some investment goals, a person can design strategies to reach those goals. For example, Aaron Hill set as one of his investment goals to achieve an average annual rate of return on investment of 8 percent over the next 16 years. Furthermore, at the end of 16 years, he wants to have saved $200,000 to pay for his daughter's college expenses.

Given this goal, Aaron begins to do research to identify an investment strategy expected to yield an average of 8 percent per year during the next 16 years. After doing the research, Aaron believes that a portfolio of investments constructed using the investment categories shown in Exhibit 11.9 will yield him his target return.

Furthermore, Aaron intends that his strategy include switching all of the funds to a savings account at the end of 14 years because savings accounts are less risky. Savings accounts pay less than 8 percent interest, so Aaron understands that during those first 14 years his return will have to average more than 8 percent to make up for not receiving 8 percent during the final two years. However, Aaron feels that the investments he has identified will achieve his overall objective.

Finally, Aaron estimates the amounts that he will need to invest initially and the amounts to add to the investment portfolio annually to reach $200,000 at the end of 16 years.

There are a number of different combinations that would reach the final goal. One of them is initially investing about $15,000 and adding another $5,000 per year.

IMPLEMENTING STRATEGIES

Implementing strategies is the point when you go into action. To accomplish implementation, it is necessary to set up accounts if they do not already exist, make deposits to the accounts, and begin to make the transactions necessary to construct the portfolio of investments identified.

A person working with an investment counselor may elect to leave the counselor in charge of much of this phase. Anyone choosing to work with an investment advisor should be sure to request regular reports and updates.

Begin saving a little each month; whether you choose a bank or investment firm, the important thing to remember is that the earlier you begin saving, the more interest your money accumulates.

Implementation is a continuous process. While you have a general strategy outlined, the specific investments that achieve that strategy may change as the economic, business, and political environment changes. Unless a person is simply managing a lump sum of money, there will normally be funds for new investment flowing into the investment accounts periodically. For example, Aaron might elect to have $200 per month automatically deducted from his paycheck and deposited into his brokerage account. As these new amounts go into Aaron's account, he will want to consider the best investments for these funds, even without revising his overall strategy.

For example, suppose that Aaron has decided to place 50 percent of his money into the stocks of large, well-known companies. Last year he felt that the future was bright for Dell Computer and bought shares of that firm. This year he believes that Hewlett Packard will be more profitable and decides to purchase stock in that company.

MONITORING PROGRESS

Investment monitoring is the ongoing process of assessing investments to determine whether they are on track to meet goals.

The monitoring process includes the following:

- Computing return on investment to evaluate investment performance
- Reviewing goals and strategies
- Evaluating current market conditions
- Reassessing any investments currently owned

Effective monitoring should lead to conclusions about the need for revising any of the investment goals or strategies. This being the case, monitoring leads

Investment monitoring
Process of assessing investments to determine if they meet goals.

investors to loop back to the prior steps in their investment programs. In doing so, it allows them to change their strategy and update their investments to be more in touch with the current investment environment.

Factors That Influence Your Investment Program

The two main factors that influence the fundamental goals and strategies in an investment program are the risk a person takes on when investing and the return that he or she wants to receive.

RISK

Some investments have only one possible return. For example, if you place your money in a bank savings account that promises 2 percent interest, you will receive 2 percent return—not more (why would a bank pay you more than it promised?), not less (because your deposits are insured by the Federal Deposit Insurance Corporation, an agency backed by the full faith and credit of the U.S. government). In other words, you are guaranteed a 2 percent return.

Riskless investment Investment with a certain future return.

We call an investment with one possible return that is a virtual certainty a riskless investment, or risk-free investment. The actual future return that the investor will receive on a riskless investment is certain. While one might argue that nothing is risk-free, examples of types of securities that are very close to being risk-free are money market securities. A money market security is a short-term, interest-bearing security issued by a very creditworthy issuer. Money market securities are considered to be very safe investments.

Money market security Short-term interest-bearing security issued by a very creditworthy issuer.

It follows that an investment with more than one possible return would be a risky investment. With a risky investment, the investor is uncertain about the return to be eventually realized.

Risky investment Investment with more than one possible future return.

Exhibit 11.10 illustrates a risky and a riskless investment. The risky investment has four possible returns: 6 percent, 8 percent, 10 percent, and 12 percent. The riskless investment has one and only one possible return: 8 percent.

A risky investment will yield one return from a number of different possible future returns. Some of those possible returns are often on the negative side, representing the possibility of losing money on an investment. Investments are riskier when they have a greater range between the lowest and the highest possible returns. For example, compare investment A, with possible returns of –4 percent and +12 percent, and investment B, with possible returns of –10 percent and +30 percent. Investment B is the riskier investment.

Risk Variation in returns on an investment.

What is risk to an investor? People have different ways of describing risk. Some say that risk is uncertainty about future returns. Others might explain that risk is the potential for losing money. For our purposes, we will say that risk is the variation in future returns. Investments have greater risk when their future possible returns vary more.

RISK: BEWARE OF PONZI SCHEMES

What is a Ponzi scheme? The term is a reference to Charles Ponzi (1882-1949), a scam artist who plied his trade during the early 1900s. The operator of a Ponzi scheme promises investors high returns and pays off investors not with profits from investments, but simply with additional funds provided by new investors.

In late 1919, Ponzi hit upon the idea of turning a profit by buying and selling International Reply Coupons (IRC). An IRC is a coupon you can buy at the post office and send to someone in another country, who can take the IRC to the post office and receive a stamp to send a letter back to you.

Ponzi found that he could buy IRCs in Italy for much less than the price of postage in the United States. His idea was to buy IRCs in Italy, ship them to the United States, exchange them for U.S. stamps, and sell the U.S. stamps for a profit. Ponzi set up the Securities Exchange Company to profit from this idea, and the company began taking on investors to finance the purchase of IRCs.

Ponzi promised investors that he would double their money in 90 days, and when early investors were paid this handsome return, others followed. By February 1920, he had taken in $5,000. Ponzi hired agents and paid them generous commissions to bring in additional funds. By March Ponzi's take had risen to $30,000, and frenzy began to develop among investors to place money with Ponzi. By May, Ponzi had taken in over $400,000 (worth more than $4 million today).

Ponzi continued to pay exorbitant returns, but most investors were content to reinvest all of their profits, so the cash kept flowing in. By July Ponzi had reaped millions, but newspaper reporters and the authorities began asking questions. Clarence Barron, publisher of the financial newspaper *Barron's,* determined that Ponzi would have had to have bought 160 million IRCs, but the post office reported that only 27,000 were in circulation.

Investors began asking for their money back, and a run on the company was in full swing. On August 11 the *Washington Post* printed a front-page article on Ponzi, exposing his conviction for forgery 13 years earlier. Ponzi had bilked investors for more than $7 million (about $70 million in current dollars).

In 2008, Bernard Madoff easily topped Ponzi's feat. Madoff's firm, founded in 1960, operated a legitimate stock brokerage and trading business. However, Madoff began to operate his investment business (separate from the brokerage business) using Ponzi methods in 1991.

Madoff had been paying investors unusually high returns, and he claimed to be able to realize those returns by investing in a complicated strategy using stock options. Instead, Madoff simply deposited investors' funds in the bank and then paid off investors with funds from new investors.

On December 10, 2008, Madoff informed his sons that his business was a fraud. The sons informed federal authorities, and Madoff was arrested the following day. The total amount that investors lost with Madoff was astounding, estimated to be around $14 billion. The amazing feature of this scheme, in addition to the large sum involved, was the length of time that Madoff was able to fool investors, auditors, and regulators.

Which of the investments in Exhibit 11.10 would you prefer? In an uncertain world, certainty is good. By similar reasoning, less risk is better than no risk. Based on that reasoning, the riskless investment is better than the risky investment. But that conclusion considers only the risk of the investment.

EXHIBIT 11.10   ILLUSTRATION OF A RISKLESS AND A RISKY INVESTMENT

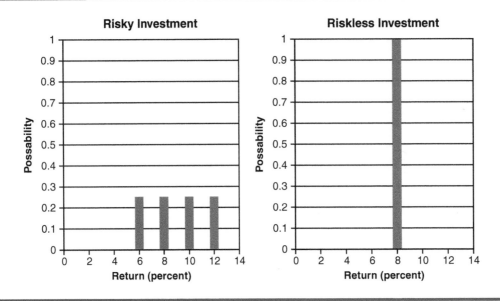

When we make investment decisions involving risk, we also need to consider the investment's expected return.

EXPECTED RETURN

Expected return The average return on an investment over the long run.

Investors recognize that risk creates a situation in which they sometimes realize high returns on their investments, and sometimes low returns. The expected return of an investment is the average return that we would receive if we were able to invest in it a number of times.

We can also view expected return as the return we would anticipate receiving on an investment over the long run. For example, suppose the expected return on a stock is 8 percent. This year it might return 14 percent, next year a slight loss at –2 percent, and the following year a gain of 12 percent. While any one year's return is not equal to the expected return, the long-run average return is the expected value.

When deciding which investments to pursue, an investor should consider the expected return on that investment. Now, the question is: Is the best investment the one that has the greatest expected return? To identify which investments you might prefer to buy, you need to consider that there is a tradeoff between risk and return.

THE TRADEOFF BETWEEN RISK AND RETURN

Every risky investment that investors consider for their investment program has both risk and expected return. The former (risk) is a characteristic they hope to avoid, while the latter (expected return) is something they hope to maximize. However, it is precisely the higher return investments that normally

THE TRADEOFF BETWEEN RISK AND EXPECTED RETURN   EXHIBIT 11.11

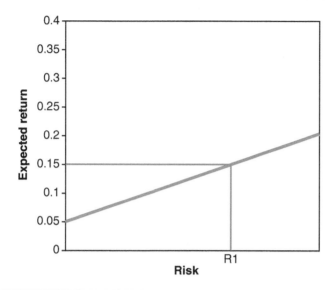

have the higher levels of risk. Or, stated conversely, the safer investments with lower risk generally have lower expected returns.

Exhibit 11.11 illustrates the relationship between risk and expected return. There is a zero level of risk that yields some minimum expected return. This would be the risk-free security. As risk rises, so does expected return. The upshot of the risk–return relationship is that when investors choose investments that will increase their expected return, they probably also increase their exposure to risk. Your goal is to find a level of risk with which you are comfortable that will also yield you a return with which you are satisfied.

Although the risk–return tradeoff may at first glance seem like a dilemma, it is no different than many situations people face every day. Consider the purchase of a new computer. Every added feature increases the utility of the computer, but also its cost. Just as the consumer needs to find the computer that provides the desired features within a certain budget, investors need to find the set of investments with returns that fit within their ability to take on risk.

Investment Decisions

Investment strategy at the phases of identifying and implementing requires investors to make a number of decisions regarding the category of investment and the actual specific investments purchased. We can classify investment decisions into two categories:

1. The asset allocation decision
2. The investment selection decision

The asset allocation decision is a broad strategy decision, while the investment selection decision is more of an implementation type of action.

ASSET ALLOCATION

Asset allocation decision
The decision of which mix of broad classes of investments will meet needs for return and risk.

The asset allocation decision involves finding the right mix of broad classes of investments that will meet your needs for achieving a particular return but that will also stay within your willingness to accept risk. In other words, in making an asset allocation decision, investors have to decide on their desired risk–return tradeoff.

In general, individuals are able to accept greater risks when they are in the early stages of their career, so they would probably be more interested in investing in securities and other investments with a relatively high expected return. People approaching retirement may want to be more conservative. They have fewer working years to recover from any losses that risky investments might experience.

Different classes of investments generally have different levels of risk. Let's consider three main types of marketable securities and their risk levels:

1. Money market securities
2. Bonds
3. Stocks

The tradeoff between risk and return for these types of securities might be as depicted in Exhibit 11.12. Money market securities are associated with almost

| EXHIBIT 11.12 | EXPECTED RISK–RETURN RELATIONSHIPS FOR DIFFERENT TYPES OF SECURITIES |

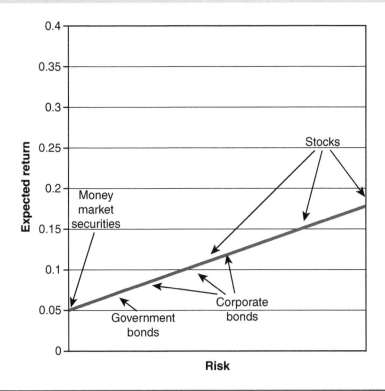

no risk, and the figure in the exhibit shows that they have the minimum expected return. Bonds promise a given rate of return, and bonds of the U.S. government are less risky than those of corporations, so the next group up the figure is government bonds, followed by corporate bonds. Stocks of companies, the riskiest group of investments shown in Exhibit 11.12, have the highest expected returns.

Of course, the exhibit does not describe all classes of investments. A speculative real estate venture, for example, may be much riskier than the average corporate stock, but its expected return should be quite high. We would expect such an investment to be represented somewhere in the far upper right of Exhibit 11.12.

INVESTMENT SELECTION

The investment selection decision entails choosing exactly which investments to purchase that will meet the targets in the asset allocation decision. An informed and profitable investment selection decision can result from performing careful research on potential investments.

Fortunately, there is a wealth of information available about stocks, bonds, and other types of investments. You can find a wide-ranging variety of information at various sites on the Internet. In addition, public libraries subscribe to services that present financial data on companies, industries, and the economy. Obviously, for those investors who prefer to leave the decision to someone else, an investment advisor can make recommendations on investments.

Exhibit 11.13 presents an example set of asset allocation decisions and the accompanying investment selection decisions. The investor in Exhibit 11.13 decided to keep 20 percent in safe money market securities, for which she

EXAMPLE ASSET ALLOCATION AND INVESTMENT SELECTION DECISIONS   EXHIBIT 11.13

Asset Allocation		Investment Selection
Asset Category	Percent Invested	
Money market securities	20%	American Century Prime Money Market Fund
Domestic stocks:	50%	Black and Decker
		Apple, Inc.
		Gap, Inc.
		Kroger Co.
		AT&T
Global stocks:	30%	Air France
		Sony
		Telefonos de Mexico

chose a money market fund. She divided the remaining 80 percent into stocks of domestic firms (50 percent) and those of global companies (30 percent), selecting stocks of individual companies to fit each category.

Managing Cash

Cash Funds available immediately.

Cash is funds that you have available to spend immediately. Currency and coin are cash, but funds on deposit in checking or debit card accounts are also cash. Depositors have immediate access to these funds without any restrictions on their withdrawal.

THE NEED TO HOLD CASH

Why do you need to hold cash? Economists usually identify three motives that explain why people have cash:

Transactions motive The need to hold cash to make purchases.

1. The transactions motive. You need cash to make purchases.
2. The precautionary motive. You should have a financial cushion to use in unforeseen circumstances, such as losing your job.
3. The speculative motive. If you expect prices to fall, you might be better off holding cash until the price falls and then buying at the lower price.

Precautionary motive The need to hold cash as a cushion for emergency use.

Speculative motive The need to hold cash to buy at lower prices in the future.

EARNING A RETURN ON CASH

Cash equivalent Investment that is available immediately like cash but also yields interest.

The problem with holding cash is that it earns absolutely no return. The alternative is to hold funds in some investment that is almost like cash but that earns some return. We call these investments cash equivalents. Cash equivalents offer the advantage of cash (immediate access) and avoid the disadvantage (of earning no return).

In order to maximize your investment return, you should have a strategy for your cash. For such a strategy, you should determine the amount of cash needed and then try to keep the least amount of that balance in true cash while holding as much as possible in interest-earning cash equivalents.

A large number of different types of cash equivalents exist. Two are popular among individual investors:

1. Interest-earning bank accounts
2. Money market funds

Bank Accounts That Earn Interest

Banks offer a number of different accounts that yield the depositor a return. Similar accounts are available at other types of depositary institutions, such as savings institutions and credit unions.

These types of accounts have the advantage of being insured by a federal agency against loss for balances up to $250,000 (the Federal Deposit Insurance Corporation (FDIC) for banks and savings institutions and the National Credit Union Administration for credit unions). Popular types of accounts include

- **Interest-bearing checking accounts.** These accounts earn interest on balances and allow the depositor to write checks against the account. Some institutions call these accounts money market accounts. These accounts are just as convenient as regular checking accounts at financial institutions, but they may have restrictions that noninterest checking accounts do not have. For example, the interest-bearing account may have a larger minimum balance requirement (with a fee imposed if the account falls below the minimum) or a maximum number of checks that may be written against the account for the month.

  Interest-bearing checking account Deposit account that pays interest and lets the customer withdraw funds by writing a check.

- **Certificates of deposit.** A certificate of deposit (often called a CD), is a savings account with a sum that the depositor agrees to leave on deposit with the financial institution for a specified period of time. There is normally a penalty charged for withdrawing the principal amount of the CD before its maturity. Interest rates on CDs are normally somewhat higher than rates available on interest-bearing checking accounts. If you normally keep a $5,000 balance, for example, for emergency purposes, it may be worthwhile to place this money in the higher-yielding CD, recognizing that should the emergency occur, you might have to pay the early withdrawal penalty.

  Certificate of deposit Deposit that earns interest for a specified length of time.

Money Market Funds

The interest rates paid on money market securities are typically slightly greater than rates on most bank interest-bearing accounts. Here are some examples of money market securities:

- **U.S. Treasury bills** are issued by the U.S. Department of the Treasury with maturities of 4, 13, and 26 weeks in minimum denominations of $1,000. Individuals can buy Treasury bills directly from the Treasury at www .treasurydirect.gov.

  U.S. Treasuring bill Money market security issued by the U.S. Department of Treasury with maturities of 4, 13, and 26 weeks in minimum denominations of $1,000.

WATCH OUT FOR PENALTIES FOR EARLY WITHDRAWAL

Banks and other institutions can charge a penalty for withdrawing savings from a certificate of deposit before its maturity date. Keep in mind the following guidelines:

- There is no law specifying that banks must charge for early withdrawal. Sometimes it is even possible to negotiate.
- Banks must disclose any penalty for early withdrawal when an account is opened.
- Penalties are usually based on interest for a specified time period or a fixed amount. For example, no interest for the last three months, or a penalty of 1 percent of the deposit.
- Some banks may impose the entire amount of the penalty even if the CD has not yet earned that much interest. For example, suppose the penalty on a $10,000 CD is 1 percent, which is $100. But the CD has only earned $25 in interest. In that case, the bank would return less than the original deposit to the depositor—a sum of only $9,925.

Commercial paper Money market security issued by corporations.

Negotiable certificate of deposit Money market security issued by large commercial banks.

Money market mutual fund Mutual fund that invests in money market securities.

- Commercial paper is issued by large corporations such as General Electric with original maturity of 270 days or less, usually in denominations of $1 million or more.
- A negotiable certificate of deposit is a security that represents a large deposit (at least $100,000) in one of the larger commercial banks with an original maturity of 1 year or less.

Since money market securities are issued in large denominations (with the exception of U.S. government issues), most buyers of money market securities are either wealthy individual investors or investing institutions such as pension funds or mutual funds.

For individual investors who wish to earn money market rates of interest on their funds, money market mutual funds provide an excellent investment vehicle. Money market mutual funds are mutual funds that invest in money market securities. They provide a way for individual investors to indirectly invest in money market securities without having to buy the large denominations.

Unlike interest-bearing accounts at financial institutions, amounts invested in money market mutual funds are not federally insured. However, to minimize any possible risk, money market funds purchase a broad portfolio of different money market securities including the types of securities listed above. They maintain a value of $1 for each share of the money market fund, so if you want to open an account and deposit $5,000, you in effect purchase 5,000 shares of the fund. Money market funds do not charge a commission for purchasing their shares.

The funds declare their interest every day and credit the interest to your account (adding additional shares) at the end of each month. The funds do issue fractional shares, so if the monthly interest (the funds call it dividends) amounts to, say, $34.23, the account will receive 34.23 additional shares.

Funds usually offer a variety of services such as the following:

- Check-writing privileges, often with a minimum per check of $500;
- Direct deposit of your paycheck or automatic deposits by way of deductions from your checking account;
- Retirement and educational accounts;
- Online or touch-tone phone access to your account with the ability to exchange your money market account shares for shares of other funds offered by the company. (For example, you might want to shift $2,000 of your funds in money market to invest in stocks. You can do this easily by trading your money market fund shares for shares of a stock mutual fund within the same mutual fund management company.)

For example, one mutual fund management company offers shares under the name of American Century Investors. This firm offers several different money market funds, one of which is the Prime Money Market Fund. Exhibit 11.14 provides sample characteristics of a money market fund using the Prime Money Market Fund.

EXAMPLE CHARACTERISTICS OF A MONEY MARKET FUND	EXHIBIT 11.14

Fund company:	American Century Investments
Fund name:	Prime Money Market Fund
Minimum investment:	
Individual account	$2,500
Individual account, automatic deposit	$50
Retirement account	$2,500
Features:	Check writing
	Direct deposit ($50 minimum)
	Online account access
	Telephone transactions
Portfolio information:	(3/31/2013)
Annual expenses as % of total assets	0.58%
Weighted average maturity	35 days
Portfolio composition:	
Commercial paper	41%
Municipal paper	31%
Corporate bonds	14%
U.S. government and agencies	14%

Source: American Century Investments, *Prospectus* 2013, Investor Class: Prime Money Market Fund, and other information from www.americancentury.com.

SUMMARY

Individuals can invest directly in businesses, or they can invest through a financial institution. Types of financial institutions include commercial banks, savings institutions, credit unions, finance companies, securities firms, mutual funds, pension funds, and insurance companies.

To invest directly in a business, individuals can purchase a partnership interest in the business. However, a more practical way of investing in businesses for most people is to purchase marketable securities such as stocks that represent ownership of a corporation.

Individuals can also invest in their government and its agencies by purchasing bonds. A convenient vehicle for investing in the U.S. government is savings bonds. Other investments popular with individuals include real estate, precious metals such as gold and silver, and collectibles.

Successful investing is an important part of anyone's financial plan and success. An investment program that includes setting goals, identifying strategies, implementing strategies, and monitoring progress should be part of everyone's financial planning. Those who want help with their investment program can access the services of an investment advisor.

Investment goals can be stated in terms of a dollar amount goal or a return on investment goal. Return on investment is the profit from an investment for each dollar invested. It is usually stated as a percentage. Individuals should identify both long-term and short-term goals.

The two most important factors that investors consider when determining their investment program are risk and expected return. A riskless investment has only one possible return, while risky investments have more than one possible future return (possibly even a loss). Risk is the variation in future returns; an investment with a greater variation in returns has more risk. The expected return on an investment is the average return over a longer period.

There is a tradeoff between risk and expected return. The greater the risk of an investment, the greater the return we should expect it to yield. All investment decisions must consider this tradeoff.

Two types of investment decisions in the investment program strategy are the asset allocation decision and the investment selection decision. Asset allocation specifies the broad investment classifications for investment, while investment selection identifies the specific investments in each classification.

When managing cash, consider how much will satisfy the three basic motives for holding cash: the transactions, the precautionary, and the speculative motives. An effective cash strategy should include cash equivalents that earn interest, such as interest-bearing checking accounts, certificates of deposit, and money market funds.

PROBLEMS

1. Sally purchases an ounce of gold for $600 and sells it one year later for $700. What is her return?

2. Armando buys an interest in his friend George's business for $5,000. After six months, George computes his profit and pays Armando $100 as his share of the earnings. At the end of the year, George's business is doing even better, and George pays Armando $300 in profits. Armando offers to sell George back his ownership in the business for $5,500, and George accepts. Compute Armando's return.

3. Karen purchases 10 shares of stock in Eastman Kodak for $28 per share. The company pays a $0.50 dividend, and the stock sells for $25 at the end of the year. Calculate Karen's return.

CASE STUDIES

COLLEGE STUDENT

We've met Kevin before; below you will find his original financial information. If you have worked on this case study from the beginning of the book, use the current financial data you have for him. If you haven't worked on this case study through the entire book, use the financial information below.

Kevin Maedor is a 19-year-old college student. He still lives at home with his parents, and he works part time at Vapor's Lane. He started his financial plan in the spring semester of 2014. He plans to graduate with a B.S. in engineering in May 2017. He has the following financial information:

- He brings home $760 a month from his job; he currently has $174 in his checking account.
- He asks his parents for $50 cash a week.
- He has a Visa card with a balance of $1,700 and a MasterCard with a balance of $800. He makes the minimum monthly payment of $15.00 on each of them.
- His cell phone bill is $85 a month.
- Last month he spent $450 on gas, $375.00 on golf, and $490.69 at restaurants.

Help him create an investment strategy:

1. Does he need to grow his investments or preserve his capital?
2. Based on your answer to question 1, set a net worth or a return on investment goal for him.
3. Are there any bills he should pay off before he invests?
4. How can he adjust his spending to accommodate an investment plan?

NEW GRADUATE

We've met Rene before; below you will find her original financial information. If you have worked on this case study from the beginning of the book, use the current financial data you have for her. If you haven't worked on this case study through the entire book, use the financial information below.

Rene Harris recently graduated with a B.S. in nursing. She lives by herself in a modest apartment. Her annual salary is $76,000 a year. Rene loves to entertain, but her apartment is too small and the neighbors complain about the slightest noise. Rene is a good neighbor, so she has been going out with friends instead. She has the following financial information:

- She brings home $4,433.33 a month from her job.
- She pays $1125.00 a month for her apartment, which includes trash service and cable.
- She used her new Visa last month for the first time and charged $600. She also opened a new Macy's charge and charged $762.78. She hasn't received her first bill for either of them; assume her minimum monthly payment will be $15.00 on each.
- She owes $30,000 in student loans and makes a monthly payment of $151.47.
- Her cell phone bill is $105.00 a month.
- She has $1,804.12 in her savings account.
- Last month she spent $275 on gas, $398.63 on food, $32.17 for her water bill, $76.18 for her electric bill, $49.98 for Internet service, $820 at restaurants, $357.82 on entertainment, $762.78 on clothing (this is her Macy's charge), and $152.75 on hair and nail services.

Help her create an investment strategy:

1. Does she need to grow her investments or preserve her capital?
2. Based on your answer to question 1, set a net worth or a return on investment goal for her.
3. How can she adjust her spending to accommodate an investment plan?
4. Are there any bills she should pay off before she invests?

CREATE YOUR OWN FINANCIAL PLAN

In this chapter you will set the goals for your investments. You will not select the personal investments yet. Once you set the goals in this chapter, you will be ready to determine which investments will help you meet those goals. Chapters 11 through 13 discuss the different investment options. As you learn about the options available to you, you can select specific needs to meet your goals. Chapter 14 covers retirement planning. Retirement planning typically involves investing for your income during retirement. You will be asked to set investment goals for retirement in that chapter. In this chapter you can set investment goals for retirement or for other reasons. You may want to consider investing for the long-term goals you set in Chapter 2 now and focus on retirement goals in Chapter 14.

1. What are you setting an investment goal for? You can use your long-term goals from Chapter 2 or create a new long-term goal. Here are a few suggestions.

   - Children's education
   - Future home purchase
   - Dream vacation
   - Wedding
   - Graduate school

2. Do you need to grow your investments (start saving) or preserve your capital (protect savings you currently have)?

3. Based on your answer to question 1, set a net worth or a return on investment goal for yourself. For example:

   - You want $20,000 in seven years.
   - You want an 8 percent return for the next 10 years.

4. Can you adjust your spending to accommodate an investment plan?

5. Are there any bills you need to pay off before you invest?

6. Use the appropriate time value of money equations to set a specific, measurable, action-oriented, realistic, and time-focused investment goal for yourself.

REVIEW QUESTIONS   CHAPTER 11

1. Describe the difference between investing directly and investing through a financial intermediary. Which would normally be the simpler and easier method? Which method might yield you a greater return in the long run?

   _____

   _____

   _____

2. List eight different types of financial institution. Classify each as depositary or non-depositary.

   _____

   _____

   _____

3. What is equity in a business?

   _____

   _____

   _____

4. Explain the difference between a commercial bank and an investment bank.

   _____

   _____

   _____

5. Describe a mutual fund. Which investor would more likely be interested in purchasing a mutual fund for investment: a person with $10,000 to invest or a person with $10 million to invest?

   _____

   _____

   _____

6. What is the difference between a retirement fund and a pension fund?

_____

_____

_____

7. Define the following terms: security, marketable security, stock, bond.

_____

_____

_____

8. Describe a convenient way for an individual to invest in real estate without actually buying real property. Identify the four elements of an investment program.

_____

_____

_____

9. List and define the two types of investment advisors based on their compensation. What are the advantages and disadvantages that the two types offer investors with a relatively small amount to invest and investors with a larger sum to invest?

_____

_____

_____

10. Your investment goals call for a return on your investments of 8 percent over the next 10 years. You are monitoring your investments and find that your average return has been 6 percent, and that your investments appear to be of lower risk than you originally estimated. What might your actions be to adjust to this situation?

_____

_____

_____

11. Is a money market security a risky or a risk-free investment? Explain your reasoning.

_____

_____

_____

12. Specify the relationship between expected return and risk.

_____

_____

_____

13. Investment A has an expected return of 9 percent and a risk of 0.25. Investment B is riskier than A. Do you expect that B's return will be less or greater than A's?

_____

_____

_____

14. Describe the asset allocation decision. You have decided to allocate your money between the money market securities and real estate categories of asset. You will put 20 percent of your funds in one and 80 percent in the other, with 20 percent going to the category with the lower risk. Identify the percentages you should allocate to each category.

_____

_____

_____

_____

_____

_____

_____

15. Define the investment selection decision and differentiate it from the asset allocation decision.

_____

_____

_____

16. Name the three motives for holding cash.

_____

_____

_____

17. List some cash equivalents.

_____

_____

_____

_____

_____

_____

_____

_____

12

Stocks

"Don't gamble; take all your savings and buy some good stock and hold it till it goes up, then sell it. If it don't go up, don't buy it."

—Will Rogers

OBJECTIVES

- Define marketable securities and list their advantages
- Describe financial markets
- Illustrate stock market indexes
- Demonstrate buying and selling securities
- Analyze common stocks
- Summarize bond investing

KEY TERMS

ADR (American Depositary Receipt)
Ask price
Bear market
Bid price
Book value
Bull market
Cash dividend
Common stock
Day order
Financial market
Floating interest bond
Form 10-K

Good-til-canceled (GTC) order
Goodwill
Initial margin requirement
Limit order
Maintenance margin requirement
Margin
Margin call
Market index
Market order
Odd lot
Open order
Preferred stock

Price-to-earnings ratio (P/E ratio)
Primary market
Proxy statement
Return on equity (ROE)
Round lot
Secondary market
Securities and Exchange Commission (SEC)
Stock exchange
Stock screening
Stock (ticker) symbol
Stockholders' equity

There are many different types of investments. Examples include buying and operating a restaurant, purchasing rental real estate, and buying silver bullion bars. In general, any asset acquired with the expectation of profit is an investment. Although each of these examples might qualify as an investment, this chapter focuses on investing in marketable securities.

Investing in Marketable Securities

It is easy and convenient to invest in marketable securities compared to other types of investments. Marketable securities offer a range of advantages that make them especially suitable for individual investors.

- Marketability and liquidity. Marketability means that there is a ready market in which investors can buy and sell these investments, and liquidity is the ability to quickly sell or buy without affecting the price. Both are desirable characteristics.
- Representing real, income-producing assets. Marketable securities usually represent ownership in a company or other organization that produces some real value. Compare this to an investment in gold; the gold can only just sit there—it never produces income.
- Availability of investment information. There is a wide array of readily available information about marketable securities and the companies that issue them.
- Relatively low expenses. It does not cost much to make transactions of stocks and bonds. The commission for selling $100,000 worth of stock (say, 2,000 shares at $50 per share) with a typical online brokerage firm would be only about $20, while selling a rental apartment for $100,000 would cost around $6,000 in commissions plus probably another several thousand in other expenses. Other investing expenses are also typically lower with marketable securities.

Many types of marketable securities are available to investors. The two most popular general types are stocks and bonds. Corporations issue stocks and bonds in order to raise capital. By selling stock to investors, corporations make the investors part owners. By selling bonds, corporations borrow from investors. This chapter deals with arguably the most popular of the two, common stocks. The material in this chapter barely scratches the surface of knowledge of stocks. If you are interested in learning more, consider taking a course in investments or reading some of the many books available on investing.

Stocks

Stocks of corporations are the most popular type of marketable security with individual investors. They represent a share of ownership in the corporation, and if the corporation makes a sufficient profit, it usually pays a portion of that profit to its stockholders as a cash dividend. A cash dividend is a periodic

Cash dividend
Corporation's cash payment to shareholders.

ADVANTAGES OF MARKETABLE SECURITIES

EXHIBIT 12.1

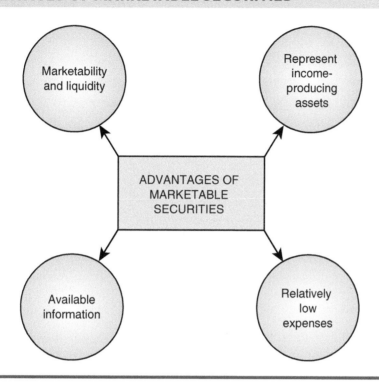

payment to shareholders by a corporation to distribute profits to shareholders. There are two types of stocks:

1. **Preferred stock** is a class of corporate stock that receives a fixed dividend. Because the dividend will not increase when the corporation's profits rise, there is very little room for price appreciation in preferred stock. Investors who buy preferred stocks are simply looking for a steady income from the dividend. For this season, preferred stock acts as if it were a bond, so we will deal with preferred stock in the bonds chapter.

2. **Common stock** is the stock that interests most investors. It allows stockholders to participate in the financial success of a company. As a corporation's profits rise, the funds available for paying cash dividends and for plowing back into the business for more profit growth increase. These benefits accrue to the common shareholders, so stocks of highly profitable companies can rise considerably, giving their shareholders a handsome gain in addition to any cash dividends.

Preferred stock Stock that receives a fixed dividend and owns a fixed amount of the corporation.

Common stock Share of ownership in a corporation.

The financial news media report prices of stocks (and other securities) daily. One of the most popular sources for business information and price quotations for stocks is various Internet sites such as Yahoo! Finance (http://finance.yahoo.com). Prices of larger companies are available in the financial newspaper *The Wall Street Journal*, published on weekdays (except holidays) plus a weekend edition. *The Wall Street Journal* carries a wealth of

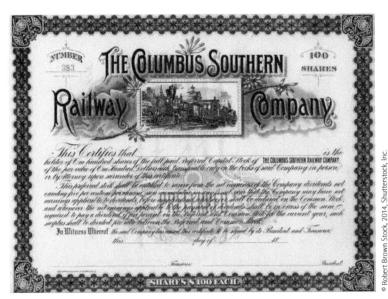

19th Century Common Stock Certificate. Presently, paper certificates are rarely issued as proof of ownership in a company.

information and data, including economic and business data in addition to detailed coverage of business and financial news. Local newspapers in many cities have some degree of coverage of the financial markets, including prices of larger stocks and mutual funds.

Markets for Securities

Financial market Market that provides the means for buying and selling securities.

Transactions of securities typically occur in one of the financial markets. Financial markets provide the means for sellers to offer securities for sale and for buyers to offer to buy. When a buyer and seller both agree on a price, a transaction occurs. Financial markets may be located in a "real" place where buyers and sellers can meet face-to-face, or in a "virtual" place where buyers and sellers match up via computer network to make transactions.

PRIMARY AND SECONDARY MARKETS

Primary market Market in which entities sell their securities to raise funds.

Secondary market Market for trading securities.

Investors sometimes categorize a transaction of a stock or bond as having occurred in either the primary market or the secondary market. There is no one place for primary markets and another place for secondary markets, but rather, the difference is that:

- When a corporation issues a security and sells it to public investors, the transaction occurs in the primary market.
- When one investor sells a security to another investor, the transaction occurs in the secondary market.

The primary markets allow firms to raise capital through the sale of newly issued securities to investors. In the primary markets, as Exhibit 12.2 demonstrates,

PRIMARY AND SECONDARY MARKET TRANSACTIONS — EXHIBIT 12.2

A Primary Market Transaction

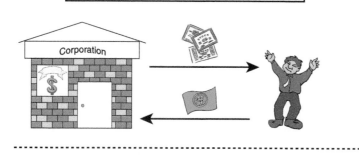

A Secondary Market Transaction

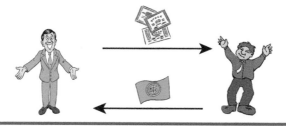

funds flow from investors to security issuers. When a corporation sells its stocks or bonds to investors, it usually enlists the services of an investment bank to handle the sale. An investment bank can act both as an advisor to the corporation (e.g., advising how much stock to sell) and as an agent to sell the stock to investors.

Once securities have been sold to investors, what do investors do with them? They hold them, and then at some point they want to sell them. How do they sell them? They do so in the secondary markets. In the secondary markets, funds flow from the buying investor to the selling investor. When investors buy or sell, they normally use the services of an investment brokerage firm, or simply a broker.

A brokerage firm receives commissions from investors in exchange for buying and selling stocks for them. Some brokerage firms also are investment bankers; the two businesses go hand in hand.

ARE MARKETS IMPORTANT?

One characteristic common to all developed economies of the world is well-functioning financial markets, both at the primary and secondary levels. They are central to the success of any free-enterprise economy. Primary markets provide the mechanism for firms to raise capital. Companies need capital to finance expansion and growth, and when companies grow, the economy grows, and there are more jobs and prosperity.

Primary markets can be successful only when they are accompanied by effective secondary markets. Investors want to have the opportunity to sell their investments. (How much would the stock of Intel be worth if you could not sell it?) They often want to shift their money to another investment or simply to raise cash, and secondary markets provide this mechanism.

STOCK EXCHANGES

Stock exchange
Organization that provides a framework and mechanisms for trading securities.

A stock exchange is an organization that provides the framework and mechanisms for trading securities. At one time, the term *stock exchange* meant that the exchange provided a physical location where stocks and bonds were traded among brokers and traders. Today exchanges that exist in a physical location share the markets with those that exist electronically. They trade billions of shares of stock every day. The principal stock exchanges in the United States are as follows:

- NYSE Euronext
- NASDAQ Stock Market

NYSE Euronext
NYSE Euronext is a corporation that operates a number of stock exchanges in the United States and other countries, principally in Europe. Markets operated by NYSE Euronext in the United States include

- NYSE Equities. The New York Stock Exchange where security dealers meet to trade stock both in a physical location and electronically.
- NYSE Arca Equities. Electronic trading system for stocks also listed on the New York Stock Exchange.
- NYSE MKT: Market for smaller companies that combines electronic trading with the additional participation of human market makers.

A company that wants its stocks to be listed (traded) in one of these markets files an application with NYSE Euronext. If the company meets the listing standards and pays the listing fee, its stock begins trading in the appropriate market. Larger companies typically list on NYSE Equities, while smaller forms might opt for NYSE MKT listing.

NASDAQ OMX

NASDAQ OMX is a corporation that owns and operates a number of markets around the world. For trading stocks, NASDAQ OMX has the NASDAQ Stock Market in the United States and seven separate equities markets in Europe. These markets maintain electronic trading venues. Listing standards for the NASDAQ Stock Market are not as stringent as those of NYSE Euronext, so smaller companies often elect to list on NASDAQ. In spite of this, a number of major corporations, such as Microsoft and Intel, have continued to trade on the NASDAQ even after growing to a very large size.

OTC MARKETS GROUP

OTC Markets Group provides three markets for trading stock in the United States.

- OTCQX allows for trading stocks of smaller companies that meet a set of financial and disclosure standards. These are companies that may not be required to file reports with U.S. regulatory agencies.
- OTCQB is a market for trading stocks of smaller firms that report regularly to one of the U.S. financial regulatory agencies (SEC, banking, or insurance[3]).
- OTC Pink offers trading of any security. There are no standards for trading in this market, so while some of these stocks are financially sound and regularly provide reliable information to investors, they are not required to do so and many report only limited or no information and may be in financial distress or bankruptcy.

Global Stock Markets

U.S. stock markets represent only a fraction of the total world market. Stock exchanges exist in virtually all of the developed countries in the world, and many of the developing nations have them. Investor interest in emerging markets has stimulated the growth of stock markets in developing countries. In addition to trading in their home countries, stocks of many international firms trade also on one of the U.S. or other global exchanges.

MARKET INDEXES

When someone asks, "How's the stock market today?" the answer is likely going to be based on whether one of the stock market indexes is up or down. A market index represents a portfolio of securities set up to measure market performance. The value for the index is an average of the stocks that make up the index.

> **Market index** Representative portfolio of securities that measures market performance.

Market indexes also serve as useful benchmarks against which investors can compare the performance of their own stocks, and they allow investors to identify market trends. Stock market tradition calls a rising market a bull market, while a market with generally falling prices is a bear market.

> **Bull market** Period when market prices rise.
>
> **Bear market** Period when market prices fall.

Many different stock market indexes exist, sponsored by a variety of financial publishing firms. There are indexes that represent the general market and subsets of the market. Exhibit 12.3 provides summary information about some of the most popular and widely referenced stock market indexes.

The Dow Jones Industrial Average, created by Charles Dow in 1884, was the first widely distributed market index. It is probably the stock market index most widely quoted by the news services. However, it is based on a small sample (only 30) of stocks, although they do represent 30 of the largest diversified companies in the United States.

Indexes constructed and published by other services are based on broader samples of stocks. For example, the S&P 500 Index is composed of 500 of the largest companies in the United States, representing a broad cross-section of industries. Even though there are only 500 companies in the index, these firms represent more than 80 percent of the total value of publicly traded stocks in the United States. Exhibit 12.4 shows the year-end values for the S&P 500 Index for 1980 to 2012.

EXHIBIT 12.3　POPULAR STOCK MARKET INDEXES

Index	Publisher	Contents
Dow Jones Industrial Average	Dow Jones	30 industrial stocks
Dow Jones Transportation Average	Dow Jones	20 transportation stocks
Dow Jones Utility Average	Dow Jones	15 utility stocks
Dow Jones Sector Titans indexes	Dow Jones	stocks representing a geographic region, country, or sector
Dow Jones Corporate Bond Indexes	Dow Jones	bonds
NASDAQ Composite	NASDAQ	all NASDAQ stocks
NASDAQ 100	NASDAQ	100 large active NASDAQ stocks
NASDAQ sector indexes	NASDAQ	stocks representing a sector
NYSE Composite	New York Stock Exchange	all NYSE common stocks
Russell 1000	Frank Russell Company	1,000 largest stocks
Russell 2000	Frank Russell Company	next 2,000 largest stocks
Russell 3000	Frank Russell Company	stocks in Russell 1000 and 2000
S&P 500	Standard & Poor's	500 of the largest stocks
S&P 400 MidCap	Standard & Poor's	400 mid-size stocks
S&P 600 SmallCap	Standard & Poor's	600 small stocks
S&P Global 1200	Standard & Poor's	1,200 stocks from 31 countries

EXHIBIT 12.4　YEAR-END VALUES FOR THE STANDARD & POOR'S 500 INDEX, 1980–2012

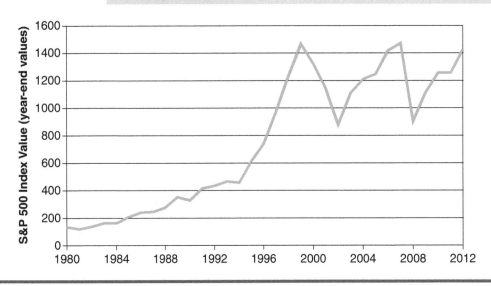

Buying Securities

To buy any security except a mutual fund, individual investors almost always use the services of an investment brokerage firm. Even with mutual funds, investors often use brokers.

SERVICES OF BROKERAGE FIRMS

Brokerage firms have four main areas of service that they offer individual investors. They

1. Handle purchases and sales of securities
2. Provide investment information and advice
3. Keep securities in a brokerage account
4. Lend customers money to buy securities

Buying and Selling

Although it is possible to buy and sell securities without the aid of a broker, doing so would normally be more costly and troublesome than it is worth. When making a securities transaction, investors pay a commission to the brokerage firm. At one time, brokerage commissions were an onerous expense to investors, but competition in the brokerage industry and the advent of online brokerage firms has driven commissions to the point where they are a very small portion of the sums that individuals invest.

Today, brokerage firms fall into the full-service and discount categories. At full-service firms, account executives attend to customers' orders and act as sales personnel. They offer a wide range of financial services and generally do not charge extra for those services; they recoup the cost by charging higher commissions.

At discount firms, customers pay a lower commission and receive a reduced level of personal service. Some firms have automated order taking through a

---

AN INDEX FOR EVERY PURPOSE

Would you like to know how the health care industry is doing? You could check the latest performance of the S&P Healthcare Index. Stock market indexes provide a good snapshot of the financial health of an economy or sector. If someone wants to know information about the current condition of a particular market or segment, chances are pretty good that a market index exists to help with the answer.

For example,

- The Dow Jones Industrial Average is an indicator of 30 large industrial firms.
- Someone wanting to know the status of the financial sector could refer to the NYSE Financial Index.
- The Wilshire 5000 Index is a good measure of stocks in the entire economy, because it includes every stock for which a quote is available.
- How are smaller companies doing in today's economy? The S&P Small Cap 600 Index might yield a clue.

touch-tone phone, with the option of personalized order taking with a live representative for a higher commission. They may have local branch offices for personal service, newsletters, and investment literature. At the extreme end of the discount brokers are the online brokerage firms. They have the lowest commission structures but offer little in the way of personal service.

STRETCH
YOUR DOLLAR

SHOP AROUND FOR A BROKERAGE FIRM

It pays to shop around when looking for a brokerage firm. Commissions vary according to the individual brokerage firm, but as a comparison, consider an order to buy or sell 1,000 shares of stock at $40 per share. Prior to May 1, 1975, you would have paid a $499 commission to make this trade. Today, commissions on this trade vary according to the type of brokerage firm, but on average, you could expect to pay about

- $200 at a full-service firm
- $30 to $50 with a broker-assisted trade at a discount firm
- $3 to $20 with an online broker

Investment Information and Advice

Full-service brokerage firms have a staff of security analysts who study stocks and make recommendations regarding which companies to buy or sell. Account executives at the full-service firms pass these recommendations on to their clients. The transactions generated by these recommendations yield commissions.

Clients of full-service brokerage firms can even give their account executives discretion over their accounts, allowing them to buy or sell stocks without a specific order from the clients. Any investor giving a broker discretion over an account should regularly monitor the investment decisions made by the account executive, because the goal of the account executive (maximizing commission income) may not be consistent with the goal of the client (maximizing investment wealth).

YOUR MONEY IS SAFE WITH A BROKERAGE FIRM

Most people know that their money deposited in a bank is insured by a federal agency, the FDIC, against the bank's financial failure. Your money is just as safe with a brokerage firm because of the SIPC, the Securities Investor Protection Corporation.

The SIPC insures customer accounts at member brokerage firms. If the brokerage firm fails and your shares of stock and cash on deposit with the firm are lost, you can recover up to $500,000, of which up to $100,000 can be for cash deposits.

Note that the SIPC does not insure customers against losing money in the stock market. If your 100 shares of Procter & Gamble took a $10 per share hit, that $1,000 loss is yours. However, if the broker where you held your stock went bankrupt and your shares could not be found, the SIPC would replace your 100 shares of the company.

Although discount and online brokers generally offer little or no investment counsel, they do often provide financial information that investors can use to help make investment decisions. For example, most online brokers allow customers to access databases containing financial results and other information about companies.

Brokerage Accounts

Just as you have a bank account to hold your money, you can have a brokerage account to hold your stock. You can keep cash in a brokerage account, too. For example, your brokerage account monthly statement might state that you have in your account $500 cash, 100 shares of Apple, and 200 shares of General Electric. It is much more convenient to keep your securities on deposit with your brokerage firm than it is to have them issued in your name. Most brokerage firms charge an extra fee for issuing securities to customers.

Brokerage firms usually pay interest on cash balances they hold, and they may also allow clients to write checks against cash balances. If a stock in your brokerage account pays a dividend (or a bond pays interest), the corporation will pay the dividend (or interest) to your brokerage firm. Your broker will then credit the amount to the cash balance in your account.

Lending

Brokerage firms allow customers to borrow funds to purchase securities. Margin is the term that describes funds that brokerage firms lend to clients. The collateral for these margin loans is securities that the clients hold in their accounts. When an investor buys stock on margin, the investor pays for a portion of the total purchase price, and the brokerage firm lends the investor the remainder.

Margin Funds that brokerage firms lend to clients using securities as collateral.

Margin lending is big business; at mid 2013, there was more than $380 billion in margin loans at NYSE-member brokerage firms. Exhibit 12.5 shows the total amount of margin debt loaned by brokerage firms from 1996 to 2012. The amount of margin debt has a close relationship with stock prices in general. Note that the level of margin debt shows peaks in 2000 and in 2007, the same years that market indexes reached highs.

The down payment that an investor has to make in a margin transaction is the initial margin requirement. The initial margin requirement is the percentage of funds that the investor has to pay in order to purchase a security with borrowed money. The board of governors of the Federal Reserve System sets the initial margin requirement for the purchase of stocks. The current initial margin requirement is 50 percent, a level at which it has remained since 1974.

Initial margin requirement Percentage of funds needed to buy a security with borrowed money.

To compute margin, use the following equation:

$$\text{margin} = \frac{\text{price} - \text{loan}}{\text{price}} \qquad \textbf{Equation 12.1}$$

The numerator in Equation 12.1 is the amount that you have to when buying stock on margin. Example 12.1 shows how to compute the initial margin for a purchase of stock. In the example, Angela Ramirez has to put up $24 per share to buy her stock, and she gets a margin loan from her brokerage firm to finance the remaining $24 per share.

| EXHIBIT 12.5 | MARGIN DEBT AT NYSE MEMBER BROKERAGE FIRMS, 1992–2008 (billions of dollars) |

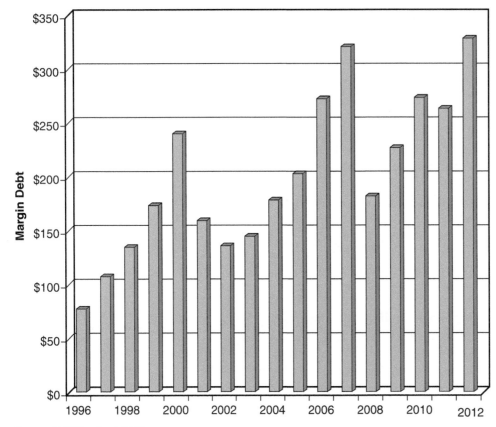

Source: *NYSE Facebook*, 2012.

| EXAMPLE 12.1 | Angela's Stock Purchase |

Angela Ramirez places an order to purchase 100 shares of Regents Oil Company at $48 per share. How much does she need to deposit with her brokerage firm to purchase the stock on margin with a 50 percent margin requirement?

Using Equation 12.1,

$$\text{margin} = \frac{\text{price} - \text{loan}}{\text{price}}$$

$$.50 = \frac{48 - \text{loan}}{48}$$

$$\text{loan} = 24.00$$

Angela gets a loan of $24 per share, leaving her to put up the remaining $24 per share, a total of $2,400 of equity in her margin account. (The popular term is to say she needs $2,400 in margin.) Her loan amount is also $24 per share for a total of $2,400. ■

Angela's Margin Percent   **EXAMPLE 12.2**

The price of Regents Oil stock falls to $30 per share (Example 12.1). What is Angela's margin percentage?

Note that the stock price had changed from 48 to 30, but the loan remains at 24, so

$$\text{margin} = \frac{\text{price} - \text{loan}}{\text{price}}$$

$$\text{margin} = \frac{30 - 24}{30}$$

$$\text{margin} = .20$$

Angela's margin percent now lies at 20 percent. ■

So, let's assume that Angela has made her purchase of Regents Oil on margin. She now has to be concerned that any drop in the price of Regents' stock will change her margin position. Changing market prices will change the price of a stock while the principal of the loan remains fixed. As market prices change, the margin percent changes. What would happen if Regents' price drops to $30 per share? Example 12.2 shows that if Regents Oil falls to $30 per share, Angela's margin percentage falls from its original 50 percent to 20 percent.

At this point, another margin requirement comes into play: the maintenance margin requirement. Regulations oblige investors to keep a certain minimum margin in their account; this is the maintenance margin requirement. If an investor's margin falls below the maintenance margin requirement, then the brokerage firm will issue a margin call asking the investor to contribute more funds to the position, thus raising the margin back up beyond the maintenance requirement.

The individual exchanges set maintenance margin requirements for their member brokerage firms. The NYSE has a current maintenance margin requirement for common stocks of 25 percent. In Example 12.2, Angela's margin of 20 percent falls below this point, and she will receive a margin call from her broker.

If an investor does not comply with a margin call, the brokerage firm will sell enough of the stock to bring the account back into compliance.

Maintenance margin requirement Margin percentage that an investor must maintain in an investment position.

Margin call Call to deposit additional funds in a margin account.

PLACING AN ORDER TO BUY OR SELL SECURITIES

Placing an order to buy or sell a stock is easy. There are a number of alternative specifications for security transaction orders, but the following list takes care of nearly everything an individual investor needs to know. Knowing the types of order is especially important if you trade through an online brokerage firm. With an order, you need to specify the following:

- Order direction (buy or sell)
- Order size (number of shares)
- Stock price (market or limit order)

© Kzenon, 2014, Shutterstock, Inc.

Buying or selling stock has become easier with online trading. Use the Internet to your advantage when researching stocks and brokerage firms.

Direction (Buy or Sell)

The first thing that you typically specify when placing an order is to identify whether you want to buy or to sell securities.

Size

Round lot Multiple of 100 shares of stock.

If you are buying or selling stocks, you need to state the number of shares for the order. Stocks normally trade in round lots. A round lot is 100 shares or any multiple of 100 shares. For example, 800 shares of Westvaco are eight round lots.

Odd lot Less than 100 shares of stock.

Any order of less than 100 shares (or a remainder less than 100) is an odd lot. For example, an order for 150 shares is one round lot and one odd lot of 50 shares. It is possible to buy and sell odd lots, but your brokerage firm may charge a higher commission.

Price

Market order Order to buy or sell a security immediately at the best-quoted price.

Finally, you need to identify any conditions related to the price of a transaction. When you place an order, you have the ability to accept the going market price by placing a market order. A market order is an order to buy or sell immediately at the best quoted price.

STRETCH
YOUR DOLLAR

NAME YOUR OWN PRICE WITH A LIMIT ORDER

Is the stock you wanted to buy for $16 selling for $17.50 a share? If so, consider placing a limit order with your brokerage firm. You place the limit order, and the brokerage firm will execute the order when (and if) the stock reaches $16. It's that easy. You don't have to keep watching the stock every day to see if it has fallen to your desired buying price.

But there is a downside. If the stock does not reach your limit, you may never buy it. If the stock keeps rising, you will have lost out on a major gain trying to save a few cents on the initial purchase.

Ask price Price for which active sellers offer to sell a stock.

If you place a market order to buy a stock, you will most likely buy it at the lowest quoted ask price. The ask price is the price for which active sellers are offering to sell the stock.

Bid price Price for which buyers are actively offering to buy a stock.

If you place a market order to sell a stock, your sales price will probably be the highest quoted bid price. The bid price is the price for which buyers are actively offering to purchase the stock.

In other words, an active market will already have potential buyers and sellers willing to take the opposite side of your transaction. There will be active buyers to whom you can sell at the bid price and active sellers from whom you can buy at the ask price. A full quote of a stock's price gives both the bid price and the ask price. For example, the quote for a stock might be 32.05 bid and 32.10 ask (stated as 32.05 to 32.10). An investor would know that he could buy the stock for 32.10 or sell it for 32.05.

If you would like to try to do better than the quoted bid or ask price, you can put in your own bid (if you want to buy) or ask (if you want to sell). You do this by placing a limit order. A limit order is an order to buy or sell at a specified price (or better). If there are no takers at your stated limit price, your order will not be executed.

Because a limit order might not be executed immediately, you must also specify the length of time that the order is to remain active. A day order remains active until the end of the trading day, at which time it is canceled. An open order (also called a good-til-canceled [GTC] order) remains active until it is canceled.

BUYING STOCKS OF FOREIGN COMPANIES THROUGH ADRS

Investing in companies around the globe has become much easier with improved communication and financial systems. Still, though, it would be quite a bit of trouble to open a brokerage account in a foreign country to try to trade stocks in that country. Fortunately, there is an easier way. Investors can share in the fortunes of global companies by investing in their stock through ADRs (American Depositary Receipts).

An ADR is a receipt for the stock of a company in a foreign country. The stock trades in the foreign country, and the shares represented by the ADR are held in trust in the foreign country. However, the ADR trades in the U.S. markets. So, for example, you can buy Sony Corporation by purchasing Sony's ADR on the NYSE instead of purchasing it on the Tokyo Stock Exchange. Purchasing ADRs instead of foreign shares offers several advantages:

- Transactions occur on a U.S. exchange through a U.S. brokerage firm.
- Investors can avoid the cost of exchanging dollars to the foreign currency for the transaction.
- Dividends are paid in U.S. dollars.

Investing in Stocks

Investing in common stocks is very popular with individual investors. Stocks give their owners the opportunity to participate in the growth of the economy and the growth of the individual companies that the investors purchase. Although stocks do fluctuate in value, over the long run they have yielded investors more return than other types of investments.

Exhibit 12.6 illustrates the return from common stocks compared to 20-year U.S. Treasury bonds and three-month Treasury bills. The exhibit uses the S&P 500 Index to represent the returns available on common stocks. It assumes that you invested $100 in each of the three types of investment at the beginning of 1985 and reinvested all of your cash dividends and interest payments in the same investment over time.

As Exhibit 12.6 shows, the original $100 would have grown to $1,603 by the end of 2012. There were years in which you would have lost money from the previous year, but that is the risk you take with investing in stocks. There was a big loss in 2008, as a result of the financial crisis that began in that year. By 2012, your wealth would have more than recovered.

Limit order Order to buy or sell at a specified price (or better).

Day order Order to trade that remains active until the end of the trading day.

Open order Order to transact securities that remains active until canceled.

Good-til-canceled (GTC) order Open order.

ADR (American Depositary Receipt) Receipt for stock of a company in a foreign country.

| EXHIBIT 12.6 | ACCUMULATED INVESTMENT IN COMMON STOCKS, TREASURY BONDS, AND TREASURY BILLS, STARTING WITH $100 AT THE BEGINNING OF 1985 |

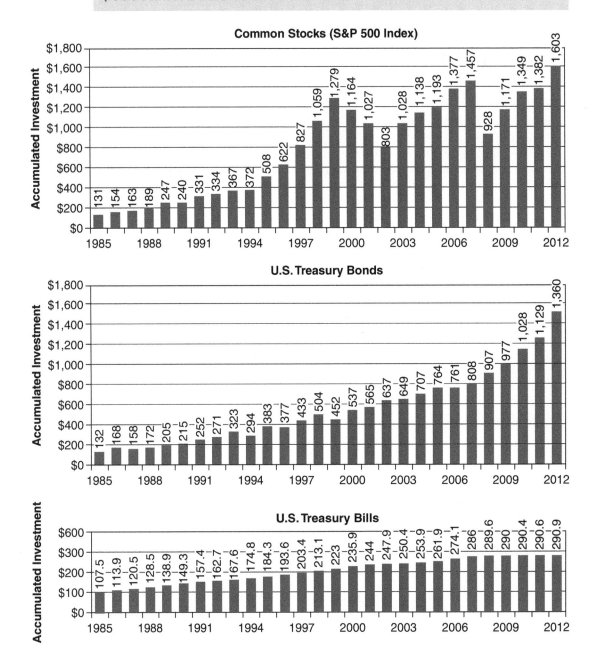

Your initial investment of $100 in Treasury bonds, a relatively safe investment whose returns can vary because of changes in interest rates (as you will see in the bond chapter), resulted in an accumulated value of $1,360 in 2012. This was almost as much as the investments in the risky stocks yielded, but note that in some previous years, Treasury bonds were well behind stocks.

Finally, the least risky of the group, Treasury bills, left you with $291 in the final year. While this amount is much less than the profits that stocks and bonds yielded, note that there was almost no variation in the steady climb of value over the years, and no year with a loss for T-bills.

The implications of Exhibit 12.6 are that carefully analyzing your prospective investments in common stocks and making the choices that fit your investment program are very important. Mistakes in choosing the wrong stocks can be costly, so you should either educate yourself to analyze and monitor your own investments or take advantage of a financial planner who can take care of your investments for you.

INVESTMENT ANALYSIS

Investment analysts conduct their investigation of the investment potential of a stock on three levels. They analyze:

1. The economy
2. The company's industry
3. The individual company

This approach provides examination of the factors over which the firm's management has no control (the economy and the industry) and those over which management has influence (conditions within the firm).

Analysis of the Economy

Analysis of the economy is a broad type of analysis. Company management has no control over economic factors, so the economic analysis usually concentrates on forecasting the economy and what effect it will have on a particular industry or company. Most events that impact the business cycle (prosperity and recession) will affect the value of the firm.

Analysis of the Industry

We can usually classify companies according to the primary industry in which they operate. Industry analysis is a blend of macro- and microanalysis; it studies the industry within the economy and the individual firms within the industry. The goal of industry analysis is to identify which industries are best poised to take advantage of the present and coming economic environment and which companies within an industry have the best investment potential.

The North American Industrial Classification System (NAICS) provides an organized coding system for classifying industries. The first two digits represent broad industries, and a progression of up to four additional digits further refines industry definitions. For example, NAICS code 44 is "Retail Trade," 448 is "Clothing and Clothing Accessory Stores," 4481 is "Clothing Stores," and 44811 is "Men's Clothing Stores."

NAICS replaces the previous standard, the Standard Industrial Classification (SIC) System. The first two digits of SIC codes represent a broadly defined industry, with the next two providing more detail. Exhibit 12.7 shows some of the NAICS classifications and their SIC counterparts.

Some companies are so large and diverse that they defy classification into one primary industry. For example, General Electric (GE) is a diversified company involved in many industries. Its products include major appliances, lighting products, industrial automation products, medical diagnostic imaging equipment, aircraft jet engines, and many others. Furthermore, GE offers services such as engineering and computer-related information services, and it delivers network television services, operates television stations, and provides cable and

---

EXHIBIT 12.7   **INDUSTRY CLASSIFICATIONS BY NAICS AND SIC**

Code	Description
NAICS: North American Industrial Classification System	
11	Agriculture, Forestry, Fishing and Hunting
21	Mining
22	Utilities
23	Construction
31–33	Manufacturing
42	Wholesale Trade
44–45	Retail Trade
48–49	Transportation and Warehousing
51	Information
52	Finance and Insurance
53	Real Estate and Rental and Leasing
54	Professional, Scientific, and Technical Services
55	Management of Companies and Enterprises
56	Administrative and Support and Waste Management and Remediation Services
61	Educational Services
62	Health Care and Social Assistance
71	Arts, Entertainment, and Recreation
72	Accommodation and Food Services
81	Other Services (except Public Administration)
92	Public Administration
SIC: Standard Industrial Classification System	
01–09	Agriculture, Forestry, and Fisheries
10–14	Mineral Industries
15–17	Construction
20–39	Manufacturing
41–49	Transportation, Communication, and Utilities
50–51	Wholesale Trade
52–59	Retail Trade
60–67	Finance, Insurance, and Real Estate
70–89	Service Industries
91–97	Public Administration

Internet services. With all of these widely different products and services, it is obvious that GE does not fit into one or even several different industries.

Analysis of an Individual Company

Individual company analysis is a microanalysis. It focuses on areas over which the firm's management can have an impact. Company analysis involves the following:

- Examining the firm's financial statements to evaluate the effectiveness of management
- Forecasting the company's future earnings and estimating the true value of the firm's stock

Forecasting financial results of an individual company often relies on a thorough economic and industry analysis. For example, a forecast of sales for the firm for the next few years depends not only on the ability of the firm's marketing efforts, but also on the conditions existing within the economy and the growth of the industry.

INVESTMENT INFORMATION

Information is the most important tool for making wise investment decisions. It supplies the building blocks that investors use to form their opinions about the investment characteristics and merits of a security. The cost of investment information ranges from free sources to those that charge hundreds or even thousands of dollars per year for a subscription or access to a database.

To illustrate the importance of accurate and timely information, consider horse races. In horse racing, betting patterns determine the payoff for the winner. That is, few people will probably bet for a horse with a slim chance of winning, so that horse will run with a high payoff, such as 50 to 1.

To win, bettors need either luck or information enabling them to place bets that win in the long run. A good bet would be one whose expected payoff is greater than the odds against winning. For example, a good bet would be one in which the true probability of the horse winning is 1 in 25 (that is, the odds against winning are 25 to 1) and the payoff is 50 to 1.

In a situation like this, a bettor would want to have any information that would help reveal the odds of the horse winning. Types of information that could give a bettor a greater chance of selecting the winner could be the direction and force of the wind, the condition of the track, the jockey riding the horse, and the breed, age, and experience of the horse.

Similar to information about horse races, information about the economy, financial markets, industry, and particular company gives investors the facts enabling a thorough investment analysis leading to an informed investment decision. The popularity of the Internet for disseminating information of all types has led to a virtual information explosion of information availability.

Information About the Economy

The main responsibility for collecting and compiling economic data lies with the government, principally at the federal level but also at the state and local levels. Important sources of economic information are the various governmental agencies that report economic data. In addition, there are private firms that conduct the business of collecting, reporting, and interpreting economic information. Exhibit 12.8 presents some examples of sources of economic information.

Information About Industries

Among the publications that provide information organized by industry are *The Value Line Investment Survey* and Standard & Poor's *Industry Surveys*. Both of these are often available in public and university libraries. *Value Line*, a weekly publication, divides its analysis by industry. Each week's publication features one or more industries. The analysis contains much information about the industry and analyses of individual companies in the industry.

Standard & Poor's *Industry Surveys* are comprehensive overviews of 50 major industries. These reports cover industry trends, developments and forecasts, major players and market share data, key ratios and statistics, comparative company analysis, general industry operations, and other information.

EXHIBIT 12.8   SOURCES OF INFORMATION ABOUT THE ECONOMY

Publication, Publisher	Web Site	Content Summary
Governmental Sources		
Federal Reserve Bulletin Board of Governors of the Federal Reserve System	www.federalreserve.gov	Extensive coverage of national economic data, including the banking system, money supply, financial markets, interest rates
Monthly Bulletin Individual Federal Reserve Banks	For links to the individual Federal Reserve Banks, check: www.federalreserve.gov.	National and regional economic data
Survey of Current Business Department of Commerce Bureau of Economic Affairs	www.bea.doc.gov	General economic and commercial data, national income and product accounts, employment data
Economic Reports Federal Trade Commission	www.ftc.gov	Analyses of various economic issues
Economic Report of the President Council of Economic Advisors	http://w3.access.gpo.gov/eop/index.html	Summary of past year's economy, discussion of coming year's areas of concern
Nongovernmental Sources		
Business Week, McGraw-Hill weekly magazine	www.businessweek.com	Current economic statistics, articles of general economic topics
The Economist newspaper	www.economist.com	British publication, international coverage
The Outlook Standard & Poor's	www.spoutlookonline.com	Summaries of general economic statistics, economic forecasts

Information About Individual Companies

There are many sources of information about individual companies. The two principal sources of company information are the company and publishers who organize and sell investment information.

Most information about individual companies, even that published by other sources, originates from the company. Companies provide information to investors through three main channels:

1. Reports to shareholders
2. News releases to the media
3. Periodic reports filed with the SEC

Companies send financial reports to their shareholders at quarterly intervals. These financial reports present financial and operating results of the company for the recent period. The final of the four reports is the annual report, and it is more detailed than the preceding three interim reports. Interested investors can usually receive copies of these reports at no charge by requesting them from the company. Many firms make them available for download from their Internet sites.

Another important source of investment information is from company news releases. Companies often announce a press release in conjunction with another type of information release. A broad announcement of information to the news media complies with the legal requirement that when a company releases information, it must do so to the broad investing public.

U.S. security law calls for regular disclosure of financial results of larger corporations and for companies whose stock trades on the public markets. The Securities and Exchange Commission (SEC), a federal government agency charged with enforcing securities laws, has a set of reports (also called "forms") that companies must file to comply with the statutes. Exhibit 12.9 gives a brief overview of some of the most common of the SEC forms.

SEC Form 10-K is the most widely used. It contains a company's annual financial statements, information about the nature of the business, identification of officers and directors, and other relevant information.

The proxy statement is another useful filing. A company must file a proxy statement whenever an issue must be put to a stockholder vote and someone (usually company management) is soliciting a proxy from shareholders. A proxy transfers the right to vote shares. The proxy statement provides shareholders with information to enable them to vote their shares or to sign a proxy designating someone else to vote their shares. For investors, one of the useful pieces of information that must be included in the proxy statement is the annual compensation of officers and directors of the corporation.

SEC filings are available from the SEC's web site, www.sec.gov. The SEC maintains a database called IDEA (formerly called Edgar) of these filings. Anyone interested in these filings can access the database via the SEC's web site.

A number of independent publishers provide information to investors about companies and their investment potential. These services range from newsletters with a few dozen subscribers to major publishing companies supplying thousands of libraries, institutions, investment advisors, and individual investors with investment information. Exhibit 12.10 shows some of these publishers and a sample of the publications they offer.

Securities and Exchange Commission (SEC) U.S. government agency charged with enforcing securities laws.

Form 10-K Corporation's annual financial statements filed with the SEC.

Proxy statement Document providing shareholders information on corporate voting proposals.

EXHIBIT 12.9	COMMON REPORTS THAT CORPORATIONS FILE WITH THE SEC

Report	Brief Description
Prospectus	Part I of the security registration statement. Contains basic business and financial information about the security issuer. Filed when needed for a new security issue.
Proxy Statement	Provides information about matters on which a stockholder vote is required. Filed when needed for a shareholder vote.
S-1	Part II of the security registration statement. Contains information not required in the prospectus such as expenses of issuance and distribution, indemnification of officers and directors, and recent sales of unregistered securities. Filed when needed for a new security issue.
3, 4, and 5	Statements filed by officers, directors, and owners of 10 percent or more of the company's stock reporting ownership or changes in ownership. Filed when needed or annually (Form 5).
8-K	Used to report the occurrence of any material corporate event or change deemed important to investors and previously not reported. Filed when needed as an event occurs.
10-K	Comprehensive overview of the company's business including audited financial statements. Filed annually within 90 days of the end of the company's fiscal year.
10-Q	View of the company's financial position including unaudited financial statements. Filed quarterly for the first three fiscal quarters within 45 days of the end of the quarter.

EXHIBIT 12.10	SAMPLE PUBLISHERS OF COMPANY INFORMATION

Publisher	Publications
Moody's Investors Services	A broad range of publications. Some examples: *Moody's Municipal and Government Manual* (information about government debt issues) *Moody's Handbook of Common Stocks* (basic description and financial information for hundreds of companies)
Standard & Poor's	A broad range of publications. Some examples: *Standard & Poor's Register of Corporations* (directory of corporations with names of officers and directors) *Standard & Poor's Stock Reports* (basic description and financial information for hundreds of companies)
Value Line	*The Value Line Investment Survey* (weekly publication, over three months covers 1,700 different companies, then repeats)

There is a wealth of investment information available on the Internet. Some is available only to subscribers, but Internet users can access much investment information at no charge. Exhibit 12.11 lists some providers of investment information via Internet and other computer-based access methods. Web sites seem to come and go regularly; the sites provided here are those that have some degree of permanence such as the sites of the Federal Reserve Banks. To locate many more sources of investment information on the Internet, simply do a search using keywords such as "investment information" or "stocks investing."

Although most information from the Internet is reliable, users should be cautious about accepting all information provided by Internet sources. Investors can confidently rely on information obtained from a commercial site that also

SAMPLE INTERNET INVESTMENT INFORMATION PROVIDERS   EXHIBIT 12.11

Data Supplier	Web Site	Summary of Information
Available at no charge		
American Association of Individual Investors (for members)	www.aaii.com	Screening tools, stock reports
Federal Reserve Board	www.federalreserve.gov	Economic data such as interest rates, exchange rates, money supply, and industrial production
Reuters	www.reuters.com	Information about the market, individual companies, stock screening
U.S. Department of Commerce, Bureau of Economic Analysis	www.bea.gov	International, national and regional economic indicators and statistics, industry statistics
U.S. Securities and Exchange Commission	www.sec.gov	EDGAR database with access to company filings with the SEC
Yahoo! Finance	finance.yahoo.com	Access to stock quotes, company financial data, historical security prices, stock screening, mutual funds
Available for subscription *fee or one-time charge*:		
Hoovers Online	www.hoovers.com	Stock screening, company financial information
Media General Financial Services		
U.S., Canadian, and Global IPO		
Executive Compensation	www.mgfs.com	20 years of company financial data and price history, IPO, executive compensation data
Standard & Poor's		
Compustat Global		
Compustat Backdata		
Research Insight		
Market Insight	www.standardandpoors.com	Fundamental and market data on 54,000 companies, available online or on storage media

publishes respected print media, such as the Yahoo! Finance site. On the other extreme, the reliability of information gleaned from Internet chat rooms or newsgroups is notoriously unpredictable, and investors should verify such information from an independent source before acting on the information.

To look up information about a company on the Internet or on terminals that brokers use, enter the stock (ticker) symbol for the company. The stock symbol is a set of one to five letters that uniquely identifies the company. Sometimes the symbol is logical; for example International Business Machines Corp. is IBM. However, be careful, TI is not Texas Instruments, it is Telecom Italia. (Texas Instruments is TXN.)

Some stock symbols have no relationship to the company name—like U.S. Steel, which has the symbol X. Sometimes companies get creative with their symbol; Brinker International (which owns and operates Chili's Grill and Bar, Romano's Macaroni Grill, and other restaurant chains) adopted the symbol EAT. VCA Antech, Inc., a company that offers veterinary services, has the symbol WOOF. Can you guess which airline has the symbol LUV?

Stock (ticker) symbol One to five letters that uniquely identify a company's stock.

FINANCIAL STATEMENTS

The study of financial statements is worthy of a lengthy book by itself, so this chapter can only introduce some of the basic definitions. The two principal corporate financial statements are the balance sheet and the income statement.

Balance Sheet

A balance sheet shows the financial position of the company on a particular date, usually the end of a quarter or of the year. The balance sheet is also called the statement of financial condition. It is a summary of what the firm owns (its assets), what it owes to outside parties (its liabilities), and what it owes to its owners (its stockholders' equity). The relationship between these items is

Stockholders' equity The net value of a corporation: assets less liabilities.

$$\text{assets} = \text{liabilities} + \text{stockholders' equity} \qquad \textbf{Equation 12.2}$$

Equation 12.2 is a logical relationship. For example, suppose Dan starts a business selling snow cones. He puts up $1,000 of his own money (stockholders' equity) and borrows another $500 (liability) from his generous brother to buy the stand, equipment, and supplies (the assets) for $1,500. Dan's balance sheet would look like Exhibit 12.12.

A balance sheet can provide much useful information. It allows investors and analysts to inspect issues such as

- Is this firm carrying too much debt?
- Does this company have enough cash to meet its near-term needs?
- Is this firm extending too much credit to its customers?

Exhibit 12.13 presents a recent balance sheet for The Gap, Inc., the retailer of casual apparel and accessories. The stock symbol for The Gap is GPS. As an example of what a balance sheet might tell us, consider The Gap's cash position. You can tell that GPS is a company with relatively little debt. In 2012, for example, it had $1.2 billion in debt. While that may seem like a large sum,

| BALANCE SHEET FOR DAN'S SNOW CONE STAND | **EXHIBIT 12.12** |

Assets	
Supplies	$200
Equipment	500
Stand	800
Total assets	$1,500
Liabilities	
Loan	$500
Stockholders' equity	1,000
Total liabilities and stockholders' equity	$1,500

it is only a small fraction of the company's $7.5 billion in total assets. From that information, an analyst would likely conclude that The Gap should easily handle its debt load.

Balance sheets let analysts and investors examine issues such as these and also compare one year's results to previous years to investigate any trends. The example Gap balance sheet shows three years of balance sheets.

Income Statement

In its income statement, a company reports its revenues (or sales) and expenses. The firm's net income is the difference between revenue and expenses. These reports often use the terms *net income*, *earnings*, and *profit* interchangeably.

© Waxen, 2014, Shutterstock, Inc.

A ticker symbol uniquely identifies a company traded on the stock market. Some companies use mnemonics for their symbol. BABY is the ticker symbol for Natus Medical Incorporated, a manufacturer of newborn care products.

| EXHIBIT 12.13 | THE GAP, INC., BALANCE SHEET (MILLIONS OF DOLLARS) |

	2012	2011	2010
Assets			
Current assets			
Cash and equivalents	$1,510	$1,885	$1,661
Inventory	1,758	1,615	1,620
Other current assets	864	809	645
Total current assets	4,132	4,309	3,926
Long-term assets			
Property, plant, and equipment	2,619	2,523	2,563
Other	719	590	576
Total long-term assets	3,338	3,113	3,139
Total assets	7,470	7,422	7,065
Liabilities			
Current liabilities			
Accounts payable	2,344	2,069	2,092
Other current liabilities		59	3
Total current liabilities	2,344	2,128	2,095
Long-term liabilities			
Long-term debt	1,246	1,606	
Other liabilities	986	933	890
Total long-term liabilities	2,232	2,539	890
Total liabilities	4,576	4,667	2,985
Total stockholders' equity	2,894	2,755	4,080
Total liabilities and equity	$7,470	$7,422	$7,065

Exhibit 12.14 shows the income statement for The Gap and provides three years of data. The main use of the income statement is to examine the profitability of the company. The next section of this chapter shows one way to analyze a company's profitability with information from the income statement.

Income statements also allow comparison to previous years' results. For example, by looking at the three years of earnings of The Gap, you can see that the firm's income fell from 2010 to 2011 but recovered some in 2012.

THE GAP, INC., INCOME STATEMENT (MILLIONS OF DOLLARS)   EXHIBIT 12.14

	2012	2011	2012
Total revenue	$15,651	$14,549	$14,664
Cost of revenue	9,480	9,275	8,775
Gross profit	6,171	5,274	5,889
Operating expenses	4,229	3,836	3,921
Operating income (loss)	1,942	1,438	1,968
Other income net of expenses	6	5	6
Earnings before interest and taxes	1,948	1,443	1,974
Interest expense	87	74	−8
Income before tax	1,861	1,369	1,982
Income taxes	726	536	778
Net income	$1,135	$833	$1,204
Common stock shares outstanding	488	533	641
Earnings per share	$2.33	$1.56	$1.88

ANALYZING STOCKS

This section will present just a few of the many techniques for analyzing the investment worth of a stock. Careful investors will use a number of methods and make their final decision based on a consensus on all the techniques they use.

Assets

One way of viewing a company's value is to examine its assets. Take Dan's Snow Cone Stand, for example. Dan has assets for which he paid $1,500. Subtract the $500 he owes his brother, and you have a business with a net worth of $1,000 based on its assets net of liabilities.

This is a number that investors call book value. For corporations, we usually state book value on a per share basis, so book value is equal to the firm's assets minus liabilities, then divided by the number of shares it has outstanding. In other words, book value is the amount of net assets behind each share

Book value Assets less liabilities behind each share of stock.

of stock. If stockholders could sell those assets at their recorded value and pay off the debt, book value would be the amount of cash they would have.

$$\text{book value} = \frac{\text{assets} - \text{liabilities}}{\text{number of shares outstanding}}$$ **Equation 12.3**

Is a company worth its book value? Ask this question: Can you sell the company's assets for their recorded value? Maybe you can sell the assets for less, maybe more—it all depends on the market value for those assets. But would you really want to sell off the assets? Maybe the company is worth more than just its assets. Maybe Dan's Snow Cone Stand has a number of loyal customers who know just where to go for a nice snow cone on a hot day. So Dan's Snow Cone Stand is worth more than $1,000 because of the business these regular customers bring in. We call this goodwill. Goodwill is the value of a business over and above its book value.

Goodwill Value of a business over and above its book value.

Although using the value of a firm's assets as a yardstick for the value of its stock has its pros and cons, it is a good starting point. You might decide that you want to purchase a stock only if its price per share is less than its book value. The famous investor Benjamin Graham, whose book *The Intelligent Investor* way back in 1949 remains a classic even today, recommended buying a stock only when its price is no more than two-thirds of book value.

Example 12.3 shows how to compute book value using financial information for The Gap. The Gap's book value was $5.93 at the end of 2012. Would Ben Graham have recommended purchasing The Gap's stock? In mid 2013, the price for a share of stock was about $40, so The Gap was selling for about 6.7 times its book value, much more than the two-thirds favored by Graham. Ben Graham would probably not have recommended The Gap.

Earnings

Earnings are the key to company growth. Rising earnings mean that the company can increase its dividend and gives investors a reason to pay more for a

---

EXAMPLE 12.3   The Gap's Book Value

Compute the book value for The Gap for 2012 using information in Exhibits 12.13 and 12.14.

To compute book value, we need the stockholders' equity and the number of shares outstanding. Stockholders' equity is on the balance sheet, Exhibit 12.13, and the number of shares follows at the bottom of the income statement in Exhibit 12.14. Using Equation 12.3,

$$\text{book value} = \frac{\text{assets} - \text{liabilities}}{\text{number of shares outstanding}}$$

$$= \frac{2,894}{488}$$

$$= 5.93$$

The Gap's book value is $5.93 per share. ■

company's stock. When analyzing earnings, investors usually use earnings per share (total earnings divided by the number of shares that the company has issued and has outstanding). Note that the income statement in Exhibit 12.14 reports both total earnings and also its earnings per share of common stock of The Gap.

One measure that investors often compute is a company's price-to-earnings ratio. The price-to-earnings ratio (P/E ratio), is simply the company's stock price divided by its earnings per share.

$$P/E \text{ ratio} = \frac{\text{stock price}}{\text{earnings per share}}$$ Equation 12.4

Price-to-earnings ratio (P/E ratio) Stock price divided by earnings per share.

Another term for the P/E ratio is the earnings multiple. The idea is that a company's stock is fundamentally worth some multiple of its earnings. Example 12.4 shows that The Gap was selling for a P/E ratio of 17.18. How do investors use the P/E ratio to help make investment choices? One way is the method recommended by Ben Graham. He said that investors should look for stocks with a P/E ratio less than twice the average yield on AAA-rated bonds.

In mid 2013, AAA-rated bonds had an average yield of about 4.25 percent, so applying Graham's rule would lead you to seek stocks with a P/E ratio less than twice that–about 8.5 percent. In mid 2013, the average P/E in the market was about 19.7, so Ben Graham would have found the average stock an unattractive purchase at that time. With a P/E of 17.18, The Gap would probably not have been on Mr. Graham's recommended list, either.

Profitability

An efficiently run company will have a high degree of profitability. Profitability is the company's capacity to use capital contributed by its stockholders (stockholders' equity), assets, or revenue to generate earnings. There are many measures of a company's profitability, but the one presented here is the return on equity (ROE).

Return on equity (ROE) Measure of company profitability equal to profits divided by equity.

The Gap's P/E Ratio	**EXAMPLE 12.4**

Compute The Gap's P/E ratio.

In mid 2013, the price for a share of The Gap stock was about $40. Exhibit 12.14 shows that The Gap's earnings per share were $2.33.

$$P/E \text{ ratio} = \frac{\text{stock price}}{\text{earnings per share}}$$

$$= \frac{40}{2.33}$$

$$= 17.18$$

The Gap's P/E was 17.18. ■

EXAMPLE 12.5   The Gap's ROE

To find out how profitable The Gap, Inc., was in 2012, compute the company's return on equity.

Find earnings in the income statement (Exhibit 12.14) and stockholders' equity in the balance sheet (Exhibit 12.13) and use Equation 12.5:

$$ROE = \frac{earnings}{stockholders'\ equity}$$

$$= \frac{1,135}{2,894}$$

$$= 0.3922$$

The Gap's 2012 ROE was 0.3922, or 39.22 percent.   ■

Return on equity represents a firm's ability to use stockholders' equity to produce profits for the company. It is equal to earnings divided by stockholders' equity.

$$ROE = \frac{earnings}{stockholders'\ equity} \qquad \text{Equation 12.5}$$

Example 12.5 illustrates the computation of The Gap's ROE for 2012. In that year, Gap showed a return of 39.22 percent on its stockholders' equity.

The most widely used method for assessing return on equity is to compare the company's ROE to the value of companies in general, or of the firm's close competitors. For example, the average ROE in 2012 was about 13.5 percent, so The Gap showed better-than-average profitability for that year. For a comparison based on The Gap's competition, Guess?, Inc., is a close competitor of The Gap in 2012. Guess? had an ROE of 14.78 percent. The Gap's ROE was much stronger and favorable than Guess? Inc.

Dividends

Dividends are the cash payments that corporations often elect to pay to their stockholders. Dividend payments allow stockholders to share in the earnings of the company. Many companies pay regular dividends every quarter or annually. A number of companies try to maintain a policy of increasing their dividend each year as long as earnings have increased.

The dividend yield is the company's dividend per share over the latest year divided by the price of the stock.

$$dividend\ yield = \frac{annual\ dividend}{stock\ price} \qquad \text{Equation 12.6}$$

Many companies pay dividends on a regular basis. The most common is a quarterly dividend. When a company's management feels that profitability has

THE GAP, INC., QUARTERLY DIVIDENDS, 2009–2013 — EXHIBIT 12.15

Year	First Quarter	Second Quarter	Third Quarter	Fourth Quarter	Total Annual
2009	0.0850	0.0850	0.0850	0.0850	0.3400
2010	0.0850	0.1000	0.1000	0.1000	0.3850
2011	0.1000	0.1125	0.1125	0.1125	0.4375
2012	0.1125	0.1250	0.1250	0.1250	0.4875
2013	0.1250	0.1500	0.1500	0.2000	0.6250

increased and can sustain an increase in the dividend payout, the company will usually raise its quarterly dividend.

Exhibit 12.15 shows quarterly dividends paid by The Gap from 2009 to 2013. Note how dividends increased each year, although not by the same amount. Example 12.6 shows that the dividend yield for The Gap in early 2013 was about 1.22 percent.

How did Benjamin Graham feel about dividends? His advice was to identify stocks whose dividend yields are at least two-thirds of the yield of AAA-rated bonds. As stated earlier, AAA-rated bonds carried an interest yield of 4.25 percent at in mid 2013, so at that time Graham's criterion would entail looking for stocks with a dividend yield greater than about 2.85 percent. It looks like The Gap's dividend yield would not have passed old Ben Graham's test.

STOCK SCREENING

Investors have a powerful tool for identifying potential investments: stock screening. Stock screening is the process of identifying a set of stocks that

Stock screening The process of identifying stocks that meet a set of desired characteristics.

The Gap's Dividend Yield — EXAMPLE 12.6

Compute The Gap's dividend yield in early 2013 based on a stock price of $40.

From Exhibit 12.15, The Gap's annual dividend for the year 2012 was $0.4875 per share. Using Equation 12.6,

$$\text{dividend yield} = \frac{\text{annual dividend}}{\text{stock price}}$$

$$= \frac{0.4875}{40}$$

$$= 0.0122$$

The Gap's dividend yield in early 2012 was 0.0122, or 1.22 percent. ■

meet a particular list of criteria that an investor identifies as desired characteristics. It uses huge databases of financial information about thousands of
companies.

Suppose that you want to know which stocks pay at least a 3 percent
annual dividend and have experienced earnings growth of at least 10 percent
annually over the last five years. You can perform a stock screen that will provide you with a list of stocks meeting those criteria.

There are a number of Internet sites that provide stock screening; some
require a monthly or annual fee, whereas others are available at no charge.
To see a list of stock screeners, simply do a search in the Internet for "stock
screener" or "stock screening software."

To see an illustration of stock screening, consider the four company characteristics presented the previous section of this chapter. For book value, P/E
ratio, and dividend yield, each subsection identified the criteria that Ben Graham suggests. Let's use his criteria. For the remaining criterion, ROE, let's say
that we want our stocks to have an ROE that is 20 percent better (greater) than
average. In early 2013, the average ROE was about 13.5 percent, so let's set the
screen to search for stocks with ROE ≥ 16.2.

Exhibit 12.16 presents a stock screen using these criteria with the screener
available from Fidelity Investments at www.fidelity.com. First of all, a total of
20 stocks were left in the screen following the inclusion of the first three criteria, but the list dropped to zero when including the price/book < .67 criterion.
So, let's adjust Ben Graham's final criterion to a value of 1.0. That leaves only
six stocks in the list, and Exhibit 12.16 reveals those stocks and how they met
the criteria. The exhibit summarizes the criteria used in the screen and presents
a list of the six companies whose stock met the criteria. A smart investor would

EXHIBIT 12.16   STOCK SCREENING EXAMPLE

ROE ≥ 16.2%

Dividend yield ≥ 2.85%

P/E ratio ≤ 8.5

Price as a portion of book value (price/book value) ≤ 1.0

Company Name	Ticker	ROE	Dividend Yield	P/E Ratio	Price as a Portion of Book Value
CBS CORP-A	CBS.A	16.66	4.39	1.20	0.36
BANCOLOMBIA-ADR	CIB	21.24	4.78	6.36	0.63
ARCELOR MITTAL	MT	24.78	5.16	2.14	0.57
OVERSEAS SHIPHO	OSG	22.17	6.95	1.83	0.41
TWIN DISC	TWIN	16.74	4.08	3.71	0.66
UTD STATES STL	X	38.18	5.15	1.24	0.55

take a closer look at each of the six companies in the list, examining other characteristics of the firms. The investor would eliminate those stocks that do not meet standards and keep those that do, ultimately deciding to invest in one or more of the stocks (or, possibly, none).

ESTIMATING A STOCK'S VALUE

If you know just how much a company's stock is really worth (that is, you know its true value), then you would have the key to investment success. Knowing a stock's true value, you can compare that value to the current market price of the stock and make an informed decision about whether you should invest in that company. If the true value of a stock is less than its market price, then the stock is undervalued in the market (i.e., other investors in the market do not realize the company's true value). However, over time, as the company exhibits its success, others in the market will come to recognize the stock's true value and will bid the price up to that value. So, if you had bought that undervalued stock, you would have some handsome returns to show for your effort.

Just how much is a particular stock worth? This is the big question, and if you could answer it with accuracy for a large percentage of stocks, you could become a very wealthy investor by using your skill. The truth is that trying to determine the real value of a stock is a very challenging undertaking. There are hundreds of professional stock analysts following most of the stocks that exist. Each analyst pores over financial statements, keeping abreast of new company developments, and watches the competition to try to forecast the company's profitability. And these professionals are not always on target.

But the potential for making investment profits is so powerful that it is often worth it to either purchase the analyses produced by others, access analyses offered by your brokerage firm, or to analyze the company yourself. There are many complex methods used by analysts to estimate a company's worth and forecast its future stock price, and it is far beyond our scope in this book to begin to consider them. However, almost all of the techniques have their basis in the fundamental valuation equation developed way back in 1938 by John Burr Williams when he stated, "Let us define the investment value of a stock as the present worth of all the dividends to be paid upon it" (John Burr Williams [1938], *The Theory of Investment Value*, Cambridge: Harvard University Press).

So, as Mr. Williams put it, all you have to do is forecast all of the future dividends that the stock will pay and discount them to present value using the concepts from this book in Chapter 1. Accomplishing that, however, is a daunting task for many reasons, including the task of forecasting future dividends and the challenge of identifying the applicable discount rate. But, if we can make some simplifying assumptions, then we can see the principles of stock valuation in action using what has become known as the dividend discount model.

Dividend discount model
An equation that specifies a relationship for valuing common stocks based on the present value of future dividends.

To specify the dividend discount model, let's assume that we know or can estimate:

- The current dividend that the stock pays or the dividend that it should pay if it does not pay one.
- The rate that the company will grow in the foreseeable future. This is the annual future growth rate of the firm's earnings (and therefore its dividends too). This will be the growth rate in the equation.
- The rate of return that investors require in order to invest in the company. This will be the required rate of return in the equation.

The dividend discount model is

$$\text{stock value} = \frac{\text{dividend} \cdot (1 + \text{growth rate})}{\text{required rate of return} - \text{growth rate}} \qquad \text{Equation 12.7}$$

Example 12.7 provides an illustration of the use of the model to estimate a stock's value. In the example, Albert estimates a share of Geltico common stock to have a value of $35.33. Albert checks the price of Geltico on his favorite investments website and finds that it currently sells for $34 per share. Technically that makes the stock undervalued based on Albert's estimates, but that market price is not much less that Albert's estimate of Geltico's true value of $35.33, so he decides not to buy the stock.

Later that week, Albert notices a news item explaining that Geltico plans to spend more money on product development over the next decade. Product development was precisely one of the factors that Albert had considered when he estimated a growth rate of 6 percent for Geltico. He believes this new information is important, and after considering the new information

EXAMPLE 12.7

Albert Bartowski is considering investing in Geltico, Inc. Based on his estimate of the company's risk, Albert wants to get a return of at least 12 percent on his investment (his required rate of return). Geltico pays an annual cash dividend of 2.00 per share, and Albert estimates that the company will grow at a rate of 6 percent for the foreseeable future. What is a share of Geltico worth to Albert?

$$
\begin{aligned}
\text{stock value} &= \frac{\text{dividend} \cdot (1 + \text{growth rate})}{\text{required rate of return} - \text{growth rate}} \\
&= \frac{2.00 \cdot (1 + .06)}{.12 - .06} \\
&= 35.33
\end{aligned}
$$

Albert's estimate of Geltico's value is $35.33 per share.   ∎

Albert Bartowski (Example 12.7) raises his estimate of Geltico, Inc.'s growth rate after considering the impact of the firm's increased focus on product development. What is the value of the firm's stock considering this revised growth rate estimate?

$$\text{stock value} = \frac{\text{dividend} \cdot (1 + \text{growth rate})}{\text{required rate of return} - \text{growth rate}}$$

$$= \frac{2.00 \cdot (1 + .07)}{.12 - .07}$$

$$= 42.80$$

Albert's revised estimate of Geltico's value is $42.80 per share. ■

in his analysis, his forecast of Geltico's growth rate increases to 7 percent. Exhibit 12.8 demonstrates the effect that this increased growth rate should have on the value of Geltico's stock.

Considering the new information, Geltico's stock has an estimated value of $42.80 per share. Albert notes that Geltico continues to sell for around $34 in the market, and he decides to buy 100 shares because he believes that he is getting good investment value for his money. He is buying shares that he believes are worth $42.80 for a price of only $34.

Many investment situations may in reality be more complicated than this example, but it illustrates the process of evaluating a company's growth prospects and using that to estimate a value. While other situations may be more complicated, their analysis usually follows the same outline and the analyst uses some expanded form of the dividend discount model to arrive at a value for the firm's stock.

SUMMARY

Marketable securities provide a convenient vehicle for investing. Advantages of marketable securities include marketability and liquidity; they represent real, income-producing assets, availability of investment information, and relatively low expenses.

Stocks and bonds are the two major types of marketable securities of interest to individual investors. Common stocks represent ownership of a corporation and increase in value when the company's profits rise and fall in value when profits decrease. Common stocks may pay a cash dividend that the corporation often increases when profits increase. Preferred stocks, by contrast, pay a fixed dividend but do not share in increases in profits. Bonds are the debt securities of corporations or governments.

Financial markets provide the means for investors to buy and sell securities. Primary markets facilitate the sales of stocks and bonds by corporations and other issuers to investors, and secondary markets allow investors to buy and sell among each other. Financial markets are important to the development and growth of free-enterprise economies.

Stock exchanges are the organizations that facilitate trading in the secondary markets. Chief among these is NYSE Euronext, which operates the New York Stock Exchange. NASDAQ is an electronic stock exchange that trades mostly stocks of smaller companies.

A market index is useful for measuring the strength and direction of market movements. Popular market indexes include the Dow Jones Industrial Average and the Standard & Poor's 500 Index.

Investors deal with securities brokerage firms to buy or sell securities. For their clients, brokerage firms can make transactions, provide investment information and advice, maintain securities in a brokerage account, and lend money against securities as collateral.

Lending money against securities is margin lending. It allows investors to purchase securities by borrowing a portion of the purchase price. The initial margin requirement defines the minimum amount of cash an investor needs to provide to purchase stock. The maintenance margin requirement defines the amount of equity investors must keep in their account. When the account falls below the maintenance margin requirement, the investor receives a margin call to deposit additional cash.

When placing an order to make a security transaction, an investor should specify the order direction (buy or sell), size, and price. Market orders tell the broker to make the transaction at the current market price, while limit orders give a specific price limit for the transaction.

When analyzing stocks for investment, investors analyze the economy, the company's industry, and the individual company. Analysis of the company involves examining the firm's financial statements and forecasting company earnings to estimate the value of the firm's stock.

Investment information is the important basis for any investment evaluation. Financial reports provide the financial information about a company. The two principal reports are the balance sheet and the income statement. Stock screening is a useful tool that screens through databases of company data to identify companies that meet criteria specified by the investor.

PROBLEMS

1. Compute the commission on the following transactions:

   a. The sale of a small rental property for $45,000 through a real estate broker who charges 6 percent commission

   b. The sale of 1,200 shares of stock at $38 per share through a full-service broker who charges a commission of $50 plus 5 cents per share

   c. The sale of 1,200 shares of stock at $38 per share through a discount broker who charges $15 plus .01 percent of the amount of the transaction

   d. The sale of 1,200 shares of stock at $38 through an online broker who charges a flat commission of $15 for trades of 2,000 shares or less and $24 for trades of more than 2,000 shares

2. The initial margin requirement is 50 percent. Compute the total amount of funds needed to purchase 800 shares of stock at $24 per share on margin.

3. If the initial margin requirement is 70 percent, how much per share would an investor need to deposit in a margin account to buy stock selling for $47 per share?

4. James has a margin loan of $7,000 and stock with a market value of $10,600. Calculate his margin percent.

5. Orin buys stock for $18 per share at 50 percent initial margin. The maintenance margin requirement is 25 percent, and Orin's stock falls to a price of $11. Will Orin get a margin call?

6. Amy Stengel places a market order to buy 100 shares of stock. The quote on the stock at the time of her order is $41.30 bid and $41.50 ask. At what price will Amy's order most likely be executed?

7. Terry places a limit order to sell stock at $43.20. The quote is $43.10 bid to $43.25 ask. Will her order be executed? If her order had been a market order, at what price would it be executed?

8. A company has total liabilities of $40,000 and stockholders' equity of $110,000. If the company has 5,000 shares of common stock outstanding, what is its book value?

9. The Glixor Corp. has the following information:

   a. Assets $200,000
   b. Liabilities   60,000
   c. Stockholders' equity   140,000
   d. Net income (earnings)   12,600
   e. Stock price   25.00
   f. Dividend per share   1.00
   g. Shares outstanding   10,000

   Using this information, compute Glixor's book value, P/E ratio, ROE, and dividend yield.

10. The P/E ratio of the S&P 500 Index is 26. You have decided to run a stock screen using the following criteria: book value < 120 percent of stock price, dividend yield of at least 3 percent, ROE greater than 8 percent, and P/E less than 80 percent of the average market P/E. Identify whether Glixor (previous problem) meets each of these criteria. Will Glixor pass your screen?

11. Artie Holmes is analyzing the common stock of Smithton Corp. and believes that investors should require a rate of return from the stock. He forecasts the company's dividends to increase at a rate of 4 percent in the future, and Smithton pays cash dividends of $4.00 per share. What is the value of a share of Smithton common stock?

12. Velma Holcomb is considering purchasing stock of Piltdown, Inc. at a price of $22 per share. She requires a rate of return of 12 percent on her investments of companies like Piltdown, and the stock pays a dividend of $1.20. Analysts forecast a growth rate of 8 percent for the company. Based on the value of Piltdown indicated by the dividend discount model, should Velma invest?

13. Piltdown, Inc. (previous problem) has just announced that as a result of a previously unobserved geological formation that was just discovered by company geologists, its properties in the Olsen Field will be less productive in future years. Velma believes that the outcome of this will be slower growth in revenues and dividends for Piltdown. Her new estimate of the company's growth rate is 6 percent. Estimate the value of Piltdown stock and make a recommendation to Velma regarding whether she should buy more, sell what she has, or hold what she has.

CASE STUDIES

COLLEGE STUDENT

Kevin Maedor is a 19-year-old college student. He still lives at home with his parents, and he works part time at Vapor's Lane. He started his financial plan in the spring semester of 2014. He plans to graduate with a B.S. in engineering in May 2017 Use the investing goals you created for him in Chapter 11.

- Suggest investments for him. Use Stock Track to research your suggestions.
- Provide a detailed explanation of why these are good investments for him.

Alternate:
   He inherited $40,000 from his grandmother.

- Recommend an investment strategy for him.
- Set a net worth or a return on investment goal for his inheritance.
- Suggest investments for him. Use Stock Track to research your suggestions.
- Provide a detailed explanation of why these are good investments for him.

NEW GRADUATE

Rene Harris recently graduated with a B.S. in nursing. She lives by herself in a modest apartment. Her annual salary is $76,000 a year. Use the investing goals you created for her in Chapter 11.

- Suggest investments for her. Use stock track to research your suggestions.
- Provide a detailed explanation of why these are good investments for her.

Alternate:
   She received a $25,000 sign-on bonus from a rural hospital.

- Recommend an investment strategy for her.
- Set a net worth or a return on investment goal for her grant.
- Suggest investments for her. Use Stock Track to research your suggestions.
- Provide a detailed explanation of why these are good investments for her.

CREATE YOUR OWN FINANCIAL PLAN

Use the investment goals you set for yourself in Chapter 11.

- Will you use stocks, bonds, or a combination of both to reach your goals?
- Use Stock Trak to research your investment options.
- Select a portfolio of stocks and bonds that will help you meet your goals.

REVIEW QUESTIONS

1. List four advantages of marketable securities compared to other investments. Give an example of each advantage, comparing a marketable security to another investment.

_____

_____

_____

_____

2. Identify and explain the two types of corporate stock. As an investor who wants to profit from long-run growth, which type of stock would you prefer to own?

_____

_____

_____

3. Contrast primary financial markets with secondary markets. Can one be successful without the other? Explain why, or why not.

_____

_____

_____

4. Explain the difference between a bull market and a bear market.

_____

_____

_____

5. Identify the four principal services offered by securities brokerage firms.

_____

_____

_____

_____

6. Explain how an investor can purchase stock by putting up only a portion of the purchase price. Include initial margin, maintenance margin, and margin calls in your explanation.

_____

_____

_____

7. Smith and Jones each buy $10,000 worth of stock. Smith pays $10,000 cash for her stock while Jones buys hers on margin. The stock rises nicely in value. Which investor makes the greater return? If the stock were to fall in value, which investor would experience the greatest loss (expressed in terms of return)?

_____

_____

_____

8. Differentiate between a market order and a limit order, including the role of bid and ask prices.

_____

_____

_____

9. Define the following:
   • Day order

   _____

   • Open order

   _____

   • Fill or kill order

   _____

10. Describe an ADR and explain why an individual investor might prefer it over its foreign counterpart.

_____

_____

_____

11. List the three levels of investment analysis.

_____

_____

_____

12. Identify the principal financial statements issued by a company and filed with the SEC.

_____

_____

_____

13. Explain the following:
   • Book value

_____

   • P/E ratio

_____

   • ROE

_____

   • Dividend yield

_____

14. What is stock screening? Identify several characteristics that you might identify for a stock screen.

_____

_____

_____

15. Find a stock screener on the Internet and use it to screen for a list of stocks using your own set of screening criteria.

_____

_____

_____

13

Bonds

"Gentlemen prefer bonds."

−Andrew Mellon
(1855−1937)

OBJECTIVES

- Describe bonds

KEY TERMS

Bond
Bond rating
Convertible bond
Corporate bond
Coupon rate
Current yield
Debenture
Default
Face value

Floating interest bond
Investment grade bond
Maturity
Municipal bond
Note
Par value
Preferred stock
Secured bond
Speculative bond

Treasury bonds (T-bonds)
Treasury Inflation-Protected
 Securities (TIPS)
Treasury notes (T-notes)
Unsecured bond
Variable interest bond
Yield to maturity
Zero-coupon bond

Investing in Bonds

Bonds are debt securities that pay interest to their holder and return the principal amount of the bond at maturity. Bonds can have maturities ranging from 1 year up to 30 years or so. Some countries have even issued perpetual bonds. Bonds with intermediate maturities (3–10 years, or thereabouts) are often called notes.

Note Bond with maturity of about 3–10 years.

The traditional bond has the following characteristics:

Par value Principal amount of a bond that is paid to the bondholder at maturity.

- The par value (or face value) of a bond is the principal owed on the bond. Traditionally, bonds have a face value of $1,000, but they sometimes are issued in different amounts such as $100.

Coupon rate The rate of interest that the bond pays each year based on the face value

- The coupon rate is the rate of interest that the bond pays each year based on the face value. Bonds typically pay interest semi-annually (i.e. every six months), although sometimes they pay monthly or quarterly interest. For example, a $1,000 bond paying a 7 percent coupon rate semi-annually would make an interest payment of $35 every six months ($70 total each year).

Maturity The date when the bond face value must be paid

- The maturity is the date when the bond face value must be paid. For example, a one-year bond matures in a year and a 30 year bond matures in 30 years.

However, bonds may have provisions that differ from these characteristics. For example:

Zero-coupon bond Bond with no interest payments sold at a discount from face.

- A zero-coupon bond makes no interest payment before maturity. It sells originally to investors at a discount from its face value and then pays the face amount at maturity. For example, a company sells 5-year $1,000 zero-coupon bonds to investors for $725. The investors receive no interest payments during the five years, but at maturity they receive $1,000, representing $725 return of their principal plus $275 interest.

Floating interest bond Bond with an interest rate that changes based on changes in an interest rate index.

- A floating interest bond (variable interest bond) pays an interest rate that changes as general interest rates change. The change in the bond's interest rate is usually linked to some interest rate index. For example, in January 2008, the National Football league issued $100 million in floating rate bonds at an interest rate that is equal to the London Interbank Offered Rate (LIBOR) plus 1.43 percent. The LIBOR rate changes every day, and the bond will adjust its rate when it pays interest, every six months.

Variable interest bond A floating interest bond.

Current yield Bond annual interest divided by its market price.

Although bonds have a fixed principal amount, their price may vary depending on market conditions, just as the price of a stock can fluctuate. A bond with a par value of $1,000 may sell for $800 in the open market. Later, as interest rates and other conditions in the economy change, the bond's price could rise to $1,100 or more. The current yield of a bond represents the annual return that the bondholder receives based on the bond's price. It is equal to the annual interest paid by the bond divided by the bond's price.

$$\text{current yield} = \frac{\text{annual interest}}{\text{bond price}}$$

Equation 13.1

Current Yield of a Bond	**EXAMPLE 13.1**

Willimco, Inc., has a 20-year bond outstanding that was issued 10 years ago. The bond makes semiannual interest payments of $35 and has a par value of $1,000. It currently sells in the market for $816. Compute the bond's current yield.

A semiannual interest payment of $35 is $70 per year.

$$\text{current yield} = \frac{\text{annual interest}}{\text{bond price}}$$

$$= \frac{70}{816}$$

$$= 0.0858$$

or

8.58% ▪

Example 13.1 illustrates how to compute the current yield of a bond.

A bond's current yield, however, does not provide a complete picture of the return that a bond will pay its owner when the price of the bond is different from the par value. Note in Example 13.1 that price is $816 for a $1,000 face-value bond. The bondholder receives 8.58 percent return or yield each year, based on the current yield.

Bondholders can receive yield that is in addition to the amount of the current yield. The source of this extra return is that the bond will pay more at maturity ($1,000) than the bondholder originally paid for the bond ($816 in the example). This $184 profit serves to increase the return that the bondholder receives from the bond over its 20-year life. The return that includes this extra return is the yield to maturity of the bond.

The yield to maturity of a bond is the total return that a bondholder receives over the life of a bond including all interest payments and profit (or loss) from the bond principal payment. The bond in Example 13.1 showed extra return for its holder because the holder bought the bond for a discount from the bond's par value. This bond's yield to maturity is 9 percent, which is even greater than the 8.58 percent current yield.

Yield to maturity The total return over life of a bond.

When a bond sells for a price that is less than its face value (a discount), that bond will have a yield to maturity that is greater than its current yield. If a bond sells for a price greater than its face value (a premium), the effect is the opposite. This bond reduces the return for the bondholder, because the holder will receive less at maturity than was originally paid for the bond. Computation of yield to maturity involves a financial calculator or compound interest tables using principles from the first chapter of this book.

A variety of issuers issue bonds. Most of the issuers fall into one of the two following categories:

1. Governments
2. Corporations

GOVERNMENT BONDS

Governments around the world help finance their operations by issuing debt. These governments include governments of virtually all nations, governments of states and provinces, and governments of counties, cities, and towns.

Bonds Issued by the U.S. Government

The U.S. Treasury issues bonds that are direct obligations of the U.S. government. Interest payments on all U.S. government debt are exempt from any state and local income taxes but are subject to federal income tax. The easiest way for individual investors to purchase Treasury bonds is through the Treasury's TreasuryDirect program, thus avoiding going through a brokerage firm. (You can also buy Treasury bills, described in Chapter 11, from Treasury-Direct.) Information about TreasuryDirect is available at its web site, www .treasurydirect.gov.

The Treasury issues several different types of bonds:

Treasury note (T-note)
Bonds issued by the U.S. Treasury with fixed interest and original maturity of 2–10 years.

Treasury bonds (T-bonds)
Fixed-interest bonds issued by the U.S. Treasury with original maturity of 30 years.

Treasury Inflation-Protected Securities (TIPS) Bonds issued by the U.S. Treasury whose principal changes according to the Consumer Price Index.

- Treasury notes (T-notes) are bonds with fixed interest issued with original maturities of 2, 3, 5, and 10 years.
- Treasury bonds (T-bonds) are fixed-interest bonds that have original maturities of 30 years.
- Treasury Inflation-Protected Securities (TIPS) provide protection against inflation. The principal of a TIPS increases with inflation and decreases with deflation, as measured by the Consumer Price Index.

STRETCH
YOUR DOLLAR

BUY U.S BONDS DIRECTLY FROM THE TREASURY

Investing your money in U.S. government savings is easy with the TreasuryDirect program. The U.S. Treasury maintains a web site at www.savingsbonds.gov. Individuals can open accounts and purchase

- Savings bonds in minimum amounts of $25
- Treasury bills, notes, and bonds in minimum amounts of $100
- Treasury Inflation-Protected Securities in minimum amounts of $100

You can also buy savings bonds at banks and other Treasury securities through a brokerage firm, but the brokerage firm will charge a commission for its services.

In addition to Treasury issues, certain government agencies such as the Federal Home Loan Bank and the Tennessee Valley Authority have the authority to issue debt. Depending on the agency, the interest and principal payments of the debt issued by the agency may be guaranteed by the U.S. government. Although some of these agency issues are technically not guaranteed by the federal government, it is doubtful that the U.S. government would allow one of its agencies to default on debt.

Bonds Issued by Other Countries

Bonds issued by foreign governments usually fall into one of two categories:

1. External bonds
2. Internal bonds

External bonds are sold to investors in other countries and are usually payable in U.S. dollars or in some other strong currency. Internal bonds are marketed in the country of issue and are payable in the local currency. The record of the external debt of many countries has not been a good one, and investors should be wary of the additional risks of foreign investing when considering foreign government bonds.

Investing your money is easy through U.S. government savings bonds.

MUNICIPAL BONDS

Municipal bonds are the debt issues of all political subdivisions within a country. In the United States, municipal bonds include issues of states, counties, cities, and other government entities such as public universities or industrial development districts.

The most distinguishing feature of municipal bonds for U.S. investors is that interest on all municipal bonds issued in the United States is exempt from the federal income tax. For this reason, the interest yield on municipal bonds is less than the yield on Treasury issues, even though the risk of municipal bonds is greater.

Municipal bond Bond issued by states, cities, etc., interest is exempt from U.S. income tax.

WHY DO CORPORATIONS ISSUE BONDS INSTEAD OF BORROWING FROM BANKS?

Corporations sell bonds to raise funds to run or expand their business. They could choose to raise funds by selling stock to investors, but often they elect to borrow instead. The main advantage of borrowing is that the interest that businesses pay on their debt is a tax-deductible expense.

Given that a company has decided to borrow money, why would it prefer to issue bonds rather than simply borrowing the money from a bank? Borrowing from a bank would be easier, but there are three main reasons why corporations often sell bonds to investors to raise capital.

1. **The total amount of the bond issue may be very large.** The total amount of bond issues for larger corporations can be hundreds of million dollars which is an amount that individual banks or even syndicates of several banks may be willing to lend.
2. **The maturity of the bond might be far into the future.** Banks tend to prefer to lend money on a shorter-term basis. Bank loans to corporations usually have a term from several months to about 5 years. To borrow money for longer periods, up to 30 years, companies need to consider issuing bonds.
3. **The interest rate available for the bond issue might be lower.** Companies are sometimes able to sell bonds directly to investors at rates slightly lower than the rate that they would have to pay for bank financing.

CORPORATE BONDS

Corporate bond
Corporations' debt issues with maturities greater than 1 year.

Corporate bonds are corporations' debt issues with maturities greater than one year. Maturities typically range from 2 to 30 years, and the standard face amount is $1,000. Because the credit risk of corporations is higher than the risk of the U.S. government, yields on corporate bonds are greater than yields on Treasury issues. Exhibit 13.1 presents interest rates on Treasury and corporate bonds and shows rates on corporate bonds higher than on Treasury issues.

An important risk associated with corporate bonds is the risk of default. Default is the condition occurring when a bond issuer fails to meet a scheduled interest or principal payment. In the best case, the bond resumes interest payments at some future date, but the bondholder's return suffers somewhat because of the delay in payments. In the worst case, default leads to eventual bankruptcy and the partial or even total loss of interest and principal payments.

Default Condition occurring when a company fails to pay interest on its debt.

Secured bond Bond collateral pledged as security in case of default.

If a bond should fall into default, bondholders will look to the security underlying the bond issue. Bonds that have some type of collateral pledged to the bondholders in case of default are secured bonds. For example, a company might pledge one of its office buildings as collateral against one of its bonds. If the bond falls into default, the bondholders can claim the building. Secured bonds have less risk than unsecured bonds, which have no security pledged against them.

EXHIBIT 13.1	INTEREST RATES ON TREASURY BONDS, AAA-RATED CORPORATE BONDS, AND BAA-RATED CORPORATE BONDS, 1993–2013

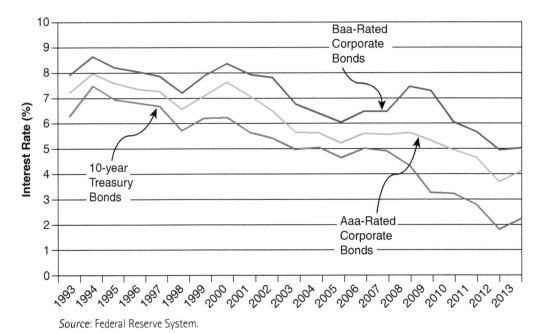

Source: Federal Reserve System.

Bonds with no pledged security are unsecured bonds (or debentures). The risk of a debenture therefore is based solely on the firm's ability to repay the bond from its cash and earnings, not on the value of any assets pledged to the bond issue.

Although default is certainly a source of loss to bondholders, most losses due to default risk do not arise because of actual default. They result from increases in the probability of default caused by a deteriorating financial condition of the

Unsecured bond Bond with no specific pledged collateral.

Debenture Unsecured bond with no pledged collateral.

STOCKS OR BONDS?

What is the best choice for you: stocks or bonds? In a thriving economy stocks usually outperform bonds, but when economic times are tough, bonds can provide a greater return than stocks. Since stocks carry more risks than bonds, they do usually yields a higher rate of return over the long haul. Stocks are a great choice to grow your money. If you have sufficient time to recover from market downturns before you need the money, you can afford the risk of the stock market and net the higher returns.

Bonds offer less risk because they are debt and not ownership of the company. If a company declares bankruptcy, its debt must be paid before its owners are compensated. Bonds are great for generating interest income once you have grown your investment. When you retire, you typically want to limit your risk and use your nest-egg to produce a retirement income. Bonds provide a good investment vehicle for this purpose, and many people move their investments from stocks to bonds as they approach retirement.

If you choose bonds to provide regular income, you can stagger their maturities so that you receive a monthly income. Bonds that pay interest twice a year follow one of the following schedules.

- JJ – January and July
- FA – February and August
- MS – March and September
- AO – April and October
- MN – May and November
- JD – June and December

You can purchase a variety of bonds with different payment schedules to generate a consistent monthly income. A million dollars will generate an annual income of $75,000 if it is invested at 7.5 percent interest. When your bonds mature, you can purchase another bond. This method will allow you to produce an income in your retirement without spending the principal you accumulated over your lifetime. This allows you to leave your accumulated wealth to your loved ones and still enjoy a nice income during your retirement years.

For example, suppose you retire with $800,000 invested in stocks. You can sell those stocks and invest the proceeds in a variety of bonds whose interest payments are evenly spread among the payment schedules identified above. If your bonds pay an average of 7½ percent, your annual income from interest would be $60,000. If the bond interest payments are evenly spread out over the payment schedules, your monthly income would be about $5,000. You can live off of the interest alone from the bonds and leave the accumulated wealth of the bond maturity values to your loved ones.

firm. If a company enters a period of financial distress, investors realize the additional risks of holding the firm's bonds, and the bond will fall in price.

Bond investors can control for default risk by identifying default risk level that they are willing to accept and then selecting bonds that meet that level of risk. While some investors will conduct their own research as part of a complete bond analysis before investing, there are bond rating services that analyze bond issues. These services assign a bond rating that is an assessment of the bond's default risk.

Bond rating Ranking that measures a bond's default risk.

The three most widely used bond rating services are

1. Standard & Poor's
2. Moody's Investors Service
3. Fitch Ratings

Exhibit 13.2 shows an abbreviated summary of the main ratings categories used by Standard & Poor's and Moody's. Standard & Poor's (S&P) highest rating for firms with the best credit is AAA. Bonds between AAA and BBB are investment grade bonds. BB bond or lower are speculative bonds. In addition, the rating agencies sometimes give ratings between the main categories. For example, S&P awards A– to firms slightly less than A, and it awards BBB+ for companies whose credit is slightly better than BBB but not quite good enough for A–. High-rated bonds have low risk; low-rated bonds have high risk.

Investment grade bond A bond of high creditworthiness.

Speculative bond Bond of issuer with risky credit (BB or lower).

EXHIBIT 13.2	**SUMMARY OF BOND RATINGS FROM MOODY'S AND STANDARD & POOR'S**

S&P	Moody's	Description
AAA	Aaa	Highest level of creditworthiness. Extremely strong capacity to pay interest and principal.
AA	Aa	Very strong capacity to pay interest and principal on debt. Only slightly less than the highest rating.
A	A	Strong capacity to pay interest and principal. Somewhat more susceptible to adverse conditions than the higher ratings.
BBB	Baa	Adequate capacity for interest and principal. Adverse conditions more likely to weaken the capacity of the issuer to pay.
BB	Ba	Somewhat speculative. Only moderate protection of principal and interest payments.
B	B	Speculative. May not provide interest and principal payments even under good economic conditions.
CCC	Caa	Very speculative. Large uncertainties exist about the issuer's ability to continue to service its debt.
CC	Ca	Highly speculative. Issuer may be close to default or presently in default. Capacity to pay interest and principal is questionable.

Yields of bonds of different issuers will vary based on their credit ratings. Other factors being equal, higher-risk bonds (those with lower ratings) should have greater yields. Exhibit 13.2 illustrates this relationship. Although interest rates varied over the time covered in the chart, yields on the lower-rated Baa bonds always averaged more than the yields on the safer Aaa bonds.

You can purchase a variety of bonds with different payment schedules to generate a consistent monthly income. A million dollars will generate an annual income of $75,000 if it is invested at 7.5 percent interest. When your bonds mature, you can purchase another bond. This method will allow you to produce an income in your retirement without spending the principal you accumulated over your lifetime. This allows you to leave your accumulated wealth to your loved ones and still enjoy a nice income during your retirement years.

For example, suppose you retire with $800,000 invested in stocks. You can sell those stocks and invest the proceeds in a variety of bonds whose interest payments are evenly spread among the payment schedules identified above. If your bonds pay an average of 7½ percent, your annual income from interest would be $60,000. If the bond interest payments are evenly spread over the payment schedules, your monthly income would be about $5,000. You can live off of the interest alone from the bonds and leave the accumulated wealth of the bond maturity values to your loved ones.

Valuing Bonds

Bonds have their face value, typically $100 or $1,000 per bond. Also, as mentioned earlier in this chapter, a bond also has a market price which may not be equal to the face value. In other words, when the bond matures, the investor who holds the bond may not get back the price the investor paid for the bond. Bondholders who originally purchased their bond for a discount will be repaid more than they originally invested, and holders who purchased bonds at a premium will receive less.

The principle of valuation for bonds is the same as it is for stocks, that is, a bond is worth the present value of all of the future payments that the holder expects to receive. The big difference between trying to value a stock and trying to value a bond is that the future payments for a bond are known (the interest payments are a stated feature of the bond), but the payments for a stock can only be estimated (future dividends might be forecastable, but they are not known with certainty). With a bond, the holder will always receive the stated interest and repayment of the face value of the bond except in cases of bankruptcy.

An example will best illustrate the value of a bond. Exhibit 13.3 presents the case of a 6 percent bond with face amount of $1,000 and 2 years until maturity. The annual interest on the bond is 6 percent of 1,000, or $60. The bond makes semiannual interest payments, so there are two interest payments per year, each being in the amount of $30.

So, the bond makes five payments, four payments of $30 in interest and one final payment of $1,000 in principal face amount. Actually, the final interest

| EXHIBIT 13.3 | **EXAMPLE COMPUTATION OF THE PRICE OF A BOND** |

<u>Characteristics of the bond</u>

Bond rating:	A
Face amount	$1,000
Coupon rate:	6%
Interest payments:	Semiannual
Years to maturity:	2
Bond yield to maturity:	8%

<u>Importance for bond pricing</u>

Bond rating is an indication of the yield to maturity
Amount that annual interest is based on
Bond pays $60 per year in interest
Bond makes two $30 interest payments each year
2 years is four semiannual interest payments
8 percent is the rate to use for computing present value, since there are two interest payment per year, the rate per period is 4 percent

963.70 = 24.84 + 27.74 + 26.67 + 25.64 + 854.80

0 (present)   1   2   3   4

Payment	Amount	PV factor	PV of amount
Interest no. 1	$30	.9615 (1)	28.85
Interest no. 2	$30	.9246 (2)	27.74
Interest no. 3	$30	.8890 (3)	26.67
Interest no. 4	$30	.8548 (4)	25.65
Face amount	$1,000	.8548 (5)	854.79

(1) Present value factor from Appendix A-2, 4% 1 period
(2) Present value factor from Appendix A-2, 4% 2 periods
(3) Present value factor from Appendix A-2, 4% 3 periods
(4) Present value factor from Appendix A-2, 4% 4 periods
(5) Present value factor from Appendix A-2, 4% 4 periods

Note: Interest payment no. 4 and the face amount are received at the same time and therefore have the same PV factor.

payment and the payment of the face amount occur at the same time, so we could say the fourth payment is the final one, and it is for $1,030.

To compute the present value of those payments, we need the appropriate discount rate. What is the appropriate rate to use to discount those payments? Recall that investors want their investments to compensate them for the risk that they take. Now, connect that concept with the idea that bond ratings represent measures of a bond's risk, and that the higher the bond rating, the lower the risk and the lower the rate of return that investors will demand for those types of bonds. So, a bond's rating should give us a good idea of the appropriate discount rate, and the discount rate is the same as the rate of return or, in bond terminology, the yield to maturity of the bond.

Getting back to the bond valuation example in Exhibit 13.3, the bond has a rating of "A." Let's assume that other bonds rated "A" at that time on average have an average yield to maturity of 8 percent. Therefore, an appropriate rate to apply to the bond would be 8 percent.

Using 8 percent as our discount rate, and applying it to the bond with semiannual interest payments (two payments per year), the 8 percent rate per year is a 4 percent rate on a semiannual basis.

We now have all of the information we need to compute the bond's price:

- Interest rate for discounting (i%) – 4 percent
- The number of periods that the payments will be received (N) – 4
- The annual interest payments (PMT) – 30
- The final future single payment (FV) – 1,000

Exhibit 13.3 shows how we can discount the payments to present value using the tables in the Appendix A-2 of this book. The value of the bond is $963.70. The bond value is at a discount from its face value. Even without computing the bond's value, we can know this because the coupon rate on the bond is less than the bond's yield to maturity.

We can also solve the problem with a financial calculator or using the financial calculator available at online at www.fin1000.com. Exhibit 13.4 shows a screenshot of the fin1000 calculator with the appropriate inputs to value the bond. To use the online calculator, fill in the variables you know and leave the one you are computing blank. Be sure to set the correct number of compounding periods (interest payments) per year (two in the example). (You might need to press the "Reset" button before inputting the numbers.)

COMPUTATION OF BOND PRICE USING FINANCIAL CALCULATOR

EXHIBIT 13.4

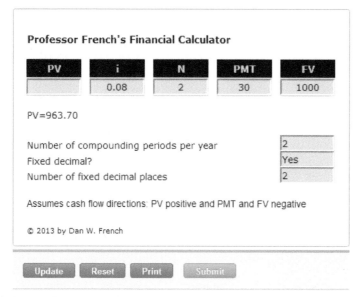

Financial calculator available at www.fin1000.com

EXHIBIT 13.5	COMPUTATION OF BOND YIELD TO MATURITY USING FINANCIAL CALCULATOR

Professor French's Financial Calculator

PV	i	N	PMT	FV
963.7		2	30	1000

I=0.08

Number of compounding periods per year	2
Fixed decimal?	Yes
Number of fixed decimal places	2

Assumes cash flow directions: PV positive and PMT and FV negative

© 2013 by Dan W. French

[Update] [Reset] [Print] [Submit]

Financial calculator available at www.fin1000.com

Financial calculators are handy to compute the yield to maturity of a bond as long as you know the price. Actually, they are almost necessary because the solution process using the tables is quite tedious. To compute the yield to maturity of a bond, input the observed market price of a bond as PV (present value) and solve for the interest rate. Exhibit 13.5 shows the fin1000 financial calculator solution to solving for the example bond's yield to maturity when we know the price is $963.70.

The main economic factor that influences the prices of bonds is the level of interest rates in general. The principal factor that influences the price of an individual bond is that bond's rating.

Investing in Preferred Stock

Preferred stock is stock that pays a fixed dividend. This contrasts with common stock that pays a dividend declared by the corporation's board of directors depending on how much profit the firm is making, how much of those profits the board wants to reinvest in the company, and how much it wants to pay to common stockholders. In general, when the corporation's profits rise, the board increases the dividend. When profits fall, the board sometimes compensates by reducing the common stock dividend. So, the most important factor that determines common stock dividends and then the value of the company's common stock is profitability.

Because preferred stock pays a fixed dividend, you might think that preferred stock is more like a bond than like common stock. If so, you are right, because preferred stock behaves more like a bond than like a stock. The main factors that influence the value of preferred stock is the level of interest rates and the rating of the preferred stock.

Yes, preferred stocks get rated too, just like bonds. The same rating agencies that rate bonds (for example, Moody's) also rate preferred stocks. The ratings are very similar. For example an A-rated preferred stock has less risk than one rated B, and the dividend yield on an A-rated preferred should be less than the dividend yield on a B-rated issue.

If preferred stocks behave like bonds, why do we call them stocks? The answer to that question lies in the way that the accountants record preferred stock on the books of the corporation. It is recorded in the same section as common stock and not as debt like bonds. In recognition of this, if the corporation goes into bankruptcy, the first creditors that get paid off are the bondholders. Next in line are the preferred stockholders, and last are the common stockholders if anything is left for them. So, preferred stock would be more risky than bonds but less risky than common stock. And, because of the fixed dividend, preferred stocks behave more like bonds.

So, a preferred stock is like a bond with no maturity date, a perpetual bond. If we apply the same valuation principle to a preferred stock that we use to value common stocks and to value bonds, then we would say that the value of a preferred stock is the present value of the perpetual stream of dividend payments that the shareholder will receive in the future. The solution is an easy formula:

$$\text{preferred stock value} = \frac{\text{dividend}}{\text{required rate of return}} \qquad \text{Equation 13.2}$$

You might note that this formula is similar to the valuation formula for common stock, just without the growth rate. The reason is that the preferred stock dividend does not grow; it is fixed. The definition of the required rate of return is the same as it is for common stock; it is the return that an investor requires to be induced to invest in the preferred stock. Note that the dividend is the annual dividend, and most preferred stock pay dividends quarterly (four times per year). If we know the market price of the preferred stock, then solving Equation 13.2 for the rate gives us the dividend yield on the preferred stock.

Example 13.2 demonstrates the use of Equation 13.2. The preferred stock paying a 25-cent quarterly ($1.00 annual) dividend and priced at $12.50 has a dividend yield of 8 percent. The preferred with the 75-cent quarterly dividend ($3.00 per year) has a value of $37.50 when the required rate is 8 percent.

EXAMPLE 13.2   Valuation of Preferred Stock

Beetle Corp. has two different issues of preferred stock outstanding. Series A pays a quarterly dividend of 25 cents per share, and Series B pays 75 cents per share quarterly. Both series have the same risk and rating. The current price of the A shares is $12.50. What is the value of a share of Series B?

First, compute the required rate of return of the A shares. The annual dividend is $1.00.

$$\text{preferred stock value} = \frac{\text{dividend}}{\text{required rate of return}}$$

$$12.50 = \frac{1.00}{\text{required rate of return}}$$

$$\text{required rate of return} = .08$$

For preferred stock, the required rate is the dividend yield, so the yield is 8 percent. Because the two series (A and B) have the same risk, the yield (and required rate) on the Series B shares will also be 8 percent. Using the 8 percent required rate, we can now compute the value of the Series B shares:

$$\text{preferred stock value} = \frac{\text{dividend}}{\text{required rate of return}}$$

$$= \frac{3.00}{.08}$$

$$= 37.50$$

SUMMARY

Bonds are debt securities that pay interest to investors. Bondholders measure their return by a bond's current yield and its yield to maturity. Corporations and governments issue bonds. Bonds of the U.S. government include Treasury notes, Treasury bonds, and TIPS. Municipal bonds, issued by states and cities, have the advantage of paying interest that is exempt from the U.S. federal income tax.

Corporate bonds may be unsecured (debentures) or secured with some type of collateral. Secured bonds have less risk for investors than do unsecured bonds or debentures. Bond ratings measure the risk of default. They identify investment grade bonds with low levels of risk and speculative bonds with high levels of risk.

Preferred stock has a fixed dividend. Because of this, preferred stock behaves more like bonds than does common stock. Like they do for bonds, rating agencies issue ratings of preferred stocks.

PROBLEMS

1. H.T. Theron Corp. has bonds outstanding with a par value of $1,000. The bonds mature in 12 years and make semiannual interest payments of $32.50. The current market price of the bonds is $1,060. Compute the current yield of the bonds.

2. Gradon Ltd. has issued 6 percent bonds that pay interest semiannually. The bonds have a face amount of $1,000 and mature in 10 years. What is the amount of each interest payment?

3. If the yield to maturity of the bond in problem 2 is 5 percent, what is the value of the bond?

4. Compute the yield to maturity of the bond in problem 1.

CASE STUDIES

COLLEGE STUDENT

Kevin Maedor is a 19-year-old college student. He still lives at home with his parents, and he works part time at Vapor's Lane. He started his financial plan in the spring semester of 2014. He plans to graduate with a B.S. in engineering in May 2017. Use the investing goals you created for him in Chapter 11. Consider the investment choices you made in Chapter 12.

- Suggest additional investments for him. Use Stock Track to research your suggestions.
- Provide a detailed explanation of why these are good investments for him.

NEW GRADUATE

Rene Harris recently graduated with a B.S. in nursing. She lives by herself in a modest apartment. Her annual salary is $76,000 a year. Use the investing goals you created for her in Chapter 11. Consider the investment choices you made in Chapter 12.

- Suggest additional investments for her. Use Stock Track to research your suggestions.
- Provide a detailed explanation of why these are good investments for her.

REVIEW QUESTIONS   CHAPTER 13

1. Differentiate between the current yield and the yield to maturity of a bond.

   _____

   _____

   _____

2. What is default? How might a secured bond protect a bondholder in the event of default?

   _____

   _____

   _____

3. Identify three types of secured bonds.

   _____

   _____

   _____

4. Explain bond ratings and how they classify default.

   _____

   _____

   _____

5. What do bond ratings measure? Do bonds with higher ratings have higher or lower yields?

   _____

   _____

   _____

6. Is preferred stock more like common stock or like bonds? Why?

   _____

   _____

   _____

Mutual Funds

"Rather than being a risk-taker as such, I consider myself and my climbing peers to be risk-controllers, and we just enjoy being in this situation and keeping risk at a reasonable level."

—Alex Lowe
(1958–1999)

© David Davis, 2014, Shutterstock, Inc.

OBJECTIVES

- Outline the laws and regulations affecting investing.
- Identify the sources of risk.
- Interpret risk measures for investments.
- Illustrate the effects of diversification.
- Describe investment companies and mutual funds.
- Relate mutual fund types to investment strategies.

KEY TERMS

12b-1 fee	Financial risk	Market risk
Aggressive stock	Growth investing strategy	Mid-cap fund
Beta	Index fund	Net asset value (NAV)
Blend investing strategy	Interest rate risk	No-load fund
Business risk	Investment company	Open-end fund (mutual fund)
Closed-end fund	Large-cap fund	Portfolio
Conservative stock	Liquidity risk	Purchasing power risk
Contingent deferred sales charge	Load	Small-cap fund
Diversification	Load fund	Standard deviation
Exchange-traded fund (ETF)	Management fee	Unit investment trust
Expense ratio	Management risk	Value investing strategy

Managing risk is an important part of investing. Government and industry regulation of the securities markets attempts to minimize the risks of fraud and market manipulation. Other risks of investing are inherent in business risks and are left to investors to manage. This chapter summarizes some of the important legislation affecting securities markets, discusses risk and how to manage risk with diversification, and introduces investing in mutual funds as a convenient vehicle for diversification.

Managing Investment Risk

Risk is the negative part of the relationship between risk and return. Just like everyone would love to find a delicious dessert with no fat or calories, investors would like to find the perfect investment that promises high return with little or no risk. To find higher returns, investors have to be willing to accept higher levels of risk. However, that does not mean that investors should indiscriminately grab for higher risk because they know that greater return should come with it. The smart investor will manage and control risk, trying to find investments that offer a suitable return but at the same time to minimize risk for the various investments in that category.

SOURCES OF RISK

Investors often identify risk by its source. Every source of risk affects the total risk of a stock. Principal sources of risk are as follows:

Business risk Variation in a firm's value due to the firm's product.

Management risk Variation in a firm's return attributable to the company's management.

Financial risk Firm's risk associated with the amount of its debt.

Market risk Variation in returns that is related to market returns.

- Business risk. The variation in a firm's value attributable to the product line or industry of the company leads to business risk. The most important factor influencing business risk is the variation in the company's sales or revenues.

- Management risk. The quality and leadership provided by a company's management can be a critical factor in the success of an enterprise. The portion of the variation in a firm's return due to characteristics and style of the company's management is management risk.

- Financial risk. A company with debt has to make its interest payments no matter whether economic times are good or bad. These interest payments make the company's earnings fluctuate even more than its sales vary, and this extra variation is financial risk.

- Market risk. Anyone observing stock prices has observed that they

Risks should be considered when making financial decisions.

© NAN728, 2014, Shutterstock, Inc.

INFLATION OUT OF CONTROL

Purchasing power risk is at its extreme when inflation is exceedingly high. Would a business in Zimbabwe promising a 100 percent return per year have been a profitable investment in 2004? In that year, Zimbabwe's inflation rate was 624 percent, so a 100 percent investment return would have been big negative real return. It would have been even worse in later years when the annual inflation rate hit

- 9,000 percent in June 2006
- 11,000 percent in June 2007
- 11,250,000 percent in June 2008
- 231,000,000 percent in July 2008
- 516,000,000,000,000,000,000 percent in November 2008

On January 12, 2009, Zimbabwe released a $50 billion dollar note. Just four days later authorities announced a $100 trillion note. In late January 2009 Zimbabwe allowed business to begin using other currencies; use of the U.S. dollar has since become common.

- often move together. On a day when the market rises, there seems to be a positive outlook, and most stocks are on the rise. On the other side, when some stocks begin to fall, others often follow the lead, and pessimism appears to be the mood of the day. This bit of market psychology explains the concept of market risk, the variation in a stock's returns that is related to market returns.

- Purchasing power risk. Purchasing power risk is the variation in real returns caused by inflation. Real returns are returns after removing the impact of inflation. As an approximation, you can subtract inflation from an investment's return to get the real return. For example, if inflation is 6 percent, an investment yielding 8 percent has a real return of only 2 percent.

  Purchasing power risk Variation in real returns caused by inflation.

- Interest rate risk. Changes in interest rates often affect the prices of securities. Any variation in returns caused by fluctuations in interest rates is interest rate risk.

  Interest rate risk Variation in return caused by changes in interest rates.

- Liquidity risk. Liquidity risk represents the risk of being unable to sell an investment immediately for its market value. Stocks are quite liquid. If you suddenly decide to sell and put your shares on the market, you will probably get something within a few cents of the previously reported trade (unless, of course, you were dumping millions of dollars' worth of the stock on the market at once). Other investments have a greater degree of liquidity risk.

  Liquidity risk Risk of being unable to immediately sell an investment at its market value.

Rare stamps, while they might be a good investment, are not so liquid. You might observe that a nice example of the first U.S. stamp (5-cent Ben Franklin issued in 1847) is going for $1,000. If you shopped it around for a while, you

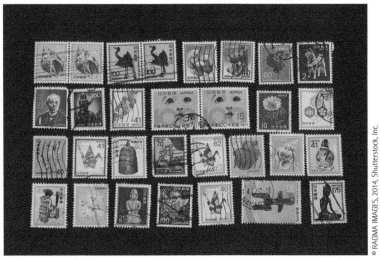

A hobby, such as this rare collection of Japanese stamps, is a good investment. However, it would be very difficult to have immediate access to its liquid value should money be needed right away.

may receive $1,000 for it. However, if you took it to a dealer and said, "I need to sell this today," you may be offered $700 for it.

HOW DO INVESTORS VIEW RISK?

Suppose that Andrea is considering investing in the stock of General Manufacturing, Inc., and she is concerned about the risk of that investment. How can Andrea view this risk, and how can she measure it?

Investors can consider risk from two different views: the individual investment view and the diversified view. To illustrate these two views, consider a forest. One tree is equivalent to General Manufacturing, and all of Andrea's investments comprise the forest.

Andrea knows that there are risks to the individual tree and risks that affect the entire forest. For example, lightning might strike one tree but not damage the forest. On the other hand, fire could pose risk to both the tree and much of the forest. Risks to the forest are also risks to the tree.

In a similar fashion there are risks that make up the risk of an individual investment and risks that are relevant for all investments. Risks relevant to all investments also affect an individual investment, so investors should consider risk both from the individual investment standpoint (the tree) and from the standpoint of how that investment fits in with all of the other investments a person owns (the forest).

MEASURING RISK OF AN INDIVIDUAL INVESTMENT

Standard deviation
Measure of variation in stock returns that measures risk.

The standard way of defining risk is that it is the variation in returns on an investment. To measure risk, we therefore use a measure of variation. The statisticians call this measure the standard deviation. So, investment analysts use the standard deviation of returns to measure the risk of an investment.

ILLUSTRATION OF STANDARD DEVIATION AND RISK   EXHIBIT 14.1

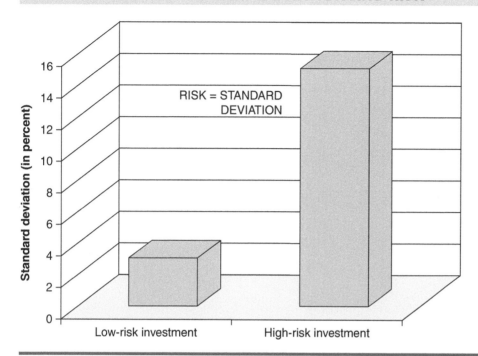

Let's leave it to the statisticians to remember the formula for computing standard deviation. For our purposes, just remember that standard deviation measures how widely returns for any one year can vary from the expected long-run return. The greater the standard deviation, the more returns can vary and the greater the risk of the investment. A lesser standard deviation means lower risk.

Exhibit 14.1 illustrates the risk of two different investments; one is a low-risk investment with a small standard deviation of returns, and the other is a high-risk investment with a large standard deviation. Now that we have a measure of risk, we can look at some actual returns and risks of some real investments to see if they really have the expected relationship that investments with greater risk tend to yield higher returns. We need to look at some returns over a long period of time; remember that risk means that any one given year can vary, so it would not be valid to compare the risk and return of some investments over just a few years.

Exhibit 14.2 has annual returns on three different investments for the 25 years from 1988 to 2012:

1. **U.S. Treasury bill.** Measured by three-month Treasury bills.
2. **Corporate bonds.** Measured by Moody's index of Aaa-rated corporate bonds.
3. **Common stocks.** Measured by the S&P 500 Index of common stocks with dividends included.

© Andresr, 2014, Shutterstock, Inc.

What is your tolerance for risk? Lessen the worry by diversifying your portfolio.

Consider the column of T-bill returns in Exhibit 14.2. Notice how the returns vary relatively little as the years proceed. The column of returns on corporate bonds tends to vary more each year when compared to T-bills (not every year, but most years). This greater variation should indicate that corporate bonds are more risky than T-bills. Corporate bonds should be more risky than T-bills— and they were, which the reported standard deviations in Exhibit 14.2 confirm. The standard deviation of T-bills was 2.4 percent, whereas it was 7.8 percent for corporate bonds.

EXHIBIT 14.2	25 YEARS OF RETURNS ON TREASURY BILLS, CORPORATE BONDS, AND COMMON STOCKS, 1988–2012

Year	U.S. Treasury Bills	Aaa–Rated Corporate Bonds	Common Stocks, S&P 500 Index
1988	6.7	14.0	16.1
1989	8.1	16.5	30.7
1990	7.5	7.2	–3.0
1991	5.4	17.8	29.7
1992	3.4	10.7	7.4
1993	3.0	17.6	9.9
1994	4.3	–7.2	1.3
1995	5.5	27.9	36.7
1996	5.0	0.9	22.4
1997	5.1	13.4	32.8
1998	4.8	12.2	28.1
1999	4.6	–8.1	20.8
2000	5.8	12.7	–9.0
2001	3.4	13.2	–11.8
2002	1.6	12.6	–21.8
2003	1.0	11.6	28.1
2004	1.4	8.1	10.7
2005	3.2	7.5	4.8
2006	4.7	1.3	15.5
2007	4.3	5.9	5.8
2008	1.3	4.7	–36.3
2009	0.2	9.5	25.9
2010	0.1	10.0	14.7
2011	0.1	8.8	2.0
2012	0.1	18.3	15.5
Average	3.6	9.9	11.1
Standard deviation	2.4	7.8	17.9

RISK AND RETURN OF T-BILLS, CORPORATE BONDS, AND COMMON STOCKS, 1988–2012

EXHIBIT 14.3

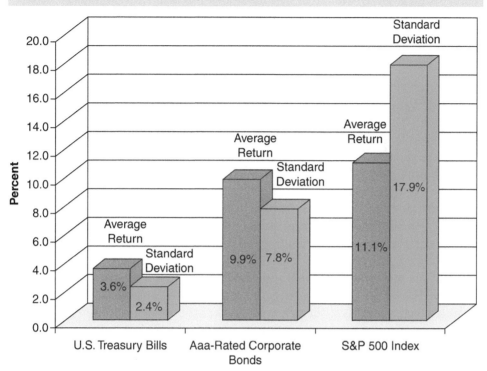

The returns and standard deviation of common stocks provide yet another example. We would expect stocks to be the most risky of these three classes of investment, but we would also expect them to return more over the long haul. The numbers in Exhibit 14.2 verify this. Exhibit 14.3 provides a summary illustration of the risks and returns of the three investment classes. Note how the return of each investment increases as the risk increases.

DIVERSIFICATION

Investors normally have more than one investment. They may concentrate on just a few investments, or they may have a large group of investments across a number of different businesses and industries. A group of investments managed together is a portfolio. A very important concept is to view the risk and return of a portfolio as a single investment, not as a collection of risks and returns of the individual investments in the portfolio.

Portfolio Set of investments that are managed as a group.

The reason that it is important to assess the risk of the portfolio is that diversification can reduce risk while not reducing return. Diversification is the act of increasing the number of investments in a portfolio. If diversification can reduce risk without reducing return, then it follows that diversification can increase return without reducing risk! That may seem like magic, but it works, and a brief demonstration will serve to show how it works.

Diversification Combining a number of investments into a portfolio.

Take a simple example of two different stocks: Halliburton (HAL, the oil-field services company), and Heartland Payment Systems (HPY, a bankcard processing service). We have the following choices:

- Invest in HAL
- Invest in HPY
- Invest in a portfolio with half our money in HAL and half in HPY

To help make this choice, we decide to pick the stock that yielded the highest return over the past five years, forecasting (and hoping) that it will continue its performance. Exhibit 14.4 presents returns on these two stocks from 2008 to 2012.

Both stocks had the same return–8.2 percent! So let's try to minimize risk by choosing the stock with the lowest standard deviation. That would be HPY, with a standard deviation of 37.8 percent.

Here is where we can see diversification work its wonders. We can construct a portfolio with half our money in HAL and half in HPY. When we do that, the return on the portfolio is equal to the average return of the two stocks. So, of course, the portfolio's return is still 8.2 percent. But, the standard deviation of the portfolio is less than the standard deviation of either stock!

The return on the portfolio is the same as the component stocks, but the risk is much less. This is the power of diversification! We can keep the benefits (returns) while getting rid of some of the regret (risk). Note that the average of the two stocks' standard deviations is 42.0 percent (computed in Exhibit 14.4), but the actual standard deviation of the two stocks in a portfolio is only 28.9 percent. Diversification reduces risk even beyond the average of the two risks.

EXHIBIT 14.4	**EXAMPLE OF HOW DIVERSIFICATION CAN REDUCE RISK WITHOUT REDUCING RETURN**

	Return on		
Year	HAL	HPY	Portfolio of both HAL and HPY
2008	−51.5%	−33.6%	−42.6%
2009	68.2	−24.5	21.9
2010	37.3	17.7	27.5
2011	−14.8	59.2	22.2
2012	1.7	22.1	11.9
Average return	8.2	8.2	8.2
Standard deviation	46.3	37.8	28.9
Average return of HAL and HPY = (8.2 + 8.2)/2 = 8.2%			
Average standard deviation of HAL and HPY = (46.3 + 37.8)/2 = 42.0%			

Note: The portfolio of HAL and HPY assumes that an equal amount of money is invested in each of the two stocks to form the portfolio (i.e., half in HAL and half in HPY).

The benefits of diversification do not stop with two stocks. Exhibit 14.5 illustrates this as a general concept and shows how the total risk of a portfolio falls as an investor adds securities to the portfolio. It is even possible to add a security whose risk is greater than the portfolio's risk, and new portfolio's risk still drops. Portfolio risk falls sharply as the portfolio grows from one to several securities. The rate of decline in risk slows down as more securities are included. The fall in risk ultimately levels off, and at this point the risk-reduction benefits of adding additional securities to the portfolio are almost nil.

It may seem surprising that most of the risk-reduction via diversification typically happens with the first two dozen or so securities. By the time that a portfolio has about 25 securities, its total risk will have fallen by about 95 percent of the total amount that it can possibly fall through diversification. Given that only a relatively small number of securities are needed for diversification, even small investors usually can effectively diversify their investment portfolios.

What is the lesson from diversification? Diversification is good. It can reduce risk without harming the expected return level of a portfolio, and it can be effectively accomplished with a relatively small number of different investments.

How does diversification work? It has to do with the fact that the returns on the individual investments in the portfolio are not always doing the same thing. Take a look again at Exhibit 14.4. In 2009, HPY had a negative return but HAL countered that with a positive year. In 2001 HAL was down but HPY

EFFECTS OF DIVERSIFICATION ON PORTFOLIO RISK	EXHIBIT 14.5

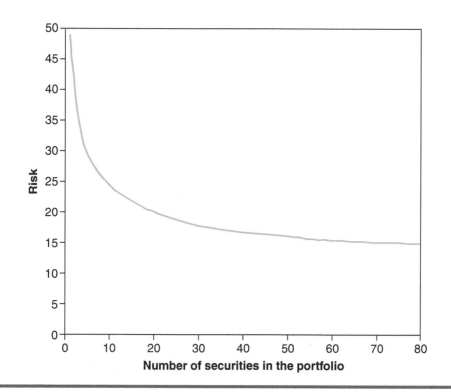

was up. The effect of this is to smooth out the rough edges of the wider swings in return. It results in a portfolio that does not vary as much as either of the two stocks but still has their average return. Diversification works because the returns on different securities are not perfectly correlated with each other.

BETA—ANOTHER WAY TO MEASURE RISK

Beta Measure of risk relative to the market.

There is another popular way to measure risk, and it can be found on many of the investment web sites where investors can look up statistics for individual stocks. The risk measure is the beta of a stock. Beta is a measure of the risk of a stock (or any investment) that quantifies the average return on the stock compared to the average return on a market index.

Let's use International Business Machines (IBM) as an example. Referring to the Yahoo! Finance web site, we find a value for the beta of the stock of IBM of 0.82. The beta of the market is equal to 1.0, so IBM, with a beta of 0.82, has a risk that is only 82 percent of the average risk in the market.

An approximation to the relationship that beta has to a stock return is as follows:

$$\text{expected return on a stock} = \text{beta} \cdot \text{expected return on a market index} \quad \textbf{Equation 14.1}$$

Example 14.1 shows how to use Equation 14.1 to estimate the return on IBM when the expected market return (measured by the return on the S&P 500 Index) is 14 percent. IBM's expected return is 11.5 percent under those conditions.

EXAMPLE 14.1

If the beta of IBM is 0.08, and you expect the return on the S&P 500 Index to be about 14 percent next year, what is your estimate of the expected return on IBM stock?

$$\text{expected return on a stock} = \text{beta} \cdot \text{expected return on a market index}$$

$$= 0.82 \cdot 0.14$$

$$= .115$$

or

$$11.5\% \quad \blacksquare$$

It is important to note that beta is an estimate; it is not an exact measure of the risk of a stock. Its value depends on the exact methods and data used to compute it, and it changes over time. If you looked up IBM's beta on Yahoo! Finance today, you will probably find that it is no longer 0.82. Also, if you found IBM's beta from another source, it might be a different number.

Conservative stock Stock with a beta less than 1.0.

Aggressive stock Stock with a beta greater than 1.0.

Stocks with betas less than 1.0 are less risky on average than the average stock. These stocks are conservative stocks. Stocks whose betas are greater than 1.0 have more risk than average, and we can say that they are aggressive stocks.

Beta already considers diversification. In other words, the risk reduction that you can get from diversifying has already been removed from beta. You will not reduce your portfolio's beta by diversifying. To reduce a portfolio's beta, add a stock with a beta that is less than the beta that the portfolio already has.

How do you compute the beta of a portfolio? It is easy; the beta of a portfolio is simply the average of the betas of the individual stocks in the portfolio. Use betas to identify and manage the risk of your portfolio. If you want to reduce your risk, buy stocks with lower betas. If you want a more aggressive portfolio, add stocks with high betas.

Investment Companies and Mutual Funds

An investment company is a company whose business is to invest in the securities of other companies. Investment companies, or funds, as they are often called, obtain their capital by selling their stock to investors. By owning a share of stock in the investment company, the investor owns a share of the portfolio that the investment company owns.

Investment company
Company that invests in a portfolio of securities.

Individual investors sometimes find it difficult to adequately diversify by purchasing individual stocks. Owning shares of investment companies allows these investors to diversify and to have their portfolio managed by the investment company.

Individual investors all over the world find investment companies a popular way to invest. Exhibit 14.6 shows that while the United States has the

GLOBAL OWNERSHIP OF MUTUAL FUNDS—PERCENTAGE OF TOTAL WORLDWIDE MUTUAL FUND ASSETS BY REGION, 2013   **EXHIBIT 14.6**

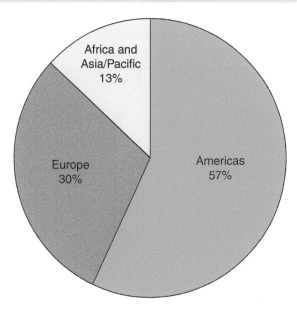

Source: Investment Company Institute.

major share of ownership in investment companies, investors in Europe, Asia, and other areas hold substantial portions of the total global ownership of investment companies.

TYPES OF INVESTMENT COMPANIES

There are four types of investment company:

1. Open-end mutual funds
2. Exchange-traded funds (ETF)
3. Closed-end funds
4. Unit investment trusts

As Exhibit 14.7 shows, mutual funds are by far the category with the most assets.

Open-End Funds

Open-end fund (mutual fund) Fund that sells and redeems shares directly to investors at net asset value.

Open-end funds, or mutual funds as they are often called, have a practice of open-ended share issuance. An investor who wants to buy shares of an open-end fund does so by purchasing directly from the fund or through a brokerage firm that obtains the shares directly from the fund. A fund holder who wants to sell shares sells them back to the fund (the fund redeems the shares.) Shares of open-end funds do not trade on secondary markets; they do not need to trade on markets. The funds stand willing to issue new shares to investors and to redeem shares from investors upon demand.

Net asset value Total net assets of a fund divided by the number of shares outstanding.

The price at which a fund issues and redeems shares is the net asset value (NAV). The net asset value is equal to the market value of the total assets of the fund divided by the number of shares outstanding:

$$\text{NAV} = \frac{\text{fund total net assets}}{\text{number of shares outstanding}} \qquad \text{Equation 14.2}$$

The numerator of NAV is the fund's net assets. Since most funds have virtually no liabilities on their balance sheet, net assets are the same as total assets. Fund assets are the securities that they own as part of their portfolio. These

EXHIBIT 14.7	U.S. INVESTMENT COMPANY TOTAL NET ASSETS, 2012

Investment Company Type	Amount
Mutual funds	$13 trillion
Exchange-traded funds (ETFs)	$1.3 trillion
Closed-end funds	$265 billion
Unit investment trusts (UITs)	$72 billion
Total U.S.	$14.7 trillion

Source: 2013 Investment Company Factbook, Investment Company Institute, 2013.

securities may be stocks, bonds, or any other type of security that the fund is authorized to own.

The issue and redemption of shares does not cause the NAV to change. Only a change in the value of the fund's portfolio results in a change in the NAV. Example 14.2 shows how a fund with $14 million in assets and 1.6 million shares outstanding has an NAV of $8.75. The fund sells new shares. The proceeds of the sale are added to the numerator and the number of new shares to the denominator. Although total fund assets increase, the fund's NAV remains the same.

Only a change in the value of the assets held by the fund causes a change in NAV. In Example 14.2, the value of the fund's portfolio falls to $14,239,500, and the NAV falls to $8.63.

Open-end mutual funds may or may not charge a commission on the sale or redemption of shares. Load funds charge a commission called a load, a fee that the fund investor pays to purchase (or sometimes redeem) fund shares. The load compensates the fund management company or a broker who handled the transaction. The fund portfolio does not receive the load.

Load fund Fund that charges a load to purchase (or possibly redeem) shares.

Load Commission to purchase a mutual fund.

MidWest Equity Fund Portfolio — EXAMPLE 14.2

The MidWest Equity Fund has a portfolio of $14 million of common stock. The fund has 1,600,000 shares of its own stock issued and outstanding. Compute the fund's net asset value (NAV).

$$NAV = \frac{\text{fund total net assets}}{\text{number of shares outstanding}}$$

$$= \frac{14,000,000}{1,600,000}$$

$$= 8.75$$

Investors purchase an additional 50,000 shares at the NAV of $8.75 per share. The fund issues new shares. Compute the new NAV.

$$NAV = \frac{14,000,000 + 50,000 \cdot 8.75}{1,600,000 + 50,000}$$

$$= \frac{14,437,500}{1,650,000}$$

$$= 8.75$$

The stock market falls, and stocks owned by the fund decrease in value to a total of $14,239,500. What is the NAV?

$$NAV = \frac{14,239,500}{1,650,0000}$$

$$= \frac{14,239,500}{1,650,000}$$

$$= 8.63 \quad \blacksquare$$

STRETCH

YOUR DOLLAR

BUY NO-LOAD MUTUAL FUNDS

Paying load fees or commissions to purchase mutual funds reduces your total return on investment. Loads range from 1 percent up to 8 percent of the fund's NAV. If you are considering buying any fund with a load, consider this: There is probably another fund available with similar objectives and expected return but that is no-load and will save you money in the long run.

A number of Internet sites are available to evaluate mutual funds and identify those with and without loads. Do an Internet search for "mutual funds" or check out www.morningstar .com.

A load is different from a commission in that a commission is added to the price of a security, whereas the load is subtracted from the price. For example, an investor buying $1,000 worth of stock paying a commission of 8 percent will pay a total of $1,080—a commission of $80 plus $1,000 worth of stock. A fund buyer who orders $1,000 of a fund will pay $1,000 and receive $920 worth of the fund ($1,000 less the $80 load).

Loads generally range from about 2 percent up to 8 percent. Some funds will charge a load to redeem the fund if the fund holder redeems the shares within a given period—for example, three years. This type of load is a **contingent deferred sales charge**.

Contingent deferred sales charge Load charged when investor redeems fund shares held for less than a specified period of time.

Load funds are usually sold through brokerage firms or insurance sales agents. Some funds have their own sales force.

Funds that do not charge a load fee are **no-load funds**. No-load funds sell their shares directly to investors, either through the mail or over the Internet, or sell shares through brokers or insurance agents. No-load funds that offer shares through agents must compensate the agent, so they charge a fee that goes into a special account that pays agents for making transactions in the fund. This fee, called a 12b-1 fee, is an annual fee paid by the fund based on net assets. It is typically about a quarter of 1 percent of the net assets of the fund.

No-load fund Fund that does not charge a load to buy or redeem shares.

Knowledgeable investors can almost always pick a no-load fund that will meet their objectives. It would be foolish to pay a load fee when buying no-load funds over the Internet is so simple.

By far the most common type of investment company is the open-end mutual fund, which comprises about 93 percent of all investment companies in the United States by total assets. Open-end funds have grown dramatically in popularity over recent decades. Exhibit 14.8 shows the growth in the total assets under management in open-end funds for 1989–2012.

Closed-End Funds

Closed-end funds have a fixed number of shares outstanding. They do not sell or redeem their shares directly with investors as do the open-end funds, but rather, their stock trades on a stock exchange, just like the stocks of other companies.

Closed-end fund Investment company with a fixed number of shares outstanding.

The price of a closed-end fund is determined just like the price of any other stock trading on the market: by supply and demand. Although the prices of

TOTAL NET ASSETS OF MUTUAL FUNDS IN THE UNITED STATES, 1990–2012

EXHIBIT 14.8

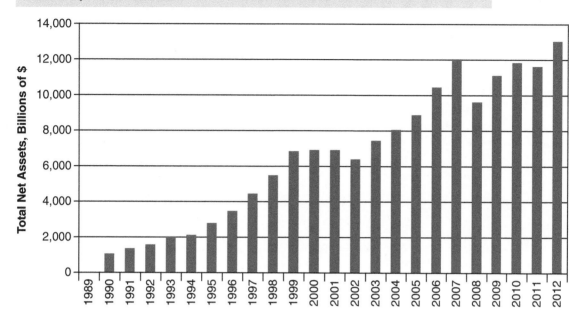

Source: 2013 Investment Company Factbook, Investment Company Institute, 2013.

closed-end funds will be close to their net asset values, the market price of a closed-end fund does not have to equal its NAV. Shares of closed-end funds may sell at a slight discount from or premium above NAV. And, of course, anyone buying a closed-end fund will pay that brokerage firm's normal commission for buying stock.

Even though closed-end funds comprise only about 2 percent of U.S. funds, they managed over $265 billion at the end of 2012.

Exchange-traded Funds (ETF)

Exchange-traded funds (ETFs) are investment companies that attempt to mirror the return of some particular market index. Their shares trade on an exchange, as do shares of closed-end funds. Unlike closed-end funds, however, the portfolio of shares is not actively managed; they simply hold shares to mimic the index they are intended to represent. Exhibit 14.9 provides a sample list of some ETFs and their associated indexes.

Exchange-traded fund (ETF) Investment company designed to mirror the return of a designated market index.

Unit Investment Trusts (UIT)

A unit investment trust has the trust form of ownership. These funds usually hold unmanaged portfolios of bonds. As the bond issuers pay off the bonds, the trustee pays off the certificate holders. When the last bond in the portfolio is paid off, the trust ceases to exist. Unit investment trusts are usually organized and sold by brokerage firms. The brokerage firms may make a secondary market in the trusts after initial issue, but the market for trusts is not active. Purchasers of unit investment trusts typically plan to hold the certificates until they are paid off.

Unit investment trust Investment company with a fixed portfolio of bonds; terminates when the final bond matures.

EXHIBIT 14.9	SAMPLE OF EXCHANGE-TRADED FUNDS

Exchange-Traded Fund	Symbol	Index
iShares Dow Jones U.S. Real Estate	IYR	Portfolio of 75 real estate investment trusts
iShares Russell 2000 Index	IWM	Russell 2000 Index
PowerShares QQQ	QQQQ	NASDAQ 100 Index
SPDR S&P 500 ETF	SPY	Standard & Poor's 500 Index
SPDR Gold Shares	GLD	Gold bullion

Expense ratio Fund expenses divided by the fund's total net assets.

12b-1 fee Fee charged to the fund to cover costs of selling the fund to investors.

Management fee Fee paid by a mutual fund to its investment advisor to manage the fund's portfolio.

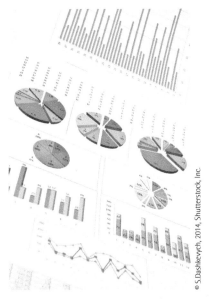

Receiving monthly statements and knowing your investments are managed by a team of professionals are just a couple of benefits when investing in mutual funds.

Fund Expenses

Funds incur expenses just as all companies do. The important issue for investors is whether the expenses that a fund pays make the fund a desirable investment. Other factors being equal, an investor should choose a fund with lower expenses. Investors can gauge a fund's expenses by inspecting the expense ratio, the annual expenses divided by net assets:

$$\text{expense ratio} = \frac{\text{annual fund expenses}}{\text{total net assets}} \qquad \text{Equation 14.3}$$

Expense ratios for funds range from about 0.1 percent up to several percentage points. The average fund expense ratio is about 1.4 percent. For individual investors, it is often a good strategy to select funds that have lower expense ratios, other factors being equal. Example 14.3 illustrates this point. Fund expenses fall into the following categories:

- **Administration costs.** Administration costs include items like shareholder recordkeeping and communication expenses.
- **Commissions paid to brokerage firms.** Funds pay brokerage commissions when they buy and sell securities. They do not itemize commissions as an expense but must disclose the amount paid in commissions in a footnote to their annual financial statements. One important point is that the commissions that funds pay are not part of the expense ratio.
- **12b-1 fees.** 12b-1 fees are annual fees paid to a fund's advisor to pay costs of selling the fund.
- **Management fees.** Management fees are annual fees paid to an investment advisor to manage the fund. Most funds retain an investment management firm to select securities and manage the fund's portfolio. The fund pays an annual fee, usually a percentage of net assets, for this service. In fact, most mutual funds are organized by investment advisory firms who arrange to serve as the advisor to the fund. Some investment advisory firms run dozens of funds. The largest fund management group, Fidelity Investments, manages more than 100 funds.

© S.Dashkevych, 2014, Shutterstock, Inc.

Lara's Mutual Funds	**EXAMPLE 14.3**

Lara is considering two different mutual funds. Both funds have similar investment styles, and Lara believes that the management of both funds is about equally capable of selecting good stocks for the long run. The Kahlo Fund has total net assets of $92 million and annual expenses of $644,000. The Rivera Fund has net assets of $28 million and expenses of $308,000. Which fund should Lara choose to invest in?

To select the fund with the lowest expense structure, compute the expense ratio for each fund. For the Kahlo Fund:

$$\text{expense ratio} = \frac{\text{annual fund expenses}}{\text{total net assets}}$$
$$= \frac{644{,}000}{92{,}000{,}000}$$
$$= 0.007 \text{ or } 0.7\%$$

For the Rivera Fund:

$$\text{expense ratio} = \frac{308{,}000}{28{,}000{,}000}$$
$$= 0.011 \text{ or } 1.1\%$$

Kahlo Fund has the lower expense ratio, so other things being equal, that fund would show better returns than the Rivera Fund, and Lara should choose the Kahlo Fund. ■

BENEFITS OF MUTUAL FUNDS FOR INDIVIDUAL INVESTORS

Mutual funds are particularly popular with individual investors and offer them a number of benefits:

- Diversification that a small investor might find it difficult to obtain purchasing individual stocks
- Shareholder services such as consolidated monthly statements, regular purchase and redemption plans, automatic dividend reinvestment, and check-writing privileges
- Savings on transactions costs, because large funds likely negotiate lower brokerage commissions than individual investors can
- Management of investments by a team of investment professionals

TAXATION OF INVESTMENT COMPANIES

Investment companies receive income from several sources:

- Cash dividends from stocks they hold
- Interest from any bonds they own
- Capital gains (or losses) from securities they sell

Corporations normally pay income tax on the income they receive. However, the U.S. tax code provides an exemption for investment companies. If an investment company or mutual fund pays out all of its income to shareholders as cash dividends, the fund pays no income taxes. Fund shareholders must still pay their own taxes at their respective tax rate on all dividends they receive from investment companies.

INVESTMENT OBJECTIVES OF MUTUAL FUNDS

Investors should choose mutual funds based on how well a fund's investment objectives meet the investor's. For example, if you wanted to receive a relatively high dividend income from your stocks, you would look for funds that invest primarily in companies that pay good dividends. The SPDR S&P Dividend ETF was yielding about 2.5 percent in early 2013, and the American Century Equity Income Fund (an open-end no-load fund) was yielding about 1.4 percent.

Every investment company must issue a statement to investors outlining its investment policy and objectives. Investment goals of mutual funds can be broadly or very narrowly defined. In addition to broad categories, many funds specialize in a particular area or within the category. For example, in the bond category, there are funds specializing in long-term bonds or short-term bonds, government bonds or corporate bonds, and low-quality bonds or high-quality bonds. Investment objectives can even be a combination of several types.

Investment Objectives by Type of Security

- **Equity.** Equity funds invest primarily in common stocks.
- **Bond.** Bond funds concentrate their investments in debt securities.
- **Balanced.** Balanced funds allocate part of their portfolio to bonds and part to stocks.

Investment Objectives by Investment Strategy

- Firm size:
  - Large-cap funds hold mostly larger firms.
  - Mid-cap funds invest in firms that are in the middle range in size.
  - Small-cap funds concentrate their holdings in stocks of smaller firms.
- Value or growth:
  - A value investing strategy involves purchasing stocks whose fundamental value is greater than the current price.
  - A growth investing strategy is based on buying stocks whose potential for growth is greater than average.
  - A blend investing strategy combines both value and growth investing.
- Index funds. Index funds have as their investment objective matching the performance of a broad market index such as the S&P 500 Index. The advantage of index funds is their lower expenses. Because their investment managers do not try to analyze and select stocks to beat the market, index funds have reduced management costs.

Investment Objectives by Country or Region

Some funds concentrate their holdings based on a geographic region or country. For example, the UltraJapan ProFund invests in stocks of Japanese firms.

Large-cap fund Fund that invests in larger companies.

Mid-cap fund Fund that invests in firms in the middle range of size.

Small-cap fund Fund that buys stocks of smaller firms.

Value investing strategy Purchasing stocks whose fundamental value is greater than the current price.

Growth investing strategy Buying stocks with potential for high growth.

Blend investing strategy Strategy combining both value and growth investing.

Index fund Mutual fund with investment objective to match the performance of a market index.

The Vanguard European Stock Index Fund purchases stocks of firms in Europe. These types of funds let investors take advantage of growth opportunities related to particular parts of the world.

Regulation of Investing

Investor protection is the main concept underlying the regulation of securities and their markets. Why would countries with a free-enterprise, market-driven economy try to regulate those markets? Many oppose market regulation and argue that laws or regulation that interferes with the natural operation of a market hinders its ability to function efficiently. Unfortunately, we have observed that when left to operate unfettered, markets tend to have periodic financial disasters that result in calls for regulation. The argument for regulation can be summarized as follows:

- The public interest is served by a growing and vibrant economy.
- Flourishing financial markets are necessary in order to have a prosperous economy.
- To be induced to participate in financial markets as investors, people must be confident that there is little risk that they might be defrauded or that the market might be manipulated against them by market insiders.
- Regulation of the securities industry is necessary to minimize the amount of market manipulation and misuse of insider power.

The purpose of regulation, therefore, is to minimize risk for investors. It is not intended to minimize the normal risk of doing business, but rather to minimize risks that some individuals might use their positions as corporate or market insiders to manipulate information or market prices to their advantage. Securities regulation attempts to create a level playing field in the financial markets so that individual investors have the same access to information that larger investors and insiders have.

Before 1933 there was no federal regulation of securities markets in the United States. Any regulation was by state governments, who were usually reluctant to meddle in the affairs of private business. The NYSE did have some self-regulatory rules that applied to member brokerage firms and companies whose stock traded on the exchange. However, these rules were generally ineffective. In addition, as often happens when an industry regulates itself, conflicts of interest arose that encouraged the self-regulators to act in their own interest rather than in the interest of the investing public.

When stock prices are rising, investors are happy and complaints of fraudulent practices in the markets are seldom heard. Investors seem to have the attitude that "If we're making money, who cares if there is a little fraud and market manipulation going on?" So a rising market often hides failing components of a system. These components become obvious once stock prices begin to fall. There were many such components in the securities markets prior to the first federal securities legislation.

For example, stock manipulation was common. Market operators, many of whom were NYSE members, would form pools to manipulate stock prices. They might buy a stock and cause its price to rise. The public would jump on

406 CHAPTER 14 MUTUAL FUNDS

the bandwagon and buy, causing the price to rise more. Meanwhile, the pool would quietly dispose of its stock. The speculative bubble would burst, the stock would fall, and the public investors would be left holding worthless stock.

More recently, the insurance giant AIG and others issued billions of dollars of financial contracts against high-risk mortgages in a largely unregulated market during the period leading up to 2008. As long as the housing market was stable, there was no problem. But once housing prices began to fall and mortgage holders defaulted on their payments, AIG could no longer stand behind its contracts. The federal government ended up spending hundreds of billions of dollars to stabilize the situation.

SECURITIES EXCHANGE ACT (1934)

The Securities Exchange Act of 1934 accomplished several important steps:

1. It created a federal agency called the Securities and Exchange Commission (SEC) to administer federal securities law.
2. It required all companies whose securities trade on public markets to file regular financial reports with the SEC.
3. It contained provisions designed to facilitate a fair market and gave the Federal Reserve Bank the authority to regulate the ability of investors to buy securities with borrowed funds.

Exhibit 14.10 outlines the four divisions of the SEC and summarizes their responsibilities.

INVESTMENT COMPANY ACT (1940)

Following a four-year investigation of investment companies and investment advisors that revealed a number of abuses, Congress passed the Investment Company Act in 1940. The act requires registration of investment companies and mutual funds. It obliges them to disclose their investment policies and provide semiannual reports to stockholders. It also prohibits anyone guilty of fraud from being associated with an investment company and forbids transactions between investment companies and their officers and directors.

INVESTMENT ADVISORS ACT (1940)

The Investment Advisors Act of 1940 requires the registration of investment advisors. The act requires only disclosure; neither the act nor the SEC makes any judgment regarding the suitability of an investment advisor. Investment advisors must disclose information to the SEC and to their clients regarding their background and business affiliations and how they compute their fees.

SECURITIES INVESTOR PROTECTION ACT (1970)

As explained in Chapter 11, the financial failure of a securities brokerage firm can result in the full or partial loss of money and securities held by the firm in customer accounts. During the 1960s, a number of brokerage firms failed,

DIVISIONS OF THE SECURITIES AND EXCHANGE COMMISSION   EXHIBIT 14.10

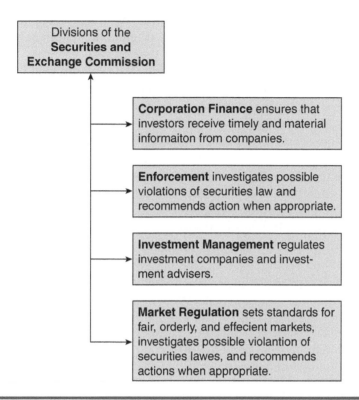

but their clients suffered no loss because the NYSE maintained a fund to reimburse clients of failed brokerage houses. By the end of the 1960s, the fund was depleted. To avert a financial disaster that would accompany failure of additional brokerage firms, Congress passed the Securities Investor Protection Act of 1970. The act created the Securities Investor Protection Corporation (SIPC) to insure customer accounts in brokerage firms, similar to the insurance the FDIC provides to depositors in commercial banks.

THE SARBANES-OXLEY ACT (2002)

The Sarbanes-Oxley Act was passed in response to a number of major corporate and accounting scandals involving prominent U.S. companies. The act had several major provisions:

- Corporations may not make personal loans to any executive officer or director.
- Chief executive officers and chief financial officers must certify the firm's financial statements.
- Corporate insiders must report their trades of company stock much more quickly (within three days) than previously required.
- Criminal and civil penalties are attached to violations of securities law.
- Longer jail sentences and larger fines are imposed for corporate executives who knowingly misstate financial statements.

SUMMARY

The main sources of risk to investors are business risk, management risk, financial risk, market risk, purchasing power risk, interest rate risk, and liquidity risk. A standard measure of risk is the standard deviation of returns, which represents the variation in returns on an investment.

One of the most useful methods for controlling risk is diversification. Diversification allows investors to reduce risk without penalizing return. Diversification reduces risk because the returns of different securities are uncorrelated, at least to some degree.

Beta is a measure of risk that compares an investment to the overall market. Stocks with betas greater than 1.0 are aggressive stocks, while those with betas less than 1.0 are conservative.

Investment companies, or mutual funds, are convenient vehicles for diversifying. The types of funds are open-end funds, closed-end funds, exchange-traded funds, and unit investment trusts. Open-end funds sell for their net asset value. If a fund is a load fund, then investors pay a load fee to purchase shares. No-load funds charge no such fee. Closed-end funds trade on an exchange for a price that may be a discount from net asset value or a premium. Investors pay the normal brokerage commission to buy and sell them. Exchange-traded funds trade on an exchange and have portfolios constructed to perform equal to some specific index. Unit investment trusts are fixed portfolios of bonds that terminate when the final bond matures.

A fund's expense ratio is equal to expenses divided by net assets. Fund expenses fall into the following categories: administration costs, commissions paid to trade securities, 12b-1 fees, and management fees.

Benefits for individual investors of investing in mutual funds include diversification, shareholder services, possible savings on commissions, and professional investment management. Funds state their investment objective based on the type of securities the fund holds, or on the fund's investment strategy.

The purpose of the regulation of securities markets is to minimize the risk of fraud and market manipulation in order to give investors the confidence to commit their funds to investing. The Securities and Exchange Commission, created by the Securities Exchange Act of 1934, is the U.S. government agency charged with enforcing securities legislation. Stock exchanges and companies whose stocks trade on the exchanges must register with the SEC. Companies must file regular financial and other reports with the SEC.

The Investment Company Act of 1940 regulates mutual funds, and the Investment Advisors Act of 1940 requires that investment advisors register with the SEC. The Securities Investor Protection Corporation insures cash and securities in brokerage accounts up to $500,000. The Sarbanes-Oxley Act of 2002 has a number of provisions intended to limit fraud and abuse by company management.

PROBLEMS

1. Jason owns 100 shares of the stock on Kameltice Corp. He has estimated the stock's beta is 0.68, and he expects that the market index will have

a return of 11 percent next year. Compute Jason's expected return on his Kameltice stock.

2. Gretchen is comparing the risk of several different stocks. She has stock D, with a standard deviation of 0.32; E, with 0.47; and F, with 0.29. Rank these stocks in order of their risk, with the lowest risk first.

3. Below is a table of returns on the stock of AmerisourceBergen Corp. (ABC), CIGNA Corp. (CI), and a portfolio containing equal amounts of ABC and CI.

Year	ABC	CI	Portfolio
2009	5.9%	40.3%	23.1%
2010	35.8	33.4	34.6
2011	9.9	23.2	16.6
2012	5.3	21.6	13.5
2013	−18.4	−78.9	−48.7
Average	7.7	7.9	7.8
Standard deviation	19.3	49.2	32.6

4. Identify the stock with the greatest expected return and the one with highest risk. Compute the average of the returns of the two stocks and the average of the standard deviations of the two stocks. How does this average return and standard deviation compare to those measures for the portfolio?

5. Compute the net asset value for a fund that has total net assets of $29.64 million and 2 million shares outstanding. If you wanted to buy this no-load fund, how much would you pay per share?

6. Fund X has total net assets of $50 million and expenses of $600,000. Fund Y, with expenses of $864,000, has net assets of $120 million. Using the expense ratio as a guide, which fund would you prefer to own, other factors being equal?

7. Paula is considering purchasing stock of Companies W (beta = 1.6), X (beta = 0.7), Y (beta = 0.9), and Z (beta = 1.2). Which of these stocks are aggressive, and which are conservative? Which is the most risky?

CASE STUDIES

COLLEGE STUDENT

Kevin Maedor is a 19-year-old college student. He still lives at home with his parents, and he works part time at Vapor's Lane. He started his financial plan in the spring semester of 2014. He plans to graduate with a B.S. in engineering in May 2017. Use the investing goals you created for him in Chapter 11 and the investment choices you made in Chapters 12 and 13.

- Suggest investments modifications or changes for him. Use Stock Track to research your suggestions.
- Provide a detailed explanation of why these are good investments for him.

NEW GRADUATE

Rene Harris recently graduated with a B.S. in nursing. She lives by herself in a modest apartment. Her annual salary is $76,000 a year. Use the investing goals you created for her in Chapter 11 and the investment choices you made in Chapters 12 and 13.

- Suggest investments modifications or changes for her. Use stock track to research your suggestions.
- Provide a detailed explanation of why these are good investments for her.

CREATE YOUR OWN FINANCIAL PLAN

Most employer-sponsored retirement plans limit your options to mutual funds or fixed investment options. However, often employers match your contributions. A common match is 50 percent of your contribution up to a maximum of 6 percent. When you participate in these plans, you receive an automatic return of your employer's match. If you invest 6 percent and your employer contributes 3 percent of your income, you instantly realize a 3 percent return on your investment. It is always wise to take full advantage of your employer's maximum match.

If you don't have the option to participate in a 401(k) now, you will probably have the option when you take your first job after graduation.

1. Use the Morningstar web site, www.morningstar.com, to research mutual funds.
2. Select 3 to 10 mutual funds you would like to invest in.
3. Allocate what portion of your investment should go to each fund. 401(k) usually require you to indicate this as a percentage.

   - Fund A – 10 percent
   - Fund B – 20 percent
   - Fund C – 15 percent
   - Fund D – 5 percent
   - Fund E – 50 percent
   - The total must equal 100 percent

REVIEW QUESTIONS

1. Outline the reasoning that underlies the existence of U.S. securities regulation.

_____

_____

_____

2. Describe the major provisions of the Securities Exchange Act of 1934.

_____

_____

_____

3. Identify the SIPC. Describe the type of risk it insures against.

_____

_____

_____

4. List and define seven sources of risk.

_____

_____

_____

_____

_____

_____

_____

5. Identify and describe two ways to measure risk.

_____

_____

_____

6. Define diversification and explain how it can reduce risk.

_____

_____

_____

7. Identify how you might distinguish between an aggressive stock and a conservative one.

_____

_____

_____

8. Describe the four types of investment companies.

_____

_____

_____

9. Explain the difference between a load fund and a no-load fund. Define a 12b-1 fee.

_____

_____

_____

10. List the types of expenses incurred by mutual funds. Identify which are included in the expense ratio.

_____

_____

_____

11. Summarize the various classifications for investment objectives of mutual funds.

_____

_____

_____

Real Estate

15

"It's tangible, it's solid, it's beautiful. It's artistic, from my standpoint, and I just love real estate."

–Donald Trump (1946–)

OBJECTIVES

- Define basic terms related to real estate
- Identify benefits of real estate investing
- Describe the ways in which individuals can invest in real estate
- Explain the use of real estate indexes
- Demonstrate the use of real estate investment trusts as real estate investments for individuals

KEY TERMS

Appraisal
Depreciation
Equity REIT
Fee simple estate

Hybrid REIT
Life estate
Mortgage REIT
Real estate

Real estate operating company (REOC)
Real estate stocks
Real property

Real estate Land and any structure attached to the land.

Real estate is a term that encompasses land and any structure attached to the land. Many people use the term *real property* synonymously with real estate, while some sources state that the concept of real property includes both the ownership rights and the real estate covered by those rights. Real property is ownership of real estate, while personal property includes items that are not attached to land such as jewelry, an automobile, household items, tools, and many other things.

Investing in real estate has become a recognized and important part of investing, and real estate is the largest class of assets in terms of total value. Real estate investment as a profession is large and includes a number of specialized jobs such as professional property managers, who manage office buildings and apartment complexes for investors who purchased them as investments. Real estate investors include pension funds, real estate investment trusts, companies, and even individuals.

Investing in real estate can be a very complex process; for example, purchasing an office building in downtown St. Louis, leasing it, and managing it as an investment is a job that requires plenty of specialized knowledge. But real estate investing need not be so complicated as to discourage individual investors from participating. There are several ways for individuals to profitably participate in the real estate market, and this chapter introduces them. Those who are interested in learning more about real estate investment should consider taking a course in real estate and reading other references on real estate investment.

Historical Real Estate Returns

Real estate has always been popular as an investment with certain types of investors. But beginning in the late 1990s, real estate investing became increasingly popular with a broad range of investors. As real estate values increased and investors received increasing returns from their real estate investments, the popularity of real estate investing increased even more. Investors came to believe prices would never fall.

However, beginning in late 2007, those returns began reversing themselves, and real estate investments became some of the big money losers. Real estate values have always fluctuated, and the downturn in real estate values in the period following 2007 is no exception. It was just larger and over a longer time period than ever experienced before.

The U.S. Federal Housing Finance Agency (FHFA) gathers information about house prices and computes indexes of housing values, which it does for all standard Metropolitan Areas in the United States as well as for the country as a whole. To illustrate returns available on real estate investment over a long historical period, Exhibit 15.1 shows housing values in the United States from 1975 to 2013 as measured by the FHFA House Price Index.

Note in the chart how housing values seemed to grow at a relatively stable rate from 1975 to the late 1990s with some minor fluctuation. Around the year 1998, housing price growth seems to have accelerated significantly. Housing prices reached a peak in the third quarter of 2007. The downward slide in house values lasted almost four years. Prices reached a cyclical low in the first

HOUSING PRICES IN THE UNITED STATES, 1975–2013   EXHIBIT 15.1

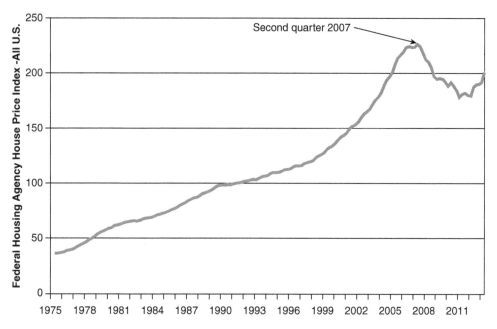

Source: U.S. Federal Housing Finance Agency.

quarter of 2011 but did not really begin to recover until a full year later in the first quarter of 2012.

To gain insight into real estate values over time, consider the impact of inflation. In fact, the reason many real estate investors invest in real estate is because real estate tends to be a good hedge against inflation. In other words, when inflation increases, real estate values also increase, so the real value of the investment remains at least constant. Exhibit 15.2 shows housing prices after adjusting for inflation.

Exhibit 15.2 reveals that home prices were very stable, with some minor ups and downs, between 1975 and the late 1990s, after adjusting for inflation. However, about 1998 housing prices began to increase more than the rate of inflation. This increase accelerated and continued through 2006 when inflation-adjusted house prices reached their peak in the last quarter of that year.

Let's divide the 1975 to 2013 period into four subperiods and compute the annual inflation-adjusted return on house prices during each subperiod:

- 1975 to 1997: 0.30%
- 1998 to 2006: 4.46%
- 2007 to 2011: -6.59%
- 2012 to 2013 (quarter 2): 5.10%

Annual inflation-adjusted returns on housing investment in 1998 to 2006 were more than 12 times the annual rate for the preceding 22-year period! These are U.S. averages. In areas where real estate investing was hot, such as Phoenix, southern California, and southern Florida, the increase was much

EXHIBIT 15.2	HOUSING PRICES IN THE UNITED STATES ADJUSTED FOR INFLATION, 1975–2013

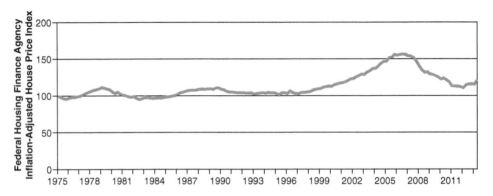

Source: U.S. Federal Housing Finance Agency and U.S. Bureau of Labor Statistics (Consumer Price Index)

THE SUBPRIME MORTGAGE CRISIS AND HOW THE U.S. GOVERNMENT DEALT WITH IT

A number of factors contributed to the real estate bubble of the mid-2000s and the decline in values that began in 2006. One of these factors was new on the scene and had not been an influence in previous real estate downturns. That factor was the subprime mortgage.

A subprime mortgage is a real estate loan to a borrower who would not qualify for a mortgage under traditional credit standards. Possibly the borrower has a low credit rating or insufficient income to qualify for a traditional mortgage. In the late 1990s and early 2000s, U.S. government policy encouraged the extension of subprime mortgage loans so that people who previously could not own a home could become home buyers. Low interest rates during that period motivated lenders to offer more of these types of loans.

The increased demand that resulted from these new buyers in the market (among other factors) pushed home prices higher and higher. As long as prices increased, most homeowners with subprime mortgages were able to continue to pay their home payments. They could even borrow more money using the increased value of their home as collateral.

However, once housing prices began to level off, these borrowers could no longer tap into ever-increasing lines of credit based on the equity in their homes. Default rates began to increase, forcing foreclosure and the sale of homes, which in turn caused further declines in house prices. The bubble had burst.

Following the collapse in house prices, the U.S. economy went into a full recession. To deal with the recession, the U.S. government instituted a number of expansionary policies to help stimulate the economy. Some of these policies were designed to help relieve the mortgage crisis and ease homeowner problems, either directly or indirectly.

Prior to the crisis, an average year might have seen somewhere around a half million home foreclosures. That number grew to more than 3 million homes each year from 2008 to 2011.

Some of the measures taken to assist homeowners and shore up the mortgage industry were:

- The Housing and Economic Recovery Act of 2008 instructed the federal government to take over two government-sponsored enterprises that operated in the mortgage market but who had basically run out of capital as a result of the crisis. These enterprises were the Federal National Mortgage Association (Fannie Mae) and the Federal Home Loan Mortgage Corporation (Freddie Mac).
- The Federal Reserve System acted to reduce interest rates and hold them low for an extended period of time.
- Government agencies created programs to assist individual homeowners during the recession. An example is the Innovation Fund for the Hardest Hit Housing Markets, which provides funding to state housing finance agencies. These agencies began to offer assistance measures such as:
  - Unemployment mortgage assistance programs that provide funds to help pay an unemployed person's mortgage payments.
  - Mortgage reinstatement programs that provide a one-time payment to bring a borrower's delinquent mortgage current.
  - Modification assistance programs facilitate modifications in the terms of a mortgage (such as reducing the interest rate) to facilitate a homeowner's being able to continue payments.
  - Transition assistance programs to help struggling homeowners transition to more affordable housing.

more. The Miami housing index showed an annual inflation-adjusted appreciation of 10.27 percent from 1998 through 2006.

In 2007 the speculative bubble in real estate prices burst, and from 2007 to 2011 prices fell at an inflation-adjusted rate of 6.59 percent per year. In the overbuilt Miami market, for example, prices fell at an annual rate of 11.4 percent over 2006 to 2011.

The lesson investors learned (the hard way) in the late 2000s was that real estate values do not always rise—and when they rise too much, they will eventually fall. There is another lesson: Real estate prices, *over the long run*, are a good hedge against inflation and should yield a return that is somewhere around the rate of inflation plus about ½ percent. Note the emphasis on the long run; over shorter periods real estate can suffer significant losses in a cyclical downturn, but historical experience shows real estate values recovering after each down cycle.

Investing in Real Estate

PROPERTY RIGHTS

Real property is real estate or the ownership rights over real estate and includes more than just the surface of the land. It includes water rights, any fixtures attached to the land (such as a house), subsurface rights to minerals, and air rights.

Real property Real estate or the ownership rights over real estate.

Although the legal descriptions of the various levels of real estate ownership and their characteristics are far beyond the scope of this chapter, some basic terms are important. The highest level of ownership of land is the fee simple estate, which represents absolute ownership of the land. When the word *fee* is part of the term, the land ownership is inheritable upon the death of its owner. Another type of ownership is the life estate, which represents ownership during the owner's lifetime, after which the land ownership reverts to the previous owner.

Fee simple estate Real property ownership that represents absolute ownership of the land.

Life estate Real property ownership during the present owner's lifetime, after which ownership reverts to the previous owner.

PROPERTY OWNERSHIP REPRESENTS INCOME POTENTIAL

Owning property carries the right to use that property to generate income. For example, an owner of real estate can use the land to farm or to build a store in which to have a business. In addition, a landowner can lease the land to someone else, who would then either occupy the land as a residence or use the land productively to generate income. The party who leases the land pays the owner rent in exchange for the use of the land.

The ability of real estate to generate income makes real estate an investment. An investor can own real estate in order to receive income from the property. The fact that real estate can generate revenue gives real estate a value. Values can rise, so the possible increase in the value of real estate represents another potential source of gain for the real estate investor.

PROPERTY VALUES

Many factors influence the value of real estate. There are macroeconomic factors such as interest rates, taxes, and the economic environment. There are microfactors, such as variables that affect the local supply and demand for real estate.

Appraisal Estimate of the value of an asset based on a market and financial evaluation.

An appraisal is an estimate of the value of an asset based on a market and financial evaluation. A thorough appraisal will examine factors such as recent transaction prices of similar real estate in the local market, potential income

Ownership of property includes any fixtures on the land. For example, this farm land contains the house, silos, fences and barns.

U.S. REAL ESTATE INDEXES

EXHIBIT 15.3

Sponsor: Name	Period	Based on	Reported for
Standard & Poor's: Case-Shiller Home Price Index	Monthly	Repeated sales (properties that have sold at least twice) of single-family homes	U.S. and 20 metropolitan regions
National Council of Real Estate Investment Fiduciaries (NCREIF): NCREIF Property Index	Quarterly	Appraised values of properties owned by NCREIF members. Computed separately for the following property types: apartments, hotels, industrial, office, and retail property	National and four U.S. regions (East, South, West, Midwest)
Federal Housing Finance Agency: House Price Index	Quarterly	Mortgage transactions of single-family homes from	U.S., nine U.S. census divisions, the 50 states and the District of Columbia and major metropolitian areas

the property could generate if it were rented, and changes in market conditions that affect real estate values.

Just as there are stock market indexes that track the performance of the stock market, real estate indexes mark the performance of real estate. There are three principal real estate indexes in the United States: the aforementioned AHFA House Price Index, the Case-Shiller Index, and the NCREIF indexes. Exhibit 15.3 identifies the content of each of these indexes. The NCREIF indexes are based on appraisals and computed for commercial property types, while the other two indexes are based on transactions and are for residential single-family housing.

All of the indexes in Exhibit 15.3 report a national aggregate index and also subindexes for various regions or states. Property values in different regions and different localities can vary because of localized demand for and supply of real estate. Sometimes the difference can be quite dramatic when, for example, house values in a particularly desirable suburb or neighborhood show several years of steep increases.

In addition, different property types can have different rates of appreciation. For example, Exhibit 15.4 shows the accumulated value of $1,000 initially invested in 1989 in apartments and in office buildings. The exhibit uses the NCREIF Property Index for each type of property and shows at the end of 2008 each $1,000 invested in apartments would have grown to $5,516, and each $1,000 invested in office buildings would have grown to $3,637. These totals include changes in the properties values and assume reinvestment of all rental profits.

Returns to real estate investors have been substantial in recent years, although the real estate slump that began in mid-2006 erased profits for most investors who invested after 2002. However, over the long haul, real estate investments have generally produced positive returns for patient investors. It is no surprise that investing in real estate has become widespread.

EXHIBIT 15.4	**VALUE OF $1,000 INITIALLY INVESTED IN APARTMENT OR OFFICE BUILDINGS**

(assumes reinvestment of all rental income and changes in property values)

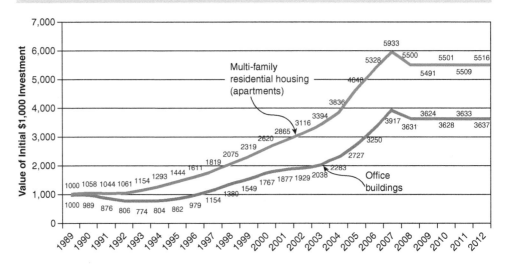

Source: NCREIF Property Indexes.

Exhibit 15.5 illustrates some real estate returns that were possible over the past several decades. Take the case of one Ellen Walker, who purchased a residential house as an investment in 1987 and let it for the next 25 years. Assume the home's value followed the Case-Shiller Home Price Index for 10 major metropolitan areas over that period. Computing Ellen's return through December 2012 considering only the increase in the value of the house (i.e., ignoring any profits from renting the house during that time), the investment produced a 4.06 percent annual return.

Of course, had Ellen been sufficiently savvy (or lucky) to have sold at the height of the market in June 2006, her return would have been much higher 16.82 percent annualized. On the other hand, the unfortunate investor who bought in June 2006 would have experienced losses at the rate of 4.28 percent per year through December 2012.

BENEFITS OF INVESTING IN REAL ESTATE

Aside from the obvious potential for positive return, there are three main benefits real estate offers as an investment:

1. Asset allocation
2. Diversification
3. Tax advantages

Asset Allocation

Recall from earlier chapters on investing that the asset allocation decision is the choice of how much to invest in the various broad asset categories. Real estate is a broad asset category, and all investors should consider including real estate as part of their investment portfolio. In 2001, Standard & Poor's recognized the

CASE-SHILLER HOME PRICE INDEX FOR 10 MAJOR U.S. METROPOLITAN AREAS, 1987–2012

EXHIBIT 15.5

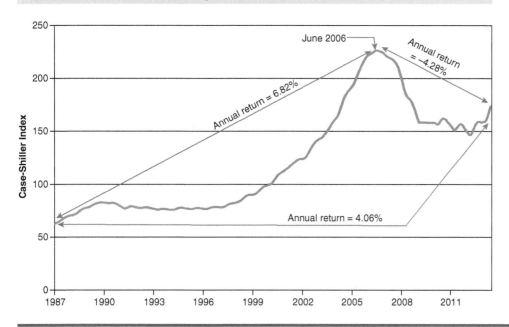

importance of real estate as a major asset type when for the first time it began including real estate stocks in its well-known S&P 500 Index of common stocks.

When informed investors make their asset allocation decisions, they consider the forecast performance of each of the different classes of asset (for example, stocks, bonds, and real estate). They will want to invest more money in asset classes they feel will perform better over the next few years and less in assets they believe will not. So, for example, if you believe real estate will perform well in the near future, you should commit more funds to real estate and less to other classes of investments.

Diversification

The earlier chapter on risk showed how diversification can benefit investors by reducing risk without sacrificing return. Real estate or securities of companies that invest in real estate offer investors additional risk-reducing possibilities.

As an example of the risk-reduction possible when adding real estate investments, consider Exhibit 15.6. The chart in Exhibit 4.6 shows the risk (standard deviation of returns) for three different investment portfolios from 2003 to 2012. The first portfolio is common stocks represented by the Standard & Poor's 500 Index. It had a standard deviation of 19.29 percent.

The second portfolio is real estate represented by the FTSE/NAREIT Index of Equity Real Estate Investment Trusts. It exhibited a standard deviation of 23.25 percent over the 10-year period from 2003 to 2012.

The third portfolio contains both common stocks and real estate; it is invested half in the S&P Index and half in the FTSE/NAREIT Index. Its standard deviation was only 9.8 percent, less than either of its components. The combination of real estate and common stocks provided effective risk-reduction benefits for investors.

EXHIBIT 15.6	RISK OF REAL ESTATE, COMMON STOCKS, AND A PORTFOLIO COMBINING REAL ESTATE AND COMMON STOCKS, 2003–2012

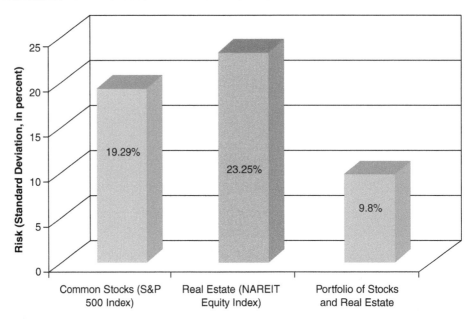

Note: Common stocks represented by annual returns on the Standard & Poor's 500 Common Stock Index, 2003–2012.

Real estate represented by the annual returns on the FTSE/NAREIT Index of Equity Real Estate Investment Trusts, 2003–2012.

Portfolio of real estate and common stocks represented by a portfolio containing 50 percent S&P 500 and 50 percent FTSE/NAREIT.

Tax Advantages

Real estate investments offer some benefits that may reduce taxes:

- For homeowners, even if no part of the home is used for rental income, the interest on a home mortgage and a second mortgage and payment of property taxes are deductible from income for U.S. federal income tax purposes.
- If you own rental property, all out-of-pocket expenses of owning and maintaining the property, including interest paid to finance the property, repairs, management expenses, and costs of maintenance, are deductible from income.
- In addition to out-of-pocket expenses, property owners who rent get to deduct depreciation on a portion of the value of the property.

Depreciation Deduction from income to represent the decline in value of an asset as a result of normal wear and tear.

Depreciation is a tax deduction that supposedly represents the decline in value of an asset as a result of normal wear and tear. The idea is that an asset has a certain amount of "use" in it, and as time passes, the value of the asset gets used. The purpose of depreciation is to let business owners deduct from income a dollar amount representing the value of their assets they have used up during the year.

DEPRECIATION RATES FOR REAL ESTATE INVESTMENTS   EXHIBIT 15.7

Property Type	Useful Life	Annual Depreciation
Residential Rental Property	27.5 years	3.6364%
Commercial Rental Property	39 years	2.5641%

An automobile is a good example of depreciation. Suppose you bought a new Toyota sport utility vehicle back in 2011. With some negotiating at the dealer, you would have paid about $30,000 for the vehicle. Assuming you drove it the typical 15,000 miles during the first year, the market value of the vehicle would have been about $25,000 one year later, in 2012. The $5,000 difference represents the depreciation of the car over the year.

The Internal Revenue Service has rules that define how much you can deduct each year for depreciation of different assets. The IRS says that you divide the value of the property by the property's useful life to get your depreciation for each year. Exhibit 15.7 shows the useful life and the resulting annual depreciation as a percentage of a property's cost.

Now, here is the great investment advantage rental real estate offers. Although most assets do fall in value as they get used, properly maintained real estate often holds its value or even increases. You get to deduct depreciation (a tax break) on an asset that has the potential for actually gaining in value!

The IRS does recognize that land does not depreciate; only the structure might depreciate in value. The depreciable value of any real estate is equal to the total value of the property less the value of the land alone. Example 15.1 shows how depreciation saves taxes for an investor renting a house.

In the example, Jason rents out a house for which he paid $140,000. Note that he can base his depreciation on only $110,000, because the land is worth $30,000. His annual depreciation on the house is $4,000, and Jason will owe $1,000 in income taxes on his rental property income. Without taking depreciation, Jason would have owed $2,000 in taxes. Depreciation saved Jason $1,000 in taxes!

RISKS OF INVESTING IN REAL ESTATE

As described in the previous section, investing in real estate can offer diversification benefits and even reduce the risk of a portfolio of investments. On the other hand, real estate does come with its particular risks. While we could discuss many detailed types of risk, there are two principal risks with owning investment real estate:

1. Risk of the loss of rental income
2. Risk of a change in the value of property

EXAMPLE 15.1 Tax Benefits of Renting a House

Jason Friedman has purchased a house he plans to rent for $850 per month. Jason paid $140,000 for the house, and the appraiser told him the land alone was worth $30,000. Jason estimates that he will pay $2,200 per year for expenses (property taxes, insurance, maintenance, and repairs). Jason pays taxes at the rate of 25 percent of his income. How much will Jason owe in taxes on his rental income? How much would Jason have owed if he had not been able to deduct depreciation?

First, let's calculate the annual depreciation amount Jason can take on his taxes:

House	$140,000
Land	−30,000
Depreciable basis	$110,000

Annual depreciation = $110,000/27.5 = $4,000

Next, compute Jason's taxable income by subtracting his expenses from his revenue:

Annual rental revenue (12 × 850)	$10,200
Expenses	−2,200
Depreciation	−4,000
Taxable income	$4,000

Then, calculate Jason's tax at 25 percent of his income:

Taxable income	$4,000
Tax (at 25% of income)	$1,000

Finally, compute Jason's taxable income and tax if he could not have taken depreciation as a deduction:

Annual rental revenue (12 × 850)	$10,200
Expenses	2,200
Taxable income	$8,000
Tax (at 25% of income)	$2,000

Depreciation saved Jason $1,000 in taxes. ■

Risk of the Loss of Rental Income

The risk associated with rental income results from rental conditions in the market where the property is located. If there are plenty of rental units available in the area, with a number of those units vacant, then the competition to attract renters may be fierce. One or more of several occurrences may cause a loss of potential rental income. These occurrences include the following:

- New renters are difficult to find when an existing occupant leaves, leaving the property vacant between renters for longer periods, resulting in reduced rental income.
- Owners offer inducements to renters such as a free month's rent or rebates at the end of a lease, all of which reduce rental income.
- Owners are forced to reduce rent to compete in the market.

Risk of a Change in the Value of a Property

Although real estate values have tended to rise over very long periods of time, real estate prices tend to follow cycles during interim periods. This cyclical nature of real estate poses a risk to investors. Risk of real estate values changing is often associated with the market in which the real estate is located.

- Real estate risk in the entire market. There is the risk that real estate, in general, in the economy can fluctuate in value. For example, suppose high interest rates cause most home buyers to put off buying a home, and home prices, in general, fall.
- Real estate risk for a geographic area such as a city. Real estate in a particular city or metropolitan region can be affected by the local economy. For example, if a large manufacturing plant closes, the loss of jobs in the city might cause property values to decline.
- Real estate risk of a neighborhood. Property values can be affected by trends and other factors in the local neighborhood. For example, if the owner of a large apartment complex allows the units to deteriorate, then the values of nearby properties can also suffer.

Real Estate Investment for Individuals

Although there are many ways to invest and investment vehicles for investing in real estate, there are three that are especially suitable for individuals who do not have special expertise in real estate yet want to participate in the investment benefits real estate offers:

1. An individual's investment in a home
2. Real estate stocks
3. Local rental property

INVESTMENT IN A HOME

The most expensive asset most people will ever purchase in their lifetime is their home. For most people, this will be their only investment in real estate. If past experience holds, an investment in a home will be a good investment for the future. Residential home prices in the United States have been on a long-term upward trend, although as Exhibits 15.1, 15.2, and 15.5 have shown, housing prices did suffer a major decline in the period following mid-2006.

House price indexes such as those listed in Exhibit 15.3 can be useful for estimating past and future house prices. For example, the U.S. FHFA

© Chin Kit Sen, 2014, Shutterstock, Inc.

Property values depreciate when neighboring homes are left to deteriorate.

computes its House Price Index every three months. Exhibit 15.8 presents year end annual values of the index adjusted so 1990 = 100.

We can use the House Price Index to estimate past and future house values using the following relationship:

$$\text{present house value} = \text{past house value} \cdot \frac{\text{present house price index}}{\text{past house price index}} \qquad \textbf{Equation 15.1}$$

Example 15.2 illustrates how to use the House Price Index to estimate the change in wealth homeowners experienced while owning and living in their home over a significant part of their lives.

The FHFA House Price Index is useful for national and regional averages. However, home prices can vary significantly depending on the local real estate

| EXHIBIT 15.8 | FHFA HOUSE PRICES INDEXES |

	Entire U.S.A	Midwest Region, WNC Division (1)	Kansas City (2)
1991	101.46	101.62	101.69
1992	104.25	106.00	104.07
1993	107.09	112.48	107.72
1994	110.19	117.53	113.00
1995	113.12	123.10	118.30
1996	116.28	128.01	124.51
1997	120.14	132.82	131.24
1998	126.97	141.31	139.99
1999	134.87	149.10	148.06
2000	144.30	158.64	157.05
2001	154.03	168.35	167.34
2002	165.87	177.81	173.25
2003	178.91	187.68	181.89
2004	197.09	198.21	189.38
2005	217.17	207.97	196.87
2006	223.84	212.41	201.73
2007	218.43	211.25	197.34
2008	197.16	202.19	186.66
2009	192.86	201.68	183.61
2010	184.88	194.82	166.55
2011	180.56	192.16	168.01
2012	190.48	200.76	175.24

1. U.S. Census Bureau Midwest Region, West North Central Division (Iowa, Kansas, Minnesota, Missouri, Nebraska, North Dakota and South Dakota)
2. Kansas City KS ad MO area

Source: U.S. Federal Housing Finance Agency.

| Example of a Home as an Investment | **EXAMPLE 15.2** |

Christos and Elise Mitrokostas saved and purchased a new home in 1994 in Kansas City, for $80,000. They purchased as much home as they could possibly afford because they felt that a home was a good investment. In 2012 they retired and decided to sell their house and move to an apartment to have less maintenance. Assuming that their house appreciated in value at the average rate according to the Kansas City House Price Index, estimate the value of Elise and Christos's home when they retired.

The "past house price index" for 1994 from Exhibit 15.8 is 113.00, and the "future house price index" for 2012 is 175.24.

$$\text{present house value} = \text{past house price} \times \frac{\text{present house price index}}{\text{past house price index}}$$

$$= 80,000 \times \frac{175.24}{113.00}$$

$$= 124,064 \quad \blacksquare$$

market. Some areas may experience robustly increasing house values, while others have home prices languish. For example, Exhibit 15.9 shows home prices measured by the Case-Shiller Home Price Indices for the Dallas and the Denver metropolitan areas. Note how Denver home prices were above Dallas prices during the 2000–2008 period covered in the chart.

| **S&P/CASE SHILLER HOME PRICE INDICES, DALLAS AND DENVER METROPOLITAN AREAS, 2000–2013** | **EXHIBIT 15.9** |

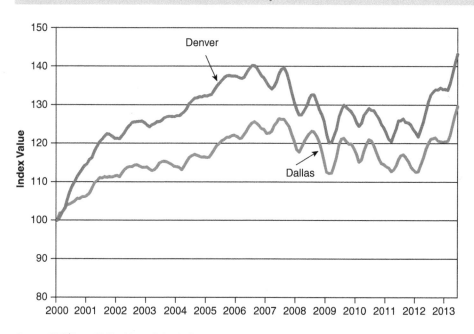

Source: S&P/Case-Shiller Home Price Indices.

REAL ESTATE STOCKS

Real estate stocks Stocks of companies that manage or invest in real estate.

Real estate stocks are stocks of companies that invest in real estate, manage real estate, and invest in mortgages used to finance real estate. There are two main types of real estate stocks:

1. Real estate investment trust (REIT)
2. Real estate operating company (REOC)

Real Estate Investment Trusts

A real estate investment trust (REIT) is a company that invests in real estate or mortgages to finance real estate. REITs as we know them today came into being in 1960, when the U.S. Congress passed legislation giving REITs an exemption from paying U.S. federal income tax as long at the REIT pays out substantially all of its income to its shareholders in the form of cash dividends.

There are approximately 150 REITs in the U.S. whose stocks trade on the public markets; most trade on the New York Stock Exchange. There are an additional 800 or so REITs that are privately held and do not trade on one of the exchanges. The publicly traded REITs provide excellent investment vehicles for individual investors who want to participate in the benefits real estate offers but do not want the responsibility of buying and managing a property. In addition to the U.S. markets, many other countries have adopted the REIT concept and have REITs trading in their local markets.

Equity REIT Real estate investment trust that owns and operates income-producing real property.

Mortgage REIT Real estate investment trust whose portfolio is invested in mortgages or mortgage securities.

Qualifications to Operate as a REIT

To operate as a REIT and qualify for the tax exemption, a company must

- Pay cash dividends of at least 90 percent of its taxable income to shareholders every year.
- Be managed by a board of directors and taxable as a corporation.
- Have at least 100 shareholders and no more than 50 percent of its stock held by five or fewer investors.
- Invest at least 75 percent of its total assets in real estate assets.
- Derive at least 75 percent of its gross income from rents from real estate property or interest on mortgages on real property.

Types of REITs

There are two main types of REIT:

1. Equity REITs own and operate income-producing real property.
2. Mortgage REITs lend money directly by lending to real estate purchasers to finance real estate or indirectly by investing in mortgages.

Equity REITs are by far the most numerous type of REIT. They hold more real estate assets than do the other types. Exhibit 15.10 illustrates the portion of total REIT property held by each type of REIT. Mortgage REITs hold 7.1 percent of the total value of all real estate owned by REITs; and hybrid REITs have only 1.4 percent.

Investing in a REIT gives everyday people a piece of the real estate market without the responsibilities of managing property.

REAL ESTATE OWNED BY REITS CATEGORIZED BY THE PROPERTY SECTOR CATEGORY OF THE REIT, JULY 2013

EXHIBIT 15.10

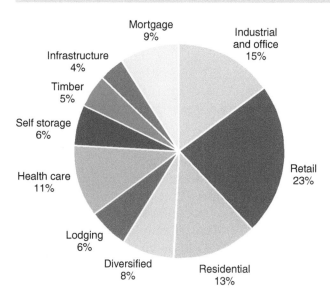

Source: National Association of Real Estate Investment Trusts.

The remaining 91.5 percent of REIT real estate is in the hands of the various equity REITS.

Benefits of REITs for Individual Investors
The potential to invest in real estate via REITs offers individual investors a number of benefits:

- Dividends. REITs pay relatively high dividend yields compared to most other stocks.
- Professional management. Real estate owned by REITs is managed by professional property managers, and REITs use professional real estate analysts to select properties to purchase.
- Liquidity. Unlike real estate owned directly, REITs are a liquid asset that the investor can sell fairly quickly to raise cash or take advantage of other investment opportunities.
- Diversification. REITs offer the diversification risk reduction benefits of real estate as illustrated in Exhibit 15.6.
- Accessibility to small investors. REITs are accessible to all investors, even those with just a few thousand (or even a few hundred) dollars to invest. Purchasing a property for direct real estate investment can require a commitment of much more money.

There are also mutual funds of REITs. These mutual funds offer a convenient way to invest in a diversified portfolio of REITs for a relatively small sum of money.

Investment Performance of REITs

As mentioned previously in this chapter, real estate tends to be a cyclical investment, so REITs will also be cyclical. REITs grew in popularity during a period of general increases in the value of real estate resulting in high returns to equity REITs during the 1990s and early 2000s.

The performance of mortgage REITs tends to follow the bond market rather than the real estate market, so mortgage REIT returns tend to be sensitive to changes in interest rates. However, the mortgage crisis that began with problems in subprime mortgages in 2007 caused a precipitous drop in values of mortgage REITs in 2007 and 2008.

Exhibit 15.11 illustrates the growth from 1994 to 2012 of a $1,000 initial investment in each of the equity REITs and in mortgage REITs. Computations use REIT indexes from the National Association of Real Estate Investment Trusts (www.nareit.com) and assume all dividends are reinvested.

As Exhibit 15.11 shows, equity REITS showed the strongest performance over the 19-year period. The $1,000 investment in equity REITs resulted in a portfolio with a value of $6,718. Compare this to an ending value of $3,944 for mortgage REITs.

EXHIBIT 15.11   **INVESTMENT PERFORMANCE OF RETIS, 1994–2012**

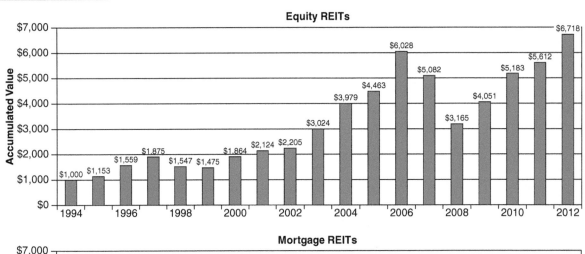

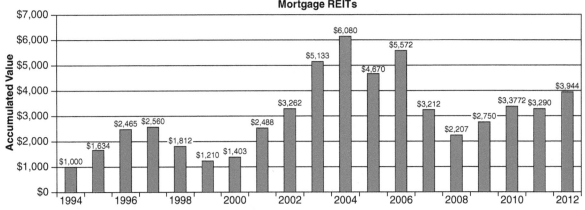

REAL ESTATE OPERATING COMPANIES

The requirements of being a REIT place restrictions on REITs; for example, they have to pay out virtually all of their earnings as dividends to shareholders. They cannot plow back any of their earnings into the company for future growth. To avoid these restrictions, a real estate company may choose not to be a REIT.

Real estate operating companies (REOCs) have greater flexibility than REITs do. The drawback of gaining this flexibility is that REOCs lose the tax exemption granted to REITs—which is a big advantage for REITs.

There are around 30 companies classified as REOCs. About half of them operate hotel chains.

> **Real estate operating company (REOC)** Real estate investment company that does not qualify for REIT status.

Investing in Local Rental Property

A final alternative for individual investors is to purchase local real estate for purposes of rental. It is possible to own, manage, and rent several local properties while maintaining full-time employment elsewhere. Many people own one or several residential rental units as a source of extra income and investment.

The market for single-family homes is particularly suited to individual investors. Commercial real estate investors (including REITs) have avoided entering the market for residential single-family rental housing. They do participate, to a large degree, in the market for multifamily and apartment rentals.

Owning local rental property can be quite profitable and rewarding. However, this is one investment that takes a substantial amount of work and oversight. Unless you contract the management of your property to an agent (which will, of course, cost you a fee), you will be responsible for finding suitable tenants, checking their credit, signing leases, and retaining and dealing with deposits at the beginning of a lease.

During the lease, you will need to attend to any repairs or maintenance the property needs, periodically check on the property, and respond to requests from tenants. All of this takes time and effort. If you are willing and able, investing in rental property can be a profitable long-term investment. If you prefer to spend your time at other pursuits, investing in real estate via REITs may be the preferable alternative for you.

SUMMARY

Real estate is land and any structure attached to the land, and the term real property is often synonymous with real estate. Real estate is the largest asset class, and real estate is a widespread and popular investment.

Real estate includes the land surface, any structures on the land, water rights, subsurface rights, and air rights. The highest level of land ownership is a fee simple estate, which gives the owner absolute ownership and inheritability. A life estate grants ownership of real property only over the lifetime of the individual.

Real estate offers two potential sources of profit: rental income and profit from an increase in the value of the property. Real estate values have experienced a long-term trend toward higher values. The benefits of investing in real estate include asset allocation, diversification, and tax advantages.

Homeowners receive a tax benefit even though they do not rent their property for income. They can deduct interest payments on their home mortgage. Investors can deduct interest and other out-of-pocket expenses, plus depreciation on the property.

There are three avenues for investing in real estate that are popular with individual investors: investing in a home, real estate stocks, and local rental property. For most people, their only investment in real estate is the purchase of a home. The experience of most U.S. homeowners in the past decades has been their home proved to be a profitable investment in addition to providing them a place to live.

A real estate investment trust (REIT) is a real estate investment company that qualifies for a federal tax exemption as long as it pays out at least 90 percent of its profits to stockholders as cash dividends. A real estate operating company (REOC) does not qualify for the tax exemption. Both provide popular real estate investment vehicles for individual investors.

There are two types of REIT: equity REITs, which invest in rental property and mortgage REITs, which lend money for real estate mortgages. Benefits of REITs for individual investors include relatively high cash dividends, professional real estate management, liquidity, diversification, and accessibility to the small investor.

Purchasing local residential property for rental is another investment possibility for individuals. However, this investment takes a significant amount of time dealing with rental and maintenance of the property.

PROBLEMS

1. Examine Exhibit 15.2 and identify periods when real estate values gained over inflation and periods when they lost ground to inflation.

2. Jerry owns a rental house for which he paid $80,500. The land on which the house sits is worth $20,000. Using the useful life of residential real estate of 27.5 years, compute the annual depreciation deduction Jerry can take on his income tax return.

3. Jerry (problem 2) rents his property for $650 per month. His expenses run to $90 per month. How much will Jerry owe in taxes on his rental income if his tax rate is 30 percent of net income? How much did the depreciation save Jerry in taxes?

4. Renell Blasingame owns a home that, in 2008, had a value of $175,000. Using the U.S. House Price Index in Exhibit 15.8, estimate the price she paid for the house when she purchased it in 1991.

5. Harvey Johnson purchased a home in Kansas City in 1994 for $68,000. Use Exhibit 15.8 to estimate the value of Harvey's home in 2012.

6. Lilian and George Harris purchased their home for $68,000 in 1997. Appraise the house in 2012 using the House Price Index for the midwest Region, west north Central Division (Exhibit 15.8).

CASE STUDIES

COLLEGE STUDENT

We've met Kevin before; below you will find his original financial information. If you have worked on this case study from the beginning of the book, use the current financial data you have for him. If you haven't worked on this case study through the entire book, use the financial information below.

Kevin Maedor is a 19-year-old college student. He still lives at home with his parents, and he works part time at Vapor's Lane. He started his financial plan in the spring semester of 2014. He plans to graduate with a B.S. in engineering in May 2017. He has the following financial information:

- He brings home $760 a month from his job; he currently has $174 in his checking account.
- He asks his parents for $50 cash each week.
- He has a Visa card with a balance of $1,700 and a MasterCard with a balance of $800. He makes the minimum monthly payment of $15.00 on each of them.
- His cell phone bill is $85 a month.
- Last month he spent $450 on gas, $375.00 on golf, and $490.69 at restaurants.

He is considering diversifying his investments. Although he won't be able to invest until after he graduates, he wants to prepare now. He needs more information about his options.
Help him consider real estate as an option:

1. Recommend which of the following would benefit him.
   - Home ownership
   - REITs
   - Rental property
2. Explain your recommendations for him.
   Students' answers will vary.

NEW GRADUATE

We've met Rene before; below you will find her original financial information. If you have worked on this case study from the beginning of the book, use the current financial data you have for her. If you haven't worked on this case study through the entire book, use the financial information below.

Rene Harris recently graduated with a B.S. in nursing. She lives by herself in a modest apartment. Her annual salary is $76,000 a year. Rene loves to entertain, but her apartment is too small and the neighbors complain about the slightest noise. Rene is a good neighbor, so she has been going out with friends instead. She has the following financial information:

- She brings home $4,433.33 a month from her job.
- She pays $1,125.00 a month for her apartment, which includes trash service and cable.
- She used her new Visa last month for the first time and charged $600. She also opened a new Macy's charge and charged $762.78. She hasn't received her first bill for either of them; assume her minimum monthly payment will be $15.00 on each.
- She owes $30,000 in student loans and makes a monthly payment of $151.47.
- Her cell phone bill is $105.00 a month.
- She has $1,804.12 in her savings account.
- Last month she spent $275 on gas, $398.63 on food, $32.17 for her water bill, $76.18 for her electric bill, $49.98 for Internet service, $820 at restaurants, $357.82 on entertainment, $762.78 on clothing (this is her Macy's charge) and $152.75 on hair and nail services.

She is considering diversifying her investments. She needs more information about her options.

Help her consider real estate as an option:

3. Recommend which of the following would benefit her.
    - Home ownership
    - REITs
    - Rental property
4. Explain your recommendations for her.
   Students' answers will vary.

CREATE YOUR OWN FINANCIAL PLAN

Do you have an interest in real estate as an option to diversify your investment strategy?

1. Which of the following interest you?
    - Home ownership
    - REITs
    - Rental property
2. When do you think you can include your choices into your plan?
    - Next year
    - Now
    - When you graduate
    - Ten years from now
3. Write a goal and include your choices in your financial plan.

REVIEW QUESTIONS   CHAPTER 15

1. Define real estate and identify the property rights that accompany ownership of real estate.

   _____

   _____

   _____

2. Describe the NCREIF Property Index and how it might be used. Identify how appraisals are relevant to the index.

   _____

   _____

   _____

3. List the three main benefits that investing in real estate offers investors.

   _____

   _____

   _____

4. Define depreciation and demonstrate with an example how it can reduce an investor's taxes.

   _____

   _____

   _____

5. Distinguish between a REIT and a REOC.

   _____

   _____

   _____

6. Identify the requirements a company must meet to qualify as a REIT.

_____

_____

_____

7. List and define the three main types of REIT.

_____

_____

_____

8. Describe the principal benefits that REITs offer as investments for individual investors.

_____

_____

_____

9. Identify some of the tasks that individuals might have to perform when they invest in residential rental property. Assess the amount of investment management work that such an investor has compared with that of a person who invests in REITs.

_____

_____

_____

Retirement Planning

"The company accountant is shy and retiring. He's shy a quarter of a million dollars. That's why he's retiring."

–Milton Berle
(1908–2002)

OBJECTIVES

- Describe the various types of retirement plans
- Distinguish defined benefit plans from defined contribution retirement plans
- Compute retirement benefits
- Describe the financial life cycle
- Select asset allocation for retirement planning using the concept of the financial life cycle
- Analyze the use of target-date and target-risk funds for a retirement plan

KEY TERMS

401(k) plan
403(b) plan
Coverdell IRA
Defined benefit plan
Defined contribution plan
Employee Stock Ownership Plan (ESOP)
Employee Retirement Income
Security Act (ERISA)

Financial life cycle
Funded plan
Keogh plan
Life cycle investing
Life cycle mutual fund
Non-contributory plan
Pension plan
Pension Benefit Guaranty Corporation

Profit-sharing plan
Rollover
SIMPLE IRA
Simplified employee pension (SEP) plan
Target-date life cycle fund
Target-risk life cycle fund
Vested benefits

Thinking about retirement is probably not the first thing that comes to your mind each day unless you are about 50 years of age or older. Although the golden years may be decades away at this point, the surest way to achieve a significant retirement nest egg is by planning for it many years in advance.

How do you visualize your retirement? Waiting until you can draw Social Security in your mid-sixties and barely getting by each month? Retiring at age 50, healthy and fit, and able to enjoy traveling and other benefits of the extra free time available? Your actions today and in the next few years or decade may determine which of these scenarios describes your future. This chapter summarizes the various retirement plans available.

Starting Early with Retirement Planning

People should start planning for retirement at the point they have steady income, either through full-time employment or self-employment. For most people, the point when planning should begin occurs in their early twenties when retirement is a distant four-plus decades away. At that age those who plan for their retirement have longevity on their side. Starting to save for retirement early allows compound interest and returns to work in the saver's favor. The example of Mike and Patrick Doyle illustrates the pitfalls of only thinking about retirement when it is around the corner.

The benefits of early retirement planning are clear. The earlier a person begins to save for retirement, the more funds will be available in the retirement years. People can plan and save for retirement through two different means:

1. Formal retirement plans
2. Saving outside of a formal plan

RETIREMENT PLANNING—MIKE AND PATRICK DOYLE

Picture twin brothers, Mike and Patrick Doyle. Both are hard-working individuals who earn a good income working in the financial services industry. Mike decided at the age of 25 that he was going to start committing some money every month to a retirement account. He looked at his personal financial situation and concluded that he could save $200 each month.

Patrick also understood the importance of proper financial planning, but he also liked the idea of having a really fun deck at his house with a pool and hot tub; after making his loan payment on those items he had no money left over to save for retirement. When Patrick turned 45, Mike finally convinced him to create a retirement investment account. Patrick realized that he was getting a late start, so he decided to save $800 each month so that he could easily play catch-up with his brother. Both brothers put their savings into a stock market account that earned 12 percent each year.

At age 65, Mike had put aside a total of $96,000 over his 40 years of making $200 monthly contributions to his retirement account. Patrick had contributed

$192,000 to his account over 20 years. Which brother had the highest retirement account balance?

Considering compound returns, Mike has $2,352,954 at the age of 65, while Patrick has much less, $791,404. Patrick has a third of the wealth of his brother, even though he saved twice as much money as Mike.

The fact that Mike started saving early, even though he didn't save a great deal each month (only $7 a day), makes all the difference. Mike becomes a millionaire by age 57 and can retire earlier than age 65 if he so desires.

Formal retirement plans are either sponsored by an employer or are sanctioned by the U.S. government. Formal retirement plans offer the advantages of a recognized structure provided by federal law and certain tax benefits.

However, people do not need a formal retirement plan in order to save for retirement. Individual savings outside a formal plan offer benefits such as added flexibility of investment choices and opportunity for early withdrawal without penalty.

Formal plans should always form the foundation of a person's retirement plan. Outside savings can provide a good supplement, but the tax advantages and legal protections offered by formal plans give them the upper hand in the advantages for retirement planning.

For U.S. taxpayers and residents, there are four principal categories of retirement programs. Although some individuals rely on only one of these, those who accumulate enough to have a comfortable retirement income usually have a combination of two or more of these plans. The retirement plan categories are the following:

1. Federal government retirement programs
2. Employer-sponsored retirement plans
3. Individual retirement accounts (IRAs)
4. Self-employed retirement accounts

Federal Government Retirement Programs

The U.S. government sponsors two retirement programs in addition to retirement programs for its own employees (which are considered employer-sponsored retirement plans): Social Security and railroad retirement.

© Rido, 2014, Shutterstock, Inc.

Begin retirement planning early to avoid playing catch up later in life. Remember the rule of compound interest.

SOCIAL SECURITY

The U.S. Social Security Administration administers several federal programs including the Old-Age, Survivors, and Disability Insurance (OASDI), Medicare, and Supplemental Security Income (SSI) programs. Medicare provides health insurance to people age 65 and older, and SSI offers payments to disabled adults, children, and individuals over age 65 who have limited income and financial resources.

OASDI is the program that most people simply refer to as "Social Security." It provides income to:

- Individuals over age 62 for reduced benefits and over age 65 to 67 for full benefits
- Surviving children or spouses of covered individuals
- Disability income to covered individuals and family members

As Exhibit 16.1 shows, the number of people receiving Social Security benefits has consistently increased over recent decades.

Social Security is a federal program that began in 1935 to serve as a financial retirement cushion for workers who become disabled and for retirees. Social Security is one of the two taxes (along with the Medicare tax) that make up the FICA tax that is withheld from employees' paychecks. The Social Security portion is 6.2 percent of an employee's gross income, up to a certain cap. This cap increases slightly each year with inflation and was $113,700 in 2013.

For example, a person earning $50,000 in a year would have $3,100 withheld from his or her paycheck to cover Social Security benefits in 2013. A person who earned wages of $500,000 will have $7,049 withheld, because the tax is due only on the first $113,700 of income.

EXHIBIT 16.1	NUMBER OF INDIVIDUALS RECEIVING BENEFITS FROM SOCIAL SECURITY

(Includes old age (retirement), survivors, and disability benefit payments.)

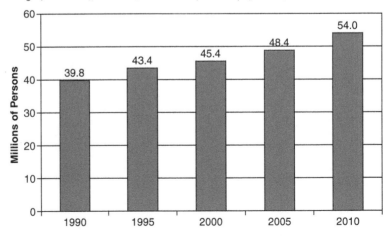

Source: Statistical Abstract of the United States, 2012.

Employers also owe Social Security tax on their employees' income at the same rate of 6.2 percent. In practice, employers match dollar for dollar all Social Security payments made by their employees.

Social Security is not a fully funded plan. A retirement plan is funded when there are sufficient funds set aside to cover the projected retirement benefits of all employees. Although payments into Social Security do go into a trust fund, the trust fund is only a cushion. The taxes that employees and employers pay today pay the benefits that current retirees are receiving. The benefits that today's workers receive in the future will be paid by future workers. Total benefits paid by Social Security have increased steadily in recent years as shown in Exhibit 16.2.

Funded plan A retirement plan that contains sufficient funds to pay all current and expected future benefits to its beneficiaries.

THE FUTURE OF SOCIAL SECURITY

In 1960, there were 5.1 workers paying into Social Security for each person receiving benefits. In 2007, that number had fallen to 3.3 workers, and in 2010 it was only 2.9. Current forecasts predict that in 2032 there will be only 2.1 workers supporting each retiree in the system.

Social Security currently takes in more funds than it pays out, and it saves the remaining money in the program's trust funds. These trust funds have large reserves now. However, with the declining numbers of workers per beneficiary, in 2017 Social Security will begin paying out more in benefits than it collects in taxes. It can continue to pay benefits by dipping into the trust funds, but unless changes are made to the system, the trust funds will be exhausted by 2041.

Possible changes that Congress might make to continue the program include:

- Raising the retirement age
- Increasing the Social Security tax rate
- Removing the cap on the Social Security tax
- Creating some sort of privatized account for employees

Workers become eligible to receive future retirement benefits from Social Security once they have earned 40 employment credits. Employees earn four employment credits for each year with at least $3,880 in income. So, most individuals will qualify for future Social Security benefits after they have worked for 10 years.

There are two ways to begin receiving Social Security benefits: retirement and death. The survivors of workers who die are eligible to receive Social Security benefits. A spouse and children are eligible for the following payments:

- A one-time payment up front to help with funeral costs, etc., of $255
- A monthly payment if the spouse is over 60, or any age if the spouse is caring for a child under the age of 16 or disabled
- A monthly payment to all children under the age of 18

Retiring is of course the more desirable way to begin receiving Social Security income. At the age of 67, those who have qualified with 40 credits can start receiving full Social Security benefits. Receiving Social Security as early as age 62 is an option, although it is at a reduced amount. A portion of this income may be taxable if the recipient has significant income from other sources during retirement years.

| EXHIBIT 16.2 | TOTAL BENEFITS PAID BY SOCIAL SECURITY |

(Includes old age (retirement), survivors, and disability benefit payments.)

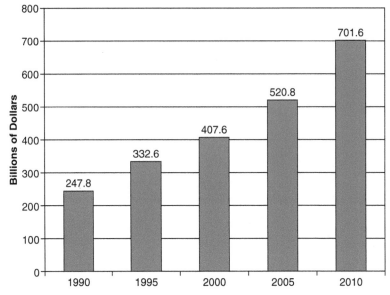

Source: *Statistical Abstract of the United States*, 2012.

| EXHIBIT 16.3 | AVERAGE MONTHLY SOCIAL SECURITY RETIREMENT BENEFIT FOR AN INDIVIDUAL |

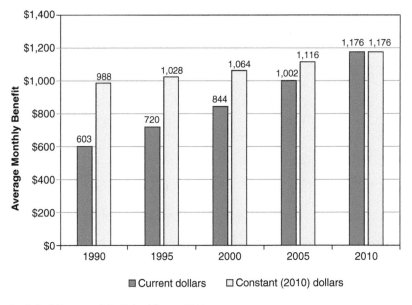

Source: *Statistical Abstract of the United States*, 2012.

The Social Security program has made a big difference for many people. For 65 percent of older Americans, Social Security provides over 50 percent of their annual income. Exhibit 16.3 (on previous page) shows average monthly Social Security retirement benefits. The average monthly payment has increased over the past several decades, both in nominal terms and in inflation-adjusted constant dollars.

The Social Security Administration sends out a letter each year to all employees detailing their estimated benefits in the future. The Social Security web site (www.ssa.gov) is also helpful for estimating future income from Social Security. Exhibit 16.4 shows an example statement of estimated Social Security benefits.

The purpose of Social Security is to be an aid to help individuals in retirement. Unfortunately, many retirees rely almost entirely on their Social Security benefits. Over half of retirees would be below the poverty line in the United States without Social Security, and this percentage is even higher for minorities and single individuals. With the level of future Social Security benefits in question, making other retirement plans beginning at an early age is even more important. Luckily, there are many retirement programs available to help people create a sufficient amount of wealth for retirement years.

EXAMPLE STATEMENT OF ESTIMATED SOCIAL SECURITY BENEFITS

EXHIBIT 16.4

Your Estimated Benefits

*Retirement	You have earned enough credits to qualify for benefits. At your current earnings rate, if you continue working until…
	your full retirement age (67 years), your payment would be about .... $ 1,543 a month
	age 70, your payment would be about .... $ 1,924 a month
	If you stop working and start receiving benefits at…
	age 62, your payment would be about .... $ 1,064 a month
*Disability	You have earned enough credits to qualify for benefits. If you became disabled right now, your payment would be about .... $ 1,411 a month
*Family	If you get retirement or disability benefits, your spouse and children also may qualify for benefits.
*Survivors	You have earned enough credits for your family to receive survivors benefits. If you die this year, certain members of your family **may** qualify for the following benefits:
	Your child .... $ 1,101 a month
	Your spouse who is caring for your child.. $ 1,101 a month
	Your spouse, if benefits start at full retirement age .... $ 1,468 a month
	Total family benefits cannot be more than.. $ 2,702 a month
	Your spouse or minor child may be eligible for a special one-time death benefit of $255.
Medicare	You have enough credits to qualify for Medicare at age 65. Even if you do not retire at age 65, be sure to contact Social Security three months before your 65th birthday to enroll in Medicare.

* **Your estimated benefits are based on current law. Congress has made changes to the law in the past and can do so at any time. The law governing benefit amounts may change because, by 2037, the payroll taxes collected will be enough to pay only about 76 percent of scheduled benefits.**

We based your benefit estimates on these facts:
Your date of birth (please verify your name on page 1 and this date of birth).. April 5, 1968
Your estimated taxable earnings per year after 2008 .... $42,181
Your Social Security number (only the last four digits are shown to help prevent identity theft) XXX-XX-1234

Source: http://www.ssa.gov/myaccount/SSA-700S-OL.pdf

RAILROAD RETIREMENT

Railroad retirement provides retirement income for employees of railroad companies. It was established at about the same time as Social Security, and railroad employees and their employers pay into railroad retirement rather than Social Security. The U.S. Railroad Retirement Board administers the program.

Employer-Sponsored Retirement Programs

Many employers offer some type of retirement program to their employees. In 2010, 50 percent of all workers in the United States participated in an employer-sponsored retirement plan.

These programs vary from employer to employer, so anyone considering accepting a job should closely examine the retirement program before taking the job. When considering employment, look past the annual salary figure because an excellent benefits package, of which the retirement plan is a large part, can easily make up for a lower salary. Retirement programs offered by employers fall into one of two categories:

1. Defined benefit plans
2. Defined contribution plans

DEFINED BENEFIT PLANS

Defined benefit plan A retirement plan from an employer that promises a certain amount of income upon retirement.

Pension plan Another name for a defined benefit plan.

Vested benefits Benefits to which employees are entitled even if they leave the employer before reaching retirement age.

Employee Retirement Income Security Act (ERISA) Federal law that sets minimum standards for retirement plans in private industry.

A defined benefit plan is a retirement plan that promises the employee a certain amount of income upon retirement. Employers and sometimes employees contribute to the plan, but the ultimate retirement benefit is based on a promised amount (which is usually based on the employee's salary and years of service), not on the amount contributed to the fund. Defined benefit plans are commonly called pension plans. About 20 percent of U.S. employees who participate in a retirement plan are in a defined benefit plan.

The investment risk with a defined contribution plan is the responsibility of the employer. If retirees in the retirement pool begin living longer than expected and/or the investment return on the pension fund is less than expected, the employer is responsible for making up the difference so that beneficiaries of the plan receive the retirement incomes promised to them.

Most pension plans of governments (federal, state, and local) are defined benefit plans. Many private employers have defined benefit plans, but a number have been changing to other types as a cost saving measure.

An important concept in pension plans is vesting. Employees who have vested benefits are qualified to receive those benefits even if they leave the employer before retirement.

The Employee Retirement Income Security Act (ERISA) originally passed in 1974 is a federal law that sets minimum standards for retirement plans in private industry. ERISA does not require any employer to establish a retirement plan. It only requires that those who establish plans must meet certain minimum standards. The law generally does not specify how much money a participant must be paid as a benefit.

When considering a new job, examine the employer's retirement program before accepting a position with the company.

ERISA does the following:

- Requires that employers provide participants with information about the plan, including important information about plan features and funding.
- Sets minimum standards for participation, vesting, benefit accrual, and funding. Employees become vested in a plan at the point in time when they become entitled to at least a portion of their retirement benefits even if they leave the employer before reaching retirement age. The law also establishes detailed funding rules that require plan sponsors to provide adequate funding for their plan.
- Requires accountability of plan fiduciaries. ERISA defines a fiduciary as anyone who exercises control over a plan's management of assets, including anyone who provides investment advice to the plan. Fiduciaries that do not follow the principles of conduct may be held responsible for restoring losses to the plan.
- Gives participants the right to sue for benefits and breaches of fiduciary duty.
- Guarantees payment of certain benefits if a defined benefit plan is terminated through a federally chartered corporation, known as the Pension Benefit Guaranty Corporation.

Pension Benefit Guaranty Corporation A federally chartered corporation that guarantees payment of defined benefit pension benefits.

The exact terms of any plan will be unique for every employer. Key factors to know about a plan are the following:

- The length of employment before the employee becomes vested in the plan
- Amount of contributions made by the employee (if required)
- How the retirement benefit is calculated
- At what age are employees eligible to begin drawing benefits

Every defined benefit plan will specify its vesting schedule. ERISA allows some flexibility, but all plan participants must be fully vested by 10 years of service to the employer. Exhibit 16.5 shows a sample vesting schedule that an employer might choose.

In addition, the plan will specify any amounts that an employee must contribute. Some plans are non-contributory, meaning that the employee makes no contribution to the plan; the employer fully funds the plan. Other plans may

Non-contributory plan A retirement plan in which employers, not employees, fully fund the plan.

EXHIBIT 16.5	EXAMPLE DEFINED BENEFIT PENSION PLAN TERMS

Vesting Schedule:

Years Employed	Percent Vested
2	20%
3	40%
4	60%
5	80%
6	100%

Employee Contributions:
    None

Retirement Benefit Formula:
    Annual retirement benefit = M x Years x Average Salary
    where: M = a multiplier such as 2.2
              Years = years of employment with the employer
              Average Salary = average annual salary for the 5 highest paid years

Retirement Age and Benefits:
    100% of benefit at age 65 with a minimum of 10 years employment
    100% of benefit at any age with 35 years of employment
    If less than age 66 and age + years of employment >= 75
        100% of benefit less 5% of benefit for each year less than 65

require that employees contribute some portion of their salary, for example, 5 percent, to the retirement plan.

Plans will also specify how the retirement benefit will be calculated. A typical plan bases the benefit on three factors:

1. A multiplier that is based on the amount of benefit that the fund can afford to pay to retirees. Multipliers are usually around a value of 2.
2. Retirees' average salary over their three or five highest paid years.
3. The number of years employed.

The sample plan in Exhibit 16.5 has benefits equal to the product of a multiplier of 2.2, the average of the employee's five highest paid years, and the number of years of employment.

The final important piece of information about a retirement plan is the age at which a participant can begin receiving monthly retirement checks. Many employers also offer an early retirement option that allows retirement at an earlier age (like 50 or 55), usually at a reduced benefit. Exhibit 16.5 provides an example.

The following are advantages that defined benefit plans offer to employees:

- **Benefits are not based on contributions.** If the fund has a less-than-average investment return, beneficiaries are still guaranteed their promised retirement income (within some limits).
- **Employers assume the risk.** Even when a beneficiary lives longer than expected, the retirement income keeps on coming.

DEFINED CONTRIBUTION PLANS

A defined contribution plan is one in which the employer and/or employee makes contributions to an investment account that the employee can then withdraw upon reaching retirement age. In a defined contribution plan, the ultimate

Defined contribution plan A retirement plan in which the employer and/or employee makes contributions to some kind of investment account that the employee can then withdraw upon reaching retirement age.

retirement benefit is a function of the amounts contributed and the investment experience of the account. Of all employees participating in an employer-sponsored retirement plan, about 80% are in a defined contribution plan.

Beneficiaries, not employers, bear the risks of defined contribution plans. Retirees who live longer than expected can draw their accounts down to zero and be without a retirement income other than that provided by Social Security. Because defined contribution plans reduce their risk, some employers have been switching from defined benefit plans to defined contribution plans. Exhibit 16.6 illustrates this trend.

It is very important for workers to understand the ins and outs of defined contribution plans and to plan their retirement withdrawals upon retirement so that they do not run their accounts down too low.

In spite of the risk, defined contribution plans do offer several advantages to employees:

- Tax break. Normally, any contributions that an individual makes to a qualified plan are not taxed until payment of retirement benefits years in the future.
- Flexible investment options. Depending on the type of plan, most participants have an array of alternative investment accounts to which they can direct their contributions. Choices are usually mutual funds offering all of the typical mutual fund opportunities such as stocks, industries, sectors, foreign stocks, index funds, asset allocation funds, bonds, etc. A smart choice of investments can build a nice retirement accumulation in a defined contribution plan. However, this flexibility does mean that the employee has the responsibility to choose appropriate investments.

NUMBER OF DEFINED-BENEFIT AND DEFINED-CONTRIBUTION RETIREMENT PLANS IN THE UNITED STATES, 1990 TO 2008

EXHIBIT 16.6

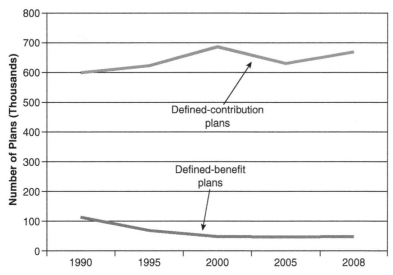

Source: Statistical Abstract of the United States, 2012.

There are several types of defined contribution plans that an employer may offer:

- 401(k) plan
- 403(b) plan
- Simplified employee pension (SEP)
- SIMPLE IRA plan
- Profit-sharing plans
- Employee stock ownership plan (ESOP)

401(K) PLAN

401(k) plan The most popular defined contribution plan allows employees to make pretax contributions and may also allow employer matching of contributions.

The most popular defined contribution plan, a 401(k) plan allows participants to make tax-free contributions. The annual contribution limit in 2013 was $17,500. The employer will identify a set of investment options for the plan, and participants can choose among them to set up the investment program that they desire in their retirement plan.

Investment alternatives usually include a family of mutual funds or the employer's stock if the company is publicly traded. However, a person should be careful about investing a large amount of the 401(k) into the employer's stock. Principles of diversification tell us that it is not a wise idea to bet both your employment income and your retirement income on the same organization. Consider the Enron employees whose 401(k) plans became virtually worthless with the fall of the firm in 2001. The double whammy is that these employees also lost their jobs.

Contributions to a 401(k) are tax free, meaning that those who contribute will not owe federal or state income tax on the amount of their contribution. Withdrawal of funds is permissible beginning at age 59½, and all withdrawals

---

STRETCH
YOUR DOLLAR

TIPS FOR 401(K) CONTRIBUTORS

1. **Start early.** If your employer has a 401(k) plan, start contributing as soon as you become eligible. Compound interest is your friend; the earlier you start, the more time your money has to grow.
2. **Know your rights.** By law, you are eligible to start contributing to a 401(k) plan after one year of service; your employer can't make you wait longer than that.
3. **Use payroll deduction.** You probably will not even miss contributions taken directly out of your paycheck and sent straight to your 401(k) account.
4. **Contribute to the max.** The more you contribute, the more your account will grow. Maximum contributions are adjusted each year; the 2013 maximum was $17,500.
5. **Don't turn down free money.** If your employer offers matching contributions, contribute as much as possible to take advantage of the match.
6. **Love those tax breaks.** Contributions are not taxed until you withdraw your money. Saving pre-tax gives you more money to invest and you will pay less to the IRS.
7. **Keep your hands out of the cookie jar.** Resist temptation to invade your retirement account. It is generally not a good idea to withdraw funds early or to borrow from your 401(k). Early withdrawals and loans not paid back within five years trigger a 10 percent penalty.
8. **Monitor your account.** Review your plan regularly to ensure that it still meets your needs as retirement approaches.

are taxable at the recipient's normal tax rate. A person can withdraw funds before the age of 59½ but will have to pay a 10 percent penalty on any early withdrawals in addition to regular federal and state taxes.

When an employer matches a portion of an employee's 401(k) contributions, the retirement fund can really grow fast. Employers are allowed to make contributions up to a 100 percent match. For example, for an employee who contributes $3,000 to a 401(k) plan, the employer can match that contribution up to $3,000. The details of the matching will differ from company to company, but the majority of employers do offer some kind of matching.

403(b) Plan

A 403(b) plan is very similar to a 401(k) plan, the only difference being that it is offered by employers that qualify as a nonprofit organization. This type of plan works the same way as the 401(k), with the same amount of maximum contributions allowed tax-free each year. Withdrawals can begin without penalties at age 59½, and recipients pay taxes on withdrawals at their normal tax rates.

403(b) plan A defined contribution plan that is very similar to a 401(k) plan but is offered by nonprofit organizations.

Simplified Employee Pension Plan

A simplified employee pension plan, or SEP, is a retirement plan for small businesses that have at least one employee. This type of plan is unique in that the employee is not allowed to make contributions; the employer must make all contributions. Employers can contribute up to 25 percent of an employee's wages up to a maximum amount. Annual maximums change, and the maximum was $50,000 in 2012.

Vesting occurs immediately with a SEP plan, so employees immediately own any contributions made on their behalf. The downside of SEP plans is that employees have no control over the amount of contribution. An employer can decide to play Scrooge any year and reduce or eliminate contributions.

Employers usually select a family of mutual funds to manage investments in the SEP, and employees can choose how much should be invested in the various funds offered. Similar to 401(k) and 403(b) plans, plan participants can begin withdrawing money with no penalty at age 59½.

Simplified employee pension (SEP) A retirement plan for small businesses that have at least one employee where only the employer is allowed to make contributions for an employee.

SIMPLE IRA Plan Contributions

EXAMPLE 16.1

Harry works for the Columbia Manufacturing Company, a small business with 50 employees. The firm has decided to establish a SIMPLE IRA plan for all its employees and will match its employees' contributions dollar-for-dollar up to 3 percent of each employee's salary. Under this option, Columbia employees who do not contribute to their SIMPLE IRA will not receive any matching employer contributions from Columbia.

Harry's annual salary is $50,000, and he decides to contribute 5 percent to his SIMPLE IRA. The financial institution partnering with Columbia on the SIMPLE IRA has several investment choices, and Harry is free to pick and choose which ones suit him best. How much is Harry's contribution, Columbia's match, and the total contribution to Harry's IRA?

       Harry's contribution is $2,500 (5 percent of $50,000);
       Columbia's matching contribution is $1,500 (3 percent of $50,000);
       Therefore, the total contribution to Harry's SIMPLE IRA is $4,000. ■

SIMPLE IRA Plan

Companies with fewer than 100 employees may have a SIMPLE IRA plan. SIMPLE is an acronym for Savings Incentive Match Plan for Employees of Small Employers. Employers have two choices for making contributions to the plan:

1. Contribute 2 percent of each employee's compensation to the plan regardless of whether the employee makes any contributions.
2. Match employee contributions dollar-for-dollar up to 3 percent of the employee's compensation only for employees who elect to contribute. Employees may contribute up to a given amount annually ($12,000 in 2013 and adjusted for inflation every year).

SIMPLE plans are easy to set up through a financial institution such as a bank or mutual fund. The institution will typically offer several different investment options for participants' funds. Just like the other types of retirement accounts, contributions are tax deductible for both the employee and the employer. Participants can begin to withdraw funds without penalty at age 59½.

Profit-Sharing Plan

A profit-sharing plan is a retirement program in which the employer makes contributions into employee accounts based on the earnings of the company. This plan encourages employees to improve job performance and aligns the interests of owners and employees. If the company does well financially, the employees will receive a greater contribution. The details of a profit-sharing plan will differ greatly from company to company, so anyone with a profit-sharing plan or considering employment with a company offering a profit-sharing plan should research the intricacies of the firm's plan carefully.

Employee Stock Ownership Plan (ESOP)

An Employee Stock Ownership Plan (ESOP) takes the idea of profit-sharing plan one step further by actually making employees the owners of the company as well. ESOPs allow employees to buy stock in their employer. In some smaller companies, employees actually end up being the majority shareholders in the company. As with a 401(k) plan, anyone who ties up a significant portion of their wealth with his or her employer is in a risky position. Bankruptcy of the company results in the loss of both job and savings.

What Happens to Your Retirement Account If You Leave Your Job?

Employees who leave their job before retirement usually have one or more of the following three options for funds that are vested with their retirement plan:

1. Leave the funds in the plan and begin to draw benefits in the future upon retirement. This option is usually advantageous for near-retirement participants of defined-contribution plans.
2. Withdraw funds from the plan and place them in another qualified plan to avoid penalty. The most common is converting the assets of a 401(k) plan to a traditional IRA in a process called a rollover IRA.
3. Transfer the plan to a new employer. A good example of a plan transfer is TIAA-CREF, a manager of defined contribution plans for many universities. Any faculty member who moves from one university to another that

participates in TIAA-CREF simply has the new institution continue making contributions to TIAA-CREF.

Most workers will not work their entire lifetime for one employer, so the question of vesting and transferability of retirement accounts is important. First of all, regardless of whether a plan is defined benefit or defined contribution, all contributions made by the employee belong to the employee and are immediately vested. Employer contributions follow a vesting schedule such as in Exhibit 16.5.

Individual Retirement Accounts (IRAs)

A rollover allows you to move your vested retirement funds to a new qualified plan should you leave your job.

Individual retirement accounts, or IRAs, are another tool for funding retirement. Actually, the official name is "individual retirement arrangement," but everyone calls them individual retirement accounts. Anyone has the right to set one up, and they are not tied to an employer. Individuals can set up an IRA in addition to whatever employer-sponsored retirement account they may have.

The tax exemption that the federal government grants to contributions to an IRA enhances their use as a retirement savings vehicle. They are yet another example of the government utilizing tax deductions as a way to encourage certain behaviors. Virtually all types of financial institution–banks, investment firms, insurance companies, and online discount brokers, to name a few–offer IRAs. There are three types of IRAs for individuals with important differences among them:

1. Traditional IRA
2. Roth IRA
3. Coverdell Educational IRA

TRADITIONAL IRA

The traditional IRA, the first kind of IRA created by tax law, is a retirement account set up by the individual rather than the employer. Anyone can set one up. Traditional IRA contributions are tax deductible and provide an incentive to save for retirement. Individuals who have an employer-sponsored retirement plan are eligible for the full deduction only if their income is less than a certain amount, $59,000 in 2013. From $59,000 to $69,000, a person gets a partial deduction and above $69,000 no deduction is allowed. For married couples living jointly these numbers are $95,000 to $115,000.

Maximum contributions were $5,500 in 2013 and are adjusted each year for inflation. Individuals older than 50 years old can contribute an additional $1,000 per year. Account holders can begin withdrawing money from their traditional IRA at age 59½ and must begin this process by age 70½. Retirees who receive income from an IRA owe taxes on the amounts they withdraw at their usual applicable tax rates. People who withdraw funds from an IRA before age 59½ pay a penalty equal to 10 percent of the withdrawal in addition to having to pay regular taxes on the withdrawal.

Traditional IRAs are available at virtually any financial institution. Before opening an IRA, an individual should research different possibilities and consider the following:

- Are there any minimum balances to open an IRA?
- Does the institution charge any fees on the IRA?
- What types of investment options are available?

Online brokerage firms are often the lowest cost option, especially for those who like to make their own investment decisions.

ROTH IRA

A Roth IRA is similar to the traditional IRA. Individuals in 2013 can contribute up to $5,500 per year for retirement, and individuals older than 50 can invest an additional $1,000 you can have both a traditional and a Roth IRA, but the combined contributions to both cannot exceed the maximum. The same range of institutions offering traditional IRAs offer Roth IRAs, so there are plenty of options available. There are several key differences between the Roth and traditional IRA:

- There is no tax deduction for contributions to a Roth IRA.
- Contributions may be withdrawn at any age tax free.
- All funds in the account may be withdrawn tax free after age 59½.

In 2013, individual taxpayers whose adjusted gross income was greater than $112,000 or married taxpayers with more than $178,000 could make reduced contributions to a Roth IRA, and individual taxpayers making more than $127,000 or married taxpayers earning more than $188,000 could not make contributions to a Roth IRA.

Comparison of Traditional versus Roth IRA

A very popular personal finance question is: Which type of IRA should I open? Individuals can have both a traditional and Roth IRA account, but they cannot contribute more than $5,500 in total to both IRAs. Both types of IRA are popular. As Exhibit 16.7 shows, a significant portion of U.S. households owned one of these types of IRA in 2007.

Like many personal financial decisions, there is no universal answer to the Roth versus traditional IRA choice. It depends on the taxpayer's situation. As a general guideline, the Roth IRA is the best choice. This is especially true for young people in their twenties or thirties whose IRA balances have many years to accumulate a tax-free balance.

Converting a Traditional IRA to a Roth IRA

Prior to 1997, only the traditional IRA was available. When Congress created the Roth IRA, it allowed individuals with traditional IRAs to convert them to Roth IRAs. Because of the long-term tax-exempt growth potential of the Roth IRA, many financial planners encourage converting a traditional into a Roth IRA. However, there are some unfavorable tax consequences with such a conversion, and it is not always the right choice.

The optimal decision to convert a traditional IRA to a Roth IRA will depend on the taxpayer's current tax rate, estimated retirement tax rate, annual rates of return expected in the future, and the time until retirement. Typically, the longer the time until retirement the more a Roth conversion will make sense. Many financial web sites have a Roth conversion calculator to assist with this decision.

PERCENT OF U.S. HOUSEHOLDS OWNING AN IRA, 2007 | EXHIBIT 16.7

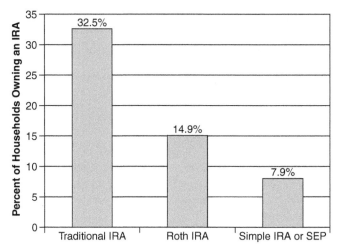

Source: *Statistical Abstract of the United States*, 2009.

Coverdell Educational IRA

A Coverdell IRA is not actually for retirement purposes, but it is for a closely related area. A Coverdell IRA is basically a Roth IRA for educational expenses. Parents can contribute up to $2,000 per year for each child, and whenever the child goes to college parents can withdraw funds tax free. Similar to the Roth IRA, there is no tax deduction upfront for a Coverdell contribution. The Coverdell can also be used for K–12 private school expenses, and amounts in the account can be switched to another beneficiary with no consequences.

Coverdell IRA An IRA that can be used to pay for your children's educational expenses.

Retirement Accounts for Self-Employed Individuals

In addition to the traditional IRA, self-employed individuals have two types of retirement plans available:

1. A Keogh plan
2. Simplified employee pension (SEP)

KEOGH PLAN

A Keogh plan allows self-employed individuals to make pretax contributions to a retirement account of up to 25 percent of their annual net income up to a yearly maximum, which was $50,000 in 2013. Other provisions of the Keogh plan such as investment options and the age for beginning withdrawals follow the traditional IRA.

Keogh plan A retirement plan for self-employed individuals that allows for pretax contributions to a retirement account.

SIMPLIFIED EMPLOYEE PENSION PLAN (SEP)

Small business owners are eligible to set up the same type of SEP as the employer-sponsored SEP discussed in a previous section. A self-employed person can contribute up to 25 percent of net income up to a maximum per year

Through a Keogh plan or a SEP, a self-employed individual has the opportunity to establish a retirement account.

($50,000 in 2013). In general, the process for setting up and maintaining an SEP for a self-employed person is much less complicated than a Keogh plan.

Retirement Planning: Investment Choices

Some people have no choice as to their retirement plan; they must go with their employer-sponsored plan. Others may have an employer-sponsored plan and still be eligible for one or more of the individual accounts. Still others may have no employer plan at all. Those in these final two categories have a choice of retirement plan or plans, and this choice can be complicated. Exhibit 16.8 provides a summary of the characteristics of the various plans.

EXHIBIT 16.8	SUMMARY COMPARISON OF RETIREMENT PLANS

	Pension Plan	401(k) plan	403(b) plan	SEP	SIMPLE IRA	Profit Sharing Plan	ESOP	Traditional IRA	Roth IRA	Keogh plan
Allows tax-free contributions		X	X	X	X			X		X
Defined benefit plan	X									
Defined contribution plan		X	X	X	X	X	X			
Allows matching by employer		X	X							
Only employer can make contributions				X						
Allows tax-free withdrawals									X	
Aligns owner and employee interests						X	X			
Designed for small businesses				X	X					
For nonprofit organizations			X							
Maximum contribution (2013, thousands)		$17.5	$17.5	$50	$12			$5.5	$5.5	$50

In addition to choosing which type of retirement plan to utilize, those planning for retirement need to decide the type and mix of financial assets for investment. With most plans there are alternatives from which to select, such as funds investing in stocks, bonds, government securities, or short-term assets like CDs and money market accounts.

The longer the period of time until retirement, the longer the period of time for investment, and the more risk a person should be able to accept. In the long run, accepting more risk should yield a greater return. This is the concept behind life-cycle investing.

Key Phases of the Financial Life Cycle

The financial life cycle is a model that divides a person's life into phases according to the earning potential, need for saving and investing, and ability to take on risk in each phase of the cycle.

Financial life cycle A model that divides a person's life into phases according to the earning potential, need for saving and investing, and ability to take on risk in each phase of the cycle.

We can divide a person's life into five main phases from a financial standpoint:

1. Education. During the educational years phase, people learn skills that they will use later in life in whatever career they choose. These years are characterized by limited income and difficulty staying out of debt. A good financial goal during the education years would be to not take on any high-interest debt for unnecessary expenses. Students should borrow no more than the funds needed to complete their education. Graduates who can start their employment years with as clean of a debt slate as possible will be in a much better financial position to plan for the future.

2. Employment. It is during this period, which usually begins in a person's late teens or early twenties, that people accumulate most of their wealth. Characteristics of this phase include increasing income, growing responsibilities and expenses, and the need for saving for future major expenses and retirement. While saving amidst all the expenses and desire for consumer goods may seem difficult, it is important to start saving early.

3. Approaching retirement. During this phase people should monitor their investment accounts to see if they have sufficient balances for their planned retirement and to ascertain that the risk of the accounts is at an appropriate level.

STRETCH
YOUR DOLLAR

START SAVING EARLY

Sharon has a goal of having saved $1,000,000 by age 60. How much would she need to invest each month in order to reach this financial milestone? Assuming a 10 percent annual return on investment, the answer depends on when she started investing. **Exhibit 16.9** shows the monthly savings needed at various ages to reach $1,000,000 at age 60.

If Sharon starts at age 20, she need invest only $158 per month. But if she waits 25 years until she is 45 years old, she will need to save more than $2,400 per month. This shows how difficult it is to play catch-up with saving for people who do not start saving early.

EXHIBIT 16.9	MONTHLY SAVINGS NEEDED TO HAVE $1,000,000 AT AGE 60

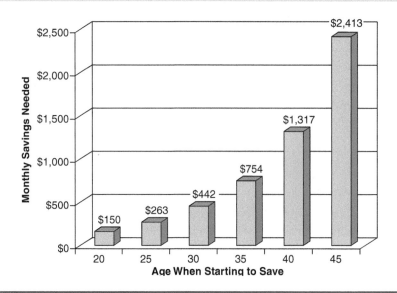

4. Retirement. During this period people begin to draw down the financial resources they have acquired during earlier phases.
5. Estate planning. During this final phase, which may even run concurrently with the previous two phases, people plan the disposition of their remaining financial resources and other assets for the period after they pass on.

INVESTMENT DECISIONS DURING A LIFETIME

Investing helps people achieve their financial goals during all phases of their lifetime. Because financial needs and planning are different in each of the phases, people will need different investment strategies to fit the different phases of the financial life cycle. People should ask themselves two principal questions during every life cycle phase:

1. Do I have sufficient liquid investments to cover financial emergencies in the short run?
2. Once I have enough to satisfy the first question, how should I invest my remaining funds to maximize value in the long run?

Investing for the Short Term
Everyone should have enough liquid investment or "cash" to cover unexpected and emergency situations that may arise. Many financial planners recommend having three to six months' regular monthly expenses saved for emergencies.

Many individuals may simply put this amount in a checking or savings account at the bank so that it is easily accessible. While this is convenient and may be appropriate for smaller balances, chances are that any interest earned on these balances will be at a lower rate than might be available from other investments.

Previous chapters of this text present a number of investment vehicles. Investments appropriate for short-term financial needs would have the following desirable characteristics:

- High liquidity (ability to convert into cash quickly)
- Very little risk or possibility of losing any of the original investment
- Return greater than a simple bank savings account

Two example investments that meet these criteria are certificates of deposit and money market mutual funds.

Investing for the Long Run

For investing for the long run, investments with more risk than certificates of deposit or money market funds are appropriate. While investments of higher risk do have a greater chance of losing money in the short run, over the long run they should yield higher returns to the investor as illustrated in earlier chapters.

Stocks and other long-term higher yielding investments should be a person's focus for long-term investing. For planning longer-term investing, the concept of life cycle investing is useful.

LIFE CYCLE INVESTING

The concept of life cycle investing matches the amount of risk that people should be able to take to the key phases of their life cycle. Using the life cycle concept you should first take care of short-term saving needs. After meeting those needs, you should then invest for the longer term. Exhibit 16.10 summarizes the investment goals and strategies during the life cycle.

Life cycle investing An investment strategy that matches the amount of risk that people should be able to take to the key phases of their life cycle.

Description of Life Cycle Investing

For any investment funds that you might have available during the education phase, a very long-term investment horizon with riskier investments is most likely appropriate. With a long time horizon, any short-term losses the investments might experience over a one- or two-year period are usually worth the risk because high-risk investments should yield more over the long run.

LIFECYCLE PHASES MATCHED WITH LIFECYCLE INVESTING   EXHIBIT 16.10

	Savings (Investment) Targets	Investment Horizon	Risk Taking Ability
Education	Spend on education	Very long term	High risk
Employment	Save as much as possible	Very long term to long term	High risk
Approaching retirement	Continue saving	Intermediate term	Balanced risk
Retirement	Withdraw savings	Short term	Low risk
Estate planning	Bequests of savings	Short term	Low risk

During the employment years, people have a long investment horizon and a high ability to assume risk. This lets them invest in higher-risk, higher-yielding investments during these years, allowing the investments to grow over a long period of time, taking advantage of compounding of returns.

As a person approaches retirement, the life cycle approach implies that he or she should begin to have a more intermediate investment time horizon and begin to reduce the amount of risk. The closer to retirement, the less risk a person should have. People approaching retirement should transfer invested funds from higher risk to lower risk investments as time passes.

To summarize the life cycle approach, individuals should begin investing in their early years in a portfolio that, on average, is of higher risk. As the years pass, funds should be gradually shifted to lower-risk investments so that by the time retirement arrives, most of the portfolio is in lower-risk, safer investments.

Implementing Life Cycle Investing

To implement life cycle investing with an investment plan, there are two main methods that individual investors can pursue:

1. Select their own asset allocation, and
2. Use life cycle mutual funds to accomplish asset allocation

SELECTING AN ASSET ALLOCATION

Recall that common stocks are riskier investments but tend to have greater long-run returns than bonds, which are then higher yielding and more risky than money-market investments. Exhibit 12.6 from back in Chapter 12 provided a good illustration: $100 invested in stocks in 1985 grew to $1,603 in 2013, while the same amount in bonds grew only to $1,380, and in money market investments $291. Consider also that those stock returns immediately followed the stock market decline associated with the financial crisis of 2007 and 2008.

The life cycle approach therefore implies that in their early years, individuals should allocate all or at least the greater portion of their investment funds to the higher-risk common stocks. As time passes, they should shift funds to lower risk stocks and to bonds. Finally at retirement they should have most of their money in bonds and money market funds.

Exhibit 16.11 presents a sample asset allocation between several different types of stocks, bonds, and money market investments for each of the phases of the life cycle. However, every individual is different, having different risk preferences and expectations about desired returns.

While individuals can accomplish their own asset allocation, the task is often better placed with a financial advisor who can offer professional advice. Financial advisors can apply the life cycle concept for given individuals by tailoring the asset allocation strategy for each client. These customized asset allocations should meet both the client's ability to take on risk and the need for a given return.

EXAMPLE ASSET ALLOCATION USING THE LIFECYCLE INVESTING APPROACH

EXHIBIT 16.11

Phase	Risk–Taking Ability	Asset Allocation	
Education	High risk	Higher risk stocks	75%
		High dividend stocks	10%
		Real estate stocks	10%
		Bonds	5%
		Money market	0%
Employment	High risk	Higher risk stocks	75%
		High dividend stocks	10%
		Real estate stocks	10%
		Bonds	5%
		Money market	0%
Approaching retirement	Balanced risk	Higher risk stocks	10%
		High dividend stocks	40%
		Real estate stocks	10%
		Bonds	30%
		Money market	10%
Retirement	Low risk	Higher risk stocks	0%
		High dividend stocks	20%
		Real estate stocks	10%
		Bonds	50%
		Money market	20%
Estate planning	Low risk	Higher risk stocks	0%
		High dividend stocks	10%
		Real estate stocks	0%
		Bonds	40%
		Money market	50%

USING LIFE CYCLE MUTUAL FUNDS

Life cycle mutual funds are funds of funds designed to make life cycle investing easier. A fund of funds is a mutual fund that invests in other mutual funds. Life cycle mutual funds invest in other funds to achieve a particular asset allocation strategy used in life cycle investing.

There are two types of life cycle funds:

1. Target-date life cycle funds. These funds have a target retirement date and set up an asset allocation strategy based on that date. With a target-date fund, you simply choose a fund with a target date as close as possible to your retirement date. The fund management alters the allocation of assets as time passes so that fund risk declines as the target date approaches.
2. Target-risk life cycle funds. These funds split into three (or more) groups according to their risk. A fund family with three funds might have an aggressive, moderate, and conservative fund. You decide how much you

Life cycle mutual fund A mutual fund that invests in other mutual funds with an asset allocation target designed to meet a certain life cycle investing goal.

Target-date life cycle fund A life cycle mutual fund with a target retirement date and an asset allocation strategy based on that date. The fund changes the asset allocation targets as the retirement date approaches.

Target-risk life cycle fund
A life cycle mutual fund that has an aggressive, moderate, or conservative asset allocation target. The individual investor decides how much to allocate to each type of fund at each phase of the financial life cycle.

want to allocate to each type of fund, and you should monitor and change allocations as time passes.

Target-date life cycle funds attract a number of investors because they make the asset allocation decision simple. You simply choose a fund whose target date matches or is very close to your planned retirement date. The fund will take care of all of the asset allocation decisions and any periodic rebalancing needed in the portfolio.

As an example of the target-date type of life cycle funds, the American Century family of mutual funds has a series of target-date funds. Exhibit 16.12 shows a summary of the different funds and their target asset allocation percentages. Note how the funds with the later dates have portfolios with greater percentages of stocks (i.e., they have more risk).

Target-risk life cycle funds have the advantage of offering investors the opportunity to adjust their own asset allocations. For example, suppose that

---

EXHIBIT 16.12   AMERICAN CENTURY TARGET-DATE LIFECYCLE FUNDS

All funds charge a $25 annual fee for investors who have less than $10,000 invested in any combination of American Century Funds. Expense ratios are based on "investor class" shares. American Century also has One Choice Portfolios with target dates of 2020, 2030, 2040, 2050, and 2055.

| Fund Name | Estimated Expenses to Net Assets Ratios | | |
	Administrative fee	Underlying Fund Expenses	Combined Total Expenses
One Choice 2015 Portfolio	0.21%	0.59%	0.80%
Target Asset Allocation			
Stocks 47%			
Bonds 44%			
Money market 9%			
One Choice 2025 Portfolio	0.21%	0.65%	0.86%
Target Asset Allocation			
Stocks 67%			
Bonds 38%			
Money market 5%			
One Choice 2035 Portfolio	0.20%	0.71%	0.91%
Target Asset Allocation			
Stocks 70%			
Bonds 26%			
Money market 4%			
One Choice 2045 Portfolio	0.20%	0.78%	0.98%
Target Asset Allocation			
Stocks 81%			
Bonds 19%			
Money market 0.00%			

Source: Prospectus Supplement, American Century Asset Allocation Portfolios, Inc., May 31, 2013.

you were approaching retirement but wanted your portfolio to have more risk than offered by the typical target-date fund. You could accomplish your objective by using target-risk funds and keeping a higher percentage of your funds invested in an aggressive target-risk fund. The Calvert family of mutual funds offers examples of target-risk funds. Exhibit 16.13 shows the asset allocation target ranges for these funds.

Although life cycle funds offer a convenient method for implementing life cycle investing principles, they have some drawbacks:

- Target-date funds do not have funds for all retirement dates. For example, the American Century Funds have target dates that are five years apart.
- Funds tend to invest only in mutual funds within their own families to the exclusion of the 10,000 or so other funds available.
- Funds of funds have a double layer of fees. Consider, for example, the Calvert Moderate Allocation Fund in Exhibit 16.13. The fund charges expenses of 0.72 percent of the value of underlying mutual fund shares it owns. In addition, the underlying funds owned by the target-risk fund charge a fee of 0.73 percent, so the total fees charged are 1.45 percent, a fairly hefty charge for a mutual fund.

ASSET ALLOCATION TARGET RANGES FOR TARGET-RISK LIFE CYCLE FUNDS IN THE CALVERT MUTUAL FUND FAMILY

EXHIBIT 16.13

				Annual Expenses as Percent of Total Assets (1)				
				Fund	Underlying Funds	Total Expenses	Fee Waiver (2)	Net Expenses
Calvert Conservative Allocation Fund				.77%	.65%	1.42%	.33%	1.09%
Target Asset Allocation								
Stocks	20%	to	40%					
Bonds	60%	to	80%					
Money market	0%	to	10%					
Calvert Moderate Allocation Fund				.72%	.73%	1.45%	—	1.45%
Target Asset Allocation								
Stocks	50%	to	80%					
Bonds	20%	to	50%					
Money market	0%	to	10%					
Calvert Aggressive Allocation Fund				.86%	.82%	1.68%	.43%	1.25%
Target Asset Allocation								
Stocks	80%	to	100%					
Bonds	0%	to	20%					
Money market	0%	to	5%					

(1) Fees listed are for Class A shares that have a front-end sales charge (load) of 4.75% of shares purchased for purchases of less than $50,000 to no sales charge for purchases of $1 million and more. Class A shares have no front-end sales charge but have an additional annual fee (12b-1 fee) of .75%. They also have a contingent deferred sales charge of 1% of the value of shares sold if they are sold within one year of purchase.
(2) Calvert currently grants a fee waiver that reduces net fees charged to fund shares for some funds.
Source: Supplement to Calvert Fund of Funds Prospectus, January 31, 2013.

ESTIMATING RETIREMENT FUND VALUES

The main components of overall retirement planning are estimating your income needs upon retirement and then computing the savings needed to reach that income level. As time passes, there are two activities that everyone should conduct from time to time to make sure that their retirement planning is on track.

- Constantly monitor your account balances. Retirement planning is not creating a plan when you are 30, and then waking up one morning when you are 55 to see if you can retire the next day. You should be analyzing your values at least every quarter and seeing if you are falling short or exceeding expectations. That way you can make small but necessary changes along the way to ensure that you will have sufficient funds upon retirement.
- Perform scenario analysis. Unless you have a crystal ball, your best estimates at age 25 of what will happen for the next 40 years will probably not be right on target. So you need to see what happens given different assumptions. For example, ask yourself the question, "What happens if I earn only 8 percent annually rather than my estimate of 11 percent?" Or, "When can I retire if I contribute $6,000 per year rather than $4,000 per year?" Perform a range of calculations to analyze the effect that changes like these will have on your retirement.

CALCULATING YOUR RETIREMENT FUND NEEDS

Hopefully, you will be able to start planning and saving for retirement early on in your life and therefore make it easy to accumulate more than enough wealth for all living expenses during retirement. In calculating how much you will need to have saved, think about the following questions:

- How much do I (we) need for living expenses each year?
- Will I need to pay for any large expenses?
- How much do I want to leave to my beneficiaries or to charitable organizations?

Based on answers to these questions and a desired life style, it is possible to estimate future monthly income needs after retirement. It is this estimate that forms the basis for determining the amount of savings you will need in the future to fund retirement.

Employees of a company with a defined benefit plan will receive a monthly income check from that plan retirement. The same applies to those who qualify for Social Security. The pension plan or Social Security can provide forecasts of monthly retirement benefits forthcoming at a future date. If you fit either or both of these categories, then you should consider that these payments will cover a portion of your estimated monthly retirement income needs.

If your employer has a defined contribution plan, if you set up an IRA, or if you otherwise make savings arrangements for retirement income, then you can forecast the value of these accounts at your future retirement date. This sum will be available to generate a monthly income. For example, a balance of $500,000 in an account earning 8 percent produces an annual income of

$40,000 without ever reducing the principal account balance. Keep in mind that a portion of most retirement income will be subject to income taxes.

When estimating retirement needs, it is good practice to be conservative and analyze worst-case scenarios. It is much better to have too much money for retirement than too little.

COMPUTING THE FUTURE VALUE OF INVESTMENTS

To estimate the amount of money that will accumulate in your investment accounts over time, apply the principles of compound return. Given an estimate of the rate of return that your investments will earn, you can estimate the value that they should have in the future using these principles.

Example 16.2 presents an example that uses compound returns to forecast the value of an investment account in the future. It assumes annual contributions.

Example 16.3, illustrates another case of using compound returns to forecast the value of an investment account in the future. This example uses monthly contributions.

Computing the Future Value of an Investment Account with Annual Contributions **EXAMPLE 16.2**

Kerri Higgins is 25 years old and planning for the future by investing in mutual funds. She believes that her long-run return will average 12 percent per year. She wants to retire in 30 years at age 55 and is saving for that by investing $2,000 per year in her funds. To supplement her company's retirement plan and Social Security, she wants to have $600,000 in her mutual fund investments by her retirement time. Will she have the desired amount in 30 years? If not, how much does she need to invest annually? Financial calculator solution:

She invests for 30 years (N=30) at 12% (I/Y=12) with a payment of $2,000 (PMT= −2,000).

30	12	0	−2,000	482,665.37
[N]	[I/Y]	[PV]	[PMT]	[FV]

Compound interest tables solution:

$$FVA = PMT \times FVAF_{N,1\%}$$
$$= 2,000 \times 241.3327$$
$$= 482,665.40$$

$2,000 per year is not enough to build the investment to $600,000. Solving for the payment that will yield a $600,000 balance:

30	12	0	−2,486.19	600,000
[N]	[I/Y]	[PV]	[PMT]	[FV]

$$FVA = PMT \times FVAF_{N,1\%}$$
$$600,000 = PMT \times 241.3327$$
$$PMT = 2,486.19 \blacksquare$$

EXAMPLE 16.3   Computing the Future Value of an Investment Account with Monthly Contributions

Alejandro contributes to a retirement fund by having $100 per month deducted from his paycheck. He has directed his investments to an aggressive mutual fund, and he estimates his investments will earn an average annual return of 15 percent compounded monthly over the next 30 years. How much should Alejandro have after 30 years?

Financial calculator solution:
Be sure the calculator is set to 12 payments per year. In 30 years, there are 360 months (N=360), the interest rate per year is 15% (I/Y=15), and the payment is $100 (PMT= -100).

360	15	0	-100	692,327.96
[N]	[I/Y]	[PV]	[PMT]	[FV]

Compound interest tables solution:
There are monthly payments, so the interest rate per month is 15%/12 or 1.25%. The factor in the table corresponding to 1.25% over 360 payments is 6923.2796.

$$FVA = PMT \times FVAF_{N,1\%}$$
$$= 100 \times 6923.2796$$
$$= 693,327.96 \quad \blacksquare$$

SUMMARY

The best time for workers to plan for an early and rewarding retirement is at the very beginning of their employment years. It is from such an early date that compound interest and returns have more time to do their work. The uncertainty regarding the future of Social Security puts more responsibility on individuals to properly plan for and fund their own retirement. Planning for retirement involves several important decisions, the first of which is what type of plan to utilize. There are a number of options from employer-based retirement programs to individual retirement accounts.

Retirement programs available include federal government programs, employer-sponsored plans, individual retirement accounts, and self-employed retirement plans. Social Security is a tax on all employees, employers, and self-employed individuals. It pays a basic retirement income beginning at age 67 (with reduced amounts possible beginning at age 62). It also provides for survivor benefits in case of death. The federal government also administers the railroad retirement.

The two types of employer-sponsored plans are the defined benefit plan and the defined contribution plan. Defined benefit plans, or pensions, provide a guaranteed income upon retirement. Defined contribution plans build a value that the beneficiary uses to produce income at retirement. Types of defined contribution plans include the 401(k), 403(b), simplified employee pension, SIMPLE IRA, profit sharing, and employee stock ownership plans.

Anyone can set up and contribute to an individual retirement accounts (IRA). These accounts include the traditional, Roth, and Coverdell educational IRAs.

A person's financial life cycle has five main financial phases, each of which is characterized by different goals and priorities. The five phases are education, employment, approaching retirement, retirement, and estate planning.

During all of these financial phases an individual has two main investing decisions: short-term investment for unexpected events and long-term investing for the future. For short-term investment, individual investors have CDs and money market mutual funds in addition to bank accounts.

Investing for the long run should follow the life cycle model of investing that recognizes that younger individuals can assume greater risk than those who are near or at retirement. Younger people should concentrate their investments in more aggressive, riskier investments with greater levels of expected return. As the years pass, they should move to a more moderate and then conservative investment portfolio.

Investors can implement the life cycle approach by choosing their own investments and making their own asset allocations. Life cycle mutual funds offer a convenient way to implement the life cycle approach. Target-date life cycle funds have a target retirement date and set up an asset allocation strategy based on that date. Target-risk life cycle funds identify investing goals as aggressive, moderate, or conservative and set an asset allocation to match that goal. Investors then decide how much to allocate to each type of fund and change allocations as time passes.

The future value of investment accounts can be estimated by using the principles of compound interest and assuming a given rate of return on the investment.

PROBLEMS

1. Gabriela plans to retire three years from now. She works for Alden Consulting and makes an annual salary of $85,000. The company has a retirement plan that pays employees an annual pension equal to the average of the employee's three highest years' wages multiplied by the number of years of employment multiplied by a factor of 2.2. Gabriela estimates that she will receive a raise of 4 percent each year for the next three years.

   a. What type of retirement plan does Alden Consulting have?
   b. Project Gabriela's annual salary for each of the next three years.
   b. Compute Gabriela's estimated annual retirement income.
   c. Suppose Gabriela decides to work an additional two years with no additional raises. Estimate her retirement income.

2. Janet is planning a supplemental investment account to add to her retirement funds. She is currently 45 years old and plans to retire at age 65. If she contributes $1,500 per year to her account that earns 9 percent, how much will she have at age 65?

3. Shah is 23 years old and wants to have $1 million is an investment account at age 65. He plans to add to an investment account earning 12 percent at the end of each year. How much does he need to deposit into the account to meet his goal?

4. Jason and Maria have a joint investment account. They are applying lifecycle investing and intend to invest in an aggressive lifecycle fund with an expected return of 12 percent for the first 15 years. How much will they have at the end of 15 years?

5. Kara deposits $300 per month in an account earning 9 percent annually compounded monthly. Compute the amount to which her account will grow after 20 years.

6. Laurence plans to contribute $375 to an investment account every month for 144 months. His account earns 1.5 percent per month. How much will Laurence end up with?

   Following are two different asset allocation targets:

   Target Asset Allocation A
   Stocks   20%
   Bonds   60%
   Money market   20%

   Target Asset Allocation B
   Stocks   70%
   Bonds   25%
   Money market   5%

   Based on life cycle investing, assign the appropriate target to Investor X who is a single 29-year-old working as an electrical engineer in a manufacturing plant and to Investor Y who is a 62-year-old manager of a retail store. Justify your choices.

CASE STUDIES

COLLEGE STUDENT

Kevin Maedor has over 45 years to retirement. He has plenty of time to provide for a comfortable retirement, and he needs a good plan. The earlier he starts saving, the more compounding will work for him. Social Security is not a dependable option. Kevin does not want to depend on any financial assistance from any future children he may have, so he wants to plan for financial security in his retirement.

Create a retirement plan for him.

1. Select appropriate options for him from the available retirement plans:

   - Pension Plan
   - 401K
   - 403b
   - SEP
   - SIMPLE IRA
   - IRA
   - Roth IRA
   - Keogh Plan
   - Profit Sharing
   - ESOP

2. Explain why the options you picked for him are appropriate for his situation.
3. Determine how much he needs to contribute to have $1,000,000 when he retires (Hint: Use the FV of an annuity equation).

NEW GRADUATE

Rene has over 40 years to retirement. She has plenty of time to provide for a comfortable retirement, and she needs a good plan. The earlier she starts saving, the more compounding will work for her. Social Security is not a dependable option. Rene prefers not to depend on any financial assistance from any children she may have in the future, so she wants to plan for financial security in her retirement.

Create a retirement plan for her.

1. Select appropriate options for her from the available retirement plans:

   - Pension Plan
   - 401K
   - 403b
   - SEP
   - SIMPLE IRA
   - IRA
   - Roth IRA
   - Keogh Plan
   - Profit Sharing
   - ESOP

2. Explain why the options you picked for her are appropriate for her situation.
3. Determine how much she needs to contribute to have $1,000,000 when she retires (Hint: Use the FV of an annuity equation).

REVIEW QUESTIONS

1. Explain the reason that retirement planning and contributions are important in the early career years.

   _____

   _____

   _____

2. List the four types of retirement programs.

   _____

   _____

   _____

3. Outline the Social Security program.

   _____

   _____

   _____

4. Identify issues regarding the financial future of Social Security.

   _____

   _____

   _____

5. Distinguish between a defined benefit and a defined contribution retirement plan. Identify who assumes the risk of the retirement plan of each type and outline the benefits of each.

   _____

   _____

   _____

6. Summarize the provisions of ERISA.

_____

_____

_____

7. Describe the three main factors that determine the benefits for a participant in a defined benefit retirement plan.

_____

_____

_____

8. Summarize the 401(k) and 403(b) retirement plans.

_____

_____

_____

9. Identify the main provisions of a SEP.

_____

_____

_____

10. Identify and describe the three types of IRAs.

_____

_____

_____

11. Describe scenario analyses and explain why it is a useful tool in retirement planning.

_____

_____

_____

12. Define the financial life cycle.

_____

_____

_____

13. List the key phases of the financial life cycle and identify the characteristics of each phase.

_____

_____

_____

14. Distinguish between the investments for short-term investing and those for long-term investing.

_____

_____

_____

15. Define lifecycle mutual funds and describe the two types of funds.

_____

_____

_____

16. Identify the benefits that lifecycle funds offer individual investors and the drawbacks.

_____

_____

_____

Estate Planning 17

"Death never takes the wise man by surprise; he is always ready to go."

—Jean De La Fontaine
(1621–1695)

OBJECTIVES

- Outline the process of estate planning
- Define a will and summarize its components
- Identify characteristics of people who benefit most from estate planning
- Describe the valuation of an estate
- Illustrate methods for minimizing estate taxes

KEY TERMS

Codicil
Durable power of attorney for health care
Estate
Estate planning
Executor
Family trust
Gift
Grantor

Guardian
Holographic will
Intestate
Irrevocable living trust
Letter of last instruction
Living trust
Living will
Power of attorney
Probate

Revocable living trust
Self-proving will
Testamentary trust
Testator
Trust
Trustee
Will

473

Estate All of the assets that an individual owns less any liabilities owed.

Estate planning Process of planning for estate distribution.

Your estate is the sum of the assets you own (less any liabilities you owe), and estate planning is the process of planning for the distribution of your estate in the manner that best accomplishes your objectives. Your primary objectives should be that your estate be settled according to your personal wishes and preferences. However, since estate taxes can be significant, you should plan your estate to minimize the impact of taxes wherever possible. Minimizing taxes will maximize the value of your estate that is available for distribution.

Estate planning is one of those things that is easy to put off for some time in the future. Younger people especially find it difficult to consider that they are only mortal and that their passing might occur sooner rather than later. However, one never knows when the unexpected might happen, and not properly planning for this event can create legal problems and result in an estate paying significantly more in taxes that it would have with appropriate planning.

Estate planning and negotiating the various federal and state laws and rules can be a complicated task. This chapter presents a few basics of estate planning but is not comprehensive, and anyone with much accumulated wealth should consult an estate planning specialist such as an attorney or a certified public accountant while making estate plans.

Will A legal document that details how a person would like the estate to be distributed after the person's death.

Testator A person making a will.

Wills

A will is a document that details an individual's wishes regarding the disposition of his or her assets after death. The individual making the will is the testator. A will is revocable during the testator's lifetime, meaning that the testator can revoke or modify the will at any time. The will specifies each beneficiary. A beneficiary is a person or organization that will receive assets from the estate.

EXHIBIT 17.1	TYPICAL RULES FOR THE DISTRIBUTION OF AN ESTATE WHEN THE DECEASED DIES INTESTATE

- If the decedent has a surviving spouse but no children, the spouse receives the entire estate.
- When a spouse and children survive, each is entitled to some portion of the estate.
- In cases where only children survive, they divide the entire estate.
- If no spouse or children survive, the decedent's parents receive the estate.
- If the parents do not survive, then the estate passes to the decedent's siblings or to their heirs.
- If the estate does not pass according to the above criteria, the estate goes to the decedent's grandparents and their heirs.
- If none of the above survives, any children of the decedent's predeceased spouse receive the estate.
- If the estate cannot pass according to above rules, the estate goes to the next of kin.
- In cases where there are no next of kin, the estate passes to the state.

| PEOPLE WHO ARE CANDIDATES FOR ESTATE PLANNING | EXHIBIT 17.2 |

Those who:

- Have estates exceeding the amount exempted from estate and gift taxes—$5.25 million in 2013
- Are in combined state and federal income tax brackets greater than 15 percent
- Have minor children
- Have dependents who have emotional, mental, or physical handicaps
- Own closely held business interests
- Own property in more than one state
- Have charitable objectives
- Have pets that are particularly important to them

A person who dies without having a will dies intestate. Dying intestate can create a complicated legal and family situation. When someone dies intestate, the court appoints an administrator who will allocate assets to beneficiaries based on the applicable state laws. This can result in the estate's not being distributed as the deceased would have liked. When a person dies intestate, it simply creates one more problem for a family already dealing with grief over the loss of a family member. Exhibit 17.1 shows some examples of typical rules for distribution of an estate when the decedent dies intestate. These rules vary from state to state, underscoring why it is advisable to consult an estate planning professional.

Intestate Dying without a will.

WHO NEEDS ESTATE PLANNING?

For some people who have few assets, a simple will bequeathing all of their assets to certain individuals or charitable organizations is all they need. However, many individuals and families need a more sophisticated approach and are candidates for careful estate planning. Exhibit 17.2 outlines situations in which a person's estate would likely benefit from estate planning.

Estate Planning Overview

The general process of estate planning includes three elements:

1. Creating a legal will
2. Properly valuing the estate
3. Minimizing estate taxes, where applicable, by properly planning gifts, trusts, and charitable contributions as appropriate

CREATE A LEGAL WILL

In order to create a valid will, a person should be:

- At least 18 or 21, depending on the state
- Mentally competent
- Clear of undue influence from others

Self-proving will A will with notarized signatures of witnesses.

Holographic will A will written and signed in the person's own handwriting.

A will should be signed, dated, and signed by at least two witnesses present who are not beneficiaries of the will. A self-proving will has notarized signatures of witnesses.

While most wills are typed, a holographic will is a will written and signed in the person's own handwriting. Some states allow unwitnessed holographic wills. A few states even recognize the validity of an oral will, which is usually dictated in front of a sufficient number of witnesses during a person's last illness.

Wills are sometimes challenged in court, especially when there is significant wealth at stake. Unwitnessed holographic wills and oral wills are much easier to challenge in court, so having a properly prepared, typed, and witnessed will is important. Although a lawyer is not necessary to create a legal will, it is often a good idea to have one involved in the creation of the will. At some point after death, the will has to be approved by a probate court, and you do not want things to go awry because of some oversight or legal technicality.

Information in a Will

The length and details included in a will can be very different from person to person. A few sentences might be all that is necessary for one person, while someone else might require a lengthy document. All wills should include the following information:

Executor An individual placed in charge of the process of distributing a deceased person's estate.

Guardian The person identified in his or her will who is responsible for the person's minor children upon the person's death.

- **Name of the executor.** The executor is the person placed in charge of the process of distributing assets according to the instructions in the will.
- **Distribution of the estate.** Specification of the beneficiaries and exactly which assets, specific dollar amounts, specific percentages, or remainders (amounts remaining after other beneficiaries have been paid) they should receive.
- **Guardian or guardians of any minor children.** Parents of minor children should name a guardian—a capable and willing person to be legally responsible for the children until they reach the age of majority.
- **Signature, date, and witnesses.**

Exhibit 17.3 illustrates a sample will with its major provisions.

© Monkey Business Images, 2014, Shutterstock, Inc.

Do you have children? If so, it's a good idea to establish a will and appoint responsible guardians in the event of your untimely death.

SAMPLE WILL

EXHIBIT 17.3

LAST WILL AND TESTAMENT OF GAYLE Z. WILLIAMS

I, GAYLE Z. WILLIAMS, of Kansas City, Missouri, declare this to be my last Will and Testament, hereby revoking all Wills and Codicils heretofore made by me.

FIRST: I direct my Executor, hereinafter named, to pay all my funeral expenses, administration, and lawful debts of my Estate.

SECOND: To my beloved daughter, ELLEN W. GUTHRIE, I give the sum of Fifty Thousand Dollars ($50,000.00).

THIRD: To my dear nephew, KELLY WILLIAMS, I give my baseball card collection.

FOURTH: To my dear niece, LISA WILLIAMS EISEN, I give all of the household goods and furnishings of my home.

FIFTH: To the West Side Community Development Center of Kansas City, I give the sum of Five Thousand Dollars ($5,000.00) to be used for the organization's general purposes.

SIXTH: I give the rest, remainder, and residue of my Estate, including all remaining and real personal property not herefore bequeathed, to the COLLEGE OF BUSINESS OF THE UNIVERSITY OF MISSOURI–COLUMBIA to be used for purposes deemed appropriate by the Dean of the College.

SEVENTH: I hereby appoint GEORGE W. GUTHRIE, of 9999 What Street, Kansas City, Missouri USA, as Independent Executor of this Last Will and Testament. If GEORGE W. GUTHRIE does not survive me or is unable or unwilling to serve as my Executor, I hereby appoint LAWSON G. ANDERSON as Independent Executor.

_____ Date: _____

Gayle Z. Williams

Witnesses:

_____ Date: _____

_____ Date: _____

The Executor

The choice of executor is one of the most important decisions in the estate planning process. The person selected should be trustworthy, competent, familiar with the decedent's business, and knowledgeable of the needs, and appreciative of the circumstances, of the beneficiaries.

When death occurs, the executor must locate the will and begin the process of probating the will. Probate is the legal process of administering the estate of a deceased person. Probate includes resolving all claims against the estate and distributing the deceased person's property to the beneficiaries. The executor may need to sell assets of the estate in order to make proper distribution. The executor is also in charge of taking care of any expenses that the estate owes. Such expenses include funeral costs, legal expenses, and administrative items that arise from distribution of the estate.

Probate The legal process of administering the estate of a deceased person.

Additions and Changes to a Will

Letter of last instruction
An inclusion in a will that presents a person's last words and discusses desired details of administering the estate.

A letter of last instruction may accompany a will. This letter is an optional document that discusses administrative details for the estate. For example, this letter might list desired details for the funeral service and any burial arrangements. It can detail the location of important documents, such as birth certificates or financial assets. The purpose of this document is to make it easier for the executor to locate assets and sell them or transfer them to the beneficiaries as efficiently as possible.

Codicil An addition to an existing will.

A person can make changes to a will at any time. The choices are to write an entirely new will or to amend an existing will. If the changes are relatively minor, then a codicil is in order. A codicil is a document added to a will that makes changes to the original document. If the changes are major, it is probably best to create a new will from scratch. When there is an issue regarding which will is valid after someone dies, the most recent will takes precedence.

VALUING THE ESTATE

Calculating the value of the estate is a very important part of the overall planning process. The value of a person's estate serves as an indicator of the need to go through special steps such as the creation of a trust that might reduce the value of the estate and thus reduce estate taxes payable. Individuals who have estates valued at more than about $5 million should consider actions to minimize the impact of estate taxes.

Valuing your estate may be very easy or extremely complicated. A key fact is that the fair market value of all property in an estate determines the estate's value, not what you originally paid for the assets. It is easy to determine the fair market value of many financial assets, such as bank accounts or shares of stock of a publicly traded corporation.

On the other hand, the valuation of many other types of assets, such as privately held businesses or real estate, can be much more difficult. It is not possible to observe a transaction of these assets to get a market value, so you have to rely on an appraisal or estimate of the value of the asset. For estimating the value of these difficult-to-value properties, it is often a good idea to retain the services of an independent appraiser who is skilled, and possibly certified, in the valuation of such assets. Estimating accurate values for all of the properties in an estate is important for determining if taxes are an issue for the estate.

© Pablo Rogat, 2014, Shutterstock, Inc.

Depending on your individual situation, calculating the value of your estate can either be simple or very complex.

MINIMIZING ESTATE TAXES

The federal government and the various state governments levy a tax on a deceased person's estate (less certain expenses of administering the estate). The federal tax is an estate tax, levied on the value of the deceased person's estate on the date of death. Some states also have an estate tax, and some have an inheritance tax, while others levy no taxes on estates. An inheritance tax is a tax on the value of assets bequeathed to a given individual by the deceased. Each individual beneficiary is responsible for any inheritance tax due.

The United States has moved to a unified estate and gift tax schedule. This means that certain larger gifts made during a person's lifetime need to be included as part of the estate for computation of the unified gift/estate tax. (See the Computing Gift and Estate Taxes section later in this chapter.)

Estates over a certain value have to pay estate taxes to the federal government. In 2013, estates valued at less than $5.25 million were exempt and owed no estate tax. Any estate in excess of $5.25 million pays tax on a sliding scale up to 40 percent of the value greater than $5.25 million. Only about 2 percent of individuals have to pay estate taxes. Exhibit 17.4 shows these rates for 2013.

People whose net worth approaches or is above the amount that is exempt from estate taxes have several ways to go about reducing the value of their estate. The main areas to focus on are the following:

- Creating a trust
- Making allowed gifts before death
- Donating to charities

UNIFIED GIFT AND ESTATE TAX RATES FOR 2013			EXHIBIT 17.4
Taxable Estate (1)	Base Tax	Plus	Of Amount Over
0–$10,000	$0	18%	$0
$10,000–$20,000	$1,800	20%	$10,000
$20,000–$40,000	$3,800	22%	$20,000
$40,000–$60,000	$8,200	24%	$40,000
$60,000–$80,000	$13,000	26%	$60,000
$80,000–$100,000	$18,200	28%	$80,000
$100,000–$150,000	$23,800	30%	$100,000
$150,000–$250,000	$38,800	32%	$150,000
$250,000–$500,000	$70,800	34%	$250,000
$500,000–$750,000	$155,800	37%	$500,000
$750,000–$1,000,000	$248,300	39%	$750,000
$1,000,000 +	$345,800	40%	$1,000,000

(1) For 2013 the taxable estate is equal to the total estate value less $5.25 million.

The fixed exemption for U.S. estate taxes is set at $5 million. Each year the exemption is adjusted for inflation, and that exemption for 2013 was $5.25 million.

Individuals can use any of these tools, whether singly or in combination, to minimize estate taxes, thus assuring that they are able to pass on the largest inheritance possible to their beneficiaries.

Trusts

Trusts are the most popular method for individuals with high net worth to avoid or minimize estate taxes. A trust is a legal entity in which one person (called the grantor) transfers assets to another individual or institution (called a trustee) charged to manage the assets for the beneficiaries of the grantor.

The selection of a capable trustee is vital to this arrangement. The trustee can be an individual that the grantor trusts or a financial institution, such as an investment firm or bank. Since many times the majority of a person's worth is tied up in financial assets, the trustee should be knowledgeable about investing.

There are several reasons people create trusts other than the reduction of estate taxes:

- Trusts are more difficult to challenge than a will.
- In a trust, funds are separate until a beneficiary reaches a certain age.
- Trusts allow professional management to invest the assets of the trust.
- Funds in a trust avoid probate, because trusts are not part of the estate.

There are two main types of trusts that are important for estate planning:

- Living trust. A trust created by a living person.
- Testamentary trust. A trust established in a will and created upon the death of the testator.

A revocable living trust allows the grantor to withdraw the assets of the trust at a later date. This type of trust is simply a different way of holding assets. The grantor still technically owns the assets, receives income from the trust funds, and pays taxes on this income. This type of trust does not reduce the value of an estate, so it will not help reduce estate taxes. The main advantage of the revocable trust is that when the grantor dies, it is easy to transfer the assets to beneficiaries, thereby avoiding the time and costs of probate.

By contrast, an irrevocable living trust creates a separate legal entity that owns the assets. The assets no longer belong to the grantor. The trustee, rather than the grantor, has control over the management of the funds in the trust. This type of trust does help reduce estate taxes, because any amounts held in an irrevocable living trust are no longer considered part of the estate. An irrevocable living trust still helps avoid probate and facilitates transfer of assets smoothly and quickly to beneficiaries.

Different from living trusts, the provisions of a will establish a testamentary trust. The event of the person's death then creates the trust according to the specifications in the will. The main purpose of a testamentary trust is to help avoid estate taxes and to have professional management of the estate's assets. The standard family trust is the most popular testamentary trust and is useful whenever one spouse dies before the other.

Trust A legal entity in which one person transfers assets to another individual or institution (the trustee) to manage for the beneficiaries.

Grantor An individual transferring assets into a trust.

Trustee The individual or institution that manages the assets in a trust for the beneficiaries.

Living trust A trust created when the grantor is living.

Testamentary trust A trust created by a person's will.

Revocable living trust A type of living trust in which the grantor still owns the assets in the trust and has control over them.

Irrevocable living trust A type of living trust that creates a separate legal entity that owns the assets.

Family trust A type of testamentary trust that holds property for beneficiaries other than the surviving spouse. The surviving spouse may receive income from the trust.

Gifts

A gift is an easy way to reduce the value of an estate. For estate purposes, a gift   **Gift** A transfer of property.
is a nontaxable transfer of property. First of all, in 2013 individuals can give up
to $14,000 free of taxes to any number of individuals each year. For example,
you could give $14,000 to each of five nieces and nephews if you wished and
owe no taxes. Married couples can pool this exemption and give up to $28,000
to each individual.

Gifts in excess of $14,000 in 2013 (or the appropriate annual exemption
amount in prior years) to any individual accrue to a person's lifetime gift/
estate tax exemption. The lifetime exemption for those who passed away in
2013 is $5.25 million. Current law requires that this exemption amount be
adjusted every year according to the rate of inflation, so the IRS publishes a
new tax schedule each year. Exhibit 17.5 shows the annual gift tax exemption
amounts from 1997 to 2013.

So, for example, a person could give $14,000 to anyone in 2013 and
that amount is exempt from gift tax. Giving additional amounts in 2013 to
that same person would then accrue to the lifetime exemption. If a person's
accrued exemption amount exceeds the lifetime exemption in any one year
($5.25 million in 2013), then the person has to pay gift taxes on the amount
that exceeds the exemption in that year.

If an estate is near or slightly above the tax-exempt estate amount, regular
annual gifts are a simple way to reduce the value of the estate. If a couple has
three children, they can give each of them $28,000 tax-free every year, for a
total of $84,000 each year.

ANNUAL GIFT TAX EXCLUSION AMOUNTS, 1997–2013   EXHIBIT 17.5

Year	Annual Exclusion Amount
1997	$10,000
1998	$10,000
1999	$10,000
2000	$10,000
2001	$10,000
2002	$11,000
2003	$11,000
2004	$11,000
2005	$11,000
2006	$12,000
2007	$12,000
2008	$12,000
2009	$13,000
2010	$13,000
2011	$13,000
2012	$13,000
2013	$14,000

Giving money to grandchildren or other family and friends can help accelerate this process. The nice part is that no paperwork is required for these gifts. Of course, no one should give away assets that provide them with needed income.

Charitable Contributions

Many individuals plan on leaving some of their estate to a charity of their choice. Although the altruism of the giving itself should be the most important reason for giving to charitable organizations, the tax benefits cannot be ignored. Any donation to a qualified charity or other tax-exempt organization is exempt from estate taxes. So a person with an estate worth $6.25 million could give $1 million to charity, leaving the rest of the estate then exempt from estate tax. Charitable contributions provide another tool for properly planning an estate.

Computing the Estate Tax

This section presents an example of a simple calculation of estate taxes with the unified gift and estate tax system. However, this is only a simple example; computation of estate and gift taxes can be extremely complicated, and anyone with a sizable estate should consult professional tax and estate planners.

Suppose that Edna Arbuckle died in 2013 with an estate valued at $8.5 million. Her will provided for a total of $3 million in bequests to charitable organizations. In addition, back in 2004 she had set up a college savings account for her granddaughter with $300,000. In 2008, she gave her son $75,000 for the down payment on a home.

Exhibit 17.6 illustrates the computation of the tax due on Edna's estate. The charitable contribution of $3 million reduced the estate to $5.5 million. The 2013 exemption was $5.25 million, but Edna had given prior gifts that

---

EXHIBIT 17.6	EXAMPLE ESTATE TAX COMPUTATION WORKSHEET

Total estate value	$8,500,000	
Less: Charitable bequests	3,000,000	
Net estate		$5,500,000
Total gift/estate tax exemption	5,250,000	
Less: Prior gifts in excess of annual gift exemption		
Year: 2004 (300,000–11,000)	289,000	
Year: 2008: (75,000–12,000)	63,000	
Year:		
Year:		
Net estate tax exemption		4,898,000
Estate taxable estate		602,000
Estate tax due (155,000 + .37 × 102,000)		192,740

exceeded her annual gift exemption. In 2004, considering the $11,000 annual gift exemption in that year (see Exhibit 17.5), her gift of $300,000 resulted in an adjustment of $289,000 to the lifetime exemption. The 2008 gift resulted in an adjustment of $63,000 after allowing for the $12,000 annual exemption effective in 2008. After these adjustments, the net tax exemption for the estate was $4,898,000. The amount of the taxable estate, after the $4,898,000 exemption, was $602,000.

To compute the tax due on a net taxable estate of $602,000 in 2013, consult Exhibit 17.4. Edna's estate was in the $500,000 to $750,000 tax bracket, so the tax is equal to $155,000 plus 37 percent of $102,000 (the amount of the taxable estate in excess of $500,000). The tax due totaled $192,740.

Other Aspects of Estate Planning

LOCATION OF IMPORTANT DOCUMENTS

It is important that more than one person know where a person's important documents and records are kept. A lawyer is normally involved with more complicated estates, but a family member or trusted friend should also know where to find all of the documents relating to the transfer of one's estate and/or the identity of the lawyer handling the estate details.

LIVING WILL

A living will is a legal document in which a person states his or her preferences in case he or she becomes seriously mentally or physically ill. For example, this document can detail whether a person wants to stay on life support under certain medical conditions. All individuals should have a living will so that their family and friends do not have to make such complicated and ethical decisions should the situation call for such decisions.

POWER OF ATTORNEY

The power of attorney grants another person the right to make decisions on your behalf in case you become incapacitated or incompetent. A durable power of attorney for health care allows another person to make health care decisions for you if you are unable to do so. A living will may not cover all possibilities, and the person given the durable power should work in conjunction with your living will to make the right decisions for you.

Living will A legal document that states a person's desires should he or she become unable to make his or her own decisions.

Power of attorney A legal document that grants another person the right to make decisions on the grantor's behalf should the grantor become incapacitated or incompetent.

Durable power of attorney for health care A legal document that allows another person to make health care decisions for the grantor of the power of attorney should the grantor become incapacitated.

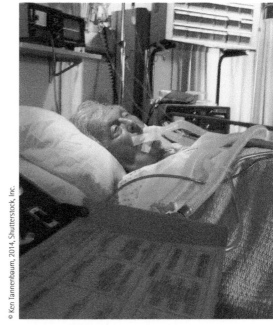

© Ken Tannenbaum, 2014, Shutterstock, Inc.

A living will is necessary in case a person becomes incapacitated and unable to convey their medical wishes.

SUMMARY

Estate planning is the process of taking steps to ensure that a person's assets are distributed as he or she prefers after death. Estate planning is important for everyone who has a positive net worth, regardless of age, to consider. The first step in estate planning is to create a will, the legal document that provides the administrative details and identifies the beneficiaries of the estate.

In the estate planning process, it is important that people know the value of their total estate. The value of an estate is based on the fair market value of the assets at the time of death, not the original cost of the asset.

There are three main ways that individuals can reduce the value of their estate in order to minimize or avoid estate taxes: place assets in a trust, give money to heirs before dying, and make charitable contributions.

A trust is a legal entity created when one person transfers assets to the trust for the benefit of another person. A trustee manages the funds in the trust. Trusts can either be created while the grantor is alive (living trusts) or after death via instructions in the will (testamentary trusts). Trusts are a vital part of estate planning for individuals with high net worth.

Tax law allows individuals to give, tax-free, up to a certain amount every year to as many different people as they wish. In 2013 this amount was $14,000. Living individuals whose estates are near the estate tax-exempt level should consider making gifts annually to their heirs in order to lower the value of their estate. These gifts require no paperwork or filings.

Donations made to qualified charities are exempt from estate taxes. Another aspect of estate planning is to make sure that some family member or legal help knows the location of important documents. Everyone should also consider making a living will, power of attorney, and durable power of attorney.

The United States has a unified gift and estate tax system so that gifts in excess of the annual gift exemption reduce the estate tax exemption. The gift/estate tax total exemption in 2013 was $5.25 million. Estates that exceed that amount pay taxes at a rate of up to 40 percent of the value in excess of the exemption.

PROBLEMS

1. Using the estate tax exemption and rates effective in 2013, compute the amount of federal estate tax that an estate valued at $7 million would owe, in 2013.
2. Assuming that the estate tax exemption is $6 million with a tax rate of 46 percent on value that exceeds that amount, compute the amount of federal estate tax that an estate valued at $7 million would owe.
3. J.A. Metz died in 2013 leaving an estate valued at $6,750,000. His will left 20 percent of his estate to his nephew and $200,000 to his housekeeper.

The remainder of the estate was bequeathed to various charitable organizations. How much estate tax was due on the estate?

4. Elsa Andrew passed away in 2013. Her total estate was valued at $12 million. Provisions in her will left $4 million to charitable organizations and the remainder to her two children. In 2013 and in each of the previous three years, she had given each child $100,000. Compute the tax due on Elsa's estate using the exhibits in the chapter.

CASE STUDIES

COLLEGE STUDENT

We've met Kevin before; below you will find his original financial information. If you have worked on this case study from the beginning of the book, use the current financial data you have for him. If you haven't worked on this case study through the entire book, use the financial information below.

Kevin Maedor is a 19-year-old college student. He still lives at home with his parents, and he works part time at Vapor's Lane. He started his financial plan in the spring semester of 2014. He plans to graduate with a B.S. in engineering in May 2017. He has the following financial information:

- He brings home $760 a month from his job; he currently has $174 in his checking account.
- He asks his parents for $50 cash each week.
- He has a Visa card with a balance of $1,700 and a MasterCard with a balance of $800. He makes the minimum monthly payment of $15.00 on each of them.
- His cell phone bill is $85 a month.
- Last month he spent $450 on gas, $375.00 on golf, and $490.69 at restaurants.

Help him prepare his estate:

1. Does he need a will now? Why or why not?
2. Which type of will would you recommend for him? Explain your decision.
3. Which, if any, of the following items do you think he needs?

- Appraisal
- Durable power of attorney for health care
- Guardian
- Irrevocable living trust
- Living trust
- Living will
- Power of attorney
- Revocable living trust

NEW GRADUATE

We've met Rene before; below you will find her original financial information. If you have worked on this case study from the beginning of the book, use the current financial data you have for her. If you haven't worked on this case study through the entire book, use the financial information below.

Rene Harris recently graduated with a B.S. in nursing. She lives by herself in a modest apartment. Her annual salary is $76,000 a year. Rene loves to entertain, but her apartment is too small and the neighbors complain about the slightest noise. Rene is a good neighbor, so she has been going out with friends instead. She has the following financial information:

- She brings home $4,433.33 a month from her job.
- She pays $1,125.00 a month for her apartment, which includes trash service and cable.
- She used her new Visa last month for the first time and charged $600. She also opened a new Macy's charge and charged $762.78. She hasn't received her first bill for either of them; assume her minimum monthly payment will be $15.00 on each.
- She owes $30,000 in student loans and makes a monthly payment of $151.47.
- Her cell phone bill is $105.00 a month.
- She has $1,804.12 in her savings account.
- Last month she spent $275 on gas, $398.63 on food, $32.17 for her water bill, $76.18 for her electric bill, $49.98 for Internet service, $820 at restaurants, $357.82 on entertainment, $762.78 on clothing (this is her Macy's charge), and $152.75 on hair and nail services.

Help her prepare her estate:

1. Does she need a will now? Why or why not?
2. Which type of will would you recommend for her? Explain your decision.
3. Which, if any, of the following items do you think she needs?

   - Appraisal
   - Durable power of attorney for health care
   - Guardian
   - Irrevocable living trust
   - Living trust
   - Living will
   - Power of attorney
   - Revocable living trust

CREATE YOUR OWN FINANCIAL PLAN

Depending on your current situation, you may or may not feel you need a will. After reading this chapter, do you now see a need for a will?

1. Which type of will best meets your current needs?
2. Which if any of the following items do you need?

   - Appraisal
   - Durable power of attorney for health care
   - Guardian
   - Irrevocable living trust
   - Living trust
   - Living will
   - Power of attorney
   - Revocable living trust

3. What life changes would affect your need to change your will?

   - Marriage
   - Birth of a child
   - Change in financial status
   - Death of another person

4. Would any of these or other life changes create a need for any of the items listed in question 2?
5. How can you prepare for these events, so during the excitement or sorrow of life you don't forget to take care of this item?

REVIEW QUESTIONS   CHAPTER 17

1. Define a will and identify the characteristics of a person legally able to write a will.

   _____

   _____

   _____

2. Name the term for a will that is in a person's own handwriting.

   _____

   _____

   _____

3. Identify and describe the main parts of a will.

   _____

   _____

   _____

4. Define a self-proving will.

   _____

   _____

   _____

5. Distinguish between an estate tax and an inheritance tax.

   _____

   _____

   _____

6. List three principal vehicles for minimizing estate taxes.

_____

_____

_____

7. Describe a trust, types of trusts, and trusts used as devices for minimizing or forgoing payment of estate taxes.

_____

_____

_____

8. Define a living will and distinguish it from a durable power of attorney for health care.

_____

_____

_____

Appendix

A-1: Future Value of $1

A-2: Present Value of $1

A-3: Future Value of $1 Per Period at the
   End of Each Period (Ordinary Annuity)

A-4: Present Value of $1 Per Period at the
   End of Each Period (Ordinary Annuity)

A-1: Future Value of $1

Periods	Rate per period 0.50%	0.75%	1%	1.25%	1.50%	1.75%	2%	3%
1	1.0050	1.0075	1.0100	1.0125	1.0150	1.0175	1.0200	1.0300
2	1.0100	1.0151	1.0201	1.0252	1.0302	1.0353	1.0404	1.0609
3	1.0151	1.0227	1.0303	1.0380	1.0457	1.0534	1.0612	1.0927
4	1.0202	1.0303	1.0406	1.0509	1.0614	1.0719	1.0824	1.1255
5	1.0253	1.0381	1.0510	1.0641	1.0773	1.0906	1.1041	1.1593
6	1.0304	1.0459	1.0615	1.0774	1.0934	1.1097	1.1262	1.1941
7	1.0355	1.0537	1.0721	1.0909	1.1098	1.1291	1.1487	1.2299
8	1.0407	1.0616	1.0829	1.1045	1.1265	1.1489	1.1717	1.2668
9	1.0459	1.0696	1.0937	1.1183	1.1434	1.1690	1.1951	1.3048
10	1.0511	1.0776	1.1046	1.1323	1.1605	1.1894	1.2190	1.3439
11	1.0564	1.0857	1.1157	1.1464	1.1779	1.2103	1.2434	1.3842
12	1.0617	1.0938	1.1268	1.1608	1.1956	1.2314	1.2682	1.4258
13	1.0670	1.1020	1.1381	1.1753	1.2136	1.2530	1.2936	1.4685
14	1.0723	1.1103	1.1495	1.1900	1.2318	1.2749	1.3195	1.5126
15	1.0777	1.1186	1.1610	1.2048	1.2502	1.2972	1.3459	1.5580
16	1.0831	1.1270	1.1726	1.2199	1.2690	1.3199	1.3728	1.6047
17	1.0885	1.1354	1.1843	1.2351	1.2880	1.3430	1.4002	1.6528
18	1.0939	1.1440	1.1961	1.2506	1.3073	1.3665	1.4282	1.7024
19	1.0994	1.1525	1.2081	1.2662	1.3270	1.3904	1.4568	1.7535
20	1.1049	1.1612	1.2202	1.2820	1.3469	1.4148	1.4859	1.8061
24	1.1272	1.1964	1.2697	1.3474	1.4295	1.5164	1.6084	2.0328
30	1.1614	1.2513	1.3478	1.4516	1.5631	1.6828	1.8114	2.4273
36	1.1967	1.3086	1.4308	1.5639	1.7091	1.8674	2.0399	2.8983
42	1.2330	1.3686	1.5188	1.6850	1.8688	2.0723	2.2972	3.4607
48	1.2705	1.4314	1.6122	1.8154	2.0435	2.2996	2.5871	4.1323
54	1.3091	1.4970	1.7114	1.9558	2.2344	2.5519	2.9135	4.9341
60	1.3489	1.5657	1.8167	2.1072	2.4432	2.8318	3.2810	5.8916
66	1.3898	1.6375	1.9285	2.2702	2.6715	3.1425	3.6950	7.0349
72	1.4320	1.7126	2.0471	2.4459	2.9212	3.4872	4.1611	8.4000
120	1.8194	2.4514	3.3004	4.4402	5.9693	8.0192	10.7652	34.7110
126	1.8747	2.5638	3.5034	4.7838	6.5271	8.8989	12.1233	41.4467
132	1.9316	2.6813	3.7190	5.1540	7.1370	9.8751	13.6528	49.4896
138	1.9903	2.8043	3.9477	5.5528	7.8039	10.9585	15.3753	59.0931
144	2.0508	2.9328	4.1906	5.9825	8.5332	12.1606	17.3151	70.5603
150	2.1130	3.0673	4.4484	6.4455	9.3305	13.4947	19.4996	84.2527
156	2.1772	3.2080	4.7221	6.9442	10.2024	14.9751	21.9597	100.6021
162	2.2434	3.3550	5.0126	7.4816	11.1558	16.6179	24.7302	120.1242
180	2.4541	3.8380	5.9958	9.3563	14.5844	22.7089	35.3208	204.5034
240	3.3102	6.0092	10.8926	19.7155	35.6328	64.3073	115.8887	*
300	4.4650	9.4084	19.7885	41.5441	87.0588	182.1065	380.2345	*
360	6.0226	14.7306	35.9496	87.5410	212.7038	515.6921	*	*

Rate per period

Periods	4%	5%	6%	7%	8%	9%	10%	12%
1	1.0400	1.0500	1.0600	1.0700	1.0800	1.0900	1.1000	1.1200
2	1.0816	1.1025	1.1236	1.1449	1.1664	1.1881	1.2100	1.2544
3	1.1249	1.1576	1.1910	1.2250	1.2597	1.2950	1.3310	1.4049
4	1.1699	1.2155	1.2625	1.3108	1.3605	1.4116	1.4641	1.5735
5	1.2167	1.2763	1.3382	1.4026	1.4693	1.5386	1.6105	1.7623
6	1.2653	1.3401	1.4185	1.5007	1.5869	1.6771	1.7716	1.9738
7	1.3159	1.4071	1.5036	1.6058	1.7138	1.8280	1.9487	2.2107
8	1.3686	1.4775	1.5938	1.7182	1.8509	1.9926	2.1436	2.4760
9	1.4233	1.5513	1.6895	1.8385	1.9990	2.1719	2.3579	2.7731
10	1.4802	1.6289	1.7908	1.9672	2.1589	2.3674	2.5937	3.1058
11	1.5395	1.7103	1.8983	2.1049	2.3316	2.5804	2.8531	3.4785
12	1.6010	1.7959	2.0122	2.2522	2.5182	2.8127	3.1384	3.8960
13	1.6651	1.8856	2.1329	2.4098	2.7196	3.0658	3.4523	4.3635
14	1.7317	1.9799	2.2609	2.5785	2.9372	3.3417	3.7975	4.8871
15	1.8009	2.0789	2.3966	2.7590	3.1722	3.6425	4.1772	5.4736
16	1.8730	2.1829	2.5404	2.9522	3.4259	3.9703	4.5950	6.1304
17	1.9479	2.2920	2.6928	3.1588	3.7000	4.3276	5.0545	6.8660
18	2.0258	2.4066	2.8543	3.3799	3.9960	4.7171	5.5599	7.6900
19	2.1068	2.5270	3.0256	3.6165	4.3157	5.1417	6.1159	8.6128
20	2.1911	2.6533	3.2071	3.8697	4.6610	5.6044	6.7275	9.6463
24	2.5633	3.2251	4.0489	5.0724	6.3412	7.9111	9.8497	15.1786
30	3.2434	4.3219	5.7435	7.6123	10.0627	13.2677	17.4494	29.9599
36	4.1039	5.7918	8.1473	11.4239	15.9682	22.2512	30.9127	59.1356
42	5.1928	7.7616	11.5570	17.1443	25.3395	37.3175	54.7637	116.7231
48	6.5705	10.4013	16.3939	25.7289	40.2106	62.5852	97.0172	230.3908
54	8.3138	13.9387	23.2550	38.6122	63.8091	104.9617	171.8719	454.7505
60	10.5196	18.6792	32.9877	57.9464	101.2571	176.0313	304.4816	897.5969
66	13.3107	25.0319	46.7937	86.9620	160.6822	295.2221	539.4078	*
72	16.8423	33.5451	66.3777	130.5065	254.9825	495.1170	955.5938	*
120	110.6626	348.9120	*	*	*	*	*	*
126	140.0234	467.5754	*	*	*	*	*	*
132	177.1743	626.5958	*	*	*	*	*	*
138	224.1820	839.6983	*	*	*	*	*	*
144	283.6618	*	*	*	*	*	*	*
150	358.9227	*	*	*	*	*	*	*
156	454.1517	*	*	*	*	*	*	*
162	574.6468	*	*	*	*	*	*	*
180	*	*	*	*	*	*	*	*
240	*	*	*	*	*	*	*	*
300	*	*	*	*	*	*	*	*
360	*	*	*	*	*	*	*	*

A-2: Present Value of $1

Rate per period

Periods	0.50%	0.75%	1%	1.25%	1.50%	1.75%	2%	3%
1	0.9950	0.9926	0.9901	0.9877	0.9852	0.9828	0.9804	0.9709
2	0.9901	0.9852	0.9803	0.9755	0.9707	0.9659	0.9612	0.9426
3	0.9851	0.9778	0.9706	0.9634	0.9563	0.9493	0.9423	0.9151
4	0.9802	0.9706	0.9610	0.9515	0.9422	0.9330	0.9238	0.8885
5	0.9754	0.9633	0.9515	0.9398	0.9283	0.9169	0.9057	0.8626
6	0.9705	0.9562	0.9420	0.9282	0.9145	0.9011	0.8880	0.8375
7	0.9657	0.9490	0.9327	0.9167	0.9010	0.8856	0.8706	0.8131
8	0.9609	0.9420	0.9235	0.9054	0.8877	0.8704	0.8535	0.7894
9	0.9561	0.9350	0.9143	0.8942	0.8746	0.8554	0.8368	0.7664
10	0.9513	0.9280	0.9053	0.8832	0.8617	0.8407	0.8203	0.7441
11	0.9466	0.9211	0.8963	0.8723	0.8489	0.8263	0.8043	0.7224
12	0.9419	0.9142	0.8874	0.8615	0.8364	0.8121	0.7885	0.7014
13	0.9372	0.9074	0.8787	0.8509	0.8240	0.7981	0.7730	0.6810
14	0.9326	0.9007	0.8700	0.8404	0.8118	0.7844	0.7579	0.6611
15	0.9279	0.8940	0.8613	0.8300	0.7999	0.7709	0.7430	0.6419
16	0.9233	0.8873	0.8528	0.8197	0.7880	0.7576	0.7284	0.6232
17	0.9187	0.8807	0.8444	0.8096	0.7764	0.7446	0.7142	0.6050
18	0.9141	0.8742	0.8360	0.7996	0.7649	0.7318	0.7002	0.5874
19	0.9096	0.8676	0.8277	0.7898	0.7536	0.7192	0.6864	0.5703
20	0.9051	0.8612	0.8195	0.7800	0.7425	0.7068	0.6730	0.5537
24	0.8872	0.8358	0.7876	0.7422	0.6995	0.6594	0.6217	0.4919
30	0.8610	0.7992	0.7419	0.6889	0.6398	0.5942	0.5521	0.4120
36	0.8356	0.7641	0.6989	0.6394	0.5851	0.5355	0.4902	0.3450
42	0.8110	0.7306	0.6584	0.5935	0.5351	0.4826	0.4353	0.2890
48	0.7871	0.6986	0.6203	0.5509	0.4894	0.4349	0.3865	0.2420
54	0.7639	0.6680	0.5843	0.5113	0.4475	0.3919	0.3432	0.2027
60	0.7414	0.6387	0.5504	0.4746	0.4093	0.3531	0.3048	0.1697
66	0.7195	0.6107	0.5185	0.4405	0.3743	0.3182	0.2706	0.1421
72	0.6983	0.5839	0.4885	0.4088	0.3423	0.2868	0.2403	0.1190
120	0.5496	0.4079	0.3030	0.2252	0.1675	0.1247	0.0929	0.0288
126	0.5334	0.3901	0.2854	0.2090	0.1532	0.1124	0.0825	0.0241
132	0.5177	0.3730	0.2689	0.1940	0.1401	0.1013	0.0732	0.0202
138	0.5024	0.3566	0.2533	0.1801	0.1281	0.0913	0.0650	0.0169
144	0.4876	0.3410	0.2386	0.1672	0.1172	0.0822	0.0578	0.0142
150	0.4733	0.3260	0.2248	0.1551	0.1072	0.0741	0.0513	0.0119
156	0.4593	0.3117	0.2118	0.1440	0.0980	0.0668	0.0455	0.0099
162	0.4458	0.2981	0.1995	0.1337	0.0896	0.0602	0.0404	0.0083
180	0.4075	0.2605	0.1668	0.1069	0.0686	0.0440	0.0283	0.0049
240	0.3021	0.1664	0.0918	0.0507	0.0281	0.0156	0.0086	*
300	0.2240	0.1063	0.0505	0.0241	0.0115	0.0055	0.0026	*
360	0.1660	0.0679	0.0278	0.0114	0.0047	0.0019	*	*

Rate per period

Periods	4%	5%	6%	7%	8%	9%	10%	12%
1	0.9615	0.9524	0.9434	0.9346	0.9259	0.9174	0.9091	0.8929
2	0.9246	0.9070	0.8900	0.8734	0.8573	0.8417	0.8264	0.7972
3	0.8890	0.8638	0.8396	0.8163	0.7938	0.7722	0.7513	0.7118
4	0.8548	0.8227	0.7921	0.7629	0.7350	0.7084	0.6830	0.6355
5	0.8219	0.7835	0.7473	0.7130	0.6806	0.6499	0.6209	0.5674
6	0.7903	0.7462	0.7050	0.6663	0.6302	0.5963	0.5645	0.5066
7	0.7599	0.7107	0.6651	0.6227	0.5835	0.5470	0.5132	0.4523
8	0.7307	0.6768	0.6274	0.5820	0.5403	0.5019	0.4665	0.4039
9	0.7026	0.6446	0.5919	0.5439	0.5002	0.4604	0.4241	0.3606
10	0.6756	0.6139	0.5584	0.5083	0.4632	0.4224	0.3855	0.3220
11	0.6496	0.5847	0.5268	0.4751	0.4289	0.3875	0.3505	0.2875
12	0.6246	0.5568	0.4970	0.4440	0.3971	0.3555	0.3186	0.2567
13	0.6006	0.5303	0.4688	0.4150	0.3677	0.3262	0.2897	0.2292
14	0.5775	0.5051	0.4423	0.3878	0.3405	0.2992	0.2633	0.2046
15	0.5553	0.4810	0.4173	0.3624	0.3152	0.2745	0.2394	0.1827
16	0.5339	0.4581	0.3936	0.3387	0.2919	0.2519	0.2176	0.1631
17	0.5134	0.4363	0.3714	0.3166	0.2703	0.2311	0.1978	0.1456
18	0.4936	0.4155	0.3503	0.2959	0.2502	0.2120	0.1799	0.1300
19	0.4746	0.3957	0.3305	0.2765	0.2317	0.1945	0.1635	0.1161
20	0.4564	0.3769	0.3118	0.2584	0.2145	0.1784	0.1486	0.1037
24	0.3901	0.3101	0.2470	0.1971	0.1577	0.1264	0.1015	0.0659
30	0.3083	0.2314	0.1741	0.1314	0.0994	0.0754	0.0573	0.0334
36	0.2437	0.1727	0.1227	0.0875	0.0626	0.0449	0.0323	0.0169
42	0.1926	0.1288	0.0865	0.0583	0.0395	0.0268	0.0183	0.0086
48	0.1522	0.0961	0.0610	0.0389	0.0249	0.0160	0.0103	0.0043
54	0.1203	0.0717	0.0430	0.0259	0.0157	0.0095	0.0058	0.0022
60	0.0951	0.0535	0.0303	0.0173	0.0099	0.0057	0.0033	0.0011
66	0.0751	0.0399	0.0214	0.0115	0.0062	0.0034	0.0019	*
72	0.0594	0.0298	0.0151	0.0077	0.0039	0.0020	0.0010	*
120	0.0090	0.0029	*	*	*	*	*	*
126	0.0071	0.0021	*	*	*	*	*	*
132	0.0056	0.0016	*	*	*	*	*	*
138	0.0045	0.0012	*	*	*	*	*	*
144	0.0035	*	*	*	*	*	*	*
150	0.0028	*	*	*	*	*	*	*
156	0.0022	*	*	*	*	*	*	*
162	0.0017	*	*	*	*	*	*	*
180	*	*	*	*	*	*	*	*
240	*	*	*	*	*	*	*	*
300	*	*	*	*	*	*	*	*
360	*	*	*	*	*	*	*	*

A-3: Future Value of $1 Per Period at the End of Each Period (Ordinary Annuity)

Periods	Rate per period 0.50%	0.75%	1%	1.25%	1.50%	1.75%	2%	3%
1	1.0000	1.0000	1.0000	1.0000	1.0000	1.0000	1.0000	1.0000
2	2.0050	2.0075	2.0100	2.0125	2.0150	2.0175	2.0200	2.0300
3	3.0150	3.0226	3.0301	3.0377	3.0452	3.0528	3.0604	3.0909
4	4.0301	4.0452	4.0604	4.0756	4.0909	4.1062	4.1216	4.1836
5	5.0503	5.0756	5.1010	5.1266	5.1523	5.1781	5.2040	5.3091
6	6.0755	6.1136	6.1520	6.1907	6.2296	6.2687	6.3081	6.4684
7	7.1059	7.1595	7.2135	7.2680	7.3230	7.3784	7.4343	7.6625
8	8.1414	8.2132	8.2857	8.3589	8.4328	8.5075	8.5830	8.8923
9	9.1821	9.2748	9.3685	9.4634	9.5593	9.6564	9.7546	10.1591
10	10.2280	10.3443	10.4622	10.5817	10.7027	10.8254	10.9497	11.4639
11	11.2792	11.4219	11.5668	11.7139	11.8633	12.0148	12.1687	12.8078
12	12.3356	12.5076	12.6825	12.8604	13.0412	13.2251	13.4121	14.1920
13	13.3972	13.6014	13.8093	14.0211	14.2368	14.4565	14.6803	15.6178
14	14.4642	14.7034	14.9474	15.1964	15.4504	15.7095	15.9739	17.0863
15	15.5365	15.8137	16.0969	16.3863	16.6821	16.9844	17.2934	18.5989
16	16.6142	16.9323	17.2579	17.5912	17.9324	18.2817	18.6393	20.1569
17	17.6973	18.0593	18.4304	18.8111	19.2014	19.6016	20.0121	21.7616
18	18.7858	19.1947	19.6147	20.0462	20.4894	20.9446	21.4123	23.4144
19	19.8797	20.3387	20.8109	21.2968	21.7967	22.3112	22.8406	25.1169
20	20.9791	21.4912	22.0190	22.5630	23.1237	23.7016	24.2974	26.8704
24	25.4320	26.1885	26.9735	27.7881	28.6335	29.5110	30.4219	34.4265
30	32.2800	33.5029	34.7849	36.1291	37.5387	39.0172	40.5681	47.5754
36	39.3361	41.1527	43.0769	45.1155	47.2760	49.5661	51.9944	63.2759
42	46.6065	49.1533	51.8790	54.7973	57.9231	61.2724	64.8622	82.0232
48	54.0978	57.5207	61.2226	65.2284	69.5652	74.2628	79.3535	104.4084
54	61.8167	66.2718	71.1410	76.4666	82.2952	88.6783	95.6731	131.1375
60	69.7700	75.4241	81.6697	88.5745	96.2147	104.6752	114.0515	163.0534
66	77.9650	84.9961	92.8460	101.6193	111.4348	122.4270	134.7487	201.1627
72	86.4089	95.0070	104.7099	115.6736	128.0772	142.1263	158.0570	246.6672
120	163.8793	193.5143	230.0387	275.2171	331.2882	401.0962	488.2582	*
126	174.9331	208.5010	250.3427	302.7049	368.4744	451.3661	556.1661	*
132	186.3226	224.1748	271.8959	332.3198	409.1354	507.1507	632.6415	*
138	198.0581	240.5674	294.7749	364.2264	453.5959	569.0551	718.7652	*
144	210.1502	257.7116	319.0616	398.6021	502.2109	637.7504	815.7545	*
150	222.6095	275.6419	344.8423	435.6378	555.3687	713.9819	924.9801	*
156	235.4473	294.3943	372.2091	475.5395	613.4937	798.5761	*	*
162	248.6751	314.0065	401.2594	518.5289	677.0501	892.4505	*	*
180	290.8187	378.4058	499.5802	668.5068	905.6245	*	*	*
240	462.0409	667.8869	989.25541	497.2395	*	*	*	*
300	692.9940	1121.1219	1878.8466	3243.5296	*	*	*	*
360	1004.5150	1830.7435	3494.9641	6923.2796	*	*	*	*

Rate per period

Periods	4%	5%	6%	7%	8%	9%	10%	12%
1	1.0000	1.0000	1.0000	1.0000	1.0000	1.0000	1.0000	1.0000
2	2.0400	2.0500	2.0600	2.0700	2.0800	2.0900	2.1000	2.1200
3	3.1216	3.1525	3.1836	3.2149	3.2464	3.2781	3.3100	3.3744
4	4.2465	4.3101	4.3746	4.4399	4.5061	4.5731	4.6410	4.7793
5	5.4163	5.5256	5.6371	5.7507	5.8666	5.9847	6.1051	6.3528
6	6.6330	6.8019	6.9753	7.1533	7.3359	7.5233	7.7156	8.1152
7	7.8983	8.1420	8.3938	8.6540	8.9228	9.2004	9.4872	10.0890
8	9.2142	9.5491	9.8975	10.2598	10.6366	11.0285	11.4359	12.2997
9	10.5828	11.0266	11.4913	11.9780	12.4876	13.0210	13.5795	14.7757
10	12.0061	12.5779	13.1808	13.8164	14.4866	15.1929	15.9374	17.5487
11	13.4864	14.2068	14.9716	15.7836	16.6455	17.5603	18.5312	20.6546
12	15.0258	15.9171	16.8699	17.8885	18.9771	20.1407	21.3843	24.1331
13	16.6268	17.7130	18.8821	20.1406	21.4953	22.9534	24.5227	28.0291
14	18.2919	19.5986	21.0151	22.5505	24.2149	26.0192	27.9750	32.3926
15	20.0236	21.5786	23.2760	25.1290	27.1521	29.3609	31.7725	37.2797
16	21.8245	23.6575	25.6725	27.8881	30.3243	33.0034	35.9497	42.7533
17	23.6975	25.8404	28.2129	30.8402	33.7502	36.9737	40.5447	48.8837
18	25.6454	28.1324	30.9057	33.9990	37.4502	41.3013	45.5992	55.7497
19	27.6712	30.5390	33.7600	37.3790	41.4463	46.0185	51.1591	63.4397
20	29.7781	33.0660	36.7856	40.9955	45.7620	51.1601	57.2750	72.0524
24	39.0826	44.5020	50.8156	58.1767	66.7648	76.7898	88.4973	118.1552
30	56.0849	66.4388	79.0582	94.4608	113.2832	136.3075	164.4940	241.3327
36	77.5983	95.8363	119.1209	148.9135	187.1021	236.1247	299.1268	484.4631
42	104.8196	135.2318	175.9505	230.6322	304.2435	403.5281	537.6370	964.3595
48	139.2632	188.0254	256.5645	353.2701	490.1322	684.2804	960.1723	*
54	182.8454	258.7739	370.9170	537.3164	785.1141	*	*	*
60	237.9907	353.5837	533.1282	813.5204	*	*	*	*
66	307.7671	480.6379	763.2278	*	*	*	*	*
72	396.0566	650.9027	*	*	*	*	*	*
120	*	*	*	*	*	*	*	*
126	*	*	*	*	*	*	*	*
132	*	*	*	*	*	*	*	*
138	*	*	*	*	*	*	*	*
144	*	*	*	*	*	*	*	*
150	*	*	*	*	*	*	*	*
156	*	*	*	*	*	*	*	*
162	*	*	*	*	*	*	*	*
180	*	*	*	*	*	*	*	*
240	*	*	*	*	*	*	*	*
300	*	*	*	*	*	*	*	*
360	*	*	*	*	*	*	*	*

A-4: Present Value of $1 Per Period at the End of Each Period (Ordinary Annuity)

Periods	Rate per period 0.50%	0.75%	1%	1.25%	1.50%	1.75%	2%	3%
1	0.9950	0.9926	0.9901	0.9877	0.9852	0.9828	0.9804	0.9709
2	1.9851	1.9777	1.9704	1.9631	1.9559	1.9487	1.9416	1.9135
3	2.9702	2.9556	2.9410	2.9265	2.9122	2.8980	2.8839	2.8286
4	3.9505	3.9261	3.9020	3.8781	3.8544	3.8309	3.8077	3.7171
5	4.9259	4.8894	4.8534	4.8178	4.7826	4.7479	4.7135	4.5797
6	5.8964	5.8456	5.7955	5.7460	5.6972	5.6490	5.6014	5.4172
7	6.8621	6.7946	6.7282	6.6627	6.5982	6.5346	6.4720	6.2303
8	7.8230	7.7366	7.6517	7.5681	7.4859	7.4051	7.3255	7.0197
9	8.7791	8.6716	8.5660	8.4623	8.3605	8.2605	8.1622	7.7861
10	9.7304	9.5996	9.4713	9.3455	9.2222	9.1012	8.9826	8.5302
11	10.6770	10.5207	10.3676	10.2178	10.0711	9.9275	9.7868	9.2526
12	11.6189	11.4349	11.2551	11.0793	10.9075	10.7395	10.5753	9.9540
13	12.5562	12.3423	12.1337	11.9302	11.7315	11.5376	11.3484	10.6350
14	13.4887	13.2430	13.0037	12.7706	12.5434	12.3220	12.1062	11.2961
15	14.4166	14.1370	13.8651	13.6005	13.3432	13.0929	12.8493	11.9379
16	15.3399	15.0243	14.7179	14.4203	14.1313	13.8505	13.5777	12.5611
17	16.2586	15.9050	15.5623	15.2299	14.9076	14.5951	14.2919	13.1661
18	17.1728	16.7792	16.3983	16.0295	15.6726	15.3269	14.9920	13.7535
19	18.0824	17.6468	17.2260	16.8193	16.4262	16.0461	15.6785	14.3238
20	18.9874	18.5080	18.0456	17.5993	17.1686	16.7529	16.3514	14.8775
24	22.5629	21.8891	21.2434	20.6242	20.0304	19.4607	18.9139	16.9355
30	27.7941	26.7751	25.8077	24.8889	24.0158	23.1858	22.3965	19.6004
36	32.8710	31.4468	30.1075	28.8473	27.6607	26.5428	25.4888	21.8323
42	37.7983	35.9137	34.1581	32.5213	30.9941	29.5678	28.2348	23.7014
48	42.5803	40.1848	37.9740	35.9315	34.0426	32.2938	30.6731	25.2667
54	47.2214	44.2686	41.5687	39.0967	36.8305	34.7503	32.8383	26.5777
60	51.7256	48.1734	44.9550	42.0346	39.3803	36.9640	34.7609	27.6756
66	56.0970	51.9070	48.1452	44.7615	41.7121	38.9588	36.4681	28.5950
72	60.3395	55.4768	51.1504	47.2925	43.8447	40.7564	37.9841	29.3651
120	90.0735	78.9417	69.7005	61.9828	55.4985	50.0171	45.3554	32.3730
126	93.3143	81.3263	71.4565	63.2769	56.4529	50.7215	45.8757	32.5291
132	96.4596	83.6064	73.1108	64.4781	57.3257	51.3563	46.3378	32.6598
138	99.5122	85.7865	74.6691	65.5929	58.1240	51.9284	46.7480	32.7693
144	102.4747	87.871	176.1372	66.6277	58.8540	52.4439	47.1123	32.8609
150	105.3500	89.864	277.5201	67.5882	59.5217	52.9084	47.4358	32.9377
156	108.1404	91.7700	78.8229	68.4797	60.1323	53.3270	47.7231	33.0020
162	110.8486	93.5922	80.0503	69.3071	60.6907	53.7042	47.9782	33.0558
180	118.5035	98.5934	83.3217	71.4496	62.0956	54.6265	48.5844	33.1703
240	139.5808	111.1450	90.8194	75.9423	64.7957	56.2543	49.5686	33.3057
300	155.2069	119.1616	94.9466	78.0743	65.9009	56.8291	49.8685	33.3286
360	166.7916	124.2819	97.2183	79.0861	66.3532	57.0320	49.9599	33.3325

Periods	Rate per period							
	4%	5%	6%	7%	8%	9%	10%	12%
1	0.9615	0.9524	0.9434	0.9346	0.9259	0.9174	0.9091	0.8929
2	1.8861	1.8594	1.8334	1.8080	1.7833	1.7591	1.7355	1.6901
3	2.7751	2.7232	2.6730	2.6243	2.5771	2.5313	2.4869	2.4018
4	3.6299	3.5460	3.4651	3.3872	3.3121	3.2397	3.1699	3.0373
5	4.4518	4.3295	4.2124	4.1002	3.9927	3.8897	3.7908	3.6048
6	5.2421	5.0757	4.9173	4.7665	4.6229	4.4859	4.3553	4.1114
7	6.0021	5.7864	5.5824	5.3893	5.2064	5.0330	4.8684	4.5638
8	6.7327	6.4632	6.2098	5.9713	5.7466	5.5348	5.3349	4.9676
9	7.4353	7.1078	6.8017	6.5152	6.2469	5.9952	5.7590	5.3282
10	8.1109	7.7217	7.3601	7.0236	6.7101	6.4177	6.1446	5.6502
11	8.7605	8.3064	7.8869	7.4987	7.1390	6.8052	6.4951	5.9377
12	9.3851	8.8633	8.3838	7.9427	7.5361	7.1607	6.8137	6.1944
13	9.9856	9.3936	8.8527	8.3577	7.9038	7.4869	7.1034	6.4235
14	10.563	19.8986	9.2950	8.7455	8.2442	7.7862	7.3667	6.6282
15	11.1184	10.3797	9.7122	9.1079	8.5595	8.0607	7.6061	6.8109
16	11.6523	10.8378	10.1059	9.4466	8.8514	8.3126	7.8237	6.9740
17	12.1657	11.2741	10.4773	9.7632	9.1216	8.5436	8.0216	7.1196
18	12.6593	11.6896	10.8276	10.0591	9.3719	8.7556	8.2014	7.2497
19	13.1339	12.0853	11.1581	10.3356	9.6036	8.9501	8.3649	7.3658
20	13.5903	12.4622	11.4699	10.5940	9.8181	9.1285	8.5136	7.4694
24	15.2470	13.7986	12.5504	11.4693	10.5288	9.7066	8.9847	7.7843
30	17.2920	15.3725	13.7648	12.4090	11.2578	10.2737	9.4269	8.0552
36	18.9083	16.5469	14.6210	13.0352	11.7172	10.6118	9.6765	8.1924
42	20.1856	17.4232	15.2245	13.4524	12.0067	10.8134	9.8174	8.2619
48	21.1951	18.0772	15.6500	13.7305	12.1891	10.9336	9.8969	8.2972
54	21.9930	18.5651	15.9500	13.9157	12.3041	11.0053	9.9418	8.3150
60	22.6235	18.9293	16.1614	14.0392	12.3766	11.0480	9.9672	8.3240
66	23.1218	19.2010	16.3105	14.1214	12.4222	11.0735	9.9815	8.3286
72	23.5156	19.4038	16.4156	14.1763	12.4510	11.0887	9.9895	8.3310
120	24.7741	19.9427	16.6514	14.2815	12.4988	11.1108	9.9999	*
126	24.8215	19.9572	16.6559	14.2829	12.4992	11.1109	*	*
132	24.8589	19.9681	16.6591	14.2838	12.4995	*	*	*
138	24.8885	19.9762	16.6613	14.2845	*	*	*	*
144	24.9119	19.9822	16.6629	14.2849	*	*	*	*
150	24.9303	19.9867	16.6640	*	*	*	*	*
156	24.9450	19.9901	16.6648	*	*	*	*	*
162	24.9565	19.9926	16.6653	*	*	*	*	*
180	24.9785	19.9969	*	*	*	*	*	*
240	24.9980	19.9998	*	*	*	*	*	*
300	24.9998	*	*	*	*	*	*	*
360	25.0000	*	*	*	*	*	*	*

Bibliography

Chapter 1 Time Value of Money

Garrison, Sharon. *The Time Value of Money*. Retrieved November 7, 2009, from www.studyfinance.com/lessons/timevalue/index.mv

Thismatter.com. "The Present Value and Future Value of an Annuity; Annuity Due, Ordinary Annuity; Time Value, with Formulas and Examples; Discount Rate." *All about Money: Credit and Debt, Bonds, Stocks, Options, Futures, Mutual Funds, Foreign Exchange, Real Estate, Taxes, Saving, Shopping, and more!* Retrieved September 28, 2009, from http://thismatter.com/money/investments/present-value-future-value-of-annuity.htm

Chapter 2 A Financial Planning Overview

CNNMoney.com. *Money 101 - Financial Advice & Lessons Made Easy*. Retrieved September 28, 2009, from http://money.cnn.com/magazines/moneymag/money101/index.html

Consumer Credit Counseling and Debt Consolidation Services. *Informative Articles on How to Budget*. Retrieved September 28, 2009, from www.consumercredit.com/budget-sheet.htm

Financial Planning Association. *Information & Resources for Financial Planners*. Retrieved September 28, 2009, from www.fpanet.org

U.S. Financial Literacy & Education Commission. "Mymoney.gov." Retrieved September 28, 2009, from www.mymoney.gov

Chapter 3 Housing

FHA. *FHA Home Loans*. Retrieved September 28, 2009, from www.myfhahomeloan.com

HomeClosing101.org. "HomeClosing101.org–Closing Costs Explained." In–*Protecting Your American Dream*. Retrieved September 28, 2009, from www.homeclosing101.org/costs.cfm

Home & Garden Television. "Home Buying: Real Estate: HGTV." In–*Decorating, Home Improvement, Landscaping Ideas, Kitchen and Bathroom Design*. Retrieved September 28, 2009, from www.hgtv.com/topics/home-buying/index.html

KC Home Programs. *Program Search Results*. Retrieved September 28, 2009, from www.kchomeprograms.com/program/all_programs.php?op=all

U.S. Department of Agriculture. "Individual and Family Opportunities." *USDA Rural Development Home Page*. Retrieved September 28, 2009, from www.rurdev.usda.gov/rhs/common/indiv_intro.htm#Guaranteed%20Loan%20Program%20(Section

U.S. Department of Housing and Urban Development. *American Dream Downpayment Initiative–Affordable Housing–CPD–HUD.* Retrieved September 28, 2009, from www.hud.gov/offices/cpd/affordablehousing/programs/home/addi

U.S. Department of Housing and Urban Development. *RESPA–Real Estate Settlement Procedures Act Home Page–HUD.* Retrieved September 28, 2009, from www.hud.gov/offices/hsg/ramh/res/respa_hm.cfm

U.S. Department of Justice. "Civil Rights Division Home Page." Retrieved September 28, 2009, from www.usdoj.gov/crt/housing/title8.php

Chapter 4 Manage Your Credit

Consumer Federation of America. *Consumer Federation of America.* Retrieved September 28, 2009, from www.consumerfed.org

"Credit Crisis." *The New York Times.* Retrieved September 28, 2009, from www.topics.nytimes.com/top/reference/timestopics/subjects/c/credit_crisis/index.html

Dash, Eric, and Vikas Bajaj. "Credit, and Trust, Needed to End Financial Crisis." *The New York Times–Breaking News, World News & Multimedia.* Retrieved September 28, 2009, from www.nytimes.com/2009/01/01/business/worldbusiness/01iht-lend.4.19036820.html?_r=1

Federal Deposit Insurance Corporation. *FDIC Law, Regulations, Related Acts–Consumer Protection.* Retrieved September 28, 2009, from www.fdic.gov/regulations/laws/rules/6500-200.html

Federal Trade Commission. *Debt Collection FAQs: A Guide for Consumers.* Retrieved September 28, 2009, from www.ftc.gov/bcp/edu/pubs/consumer/credit/cre18.shtm

myFICO.com. *How Your FICO ® Credit Score Is Calculated.* Retrieved September 28, 2009, from www.myfico.com/crediteducation/WhatsInYourScore.aspx

Wikipedia. *Subprime Mortgage Crisis.* Retrieved September 28, 2009, from http://en.wikipedia.org/wiki/Subprime_mortgage_crisis

Chapter 5 Spending Wisely

Board of Governors of the Federal Reserve System. *Publications.* Retrieved September 28, 2009, from www.federalreserve.gov/publications/default.htm

Board of Governors of the Federal Reserve System. *Vehicle Leasing: Quick Consumer Guide.* Retrieved September 28, 2009, from www.federalreserve.gov/pubs/leasing/default.htm

The Digital TV Transition. *What You Need to Know About DTV.* Retrieved September 28, 2009, from www.dtv.gov

Federal Trade Commission. *Buying a New Car.* Retrieved September 28, 2009, from www.ftc.gov/bcp/edu/pubs/consumer/autos/aut11.shtm

Federal Trade Commission. *Energy Guide: Appliance Shopping and Using the Energy Guide Label.* Retrieved September 28, 2009, from www.ftc.gov/bcp/edu/pubs/consumer/homes/rea14.shtm

Federal Trade Commission. *Warranties.* Retrieved September 28, 2009, from www.ftc.gov/bcp/edu/pubs/consumer/products/pro17.shtm

High Speed Internet Deals: Learn and Compare. *Wireless High Speed Internet Service.* Retrieved September 28, 2009, from www.highspeedinternetdeals.com/wireless-broadband.html

MDCIS. *Study of Broadband in Michigan.* Retrieved September 28, 2009, from www.dleg.state.mi.us/mpsc/comm/broadband/start.htm

U.S. Food and Drug Administration. *How to Understand and Use the Nutrition Facts Label.* Retrieved September 28, 2009, from www.fda.gov/Food/LabelingNutrition/ConsumerInformation/ucm078889.htm

Chapter 6 Tax Planning

CATO Institute. *Follow the Math.* Retrieved September 28, 2009, from www.socialsecurity.org/pubs/articles/tanner-050114.html

Internal Revenue Service. *Education-Related Tax Changes.* Retrieved September 28, 2009, from www.irs.gov/formspubs/content/0,,id=178787,00.html

Internal Revenue Service. *Forms and Publications.* Retrieved September 28, 2009, from www.irs.gov/formspubs/index.html

Internal Revenue Service. *Home/Residence-Related Tax Changes.* Retrieved September 28, 2009, from www.irs.gov/formspubs/content/ 0,,id= 178791,00.html

Social Security Online. *Actuarial Publications.* Retrieved September 28, 2009, from www.socialsecurity.gov/OACT/solvency/provisions/wagebase.html

Social Security Online. *Contribution and Benefit Base.* Retrieved September 28, 2009, from www.socialsecurity.gov/OACT/COLA/cbb.html#Series

Spriggs, William E., and Price, Lee. "Productivity Growth and Social Security's Future." *Economic Policy Institute.* Retrieved September 28, 2009, from www.epi.org/publications/entry/ib208

White House. "*Budget 2009–Summary Tables.*" Office of Management and Budget. Retrieved September 28, 2009, from www.whitehouse.gov/omb/rewrite/budget/fy2009/summarytables.html

Chapter 7 Property and Casualty Insurance

Insurance Information Institute. *Catastrophes: Global.* Retrieved September 28, 2009, from www.iii.org/media/facts/statsbyissue/catastrophesglobal

Insurance Information Institute. *Compulsory Auto Uninsured Motorists.* Retrieved September 28, 2009, from www.iii.org/IU/Compulsory-Auto-Uninsured-Motorists

Insurance Information Institute. *Property/Casualty Financial Data.* Retrieved September 28, 2009, from www.iii.org/policymakers/pcfin/#

U.S. Department of Labor, Census Bureau. *The 2009 Statistical Abstract: Finance and Insurance Industries.* Retrieved September 28, 2009, from www.census.gov/compendia/statab/cats/banking_finance_insurance/finance_and_insurance_industries.html

Chapter 8 Health and Disability Insurance

American Medical Student Assoication. *Universal Health Care PowerPoint Presentations.* Retrieved September 28, 2009, from www.amsa.org/uhc/presentations.cfm

Citizen Wells. *Obama Health Care, ObamaCare, Hidden Truth*, YouTube video (Nancy Pelosi, shutting out public, abuse of power), August 1, 2009. Retrieved September 28, 2009, from http://citizenwells.wordpress.com/2009/08/01/obama-health-care-obamacare-hidden-truth-youtube-video-nancy-pelosi-shutting-out-public-abuse-of-power

Council for Disability Awareness. *2008 CDA Long-Term Disability Claims Review.* Retrieved September 28, 2009, from www.disabilitycanhappen.org/surveys/CDA_LTD_Claims_Survey_2008.asp

Crawford, Steve. *About Disability Insurance.* Retrieved September 28, 2009, from www.about-disability-insurance.com

Dingell, Rangel, Waxman, and George Miller. *America's Affordable Health Care Act, 2009.* 111th Congress 1st Session H.R. (Healthcare Reform) (July 14, 2009). Retrieved September 28, 2009, from http://docs.house.gov/edlabor/AAHCA-BillText-071409.pdf

Fletcher, Michael A., and Shailagh Murray. "Senators Explore Alternatives to Government-Run Plan on Health Care." washingtonpost.com, June 12, 2009. Retrieved September 28, 2009, from www.washingtonpost.com/wp-dyn/content/article/2009/06/11/AR2009061104257.html

Freeman, Mark. "Obama's Healthcare Plan Needs to Be Rethought–Opinion." *Collegian.* (September 22, 2009). Retrieved September 28, 2009, from http://media.www.smccollegian.com/media/storage/paper841/news/2009/09/22/Opinion/Obamas.Healthcare.Plan.Needs.To.Be.Rethought-3779820.shtml#4

House Committees on Ways and Means, Energy and Commerce, and Education and Labor. *America's Affordable Health Care Choice Act.* (June 14, 2009). Retrieved September 28, 2009, from http://waysandmeans.house.gov/media/pdf/111/exchange.pdf

Hilzenrath, David. "Health-Care Reform–What It Means for You." washingtonpost.com, July 6, 2009. Retrieved September 28, 2009, from www.washingtonpost.com/wp-srv/package/health-care-reform09/what-it-means-for-you/health-care-reform-2009.html

The Henry J. Kaiser Foundation. *How Private Health Coverage Works, A Primer 2008 Update.* Retrieved September 28, 2009, from www.kff.org/insurance/upload/7766.pdf

Internal Revenue Service. *Publication 969 (2008), Health Savings Accounts and Other Tax-Favored Health Plans.* Retrieved September 28, 2009, from www.irs.gov/publications/p969/ar02.html

Klein, Ezra. " Health Insurance Exchanges: The Most Important, Undernoticed Part of Health Reform." Blog Directory, washingtonpost.com, June 16, 2009. Retrieved September 28, 2009, from http://voices.washingtonpost .com/ezra-klein/2009/06/health_insurance_exchanges_the.html

Lee, Christopher. "Rise in Cost of Employer-Paid Health Insurance Slows. washingtonpost.com, September 12, 2007. Retrieved September 28, 2009, from www.washingtonpost.com/wp-dyn/content/article/ 2007/09/11/AR2007091100666.html

Lucas, Fred. "Republicans Offer Alternative to Obama Health Care Plan." CNSNews.com, May 28, 2009. Retrieved September 28, 2009, from www.cnsnews.com/news/article/48709

Medical Expenditure Panel Survey. *Medical Expenditure Panel Survey Insurance Component National-Level Summary Tables Search.* Retrieved September 28, 2009, from www.meps.ahrq.gov/mepsweb/ data_stats/quick_tables_search.jsp?component=2&subcomponent=1&ty ear=2002&tableSeries=1&tableSubSeries=CDE&searchText=& searchMethod=1

Moffit, Robert E. "The Rationale for a Statewide Health Insurance Exchange." The Heritage Foundation, October 5, 2006. Retrieved September 28, 2009, fromwww.heritage.org/research/healthcare/wm1230.cfm

NCHC. *Facts About Healthcare–Health Insurance Costs.* Retrieved September 28, 2009, from www.nchc.org/facts/cost.shtml

O'Reilly, Bill. "Health Care Alternative." Talking Points, Fox News. Retrieved September 28, 2009, from www.facebook.com/video/video.php?v= 1170447573904

Silva, Chris. "AMNews: Aug. 10, 2009. Debate Flares over What 'Essential' Benefits Include." American Medical Association, August 10, 2009. Retrieved September 28, 2009, from www.ama-assn.org/amednews/ 2009/08/10/gvsb0810.htm

Social Security Online. *Disability Planner: What We Mean by Disability.* Retrieved September 28, 2009, from www.ssa.gov/dibplan/dqualify4.htm

Tully, Shawn. "You'll Lose 5 Key Freedoms under Obama's Health Care Plan." CNNMoney.com, July 24, 2009. Retrieved September 28, 2009, from http://money.cnn.com/2009/07/24/news/economy/health_care_reform _obama.fortune

U.S. Department of Labor. *COBRA Continuation Coverage Assistance Under the American Recovery and Reinvestment Act of 2009.* Retrieved September 28, 2009, from www.dol.gov/ebsa/COBRA.html

U.S. Department of the Treasury. *hp-975: Treasury, IRS Issue 2009 Indexed Amounts for Health Savings Accounts,* March 13, 2008. Retrieved September 28, 2009, from www.treas.gov/press/releases/ hp975.htm

U.S. Office of Personnel Management. *"High Deductible Health Plans (HDHP) with Health Savings Accounts (HSA)."* Retrieved September 28, 2009, from www.opm.gov/insure/health/hsa/hsa.asp

Chapter 9 Life Insurance

Baldwin, Ben G. *The New Life Insurance Investment Advisor: Achieving Financial Security for You and your Family Through Today's Insurance Products.* New York: McGraw-Hill, 2002.

Insurance Information Institute. *Life* Insurance. Retrieved November 7, 2009, from www.iii.org/individuals/LifeInsurance

Kelly, Ed. 2008. *Life Insurance for the American Family: Most of What You Know About Life Insurance Is Wrong.* Retrieved November 7, 2009, from IUniverse.com

Leimberg, Stephan J., and Robert J. Doyle, Jr. *Tools and Techniques of Life Insurance Planning*, 4th ed. Cincinnati: National Underwriter Co., 2007.

Chapter 10 Entrepreneurship

ALMIS. *State Projections.* Retrieved September 28, 2009, from www.projectionscentral.com

Berry, Tim. "Business Plan Samples, Writing a Business Plan." *Business & Small Business.* Retrieved September 28, 2009, from www.entrepreneur.com/businessplan/index.html

Entrepreneur.com. *Business & Small Business.* Retrieved September 28, 2009, from www.entrepreneur.com

Find a Sponsor. *Athletic Sponsorship.* Retrieved September 28, 2009, from http://findasponsor.com/athletic-sponsorship.html

LiveCareer."Free Online Career Assessment, Counseling & Development Test Center, Help to Find a Career" Career Test–Aptitude Test–Career Aptitude Test–Career Tests–Career Quiz. Retrieved September 28, 2009, from www.livecareer.com/default.asp?lp=st03&cobrand=CLEAR#

Love, Joe. *The Entrepreneurial Spirit.* Retrieved September 28, 2009, from http://ezinearticles.com/?The-Entrepreneurial-Spirit&id= 86369&opt =print

Small Business Administration. *Office Locator.* Retrieved September 28, 2009, from www.sba.gov/aboutsba/sbaprograms/sbdc/sbdclocator/index.html

Strauss, Steve. "Counselors to America's Small Business." *SCORE.* Retrieved September 28, 2009, from www.score.org/index.html

U.S. Chamber of Commerce. *U.S. Chamber of Commerce Small Business Center.* Retrieved September 28, 2009, from www.uschamber.com/sb/default

U.S. Bureau of Labor Statistics. *Occupational Outlook Handbook, 2008–09 Edition.* Retrieved September 28, 2009, from www.bls.gov/OCO

U.S. Bureau of Labor Statistics. *Tomorrow's Jobs.* Retrieved September 28, 2009, from www.bls.gov/oco/oco2003.htm

Chapter 11 Investing

Doroghazi, Robert M. *The Physician's Guide to Investing*, 2nd ed. Totowa, NJ: Humana Press, 2009.

Foundation for Investor Education. *ABCs of Investing.* Retrieved November 7, 2009, from http://www.pathtoinvesting.org/invbasics/abc/abcs_index.htm

Morris, Virginia, and Kenneth Morris. *Standard & Poor's Guide to Money and Investing.* New York: Lightbulb Press, 2005.

U.S. Financial Literacy and Education Commission. *Saving and Investing.* Retrieved November 7, 2009, from http://www.mymoney.gov/saving.shtml

U.S. Securities and Exchange Commission. *Publications for Investors.* Retrieved November 7, 2009, from www.sec.gov/investor/pubs.shtml

Chapters 12 and 13 Stocks and Bonds

American Association of Individual Investors. *Investing Basics: Successful Investing for Beginning (and Advanced) Investors.* Retrieved November 7, 2009, from http://aaii.com/basics

Brandes, Charles H. *Value Investing*, 2nd ed. New York: McGraw-Hill, 1998.

Dorsey, Pat, and Joe Mansueto. *The Five Rules for Successful Stock Investing: Morningstar's Guide to Building Wealth and Winning in the Market.* Hoboken, NJ: John Wiley & Sons, 2004.

Faerber, Esmé. *All About Bonds, Bond Mutual Funds, and Bond ETFs: The Easy Way to Get Started*, 3rd ed. New York: McGraw-Hill, 2009.

Greenwald, Bruce C. N., Judd Kahn, Paul D. Sonkin, and Michael van Biema. *Value Investing: From Graham to Buffett and Beyond.* Hoboken, NJ: John Wiley & Sons, 2004.

Kelly, Jason. *The Neatest Little Guide to Stock Market Investing.* New York: Plume, 2009.

Thau, Annette. *The Bond Book: Everything Investors Need to Know About Treasuries, Municipals, GNMAs, Corporates, Zeros, Bond Funds, Money Market Funds, and More.* New York: McGraw-Hill, 2001.

Chapter 14 Mutual Funds

Benz, Christine. *Morningstar Guide to Mutual Funds: Five-Star Strategies for Success*, 2nd ed. Hoboken, NJ: John Wiley & Sons, 2007.

Bogle, John C. *Common Sense on Mutual Funds.* Fully Updated 10th Anniversary Edition. Hoboken, NJ: John Wiley & Sons, 2009.

FINRA. "Avoid Investment Fraud." Retrieved November 7, 2009, from http://www.finra.org/Investors/ProtectYourself/AvoidInvestmentFraud

Investment Company Institute. *Investor Education.* Retrieved November 7, 2009, from http://www.ici.org/#investor_education

Trivoli, George W. *Personal Portfolio Management.* Upper Saddle River, NJ: Prentice-Hall, 2000.

Chapter 15 Real Estate

Block, Ralph L. *Investing in REITs: Real Estate Investment Trusts*, 3rd ed. New York: Bloomberg Press, 2006.

Fisher, Steven D. *The Real Estate Investor's Handbook: The Complete Guide for the Individual Investor.* Ocala, FL: Atlantic Publishing Group, 2006.

Jacobus, Charles J. *Real Estate Principles.* Florence, KY: South-Western Educational Publishing, 2009.

National Association of Real Estate Investment Trusts. "Guide to REIT Investing." Retrieved November 7, 2009, from http://www.reit.com/IndividualInvestors/GuidetoREITInvesting/tabid/109/Default.aspx.com

Chapter 16 Retirement Planning

Carlson, Robert C. *The New Rules of Retirement: Strategies for a Secure Future.* Hoboken, NJ: John Wiley & Sons, 2005.

Lange, James. *Retire Secure!: Pay Taxes Later–The Key to Making Your Money Last*, 2nd ed. Hoboken, NJ: John Wiley & Sons, 2009.

Slesnick, Twila, and John Suttle. *IRAs, 401(k)s & Other Retirement Plans: Taking Your Money Out.* Berkeley, CA: Nolo, 2009.

U.S. Financial Literacy and Education Commission. "Retirement Planning." Retrieved November 7, 2009, from http://www.mymoney.gov/retirement.shtml.

U.S. Internal Revenue Service. "Retirement and Savings Initiatives." Retrieved November 7, 2009, from http://www.irs.gov/retirement/article/0,,id=212061,00.html

U.S. Social Security Administration. www.ssa.gov

Chapter 17 Estate Planning

Clifford, Denis. *Plan Your Estate: Protect Your Loved Ones, Property & Finances*, 9th ed. Berkeley, CA: Nolo, 2008.

Cullen, Melanie, and Shae Irving. *Get It Together: Organize Your Records So Your Family Won't Have To*, 3rd ed. Berkeley, CA: Nolo, 2008.

National Association of Estate Planners and Councils. *Plan Your Estate, or the State Will Do It For You.* Retrieved November 7, 2009, from http://www.naepc.org/doc_13.web

Randolph, Mary. *Executor's Guide: Settling a Loved One's Estate or Trust*, 3rd ed. Berkeley, CA: Nolo, 2008.

Ventura, John. *Kiplinger's Estate Planning: The Complete Guide to Wills, Trusts, and Maximizing Your Legacy.* New York: Kaplan Publishing, 2008.

Glossary

12b-1 fee Fee paid by some mutual funds to cover fund selling expenses.

401(k) plan The most popular defined contribution plan, allows employees to contribute up to $15,000 pretax and may also allow employer matching of contributions.

403(b) plan A defined contribution plan that is very similar to a 401(k) plan but is offered by nonprofit organizations.

Accidental death life insurance A special form of term life insurance in which the beneficiary receives payment only if the insured's death was the result of an accident.

Actual cash value Insurance coverage that pays the cost of replacing a loss less any depreciation.

Adjustable rate mortgage (ARM) A mortgage with an initial fixed rate for 3, 5 or 7 years which adjust annually after the initial period. The new interest rate is calculated based on the index, the lenders margin, and the caps associated with the loan.

Adjusted gross income (AGI) The amount of income that you have after taking into account any applicable adjustments on the first page of the 1040 form.

ADR (American Depositary Receipt) Receipt for stock of a company in a foreign country.

Aggressive stock Stock with a beta greater than 1.0.

Annuity A series of periodic payments.

Annuity due An annuity in which payments are at the beginning of each period.

Any-occupation disabled Under this policy you will not be considered totally disabled if you can work in another occupation.

Appraisal Estimate of the value of an asset based on a market and financial evaluation.

Ask price Price for which active sellers offer to sell a stock.

Asset allocation decision The decision of which mix of broad classes of investments will meet needs for return and risk.

Assets Everything you own with value.

Automobile insurance Protects the policyholder in the event that his or her vehicle is damaged or he or she is in an accident that damages another car.

Balance sheet Lists your assets and liabilities on a specific date.

Basis The amount you paid for a security; used in the capital gain calculation.

Bear market Period when market prices fall.

Beneficiary The person or organization designated to receive the death benefit of a life insurance policy.

Beta Measure of risk relative to the market.

Bid price Price for which buyers are actively offering to buy a stock.

Blend investing strategy Strategy combining both value and growth investing.

Bond A security representing debt of the issuer; debt security that pays interest periodically and returns the principal at maturity.

Bond rating Ranking that measures a bond's default risk.

Bonds Issued debt from a government or company.

Book value Assets less liabilities behind each share of stock.

Brands Indicate who the product was manufactured by or for.

Budget method A method of calculating how much life insurance coverage a person needs by taking into account expected future income and expenses.

Bull market Period when market prices rise.

Business risk Variation in a firm's value due to the firm's product.

Capital gain Whenever you sell an asset for more than you paid for it, a tax is owed on this gain.

Captive finance company A finance company owned by a parent company. The purpose of the finance company is to provide financing to customers of the parent company for purchase of the parent company's products or services.

Car leasing When you lease a car you agree to pay for the value of the vehicle used during the lease.

Career test Tests that ask you a series of questions about your preferences between specific tasks. They use your interests to suggest appropriate careers that would utilize those interests.

Cash Funds available immediately.

Cash dividend Corporation's cash payment to shareholders.

Cash equivalent Investment that is available immediately like cash but also yields interest.

Cash flow statement Lists your income and expenses.

Certificate of deposit (CD) A savings instrument issued through a financial institution. It is issued for a specified amount of time, typically 90 days to five years.

Chronological resume Lists your information from most recent to the oldest.

Claim The official process of notifying the insurance company you have suffered a loss.

Closed-end credit A loan for a specific amount that must be paid back on or before an agreed upon date.

Closed-end fund Investment company with a fixed number of shares outstanding.

Closing costs Unsettled costs associated with the loan and title transfer of the property. These are paid when the final documents are signed.

COBRA Act of 1986 Requires companies to allow employees to continue in a company-sponsored health insurance plan for 18 months to three years after leaving the company.

Codicil An addition to an existing will.

Co-insurance The percent of cost sharing between the policy holder and the insurance company.

Collateral An item of value used to secure a loan. The lender has the right to repossess collateral if the borrower fails to pay the loan back.

Collision insurance A type of automobile insurance that provides compensation if the covered vehicle is involved in a collision.

Commercial bank A financial institution that accepts deposits and makes loans.

Commercial paper Money market security issued by corporations.

Commission-based investment advisor Advisor compensated by commissions from the investments sold to clients.

Common stock Share of ownership in a corporation.

Compound interest Interest computed in the second period is interest on the original principal plus interest on the previous interest.

Comprehensive insurance A type of automobile insurance that provides compensation in case of losses stemming from non-collision events such as weather, theft, or vandalism.

Conservative stock Stock with a beta less than 1.0.

Contingent beneficiary A person who receives policy benefits if the primary beneficiary is not able to receive benefits.

Contingent deferred sales charge Load charged when investor redeems fund shares held for less than a specified period of time.

Convertible bond Bond that is exchangeable into stock.

Convertible policy Provision that allows a term life insurance policy to be converted into some kind of whole life plan.

Co-payment A payment the policyholder makes for each medical service received.

Corporate bonds Corporations' debt issues with maturities greater than 1 year.

Corporate sponsorship Business arrangement where an athlete receives funds and the business receives advertisement.

Coupon rate The rate of interest that the bond pays each year based on the face value

Cover letter A resume's introduction; it states which position you wish to apply for, tells how you fit the position, and asks for an interview.

Coverdell IRA An IRA that can be used to pay for your children's educational expenses.

Credit A contract that allows the borrower to accept something of value with the promise to pay the lender back later.

Credit union A financial institution that is owned by its members. Members finance the credit union by making deposits, and the credit union extends loans to its members.

Current liabilities Debts you expect to pay off within the next year.

Current yield Bond annual interest divided by its market price.

Day order Order to trade that remains active until the end of the trading day.

Debenture Unsecured bond with no pledged collateral.

Debt-to-income ratio Total monthly debt payments divided by gross monthly income.

Decreasing term policy A term insurance policy in which coverage decreases.

Deductible The amount of money the policyholder pays for a loss before the insurance coverage takes over.

Default Condition occurring when a company fails to pay interest on its debt.

Defined benefit plan A retirement plan from an employer that promises a certain amount of income upon retirement.

Defined contribution plan A retirement plan in which the employer and/or employee makes contributions to some kind of investment account that the employee can then withdraw upon reaching retirement age.

Dental insurance Covers expenses such as dental checkups, miscellaneous dental work, or orthodontics.

Dependent Normally applied to children or family members for which a taxpayer is providing at least half of the living expenses.

Depositary financial institution Raises funds by accepting deposits from customers.

Depreciation Deduction from income to represent the decline in value of an asset as a result of normal wear and tear.

Dial-up An internet service provider. Your computer literally places a call or dials up a local server.

Disability income insurance An insurance policy that provides income to an individual in the event that he or she becomes disabled.

Diversification Combining a number of investments into a portfolio.

Dividend Income received from companies or mutual funds that you have invested in.

DSL (Digital subscriber line) Like dial up requires the use of a phone line, but unlike dial up DSL allows the consumer to use both their phone and connect to the internet at the same time.

Durable power of attorney for health care A legal document that allows another person to make health care decisions for the grantor of the power of attorney should the grantor become incapacitated.

Elimination period A waiting period that is the length of time from the original disability-causing event to the time when the policy begins to make payments.

Employee Retirement Income Security Act (ERISA) Federal law that sets minimum standards for retirement plans in private industry.

Employee Stock Ownership Plan (ESOP) A retirement plan that encourages employees to become owners of their employer's business through stock ownership.

Endorsement A type of corporate sponsorship where the athlete actually participates in ad campaigns.

Energy guide label A label on an appliance that shows estimated energy consumption, estimated annual energy cost for the appliance, and a comparison of energy costs to other similar appliances with the same features.

Entrepreneur Person who takes a vision and makes it a reality.

Entrepreneurial spirit The drive behind a successful person.

Equity Funds that owners have invested in their business.

Equity REIT Real estate investment trust that owns and operates income-producing real property.

Escrow account An account to hold funds for a future use. The escrow account on a mortgage is used to pay real estate taxes and homeowners' insurance.

Estate All of the assets that an individual owns less any liabilities owed.

Estate planning Process of planning for estate distribution.

Estate tax Tax based on the value of the total estate of a deceased person.

Eviction The process of forcibly and immediately removing a tenant from the rental property for violation of the lease.

Exchange-traded fund (ETF) Investment company designed to mirror the return of a designated market index.

Excise tax Tax imposed on certain purchases, such as gasoline, alcohol, or cigarettes.

Executive summary The first page of the business plan that clearly highlights all the important points of your entire plan.

Executor An individual placed in charge of the process of distributing a deceased person's estate.

Expected return The average return on an investment over the long run.

Expense ratio Fund expenses divided by the fund's total net assets.

Extended replacement cost Insurance coverage that compensates for the full replacement value even when that value exceeds the maximum coverage of the policy.

Face value Principal amount of a bond that is paid to the bondholder at maturity.

Family trust A type of testamentary trust that holds property for beneficiaries other than the surviving spouse. The surviving spouse may receive income from the trust.

FDIC Insurance that protects the depositor against loss in the event the financial institution was to fail.

Fee simple estate Real property ownership that represents absolute ownership of the land.

Fee-based investment advisor Advisor who charges a fee for services rendered.

FICA The combination of Social Security and Medicare taxes.

Finance company A financial institution that extends loans to its customers but raises funds from investors rather than accepting deposits.

Financial assets Typically represented by a written document, an interest in something of value.

Financial independence The ability to afford a preferred lifestyle.

Financial institution A business that accepts funds from investors and provides these funds to users of capital.

Financial intermediaries Any financial institution that collects funds from investors and supplies these funds to businesses and other entities (e.g., a government) that need funds.

Financial intermediation The process by financial institutions of acquiring funds and channeling them to users of funds.

Financial life cycle A model that divides a person's life into phases according to the earning potential, need for saving and investing, and ability to take on risk in each phase of the cycle.

Financial market A market that provides the means for buying and selling securities.

Financial risk Firm's risk associated with the amount of its debt.

Fixed interest loans Has a constant interest rate throughout the life of the loan.

Fixed-rate mortgage A mortgage with a fixed interest rate for the life of the loan.

Flexible spending account An employer-offered benefit allowing employees to contribute tax-deductible dollars to an account to be used for medical expenses.

Floating interest bond Bond with an interest rate that changes based on changes in an interest rate index.

Form 1040 The standard tax form used to file an individual federal tax return.

Form 10-K Corporation's annual financial statements filed with the SEC.

Fraternal societies Organizations whose members have a common pursuit.

Functional resume Resume that does not use chronological order; it highlights specific skills aimed at a specific occupation.

Funded plan A retirement plan that contains sufficient funds to pay all current and expected future benefits to its beneficiaries.

Future value The ending balance in an account or the future worth of a present balance.

General credit card Credit issued by finance companies, credit unions, or banks.

Gift A transfer of property.

Gift tax A federal tax on gifts received. Gifts valued over $13,000 in 2009 are subject to gift tax.

Good-til-canceled (GTC) order Open order.

Goodwill Value of a business over and above its book value.

Grantor An individual transferring assets into a trust.

Group term insurance Term insurance that is offered to individual members of a group.

Growth investing strategy Buying stocks with potential for high growth.

Guardian The person identified in his or her will who is responsible for the person's minor children upon the person's death.

Hazard Increases the chance of a risk occurring, such as icy roads and drunk drivers.

Health insurance Provides benefit payments for health care expenses.

Health maintenance organization (HMO) A managed health care plan that allows its members medical services performed by approved doctors and hospitals.

Health savings account (HSA) A savings account funded with tax-deductible dollars to be used for medical expenses for people who have a catastrophic health insurance plan (HDHP).

High deductible health plan (HDHP) This health insurance is also referred to as catastrophic health insurance, since it pays only if you have a medical catastrophe. It is best for healthy individuals who don't require frequent doctor visits.

HIPAA Act of 1996 Prohibits insurers from denying health insurance coverage based on the health status of an individual with preexisting conditions.

Holographic will A will written and signed in the person's own handwriting.

Home equity loan Revolving credit account available to homeowners.

Homeowners' insurance Insurance that covers a homeowner for damage to the home. Homeowners' insurance can also cover personal property in the home.

Hope Credit An educational credit that is available to use for the first four years of college if the student is full-time.

Housing-expense ratio The total housing payment, including insurance and property taxes as a percent of the borrower's income.

Hybrid REIT Real estate investment trust whose portfolio contains investments in mortgages and in real property.

Implied warranties A product warranty created by state law, and all states have them. Almost every purchase you make is covered by an implied warranty.

Income method (needs approach) A method of estimating life insurance needs applying a multiple to a person's annual earnings.

Income replacement policy This policy provides income if the policyholder is unable to perform the job duties of his or her current occupation and he or she is not employed in another occupation.

Income statement A financial statement used to show a company's profitability.

Indemnity plan A private health care plan in which the policyholder is free to select his or her own health care provider.

Independent insurance sales agent An insurance sales agent who represents more than one insurance company.

Index fund Mutual fund with investment objective to match the performance of a market index.

Individual retirement account (IRA) Account that allows the investor to deposit money tax deferred.

Inflation The increase in the price of goods over time.

Inheritance tax A tax on a deceased person's property based on who receives the bequest and the amount of the bequest.

Initial margin requirement Percentage of funds needed to buy a security with borrowed money.

Installment loan Loan that is paid back in periodic payments for a specified period of time until paid off.

Installment payments Life insurance proceeds received as an annuity.

Insurance policy Lists covered services and maximum benefit amounts.

Insured The person whose life is covered by a life insurance policy.

Interest The cost of credit. The interest rate is expressed as a percentage per year.

Interest income Taxable interest you received, common sources of taxable interest are savings accounts, tax accounts, personal loans you made, CDs, federal and corporate bonds.

Interest rate Amount of interest per year expressed as a percentage of the amount borrowed.

Interest rate risk Variation in return caused by changes in interest rates.

Interest-bearing checking account Deposit account that pays interest and lets the customer withdraw funds by writing a check.

Intestate Dying without a will.

Investment bank A securities firm that assists corporations and other entities to raise capital by selling the corporations' securities to investors.

Investment company Company that invests in a portfolio of securities.

Investment grade bond A bond of high creditworthiness.

Investment monitoring Process of assessing investments to determine if they meet goals.

Irrevocable living trust A type of living trust that creates a separate legal entity that owns the assets.

Itemized deductions Specific expenses that you can deduct before arriving at taxable income; used when their total is greater than the standard deduction.

Keogh plan A retirement plan for self-employed individuals that allows for pretax contributions to a retirement account of 25 percent of annual net income, up to a yearly maximum of $42,000.

Key person life insurance Life insurance policy on an important employee or owner of a business, and the business is the beneficiary.

Laddering A process of buying staggered maturity date CDs.

Landlord The owner of rental property.

Large-cap fund Fund that invests in larger companies.

Lease A legal document specifying the terms of rental of a property.

Letter of last instruction An inclusion in a will that presents a person's last words and discusses desired details of administering the estate.

Level term life insurance Term life insurance with constant coverage amount over the life of the policy.

Liabilities Debt.

Liability coverage A type of automobile insurance that pays for damages to another person's vehicle and/or medical bills should the insured be at fault in an automobile accident.

Life cycle investing An investment strategy that matches the amount of risk that people should be able to take to the key phases of their life cycle.

Life cycle mutual fund A mutual fund that invests in other mutual funds with an asset allocation target designed to meet a certain life cycle investing goal.

Life estate Real property ownership during the present owner's lifetime, after which ownership reverts to the previous owner.

Life insurance Insurance that provides a monetary payment to a specified beneficiary in the event that the policyholder dies.

Lifetime Learning Credit An educational credit that is available for any college student who doesn't claim the Hope Credit.

Lifetime maximum benefit The maximum amount the insurance company will pay for claims over the policy holder's life.

Limit order Order to buy or sell at a specified price (or better).

Liquidity The ability to turn an asset into cash quickly at the current market value.

Liquidity risk Risk of being unable to immediately sell an investment at its market value.

Living trust A trust created when the grantor is living.

Living will A legal document that states a person's desires should he or she become unable to make his or her own decisions.

Load Commission to purchase a mutual fund.

Load fund Fund that charges a load to purchase (or possibly redeem) shares.

Loan application fee A fee paid to the lender for loan application and documentation costs.

Loan origination fee A percent of the amount of the loan paid at the beginning of the loan. The fee is extra interest on the loan.

Long-term disability policy Disability insurance policy with a waiting period of several weeks to several months that pays benefits for periods from several years to as long as the lifetime of the insured.

Long-term gain A capital gain that occurs when you hold the security for more than one year.

Long-term liabilities Debts you expect to pay off more than one year from now.

Lump-sum distribution Life insurance proceeds received in one payment.

Maintenance margin requirement Margin percentage that an investor must maintain in an investment position.

Managed health care plan A plan that requires you to choose medical providers who are a part of your provider's network.

Management fee Fee paid by a mutual fund to its investment advisor to manage the fund's portfolio.

Management risk Variation in a firm's return attributable to the company's management.

Margin call Call to deposit additional funds in a margin account.

Margin Funds that brokerage firms lend to clients using securities as collateral.

Market index Representative portfolio of securities that measures market performance.

Market order Order to buy or sell a security immediately at the best-quoted price.

Market risk Variation in returns that is related to market returns.

Marketable securities Securities that trade on open financial markets.

Maturity The date when the bond face value must be paid

Medicaid A government-sponsored health insurance plan for individuals and families with limited income and assets.

Medical insurance An insurance plan that covers medical expenses; often called health insurance.

Medical payments coverage Provides compensation to anyone riding in your vehicle and when you are driving someone else's vehicle.

Medicare A government-sponsored health insurance program for individuals over 65 and disabled persons.

Mid-cap fund Fund that invests in firms in the middle range of size.

Mitigate To transfer all or part of the risk to another.

Money market account Savings account that bear a higher interest rate than standard savings accounts.

Money market mutual fund Mutual fund that invests in money market securities.

Money market security Short-term interest-bearing security issued by a very creditworthy issuer.

Money markets Pooled funds that are invested in short term securities.

Mortgage loan A loan with the home serving as collateral; the type of loan used to purchase a house.

Mortgage REIT Real estate investment trust whose portfolio is invested in mortgages or mortgage securities.

Municipal bond Bond issued by states, cities, etc., interest is exempt from U.S. income tax.

Mutual fund Financial institution that raises funds by selling its stock to investors and investing those funds in securities such as stocks and bonds of other companies.

Mutual funds Pooled investments; funds take deposits from multiple investors and use the combined funds to purchase stocks, bonds, or short-term securities.

Mutual life insurance company Life insurance issuer owned by its policyholders.

National brands Common household name brands.

Negotiable certificate of deposit Money market security issued by large commercial banks.

Net asset value Total net assets of a fund divided by the number of shares outstanding.

Net weight The total weight minus the weight of the package

Net worth The value of your total assets minus the value of your total liabilities.

No-fault insurance A system of automobile insurance that requires drivers to carry insurance for themselves and places limits on their ability to sue other drivers for damage.

No-load fund Fund that does not charge a load to buy or redeem shares.

Non-contributory plan A retirement plan in which employers, not employees, fully fund the plan.

Non-depositary financial institution Obtains funds by methods other than accepting deposits.

Non-forfeiture clause A provision in a whole life policy stating that the cash value in the account is owed the policyholder even if the policy is canceled.

Note Bond with maturity of about 3–10 years.

Odd lot Less than 100 shares of stock.

Open order Order to transact securities that remains active until canceled.

Open-end fund (mutual fund) Fund that sells and redeems shares directly to investors at net asset value.

Opportunity cost The value of foregoing the opportunity to have a given good, service, or activity.

Opportunity costs The consequences of choices.

Ordinary annuity An annuity in which payments occur at the end of each period.

Out-of-pocket limit The maximum out-of-pocket expenses you must pay for covered services before your insurance pays 100 percent of your covered medical expenses for an entire year.

Owner's equity Net worth in a personal balance sheet.

Own-occupation disabled A policy that provides income if the policyholder is unable to perform the job duties of his or her current occupation.

Paid-up 65 life insurance policy Life insurance with premiums paid up to the age 65 after which the life insurance continues in effect.

Par value Principal amount of a bond that is paid to the bondholder at maturity.

Participating policy Policy that pays a dividend to its policyholder when the insurance company has a surplus.

Pension Benefit Guaranty Corporation A federally chartered corporation that guarantees payment of defined benefit pension benefits.

Pension fund A fund holding and investing funds contributed by companies and/or their employees to provide an income for employees who retire.

Pension plan Another name for a defined benefit plan.

Personal financial plan Your personal goals and the activities to achieve those goals.

Personal injury protection (PIP) No-fault insurance coverage.

Personal property rider If your personal property is worth more than the insurance cap, a rider will cover the excess.

Personal property tax Tax paid to your municipality or county of residence that are based on the assessed value of real property like motor vehicles and boats.

Point-of-service (POS) plan A health insurance plan with combined components of indemnity plans, HMOs, and PPOs.

Points Interest paid up front on a loan to buy down the interest rate offered on the loan.

Portfolio Set of investments that are managed as a group.

Power of attorney A legal document that grants another person the right to make decisions on the grantor's behalf should the grantor become incapacitated or incompetent.

Preapproval A guarantee for a mortgage loan for a specified amount of time.

Precautionary motive The need to hold cash as a cushion for emergency use.

Preferred provider organization (PPO) A managed health care plan that offers medical benefits through a list of approved providers.

Preferred stock Stock that receives a fixed dividend and owns a fixed amount of the corporation.

Premium The amount you pay an insurance company for an insurance policy.

Prequalification An estimate of what you might be able to afford for a mortgage payment.

Present value The beginning balance or the present worth of a future balance.

Presumptive disability A provision that provides immediate benefits for severe and sudden disabilities, such as loss of sight, hearing, speech, or two limbs.

Price-to-earnings ratio (P/E ratio) Stock price divided by earnings per share.

Primary market Market in which entities sell their securities to raise funds.

Principal The amount borrowed.

Private health insurance Any health insurance policy purchased from a private insurance company.

Private mortgage insurance (PMI) Insurance purchased by the borrower that covers the lender in case of default.

Private sponsorship Financial support from family, friends and fans.

Probate The legal process of administering the estate of a deceased person.

Probationary period The length of time from initial application for disability insurance to the time when coverage takes effect.

Profit-sharing plan A retirement program in which the employer makes contributions into employee accounts based on the earnings of the company.

Progressive A tax characteristic, meaning that as you have greater income, you will pay a higher percent of income tax.

Property and casualty insurance Broad terms describing insurance that provides compensation for loss due to damage, theft, or liability.

Property taxes Taxes based on the value of real estate.

Proxy statement Document providing shareholders information on corporate voting proposals.

Purchasing power risk Variation in real returns caused by inflation.

Real estate Land and any structure attached to the land.

Real estate investment trust (REIT) A company that invests in income-producing real estate property.

Real estate operating company (REOC) Real estate investment company that does not qualify for REIT status.

Real estate stocks Stocks of companies that manage or invest in real estate.

Real estate tax Similar to personal property taxes but for land or homes that you own.

Real property Real estate or the ownership rights over real estate.

Renewable policy A term life insurance option that offers a guaranteed life insurance policy, albeit at higher premiums, after your current one expires.

Renters' insurance An insurance policy that covers the personal property in a rented residence.

Replacement cost Insurance coverage that covers the full cost of replacing a loss.

Retirement funds Accounts that hold investments to provide retirement income.

Return on equity (ROE) Measure of company profitability equal to profits divided by equity.

Return on investment Profit per period for each dollar invested. Often expressed as a percentage.

Revocable living trust A type of living trust in which the grantor still owns the assets in the trust and has control over them.

Revolving credit A credit line that allows the borrower to borrow up to a maximum limit.

Rider An addendum to an insurance policy that changes the features of the policy.

Risk The danger of a loss; variation in returns on investment.

Riskless investment Investment with a certain future return.

Risky investment Investment with more than one possible future return.

Rollover The process of converting the assets in a 401(k) or other defined benefit plan into a traditional IRA.

Roth IRA After-tax investment.

Round lot Multiple of 100 shares of stock.

Sales tax Tax paid on all purchases that you make. This tax goes to the city, county, or state where you are making the purchase.

Savings account An account at a commercial bank that pays the depositor interest.

Schedule A The federal tax schedule for itemized deductions.

Schedule B The federal tax schedule for totaling your interest and dividend income amounts.

Schedule D The federal tax schedule used to input capital gains.

Secondary market Market for trading securities.

Secured bond Bond collateral pledged as security in case of default.

Securities and Exchange Commission (SEC) U.S. government agency charged with enforcing securities laws.

Securities brokerage firm Securities firm that acts as an agent to transact securities from one investor to another.

Securities firm Financial service firm that sells securities to investors.

Security Documented financial interest in a company or fund.

Security deposit A deposit paid at the beginning of a lease to deter renters from abusing the premises.

Self-proving will A will with notarized signatures of witnesses.

Service contract (extended warranty) A promise to perform (or pay for) certain repairs or services. Sometimes called an "extended warranty," a service contract is not a warranty as defined by federal law.

Short-term disability policy Disability insurance policy with a waiting period of 0 to 14 days that pays benefits for up to two years.

Short-term gain A capital gain that occurs when you hold the security for less than one year.

Simple interest Interest paid one time on a balance of funds for a period of time, usually one year or less.

SIMPLE IRA An IRA for small businesses in which the employer matches employee contributions.

Simplified employee pension (SEP) A retirement plan for small businesses that have at least one employee where only the employer is allowed to make contributions for an employee.

Small-cap fund Fund that buys stocks of smaller firms.

Social Security An insurance program run by the government that provides for everyone in the case of death, disability, health issues, or retirement.

Speculative bond Bond of issuer with risky credit (BB or lower).

Speculative motive The need to hold cash to buy at lower prices in the future.

Sponsorship Money provided for education, travel, and living expenses for students, often athletes.

Standard deduction A fixed amount that is subtracted from AGI before you arrive at taxable income.

Standard deviation Measure of variation in stock returns that measures risk.

Stock Ownership in a company.

Stock exchange Organization that provides a framework and mechanisms for trading securities.

Stock life insurance company A life insurance issuer owned by stockholders.

Stock (ticker) symbol One to five letters that uniquely identify a company's stock.

Stock screening The process of identifying stocks that meet a set of desired characteristics.

Stockholders' equity The net value of a corporation: assets less liabilities.

Straight life insurance (ordinary life) Permanent life insurance that accumulates a cash value and has a level premium. Also known as whole life insurance or ordinary life insurance.

Sublet A lease contracted by a person who is also a tenant of the property.

Tangible assets Assets you can touch—they have a physical form.

Target-date life cycle fund A life cycle mutual fund with a target retirement date and an asset allocation strategy based on that date. The fund changes the asset allocation targets as the retirement date approaches.

Tax deferred Depositor doesn't have to pay taxes on the amount deposited until it is withdrawn.

Tax liability The amount of federal income taxes that you owe for the year.

Taxable income The income on which you owe federal income tax.

Tenant A person who rents and occupies rental property.

Term life insurance Provides life insurance for a certain amount of years, usually ranging from ten to thirty years, at one constant premium.

Testamentary trust A trust created by a person's will.

Testator A person making a will.

Tiered interest schedule As you reach a higher level of minimum deposit, you earn a higher interest rate.

Title insurance Insurance coverage against losing property, should issues arise concerning the legal ownership of the property.

Transactions motive The need to hold cash to make purchases.

Treasury bond (T-bond) Fixed-interest bond issued by the U.S. Treasury with original maturity of 30 years.

Treasury Inflation-Protected Securities (TIPS) Bonds issued by the U.S. Treasury whose principal changes according to the Consumer Price Index.

Treasury note (T-note) Bonds issued by the U.S. Treasury with fixed interest and original maturity of 2–10 years.

Trust A legal entity in which one person transfers assets to another individual or institution (the trustee) to manage for the beneficiaries.

Trustee The individual or institution that manages the assets in a trust for the beneficiaries.

U.S. Treasuring bill Money market security issued by the U.S. Department of Treasury with maturities of 4, 13, and 26 weeks in minimum denominations of $1,000.

Uninsured motorist coverage A form of automobile insurance that provides compensation should the policyholder or passengers suffer from injuries in an accident with an uninsured driver who is at fault.

Unit investment trust Investment company with a fixed portfolio of bonds; terminates when the final bond matures.

Unit price The price per ounce (oz) or pound (lb).

Universal life insurance A hybrid of a term insurance policy and whole life policy.

Unsecured bond Bond with no specific pledged collateral.

Value investing strategy Purchasing stocks whose fundamental value is greater than the current price.

Variable interest bond A floating interest bond.

Variable life insurance A type of universal life that lets the policyholder make certain investment decisions.

Variable rate loan Loan where the interest rate can adjust both up or down over the life of the loan.

Vested benefits Benefits to which employees are entitled even if they leave the employer before reaching retirement age.

Vision insurance Provides coverage for optometry visits, contacts, glasses, and other eye-care needs.

W-2 A federal tax sheet that you receive from any employer that you worked for during the year that lists your income and other tax amounts.

Warranty A promise by the manufacturer or merchant to stand behind their product.

Warranty of fitness A warranty for a particular purpose. When you buy a product on the seller's advice, the implied warranty holds the seller accountable for a particular use.

Warranty of merchantability A warranty implies the product will do what it is supposed to do.

Whole (permanent) life insurance Permanent life insurance that accumulates a cash value and has a level premium. Also known as ordinary life insurance or straight life insurance.

Will A legal document that details how a person would like the estate to be distributed after the person's death.

Yield to maturity The total return over life of a bond.

Zero-coupon bond Bond with no interest payments sold at a discount from face.

Index